Masterpieces and Dramas
of the Soviet Championships

Volume I (1920-1937)

Sergey Voronkov

Masterpieces and Dramas of the Soviet Championships: Volume I (1920-1937)

Author: Sergey Voronkov

Translated from the Russian by Alexei Zakharov

Typesetting by Andrei Elkov (www.elkov.ru)

Photos provided from the archives of the Russian Chess Museum, magazines *Chess in the USSR (Shakhmaty v SSSR)* and *64*, and personal archives of the author, Yuri Averbakh, David Bronstein, Irina Alatortseva, Nikolai Izmailov and Andrei Eremenko

Front cover: Levenfish versus Botvinnik, game 11 of their match, 1937

The English 2020 version is updated and expanded. The computer analysis was mostly carried out prior to the publication of the Russian version in 2007. For the English 2020 version only critical changes were made to the analysis. It was not the author's intention to exhaustively analyze the games for what is a historical book.

Follow us on Twitter: @ilan_ruby

www.elkandruby.com

ISBN 978-5-6041769-3-1 (paperback), 978-5-6044692-8-6 (hardback)

About the Author

Sergey Voronkov was born in 1954 and lives in Moscow. He is a leading Russian chess historian, journalist and author. Sergey has written 10 books in Russian and numerous articles on Russian chess history.

He graduated in Journalism from Moscow State University and edited over 100 chess books for *Fizkultura i Sport* publishing house in 1978-1991. He was Deputy Chief Editor of *Chess in Russia* in 1992-1999 working under Yuri Averbakh. As an editor of *Ripol Klassik* publishing house in 2002-2015 Sergey increased the total number of books edited by him to around 150, including 14 written by Garry Kasparov. He regularly contributes articles to the ChessPro website.

For his first book *David Janowski* (1987 in Russian, with Dmitry Plisetsky) Sergey won the prize for Best Chess Book from the USSR Sports Committee. His other books include *David Versus Goliath* (2002 in Russian, with David Bronstein, published in English as *Secret Notes*, 2007), *Russians Versus Fischer* (2004 in Russian, with Dmitry Plisetsky, English editions published in 1994 and 2005, Italian edition published in 2003), *Fyodor Bogatyrchuk: the Dr. Zhivago of Soviet Chess* (2013 in Russian, in two volumes), *Masterpieces and Dramas of the Soviet Championships* (2007 and 2019 in Russian, in three volumes) and *The Russian Sphynx. Alexander Alekhine* (2020 in Russian).

CONTENTS

Index of Games

Game	White	Black	Opening	Year
40	Freymann	V. Makogonov	Queen's Gambit	1927
41	Verlinsky	Kan	Nimzo-Indian Defense	1929
42	Kan	Verlinsky	French Defense	1929
43	M. Makogonov	Freymann	Indian Defense	1929
44	Kan	Botvinnik	Evans Gambit	1929
45	Botvinnik	Silich	Fragment	1929
46	Izmailov	Grigoriev	Fragment	1929
47	Riumin	Rauzer	Fragment	1929
48	Silich	Rokhlin	Fragment	1929
49	Rauzer	Rokhlin	Fragment	1929
50	Izmailov	Botvinnik	Queen's Indian Defense	1931
51	Botvinnik	Sorokin	Fragment	1931
52	Sorokin	Riumin	Fragment	1931
53	Botvinnik	Riumin	Semi-Slav Defense	1931
54	Riumin	Yudovich	Fragment	1931
55	Lisitsin	Yudovich	Fragment	1931
56	Goglidze	Budo	Fragment	1931
57	Bogatyrchuk	Goglidze	Fragment	1931
58	Alatortsev	Zamikhovsky	Fragment	1931
59	Ilyin-Zhenevsky	Botvinnik	Fragment	1931
60	Bogatyrchuk	Botvinnik	Fragment	1933
61	Rauzer	Botvinnik	Sicilian Defense	1933
62	Romanovsky	Bogatyrchuk	King's Indian Defense	1933
63	Levenfish	Romanovsky	Fragment	1933
64	Verlinsky	Levenfish	Fragment	1933
65	I. Rabinovich	Riumin	Dutch Defense	1933
66	Botvinnik	Riumin	Fragment	1933
67	Alatortsev	Bogatyrchuk	Fragment	1933
68	Lisitsin	Goglidze	Fragment	1933
69	Levenfish	Yudovich	Fragment	1933
70	Savitsky	Botvinnik	Indian Defense	1933
71	Chekhover	V. Makogonov	Fragment	1934/35
72	Levenfish	Kan	Fragment	1934/35
73	Levenfish	Ragozin	Fragment	1934/35
74	Veresov	Levenfish	Fragment	1934/35
75	Belavenets	I. Rabinovich	Benoni Defense	1934/35
76	Bogatyrchuk	Riumin	Fragment	1934/35
77	Lisitsin	Bogatyrchuk	Reti Opening	1934/35
78	Mazel	Riumin	English Opening	1934/35
79	Riumin	Ragozin	Queen's Gambit	1934/35
80	Belavenets	Veresov	Slav Defense	1934/35

Game	White	Black	Opening	Year
81	I. Rabinovich	Savitsky	Ruy Lopez	1934/35
82	Bogatyrchuk	Freymann	Ruy Lopez	1934/35
83	Rauzer	Alatortsev	French Defense	1934/35
84	Bogatyrchuk	Savitsky	Ruy Lopez	1934/35
85	Konstantinopolsky	I. Rabinovich	King's Indian Defense	1937
86	Panov	Bondarevsky	French Defense	1937
87	Levenfish	Goglidze	Nimzo-Indian Defense	1937
88	Levenfish	Ilyin-Zhenevsky	Fragment	1937
89	Panov	V. Makogonov	Fragment	1937
90	Panov	Yudovich	French Defense	1937
91	Belavenets	Lisitsin	Queen's Pawn Game	1937
92	Rauzer	Ilyin-Zhenevsky	Philidor Defense	1937
93	Ragozin	Lilienthal	Fragment	1937
94	Budo	V. Makogonov	Grunfeld Defense	1937
95	Ragozin	Alatortsev	Fragment	1937
96	Kan	Levenfish	Fragment	1937
97	Belavenets	V. Makogonov	Fragment	1937
98	V. Makogonov	Chekhover	Fragment	1937
99	Goglidze	Kasparyan	Fragment	1937
100	Ebralidze	Ragozin	Fragment	1937
101	Levenfish	Botvinnik	Queen's Indian Defense	1937
102	Botvinnik	Levenfish	Grunfeld Defense	1937
103	Levenfish	Botvinnik	Nimzo-Indian Defense	1937
104	Botvinnik	Levenfish	Fragment	1937
105	Botvinnik	Levenfish	Grunfeld Defense	1937
106	Botvinnik	Levenfish	English Opening	1937
107	Levenfish	Botvinnik	Grunfeld Defense	1937

Foreword to the English Edition: Chess in the Context of Time

Sergey Voronkov edited the Russian edition of *My Great Predecessors*; maybe that's what gave him the idea of creating his own huge project, *Masterpieces and Dramas of the Soviet Championships*. I wanted to show the historical development of modern chess through analyzing the games of world champions and those who got close to their level. He is trying to write the history of the Soviet chess school through the prism of the Soviet championships.

Over the years that have passed since his first book, *David Janowski* (with Dmitry Plisetsky, published in Russian in 1987), Sergey has grown into a top Russian chess historian. Small wonder: he worked with Yuri Lvovich Averbakh for a number of years and classes him as his teacher. And then Sergey gained experience of chess analysis when working with David Bronstein on their book *Secret Notes*.

As in his other books, *Masterpieces and Dramas of the Soviet Championships* is based on documents: periodicals, tournament bulletins, games collections, eyewitness accounts... And, as a classic said, "analysis of what's happening in the world based on documentary evidence is a thousand times more demonstrative than any dramatization of this world."

Another attractive feature of this book is the great game selection. I know from experience how difficult and laborious this task is: to choose, out of hundreds of worthy games, the most wholesome and beautiful, the most important for each championship, and to demonstrate the development of chess as a whole. In this sense, the idea of combining "masterpieces" with "dramas" was very clever, allowing him to include a number of historically valuable games that influenced the course of tournaments in crucial ways.

Most of the games were annotated by the players themselves. On the one hand, this makes the author's job easier, but on the other hand, it becomes more challenging ethically. There are quite a few erroneous lines and evaluations in the original annotations, which necessitates computer evaluation. But if we point out all the errors and inaccuracies, this might ruin the notes themselves and give readers the wrong idea about the masters' playing strength and analytical skills. These days, you immediately get to see any error on the screen, but back then, the analysis of a game required blood, sweat and tears... And what to do with the opening recommendations, oftentimes very obsolete? To throw them away entirely is to break the linkage of time, to dilute the development of opening thought, deprive it of its roots, and devalue the work of our predecessors. But if we don't challenge the archaic recommendations at all, the opening part of the games will become essentially useless for modern players...

It's hard to find the right balance between the analytical facts and historical truth. The author was helped by chess master Dmitry Plisetsky, who helped me to write *My Great Predecessors*. So, you can be sure that the chess part of Sergey's book is high-quality as well.

Trying to shoulder alone such a burden as the history of the Soviet chess school is a heroic act. Sergey has already published three volumes in Russian that encompass 20 championships (1920–1953). 38 more are ahead... Will he manage to complete his project? Each championship requires meticulous work. I can only imagine how many tons of chess and literary "ore" the author had to dig through, how much information he had to interpret and structure to create a seamless picture of the first ten championships! Despite its academic adherence to documents, this book virtually resembles a novel: with a mystery plot, protagonists and supporting cast, sudden denouements and even "author's digressions" – or, to be exact, introductions to the championships themselves, which constitute important parts of this book as well. These introductions, with wide and precise strokes, paint the portrait of the initial post-revolutionary era, heroic and horrific at the same time. I've always said that chess is a microcosm of society. Showing chess in the context of time is what makes this book valuable even beyond the purely analytical point of view.

Garry Kasparov
New York, July 2020

Introduction: Through the Lava of Time

"In Russia, when you talk about history, you are always alluding to current times, while a historian is a prophet who predicts retrospectively."
Dmitry Bykov, *Boris Pasternak*

It's such a pity that David Ionovich Bronstein won't see this book. His ideas demonstrated an amazing ability to grow through the lava of time. I remember sitting at his kitchen, and him showing me one of his games from a Soviet Championship. "Why has nobody published a collection of the best games of our championships?" Bronstein suddenly wondered. "Annotated by the players themselves, eight world champions among them. This would be an instant bestseller!" He disliked the term, or maybe the very concept of "Soviet Chess School" ("How can you unite such stylistically disparate players as Romanovsky, Botvinnik, Tal, Kholmov and Spassky under the same banner?!"), so he probably didn't even imagine that this question, asked in passing, would grow into a multi-volume monument to that very school...

Barely a year had passed, and Rome-based publisher Yuri Garrett, inspired by the success of the Italian version of *Russians Versus Fischer*, asked me and Dmitry Plisetsky to create... a collection of Soviet Championship games for him! This coincidence made me very happy, and I offered to simply publish all the masterpieces, adding, "This would be an instant bestseller!" Yuri's reply surprised me, however. "No," he said with a smile, "it's too easy for you and Dima, anyone can write such a book. I would like you to find games that directly influenced the results of the tournaments, that have some dramas, sensations, scandals behind them..." We held a discussion over some drinks (this happened in Moscow), and ultimately came to a healthy compromise: collect one volume of masterpieces and another volume of sensations and dramas.

However, the compensation offered for the amount of work required was too unexciting, and the idea quickly fizzled out. Time went on, I almost forgot about that conversation, but suddenly Artur Avetisyan, the creator of the great site Chesspro.ru, called and asked me to write columns about... Yes, you guessed right, the Soviet Championships! I could barely contain my laughter... This time, the money offer was much more attractive, and in March 2005 I wrote my first article for the column called *Masterpieces and Dramas of the Soviet Championships*. In the subsequent two years, I wrote eleven articles that became the backbone of this volume, although the book version is substantially different from the online one.

I hope that David Ionovich would have liked this book. It's first and foremost about people, whereas the "Soviet Chess School" is a secondary topic; this wasn't a conscious decision – it's simply because in chess, as in life, I was always more interested in individual people than in abstract chimeras of "schools" or "trends". My articles, fully based on documentary sources, were criticized because I dared to state my own opinion, even though "a chronicler should be above the fray". Please don't get confused: I'm not a chronicler, my genre is closer to a documentary movie. And as Mikhail Romm, creator of *Triumph Over Violence*, once said, "A documentary is a peculiar form of *auteur* cinema."

Some people think that it's awfully easy to work in this genre: just find a bunch of quotes, and here you go. They are blind! If you have no idea, the pile of colored glass shards will remain exactly that – a pile; you need a lot of work and faith to breathe life into these shards and create a stained glass window depicting the epoch.

I think that the only thing Bronstein wouldn't have approved of is computer analysis of the games. But what else could I do? Of course, if he was still around, as in the wonderful times when working on *David Versus Goliath[1]*, I wouldn't even have thought about it. Back then, we decided to calculate all lines purely with our human brains, but... David was the only one who could do that! The modern Goliaths of machine analysis have probably already forgotten the delights of that multiple-hour search for the truth, and just how exciting it is to slowly push around the ordinary wooden pieces on an ordinary wooden board...

I don't know whether I'll have enough persistence and inspiration to finish the project. There are still about fifty championships ahead, and each one takes two to three weeks of painstaking work.[2] Without the site, I probably wouldn't have even finished the first volume. People's lively interest, their feedback, from very enthusiastic to (thankfully, much rarer) very negative, helped me to overcome the tiredness and burnout which are unavoidable in any long-term undertaking. I want to thank those who supported me in word and deed on my way: Artur Avetisyan, Yuri Averbakh, Dmitry Plisetsky, Emil Sutovsky, Genna Sosonko, Ilya Odessky, Anatoly Matsukevich, Andrei Eremenko, Vasily Lebedev... Thank you!

Sergey Voronkov
Moscow, March 2007

---

[1]   The Russian name of our book *Secret Notes*

[2]   At the time of publication of the English version you are reading (2020) 3 volumes of this work had been published in Russian covering the first 20 Soviet Championships. Elk and Ruby plans to publish the second and third volumes in English as well

A Chess Feast During the Plague

All-Russian Chess Olympiad: Moscow, 4th – 24th October 1920

"Let's light the lamps, let's pour the drinks,
Let's drown our sorrows in the kegs,
Let's feast, and dance, and do all things
To praise the kingdom of the Plague"
Alexander Pushkin, *Feast During the Plague*

Just like any truly great undertaking – and the Soviet Chess Championships are a phenomenon of planetary scale – this one owes its existence to a random, almost trifling coincidence. Had the Leninist revolutionary Ilyin-Zhenevsky not been a passionate chess fan, who knows how many years would have passed before the Bolsheviks took note of the "royal game". Really, can you call that anything but a miracle? The Russian Civil War is still raging in the outskirts of the country, devastation and hunger are rampant, conspiracies abound, the Red Terror is in full swing – and then, suddenly, there's an All-Russian Chess Olympiad! How could such a thing have happened in 1920?

Oh, this was such an unbelievable chain of coincidences that it might really make you believe in an old adage: any random occurrence is actually a manifestation of some unknown pattern. It all began when Alexander Fyodorovich Ilyin-Zhenevsky... well, we can let him speak for himself. He described it so vividly in his book *Memoirs of a Soviet Master* that it would be a crime to retell it in my own words. Alexander Alekhine, Fyodor Bogatyrchuk, Grigory Levenfish also gave such great descriptions of the era that I should perhaps refrain from speaking at all, unless absolutely necessary, and let the participants and witnesses of those events tell us about the time and themselves.

Mobilization

Ilyin-Zhenevsky: "In early 1920, I got a job in the head office of the Vsevobuch *(VSEobschee VOennoe OBUCHenie, Universal Military Training)*[3] and was soon promoted to commissar. I worked together with great physical education specialists to develop pre-conscription training programs for workers, and I suggested including chess training in these programs... The

---

[3]   Henceforth, all italic text in this book, including game annotations, is mine unless otherwise stated (S.V.)

main value of sports, they said, was that it developed qualities that were very important for a soldier. I thought that this was true for chess as well. Chess training often develops the same qualities in people as any other sport training – bravery, resourcefulness, composure, willpower – and also, unlike sport, it develops strategic skills. My suggestion was accepted and approved by the chairman of Vsevobuch, Comrade N. I. Podvoisky. Soon after, all regional Vsevobuch heads received a decree to cultivate chess and organize chess circles..." (From the book *Memoirs of a Soviet Master.*[4])

Alekhine: "The Moscow chess players, moving from place to place, from one flat to another, with their entire library and equipment, despite the fuel crisis and many other insurmountable obstacles, managed to survive until 1919, and then, one of the most influential members of the Soviet government appeared on the horizon. And even though he was the brother of the even more famous Raskolnikov, the leader of the sailors, he had a different pseudonym, Ilyin-Zhenevsky (from the city of Geneva). He was a decent player and a fervent chess enthusiast, and his authority, both as Raskolnikov's brother and his position as the Vsevobuch head commissar, was instrumental in making the Red government drastically change its attitude towards the 'royal game'. In their eyes, chess turned from "bourgeois leisure" into a "high and useful art that develops the intellectual strength of the growing generation" (a quote from the resolution of the Moscow region Vsevobuch officials' convention, which took place in April 1920). Because of this change of stance, Moscow chess players were suddenly treated to a real cornucopia. Above all, they were allocated excellent six-room premises in the Vsevobuch Central Military Sport Club; the Moscow Chess Club was officially turned into a "department" of that institution. Also, they received funding of 100,000 rubles (which had a purchasing power of 1 million rubles now!) to organize serious tournaments. And, finally and most importantly, they got to organize the "All-Russian Chess Olympiad", which was held in October 1920." (From the book *Chess Life in Soviet Russia* by A. von Alekhine, originally published in the German language in Berlin, 1921.)

> Ilyin-Zhenevsky's authority was so great that chess players referred to him as "our president". The Leningrad master **Andrei Batuev** was a schoolboy back then and first saw Alexander Fyodorovich later, but he may as well have been referring to the 26 year-old Vsevobuch commissar:

---

[4]   The full bibliography is included at the end of the book.

"He was an incredibly handsome and unique man, with blue eyes, delicate, a girl-like blush and curly auburn hair. He was shell-shocked in the war and made funny grimaces, turning his head to the side and smacking his trembling lips. Interestingly enough, Ilyin-Zhenevsky lost his memory after a contusion, and he had to relearn chess from scratch." (*Neva* No. 9, 1984)[5]

Alexander Ilyin-Zhenevsky. "He was a decent player and a fervent chess enthusiast, and his authority, both as Raskolnikov's brother and his position as the Vsevobuch head commissar, was instrumental in making the Red government drastically change its attitude towards the 'royal game'." (Alekhine.) From the author's archive (64, No. 7, 1924).

Ilyin-Zhenevsky: "In spring 1920, talks started among Vsevobuch officials to organize an All-Russian Sports Olympiad in the autumn. I used that occasion to propose holding a chess tournament along with the sports competition, as was done at the Stockholm Olympics in 1912. My proposal was accepted, and I immediately assembled an organizing committee, which included N. D. Grigoriev, N. I. Grekov, A. A. Alekhine and me. The sports olympiad never materialized, but the chess event, which was named "All-Russian Chess Olympiad" and included the Russian SFSR championship (back then, the Russian SFSR was synonymous with the USSR), still took place...

The most daunting task for the organizing committee was to find all the strongest Russian chess players and transport them to Moscow. The information we had was woefully inadequate. We had to use the Vsevobuch system to initiate a military mobilization of chess players, if you could call it that. As an example, I'll quote a telegram that was sent to all Vsevobuch regional district departments:

Chess tournament to take place in Moscow on 1st October. I order you to notify the district about the upcoming tournament. Accommodation and food

---

[5]   All small-font insertions, including the ones in quotes, are mine unless otherwise stated (S.V.)

provided by Moscow. No later than on 15th September, send to the Vsevobuch Head Office in Moscow the information on players willing to take part: first name, last name, work address, job, how indispensable to the job, birth year, chess experience, name of chess club, which tournaments played in, which places taken, need for accommodation in Moscow. The tournament participants will be notified by telegraph. 17th August 1920, No. 648/1516.

Deputy Head of the Vsevobuch

Concurrently with this telegram, the organizers sent a list of the strongest Russian players to be personally invited to the Russian SFSR championship. You can see how woefully inadequate the information available to the organizing committee was at the time by the fact that personal invitations were also sent to Rubinstein, Bernstein, Bogoljubov and Selezniev, who lived outside Russia."

Bogatyrchuk: "In early autumn, I was told that there was a poster on one of the houses on Khreshchatyk[6], telling me to immediately come to the local Physical Education Department to discuss my participation in the Soviet Russian chess championship. Of course, I was very excited and immediately ran to the address written on the poster. The representative told me that a tournament of the country's best chess players was going to be held in Moscow in October, and I was personally invited. "Alekhine is going to take part in the tournament," he added.

The representative told me that he was authorized to offer me 15,000 rubles to cover my travel expenses. Accommodation in Moscow would be funded by the Physical Education Department, separately from that sum. I could leave a large part of that sum to my family. All in all, the offer was very tempting from any point of view – especially the opportunity to play chess again. I agreed, received the money and went home to tell my wife the news ...

But the closer I got to home, the weaker my enthusiasm became. I had overlooked a very important consideration: could I be sure that while I was away, the current authorities of Kiev wouldn't be overthrown *(Bogatyrchuk recalled that during the years of the Russian Civil War, power in Kiev changed ten times!)*, cutting me off from my family and my favorite job?

When I told all that to my wife, she had another objection: she said that I hadn't recovered from typhus yet, and it would be too difficult for me to withstand the strain of travel and tournament play. We weighed all the pros and cons for a long time and ultimately decided not to take the risk. My wife

---

[6]   The main street in Kiev

took all the money and went to the representative instead of me. I don't know what surprised him more: the explanation for my refusal (my wife, of course, only said that she feared for my health), or the fact that the wad of money was untouched. But he accepted my refusal, and plans for my participation ended then and there." (From the book *My Life Path to Vlasov and the Prague Manifesto*, San Francisco, 1978. The motto of its publisher, Russian National Publishing House Globus, was prophetic: "Communism will die, Russia will not die".)

The Bread Revolt

From the press: "16 players took part in the main tournament *(masters in italics)*: *Alekhine*, Grigoriev, Zubarev, N. Pavlov-Pianov, Tselikov, Ilyin-Zhenevsky (all Moscow), Golubev, *Levenfish, I. Rabinovich*, Romanovsky (all Petrograd), A. Kubbel (Yamburg), Daniuszewski (Nizhny Novgorod), Mund (Lodz), *A. Rabinovich* (Vilno), *Blumenfeld* (Saratov), and D. Pavlov (Mogilev).

Unfortunately, a number of the strongest Russian players could not take part – Bernstein, Rubinstein, Duz-Khotimirsky, Salwe, Znosko-Borovsky, Bogoljubov, Bogatyrchuk, Levitsky, Selezniev, Grekov, etc., but even with the aforementioned line-up, the tournament was a very interesting, important and instructive event for the Russian chess art, which has suffered major damage in recent years.

27 amateurs from many different regions of Russia took part in the "B" tournament." (*Listok Shakhmatnogo Kruzhka Petrogubkommuny*, 8th May 1921.)

It was *Listok Petrogubkommuny*, the first issue of which was published in April 1921, that saved some games – unfortunately, not too many – of the All-Russian Chess Olympiad. The story of how this publication came into being, despite the paper shortages, was told by **Peter Romanovsky:**

"Vainstein and I went to an appointment with the Petrogubkommune chairman, A. Badaev. Our campaign group thought that it would be too much to ask for paper to print a whole magazine, so at first we wanted to get permission to print the *Listok Shakhmatnogo Kruzhka Petrogubkommuny*.

Badaev heard our proposal (it was well-reasoned, by the way: there were 12 chess circles working in Petrograd alone) and said that he might provide some paper for such an endeavor. Then he added that he liked to play chess in his spare time, too. Badaev immediately called for his subordinate who managed the distribution of paper, asked him "not to hurt" the chess players and to provide some paper for the *Listok*...

The majority of the 200-copy press run was sent to Moscow, Voronezh, Novgorod and other cities where chess lovers already knew that *Listok* would be released soon, and, of course, waited impatiently for it." (*Shakhmaty v SSSR*, No. 1, 1964.)

Alekhine: "On the 1st October, about 35 players came to Moscow to take part in two tournaments... The players conference, held before the start, was quite turbulent; there were moments when it seemed that the non-Moscow players would refuse to take part and just go home. There were two main reasons for misunderstandings and disagreements, two points that weren't stated clearly enough in the tournament program: 1) prizes and 2) food rations at the tournament.

After long arguments, during which the non-Moscow players delivered an ultimatum and sent a delegation to the Vsevobuch chairman Podvoisky to voice their demands, both of those points were addressed in a satisfactory way:

a) Money prizes were abolished, and bonuses for wins were established instead: 2,000 rubles in the main championship, 1,000 rubles in the amateurs final group, and 500 rubles in the preliminary groups. Silverware served as prizes, and the championship winner also got a special prize from the organizers: a Chinese chess set made of ivory.

b) The food rations were increased: in addition to one pound of bread *(Levenfish wrote that it was just a half-pound)* and a "Soviet dinner" (dried-vegetable soup and either a herring head or a herring tail), every participant got some tea (of course, "Soviet", too), cheese and saccharine during the game.

After satisfying these modest demands, lots were drawn, and the tournament regulations were finally approved."

Ilyin-Zhenevsky: "It was incredibly hard to procure food for the players. Grigoriev and I were trying to do a million things at the same time, because Grekov distanced himself from working on the project, and Alekhine said proudly that he wasn't going to take part in organizational work after the tournament began. Since the players were mostly fed with meager Red Army meals, we put a lot of effort into procuring additional provisions. I remember finding some big round cheese, a delicacy at the time *(as Levenfish recalled, "they gave 200 grams to each player")*. Still, an unfortunate incident happened that disturbed us a great deal. One fine, or should I say, not really fine day, a group of players went on strike and presented a number of demands to me, as the chairman of the organizing committee. I still keep this curious document, very characteristic of the time, in my private archive.

PETITION
by the Participants of the All-Russian Chess Olympiad

Due to the drastic deterioration of food quality we deem it necessary to state that in the current conditions we are unable to continue the tournament and will be forced to quit on Sunday, 17th October, if the following demands are not satisfied:

1) Pay 15,000 rubles per person in advance.

2) Immediately distribute all the remaining cheese among the players.

3) Increase the bread quota or compensate the lack of bread through other means.

4) Immediately distribute cigarettes among the players.

P. Romanovsky, A. Kubbel, I. Rabinovich, I. Golubev,
D. Daniszewski, Mund, G. Levenfish

Curiously, Alekhine, a member of the organizing committee himself, instead of trying to smooth the conflict or give us advice, only poured more fuel on the fire, saying that he would refuse to play too, because "he couldn't play against famished opponents". We managed to convince the players to continue, finding a way to partially satisfy their demands."

The tournament was held in the "great six-room premises" mentioned by Alekhine. This chess and checkers club was opened in May 1920 with help from the Moscow Military District Vsevobuch head, checkers master V. Russo; it was located on the second floor of the building on the corner of Kamergersky Lane and Bolshaya Dmitrovka. **Vladimir Lezerson**, a participant of the 1919 Moscow championship and one of the arbiters of the Olympiad, recalled:

"The tournament participants dined in a mansion in Skatertny Lane, where the Vsevobuch courses were located. The food was procured with the help of Moscow chess circle member, old Bolshevik Alexei Sergeevich Butyagin, later a professor and rector of Bauman Technical University and then Moscow State University. Back then, he was a member of the Moskommune board, which controlled Moscow's food supply.

There weren't many spectators at the tournament – the games started in the morning, and there wasn't much publicity, but everyone involved with the Moscow chess circle would regularly come to the tournament and watch the games intently." (*Shakhmaty v SSSR* No. 4, 1972.)

The organizers tried as hard as they could. According to a participant in the amateurs tournament, future Professor of Asian Studies Kharlampy

Baranov, "those who lived or worked far away were brought specially to the tournament hall." (*Central Chess Club Bulletin* No. 9, 1970.)

Levenfish: "To add something to the meager cadet's allowance, the Petersburg players chose Vanya Golubev as their "supply officer": he was considered a good bargainer. He occasionally managed to get some extra food from the black market in exchange for cigarettes... The lack of calories was compensated by youthful fervor and love for chess. We played "for fun", without pressure of having to qualify for the next tournament. Our play was energetic and attacking, there were many good games, but, sadly, most game scores have been lost" (from the book *Selected Games and Memories*).

The Winners and the Prizes

From the press: "Most of the participants of the main event played after a long hiatus, and so couldn't fully demonstrate their skills on the chess

Romanovsky – Alekhine in round 12. We can even determine exactly when the photo was taken: after 6.e5 (this game was the shortest one in the whole tournament among those whose score survived: 1.e4 e5 2.♘f3 ♘c6 3.♘c3 ♘f6 4.♗b5 ♘d4 5.♘xd4 exd4 6.e5 dxc3 7.exf6 ♕xf6 8.dxc3 ♕e5+ 9.♕e2 ♕xe2+, draw agreed).
I got this unique photo from David Bronstein (for my book on Alekhine), and he himself obtained it when he worked for Izvestia as a chess reporter. The photo would have been lost in the newspaper archive, but the renowned photographer Viktor Akhlomov preserved it: seeing a random old "chess" photo, he decided to save it from oblivion and gave it to the famous grandmaster as a gift.

battlefield. Without a doubt, Alekhine didn't play his best, and managed to win only with a great effort and good share of luck. By contrast, Levenfish, who played better than everyone else, took only third place because at the very beginning of the tournament, when he hadn't hit his stride yet, he drew and even lost some games despite having completely won positions... Romanovsky played unexpectedly well, taking second place, ahead of three maestros." (*Listok Petrogubkommuny*, 8th May 1921.)

The comment about Alekhine is quite remarkable! As you might see, the opinion that he "effortlessly" and "brilliantly" won first prize only took hold years later, not immediately. I initially blamed his biographers, Vasily Panov and Alexander Kotov, but then I found the original source – Levenfish's words in 1925: "Alekhine won the 1920 Olympiad without any effort." Yes, if we look into the table, such an evaluation looks pretty convincing. But an analysis of Alekhine's games (even though only ten of them survived) shows that the victory indeed didn't come easy to him. Years later, Zubarev wrote about that, too: "The tournament ended with Alekhine's victory, however, this win wasn't completely overwhelming. Alekhine played with great strain, but despite that, he still had lost positions in several games, and Blumenfeld agreed to a draw with him despite having an obvious win." (*Shakhmaty v SSSR*, No. 11–12, 1937.)

However, we shouldn't take the *Listok*'s words at face value, either: as it soon (in No. 9) became known, there was a conflict of interest, since the magazine's editorial board included both Levenfish and Romanovsky. In this context, the remark about "Levenfish, who played better than everyone else" looks kind of improper...

I'll finish the introduction of the winner with a quote from a humorous poem about the Olympiad, written by a Moscow chess player **Boris Grigoriev**, well-known in his time. The poem is certainly not a masterpiece, but Alekhine's image is so different from the generally accepted one ("even though he doesn't create his own plan...") that this alone redeems all technical flaws. As the years go by, accounts about people written **before** they became famous geniuses and everyone started writing about them with reverence, become increasingly valuable.

Alekhine is our grandmaster.
Want to introduce him? What for?
The fame is like glue,
If it sticks to you, you can't get it off.
He doesn't need recommendations
From anyone,
And the prize – a bundle of money –
He said himself, "I'll take it!"
So, what's your opinion
About his creativity?

The general consensus
Is currently this:
Even though he doesn't create
His own plan,
And only searches for flaws,
You should beware if he finds one...
He drills into your weakness,
He hits you like a hammer!
He'll beat your pieces into a pulp,
Nobody can survive that!
He is also able
To catch the thread of play
And then think intently
On further developments...
He's a demon of destruction,
A very dangerous microbe
Of decay and dissolution,
And this is not slander!
His openings are shaky
(The theory is strict!),
But as soon as you make a smallest mistake,
Woe is you![7]

Alekhine: "The success of the young Peter Romanovsky, who earned the master's title *(it was awarded either to the champion or to the runner-up in case Alekhine won – he was essentially playing* hors concours) was well-deserved and not in any way surprising. He already looked promising in Mannheim 1914, and now, when his health has improved, Romanovsky's play has become more consistent, and he's now undoubtedly one of the strongest Russian masters.

Levenfish, who hasn't studied chess all that much in recent years due to a lack of time (he's the head of the central chemical lab of the Petrogubkommune), had a poor start, losing two games, but then he came around and finished third, without losing any more games.

Petrograd pinned particular hopes on I. Rabinovich; however, he hasn't exactly lived up to them. He grew up in the traditions of the positional school, and sometimes he would get confused in situations rife with tactical opportunities and occasionally get losing positions even against weaker opponents: this is a trait (alas, almost the only one) that he shares with Rubinstein!

Ilya Rabinovich "was considered Alekhine's main competitor for first prize and the Russian SFSR champion's title." (Ilyin-Zhenevsky.) From the Russian Chess Museum archive (64. Shakhmaty i Shashki v Rabochem Klube ("Chess and Checkers in the Workers Club"), No. 1, 1925). Published for the first time.

---

[7]   The original rhymed

Ilyin-Zhenevsky: "Ilya Leontyevich Rabinovich is one of our most outstanding players. Like Bogoljubov, he was interned in Germany during the war, and there, almost constantly playing in tournaments with his fellow Russian internees, developed the necessary chess strength and endurance. Furthermore, he has studied theory for many years, becoming one of our best chess theoreticians. At the 1920 All-Russian Chess Olympiad, he was considered Alekhine's main competitor for first prize and the Russian SFSR champion's title." (From the book *International Chess Tournament in Moscow.*)

Concerning the trio that shared the last prizes *(5th–7th)*, I should first draw attention to the Vilno master A. Rabinovich. At first, it seemed that he had excellent prospects because he won his first four games in great style and briefly led the tournament. The fact that A. Rabinovich fell behind afterwards can be explained by his tiredness and lack of practice, but there was another thing as well: in the Exchange Variation in the Ruy Lopez, which he seems to loathe, he lost four (!) games with black without much resistance.

Levenfish: "Master A. I. Rabinovich loved chess fanatically. After the Olympiad, he soon moved to Moscow. He had a job as an accountant in the porcelain trust, and then worked for many years as the chess reporter for *Vechernaya Moskva*. Verlinsky was his constant companion. Over the board, Abram Isaakovich would forget about everything else.

Once, when he was still living in Vilno, Rabinovich, who was a very hospitable and welcoming man, threw a party to celebrate the birth of his first son. About twenty guests gathered at his home in the evening. However, the host himself was late. The guests waited for several hours, but to no avail, and the party had to be canceled. It turned out that Rabinovich had met a traveling chess player in the street. They went to the hotel to play a couple of casual games, and Rabinovich only remembered about his guests the next morning.

Despite his unquestionable tactical talent, Rabinovich failed to achieve big tournament successes – he lacked stamina and patience. He could come up with interesting lines in the opening, but it was quite difficult to analyze with him. Rabinovich would only admit that a line was refuted if he got checkmated; a loss of a pawn or piece was not enough to convince him."

N. Grigoriev is, without a doubt, one of the brightest stars in the current chess landscape. A player of diverse knowledge (this especially showed in his pawn endgames) as well as great over-the-board strength, almost at master

Nikolai Grigoriev "is, without a doubt, one of the brightest stars in the current chess landscape." (Alekhine.) (Shakhmatny Listok, No. 21, 1927).

level, Grigoriev is first and foremost a tireless and fanatical promoter of the chess art. Despite his youth (he's 26), in the difficult years of 1917–1919, he was basically the only one whose energy kept the fire in the Moscow chess players' hearts alight, despite all the tragic events in the world. Now Grigoriev is the chairman of the Moscow Chess Club and the head of the Vsevobuch chess section... His start at the Olympiad was poor, but he won three games at the end, which allowed him to win a prize.

Arvid Kubbel is also a strong, almost master-level player; his success was mostly due to his level, calm personality that allowed him to defeat most *dii minores ("lesser gods, in Latin")*; however, he scored only a point against all the other prizewinners.

Among the non-prizewinners, I should mention Blumenfeld, who has managed to develop consistency in his play over the years; this is evident in the fact that he recorded fewer defeats than everyone else. Had he not lost a won position against Ilyin-Zhenevsky in the last round, he would have deservedly won fifth prize.

Ilyin-Zhenevsky: "The worries and troubles of this tournament greatly undermined my play. Shortly before the finish, I was bedridden. The old contusion caused nerve paralysis in my left leg. Still, I continued the tournament. I played the two last games lying on my bed: I lost one (to Levenfish) and even managed to win the other one (against Blumenfeld). All in all, my result was distinctly average."

Alekhine doesn't mention Ilyin-Zhenevsky's play in his article, but, as it turns out, he was a direct influence. "I have to say," Alexander Fyodorovich remembered, "that I don't like to play unfamiliar lines. I was punished repeatedly in 1920 when I played some new lines recommended by Alekhine."

Alekhine didn't say anything about Dawid Daniuszewski either, who shared 9th–10th places with Ilyin-Zhenevsky. **Yudovich:** "An ethnic Pole,

Mikhail Klyatskin, the "godfather" of the Alekhine Defense. The future world champion borrowed the idea of his famous opening, 1.e4 ♘f6!, from him. (64. Shakhmaty i Shashki v Rabochem Klube, No. 8, 1926.)

А. А. АЛЕХИН (Харьков).

Alexei Alekhine took third place in the amateurs tournament. (Novaya Vechernaya Gazeta, Leningrad, 1925.)

he lived in Lodz previously, took part in tournaments, often finishing above G. Salwe. In 1909, he played in the All-Russian Amateurs' Tournament *(where he defeated Alekhine)*. Soon after the Olympiad, D. Daniuszewski returned to his homeland. A passionate admirer of M. Chigorin's talent, Daniuszewski had been collecting his games his whole life. Shortly before his death *(1944, in the Lodz ghetto)*, he sent a valuable handwritten collection of Chigorin's games as a gift to the Soviet chess players." *(Shakhmaty,* Riga, No. 1, 1967.) This collection, 1,218 pages long (!), is now kept in the Russian Chess Museum.

27 players took part in the amateurs tournament; there were three preliminary groups before the final. After a fierce struggle, two winners emerged: Vygodchikov (from Smolensk) and Klyatskin. The former is well-known to Russian chess players because of his success in the 1911 Moscow championship (third, behind Dr. Bernstein and Selezniev), while the young Klyatskin is a promising talent from Moscow. The experienced Vygodchikov won the first-place play-off match 2-0 *(and earned the right to compete in the next championship)*. Alexei Alekhine *(Alexander's brother)* took third place in the amateurs tournament."

Zubarev: "Mikhail Gertsovich Klyatskin had a very original, distinctive chess talent. The author spent many

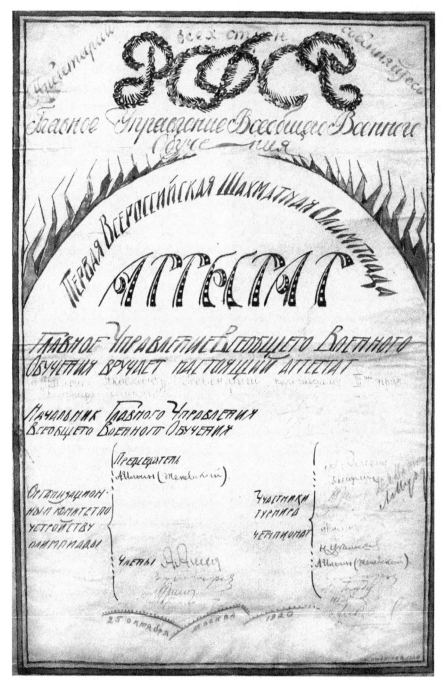

The diploma for third place in the All-Russian Chess Olympiad, awarded to Grigory Levenfish and signed by all organizing committee members and tournament participants. This unique document is now kept in the Russian Chess Museum.

evenings with M. G. , who died an untimely death in 1926, watching his constant search in all areas of chess creativity. No chess dogmas existed for M. G., and, as a result of his critical approach to the seemingly established truths, new, completely unexpected ideas were often born.

It's enough to say that the Alekhine Defense, which is now a fully-established opening, was first discovered and tested in practice by M. G.. I remember how insistent he was, how hotly he debated the appropriateness of this knight move, in defiance of all established views of opening theory. M. G. also worked a lot on the Sicilian Defense line 1.e4 c5 2.♘f3 ♘f6, bringing a lot of new thought to it. M. G.'s endgame studies and his interpretation of the middlegame were also very distinct and individualized." (*Shakhmaty v SSSR*, No. 11-12, 1937.)

Levenfish: "The problem with prizes was the easiest one to solve. When White emigrees fled abroad, they left a lot of valuable items in pawnshops, and they were all confiscated by the government. The organizing committee received three silverware items from the pawnshops. The means of distribution were quite original. The prizes were placed in a separate room. Alekhine entered first. He emerged with a huge vase in his hands, saying, "It seems that I chose the right weight." Romanovsky followed him, and then I took what remained. The prizewinners were awarded diplomas. My own diploma survived. It was drawn on a sheet of poor drawing paper which was found somewhere – printing the diploma was impossible."

> **From the press:** "The winners of the 1921 Moscow championship tournament received the following prizes from the Moscow Vsevobuch military district: a leather jacket for the champion; American boots for the runner-up; the top part of a Red Army uniform for 3rd place; the bottom part of a Red Army uniform for 4th place. Also, all prizewinners received hand-written diplomas." (*Listok Petrogubkommuny*, 27th November 1921.)

Alekhine: "The award ceremony was held in the concert hall, where famous Moscow artists once performed. We received our prizes and diplomas, specially ordered from Soviet artists and signed by the Vsevobuch head commissar and other luminaries, and then – a miracle! – we saw tea and apple tarts made with real white flour; this was a most inspiring closing chord of the Chess Olympiad for everyone."

So, What's Next?

Romanovsky: "After the tournaments, we held a one-day conference, essentially discussing one question: the future of the Soviet chess movement and forms of organization most suitable for its further development.

The delegation from Petrograd, headed by the well-known chess promoter S. Vainstein (by the way, he was the board secretary of the pre-revolutionary All-Russian Chess Union), proposed creating a new All-Russian Union, basing its charter on that of the old All-Russian Chess Union.

A. Alekhine and A. Ilyin-Zhenevsky spoke up against this proposal. In particular, the future world champion took a principled stance: he said outright that the future existence of chess is only possible if state organizations take care of it and govern it *(highlighted by me – S.V.)*.

Ilyin-Zhenevsky said that the Chess Union format was likely unacceptable – the Union would be incapable of supporting the mass chess movement, which needs vast funding.

The conference didn't adopt any special resolutions. However, Ilyin-Zhenevsky gave a valuable instruction in his speech: to create chess magazines in Russia. At the time, he'd already organized the first chess column in the Vsevobuch magazine, *K Novoi Armii ['For a New Army']*." (*Shakhmaty v SSSR*, No. 6, 1957.)

The Ruins of Former Greatness

"Unfortunately, the plans to publish a tournament book fell through because of the paper shortage in Russia," Alekhine wrote, and then explained ironically, "because only works that further Communist propaganda, directly or indirectly, can count on being printed: the state has a monopoly on paper." And so, out of 120 games played at the Olympiad, only 50 survived (including 12 in Alekhine's notes found in Alexander Kotov's archive – see my new book on Alekhine in Russian published in Moscow in 2020 *The Russian Sphynx* for details). I wonder where the tournament scoresheets went, one of which (the game Pavlov-Pianov – Alekhine) is now in my archive. They couldn't just throw them all away, could they?! And if one of the tournament's organizers had the game sheets, why couldn't they just print all the games a year later in the *Listok Petrogubkommuny*, or later still, in the *Shakhmaty* or *Shakhmatny Listok* magazines?

We can only speculate how many original ideas, tactical fireworks and subtle endgames were lost forever. For despite the Spartan conditions, the players, according to Romanovsky, pulled all the stops: "I remember we went on strike at the Moscow Olympiad in 1920 because of a lack of cheese and cigarettes, we wore torn boots and ran to the market to exchange bread for cigarettes, but we played making a real effort, with fervor and zeal, fought each other with great excitement and energy." (*Shakhmatny Listok*, June 1928.)

Alekhine's Hint

Let's begin with the most dramatic game of the entire Olympiad. It was played at the very start, but its result ultimately determined the final standings and brought the master's title to Peter Romanovsky. Still, years later, he would write, "This accidental victory did not make me happy. I realized that this tournament would be a hard test for me."

No. 1
Romanovsky – Levenfish
Moscow 1920, round 1
Annotated by G. Levenfish

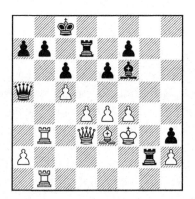

33...♛xa2. 33...♛d8 34.♛a6! ♛g8 35.e5 (35.♛xc6+ ♚d8!) 35... ♛g4+ 36.♚e4 ♛g6+ 37.♚f3 ♜xh2 or 37...♛xb1 won as well.

While my opponent thought over his move, I took a walk. Alekhine walked around the hall, too. He looked at my game, and then, walking beside me, said, "Aha, so you're preparing mate on g2!"

34.e5. Romanovsky clearly saw the rook sacrifice. For instance, 34.♜a3 is met with 34...♜g3+ 35.hxg3 ♛g2+ 36.♚g4 ♜d8 37.♗g1 ♜h8 38.♜xa7 ♜h4# *(37.f5 ♜g8+ 38.♗g5 ♗xg5 39.♛f3 ♗e3+ would only prolong the struggle)*. The game move prevents this combination.

Black could win in numerous ways now. The simplest one was 34...♜d8, again threatening ♜g3+, or 34...♗h4, or 34...♜xh2, without any fancy stuff. But, hypnotized by Alekhine's words, I came to the board and immediately sacrificed the rook, without even writing the move down!

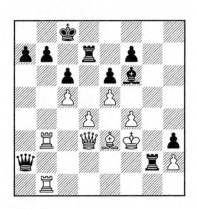

34...♖g3+??   35.hxg3   *(35.
♔xg3??   ♛g2#)*   **35...♛g2+
36.♔g4.** I didn't expect this move
at all. Curiously, Lasker suffered
from a similar hallucination in the
game against Bernstein at the St.
Petersburg 1914 international
tournament.

*Indeed, it's very similar. Here's
the position in the game Bernstein –
Lasker after 35.♘e2-d4.*

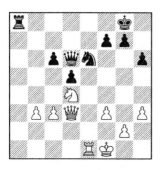

*35...♛h2? "A hallucination," wrote
Tarrasch. "Black thought that he could
checkmate his opponent on move 38
by moving the queen to g1, but missed
the fact that the white king could
escape to g3. After 36.♘xe6 ♖a2
37.♖e2 ♖a1+ 38.♔f2 fxe6 39.♛g6!
♛c7 40.♛xe6+ ♔h8 black was down
a pawn and ultimately lost.*

36...♖d8   37.♛h7! (That's
why white played 34.e5) **37...
♖h8 38.♛xh8+ ♗xh8 39.♖xb7
♛e2+ 40.♔h4 ♛a6 41.♖b8+ ♔c7
42.♗d2.** Black resigned.

I was punished for my
complacency. Because of this game,
I finished third in the tournament,
while Romanovsky took second
place.

A Double Mistake

In the aforementioned episode,
Levenfish was absolutely right. We
can't say the same about his game
with Alekhine, though, where, as
Grigory Yakovlevich would say
later, he missed an opportunity to
checkmate the eventual winner.

No. 2
Alekhine – Levenfish
Moscow 1920, round 6[8]

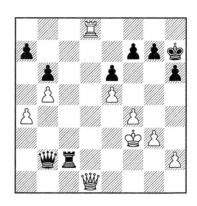

32.♔g4!! "The only path to a
draw," Alekhine exclaims. "If white
first plays 32.♛d3+ g6 and only
then 33.♔g4, there's 33...f5+ 34.exf6
h5+, winning." Kotov, in *Alexander
Alekhine*, explains how exactly
Black would win: "After the only
move   35.♔h4!   (35.♔g5 ♖c5+),
black won with the following: 35...
♛xf6+ 36.♔h3 ♛b2! 37.♔h4! ♔h6!
38.♖h8+! ♔g7!"

---

8   If the annotation's author is not
stated, the games were annotated by
me (S.V.).

A fragment of Alekhine's notes with games from the 1920 All-Russian Chess Olympiad. The surprise was that of the 25 games contained in them, 12 were previously unknown, including 2 of Alekhine's own games! From A. Kotov's archives. The superimposed pencil writing is Kotov's.

You'll probably laugh, but... this is wrong! Don't believe me?

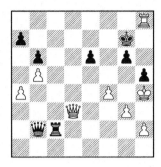

It's enough to extend this line with five exclamation marks by just one more move, 39.♕d8!, and the draw becomes obvious: 39...♖c8 40.♖g8+ ♔h7 41.♕xc8 ♕xh2+ 42.♔g5 ♕xg3+ 43.♔f6 ♕xf4+ 44.♔e7 ♕h4+ or 39...♕f6+ 40.♕xf6+ ♔xf6 41.♖f8+ ♔e7 42.♖a8 ♖xh2+ 43.♔g5 ♖g2 44.♖xa7+ etc.

Whereas the bracketed move 35.♔g5, which, after the "deadly" 35...♖c5+ should be eschewed in horror, actually wins:

36.f5 ♖xf5+ 37.♕xf5!! (obviously not 37.♔h4 ♕xh2#) 37...gxf5 38.♖d7+ ♔g8 39.♔g6!, and black can only save himself from mate by sacrificing his queen! (I was very

proud of my findings until I learned that L. Veretnov, a coach from Krasnoyarsk, had already found these lines in 2002.)

What's even more amazing, Alekhine's line is doubly wrong. First of all, as we have just seen, it was losing, rather than winning. Secondly, after 32.♕d3+ g6 33.♔g4 f5+, Levenfish showed a simple path to the draw in the *Listok Petrogubkommuny*:

34.♔f3! ♖c3 35.♖d7+ ♔h8 36.♖d8+ with perpetual check. However, he too thought that 34.exf6 lost to 34...h5+.

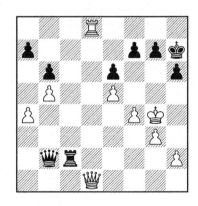

32...♖xh2. "A pity!" Levenfish laments in *Selected Games and*

Memories. "By playing 32...h5+! 33.♔xh5 (33.♔g5 f6+) 33...♖xh2+ 34.♔g4 ♕g2 35.♕d3+ (if 35.♖d7, then 35...♖h6!) 35...g6 36.♖d7 (or 36.♔g5 ♔g7 37.♖d7 ♖h5+ 38.♔g4 ♖h4+!, mating) 36...♔h6! 37.♖xf7 ♖h4+! 38.♔xh4 ♕h2+ 39.♔g4 ♕h5#, black finishes this battle in style."

It looks pretty indeed. But why then did Alekhine, who after 32...g6 showed the line 33.♖h8+!! ♔xh8 34.♕d8+ ♔h7 35.♕e7! with a draw, have only this to say about the pawn check?: "If 32...h5+, then white can simply play 33.♔xh5!" Did he make a mistake again?

No, this time, his analysis was spot on.

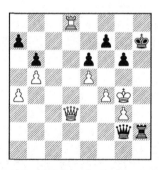

In Levenfish's line above it turns out that white is not forced to play 36.♖d7? (36.♖f8? ♕h3+ 37.♔f3 ♖g2 38.♖xf7+ ♔h6 39.♔e4 ♖xg3 is bad as well). The bracketed 36.♔g5! ♔g7 actually leads to a draw: instead of 37.♖d7?, there's 37.♕a3! ♖h5+ 38.♔g4 ♕e2+ (or 38...♔h7 39.♖h8+! ♔xh8 40.♕f8+ ♔h7 41.♕xf7+ ♔h6 42.♕f8+) 39.♕f3 ♕h2 40.♕a3 with repetition.

33.♕d3+ g6 34.♖d7! ♔g7 (34...♖h4+? 35.♔f3!) **35.♖xf7+.** Draw.

Dedicated to Grigoriev

Alekhine got into trouble several times at this tournament, but always found a way to extricate himself. He was especially proud of his game against Ilyin-Zhenevsky, which was among the handful that he included in the book *Chess Life in Soviet Russia*; here, his annotations have been taken from that book and supplemented with short comments made by Alekhine in post-mortem analysis and first published by Kotov. Ilyin-Zhenevsky's annotations are taken from the *Listok Petrogubkommuny* and his book *Memoirs of a Soviet Master*.

No. 3. Ruy Lopez C77
Ilyin-Zhenevsky – Alekhine
Moscow 1920, round 7
*Annotated by A. Alekhine
and A. Ilyin-Zhenevsky*

1.e4 e5 2.♘f3 ♘c6 3.♗b5 a6 4.♗a4 ♘f6 5.d3 d6 6.c3 g6 7.0-0 ♗g7 8.♖e1 0-0 9.♗g5 h6 10.♗h4 ♗d7 11.♘bd2 ♕e8. This plan, with the subsequent bishop and knight trade, is not too sound, because the trades don't improve black's position **(IZh).**

Fritz proposes 11...g5 12.♗g3 g4 13.♘h4 ♘h5.

12.♘f1 ♘d4. It was better to prepare the break f7-f5 with 12... ♘h7 **(A)**.

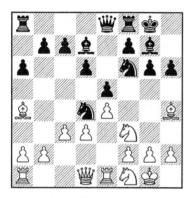

After Alekhine made his move, he excitedly jumped up and went for a walk. I soon saw him with a group of players, and he was hotly explaining something to them. Everyone else was excited too. "Piece! Piece!" was the only thing I heard. Some players approached the board, looked at the position and walked away. "Am I losing a piece?" I thought. However, no matter how hard I looked, I saw nothing of the sort. Then everything quietened down. Romanovsky, smiling, approached my board. "What's the matter? What's happening?" I asked him. "Nothing," he said. "A false alarm. Alekhine thought he'd blundered a piece." Soon, Alekhine calmed down and returned to his seat as well **(IZh)**.

13.♗xd7 ♘xf3+ 14.♕xf3 ♘xd7 (this trade is more beneficial for

white – **A) 15.♘e3 c6 16.♖ad1 ♕e6.**

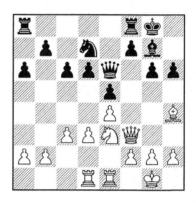

17.g4! Preventing f7-f5. After 17...♕xa2, white could play 18.♘c4 with various strong threats **(A)**.

17...♗f6! Black should go for further trades to hinder the development of the opponent's initiative **(A)**.

18.♗xf6 ♕xf6 19.♕g3 ♘c5 20.♘g2 ♘e6 21.♖f1 ♘f4. Or else f2-f4 – **IZh**.

22.♘xf4 exf4 23.♕f3. It was better to trade queens. Now black gets a better game, because the f4 square becomes a weakness in white's position **(A)**.

23...♔g7 24.♔g2 h5 25.h3 (of course, not 25.gxh5 due to 25...♖h8 – **A) 25...♕g5.** This maneuver leads to nothing. It was better to play 25... ♖h8 and then ♖ae8-e5 **(A)**.

26.♖h1 f5. It was necessary to play 26...♖ae8 27.♖dg1 d5, and white likely wouldn't get enough counterplay **(A)**.

27.exf5 gxf5.

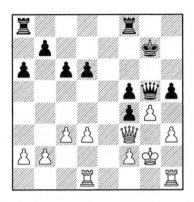

28.♖dg1! (the saving move – **A**) **28...fxg4 29.hxg4 h4.** *Ilyin-Zhenevsky assigns a question mark to this move:* "It was necessary to play 29...hxg4, agreeing to a draw: 30.♔f1 gxf3 *(Kotov's move 30...g3 is bad: 31.♖h5 ♕g6 32.♖h4! with an advantage for white)* 31.♖xg5+ ♔f6 32.♖gh5 ♖ae8 33.♖h6+".

The computer proposes preparing the pawn push with 29...♖h8.

30.♔h3! ♖ae8 31.♖e1 ♔g6. Hoping for 32.d4 ♕d5! 33.♕d3+ ♔g5 34.c4 ♖e3+!! 35.♕xe3 ♕xh1+, and black should win. But white can play simpler and stronger.

31...♖e5 was more cautious, seizing the open file **(A)**.

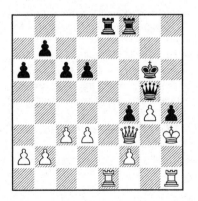

32.♖e2! Now, white gets there faster than his opponent **(A)**.

However, his opponent accords the move a question mark: "White should have played 32.♖e4, and if 32...d5, then 33.♖e2 with the subsequent ♖he1, with good winning chances for white." *Curiously, the computer agrees:* *33...a5 34.♖he1 ♖xe2 35.♕xe2 ♕f6 36.♕e7 or 33...♖g8 34.♖he1 ♔f7 35.d4 ♕f6 36.♕e5 ♖xe5 37.♖xe5 etc.*

32...♖xe2 33.♕xe2 ♕e5! Were the black pawn already on d5, this equalizing move would have been impossible **(IZh)**.

34.♖e1 ♖e8 35.♕e4+ ♕xe4 (35...♔g5? 36.♕h7! ♕xe1 37.♕g7# **IZh**) **36.♖xe4.** After I made that move, the bell rang, announcing the break *(not after 38.f3, as Kotov wrote)*. I wanted to wait until Alekhine sealed his move, but he thought so intensely and for so long that I ultimately left alone. I was in a great mood. I had no doubt that my position was won. Indeed, if Alekhine exchanges rooks, I have a clearly won pawn ending. And if he plays 36...♖f8, I give a check on e6, and then capture the d6 pawn. Alekhine seemingly can't save the game after that.

What was Alekhine doing after I was gone? I'll tell you what I heard from Grigoriev. Alekhine sat at the board for about an hour, then sealed his move and left. Shortly before the break's end, he returned to the club, happy and beaming. When he met Grigoriev, he handed him a full

Scoresheet of the game Pavlov-Pianov – Alekhine, played in round 5. The Russian abbreviation that it contains ("M.Sh.K.") means that this sheet belonged to the Moscow Chess Circle. Where is it from? There were a lot of old chess books and magazine binders in the library of the Fizkultura i Sport publishing house, where I worked as an editor for many years, and I found this sheet in one of the books – it was used as a bookmark...

And recently, from Isaak Romanov's article (Shakhmaty, Riga, No. 9, 1972), I learned the fate of Nikolai Pavlov-Pianov's archive: "His widow gave his entire archive to me – the scores of the games he played between 1908 and 1938. Here are the authentic sheets of the pre-revolutionary Moscow Chess Circle, the first Soviet championships..." The subsequent fate of these papers is unclear.

The game score: 1.d4 e6 2.e4 d5 3.exd5 exd5 4.♘f3 ♗d6 5.♗d3 ♘e7 6.c3 ♗g4 7.♗g5 ♘d7 8.♘bd2 ♘f8 9.♗xe7 ♕xe7+ 10.♕e2 ♘e6 11.h3 ♗h5 12.♗f5 0-0 13.0-0-0 ♕f6 14.♗c2 ♘f4 15.♕f1 ♗g6 16.♘e1 ♖ae8 17.g3 ♖xe1 18.♖xe1 ♗xc2 19.gxf4 ♗g6 20.♖e5 ♗xe5 21.fxe5 ♕f5 22.♕d1 c5 23.dxc5 ♕xf2 24.♖e1 ♕xc5 25.♘b3 ♕f2 26.♘d4 ♕g3 27.♖e3 ♕xe3+ White resigned.

notebook scribbled with lines written down at home, and said, "I dedicate this ending to you, as the expert on pawn endgames." Indeed, Alekhine took a risk and transitioned into the pawn endgame, calculating the only moves that led to a draw **(IZh)**.

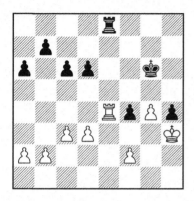

36...♖xe4! 37.dxe4 ♔g5 38.f3 a5!! The only move that saves the game. Both 38...d5? 39.exd5 cxd5 40.b4! and 38...c5? 39.a4! b5 40.axb5 axb5 41.b3 are mistakes, as is 38...b6? 39.a4 b5 40.a5 c5 41.b3 **(A)**.

39.c4. After 39.a4, there's 39...b5 40.b3 bxa4 41.bxa4 d5 with equality; 39.b3 b5! 40.a3 c5 leads to the same result.

39.b4? was a mistake due to 39...axb4 40.cxb4 d5, winning **(A)**.

39...b5 40.cxb5 cxb5. Draw.

Fritz is Envious!

And this game was basically won in the opening. The sharp combinational vision of the championship runner-up manifested itself clearly.

No. 4. Two Knights Defense C56
Romanovsky – A. Rabinovich
Moscow 1920, round 5
Annotated by P. Romanovsky

1.e4 e5 2.♘f3 ♘c6 3.♗c4 ♘f6 4.d4 exd4 5.0-0 ♘xe4 6.♖e1 d5 7.♗xd5 ♕xd5 8.♘c3 ♕c4. The queen can also retreat to d8, h5, f5 and a5. The question of which move is best hasn't been answered by theory yet.

It now has – the best move is to a5! However, you won't find the move to c4 in any opening book. Maybe because of this game?

9.♘xe4 (*9.♖xe4+ ♗e6 10.♘xd4 0-0-0, and after 11.♗e3, there's 11... f5 12.♖xe6 ♘xd4*) **9...♗e6 10.♗g5 ♗b4.** *It's time to think about the king's safety: 10...h6 11.♗h4 g5 12.♗g3 0-0-0.*

11.b3 ♕a6. It was better to play 11...♕d5 (if 11...♕b5, then 12.♘xd4! ♘xd4 13.♕xd4, threatening ♕xg7 with a crushing attack), which white would meet with 12.c3, regaining the pawn at the very least: 12...♗a5 (12...

dxc3? 13.♘f6+, winning the queen; 12...♗c5 13.c4 ♕f5 14.♘h4, winning a piece) 13.♗f6 etc.

However, 12...f5! equalized the game: 13.♘d6+! (best) 13...♗xd6 14.c4 ♗xh2+! 15.♘xh2 ♕d6 16.♕e2 ♔f7 17.♗f4 ♕d7 18.♕h5+ ♔g8 etc.

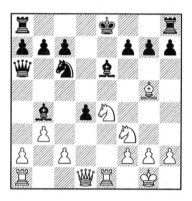

12.♘xd4! 0-0. If 12...♗xe1, then 13.♘c5 ♕b6 14.♘dxe6 ♗xf2+! 15.♔xf2 fxe6 16.♕d7+ ♔f8 17.♔g3! *(from afar, the machine only sees 17.♔e2, evaluating the position as slightly better for white)* 17...♕xc5 18.♖f1+ ♕f5 19.♖xf5+ exf5 20.♕xf5+ ♔g8 21.♕e6+ ♔f8 22.♗e3! ♖e8 23.♗c5+ ♘e7 24.♕f5+ ♔g8 25.♗xe7 ♖xe7 26.♕c8+, winning. *A brilliant 14-move line! Even the fastidious Fritz couldn't find a single flaw in it.*

13.♘xe6 fxe6 14.c3 ♗a3. It was relatively better to retreat to d6, giving up the pawn. 14...♗a5 is met with 15.b4 ♗b6 16.a4, after which black seems to lose a piece as well.

Not 14...♗e7 15.♗xe7 ♘xe7 16.♕d7 ♘g6 17.♘c5 ♕b6 18.♕xe6+.

15.b4! ♖f5 16.♕b3.

16...♘e5. It's impossible to save the piece. After 16...♖e8, there's 17.♘c5 ♖xc5 *(17...♘a5 18.♕xa3 ♕c6 19.♗e3)* 18.♖xe6! ♖xe6 19.♕xe6+ ♔f8 20.♖e1, winning.

Black tries to give up the piece in the best possible circumstances.

17.b5 ♘f3+ 18.gxf3 ♖xb5 19.♕d1 ♗b2 20.♖b1 ♗xc3 21.♖xb5 ♕xb5 22.♖e3 ♗a5 23.♖d3 c5 24.♖d7 c4? Paying no attention to white's plan.

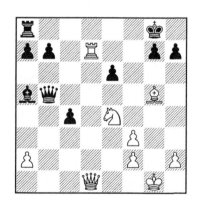

25.♗h6! ♕h5. If 25...gxh6, there's 26.♘f6+, with mate next move.

26.♗xg7 ♕g6+ 27.♔f1 ♗d8 28.♗c3 ♗h4 29.♕d4. Black resigned.

Inspired by this win, I played well

afterwards, even competing for first place with Alekhine for a while.

Simple, But Tasteful

In addition to sharp opening fights, there were pretty finishes at the Olympiad as well. They mostly occurred in already won positions, which diminishes their impressiveness a bit. Still, the combinations are beautiful.

No. 5
Grigoriev – Alekhine
Moscow 1920, round 1
Annotated by A. Alekhine

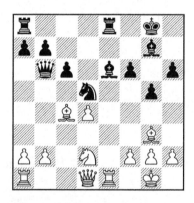

18.♘e4? The decisive mistake. White should have played 18.♘b3, with a defensible position.

18...f5! 19.♘c5. 19.♘d6 is met with the simple 19...f4 *(20.♘xe8 ♖xe8 21.♕h5 ♕d8, and black has two pieces for the rook and an overwhelming position).*

19...♗f7. Now white has to save his bishop, and he loses a pawn in the process.

20.♗d6 ♕xb2 21.♗xd5 ♗xd5 22.♖b1. This counterplay attempt is fatal, because black suddenly gets an opportunity to stage a mating attack. Still, white's position was lost anyway.

22...♕xd4 23.♖xb7.

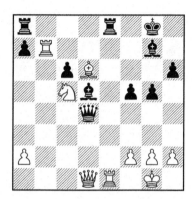

23...♕g4! An unexpected finishing maneuver.

24.f3 (or 24.♗g3 ♕xd1 and f5-f4) **24...♗d4+ 25.♔h1 ♗xf3!** White resigned: after 26.♖xe8+ ♖xe8 27.gxf3, there's a mate in two.

No. 6
Zubarev – Romanovsky
Moscow 1920, round 15

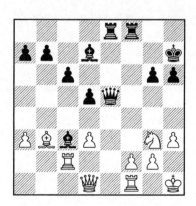

In a lost position, white decides to go for a combination: he thought he could win a piece.

27.f4?! ♖xf4 28.♖xf4 ♕xf4 29.♘e2 ♕f2! (this refutes his opponent's plan) **30.♘g1 ♕f6 31.♘f3.**

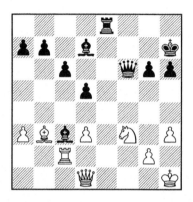

Abram Rabinovich "fanatically loved chess. Soon after the Olympiad, he moved to Moscow. He worked as an accountant in the porcelain trust, and then edited the chess column in Vechernaya Moskva for years." (Levenfish.) From the author's archive. Photo dates to 1937. Published for the first time.

31...♖e1+! "A very elegant ending to a very consistent game by black" (Alekhine).

32.♘xe1 ♕f1+ 33.♔h2 ♗e5+ 34.g3 ♕xh3+ 35.♔g1 ♗d4+ 36.♖f2 ♕xg3+ 37.♘g2 ♗xf2+. White resigned.

A Gift from Kubbel

There were some true endgame studies as well. In a book about Leonid Kubbel, the classic chess composer (published by Yakov Vladimirov and Yuri Fokin in 1984), I by chance came across a quote by one Leningrad player: "I remember how enraptured Kubbel was when he analyzed the queen play in the ending of the game Ilyin-Zhenevsky – Rabinovich at the 1920 All-Russian Chess Olympiad, and he said that we should admire it too. He classified this finish as a problem-like position."

No. 7
Ilyin-Zhenevsky – A. Rabinovich
Moscow 1920, round 3
Annotated by P. Romanovsky

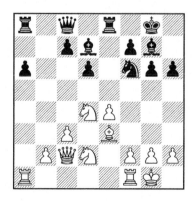

18.♖a5. The reason for the subsequent suffering. It was better to play 18.♖fe1, and the e4 pawn could be defended by various means.

Another good move was 18.f3, for instance: 18...d5 19.♘4b3 or 18...a5 19.c4 a4 20.♖fd1.

18...♕b7 19.f3 d5 20.♘4b3 dxe4 21.♘c5 ♕b6 22.♖fa1. 22.♘c4 ♕c6 23.♘xd7 ♘xd7 etc. was no better.

22...exf3   23.♖xa6   ♖xa6 24.♖xa6.

24...♗f5! *The exclamation mark was awarded by Romanovsky. Fritz thinks that the immediate 24...♕b5! 25.c4 ♕b4 was even stronger, for instance: 26.♖xf6 (26.♘xd7 ♘xd7 27.♖a4 ♕xb2 28.♕xb2 ♗xb2, winning) 26...♖xe3 27.♘d3 ♖xd3 28.♕xd3 ♗xf6 29.♕xd7 ♕b6+ etc.*

25.♕c1 ♕b5 26.c4 ♕b8. This queen manoeuvre was made to leave the d4 square unprotected by the pawn – this was necessary for a pretty finishing combination.

27.♘xf3 ♘g4.

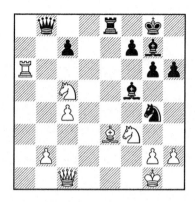

28.♗d4? *Of course 28.♗d2 was better, but then we wouldn't have seen this small masterpiece!*

28...♗xd4+   29.♘xd4   ♕xb2! White resigned: 30.♕d1 is met with 30...♕xd4+! *For a fuller picture, there's another line: 30.♕f1 ♕xd4+ 31.♕f2 ♖e1# or 31.♔h1 ♕f4 32.♕g1 ♖e1.*

The Gem of the Tournament

We end our compilation with another study-like finish. However, there were some pitfalls along the way for black...

No. 8

I. Rabinovich – Alekhine
Moscow 1920, round 13
Annotated by A. Alekhine

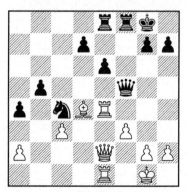

26...e5! Beginning a number of interesting complications. The bishop cannot capture the pawn because of 27...d5!, and the line 27.♗c5 d5 28.♖xc4 bxc4 29.♗xf8 ♕xf8 is better for black as well.

The cunning 28.♖d4!? is met with a spectacular rook sacrifice:

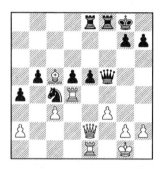

28...exd4!   29.♕xe8   ♖xe8 30.♖xe8+   ♔f7   31.♖f8+   ♔g6 32.♖xf5 dxc3!! 33.♖f4 c2 34.♖xc4 dxc4, and the bishop is helpless against the black pawn armada.

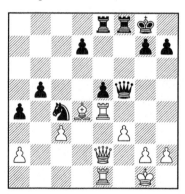

27.f4! Relatively best. White is counting on the line 27...d5 28.♖xe5 ♘xe5 29.♗xe5 with a defensible position.

27...d6. Defending the e5 pawn with a mate-in-2 threat after 28.fxe5 dxe5 29.♗xe5? ♘xe5 30.♖xe5 ♖xe5 31.♕xe5 ♕f2+.

28.h3. Again threatening the e5 pawn; black defends it indirectly.

28...♖e6! 29.fxe5 dxe5 30.♗c5! Not 30.♗xe5 ♖fe8 31.♖f1 ♕g6 32.♖xc4 ♖xe5!, and black wins.

The game move looks promising, because the black rook cannot leave the f-file. For instance: 30...♖d8 31.♖f1 ♕g6 32.♖g4 ♕h6 33.♕f3!, winning.

But the paradoxical trade of the queen for rook and bishop is stronger: 32...♕e8! 33.♖f8+ ♕xf8 34.♗xf8 ♖xf8, creating a kind of fortress.

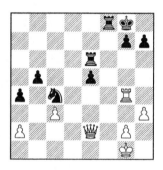

If white wants to destroy it with 35.♖xc4 bxc4 36.♕xc4, then after 36...♖ff6 37.♕xa4 e4 black will get good counterplay because of his passed pawn in the center.

30...♖f7! Beginning a combination to create a decisive attack. It was enough to play 30...♖ff6 for defense, because white can't play 31.♖b1 due to 31...♘d2!

31.♖b1. Regains the pawn, and the position is seemingly good, because now 31...♘d2 can be met with 32.♕xd2.

31...h6. Parrying the mating

threat and pulling my opponent even further along the dangerous path, where he loses.

32.♖xb5 ♘d2!

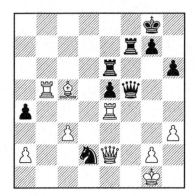

33.♖xa4. White has no defense. After 33.♖g4, black could play the same move as in the game, while after 33.♖e3 the finish would have been rather spectacular: 33...♖g6 (that's why black played ♖f7 rather than ♖f6 on move 30) 34.♖b8+ (34.♕xd2? ♕f1+ and ♕xb5) 34...♔h7 35.♖b2 (or 35.♕xd2 ♕f1+ 36.♔h2 ♖f2, winning) 35...♘f3+! 36.♔h1 ♕xh3+! etc.

However, 34.♖b8+ is obviously not the strongest move in this line. All white's woes are caused by the fact that the bishop does not control the f2 and g1 squares.

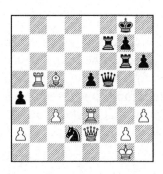

White still had chances to hold after 34.♖d3! ♕f1+ 35.♕xf1 ♖xf1+ 36.♔h2 ♖d1 37.♖b8+ ♔h7 38.♖dd8, getting some counterplay.

33...♕c2! After this move, which explains the sacrifice of two pawns, black wins, because the white rooks cannot defend the first rank.

34.♖b8+ ♔h7 35.♔h1 ♖f1+ 36.♗g1.

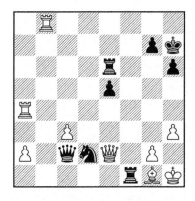

36...♖xg1+! (a pretty finish) **37.♔xg1 ♕c1+ 38.♔f2 ♖f6+ 39.♔e3** (39.♔g3 ♘f1+; now black either checkmates white or win the queen) **39...♘b1+!** White resigned.

The Shakhmaty magazine, publishing the game in 1924, was most complimentary in its assessment: "This deep, brilliant game by Alekhine, ending in a spectacular attack, was the best one in the tournament."

A Chervonets from the Proletarian Dictatorship

All-Russian Championship Tournament: Petrograd, 8th – 24th July 1923

"Stop it," the old woman said, "or is capitalism coming:
the soul parts with Soviet power.
We'll finish 'em off[9]: dry your eyes, will ya?"
Andrei Platonov. *Juvenile Sea*

Alekhine, leaving Russia in April 1921, didn't believe much in the country's chess future. Or maybe he didn't even believe in it at all. The picture he saw was too dreary. "In the latest news," he wrote in the aforementioned book *Chess Life in Soviet Russia*, "the chess players of Petrograd, Kazan and Kharkov have started to organize, but even there, as everywhere, everything depends on the personal influence of some government official – chess in Moscow flourished briefly solely because of Ilyin-Zhenevsky. It seems improbable that you can build something solid on such a precarious foundation." The foreword to the book of "Muscovy chess's ex-dictator" was written by Savielly Tartakower, and he mocked the efforts to introduce chess to the common folk in the same manner as potato cultivation: "Like the wild animals in the saga of Arion, the Bolshevik rulers proclaimed the coming of a chess miracle."

Pardon me, but what chess are you even talking about? As recently as in winter 1919, all the wooden houses in Petrograd had been dismantled for firewood, bread was rationed, the "contras" and illegal traders were shot on sight, and the requisition squads were sent to villages to find food for the dying cities... "Nothing like this Russian downfall has ever happened before. If it goes on for a year or so more the process of collapse will be complete. Nothing will be left of Russia but a country of peasants; the towns will be practically deserted and in ruins, the railways will be rusting in disuse." This is H.G. Wells, *Russia in the Shadows*. When was it written? October 1920. When the great sci-fi writer came to the Kremlin to meet Lenin, the All-Russian Chess Olympiad was in full swing...

Why, then, did the apocalypse not happen? Where did they get food for the shops, how did light and warmth return to the houses? How did printing houses return to work, how did they restart the trains? Why were restaurants and cinemas opening, one after another? How, after the *Listok Petrogubkommuny* folded, did Moscow and Petrograd almost simultaneously – in summer 1922 – start printing their own chess magazines? How did they

---

[9]   Referring to the bourgeoisie

manage to resurrect the All-Russian Chess Union and hold a new national championship a year later?

The Kronstadt sailors and Tambov peasants were the ones who saved the country from plunging into the depths of military communism. Powerful popular uprisings sobered up even the most zealous builders of the shining future. To save his power, the "Dreamer in the Kremlin" had to back down...

What were You Fighting for, Comrades?

Bogatyrchuk: "In March 1921, the Soviet citizens were stunned by the so-called New Economic Policy (NEP), which was proclaimed by Lenin out of the blue at the 10th VKP(b) *(i.e. Bolshevik)* conference. We couldn't believe our eyes. Essentially, NEP was a blatant return to the very capitalism that the Bolshevik "social" revolution fought against. Free trade was again legalized, hard currency was issued – the chervonets, equal to 10 golden rubles and backed by the State Bank gold reserve. *(The buying power of the chervonets can be demonstrated by the price of the* Shakhmaty *magazine in 1922: the October issue cost 2.5 million rubles, and the November one cost 40 golden kopecks!)*

We in Ukraine knew how quickly a country could bounce back after returning to capitalism, and we saw the same thing in Russia. NEP resurrected one of the most powerful stimuli of capitalism: private initiative. Shops and businesses popped up like mushrooms. Back then, the Russians could still believe the spoken word, so they took Lenin's assurances that NEP was here "for the long haul" at face value. Instead of many problems facing the blue and white collar workers, they now had only one: where to get the chervonets that could buy you anything. To maintain the exchange rate, the Soviet authorities had to limit the issuance of the currency, and so only well-connected government officials were well-paid; the common workers had to take work on the side to make ends meet...

While we all relished the reprieve given to us by NEP, the Bolsheviks used it to strengthen their police power over our citizens. On the surface, there was nothing dangerous. The Cheka (the secret police) was renamed the GPU (State Political Directorate), and the latter didn't show yet how strong its grip on all of us actually was...

In 1923, I was invited to take part in the Second All-Union chess championship in Petrograd. In addition to purely sporting interests, I wanted to take a look at the former capital, so I accepted the invitation.

How squalid the city of the "great" Lenin looked in comparison to Peter the Great's city I had seen a decade earlier! It was two years since NEP had been introduced, and you could only imagine how horrible it must have been before that. The shiny Nevsky Prospect, immortalized by Gogol, with its glittering shop windows, had turned into a mundane street, with the only difference between it and the main street of provincial towns being its great width. Where had the St. Petersburg citizens disappeared to, in their European clothes, with grammatically and syntactically correct speech? Instead of them, I saw poorly-dressed individuals, who spoke in an uneducated way and were always in a rush. The women's dresses struck me as especially wretched, only worn to cover their bodies with something. Many times, I wanted to walk to the middle of the street and scream heartrendingly, "What were you fighting for, comrades? This squalor?" The theaters were only finding their feet back then, and the repertoire was obviously chosen by censors. It was somewhat better with museums; however, even there the guides were instructed to emphasize the horrors of capitalism and the joys of life in a proletarian state. But here, the Bolsheviks at least couldn't draw a red tie on some Rembrandt character." (From the book *My Life Path to Vlasov and the Prague Manifesto*.)

We Need a New Union!

From the press: "In the last eight years, the chess art in Russia has declined significantly (no chess books have been printed since 1914, even though demand, especially among beginners, is great), which can chiefly be explained by the conditions and consequences of the imperial and civil wars; on the other hand, Russian chess players still cannot find a state organization which will take care of them. In 1920, Vsevobuch stepped in. Despite organizing the All-Russian Chess Olympiad, which caused a spike of interest in chess in the whole of Russia, Vsevobuch failed in its task, even though it did organize around 40 chess circles in Russia; due to a lack of funding, they all either folded or separated from Vsevobuch. Now each Russian city has 1 or 2 chess circles, which are relatively successful, but they are all organized haphazardly, depending on local conditions – mostly around party or professional organizations.

Bogatyrchuk: "After Soviet power won, chess life in Kiev got going as well. Chess players started to gather, hold tournaments, matches, etc. In 1920, Vsevobuch asked me to work as a chess organizer. They issued me with a warrant, and I went searching for a suitable building for our base... In the 4–5 months of our base's existence, we played a lot of tournaments and matches, even though they were all held in winter, in an unheated hall lit by oil lamps. Nobody even dreamed of asking for a vacation to play in a tournament. However, the base was short-lived: Vsevobuch was disbanded, and chess again lost its shelter.

In 1923, a group of chess players finally decided to self-organize. We got down to business and obtained permission to open a club, which existed for about a year..." (*64*, 5th January 1936.)

Only now, when the RSFSR is firmly on the way to peaceful economic and cultural development, does the question of revival and organization of chess life arise insistently." ("Shakhmatny Listok" in *Krasnaya Gazeta*, 6th December 1922. This was a separate section of the KG newspaper, which only appeared twice, and had nothing to do with the chess magazine of the same name.)

S. Vainstein: "The development of chess life in Russia has necessitated the issue of creating a single powerful organization to lead and control this life. The All-Russian Chess Union should be such an organization; it previously had more than 800 members and ceased to exist in the difficult war years. And Petrograd, as one of the main chess centers, needs to show some initiative. Traditions compel us, as well as seven years of work (1907–1914) to create the old union...

> **From the press:** "In just one decade (1905–1914), we witnessed a number of outstanding competitions: two international tournaments in 1909 and 1914 with the world's strongest players taking part, the All-Russian tournaments of 1905, 1909, 1911 and 1913, where new Russian maestros came to prominence, travels of those maestros abroad, to international tournaments, annual championship tournaments, matches with Moscow, publishing of many valuable chess books – that's the brilliant result of the work of energetic chess promoters whose names are unforgettable to any chess fan. B. E. Malyutin, brothers S. A. and E. A. Znosko-Borovsky, P. P. Saburov, Y. O. Sosnitsky, N. S. Tereschenko, and N. I. Maksimov, with friendly support from the capital city's chess players, managed to make the Petrograd assembly a focal point of all Russian chess life. The storm of world war and revolution destroyed the fruits of many years of labor. The generation that created a whole era in Russian chess life stepped off the stage. "Some are no longer with us, others are far away..." (*Listok Petrogubkommuny*, 9th October 1921.)

The most important goal for the young union should be organizing an <u>All-Russian tournament</u>, using efforts and funds from the whole of Russia. If this happens, the tournament won't be a random occurrence: it will be a true congress of Russian chess players that can be held periodically. In addition to this "high-profile" work, the union will have its daily work cut out. The union will have to open its branch offices in all cities with chess circles, organize oblast-level associations, as well as attract interest to chess by organizing simultaneous displays, lectures, and tours for our masters. We have to raise interest in chess problems and studies – this area of chess art is now in sharp decline. We also have to think about reviving correspondence chess, which was popular in Russia before. Finally, in those years of stagnation, new talents may have emerged, patiently waiting for their time to come, and the union should now find and help them...

Caption under the drawing: "S. O. Vainstein – the soul of all tournaments." Cartoon by N. Radlov, from his archive. Published for the first time in Krasnaya Gazeta (Leningrad, 7th September 1925).

In addition to domestic work, the union would have to do much on the external front. It's necessary to immediately resume international contacts – the union should declare an international problem and study composing competition and, at the same time, do everything that's necessary to send our masters abroad for tournaments. Inviting foreign masters to Russia is not out of the question either, and ideally, we need to hold an international tournament." (*Shakhmatny Listok*, September 1922.)

> Incredibly, all the plans on the "external front" came to fruition! They organized a problem and study competition, sent masters abroad, Lasker came to the USSR in January 1924, and Moscow hosted an international tournament with world stars taking part in late 1925.

Grekov: "Now that interest in chess has been spontaneously renewed, and the pulse of chess life is again noticeable all around Russia, when chess art has regained its important place in public life, it's imperative to pose the question of restoring the All-Russian Chess Union. Petrograd has again stepped in first. At the end of last year, the Bureau for Organization of the All-Russian Chess Union was created, chaired by the tireless S. O. Vainstein. Its efforts were quite energetic, and in just a few months it managed to gather about 700 chess players under its banner. *(By July 1923, that number had grown to 1,159.)*

The Bureau's work has been so productive that the 1st Congress of the All-Russian Chess Union is going to be held soon." (*Shakhmaty*, May 1923.)

Where is the "Chess Capital"?

The new Bureau of the All-Russian Chess Union included I. P. Golubev – the very same Vanya Golubev who procured extra food at the 1920 Olympiad in exchange for cigarettes. We will encounter him again several times in this book, but as an organizer and journalist. Information about him was dug up by St. Petersburg historian **Vadim Faibisovich** (in an article entitled "Luka Lukich and Uncle Vanya", e3e5.com website, 2019).

Ivan Petrovich Golubev was born in 1891 in St. Petersburg in a rich merchant's family ("by early 1917 his father owned seven shops and three rented out buildings on Vasilevsky Island"). He studied at the Polytechnic Institute and then served in the army. He participated in four city championships in the 1920s, and in a tournament in which Bogoljubov also participated (1925). A member of the editorial board of *Shakhmatny Listok*. He gave up playing in tournaments towards the end of the 1920s and became a professional chess administrator specializing in tournaments with a large number of players – such as the Leningrad vs Moscow "trade-union" matches (1930 and 1934), where battle was waged over several hundred boards. Shortly before the War began he completed All-Union courses for chess instructor-organizers, and in 1940 was appointed head of the circle in the Pioneers House of the Petrograd Region. He died in the first winter of the Siege, in January 1942...

Golubev: "On that memorable day of 7th July 1923, with representatives from 27 cities and many spectators gathered, the 1st Conference of the USSR Chess Union was opened in the Petrograd Chess Assembly.

A big point of principle! *Shakhmatny Listok* in Petrograd referred to the competition as the "Soviet Championship Tournament". However, the Moscow-based *Shakhmaty* (edited and published by Nikolai Grekov) referred to the new union and tournament as "All-Russian" and to the conference as a "congress", ignoring Romanovsky's instructions "about the ideological foundation on which chess art should be based". Should we wonder why the former magazine eventually turned into *Shakhmaty v SSSR*, while the latter one folded in the late 1920s?...

Ivan Golubev's best achievement was second place in the 1920 Petrograd championship, where he defeated I. Rabinovich and Levenfish. From V. Faibisovich's archive.

Greeting the esteemed guests, the chairman of the Chess Assembly board, Prof. B. M. Koyalovich, pointed to the immeasurable importance of this conference in the matters of uniting the chess players and developing the art of chess. Afterwards, I. P. Golubev greeted the conference on behalf of *Shakhmatny Listok* and, giving a short description of *Shakhmatny Listok's* efforts at dissemination of the idea of a Union and organizing this conference, expressed his hope that the "gates to Europe" would soon be opened for our best players. *(If only he knew how quickly these "gates" would be closed off for everyone except Botvinnik, and that in the mid-1930s even publishing chess problems in "bourgeois" magazines would be forbidden!)*

Then Tselikov, the chairman of the Moscow chess circle, and Krylov, representing Ivanovo-Voznesensk, cheerfully informed us of the rising popularity of chess among the common folk and military personnel, which makes chess not only a pastime (at times) for the rich, but also a source of mind development and horizon expansion for workers and peasants...

Visual propaganda, exhibit 1. Here's how two participants of the 1923 All-Russian tournament raised the popularity of chess "among the common folk and military personnel":

"On 11th September, a "living chess" game took place at the stadium of the foreign department of the Agricultural Exhibition. As far as we know, this is the fourth attempt to popularize chess in Russia in this way. The first such game was played back in 1921 in Smolensk, then Kerch repeated it this spring, and on 19th August, the "Immortal Game" between Anderssen and Kieseritzky was played out in Omsk; at the same time, this was a dramatization of the struggle between Labor (the "Reds" – playing white) and Capital (the "Whites" – playing black). In the event of one piece capturing another, they fought with bayonets or sabers, and the captured piece fell to the ground.

Leningrad, Uritsky Square, 20th July 1924. A "living chess" game between Peter Romanovsky (on the photo) and Ilya Rabinovich. The Red Navy in white sailor suits played against the Red Army. The moves were transmitted by phone and announced through a megaphone, so that all eight thousand spectators could hear them. The game ended in a draw on move 67.

Writing on the back of the award badge:
"To S. O. Vainstein, the organizer of the 1st All-Russian Chess Union conference and its first chairman, from the grateful tournament participants and congress delegates. 8th – 23rd July 1923." From M. Serebryansky's archive.

After the black king (Capital, wearing a top hat) got checkmated, all the black pieces fell, while the white pieces (the "Reds"), with cries of "Hurrah", ran up to the defeated king and posed as a living picture. Labor (the worker king), with hammer aloft, stands with his foot on the prostrate Capital, with white pieces all around him: Red Army soldiers (pawns), Red commanders (bishops), and a working woman (the queen).

In Moscow, Nenarokov and Grigoriev played an actual game, which started with the Sicilian Defense and lasted for 1 hour 10 minutes. Both armies wore costumes of two different eras, and horses (knights) and camels (rooks) were used as pieces. The moves were announced through a loud hailer, and "traffic controllers" showed each piece where to go." (*Shakhmatny Listok*, August 1923[10].)

Visual propaganda, exhibit 2, for export. "Petrograd. The State Porcelain Factory has produced a porcelain chess set symbolizing the proletariat's struggle against Tsarism (with workers in chains as pawns, etc.). At the end of April, the price for this artistic chess set was 3,000 rubles." (*Shakhmatny Listok*, April 1923).

---

[10] Publications often appeared late, allowing them to include later reports, hence the "August" issue reports an event from September

This chess set was made by the sculptor Natalia Danko. The "revolutionary" red color scheme represents the radiant world of work: the worker with a hammer as the king, the village girl with a bunch of field flowers as the queen, soldiers in early Red-Army *budenovka* hats as bishops, the horses (knights) are adorned with huge stars, there are stars with the Soviet insignia on the rooks as well, and pawns are peasant women with wheat sheaves and sickles in their hands. They are opposed by the decaying world of capital: Death in royal armor holding a bone-like scepter as the king, a half-naked woman with a sack of gold as the queen, handsome officers as bishops, the faces of the horses are hidden behind black masks, the rooks have sails that look like knights' shields with crests, and, finally, proletarians in chains as pawns (there were even sets with African workers as pawns!). In the first sets produced, the trousers and cap of the hammer-wielding king were checkered, and his shirt was covered with pictures of chess pieces...

The visual propaganda was striking, but the only people who could actually *buy* these "propaganda" or "agitation" chess sets, which were mostly sold for export, were "NEPmen" or rich foreigners. To put its price in context, the winner of the All-Russian tournament received 4 chervonets, or 3,200 rubles – just enough to buy one set!

This conference will be the foundation to build the Union; the sustainability and range of activities of this Union depend on its effectiveness. If the Union is to exist as an independent organization, we cannot be sure about its future, because its activity will be fully dependent on the Union leaders' enthusiasm. To avoid this abnormal situation, we should strive to include chess in the government structures *(as you remember, Alekhine said the same thing after the Olympiad)*. The year 1920, when Vsevobuch managed to organize chess circles all around Russia and held the All-Russian tournaments at the peak of hunger, is an ideal we should strive to observe. So, we welcome the Moscow chess players' talks with the All-Union Central Council of the Trade Unions (VtsSPS) to create chess sections everywhere, but we will merge with the trade unions only if they are able to satisfy our minimal demands. For now, at the 1st Conference, we should prepare the grounds for the 2nd Conference and do everything in our power to raise the status of chess. Currently, the Union has 32 branches with 1,159 members. If the whole mass of chess players joins the Union, it will gain ideological foundation and material sustainability, which, in turn, will show its cultural necessity and bring it closer to state support...

After discussing the new Union's charter, the new board was elected. It consisted of S. O. Vainstein (chairman), P. A. Romanovsky (1st secretary), I. P. Golubev (treasurer) from Petrograd; N. D. Grigoriev (deputy chairman), Panchenko and Geiler (secretaries) from Moscow; A. A. Alekhine from Kharkov *(Alexei Alekhine)*, Shukevich-Tretyakov from Minsk, and Diakonov from Saratov. The conference also decreed Petrograd to be considered the chess "capital" until the next conference.

> **Grekov:** "The topic of the "chess capital" – should Moscow or Petrograd be named as such? – was hotly debated. It was decreed to leave Petrograd as the Union's administrative center and defer the resolution until the 2nd Congress, planned for summer next year in Moscow." (*Shakhmaty*, August 1923.)

Finally, we should mention the beautiful idea by N. P. Tselikov – to visit the grave of M. I. Chigorin and there, at the Volkovo Cemetery, pay tribute to the person who first brought up the idea of a union, and whose behest we follow as best we can." (*Shakhmatny Listok*, July 1923).

FROM THE CONFERENCE PROGRAM

A. Championship Tournament

Maestros and first-rate Russian players who formally do not have this title may take part. The winner is awarded the title of RSFSR Champion (until the next conference) and is sent to an international tournament within a year, with the Union's support...

The number of competitors is 12 *(ultimately, 13 players took part)*. The prizes are 4, 3, 2, and 1 chervonets. Travel costs are covered by local organizations. To compensate the living costs in Petrograd, all players from other cities receive a sum equal to 1.5 chervonets. The visitors can be accommodated for free in the apartments of Petrograd players...

Playing time is 7 hours a day, 6 to 10 p.m. and 11 p.m. to 2 a.m. The play-off days for adjourned games are after rounds 5 and 10. Time regulation: 2 hours for the first 30 moves, 1 hour for each subsequent 15 moves.

If at least six maestros take part, the non-maestro prizewinners are awarded the USSR maestro title...

B. Tournament of the Strongest Amateurs

The strongest local amateur players may take part, mostly champions of provincial towns and prizewinners in tournaments of big centers. Priority is given to players whose nominations are supported by organizations...

The winner of the amateur tournament is awarded the USSR maestro title, which he must defend in one of the subsequent championship tournaments...

From the press: "Invitations to the championship tournament were sent to *(masters in italics)*: G. Y. Levenfish, I. L. Rabinovich and P. A. Romanovsky (Petrograd), N. D. Grigoriev, F. I. Duz-Khotimirsky, N. M. Zubarev, A. F. Ilyin-Zhenevsky *(he had already moved to Petrograd by the time of the tournament)* and V. I. Nenarokov (Moscow); from other cities: Arv. Kubbel (Yamburg), F. P. Bogatyrchuk (Kiev), K. A. Vygodchikov (Smolensk, *as the winner of the amateur tournament of the 1920 Olympiad*), S. M. Levitsky (Nizhneturinsky Factory, Ekaterinburg gubernia), A. A. Smorodsky (Tiflis), S. N. Freymann (Tashkent). The first reserve is S. K. Rosenthal (Minsk), and the second reserve is Y. S. Vilner (Odessa).

The top four players of the All-Russian tournament shared two such banknotes between them: 4 (i.e. for first place) +3+2+1 = 10 chervonets in total

There were more than 50 applications for the amateurs' tournament..."
(*Shakhmatny Listok,* June 1923).

The Tournament through the Eyes of an Amateur

Almost half a century later, the Riga magazine *Shakhmaty* (No. 20, 1970) published the recollections of one of the amateur tournament participants, M. Segal from Kazan. Since both tournaments were held in the same hall, he could come to the masters' tables and watch their games.

M. Segal: "As a true provincial, I arrived just three days before the tournament, but everything was ready. I registered quite quickly and went to the dormitory of one of the Petrograd colleges, I think it was the Technological Institute, which was empty in the summer. I was settled in a good, clear room. I lived there alone for a day and a half. When other players arrived, Kutuzov lodged with me. He was a nice, quiet companion, we were on friendly terms.

The accommodation was good, but food was another matter. NEP was in full swing. There were fashionable restaurants around, but I didn't dare to go there. The meals in some private cafeteria did consist of three courses, but they were all frankly a joke... The food improved only after S. O. Vainstein reached an agreement with the Dominik restaurant, and we received standard

Petrograd, 1923. The participants of the All-Russian Championship Tournament and the strongest amateurs tournament. Sitting (left to right): K. Vygodchikov (Smolensk), V. Nenarokov, N. Zubarev (both Moscow), F. Bogatyrchuk (Kiev), A. Ilyin-Zhenevsky, P. Romanovsky (both Petrograd), Y. Vilner (Odessa), G. Levenfish, I. Rabinovich, S. Vainstein (all Petrograd). Standing, first row: I. Lebedev (Kostroma), N. Krylov (Ivanovo-Voznesensk), N. Grigoriev (Moscow), N. Shesterikov (Saratov), B. Verlinsky (Moscow), A. Kubbel (Yamburg), N. Sorokin (Kiev), L. Travin (Slutsk), A. Iglitsky (Odessa), G. Burmistrov (Krasnodar). Standing, second row: G. Lastovets (Poltava), F. Duz-Khotimirsky (Moscow), P. Komarov (Novo-Nikolaevsk), A. Sergeyev (Serpukhov), V. Sozin (Novgorod), K. Lerner (Odessa), N. Kutuzov (Arkhangelsk), M. Segal (Kazan). (Shakhmaty, No. 7–8, 1923).

meals there during the day. However, the Dominik meals were too expensive for some players, and I saw them eating plain white bread between games.

The delegation from Moscow arrived shortly before the start of the tournament: the charming N. P. Tselikov, the famous N. D. Grigoriev, B. M. Verlinsky, whom I'd also heard of for some time already, A. S. Sergeyev (the eventual tournament winner), sparkling with health, Panchenko, and Slonim. Tselikov, who died recently, was well built and full of strength back then. He organized a guided tour of Petrograd.

Boris Markovich Verlinsky took part in the tour as well. Even back then, he wasn't particularly healthy or robust. The tour proved to be too much for him, and he felt unwell in the evening. Vainstein asked me to escort Verlinsky to our dormitory. You may think that helping a comrade to walk (public transport was no option) was a very simple thing. But it was not so.

We would frequently sit down and rest. As any hearing-impaired person, Verlinsky couldn't control his voice: he would speak in almost a whisper, and then he would scream, tell something very expressively, waving hands. He spoke of things completely alien to laymen: kings, elephants *('slony', the Russian word for bishops)*, and horses, which went somewhere and punched someone. The evening was warm, many people walked by, and we attracted a lot of attention each time we stopped, some even pointing at us. I feared it wouldn't end well if we met a policeman. Verlinsky, of course, never noticed anything and continued talking about chess games or his unfortunate life. He regretted moving to Moscow too late, said that "Odessa is a grammar school, and Moscow is a university", that it's now too late to achieve the things he dreamed of. I think that he was wrong in this regard. At least two triumphs awaited him in the future: winning the 6th Soviet Championship and defeating Capablanca at the 1925 Moscow International Tournament. Finally, to my great relief, we reached our dormitory.

All games were held in the same hall, with tables arranged in a U-pattern; masters sat along one of the sides. We could freely approach their tables. I've never enjoyed such a privilege since.

I vividly remember F. I. Duz-Khotimirsky, a young man back then; he came almost an hour late to his game, but still couldn't help but chat a bit with his friends. I'll forever remember A. F. Ilyin-Zhenevsky's spectacular arrival with his wife: they entered the hall shortly before the official part started. They had just returned from abroad. Now, on such a momentous occasion, there would be a lot of people in fine clothes, but back then, with very few exceptions, our clothes were very modest, and they, in their foreign attire, stood out sharply among the others. Ilyin-Zhenevsky was well-beloved, and everyone greeted him warmly.

I had a striking impression of G. Y. Levenfish. He was 35 then *(34, in fact)*. Tall, rugged, well-built, probably a strong man. I felt energy radiating from him. I watched him play a well-known opening (the Two Knights Defense with a bishop sacrifice on h2) against I. L. Rabinovich. I remember how S. M. Flohr wrote about one of his games against Alekhine that he almost physically sensed the strength of his game. I had a similar feeling on this occasion.

Many years have passed since then, but I still remember the scene well. Levenfish was sitting relatively far from the table, and he stooped to lean on it. His black bishop had just captured the h2 pawn. Rabinovich, by contrast,

---

[11]   One of the Russian words for capture in chess is *"pobit"*, literally "to punch" – *Translator*

sat very close to the table. Of course, he knew how dangerous his position was. He was clearly anxious and intently searched for a way to extricate himself. I never saw Levenfish again, but I looked through his games many times, and the more I study his games, the more I like his playing style.

I also remember the three Kubbel brothers well. I first saw them in the hall before the tournament. I recognized Leonid Ivanovich from the photos. Someone from Petrograd, knowing that I'm from another town, showed me the other two brothers, too. The older brother, Arvid Ivanovich, played in the masters tournament. He was one head taller than anyone in the crowd. A. I. looked very respectable and even a bit cold. However, I once heard how he told something to his friends, in a very informal tone, and I understood that A. I. was actually a very simple and sweet man.

It was interesting to watch S. F. Lebedev (Simbirsk). A vigorous, mobile man despite his gray hair, he didn't look like an old man at all. He was one of the few surviving players of the old chess Russia. I knew that he wasn't a pleasant man, so I was somewhat wary of talking to him. However, everything went well, and Lebedev even praised me for the game I won against Slonim...

I regret that I didn't take more opportunities to watch the masters' games more closely, but I must say that we had to play three rounds and the adjournment sessions in two days, so there were only a few opportunities to watch others' games or walk around Petrograd."

The Malaria Victim

Grekov: "The All-Russian championship tournament and the tournament of the strongest amateurs were held simultaneously with the congress. Almost all the best Russian players were invited; some of them, unfortunately, were absent, for instance, Blumenfeld, A. Rabinovich, Freymann and Smorodsky. Levitsky came to Petrograd, but fell very ill on the way and couldn't take part.

> **From the press:** "Maestro S. M. Levitsky was very ill when he arrived at the tournament. Suffering from a stomach illness *(stomach cancer)* for two years, he had felt ill back in Ekaterinburg, where he gave a blindfold 6-board simultaneous display; as soon as he got to Petrograd, he was sent to the Mariinskaya hospital, where he stayed until 28th July... A fundraiser was held on the day of the general conference, yielding 1,148 rubles, which were all given to him. On 25th July, F. I. Duz-Khotimirsky gave a 24-board simultaneous display and donated all proceeds to the sick maestro as well." (*Shakhmatny Listok*, July 1923.)

Even in his hospital bed, Stepan Mikhailovich was very interested in the tournament's progress and managed to play some casual games. Then, "due to an improvement in his health, doctors advised him to go back home to the Urals" (*Izvestia*, 12th August 1923). But remission did not last for long, and he died on 3rd April 1924...

The main sporting question was, of course, who was going to win the championship. In the "chess spheres" of Moscow and Petrograd, it was thought that the main favorites were Petrograd maestros G. Y. Levenfish and I. L. Rabinovich, and Moscow maestro V. I. Nenarokov. To some extent, the tournament was considered a battle between those "matadors", made even more interesting by the fact that Nenarokov had never played his Petrograd rivals before. However, as often happens, there were many surprises at the tournament, and many predictions turned out to be wrong...

Levenfish's first-round win against Romanovsky went more or less unnoticed – nobody thought that this would be the only defeat of the future Russian champion *(see game 13)*. The games between the "favorites" were eagerly awaited. They took place in rounds 5 and 8, and Nenarokov defeated both his opponents with deep positional play *(including game 10)*. It might have seemed that Nenarokov, who had already played the hardest games and had not suffered a single defeat, was poised to win the tournament – but this was not to be; circumstances that have nothing to do with chess played a role.

Golubev: "The Moscow lion (Nenarokov) was very strong in the first half of the tournament, but then his strength fell drastically. The form of malaria he suffered from played a cruel joke on him, and we can only marvel at the phenomenal tenacity shown by the likable player: that he still managed to complete the tournament. His tenacity helped

The "Moscow lion" Vladimir Nenarokov enjoyed a great start, but a bout of chronic malaria pushed him down the table. (64, No. 1, 1924.)

him to play a hundred-move game despite his illness; he kept his cool even after undeserved losses. Such wonderful self-control should be recommended to most of us." (*Shakhmatny Listok*, July 1923.)

Meanwhile, P. A. Romanovsky wins one game after another following that first loss and ultimately finishes first!" (*Shakhmaty*, August 1923.)

Romanovsky: "Throughout the first half of the year, I played in first-category tournaments, training games, matches, etc. The abundance of practice mobilized my strength, and, even though I was behind most of my opponents in opening theory, I considered myself well-prepared for the championship. I also put a lot of focus on my daily routine during the tournament, it was very strict and monotonous. The distance between my flat and the tournament hall was roughly four and a half kilometers. The rounds started at 6 p.m., and I got to the venue by foot, leaving home an hour and a quarter before the game *(so, that's who Botvinnik's role model was!)*. I would regularly get up at 10 in the morning. On the game days, I wouldn't touch chess at all at home, didn't prepare specifically for the next game, and chose the opening after sitting at the board if I had white.

I was physically very well, played without much strain, and I didn't feel exhausted after the championship despite the tight schedule: there was only one rest day for the entire championship." (From his book *Selected Games*.)

If only you knew what an outstanding personality hid behind this ascetic "self-portrait"! We'll meet Romanovsky many more times on this book's pages, but for now I'll show you a "slice of life" description by **Yakov Rokhlin** – a well-known chess master and organizer in his own right, the man who coined the quote supposedly attributed to Lenin "Chess is the gymnastics of the mind":

"I first got to know Romanovsky in spring 1923. He was a man of rare, natural talent, an artist and teacher by calling, he managed to rally a big group of young, knowledge-hungry chess players around himself... I remember his energetic figure, wearing a sweatshirt, always with a cigarette between his teeth. To me, he looked like a hero of the new times, a bit like Rakhmetov from *What Is To Be Done?*

...In the summer, he would move, together with his family, to his small dacha at Krestovsky Island, which in the evenings turned into the "headquarters" of young chess fans, where his wife and three daughters were the perfect hostesses. We were usually met by a boiling samovar and fresh "French" buns either on the veranda or in the lounge, but visitors had to bring their own sugar (back then, food supply in Piter *(Petrograd)* was still shaky). We would get to Krestovsky Island by bicycle, usually without telling him in advance – there was no phone at the dacha, but the cheerful host was always glad to welcome guests." (*Shakhmaty v SSSR* No. 4, 1977.)

Golubev: "Our champion P. A. Romanovsky showed great composure and special tournament skills, which, coupled with his combinational talent and great endgame knowledge, brought him the deserved victory. P. A.'s tournament qualities will surely prove even more useful when he gets to travel abroad.

G. Y. Levenfish, the 1922 Petrograd champion, took second place. He's a player of an original, distinct style, close to the modern, which, for some reason, didn't quite

Peter Romanovsky. "He was a man of rare, natural talent, an artist and teacher by calling, he managed to rally a big group of young, knowledge-hungry chess players around himself." (Rokhlin.) From the brochure International Chess Tournament in Moscow, 1925, and its Participants.

manifest itself in this tournament. A couple of poor games, with a veneer of tiredness, pushed G. Y. back to second place, which he took deservedly, finishing 1.5 points (!) ahead of his competitors."

A Gift from Black Earth

Grekov: "I. L. Rabinovich's performance was unexpectedly poor – he's a strong player who should have been competing for one of the top places. N. D. Grigoriev, the Moscow champion, recorded a poor start and couldn't achieve a good result afterwards; however, Grigoriev's play had also been inconsistent before, and so we might expect him to take a higher place in subsequent tournaments. We could also expect more from N. M. Zubarev.

Ilyin-Zhenevsky: "Zubarev is a very interesting and strong chess player. He has a rounded chess talent. He tends to play defensively, but doesn't shun aggressive chess either, has a good understanding of complicated positions, and if he gets an attack, it's usually well thought-out and energetic." (From the book *International Chess Tournament in Moscow.*)

Maestro F. I. Duz-Khotimirsky, whose performance at recent Moscow tournaments was quite poor, exceeded expectations. A. I. Kubbel, as at the 1920 Olympiad, showed solid playing strength and proved that he's a dangerous adversary for anyone over the board.

Ilyin-Zhenevsky: "Stylistically, Duz is one of the sharpest chess players. His element is difficult and complicated positions, which he plays very well. Unfortunately, his interesting and inventive play is often marred by his eccentricity, which manifests itself both in everyday life and at the board. In life, because of his funny demeanor and anarchist leanings, he has occasionally got into absurd situations. In chess, he has often got carried away by some original, but wrong idea and thrown away well-played, sometimes even won games."

Fyodor Duz-Khotimirsky "Stylistically, Duz is one of the sharpest chess players. His element is difficult and complicated positions." (Ilyin-Zhenevsky.) (64. Shakhmaty i Shashki v Rabochem Klube, No. 24, 1925).

The performance of the young Kiev player Fyodor Parfenyevich Bogatyrchuk deserves special mention. A relatively unknown player, who, because he lives in the provinces, rarely plays in big tournaments, F. P. earned the coveted maestro title and, what's even more important, played a number of great games. Despite his almost total lack of practice, he successfully fought against experienced tournament players, because he had a weapon more powerful than experience and technique: <u>chess talent</u>.

Golubev: "Bogatyrchuk is a mighty gift from Little Russia's *(Ukraine's)* Black Earth region, who is able to crush his opponents in attack, but lacks the proper training in endgames and patience in defense. Years of experience, coupled with great love for chess and natural talent, should turn him into a world-class player. He was the only one to win the maestro title – and he was the only one who deserved it."

Bogatyrchuk: "My attacking style, which I'd cultivated since 1910, finally came to fruition at this tournament. I gained the master's title, and many people enjoyed my enterprising play. The chess critic I. Golubev referred to me as a "mighty gift from Little Russia's Black Earth region." You just can't put it any better!"

Fyodor Bogatyrchuk was the only player to earn a maestro's title at this championship. (64. Shakhmaty i Shashki v Rabochem Klube, No. 24, 1925.)

Concurrently, the tournament of the strongest amateurs was held, featuring 36 players divided into three groups..." (*Shakhmaty*, August 1923.)

Golubev: "Looking at its winners, we should immediately point out the big blunder of those who like to predict the standings before the tournament begins. As unexpectedly as he won the South-Russian tournament in 1910, Verlinsky took second place this time. The happy winner of the tournament, maestro Sergeyev, made a good impression with his style. He lacks brilliancy in attack, perhaps, but he understands the position quite well, and this alone is proof of his playing strength..." (*Shakhmatny Listok*, July 1923.)

DISTRIBUTION OF PRIZES

Before the very start of the conference, a number of special prizes and donations arrived, the biggest of which were these:

1.   20,000 rubles (25 chervonets) from the USSR Central Executive Committee.

2.   30 chess books from the prominent German philanthropist and book publisher Bernhard Kagan from Berlin *(he was the one who published Alekhine's book* Chess Life in Soviet Russia*)*.

3.   2 debentures from L. K. Veman (Novo-Nikolaevsk).

This allowed them to increase the prizes for the championship tournament and distribute them in the following way:

First: the USSR Champion title, 4 chervonets and a silver watch – to P. A. Romanovsky.

Second: 3 chervonets – to G. Y. Levenfish.

Third, fourth, fifth: 2,000, 1,500 and 1,000 rubles were shared by F. P. Bogatyrchuk, F. I. Duz-Khotimirsky and V. I. Nenarokov...

From the press: "During the tournaments, numerous interesting photos were taken by photographers from periodicals including *Pravda, Krasnaya Panorama* and *Ogonyok*. You can obtain them through the *Sh. L.* editor's office for 60 golden kopecks – 1 golden ruble per piece plus delivery costs. The tournament reports are printed in all Petrograd newspapers.

On 24th July, the awards ceremony was held, and the conference was closed. Afterwards, in a private apartment (all restaurants were closed that day), a farewell party was arranged, which lasted until morning." (*Shakhmatny Listok*, July 1923.)

Beauty is a Fearsome Power

Even though *Shakhmatny Listok* reported that "a decision was taken to publish the conference's games, further information on the nature of the collection and preorder conditions shall be revealed at a later date," the book never materialized, and even fewer games survived from this championship than from the All-Russian Olympiad: just 30. You can't call it anything other than horrible mismanagement: the country had already recovered from the Civil War collapse, and, unlike 1920, when there were no chess periodicals, two professional chess magazines were active in 1923.

Thankfully, best games with annotations by the winners were still published. Let's begin with the top three brilliancy prizes.

First Brilliancy Prize:
2 debentures and a chess book

In this game, Romanovsky, by his own words, "had to face Alekhine's brilliant opening discovery." In the next championship, he tried this defense for black, but got under attack; even though he even managed to win *(see game 23)*, Peter Arsenyevich admitted later, "For some time, I have preferred to play the Alekhine Defense with white – I'm much better at it."

No. 9. Alekhine Defense B02
Romanovsky – Vilner
Petrograd 1923, round 8
Annotated by P. Romanovsky

1.e4 ♘f6 2.d3. By playing this move, you can't count on any opening advantage. But I knew that 2.e5 led to sharp lines that were studied by my opponent by some degree, so I decided to avoid that move.

2...d5 *(2...e5 3.f4 ♘c6! 4.♘f3 d5! Maroczy – Alekhine, New York 1924)* **3.e5 ♘fd7 4.f4 e6 5.♘f3 ♗e7.** Vilner's playing style was enterprising, he liked sharp positions with combination opportunities. He doesn't want to play the prophylactic move c7-c5, and instead waits until I play d3-d4, before playing the pawn break c7-c5, like in the French Defense. White follows his lead.

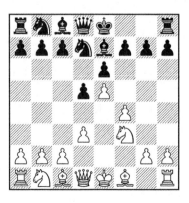

6.d4. If I liked some move during concrete calculations, I made it without thinking about whether it led to a tempo loss or violated some other positional principles. My observations show that this trait of my play caused my opponents the most trouble.

6...c5 7.c3 ♘c6 8.♗e2 ♕b6 9.0-0 f6! Vilner doesn't go for the "combination" 9...cxd4 10.cxd4 ♘xd4 11.♘xd4 ♗c5 12.♗e3 ♕xb2 13.♕d2! ♕xa1, since after 14.♘c3 white wins material.

10.♔h1 0-0 11.b3.

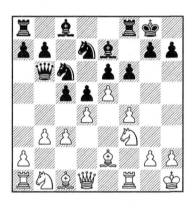

11...a5. Black overlooks the combined center and kingside attack by white. He should have eliminated tension in the center with two trades – cxd4 and fxe5, and only then gone for queenside diversions.

The exchange sacrifice for two pawns also led to sharp play with mutual chances: 11...cxd4 12.cxd4 fxe5 13.fxe5 ♖xf3 14.♗xf3 ♕xd4 15.♕xd4 ♘xd4 16.♗d1 ♘xe5 etc.

12.♗a3! ♖e8. *Romanovsky didn't annotate this move at all. However, black had an opportunity to defuse* *the situation: 12...fxe5 13.fxe5 cxd4 14.♗xe7 ♘xe7 15.cxd4 ♘f5 16.♕d2 ♘b8, intending ♘c6 and ♗d7.*

13.♗d3 f5? And this is a fatal mistake. Black had to play 13...♘f8, putting up with the trade 14.exf6 gxf6 as a necessary evil.

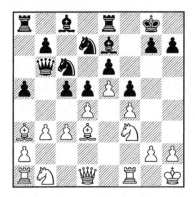

14.g4! ♘f8. It was no better to play either 14...fxg4 15.♘g5 ♗xg5 16.fxg5 cxd4 17.♕xg4 with a crushing attack, or 14...g6 15.gxf5 gxf5 16.♖g1+ ♔h8 17.♘g5 ♗xg5 18.♖xg5 cxd4 19.♕h5 ♕d8 20.♘d2 ♖g8 21.♖xg8+ ♕xg8 22.♖g1, winning.

15.gxf5 exf5 16.c4 ♗e6 17.cxd5 ♗xd5 18.♘c3! White sacrifices a pawn to make his attack even stronger *(18.♗xf5? ♘xd4).*

18...♗xf3+ 19.♕xf3 ♘xd4 20.♘d5 ♕d8. After 20...♘xf3 21.♘xb6 black lost the exchange. It's easy to see that everything was forced from move 14.

21.♕g2. White has a very strong position in the center, the bishop pair, a strong passed pawn and open lines to attack the opponent's queen and king for the sacrificed pawn.

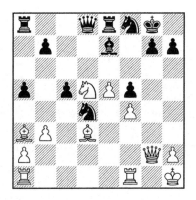

21...b5. Inventive! Black threatens ♖a8-a6-g6. 21...♖c8 was noted as the strongest move, however, after 22.♘e3 ♕d7 23.♖ad1, the f5 pawn falls.

22.♖ad1! Preparing the finishing combination. Black can't save the game. Some commentators recommended 22...♔h8 as a possible defense, but this is met with 23.♗b2 ♘fe6 24.♘e3, and white, attacking the b5 and f5 pawns, wins one of them, keeping a significant positional advantage.

22...♖a6 23.♘f6+! ♗xf6 24.♗xc5 ♘fe6. *It seems that only this move was the decisive mistake. In Fritz's opinion, black could still hold with 24...♗xe5! 25.fxe5 ♖g6 (the gun loaded on move 21 finally fires!) 26.♕b7 ♖c6!*

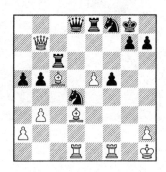

27.♗d6!   *(27.♗xd4?*   ♕*d5+ 28.♔g1 ♖g6+, and black wins!) 27... ♕c8 28.♕xc8 ♖cxc8 etc.*

25.♗xd4   ♘**xd4**   (25...♕xd4 26.♗xb5 is completely crushing) **26.♗xb5.** White is a piece down, but four (!) black pieces are hanging, and he loses a rook at the very least. Vilner prefers to give up the queen for a rook and bishop, but black's pieces are so poorly positioned that new losses are unavoidable.

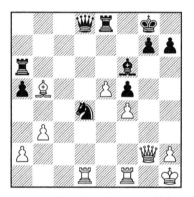

26...♘xb5 *(the alternative is no better: 26...♗xe5 27.♗xe8 ♗f6 28.♖fe1 ♖b6 29.♗a4)* **27.♖xd8 ♖xd8** (or 27...♗xd8 28.♕d5+) **28.♕b7!** This is stronger than 28.exf6 because it keeps the passed e-pawn on the board

28...♘c7 (28...♖a7 29.♕xb5 is hopeless as well) **29.♕xc7.** Black resigned.

Second Brilliancy Prize: a metallic watch from Petrosovet

Many consider this game, not the previous one, to be the best in the championship; it caused heated polemics in the press. In response to Nenarokov's annotations in *Shakhmaty*, Levenfish from Petrograd printed the game in *Shakhmatny Listok* – a reflection of the old struggle between Moscow

Sitting: Bogatyrchuk, Nenarokov, Vilner, S. Vainstein and I. Rabinovich. Standing: left – Romanovsky and Ilyin-Zhenevsky, right – Grigoriev. Photo by A. Bulla (Petrograd, No. 5, 1923).

and Petersburg-Petrograd for leadership in Russian (and then Soviet) chess. Nenarokov from Moscow picked up the gauntlet... and tore Levenfish's work apart, piece by piece: "Even a cursory glance shows that G. Y. Levenfish's analysis is rife with serious mistakes, and the "new annotations" cast the wrong light onto the game."

So, let's see who was closer to the truth. In a historical context, the game is very interesting because it was quite topical back then. Shortly afterwards, *Shakhmaty* printed Nimzowitsch's thought piece "'Losing the center' is a preconception". Here's a quote from the afterword: "Especially instructive for the "philosophy of the center" is the game Nenarokov – Rabinovich, where white first "helped" black to create an "arithmetically" powerful center, and then upset black's position and won the game in a brilliant way... It's better to have no center than a weak one, but it's better to have a strong center than no center!"

No. 10. Queen's Pawn Game A45
Nenarokov – I. Rabinovich
Petrograd 1923, round 5
Annotated by V. Nenarokov

1.d4 e6 2.c3 ♞f6 3.♗g5 b6 4.♞d2 ♗b7 5.♕c2 c5. Black's development system with c7-c5 is hardly satisfactory. The resulting pawn structure is not solid enough and vulnerable to white's attacks.

6.e3 ♗e7 7.♞gf3 ♞c6.

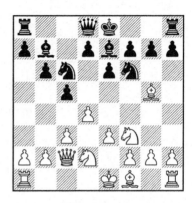

8.dxc5! Black probably didn't consider the consequences of this move, because at first glance he gets a strong pawn center. However, as the course of the game shows, white can weaken and break down this center.

8...bxc5. After 8...♗xc5, black's center is still weak, because 9...d5 can be met with 10.♖d1, threatening to push the e-pawn.

Levenfish: "White's previous move, weakening the center, was dubious, but now it pays off: after d7-d5, black gets hanging, awkward c5 and d5 pawns. It was better and calmer to play 8...♗xc5 9.♗e2 (9.♞e4 ♞b4! 10.cxb4 ♗xe4 11.♕c4 ♗d5) 9...d5 10.0-0 ♗e7 11.♖ad1 ♕c8 with a great position."

Nenarokov: "Instead of the passive and weak 9.♗e2?, it was easy to play 9.♗d3, the move I made in the actual game.

The position changes significantly. White threatens to eventually play e3-e4, and it's enough to look at the board to see who actually has a "great" position."

9.♗d3 does look more active. 1–0 to Nenarokov.

9.♗d3 h6 10.♗h4 d5 11.0-0 0-0 12.♖ad1.

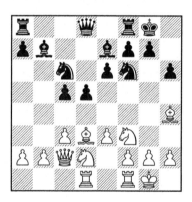

12...♘d7. Probably the best move. Black can't play 12...e5 13.e4 d4 because of 14.♗b5!, threatening ♗xc6 and ♘xe5. Black has no good defense, for instance: 14...♘d7 15.♗xc6 ♗xc6 16.♗xe7 ♕xe7 17.cxd4 exd4 18.♘xd4 or 14...♕c7 15.♗g3 ♗d6 (15...♘d7? 16.cxd4 etc.) 16.♘c4!, and black loses material.

13.♗xe7 ♕xe7 14.e4 d4. Any other move is met with 15.exd5, weakening the black pawns.

Levenfish: "This move is not well thought-out. Black tries for a c5, d4, e5 structure, but this proves to be impossible, and black's center becomes very shaky."

Nenarokov: "The commentator does not show any "well thought-out" moves, and it's easy to see why: the only way to avoid the threat exd5 is to play d5-d4."

The computer, after a bit of thought, also prefers 14...d4. 2–0 to Nenarokov.

15.♗b5! Preventing 15...e5, which will be met with 16.♗xc6 ♗xc6 17.cxd4 exd4 18.♘xd4, winning a pawn.

15...♖fc8 16.♗xc6 ♗xc6.

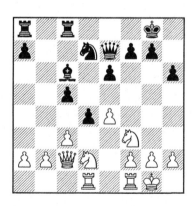

17.e5! White's plan turns out to be correct: black's center is crumbling, while white will retain the strong central e5 pawn.

17...♖ab8 18.♖fe1. If 18.b3, intending cxd4 and ♕b2, then 18...♗b5 19.♖fe1 d3 20.♕c1 c4, and white's queenside is compromised.

Levenfish: "A serious mistake that deprives white of all the advantage. 18.b3 was correct, and if 18...♗b5 19.♖fe1 d3 20.♕c1 c4, then 21.♘xc4 ♗xc4 22.bxc4 ♘c5 23.♕a3 ♕b7 24.♖d2, and white, threatening ♘f3-d4-b5, retains his extra pawn."

Nenarokov: "What's possible in bad analysis is impossible when playing against a strong opponent.

Indeed, what would I have done had Rabinovich, instead of Levenfish's suicidal move 23...♕b7??, shutting down both black rooks, just played 23...♖b6 here, threatening ♖cb8 and ♖a6? Perhaps I could still have achieved a draw, but certainly nothing more, for instance: 24.♘d4! ♖a6 25.♕b2 ♖b6, etc."

Fritz and Junior, as if by prior agreement, offer a healthy compromise – they consider both the "suicidal" 23...♕b7 and 23...♖b6 equally good. Moreover, they don't even see much difference between 18.♖fe1 and 18.b3, evaluating both positions as roughly equal.

So, this round ends in a draw. Nenarokov leads 2.5–0.5.

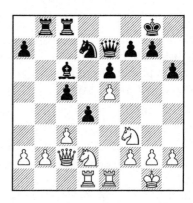

18...d3! (forced, because 19.b3 is now a threat) **19.♕xd3 ♖xb2 20.♕a6 ♖bb8 21.♘e4 ♖c7 22.h3!** To escape with the king to h2 after 23.♖d6 ♗xe4 24.♖xe4 ♖b1+.

22...♘b6 23.♖d6! This move, constricting black's position, required precise calculation, because 23...♗d5 cuts off the rook.

23...♗d5 24.♕e2.

24...f6. *Nenarokov has no commentary on this important move.*

Levenfish: "Rabinovich swallows simple bait. By just winning one tempo after another, black could gain an advantage: 24...♘c4 25.♖a6 ♖d7 26.♕c2 ♖b2 27.♕c1 ♖db7 28.♘d6 ♗xf3! 29.♘xc4 ♖b1! 30.♕xb1 (30. ♕e3 ♕g5!) 30...♖xb1 31.♖xb1 ♗e2 32.♖a4 ♕d7 33.♖b8+ ♔h7 34.♘b2 ♕d2, and black should win."

Nenarokov: "Winning "one tempo after another" – the commentator just takes away my queen, no big deal. Or is it? I think if this line had occurred in the game, I wouldn't have been as profligate, and instead of 28.♘d6??, I would have played 28.♕f4, saving the endangered queen and retaining the center and kingside pressure, as in the game.

Levenfish's line is too long to be absolutely correct. And Nenarokov is probably right about 28.♕f4 (black has an inventive reply 28...♖b1 29.♔h2 ♖xe1 30.♘xe1 f5!? 31.exf6 ♕c7 32.♕xc7 ♖xc7, but after 33.f3 ♗xe4 34.fxe4 gxf6 35.♖xe6 ♔f7 36.♖a6 it's unlikely he'd hold this endgame a pawn down). But there's another problem! After 24...f6?, the king's position was severely weakened, while 24...♘c4 25.♖a6 ♖d7 26.♕c2 ♖b6!? gave black good counterplay.

For instance: 27.♖xb6 axb6 and ♖a7 or 27.♖a4 ♘b2 28.♖a5 (28. ♖a3? ♘d3!) 28...c4 etc.

Levenfish narrowed the gap after this round, 2.5–1.5.

25.♖d1! Protecting the d6 rook in case of the exchange on e5. 25.exf6 is bad, since after 25...gxf6, black threatens f6-f5.

25...♘c4.

Levenfish: "Here, black could still correct the mistake made on the previous move: 25...f5! 26.♘ed2 ♘a4 27.♖c1 c4, and black is better."

Nenarokov: "Again, the inexplicably bad move 26.♘ed2? Why not 26.♘g3!, after which black's position is quite difficult. No rook can go to the d-file because of the threat c3-c4 after the rook exchange. The knight cannot attack the rook either, for example:

26...♘c4 27.♘xf5 ♕f7 (27... ♕f8? 28.♖6xd5! exd5 29.♘3h4 and so on) 28.♘3h4 (threatening ♖xd5) 28...♘xd6 29.exd6 ♖d7 30.♘e7+ is to white's advantage. This variation alone demonstrates just how strongly the rook stands on d6 and that white has so many options in this position."

Unfortunately, this variation alone doesn't prove anything. Instead of the cooperative 26...♘c4? black could have perfectly well played 26...♖d7 (as white cannot reply 27.♖xd7? ♕xd7 28.c4? ♗xc4!), but 26...♖f8 or 26...♕e8 are even more interesting, and black's chances are nevertheless better.

After a languid start Levenfish has fought back hard – 2.5:2.5!

26.exf6.

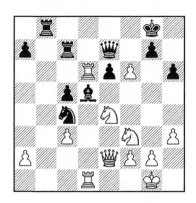

26...♕f7! The immediate 26... gxf6 is met with 27.♖1xd5! exd5 28.♘xf6+ with a crushing attack: 28...♔g7 (28...♔f7 29.♘g5+! hxg5 30.♕h5+ with a mate in three) 29.♘h5+ ♔f7 30.♘g5+! ♕xg5 (30... hxg5 31.♕f3+ ♔g8 32.♕xd5+ etc.) 31.♕e6+ ♔f8 32.♖xd5, winning the queen.

27.♖a6   ♖b2!   28.♕d3   ♖b6 29.♖xb6 axb6 30.♖e1 gxf6 31.♘fd2 ♘xd2 32.♕xd2.

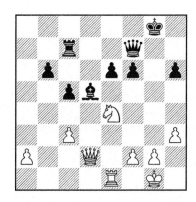

32...♕g6. After 32...♗xe4 33.♖xe4, black has no good defense against ♕xh6 or ♕d6.

Levenfish: "There was only one way to save the game: 32...f5! 33.♘g3 ♕g7."

Nenarokov: "The commentator doesn't notice that after the next move 34.c4, which was decisive in the actual game as well, black could only look at the board one last time and... resign, for instance: 34...♗xc4 35.♘h5 ♕g5 (relatively best) 36.f4 ♕e7 37.♖e3, threatening ♕c3 and ♖g3+, and white's attack is irresistible.

Yes, it is irresistible after 36... ♕e7?, but what should white do after 36...♕h4!

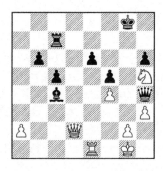

For instance: 37.♖e3 ♗d5 38.♖g3+ ♔h7 39.♕e2 ♖d7! (white threatened the cunning 40.♕e5!), white's attack fizzles out, and black has a healthy extra pawn.

And so, with a great finishing spurt, Levenfish manages to win this analytical dispute – 3.5–2.5! However, this does not diminish the creative achievements of his competitor: Nenarokov's play in the game was very strong, inventive and bold.

33.c4! ♖g7 34.♘xf6+! ♕xf6 35.cxd5 ♕f3! 36.g3 exd5. Black defends very well. He manages to trade off almost all the pieces without losing material, but the black king's position is poor, and he can't save the game.

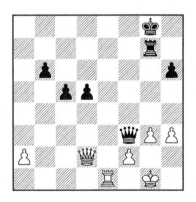

37.♖e8+! ♔f7. *After 37...♔h7 38.♕c2+ ♖g6 39.♖e7+ black loses a rook.*

38.♖e1 ♕f6 39.♖b8 ♕d6 (39... ♔g6 40.♕b1+!, winning) **40.♕e8+ ♔f6 41.♖d8 ♕e6 42.♕f8+ ♕f7.** If 42...♖f7, then 43.♕xh6+ ♔e5 44.♖e8 etc.

43.♕d6+ ♕e6 44.♕f4+. Black resigned.

A unique game. Ilyin-Zhenevsky, for the only time in his tournament practice, risked using the Budapest Gambit, and Bogatyrchuk – again, for the only time in his career – faced this rare opening. The opening experiment turned out to be a disaster for the experimenter.

No. 11. Budapest Gambit A52
Bogatyrchuk – Ilyin-Zhenevsky
Petrograd 1923, round 5
Annotated by F. Bogatyrchuk

1.d4 ♘f6 2.c4 e5 3.dxe5 ♘g4 4.e4 *(the best move, in Alekhine's opinion)* **4...♘xe5 5.f4 ♘g6.** *Playing with fire. The simple 5...♘ec6 is better.*
6.♘f3. White doesn't play 6.♗e3, instead allowing the black bishop to reach c5. In this case, as in the actual game, he planned to castle long.

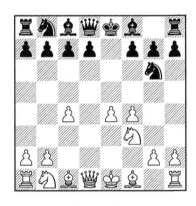

6...♘c6. *After 6...♗c5?! 7.f5! ♘h4 (7...♘e7!?) 8.♘g5!, Alekhine in his game against I. Rabinovich (Baden-*

Baden 1925) created a quick attack: 8... ♕e7 9.♕g4 f6 10.♕h5+! g6 11.♕xh4 fxg5 12.♗xg5 ♕f7 13.♗e2 etc.

7.a3 ♗e7 8.♘c3 d6 9.♗e3 ♗g4 10.♗e2 ♗f6? Black was counting on 11.♕c2, to put pressure on the e4 pawn after 11...♗xc3+ 12.♕xc3 ♕e7 13.♕c2 0-0 14.0-0 ♖fe8 with a better position.

However, after 15.♖ae1! (15.♗d3 f5!), attempting to capture the pawn is dangerous: 15...♕xe4?! 16.♗d3 ♕e7 17.f5 ♘f8 18.f6!, forcing 18... gxf6 (18...♗xf6? 19.♗g5).

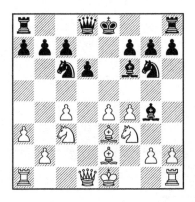

11.♘d5! An unexpected move, exposing the weakness of black's last move. Black now can't play 11... ♗xb2? because of 12.♖b1 ♗xa3 *(12...♗f6 13.♖xb7 ♖c8 14.c5! is no better)* 13.♖xb7 ♖c8 14.♕a4, and white wins.

11...0-0 12.♕d3 a6 13.0-0-0 ♖e8 14.♕c2 ♗d7 15.h4. *Fritz recommends 15.♘xf6+!, destroying the king's position (15...♕xf6? 16.f5!).*

15...♖b8 *(losing a tempo; 15... ♘f8!?)* **16.♘g5.** Threatening 17.♘xh7 and h4-h5.

16...♘f8 (16...h6 is bad due to 17.♘xf7! ♔xf7 18.♗h5 with a strong attack) **17.♗d3.**

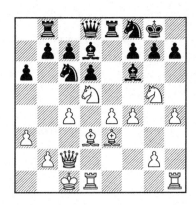

17...h6. *Black's last chance was 17...♗d4!? 18.e5 ♗xe3+ 19.♘xe3 g6, and, for instance, the straightforward 20.h5 can be met with 20...♘xe5!, complicating things.*

18.e5! ♗xg5. If 18...dxe5, then 19.♗h7+ with a mate in two. *Or 18...hxg5 19.exf6 gxf4 20.♗xf4 ♘e6 21.♗g5.*

19.hxg5 dxe5 20.gxh6 g6 21.h7+! ♔h8 22.fxe5 ♘xe5 23.♕c3! c6.

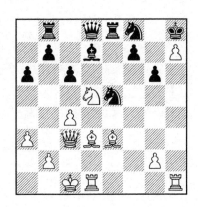

24.♗h6! Forcing his opponent to open the h-file *(threatening 25.♗g7+*

♔xg7 26.h8♕#). The previous queen move was to prevent 24...♘e6.

24...♘xh7 25.♗f4 f6 26.♗xg6 cxd5 (26...♘xg6 27.♗c7, winning) **27.♖xh7+ ♔g8 28.♕g3 ♗g4 29.♗xe5.** Black resigned. After 29...♖xe5, there's 30.♕xg4 ♖g5 31.♕e6+, and if 29...♕c8, then 30.♗f7+! ♔xh7 31.♕h4+ etc.

A Psychological Thriller

The officially-recognized masterpieces have ended. But this does not mean that there were no more masterpieces in the tournament. The creators of this gem of a draw annotated their game separately (Bogatyrchuk in *Shakhmaty*, Levenfish in *Shakhmatny Listok*), but together, they created a true psychological thriller, in which the opponents are trying to predict each other's intentions on each move – and sometimes they succeed!

No. 12

Levenfish – Bogatyrchuk

Petrograd 1923, round 2

Annotated by F. Bogatyrchuk and G. Levenfish

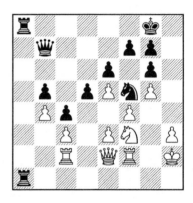

31.♘d4! The knight finally reached its desired destination – the

Left: the game Romanovsky (1) – Ilyin-Zhenevsky (2). Right: Levenfish (1) – Bogatyrchuk (2). Watching: Ilyin-Zhenevsky, I. Rabinovich, Nenarokov, S. Vainstein. Photo by S. Magaziner (Krasnaya Panorama, No. 8, 1923.)

d4 square, which it's been trying to occupy for 15 moves. However, at that moment, black prepared to win the queen for rook and knight. White intentionally allows that, thinking that the small material disadvantage is well-compensated by the knight's excellent position **(L)**.

31...♖h1+. Black is better. Now he faced a dilemma: win the queen or trade the knights and then break through along the a-file? The second continuation didn't promise any concrete opportunities: 31...♘xd4 32.exd4 ♖8a3! 33.♖f1! ♖xf1 34.♕xf1 ♕a6 35.♕c1 ♕a4 36.♕d2 ♕b3 37.♕c1 ♖a1 38.♕xa1 ♕xc2+ 39.♔g3, and there's no win in sight **(B)**.

Maybe it was better to continue the attack with major pieces – 31...♖8a3, however, after 32.♘xf5 gxf5 33.♕d2 and ♕d4, black probably had nothing substantial **(L)**.

The computer is having none of those tantalizing thoughts: if the opponent gives you the queen, take it. It immediately shows a line and flickers in sweet anticipation...

32.♔xh1 ♘g3+ 33.♔g2 ♘xe2 34.♖fxe2.

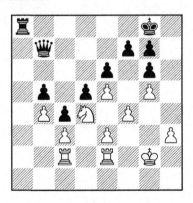

34...♖a3! In addition to the game move, black had another plan: put the queen on a6, completely seizing the a-file, then send the king to defend the b5 pawn, and only then commence operations on the a-file. This plan has a flaw, however: the rook is behind the queen, and so white could have put his e-rook on d2 and, as the black king passed the d-file, played e3-e4, significantly improving his position.

With the game move, black executes the same plan with the king walk, but with a difference: his rook would be free to move, constantly threatening to invade along the first rank **(B)**.

Black's plan is clear: ♕b7-a6-a4, then ♔g8-f8 until b6, then ♖a3-a1 and a queen invasion into the opponent's camp **(L)**.

35.♖a2! But white's move shows that his evaluation was right. Black can hold the a-file only if he exchanges rooks; but having only the queen against rook and knight, with the king out of play, he wouldn't get much **(L)**.

White wants to extricate himself from his cramped position, but he doesn't notice the opponent's hidden threat **(B)**.

35...♖xc3! 36.♖a5. Very logical. Black's position becomes dangerous: he loses the b5 pawn, the b4 pawn can move forward now, and there's also a threat of... back-rank mating combinations.

It was less logical, but more

prescient to play 36.♔f2, which more or less forces black to play for a draw immediately: 36...♖d3 37.♖a5 ♖xd4 38.exd4 ♕c6 39.♖a3 c3 40.♖c2 ♕c4 41.♖cxc3! ♕xd4+ 42.♔g3, and black, due to the threats of ♖a8+ and ♖c3-c8, has to give perpetual check **(L)**.

The computer disagrees with "playing for a draw immediately". Instead of 37...♖xd4, it confidently plays 37...c3! 38.♖xb5 ♕a6 39.♖c5 ♕a1 40.b5 ♔h7 41.b6 ♕h1! – the white pawn can't run too far anyway:

42.♘f3 (42.b7 ♕h2+, with a mate in nine) 42...d4! 43.b7 ♕b1 44.exd4 ♕xb7 45.♖e3 ♕b2+ 46.♖e2 ♕a3! (a great find) 47.♖e3 ♖xe3 48.♔xe3 c2+ 49.♔d2 ♕xf3 and curtains.

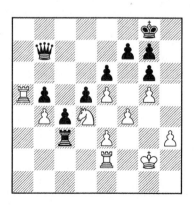

36...♖xe3‼ *Seeing this move, my silicon friend was literally flabbergasted, after a long think showing "=". Only later did it finally understand that black's position was better...*

A genius idea! The sudden rook sacrifice deprives the knight of its defender, and the two passed pawns, c and d, become very strong **(L)**.

This move disorganizes white's whole position **(B)**. *Annotating the game in 1937 (in an article about the Levenfish – Botvinnik match), Bogatyrchuk wrote:* "One of those sudden sacrifices that can upset the opponent's psychological balance. But Levenfish is unfazed – he immediately reverts to defense."

37.♖xe3 ♕b6 38.♖a8+‼ A great, subtle move by white, preventing the king from joining the queen in attack; its value will clearly tell after move 48 **(B)**.

38...♔h7.

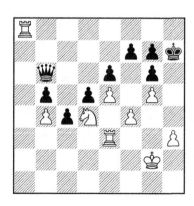

39.♘c2. White intended to force a draw with 39.♖g3 ♕xd4 40.♖g4

♕d2+ 41.♔f1, but noticed in time that 41...♕d3+! 42.♔g2 ♕e2+ 43.♔g3 ♕e1+ wins for black. Still, the check on a8 proved to be useful **(L)**.

39...d4 40.♖f3 d3 41.♖a3! *Levenfish's exclamation mark; Bogatyrchuk calls this move "the best chance!" in his 1937 annotation. The computer disagrees, however: 41.♘e3! c3 42.♖c8 ♕d4 43.♖g3! (with a pretty threat 44.♖g4 and ♘h4#!), and black is forced to play 43...d2 44.♖g4 d1♕ 45.♘xd1 ♕d5+ 46.♔g3 ♕d3+ with perpetual check.*

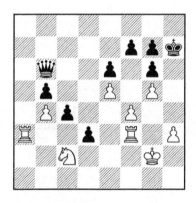

41...dxc2. *Both opponents, as though acting in concert, skip commentary until move 46 – they either decided to take a rest or thought that everything was forced.*

However, Junior is sure that black missed a win at this very moment, and it gives us a lesson in computer geometry, with the goal of winning the b-pawn: 41...♕c6 42.♖c3 ♕a8! 43.♖a3 ♕f8! (43...dxc2 44.♖xa8 c1♕ changes nothing) 44.♖c3 dxc2 45.♖xc2 ♕xb4 46.♖fc3 ♕c5!

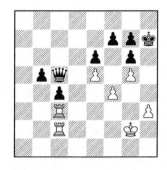

It's done – now white has to give up his rook for the pawns: 47.♖c1 b4 48.♖xc4 ♕d5+ 49.♔g3 b3 50.♖4c3 ♕d2 51.♖xb3 ♕xc1 etc. Yes, the silicon guys never cut us any slack!

42.♖ac3 ♕d4 43.♖xc2 ♕d1 44.♖ff2 ♕e1 45.♖cd2! (Bogatyrchuk) **45...♕e4+ 46.♔h2.**

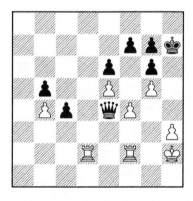

46...c3. Black had the following plan: limit the rooks' movement along the second rank with this pawn move, protect the pawn with the queen and then move the king to the queenside. Black cannot execute this plan without c4-c3, because otherwise the rooks retain their freedom of movement and can always stop the black king **(B)**.

This looks like a decisive move, however, it only leads to a draw. Black had better chances after 46...f6! 47.gxf6 gxf6 48.exf6 ♔g8 49.♖de2 ♕d4 50.♔g3 ♔f7 51.♖e5 c3 52.♖c5 ♔xf6 53.♖f3 ♕g1+ with complicated play **(L)**.

46...f6 led to a draw even faster: white only had to play 49.♖d7! c3 50.♖a2.

47.♖c2! (Bogatyrchuk) **47... ♕d3.** If 47...♕xb4, then 48.♖f3 and ♖cxc3, and the b-pawn alone cannot break through the white rooks' suppressive fire along the third rank. Now black is threatening to win the game outright with ♔h7-g8-f8-e7-d7-c6-d5-c4 **(L)**.

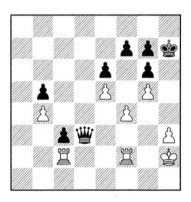

48.♖a2! Parrying the threat: after 48...♔g8, there's 49.♖a8+ ♔h7 50.♖aa2. Another way to break through with the king is dangerous for black: 48...f6 49.exf6 gxf6 50.♖a7+ ♔g8 51.♖fa2! e5! (51...fxg5 52.♖a8+ ♔f7 53.♖2a7+ ♔f6 54.♖f8#, while 51...♔f8 loses the queen) 52.♖b7 ♕d8 53.gxf6. So, he tries to win a tempo for the king's incursion **(L)**.

Now it's clear why the check on move 38 was so valuable: if not for it, black could have immediately played 48...♔f8 **(B)**.

48...♕e3 49.♖ae2! The only move. After 49.♖ac2 ♔g8 50.♖a2 ♔f8, black wins **(L)**.

49...♕d4 50.♖c2 ♕d3 51.♖a2!

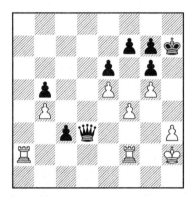

Grigory Levenfish "Tall, rugged, well-built, probably a strong man. I felt energy radiating from him." (Segal.) (64. Shakhmaty i Shashki v Rabochem Klube magazine, No. 24, 1925).

Black cannot win a tempo for the king move. If he doesn't attack the b4 pawn, white puts the rook on a2, not letting the black king out; if the queen attacks the b4 pawn, white plays ♖c2, threatening ♖f3. An outstanding position! If black tries 51...f6, there follows 52.exf6! gxf6 53.♖a7+ ♔g8 54.♖fa2 fxg5 55.♖a8+ ♔f7 56.♖2a7+ ♔f6 57.♖f8# **(B)**.

Why walk straight into mate? After 54...e5!, the king is not under any threat.

51...♕e3. Black could try to win a tempo with 51...♕c4 52.♖ac2 ♕b3. White has only one move, 53.♔g3, and if 53...♔g8, then 54.♖c1!, and black loses the c3 pawn **(L)**.

52.♖ae2 ♕d4 53.♖c2 f6 54.gxf6 gxf6 55.♖f3. Draw. One of the most interesting games in the tournament! **(L)**.

An Exception to the Rule

Romanovsky: "In the very first round, as at the All-Russian Olympiad, I was paired up against Levenfish. I lost after some intense struggle. I didn't make major mistakes in the game – I think that I just played too formulaically, and my plans weren't concrete enough. My opponent, however, played brilliantly, showing the best aspect of his creativity in the game."

No. 13
Romanovsky – Levenfish
Petrograd 1923, round 1
Annotated by G. Levenfish

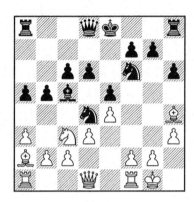

White's plan is clear. After castling, he's going to start operations in the center. Since the main strategic principle states that flank attacks are doomed to fail if a central counterblow is possible, white probably wasn't afraid of g7-g5 in the least.

13...g5! (nevertheless!) **14.♗g3 ♕d7 15.♘e2 h5 16.♘xd4 ♗xd4 17.c3 ♗b6.**

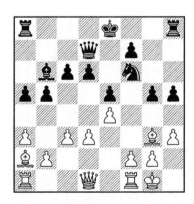

18.♕f3. *There was an alternative: 18.♔h1 h4 19.♗h2 g4 20.f4!*

gxh3 21.fxe5 hxg2+ 22.♔xg2, but 19...0-0-0! is stronger, and if 20.f3 (20.♕f3 ♖h6!), then 20...♘h5 21.♕e1 f5 with an initiative for black.

18...♗d8! A difficult move, keeping the king in the center for a while. White could meet 18...♖h6 with 19.h4! g4 *(19...gxh4!? 20.♗xh4 ♕g4 21.♕xg4 hxg4)* 20.♕e2. Black's kingside attack is stalled, and white's counter-strike in the center is imminent.

Now, however, 19.h4 is met with 19...♘g4 20.hxg5 ♗xg5 and then h5-h4.

I hope that Grigory Yakovlevich forgives me and Junior, but it seems that 18...♗d8 was just a tempo loss (see black's 21st move). He could have played according to Steinitz's guidelines: 18...♔e7! 19.d4 g4 20.hxg4 hxg4 21.♕e3 ♖h5 22.f4 exd4 23.cxd4.

If we compare this position with the one that occurred in the game after 23.cxd4, we see a significant difference: the black rook is already on h5, and he can immediately play 23...♖ah8. For instance: 24.♖ad1

d5! 25.exd5+ ♔f8, and now both 26.dxc6 ♕xc6 27.♖fe1 ♘e4 28.♕xe4 ♕xe4 29.♖xe4 ♖h1+ 30.♔f2 ♖xd1 and 26.♖fe1 ♘xd5 27.♗xd5 ♖xd5 28.♗f2 ♖dh5 29.♔f1 a4 are bad.

19.d4! g4 20.hxg4 hxg4.

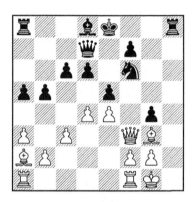

21.♕e3. The queen trade (21. ♕f5) is inconsistent with white's main plan, and after 21...♕xf5 22.exf5 ♘h5 23.♖fe1 f6 24.♖ad1 ♗b6 with the threat of 25...d5 and e5-e4, black is better.

21.♕d3 ♘h5 22.dxe5 ♘xg3 23.♕xg3 looks tempting, but the subtle reply 23...f6! with the threat ♕h7 drastically changes everything. After the forced 24.♖fe1 fxe5 and then ♗h4, 0-0-0 and ♖df8, black should win.

White's move is well thought-out. If black now plays 21...♘h5, then 22.dxe5 ♘xg3 23.fxg3! ♖f8 24.♖f5 *(24.e6! is curtains)* 24...♖b8 25.♔f1, and white is clearly better.

23...♕a7!? doesn't help either: 24.♗xf7+ ♔d7 25.e6+ ♔e7 26.♕xa7+ ♖xa7 27.♔f2 ♗b6+

28.♔e1 ♖h2 29.♖d1!, and if 29...♖xg2, then 30.♗g8!

21...♗b6! Threatening to castle long, then play ♖h5 and ♖dh8. Romanovsky showed the following plan for white: 22.♖fe1 0-0-0 23.a4 ♖h5 24.axb5 ♖dh8 25.♔f1 cxb5 26.♗b3 ♖h1+ 27.♔e2 ♖xe1+ 28.♖xe1, but even then black maintains a strong attack with 28...♖e8.

Here, after 29.♔f1 exd4 30.♕d3! d5 (30...dxc3? 31.♕xc3+) 31.exd5 ♖xe1+ 32.♔xe1, black would still need to make a lot of effort.

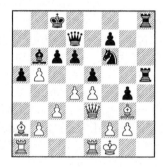

However in the above position 25...c5! 26.♗c4 (26.dxe5? ♕xb5+) 26...cxd4 27.cxd4 ♗xd4! almost wins by force: 28.♕c1 ♔b8 29.♕c2 (29.♖xa5 ♕c7) 29...♕b7 and so on. Black would also win with the computer line 27...exd4 28.♕f4 ♘xe4! – you can check your tactical skills yourself after 29.♖xe4, 29.♕xe4 or 29.♖ac1.

22.f4 exd4! Black prevents the opening of the f-file and attacks the weak d4 square.

23.cxd4.

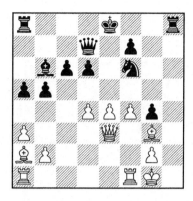

23...0-0-0 24.♖ad1 d5! 25.e5 ♘e4. Threatening to double rooks along the h-file. White's reply is forced.

26.♗b1 f5 27.exf6. Otherwise, after the forced trade on e4, black would have played dxe4, and the d4 pawn would soon fall.

27...♖de8   28.♗xe4   ♖xe4 29.♕c3 ♔b7 30.♖fe1 ♕h7.

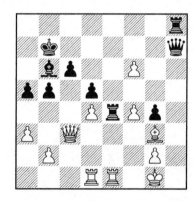

31.♔f2. Or 31.♖xe4 ♕h1+ 32.♔f2 ♕xd1 33.♖e7+ ♔a6 34.♕xc6 ♕xd4+ *(34...♕d2+! 35.♔g1 ♕xd4+ 36.♔f1 ♕d3+ 37.♖e2 ♖h1# is even simpler)* 35.♔e2 ♕xb2+ 36.♔d3 ♕xa3+ 37.♔d2 ♕b4+ 38.♔c2 ♕c4+ etc.

But white is not forced to play 34.♕xc6?

White could still hold with 34.♔e3! ♕g1+ 35.♔d2 ♕xg2+ 36.♔c1 ♕f1+ *(but not 36...♖h1+? 37.♗e1!) 37.♔c2 etc. So, after capturing on e4, white could probably still put up some resistance. However, after 31.♔f2, it's the end.*

31...♖he8 32.♖xe4 ♖xe4 33.♔g1 *(black threatened 33... ♖xd4! 34.♖xd4 ♕e4 35.♕d2 ♗xd4+ 36.♔f1 ♗xf6)* **33...♕h8.** Preventing 34.f7 because of 34...♖xd4.

34.♗f2 ♖xf4.

35.♗e3. White had an interesting combination at his disposal: 35.♗h4!, and if 35...♕xh4, then 36.g3.

However, there was a refutation: 35...♖xd4! 36.♖xd4 ♕xh4 37.f7 g3 38.f8♕ ♗xd4+.

35...♖xf6 36.♖f1 g3 37.♖xf6 ♕xf6 38.♕d3 ♗c7 39.b3 ♗f4 40.b4 axb4 41.axb4 ♕h6 42.♗xf4 ♕xf4 43.♕f3 ♕c1+, with a mate in three.

This game is interesting from the strategic point of view. How did I manage to win with a flank attack? Has the main strategic tenet, of a flank attack being refuted by a central counterblow, become obsolete? No, it's still as significant as ever. I decided to play 13...g5 for two reasons: the white king was on the kingside, and white had also played h2-h3, which made opening the h-file easier. However, even taking these two factors into account, the attack required exceptional precision and literally hung by a thread (see the line after 21.♕d3). Many games are decided by a flank attack while the center is closed off, but there are only a few games similar to this one. Another example would be the great game Vidmar – Nimzowitsch from the 1924 New York tournament.

P.S. *As I learned from Mark Dvoretsky's article "Flank Attack with an Open Center" (e3e5.com website), he prepared his own annotations of this game "a long time ago and would sometimes show it to the pupils". The next phrase, I must admit, was very flattering for me: "But recently, I saw high-quality annotations by Sergey Voronkov on chesspro.ru, with a number of lines significantly improved."*

The Smile of Fortune

Romanovsky probably remembered the dramatic finale of the next game quite well. Of course, he couldn't have known when he played it that this smile of fortune would determine his tournament result. The game was played in round 6, and had it ended as it should have, Romanovsky's morale would have suffered. However, after a 5-win streak in rounds 4 to 8, he took the lead and never relinquished it!

No. 14
Romanovsky – A. Kubbel
Petrograd 1923, round 6

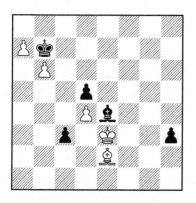

This is, plain and simple, an endgame study on the board! You might think that it doesn't matter which pawn black should push to promote. However, he moved the wrong pawn and paid the ultimate price! What's most astonishing is the fact that the black player was... a well-known chess composer!

41...h2?? 42.♗a6+! It's unknown exactly when black resigned. Probably he did it immediately: a chess composer would have surely seen the line 42...♔a8 43.♗b5!! ♔b7 (43...h1♕ 44.♗c6#) 44.♗c6+ ♔xc6 (44...♔xb6 45.a8♕ h1♕ 46.♕b7+ ♔a5 47.♕b5#) 45.a8♕+ ♔xb6 46.♕b8+ etc.

Black would have won with 41...c2!! (the difference is that this pawn promotes with a check) 42.♔d2 c1♕+ 43.♔xc1 h2, and white now lacks the one tempo necessary to execute that beautiful idea.

Who is Not With Us is Against Us

3rd Soviet Championship Tournament: Moscow, 23rd August – 15th September 1924

"The future will not come by itself,
If we don't take measures.
Grab it by the gills, Komsomol!
Grab it by the tail, pioneer!"
Vladimir Mayakovsky, *Grab the Future!*

The entire first half of the year 1924 was spent in a vicious fight to the death between the Central Chess Section, created in Moscow and headed by N. Krylenko, and the All-Russian Chess Union, headed by S. Vainstein, I. Golubev and P. Romanovsky from Leningrad. The fight was more or less one-sided. The Union, private, organizationally weak, funded only by membership fees, could not withstand the onslaught of the powerful state-backed organization, created under the auspices of the Highest Physical Education Council (VSFK). Even having their own press organ didn't help the Union. The loyal Leninist, Russian SFSR prosecutor Nikolai Vasilyevich Krylenko, knew well that the main fight would take place at the conference, and the conference, as we know, is usually won by those organizing it. And now guess who was the head of the organizing committee? The game was won before it started.

Declaring that they "considered the chess art a political weapon", the new chess authorities acted in the Bolshevik way, in a fierce attacking style. They created chess sections everywhere, absorbing the Union branches. In May, the Leningrad organization ceased to resist. The ARCU board sent a letter to the Moscow comrades, where they "greeted the conference organization work warmly", promised to "support the Chess Section and propose reorganizing the All-Russian Chess Union at the conference", and... asked to join the organizing committee. The comrades answered, requesting that the ARCU "send a representative to Moscow for 2–3 days to take part in the organizing committee meeting."

You can see how significant this conference was, where the state monopoly on chess was to be officially declared, by a quote from the editorial of the 16th issue of *Shakhmatny Listok* – the last one with "Organ of the All-Russian Chess Union" printed on the cover: "We are on the verge of the greatest chess event known not only to the Soviet Republic, but Russia as a whole, and, by extension, the entire world. The Third All-Union Chess Conference, starting in Moscow on 20th August, opens a new era in development of the chess art, not only Russian, but international as well. The same banner will be waving over this conference as over the other conferences of the Republic: the red banner of work, the red banner of proletarian unity..."

Essentially, everything was decided beforehand. The only thing up for discussion was the form of the surrender. Krylenko's personal involvement wasn't even necessary: before the conference, he went on vacation, leaving his closest assistants to deputize: checkers player Vasily Russo (one of the 1920 Olympiad organizers), trade union official (and chess problemist) Semyon Levman, and chess player Nikolai Grigoriev. The role of "collective agitator and propagandist" was to be played by the fortnightly chess and checkers magazine *64* edited by Krylenko himself; the first issue was published shortly before the conference.

The Proletarianization of Chess

Grekov: "On 20th August, at 8 p.m., in the hall of the former Hunting Club on Vozdvizhenka, V. N. Russo, in the presence of about 150 delegates arriving from all parts of the USSR, declared the conference open.

> "With the first word, V. N. Russo proposed paying respects to the great late leader of the USSR, Comrade V. I. Lenin, who played chess in his rare hours of leisure, by standing up." (*64*, August 1924.)
>
> Strangely, this was the first ever mention of Lenin's death in a chess magazine (or maybe even the very first mention of Lenin at all in a chess magazine). Both *Shakhmaty* and *Shakhmatny Listok* left this "globally historical" event unnoticed in January; there was also no mention of Comrade Russo's proposal in the conference reports.

In the introductory speech he said that this conference, convoked by the chess and checkers section of the VSFK, was significant in the sense that it was the start of chess development on a state scale, which, in turn, was made possible by recognizing chess as a new cultural force...

After further greetings, N. D. Grigoriev read the letter of the organizing committee chairman N. V. Krylenko, who had left Moscow shortly before the conference started.

> This official "Letter to the Conference", the reading of which took at least an hour, was printed in its entirety by *64*, quoted in places in *Shakhmatny Listok*, and only mentioned briefly in *Shakhmaty*. Such limited pluralism was

still tolerated. However, the letter itself left no doubt that any pluralism would be quashed quite soon. Everyone would have to make a choice. Nobody would be able to sit out the fight, citing the "pure art" excuse!

"...Two organs, comrades, have taken the business of chess under their high auspices. They are the VTsSPS (Central Council of the Proletarian Trade Unions) – a powerful coalition of the united working class – and the Highest Physical Education Council, a proletarian organ whose goal is to further the physical and cultural development of the working masses. Chess is one of the tools for such development, and, as a tool, should be used by us for the same purpose...

In any reading house, in any factory club, chess sets should be on the table together with newspapers – this is the slogan and motto we should base our work on, and we all should make efforts in this direction.

The adepts of "pure art" in chess might argue, "This is all well and good, this is all right – but why should we be doing all that? Let the trade unions do this, let physical education organs do this, let us just live with our chess, our fights, our theory. Let us study chess like science, do not burden us with popularization of chess basics among people who cannot play..."

We understand the passion for pure mathematics, we wholly understand and value the similar passion for chess. But understanding does not mean forgiving...

"Go with chess into the thick of life, do not retreat from life into chess" – that's how the conference should formulate the slogans of practical work...

And last but not least. The caste spirit of patented maestros, looking down on the "lowest of the low", the trouble-making, petty psychology of circus wrestlers plaguing many first- and second-category players, petty haggling for appearance fees, which goes as far as directly putting one's name and talent for sale and occurs even among the Grossmeisters *(surely not an allusion to Bogoljubov, the only grandmaster taking part in the tournament?!)*, mutual feuding and envy – all these dredges of the bourgeois world are, sadly, inherent in the chess environment. Our conference should stamp all of this out mercilessly...

With sincere comradely greetings, **N. Krylenko**

Comrade Krylenko was elected the honorary chairman of the conference; and comrades Rykov, Trotsky and Semashko elected honorary board members..." (*Shakhmatny Listok*, September 1924). Some explanation is in order: Nikolai Semashko, People's Commissar of Health, was the chairman of the VSFK as well.

The morning session on 21st August started with S. S. Levman's presentation on the functional principles of the new chess organization. "Chess is not art for art's sake, it's one of the means of raising the general cultural level. This is the main and principal difference between our views on chess and the policy of the All-Russian Chess Union, organized similarly to the bourgeois unions. Up till now, chess was a pure sport, a fistfight on the chess board... We, by spreading chess among the working masses, want to give the workers a new weapon in their fight for culture, so for us, increasing the general playing level is more important than developing individual talents or studying the subtleties of theory. And here's a practical conclusion: one workers' tournament is more important than a dozen championships. But we do not want to push away the chess specialists; our goal is to make them work for us."

> Two key phrases of this presentation were printed only by *64*: "The Moscow Chess Section was the first one to turn towards the proletarianization of chess" and "No independent chess unions should exist".

The third report was given by the ARCU chairman S. O. Vainstein. He described the history of the Union, whose goal was to unite Russian chess players. At first, the Union had advocated the idea of pure chess art, however, at the previous year's conference, they passed an important resolution: chess art should be widened, not only deepened. The conference itself gave a great impetus for the development of the grassroots movement we're seeing now; this is a big accomplishment of ARCU... "A number of oblast-level tournaments were organized, contact with the West was established, many things were achieved in the publishing business. In all of its forms, ARCU was essentially a temporary organization, and our goal was to join some state-backed organization... We do not disavow the Moscow program, but we should not strike out the Union's work, we should not talk about its liquidation – it would be more right to talk about reorganization..."

At the morning session on 22nd August, after a short discussion, resolutions on all reports were passed. In essence, they boiled down to the following:

"The conference deems the line of the All-Union Chess Section correct, but acknowledges the positive role ARCU played in uniting the chess players. However, as of now, ARCU's work is complete, it should be reorganized, and its branches merged with local physical education councils' chess sections... The chess associations should be based on the circles in workers', soldiers' and students' clubs, and also in schools, dormitories and reading houses. All associations answer to the All-Union Chess Section."

III-й ВСЕСОЮЗНЫЙ ШАХМАТНЫЙ СЪЕЗД В МОСКВЕ.

ВСТРЕЧА ЗАГРАНИЧНЫХ ГОСТЕЙ.

И. П. Голубев (слева направо), С. О. Вайнштейн, В. И. Ненароков, И. Л. Рабинович, Е. Д. Боголюбов, А. С. Селезнев, В. М. Нейштадт.

"Meeting the foreign guests". Efim Bogoljubov and Alexei Selezniev returned to Russia for the first time after a ten-year absence. (Shakhmatny Listok, No. 17, 1924.)

The conference expressed a desire to organize an international tournament during the next, 4th conference in 1925.

On the evening of the same day, assemblies of tournament participants were held *(two cities' tournaments and tournaments for workers and soldiers were held concurrently with the championship)*, and lots were drawn to determine the pairings in the championship *(masters in italics)*: 1. V. I. Nenarokov (Moscow), 2. S. K. Rosenthal (Minsk), 3. *P. A. Romanovsky* (Leningrad), 4. *G. Y. Levenfish* (Leningrad), 5. Y. S. Vilner (Odessa), 6. N. D. Grigoriev (Moscow), 7. V. I. Sozin (Novgorod), 8. *A. A. Smorodsky* (Tiflis), 9. *F. P. Bogatyrchuk* (Kiev), 10. *I. L. Rabinovich* (Leningrad), 11. *E. D. Bogoljubov* (Triberg, Germany), 12. B. M. Verlinsky (Moscow), 13. A. S. Sergeyev (Moscow), 14. *S. N. Freymann* (Turkestan), 15. A. F. Ilyin-Zhenevsky (Leningrad), 16. *A. I. Rabinovich* (Moscow), 17. *A. S. Selezniev* (Triberg, Germany), 18. *F. I. Duz-Khotimirsky* (Moscow).

All tournaments began on 23rd August." *(Shakhmaty, August 1924.)*

"Bogoljubchenko" and Prince Myshkin

Bogatyrchuk: "I was already a "capitalist" when I came to Moscow to take part in the third All-Union championship *(Bogatyrchuk was a radiologist and had a private laboratory in Kiev)*. The three years of NEP changed the capital city for the better. Even though there weren't too many goods in the shops, and their quality wasn't exactly the best, they were at least present in the shops, and you could buy them without food stamps. Policemen appeared at the big crossroads, controlling the traffic. People started to dress much more neatly, you could even see some elegant clothes. All in all, life was recovering nicely.

Fyodor Bogatyrchuk (left) and Efim Bogoljubov at the 1914 match tournament in Kiev. Alexander Evenson and Nikolai Grekov also took part. From F. Bogatyrchuk's archive.

Masters E. D. Bogoljubov and A. S. Selezniev came from Germany to take part in the tournament.

Bogoljubov hadn't taken out German citizenship yet – he had probably decided to check out his old country first. Both newcomers were dressed impeccably, contrasting sharply with our shabby clothes. Bogoljubov stood out especially. I remembered him back in Kiev, studying in the seminary, he was very humble and shy. The only thing he was very sure of back then was that he would definitely become one of the world's leading chess players. This boasting was so unfitting for his appearance that we used to mock him. But now, any mockery was out of the question. As any Slavic person, he had a natural affinity for languages, and after spending some years in Germany, he spoke like a true German.

The Chess Section couldn't afford hotels back then, so we were accommodated in private apartments. Engineer Y. G., a great specialist in some area who earned a lot of money, took me, Bogoljubov and Selezniev in. He and his wife were very hospitable, throwing money around like old Moscow merchants. Not even the revolution had corroded this hospitability: the couple treated us like royal princes were usually treated abroad.

The observant, inquisitive Bogoljubov instantly understood the situation in the country. An incident with me opened his eyes to many things.

Here's what happened: my wife dreamed of a fur neckpiece, and I decided to buy one in Moscow. Since fur shops were few and far between, and their prices were astronomical, I, as it became customary, tried to find a private seller. A few days later, I read a classified ad in some newspaper selling the thing I needed, and I went to the address. The apartment was big, with many dwellers, and I had to ring the doorbell a certain number of times to reach the person I needed. I rang the bell. The door was opened by some young man who, without saying a word, beckoned me into a room opposite the entrance door. As I entered, I couldn't understand what was going on. The room, probably a former lounge, was filled with people. There were many kids. I was immediately told that I had walked into a GPU ambush. They were waiting for some man who was going to visit one of the dwellers. There were many kids because a prominent children's music teacher lived in this apartment as well. The kids went to his lesson in the morning, they got detained, soon their alerted moms and dads came and got detained too, and now they all awaited the arrival of the unknown criminal together.

I also had to wait, even though the seller of the neckpiece had no links to that criminal. There was a GPU guard at the door, whose stony face clearly showed that he wasn't going to put up with any complaints or questions. The famous Russian hospitality helped to pass time here as well. Coffee with tasty buns appeared out of nowhere, and we satisfied our hunger. New people constantly entered the room, but the man who was expected never arrived. My annoyance and outrage were compounded by the fact that the neckpiece I was offered was of very low quality: it was probably made out of fur of some domestic animal.

But everything passes under the sun, and our absurd sojourn ended, too. Around four o'clock, some higher-ups came, and after a thorough interrogation and clarifying our intentions, we were allowed to leave.

I arrived at my game 20 minutes late, and my clock had already been started. I must explain to non-chess players that had I not arrived at the game within the first two hours, I

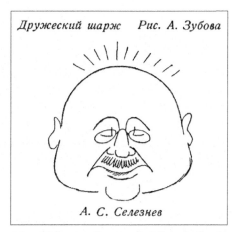

Дружеский шарж   Рис. А. Зубова

А. С. Селезнев

Alexei Selezniev. Bogatyrchuk thought that he "resembled Prince Myshkin from Dostoevsky's The Idiot; just like Prince Myshkin, he was a very clever man." Cartoon by A. Zubov (64. Shakhmaty i Shashki v Rabochem Klube, No. 21, 1927).

would've lost by forfeit. But I was enraged by what had just happened and played so fiercely that I even managed to win.

During the evening chat with my hosts, I learned that the apartment ambush method was often practiced by the GPU and was considered quite effective in catching "enemies of the people". But what about the civil rights of the detained innocent people, including minors? Reader, don't laugh! The authorities never investigated such rights violations. Our Bogoljubchenko (we often called him this Ukrainian-sounding endearment because of his Ukrainian origins) just scratched his head, probably thinking, "Such police-state measures are unthinkable in Germany!" But everything described here about the GPU's methods was just the beginning, you shall see much more.

The same evening, to console me, Alexei Selezniev pleased our ears with his beautiful musical performance. The son of rich Moscow merchants, he had received a fantastic education, spoke all European languages and was a great piano player. Because of his gentle personality, this bachelor, who never married his entire life, resembled Prince Myshkin from Dostoevsky's *The Idiot*; just like Prince Myshkin, he was a very clever man. All chess players of the world know Selezniev for his endgame studies, many of which are nothing short of genius." (From the book *My Life Path to Vlasov and the Prague Manifesto*.)

This is No New Vasiuki[12]!

Reading Bogatyrchuk, you as though travel back in time, and sit with him in a comfortable Moscow lounge, listening to the gentle Selezniev's piano play, while Bogoljubov sits opposite you, smoking a cigarette... They don't know yet that they will all sooner or later leave their motherland forever and die in foreign countries. Their names will be struck from their country's chess history for years. I remember coming across their photos in my youth and looking at faded, blurry pictures, as though they could tell me something about those men's fates...

Do you know, by the way, how fun it is to leaf through old magazines and suddenly, instead of a boring "professional" article, find a reporter's vivid sketch, filled to the bream with the realities of that bygone era – with all those "life details", without which any story is dead – even a chess one?

This was how I felt after reading the article by **Boris Pereleshin** – a popular feuilletonist who, together with Ilya Ilf, Evgeny Petrov and Yuri Olesha, created the famous "fourth page" of the *Gudok* newspaper. The son of a state counsellor, a student of the historical-philological faculties of St. Petersburg and Tomsk universities, he was a close friend of Ilf. Pereleshin Lane in *The Twelve Chairs* is named after him... Boris Nikolaevich suffered a tragic fate: he was accused of belonging to a "spying terrorist SR organization" in 1938 and shot.

Judging by the text, the author had good knowledge of our game. Read and enjoy – you don't get such a colorful tournament report every day.

At the Tournament
(A Spectator's Impressions)

"The Hunting Club. First, there's a row of smoky, cool rooms, a cramped assembly of robust, striped-breasted fellows, Komsomol girls in vibrant sweaters, a whole buzzing, gray-eyed city set alight by sport. There are other rooms, too, chess pieces glistening like evil black and yellow lights. The slimmest, chiseled wooden sets, "Chigorin" style, and the special "Staunton" tournament sets, are sold in the corner. The shelves are brimming with chess publications.

Stop. Keep absolute silence. Do not make a noise scraping the floor.

---

[12]   A fictitious town from the book *The Twelve Chairs* by Ilf and Petrov where the hero Ostap Bender plays chess

The energetic signboard, the voracious crowd pushing at the barrier, the fighters behind the barrier sitting completely still, in wooden silence.

The Soviet Championship Tournament.

The seriousness of this mental fight can be clearly seen. Its grandiosity is shown on posters and diagrams.

These ten or twenty people are fighting bitterly for the title of the <u>first</u> chess player of the Soviet Union.

But an amateur, just standing there, can't immediately feel all the drama and tension of this struggle.

Behind the barrier, there's an academy of silence and immobility.

Moves are sometimes played only every 10 or 15 minutes.

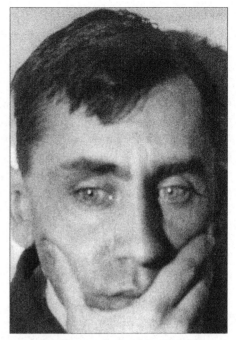

The only known photo of Boris Pereleshin, taken by his friend Ilf.

The amateur chess game with constant piece captures and mad swings of fortune from one side to the other is as different from an elite chess game as a random street fight (that includes the senior street-sweeper and ends up with the arrival of a policeman) is different from the great Battle of the Somme or at Aisne.

Here, all the pieces stand side by side squaring up to the enemy, join each other in tight strike groups, their muscles retract into their shoulders, everything on the board waits, and the opponents make some extraneous maneuvering moves, completely incomprehensible to an amateur, because they aren't fighting for a piece, or even a pawn, or the position, but for an infinitely-small part of the piece or position.

But how quickly the entire game comes crashing down as soon as this smallest part is lost.

And how much work, almost physical strain, is needed to achieve this infinitesimal advantage.

And to get that advantage, even Grandmaster Bogoljubov (the name signs over other tables read "<u>Maestro Nenarokov</u>" or "<u>Maestro Romanovsky</u>", or some other maestro, but over Bogoljubov's table, there's the harsh, embossed

"Grandmaster Bogoljubov") has to lean over the table with his entire body, eyeing the board for ten or fifteen minutes, looking at every piece, almost diving into the crease that divides the board into two halves; he squints at the clock face, flickering alarmingly near his elbow, then looks at all the pieces again, finds a cigarette in his pocket without taking his eyes off the board, puts it into his mouth the wrong away, winces, turns it around, smokes it in two puffs, stubs the butt into an ashtray, and then suddenly moves a piece with a short motion, pushes the clock and writes the move down.

But still, even after recording his move and walking several steps away from the table, he puts his hands deep into his pockets and looks at the diagram of his game through the cigarette smoke (a sleepy boy, as soon as the move is made, moves a piece on a huge demonstration board over each table); then he comes to some other player's table, looks at the game with one eye and then takes a long look across the hall at his game again.

The grandmaster is perfection. In everything, from his huge, square-jawed head to blunt-nosed, cubic shoes, a short, very podgy man, perfectly square, perfectly precise like all 64 squares of the board at once. He walks with straight, measured moves.

Romanovsky is the 1923 Soviet champion, with long parted hair, with the incomparable face of a fanatic, a liberal teacher of the 1860s, a selfless sportsman and, of course, an artist.

Grigoriev, thin, terribly mobile, like black fire, always swift, always hurrying.

The grandmaster is terrifying. He laughs with one corner of his mouth, his face unmoving as though made of stone, the hollow laugh flies out of his powerful chest. He listens to offers for simultaneous displays with one ear and mutters his acceptance or refusal. Bogoljubov started playing chess relatively late. His talent is immense. Fifteen or so years ago, in Kiev, when he was a beginner and lost to Bogatyrchuk and others, Bogoljubov, then not as fat as now, said seriously that he was going to become world champion – and during Emanuel Lasker's last visit to Moscow, the latter said quite ornately about Bogoljubov, 'I foresee a world champion's crown on his brow.'

Meanwhile, the clock is ticking almost noiselessly. It calls the grandmaster back to his table. The clock is the chess player's destiny. As any destiny, the chess player's destiny is unpredictable. And the tournament organizers are at fault if the mechanism of this destiny is not working properly. Unfortunately, this phenomenon manifests itself at every tournament. The clocks would go too fast or too slow at the New York tournament, the clocks would go too fast or too slow at the Soviet Championship Tournament as well. In the game Selezniev – Sergeyev, the clock, as it turned out, was wrong by 1 hour and 40 minutes. Speaking of clocks, we should also remember the carpets – or rather, the lack of them. The noise from the shuffling crowd disturbed the players. For this oversight, the organizers were punished with almost medieval brutality. They had to stand in the tournament hall at all times, occasionally crying out desperately, "Do not scrape the floor!"

The "wooden curtain" of 64 squares, separating the leading chess players from real life and gathering them all into a tight circle of chess interests and chess conversations, is swaying from external blows. The huge crowd, holding their breath, jostle at the barrier, climbing the benches to watch the demonstration boards on the walls. Bogoljubov makes a move. His wooden army goes into a resolute attack. The thunder of the wooden artillery, the clouds of dust, the neighing of wooden horses all reach the sky. In chess conversations, we can briefly hear the city names: Hastings, New York, Triberg. There's an atmosphere of extreme sporting tension and interest in this Hunting Club hall, indicating the full resurrection of elite chess sport in the USSR, this peculiar form of art." (*Shakhmaty*, September 1924.)

The Appearance of Bogoljubov before the People

Golubev: "The outcome of this meeting of European professionalism with our best amateurs leads us to rather bitter thoughts, and we should fully admit our defeat. It's not that we didn't expect Bogoljubov to win – it was certainly possible – but we didn't expect him to win that easily and in such a style that makes us doubt that the Russian chess art has really progressed. Bogoljubov didn't win with subtle combinations that he's so good at, didn't win with a stubborn struggle for the smallest positional advantage – no, pure technique was enough to win him the tournament...

Of course, in addition to that ideal technique, there was another factor in this brilliant victory: the briefcase with theoretical "baggage" that the professional maestro always carries with him, which probably has numerous secret compartments as well. The most interesting games from the fighting point of view – against Romanovsky, Bogatyrchuk and Levenfish – were won in the opening and then just "concluded" after less important moves. Only Sozin managed to draw from a worse position. Our maestros should come to their own conclusions from Bogoljubov's convincing win, and we can only wish that Bogoljubov himself, as the new Soviet champion, will achieve more success at international tournaments, without besmirching the workers' banner of the Republic." (*Shakhmatny Listok*, September 1924.)

Bogoljubov: "Even when I was still abroad, I still had some information about the incredible interest in chess in the USSR, but the wide interest in the championship shown by the public exceeded my wildest expectations; it's especially pleasing to see young chess fans, sometimes even children...

The organization of the championship, in addition to its main purpose, was also helpful in another regard – it increased interest in chess, both among those who can play and those who cannot... However, the best way to raise interest in chess is to hold a competition between the best representatives of the chess arts; therefore, we should give our utmost support to the project to hold an international tournament in Moscow next year, inviting the best Soviet players too, of course.

Efim Bogoljubov. The championship participants "were rather surprised to meet a modern European, clothed like a London dandy and smoking very expensive cigars from time to time." (Bogatyrchuk)

Without a doubt, we could attract the best European masters, along with Em. Lasker and Capablanca.

The Championship Tournament indeed united almost all the best Russian chess forces. Only A. A. Alekhine and O. S. Bernstein were absent; the latter, however, hasn't played in any tournament since the war.

Unlike the apolitical Bogoljubov, who, like a gentle calf, indeed managed to "suck on two cows" for a time, Alekhine immediately expressed his opinion of the new government as soon as he went abroad; he ended his book *Chess Life in Soviet Russia* with the following words: "Currently, the Russian players can only hope for chance opportunities and, of course, use them as productively as possible until the thing that is awaited by the Russian chess public with the same burning hope as the whole honestly-thinking Russia, finally happens." He meant the fall of the Bolsheviks, of course. After such a statement, the Kremlin realized that Alekhine had burned his bridges and never sent him tournament invitations; however, they weren't in a hurry to declare him a "White Guard", either. Maybe they hoped that he would come around eventually?

The Leningrad maestro I. L. Rabinovich was quickly out of contention for the championship; however, with good play in the second half of the tournament, he even managed to take fifth prize.

A. S. Selezniev, who had recently achieved major success at the Moravska Ostrava tournament, taking fourth prize, didn't play particularly well, either; perhaps he didn't expect to meet such stiff competition in the championship. The Moscow champion, V. I. Nenarokov, didn't play at his full strength either, hampered by his poor health. However, until the last rounds, he had a chance to take one of the top places, and only losses against weaker opponents pushed him further down the table. Nevertheless, Nenarokov is a dangerous opponent for anyone in the tournaments. It's a pity that he hasn't had a chance to prove himself in international tournaments yet.

> **Golubev:** "I. L. Rabinovich, a player of a "stone" style who has it especially bad in this era when old theory is taken apart, still passed his test with flying colors, and he played the last third of the tournament so well (5/6!) that he even managed to take fifth prize. An achievement after such a poor start!
>
> The other guest from abroad, A. S. Selezniev, played quite dull chess. Games where one player just strives to draw against a strong opponent cannot be considered a worthy piece of chess art.
>
> Ill fate plagues the Moscow champion, V. I. Nenarokov. His style is very good, however, Vladimir Ivanovich, along with some brilliant examples of chess creativity, played some very weak, apathetic games, marred with blunders.

We could have expected more from A. F. Ilyin-Zhenevsky – his play was solid, but he failed to obtain good results – and N. D. Grigoriev. The latter would occasionally overestimate his position and go into reckless attacks. Grigoriev was the only one who managed to gain a won position against me *(see game 19)*.

P. A. Romanovsky, who took second place, showed great composure and outstanding inventiveness. At the start of the tournament, he got some poor positions, but because of his calmness and relatively high playing ability, he managed to save them. I am sure that he would perform well at an international tournament if he's in form. His interesting and original style reflects his unusual trait of personality; in this tournament, he was too eager in following Reti's opening advice.

> **Golubev:** "Looking at the tournament results in the Soviet sphere, we should praise the "deputy champion", P. A. Romanovsky. He took second

place at the Olympiad, behind Alekhine, then won the 1923 championship in Petrograd, and now he's the runner-up again – mathematically, he has the full right to call himself the best chess player inside the USSR. This wouldn't be enough, however, if we didn't add his <u>creativity</u> to the mix, which cannot be measured by numbers, but is still very important for the evaluation of individual qualities."

Ilyin-Zhenevsky: "Romanovsky's career is interesting not only because of external successes (he has suffered from some serious setbacks as well), but because of his rich, diverse ideas that he created in his chess journey as well. Probably no Soviet player has brought to their logical conclusion so many brilliantly won games as Romanovsky." (From the book *International Chess Tournament in Moscow.*)

"P. A. Romanovsky, who took second place, showed great composure and outstanding inventiveness." (Bogoljubov.) (64, No. 3, 1924).

Levenfish's "playing style is solid and balanced... he can create positions that make beautiful combinations possible." (Bogoljubov.) (64, No. 1, 1924).

The Leningrad champion G. Y. Levenfish showed great composure. His playing style is solid and balanced; this should lead him to success in future international tournaments, because these qualities are prerequisites for success against serious competitors. Stylistically, he is similar to Reti and Spielmann, but he is free of those masters' flaws: Spielmann's unnecessary fervor, which has spoiled the results of many tournaments for him, and Reti's excessive propensity for positional play. In addition to solidity and balance, Levenfish's play is elegant; he can create positions that make beautiful combinations possible.

Golubev: "Levenfish is one of those darlings of fortune who has received great gifts from Caissa. With his great tactical prowess, he executes his plan, wearing down his opponents with a number of subtle moves. Being a good strategist and firmly believing in his creative strength, Grigory Yakovlevich often misevaluates the position while creating his plans, which occasionally leads to poor results. Great theoretical knowledge and its careful application helps him greatly..."

Levenfish: "Despite the fact that Bogoljubov came from Germany to play in the tournament, I was quite optimistic, but was proven wrong. I lost two games, sharing 3rd–4th places... It turned out that the Soviet masters, cut off from chess life abroad, have fallen behind in both opening theory and technique." (From the book *Selected Games and Memories*.)

F. P. Bogatyrchuk, together with whom I started my chess career in Kiev, was a very dangerous opponent even back then (1911–1914). He won one of the tournaments at the time, with a very strong line-up; Izbinsky took second, I was third, and Evenson took fourth place. However, Izbinsky died prematurely in 1912, then I left Kiev, and then Evenson, a talented and brilliant player, also tragically died an untimely death, so he didn't have many strong opponents left. However, despite the lack of practice, his great combinational talent manifested itself, showing fully in a number of great games in this competition. I'm sure that his chess development is far from over.

Golubev: "There were a number of cities in the old Russia that had their own recognizable faces in the chess world. We know Lodz with its solid positions, Riga with subtle analysis, Kiev with its "all-out attacking style". Bogoljubov and Bogatyrchuk are the best sons of their native Kiev. Bogatyrchuk has improved considerably over the last year, creating some attacking brilliancies; his positional skills have got better as well, and his only weakness is endgames. If he manages to improve those as well, Bogatyrchuk will get very close to the first two artists."

Grekov: "Bogatyrchuk could have shared second place with Romanovsky had he defeated Duz-Khotimirsky in the last round, but he had a bad day: after a sharp, very intense struggle, he managed to obtain an advantage, but in the decisive moment he lost an important tempo. Duz-Khotimirsky, whose defense was very inventive, exploited this error and gained a winning position..." (*Shakhmaty*, September 1924).

Of the new players who didn't have maestro titles yet, we should highlight Y. S. Vilner and B. M. Verlinsky, whose play looks very accomplished and solid. But we should pay special attention to V. I. Sozin, who, despite playing in such a serious competition for the first time, immediately showed good playing ability and was even in the leading group for a while. I wish him the right conditions to obtain experience and composure, which are necessary even if you are talented.

The lack of practice was quite detrimental for the old maestros F. I. Duz-Khotimirsky and A. I. Rabinovich, but A. A. Smorodsky and S. N. Freymann, well-known pre-war players, were hit especially hard: in the last ten years they haven't played in any serious competitions and, living in remote places, have been almost completely cut off from the chess world.

Freymann lived in the Kushka fortress, on the border with Afghanistan, and only moved to Tashkent after the tournament. He didn't move to that "remote place" by accident: Red Terror forced many noblemen to escape either abroad or to the very outskirts of the empire.

Levenfish: "His full title was Baron von Freymann, but there was nothing "baron-like" in Sergei Nikolaevich. I remember that when we first met, he introduced himself to me as "Freymann, student from the last century," which was true – he enrolled in college in 1899.

To succeed in chess, in addition to talent, you have to have tenacity, willpower, composure. Freymann lacked those qualities. He would play brilliantly occasional games or parts of games, but then just crumble and lose. For instance, he lost a strategically won game against Lasker in the 1909 international tournament in that way. His status of a perpetual student could also be explained by the weak will of this very talented player." (From the book *Selected Games and Memories*.)

S. K. Rosenthal and A. S. Sergeyev didn't prove themselves at the tournament; evidently, they still lack experience, but I should say that they both played better in the second half of the tournament than in the first.

This was the sole Soviet Championship appearance for Professor Solomon Konradovich Rosenthal, MD. He played in the 1911 All-Russian Amateur Tournament, took prizes in "B" tournaments in Hamburg (1910) and Breslau (1912); after the revolution, he won the Belorussian championship three times (1923–1925), and in 1933, he achieved his old dream, winning the first-category tournament in Leningrad and gaining the master's title. After that, he retired from chess...

Concerning my own success, I should say that my result is quite flattering for me, because the competition level was very high. I was in form at this tournament, which, unfortunately, I cannot always say about my performances." (*Shakhmaty*, September 1924.)

Bogatyrchuk: "Bogoljubov played brilliantly in the tournament and, showing his obvious superiority, won the first prize easily...

In the same year, I heard about the elevation of the new dictator – Stalin. In the first months after Lenin's death, the party's regime weakened somewhat, and we watched with joy (alas, premature) the struggle between the party higher-ups in the *Diskussionniy Listok*, a supplement to the *Pravda* newspaper. In those years, everyone was still hoping for something, waiting for something good. Meanwhile, Stalin and company entangled the country. People's thoughts and hearts were covered by a ubiquitous web that submitted us to their will."

P.S. Every Cloud Has a Silver Lining

In early October, Romanovsky, vexed by the loss of the Soviet champion's title, challenged Bogoljubov to a match. The essence of his convoluted letter was such: "Based on my achievements in three All-Russian tournaments, I believe that you would not refuse me the right to ask you to compete with me separately and perhaps allow another opportunity for both of us: you could prove your champion's title that you won at the recent tournament, and I could retain the title that I won in 1923 but had to relinquish to you this year because of your excellent play..."

He shouldn't have done that. The result of the match (Leningrad, 30th November – 28th December) didn't leave any doubt about Bogoljubov's superiority: +5−1=6 (the match was played until a player gained 6 points, but the first 4 draws did not count). His colleagues tried to explain that result in various ways. Golubev said that "Romanovsky is not a match player, he's a dangerous tournament player," and even called him "an amateur maestro." Levenfish replied that the critic overlooked the main reason for his loss: "his opponent's superior technique." Creatively, Romanovsky was on top of his game: "Bogoljubov never outplayed him with combinations in any games, and that wasn't because his style changed. I'm sure that against

Rubinstein, Bogoljubov will show his brilliancy and temperament again. But Romanovsky's combinational skills, characteristic of the masters of the Russian school founded by Chigorin, are quite high, and there aren't many players able to defeat him on these grounds."

Romanovsky also showed great fighting qualities. Despite being crushed in the first half of the match (−4=2), he didn't lose heart and still fought on. The result of the second half was much better: +1−1=4. Moreover, he was the only player to defeat Bogoljubov in the subsequent Leningrad tournament!

...The saying "every cloud has a silver lining" has a kernel of truth about it. The disappointing results of the tournament and match allowed **Nikolai Grekov** to question the main proposition of the past conference – "one workers' tournament is more important than a dozen championships":

"There is even an opinion that chess should be solely a tool to improve the general cultural level. But this view of chess contradicts its very essence. Chess is an art, first and foremost; as such, it provides an opportunity for limitless achievements. This is the nature of chess. This is the main charm of chess, and its main power as a cultural factor. If you don't view chess as an art, it will lose its glamour and degenerate. So, in addition to widening the reach of chess, we should also work on its depth. As well as the tournaments for beginners and weaker players, we need more showcase tournaments, maestro tournaments. The elimination of illiteracy and the building of elementary schools are not the only things that are necessary – we need universities as well!...

Admitting the necessity of such work in the area of chess art will produce a number of serious competitions. They will promote more in-depth study of chess and give our best players the training necessary to increase their playing strength. Such competitions, compounded by more frequent meetings with West European maestros, will become the foundation of our maestros' success in their future international endeavors." (*Shakhmaty*, December 1924.)

Money Can't Buy Happiness

Amazingly, no games collection of this championship was published either, even though everyone at the conference was talking about the propaganda of chess art and little else. Maybe they thought that such a book would be too difficult for the "wide working masses" and would only put them off chess, while for everyone else, wouldn't the best games published in the three magazines be enough? If you have only just started playing, read *64*: everything is simple and clear, the lines aren't longer than 1 or 2 moves. The solid players have a choice: subscribe to either *Shakhmatny Listok* or *Shakhmaty*. The former of these two, like *64*, is rather politicized, flirts with the authorities and adopts a general "proletarian" image, while the latter is pointedly academic and European-class, but the chess annotations are good in both magazines...

But maybe it was even simpler? Maybe one of the decision-makers was just annoyed that a visiting star from Germany had become the champion, rather than one of the USSR's "own" players. And maybe he said, with all his revolutionary directness, "Comrades, we should not publicize the successes of a bourgeois grandmaster! He should first prove that he's one of ours, a Soviet man!"

Be that as it may, only 63 games survived out of 153 played in the championship. However, almost all of them were thoroughly annotated, so I had a good choice.

By tradition, I'll open the selection with the three games that were awarded brilliancy prizes by the high jury – Bogoljubov, Nenarokov and A. Rabinovich. However, the brilliancy prizes themselves aren't mentioned in any magazines. The tournament prizes were unmentioned as well, except for a brief sentence in the June issue of *Shakhmaty*: "There would be 4 or 5 prizes, the first prize

is 250 rubles." The reason for such secrecy was simple: playing "for money" was considered a bourgeois vestige. Here's a resolution passed at the conference: "Abolish money prizes in all competitions organized by the VSFK chess sections, give the All-Union Chess Section the right to allow money prizes in each individual case if necessary."

First Brilliancy Prize

Bogoljubov: "This game, which started with a quiet opening, seemed drawish to all spectators and masters watching it, but Levenfish managed to prepare a stunningly beautiful, well-calculated rook sacrifice that ended in a spectacular finale; this game deservedly received the brilliancy prize."

Moreover, the American sci-fi writer Isaac Asimov included it in his novel *Pebble in the Sky*; I think this is the only game from Soviet Championships that have earned the honor to be featured in fiction!

No. 15. Ruy Lopez C84
Verlinsky – Levenfish
Moscow 1924, round 15
Annotated by G. Levenfish
1.e4 e5 2.♘f3 ♘c6 3.♗b5 a6 4.♗a4 ♘f6 5.♘c3 *(an old move that is now considered quite harmless and isn't played much)* **5...♗e7 6.0-0 b5 7.♗b3 d6 8.d3.** *8.♘d5!? was more energetic, intending 8...♘a5 9.♘xe7 ♕xe7 10.d4.*

8...0-0 9.♘d5 (9.a4 is better) **9...♘a5 10.♘xe7+ ♕xe7 11.♘e1.** White's plan – prepare the push of the f-pawn – is not well thought-out, and its execution is poor, because it hinders the a1 rook's development. I think that white should have played on the queenside, for instance: 11.♘d2 ♘d7 12.a4 ♘xb3 13.♘xb3 f5 14.f3 etc.

11.♗g5 h6 12.♗xf6 ♕xf6 13.♘d2 ♗d7 14.f3 ♘xb3 15.axb3 led to a rather quick draw (Spassky – Beliavsky, Tilburg 1981).

11...♘xb3 12.axb3 ♘d7 13.f4. White should have played 13.♗e3 f5 14.f3, then c2-c3 etc. Notably, after f2-f4, white can't cope with the arising problems.

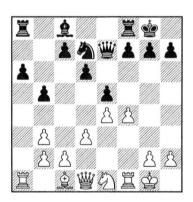

13...f5! Opening of the f-file is beneficial only to black, who can quickly get his rooks into the game. And, what's even more important, by removing the e4 pawn, he gets the long diagonal for his bishop.

Strategically, the game is easy to understand, but the tactics are rather interesting.

14.exf5 ♖xf5 15.♘f3. Trying to rectify the error. 15.♕f3 ♖b8 16.♕c6 ♘c5 gained nothing because of the threat ♗b7; 15.fxe5 ♖xf1+ 16.♔xf1 ♘xe5 17.d4 ♗g4 18.♕d2 ♖f8+ 19.♔g1 ♕f7 etc. is even worse.

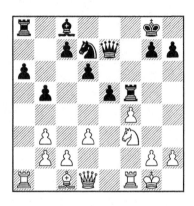

15...♗b7! Of course, not 15...exf4 16.♘d4, then ♗(♖)xf4, and white is safe.

16.♗d2. White hurries to connect the rooks, planning a drawing combination. 16.fxe5 ♘xe5 17.♘xe5 ♖xe5 and then ♖e2 lost immediately.

16...exf4 17.♘d4 ♖g5 18.♘f3. White's defensive plan hinged on this. It seems that he regains the pawn or forces a draw by repetition.

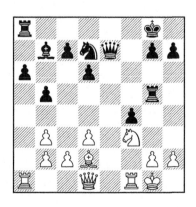

18...♖g4! Starting the decisive combination. Black threatens 19... ♘e5 and ♖f8.

19.h3 ♖xg2+!! 20.♔xg2 ♕g5+ 21.♔h1. The only move (21.♔f2 ♕g3+ 22.♔e2 ♕g2+ 23.♔e1 ♖e8+; *21.♔h2 ♕g3+ 22.♔h1 ♕xh3+ 23.♔g1 ♕g4+ 24.♔h2 ♘e5*).

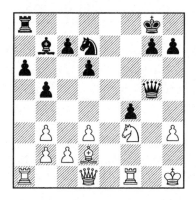

21...♘e5. Not 21...♕g3 due to 22.d4, and black can't get the a8 rook into play because of the threat d4-d5.

Was it a hallucination? It didn't even go away years later: in the book Selected Games and Memories, *Levenfish repeats the same idea. Actually, after 22...♖f8! white can't save the game: 23.♗xf4 (23. d5 ♗xd5) 23...♖xf4 24.d5 ♕xh3+ 25.♔g1 ♕g3+ 26.♔h1 ♘e5 or 23.♕e2 ♕xh3+ 24.♔h2 ♗xf3+ 25.♔g1 ♕g4+ 26.♔f2 ♘f6.*

22.♕e2. After 22.♗e1 (preparing ♔h2), black had a pretty win: 22... ♕h5 23.♔g2 ♖e8!, for instance: 24.d4 ♘xf3 25.♖xf3 ♖xe1 or 24.♗c3 ♘xf3 25.♖xf3 ♗xf3+ 26.♕xf3 ♖e2+.

To give you the full experience, I'll also add 22...♘xf3! 23.♖xf3 ♖e8

24.♗f2 ♖e3! 25.♔h2 (25.♗xe3 ♕g3) 25...♖xf3, crushing.

22...♕g3 23.♕g2 ♘xf3! Threatening 24...♕xg2+ and ♘xd2+.

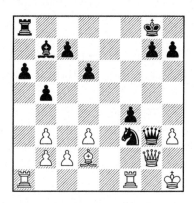

24.♗c3. The only way to prolong the game was 24.♕xg3 fxg3 25.♖xf3 ♗xf3+ 26.♔g1, but after 26...g2 the endgame, despite the opposite-colored bishops, is hopeless for white.

24...♘d4! The final combination, forcing checkmate.

25.♕xb7 ♕xh3+ 26.♔g1 ♘e2+ 27.♔f2 ♕e3+. *A funny detail: annotating the game for* Shakhmatny Listok, *Levenfish shows 28.♔e1 ♘xc3# as the finale; however, his annotations for* Shakhmaty *end with the words "and mate in two", i.e. 28.♔g2 ♕g3+ 29.♔h1 ♕h3#. A split personality?*

Second Brilliancy Prize

In this game, black followed in the footsteps of the inventor of this entire development system (and not only the move 1...♘f6, as many think!): the talented Moscow chess player Mikhail Klyatskin, who, according to Ilyin-Zhenevsky, also "preferred to capture with the c-pawn on move 5, opening a line for the queen's rook."

No. 16. Alekhine Defense B03
Bogatyrchuk – I. Rabinovich
Moscow 1924, round 1
Annotated by F. Bogatyrchuk

1.e4 ♘f6 2.e5 ♘d5 3.c4 ♘b6 4.d4 d6 5.exd6. The simplest way to get a quiet game with a small advantage: black is behind in queenside development, and his knight is placed poorly on b6.

Alekhine considered the Four Pawns Attack, 5.f4, the most dangerous line for black.

5...cxd6. Black usually captures with the e-pawn. The game move is dubious, because it weakens the queenside, and white can get three pawns versus two at any moment.

Tournament practice has questioned this abstract evaluation many times, but the capture 5...exd6 is indeed considered more solid for black.

6.♗e3 g6 7.♘c3. Perhaps it was better to play 7.d5 with the subsequent ♗d4. *In the 1990s, this logical idea was executed either immediately with 6.d5, or after 6.♘f3 g6.*

7...♗g7 8.♘f3 0-0 9.h3 ♘c6 10.♕d2.

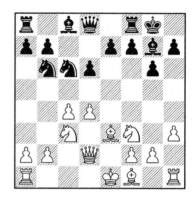

10...d5. Black sharpens the queenside and center too prematurely, which, as we'll see from the course of the game, is detrimental for him. It was better to play 10...♖e8, which is met with 11.b3. *But here, Fritz is afraid of the reply 11... e5!, so it recommends 11.d5! ♘e5 12.♘xe5 ♗xe5 13.a4 instead.*

What should black have played? It seems that he could have kept equality with the other break in the center, 10... e5!

11.c5 ♘c4 12.♗xc4 dxc4 13.0-0 ♗f5. *So many things depend on a single move! Almost the same position occurred in the game Pytel – Gipslis (Lublin 1969), but instead of 10.♕d2(!), white played 10.♖c1.*

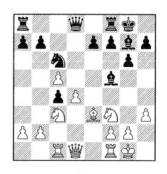

The difference looks tiny, but it was enough for black to get good counterplay: 14.♕a4 (14.d5 ♘b4; 14.b3 ♗d3) 14...e5! 15.dxe5 ♗d3 16.♖fd1 ♕e8 17.b3 ♘xe5 18.♘xe5 ♗xe5 19.bxc4 ♕xa4 20.♘xa4 ♖fd8 with equality.

14.♖fd1. *14.d5 was tempting as well.*

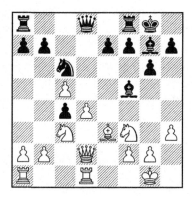

14...♘b4. Looks threatening, but gains nothing for black. 14...♗d3 was no better due to 15.b3. Black should have played 14...♖e8.

And after, say, 15.b3 (the immediate 15.d5 is stronger) 15...b6 16.d5, black has an interesting way to equalize: 16...cxb3! 17.dxc6 ♕xd2 18.♗xd2 b2 19.♖ab1 ♗xb1 20.♖xb1 ♖ac8 etc.

15.♗h6 b6 16.♗xg7 ♔xg7 17.a3.

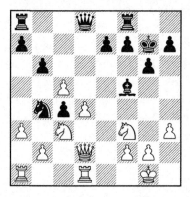

17...♘d3? The knight occupies a seemingly very strong position, but this is the losing move, because white, constantly threatening b2-b3 and g2-g4, has enough time to create an attack. It was better to play 17...♘d5, and there could follow 18.♕e2 ♗d3 19.♕e5+ ♘f6 20.c6 with a better position for white.

Perhaps black had better chances to hold after 18...♘xc3 19.bxc3 ♕d5!, and if 20.♕xe7, then 20...♖fe8 21.♕d6 ♕xd6 22.cxd6 ♖ed8.

18.c6! Unexpected and very strong. The c6 pawn only looks weak, as black can't play 18...e6, stopping d4-d5, because of 19.g4.

18...♕d6 19.d5 ♕f6.

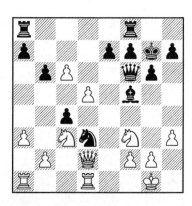

20.♕e3! Black is forced to accept this pawn sacrifice, because otherwise white plays 21.♖d2, quickly getting all his pieces into play.

20...♘xb2. *It seems that only this move was the decisive mistake. Instead of the "forced" capture, the skeptical Fritz recommends... a counter-sacrifice: 20...♖ad8 (it* *wouldn't work on the previous move because of 20.♘d4!) 21.♖d2 e6!*

And if 22.g4 (22.c7 ♖d6!; 22.d6 ♖xd6 23.g4 ♖xc6 24.gxf5 exf5 with three pawns for the bishop), then 22...exd5 23.gxf5 (23.c7 ♖de8) 23...d4, regaining the piece.

21.♖d4. The rook occupies an excellent position, which it holds almost until the end.

21...b5 22.g4 ♗d3. The only move. 22...♗c8 is met with 23.♘e4, winning the queen.

23.♘xb5 g5 (White threatened ♖f4) **24.♘e5! ♖fd8 25.f4!** *(a dual – 25.d6!)* **25...h6.**

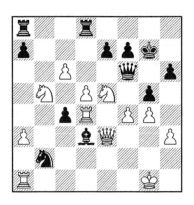

26.♘d7. *White is not tempted by the "tightrope dancing" that required*

very precise calculations: 26.c7! ♖e8 (26...♖dc8 27.♘d7 ♕a6 28.♕e5+ ♔g8 29.d6! or 27...gxf4 28.♕f2! ♕g5 29.♕xb2) 27.d6 exd6 28.♘xd6 ♖e6 29.♕f3 ♖f8 30.♘dxf7! ♖e7 31.♖d6 etc.

26...♖xd7 27.cxd7 ♖d8. It seems that winning would be quite hard for white because black has a strong passed pawn on c4, and the movement of the d4 rook is limited.

However, white manages to find a winning combination.

28.fxg5 hxg5 29.d6! ♖xd7 30.♘c7 ♔f8.

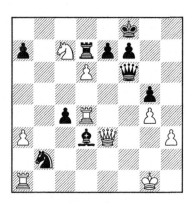

31.♖e1! Wins by force: white threatens 32.dxe7+, winning the rook. Black can't play 31...exd6 because of 32.♕e8+ ♔g7 33.♘e6+! 31...♖xd6 is bad as well due to 32.♘d5 with an irresistible attack.

31...e6 32.h4! gxh4 33.♖f4 ♕g6 34.♕e5 ♕h6 35.g5. Black resigned.

Third Brilliancy Prize

Even in tournaments where Ilyin-Zhenevsky's performance was poor, he would still play a couple of beautiful games. Positions with an initiative were his specialty, and he played them very energetically, so his opponents were quite wary of going for such positions against him.

No. 17. French Defense C15
Ilyin-Zhenevsky – Sergeyev
Moscow 1924, round 10
Annotated by A. Ilyin-Zhenevsky
1.e4 e6 2.d4 d5 3.♘c3 ♗b4 4.♗d3 c5 5.a3 ♗a5 *(5...♗xc3+!?)* **6.exd5 exd5.** After 6...♕xd5, white wins a piece with 7.b4 ♕xd4 (7...♕xg2 8.♗e4) 8.♘ge2.
7.dxc5.

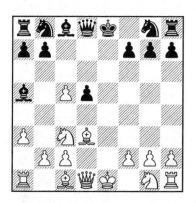

7...♗xc3+ *(there was an alternative: 7...d4 8.b4 dxc3 9.bxa5 ♕xa5)* **8.bxc3 ♕a5 9.♘e2 ♘f6.** Had black regained the c5 pawn, he would have gifted his opponent a tempo after 10.♗e3.

10.0-0 0-0 11.♗e3. Now black can't regain the pawn without giving up further material.

11...♘c6. If 11...♘bd7, then 12.♗d4! ♘xc5 13.♗xf6 gxf6 14.♘f4 with a strong attack on the black king's position, for instance: 14...♘xd3 15.♕xd3 ♗e6 16.♘h5, threatening ♕g3+.

12.♗d4 ♘d7. *The only chance to fight back at all was 12...♗g4, intending to weaken the attack with trades. But now, a Lasker-like combination with a double bishop sacrifice is brewing...*

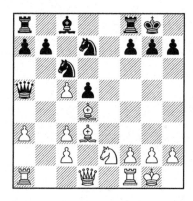

13.♖b1! a6. If 13...♕xa3, then 14.♖a1 ♕b2 15.♕d2, and the queen is lost.

14.♘f4 ♘xd4. After 14...♘xc5, there followed 15.♗xh7+! ♔xh7 16.♕h5+ ♔g8 17.♗xg7! ♔xg7 18.♕g5+ ♔h7 19.♘h5 ♕xc3 20.♘f6+ ♕xf6 21.♕xf6, and white wins because of the black king's poor position.

15.cxd4 ♘f6 16.♖b6. Cutting off the queen from the kingside and threatening a sacrifice on f6.

16...♗g4   17.♕c1   ♕a4.
Intending to meet 18.c3 with 18... ♕d7, centralizing the queen and defending all the weak squares. But white now executes a decisive exchange sacrifice.

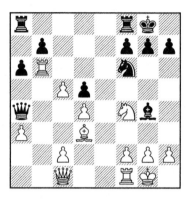

18.♖xf6! gxf6 19.♘xd5 ♗h5 (leads to mate) **20.♘xf6+.** Black resigned: 20...♔h8 21.♕h6 ♗g6 22.♗xg6 fxg6 23.♕xh7#.

The Workaholic Queen

The new USSR champion thought it would be unethical for him to nominate one of his own games for the brilliancy prize, so let's begin our "non-brilliancy" selection with an instructive game from Bogoljubov; his queen ran around as much as the king's knight in the Alekhine Defense.

No. 18
I. Rabinovich – Bogoljubov
Moscow 1924, round 3
Annotated by E. Bogoljubov

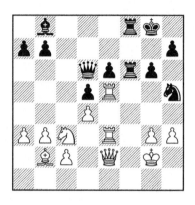

24...♕d8! 25.♘d1. White is forced to give up the exchange, because after 25.♖xe6 black wins with 25...♗xg3! *(for instance: 26.♖xf6 – black threatened ♘f4+ – 26...♕xf6 27.♕f3 ♕g5! 28.♕xd5+ ♕xd5+ 29.♘xd5 ♖f2+ 30.♔g1 ♖xc2)*, while 25.♖g5 is met with 25... ♖f2+.

25...♗xe5 26.dxe5 ♖f4! 27.♔h2 ♖f1 28.♗d4 b6 29.♖c3 ♖1f7 30.♘f2 ♖c7 31.♖d3.

31...♕g5 (The subsequent queen invasion is decisive) **32.c3 ♕c1 33.a4 ♕b1 34.b4 ♕a1 35.♕c2 ♕f1! 36.♖d1 ♕c4.** It was possible here to play 36...♖xc3 37.♕d2 ♖xf2+ *(37...♘xg3!)*, but the game move is even more convincing.

37.♖d3. Preventing 37...♖f3. Of course white has no good defense anymore.

37...♕xb4 38.♘g4 ♖f1 39.♕e2 ♕b1 40.♗f2 ♖c1 41.♕f3 ♖h1+. White resigned.

A Lost Opportunity

However, the visitor from abroad didn't always have it that easy. Especially in the second half of the tournament, when Bogoljubov got "bored with victories", started slacking a bit and was barely able to save several games. And he almost got checkmated in the penultimate round...

No. 19
Grigoriev – Bogoljubov
Moscow 1924, round 16

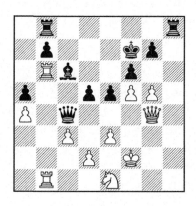

33.d4!? Under positional pressure, Grigoriev realizes that the queen exchange is only good for black and tries to complicate the game with a pawn sacrifice. And unexpectedly succeeds!

33...♕xc3 34.♘f3 ♕c2+ 35.♔g3 ♔f8 36.♘h4 exd4.

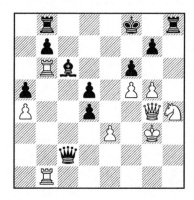

37.♕f4? Losing the chance to become the hero of the tournament, the only player to defeat Bogoljubov: 37.gxf6!! ♖h7 38.♕f4! ♖e8 39.♖xb7 ♗xb7 40.♖xb7 ♖xe3+ 41.♕xe3! dxe3 42.♘g6+, with a mate in two. Now white is worse.

37...♖e8 38.♖1b3. Capitulation. 38.♘g6+ ♔g8 39.♖6b2 ♕c3 40.♖b3 fxg5! 41.♕xd4 ♕xd4 42.exd4 etc. was more resilient.

38...fxg5 39.♕xg5 ♖h6. A pretty computer dual: 39...dxe3 40.♖xe3 ♖xh4! 41.♖xe8+ ♗xe8 42.♕xh4 ♕c7+ or 42.♔xh4 ♕f2+, snatching the b6 rook.

40.exd4 ♕d1 41.♘f3 ♕f1. White resigned.

It's Never Too Late to Resign

There were actually a lot of tactical miscalculations, mistakes and even one-move blunders in the tournament. Smorodsky set some sort of a record, resigning against Verlinsky on move 9! There were some premature resignations as well.

No. 20
Sozin – Freymann
Moscow 1924, round 3

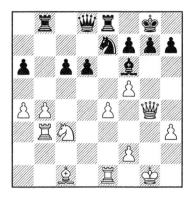

Veniamin Sozin, "even though it was his first competition at such a level, immediately showed decent ability and was among the leaders for quite a while." (Bogoljubov.) From the Russian Chess Museum archive (64, No. 3, 1924). Published for the first time.

25...♖xb4. Intending to win a piece...

26.♖xb4 ♗xc3 27.♗b2! Black obviously overlooked this great reply (now both rooks are taboo because of the mate on g7), got upset and immediately resigned. However, he could still have put up some resistance after 27...h5! 28.♕g5 f6 29.♕g3 ♗xb2 30.♖xb2 ♘xf5, for instance: 31.♕g6 ♖e5! 32.f4 ♕e8 33.♕xe8+ ♖xe8 34.♖b6 ♘d4 etc.

What a Pawn!

Ilyin-Zhenevsky: "Today, one of the most likable participants of this tournament plays against me – Fyodor Parfenyevich Bogatyrchuk. He's considered one of the sharpest and most brilliant Russian masters. His play is similar to that of Romanovsky, in a way... Bogatyrchuk's ability to suddenly sharpen the position and launch a swift attack showed clearly in my game against him. Each of his moves, in addition to direct threats, also contained a number of subtle and interesting traps..."

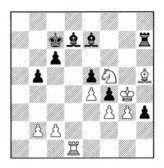

No. 21
Ilyin-Zhenevsky – Bogatyrchuk
Moscow 1924, round 6
Annotated by F. Bogatyrchuk

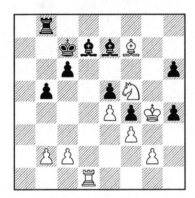

44...h5+   45.♗xh5   ♖h8! A curious position: white has no good moves. For instance: 46.♗f7 h3! 47.g3 (black threatened ♖h4#) 47... ♖h7 48.♗h5 ♖xh5 49.♔xh5 ♗xf5 50.exf5 fxg3, and black wins. It was possible to prolong the struggle, but not to save the game, with an exchange sacrifice *(47.♖xd7+ ♔xd7 48.gxh3)*.

Bogatyrchuk probably annotated this game from memory. Otherwise, he would have surely noticed that at the end of his line, it's black, rather than white, who has to resign! After the obvious 51.♔g4 h2 52.♔xg3, both dangerous passed pawns fall. So, is the combination wrong? No, it isn't, but Bogatyrchuk mixed up the move order.

Instead of 48...♖xh5?, black wins with 48...♗xf5+! 49.exf5 fxg3 50.♔xh3 ♖xh5+ 51.♔xg3 ♖xf5 etc.
   46.♖h1.

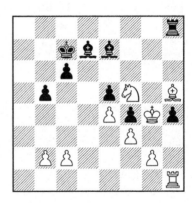

46...h3!! A rare pawn sacrifice for an actual game. White can't capture it because he loses a piece *(after 47...♖g8+ if white captures with the pawn or rook)*. Only his rook can move; the black king and queenside pawns quickly decide the game.
   47.c3   ♔b6   48.b4   c5   49.gxh3. White prefers a quick demise.
   49...♖g8+   50.♗g6   ♖xg6+ 51.♔h5   ♗e8   52.♘xe7   ♖g1+. White resigned.

The Chess Le Corbusier

Unfortunately, Alexei Selezniev, the renowned study composer, didn't perform too well at the tournament. However, his best games were quite brilliant.

No. 22
Selezniev – Ilyin-Zhenevsky
Moscow 1924, round 14
Annotated by A. Selezniev

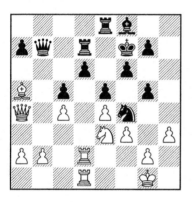

31.b4! (Starting an attack on d6) **31...♞e6 32.♖d5! ♖c8.** White threatened 33.bxc5 ♞xc5 34.♖xc5. If 32...♞f4, then 33.♖xc5.

Did masters indeed annotate the games for magazines without the board? In the second line, a Zwischenschach 33...♞e2+ 34.♔f1 ♞c3 (fork!) won the game for black. I think that instead of 33.♖xc5?, Selezniev meant another capture, 33.bxc5, and if 33...♞xd5, then 34.c6! ♞b6 35.♕b5, winning.

33.bxc5 ♞xc5 34.♕a3 g6. To stop the knight from invading on f5.

35.♗b4 (again threatening ♗xc5 etc.) **35...♖dc7.**

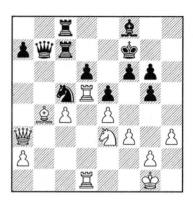

36.♖1d2! A very important move, preparing to seize the b-file. The immediate 36.♖b1 wasn't as good, because the b4 bishop would have been pinned.

36...♖c6 37.♗xc5 ♖xc5 38.♖b2 ♕d7 39.♖b4 ♖8c7. *Black had one last-ditch chance to complicate things: 39...g4!? 40.♞xg4 (40.hxg4 ♗h6) 40...♖xc4 41.♖xc4 ♖xc4 etc. Now white is clearly better.*

40.♕b3 ♕c6 41.♖b5. *It's clear that a composer is playing white. How can you deny the pleasure of making such a construction out of major pieces?*

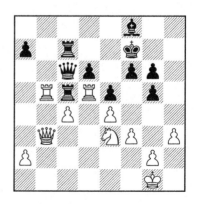

41...♕a6 42.♖dxc5. The closing, decisive maneuver.

42...♖xc5. After 42...dxc5 43.♘d5 and the subsequent push of the a-pawn black was lost as well, but he could have prolonged the resistance.

43.♘d5 f5. There is no salvation for black. After 43...♖xb5 44.cxb5, there's a threat of discovered check. After 43...♗g7, there follows 44.♖b7+ ♔g8 45.♘c7 ♕xc4 46.♘e6 ♕xb3 47.♖xg7+ and 48.axb3.

44.♖b7+ ♔e6 45.♘c7+ ♖xc7 46.♖xc7 ♔f6.

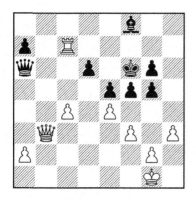

47.♕b7! The simplest: after the queen trade, black loses another pawn. It's much less clear after 47.c5 ♗e7, because black gets some chances for a perpetual check.

47...♕xb7 48.♖xb7 d5 49.cxd5 ♗c5+ 50.♔f1 g4 51.hxg4 fxg4 52.♔e2 gxf3+ 53.gxf3. Black resigned. This was my best game in the tournament.

Fiesta

Unlike the somewhat dry creations of Selezniev, Romanovsky's games, as usual, looked like a corrida. He would go for wild complications, risking to be gored by the "bull" numerous times, but, like an experienced matador, kept his cool even in the most desperate situations.

No. 23

Rosenthal – Romanovsky
Moscow 1924, round 4
Annotated by P. Romanovsky

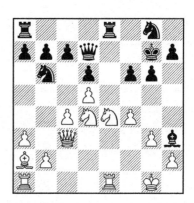

25.♘g5! ♘a4. If 25...fxg5, then 26.♘e6+ ♔h6 27.fxg5+ ♔h5 28.♕d4! ♗g4 29.h3, winning (*there's an even more spectacular line: 29.♕xg4+! ♔xg4 30.♖e4+ ♔f3 31.♖ae1! ♖xe6 32.♖f4#*).

26.♘ge6+ ♗xe6 27.dxe6 ♕e7 28.♕c2 ♘b6 29.f5 ♘h6 30.g4. A venturesome move. The preparatory 30.h3 maintained a strong attack.

30...♘xg4 31.♕g2 ♘h6 32.fxg6 hxg6.

33.♕xb7? Why? After 33.♗b1, white maintained a very strong attack and could at least regain the pawn without simplifying the position *(33...g5 34.♕e4)*.

33...c5 34.♕xe7+ ♖xe7 35.♘b5 ♘g4! (with a double threat after ♘e5) **36.♖ed1 ♖h8! 37.♖xd6 ♖xh2 38.b4.**

38...♖e2? Black missed a beautiful win here. He should have played 38...f5!! 39.bxc5 ♔f6! 40.cxb6 ♖eh7 41.e7+ ♔g5! 42.♖xg6+! ♔f4 43.♖f1+ ♔g3 44.♖f3+ ♔xf3 45.♘d4+ ♔f4 46.♘e6+ ♔g3 with an unavoidable mate. I calculated all that over the board.

However, I decided against the combination, because I thought that after 38...f5 39.bxc5 ♔f6 40.♘d4 ♖eh7 41.e7+ I couldn't capture the e7 pawn with the king due to 42.♖ae1+ and ♖d7+, forgetting that in this line, my b6 knight was not captured yet, so white can't give the check on d7.

39.bxc5 ♘c8 40.♘d4. 40.♖d8 ♖7xe6 41.♖xc8 ♖6e3! was bad for white.

40...♖e4! 41.♖d7. *Junior shows a curious line: 41.♖d8 ♘e5 42.♘b5 ♖xe6 43.♖xc8 ♘f3+! 44.♔f2 ♖e2+ 45.♔xf3 ♖6e3+ with perpetual check.*

41...♘e5.

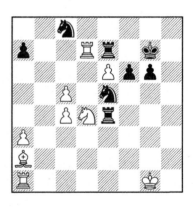

42.c6? A blunder that ends the game immediately. The only move was 42.♖d1, with the possible continuation 42...♖xd4 43.♖7xd4 ♘f3+ 44.♔f2 ♘xd4 45.♖xd4 ♖xe6 etc. Of course, white couldn't even dream of winning after that.

42...♖xd4! 43.♖xd4 ♘f3+ 44.♔f2 ♘xd4. White resigned.

For the Title of Soviet Champion

Romanovsky was obviously Caissa's favorite. In the previous championship, she helped him against Kubbel, and she saved him from certain doom in this championship as well. And he ultimately finished just one point ahead of Levenfish and Bogatyrchuk. Imagine what would have happened had Peter Arsenyevich not taken second prize? He would have lost the title of the "best chess player inside the USSR" and the moral right to challenge Bogoljubov as well.

The following titanic fight was, in everyone's opinion, the best in the match between the two.

No. 24. Grunfeld Defense D90
Bogoljubov – Romanovsky
Leningrad (m/5) 1924
Annotated by E. Bogoljubov and
P. Romanovsky
1.♘f3 ♘f6 2.c4 d5. This attempt was succesfull when first made by Marshall against Reti in New York (1924); however, it has certain positional drawbacks, because black loses far too soon his chance to create a pawn center **(B)**.

"It was better to prepare d7-d5 with c7-c6." (Alekhine)

3.cxd5 ♘xd5 4.d4. 4.e4 is probably good as well, but it commits white to playing sharply **(B)**.

Alekhine, annotating the Reti – Marshall game, attaches a question

mark to 4.d4, pointing out that white "could use the slow approach 4.g3 and 5.♗g2 to his advantage, or immediately seize the center with 4.e4 ♘f6 5.♘c3 with the subsequent d2-d4."

4...g6. Marshall played 4...♗f5, preventing 5.e4, which is I think more fitting for this opening **(B)**.

This defense makes black's position difficult. Maybe it was better to play 4...♗f5, and if 5.♘c3, then 5...♘xc3 6.bxc3 ♕d5! 5.♕b3 gained nothing for white, because black can go for a pawn sacrifice: 5... ♘c6 6.♕xb7 ♘db4! etc. **(R)**. *But the move 6.♕xb7? is more or less cooperative: after 6.♘bd2! ♘b6 7.e4, white is better.*

The strangest thing here is that 4...g6 was deliberately played by Romanovsky, who experimented a lot back then. The game Reti – Marshall was published in Shakhmatny Listok *with annotations by Tarrasch, and Romanovsky should have known his evaluation of the move 4... ♗f5: "Marshall now prevents e2-e4, strengthening the knight's great position for quite a while."*

5.e4. *If the knight were on c3, like in a "normal" Grunfeld, black could have traded the knights and then made the standard move c7-c5. But now he has to retreat. It's just move 5, and Bogoljubov has already outwitted his opponent!*

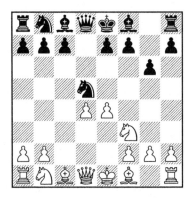

5...♘f6 6.♘c3 ♗g7 7.h3 0-0 8.♗e3. White plays his opening in a classical style, without creating any weak points in his position. It's hard to find a plan for black, however. He literally has nothing to play for **(R)**.

8...c6. Another possible move is 8...b6, developing the c8 bishop **(B)**.

9.♕d2 ♖e8 10.♗d3 ♘bd7. Another possible plan was to develop the bishop on b7 after b7-b6. However, the c-file is open, and the weakness on c6 would have eventually made itself felt **(R)**.

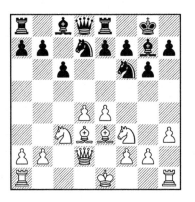

11.e5! (Bogoljubov) **11...♘d5 12.♘xd5 cxd5 13.0-0?** Black's position is poor, but this move allows

him to create some sharp play with mutual chances. It was better to play 13.♘h4, to meet 13...f6 with 14.f4 fxe5 15.fxe5 ♖f8 16.♔e2! with the subsequent ♖af1 – white's attack can hardly be stopped **(R)**.

A vivid example of Romanovsky's subjectivity. He attaches a question mark to a good developing move, even though the line he showed was not forced. Black doesn't have to open the f-file for his opponent: it's better to play 14...♘b6, finishing development.

13...f6! Black couldn't wait, because white threatened to move the knight away and then play f2-f4 **(R)**.

A necessary move, otherwise black has no counterplay **(B)**.

14.♗h6 fxe5 (Black can't play 14...♗h8 due to 15.e6 with the subsequent ♗b5 – **B)** **15.♗xg7.**

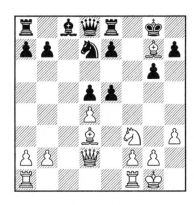

15...♔xg7. 15...e4 was very risky because of 16.♕h6! exf3 17.♗xg6 hxg6 18.♗h8 ♔f7 19.♕g7+ ♔e6 20.♖fe1+ ♔d6 21.♕xg6+ e6 (of course, not 21...♔c7 22.♖ac1+ ♔b8 23.♕g3+ etc.) 22.♕g3+ ♔c6 (if 22...♔e7, then 23.♖xe6+!) 23.♖ac1+

♔b5 24.♕d6!, and the black king's position is hopeless **(B)**.

This slight sloppiness in annotation is characteristic of Bogoljubov; you don't often see similar slip-ups in Alekhine's commentary. The computer catches such mistakes immediately.

Instead of 24.♕d6?, which, after 24...♕e7!, cedes the advantage to black (25.♕c7 a5 or 25.a4+ ♔xa4), white should play 24.♕xf3 ♔a6 25.b4 b5 26.♖c6+ ♔b7 27.♖cxe6 ♖xe6 28.♖xe6, even though it's unclear whether white still has a win after 28...♘b6 or even 28...♕xh8.

But that's not even the main point:

Instead of 22.♕g3+?!, there's a much better move: 22.♖ac1!, not letting the king out of its cage:

1) 22...♘b6 23.♗f6! ♖e7 24.♕g5

fxg2 25.♗xe7+ ♕xe7 26.♕e5+ ♔d7 27.♖c7+;

2) 22...♘f8 23.♕g3+ ♔d7 (23... e5 24.♖xe5) 24.♗e5!;

3) 22...fxg2 23.♕g3+ ♔e7 24.♖xe6+ etc.

16.dxe5 ♘c5 17.♘d4! This move forces black to play 17...♘e6 – otherwise, the white knight on d4 is very dangerous **(B)**.

Black is worse out of the opening, but, at any rate, he has managed to avoid direct threats. The next part of the game turns into a fight over the d4 square **(R)**.

17...♘e6 18.♘e2. *It seems that white did lose some advantage with his last two moves.*

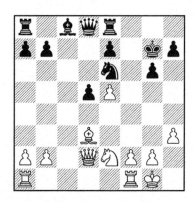

18...♖f8. A waste of time. Of course, the rook is better on f8 than on e8, but you should not make quiet positional moves in such positions. Black immediately had to play 18... ♕b6 19.♔h2 ♗d7 (not 19...♘d4 due to 20.♗xg6) 20.f4 ♘c5! (threatening ♘xd3 and ♗b5) 21.♘d4 (21.♗c2 ♗b5) 21...♘e6!, and if 22.♘f3, then 22...♘d4 etc **(R)**.

However, instead of 19.♔h2, Junior recommends the energetic 19.a4!? ♗d7 (19...a5 20.♗b5) 20.a5 ♕c7 21.f4, and it's hard to disagree with it.

19.f4   ♕b6+   20.♔h2   ♘d4? Again, a weak move. Black should have played 20...♘c5, and if 21.♘d4, then the knight goes back to e6 **(R)**.

Now that black has seemingly defended against the threat f4-f5, he can get the bishop out as well, and afterwards, he would have no further difficulties **(B)**.

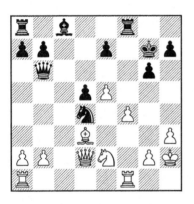

21.♘c3! This apparently modest move is the key to unlocking black's position, because the natural 21... ♗e6 is met with 22.♘a4! ♕c6 23.b3, threatening both ♗xg6 and ♖ac1 **(B)**.

23.♕b4! ♘f5 24.♖ac1 is even stronger. His opponent also gave 21.♘c3 an exclamation mark.

21...e6? This and the next move constitute positional capitulation. Black should have sacrificed a pawn with 21...♗f5 22.♗xf5 (22.♘xd5 ♕d8! 23.♗xf5 ♕xd5 with the threat ♘f3+ is more dangerous) 22...♘xf5 23.♘xd5 ♖ad8 – black has good

drawing chances. Instead, he holds on to the pawn and ultimately gets a position he'd rather give up ten pawns to get rid of **(R)**.

I wonder what Bogoljubov would have thought about "good drawing chances" in this position – he was an excellent technical player. Perhaps Romanovsky meant the simplifying line 24.♖fd1 ♖xd5 25.♕xd5 ♘e3. But after 26.♕d7! ♕xb2 27.♕xe7+ ♖f7 28.♕g5 ♘xd1 29.♖xd1 or the simple 26.♕d4 ♘xd1 27.♖xd1! ♕xd4 28.♖xd4 and ♖d7 white has a healthy extra pawn in the rook ending, with every chance of winning.

22.♖ad1 ♘f5? White threatened 23.♗xg6, but it was much better to retreat with the knight to c6, not ceding the crucial d4 square **(R)**.

After 22...♘c6, white could use the fact that the knight is too far from the kingside and launch a strong attack: 23.h4 (with the subsequent ♔g3). The maneuver ♘c3-b5-d6 is also certainly possible **(B)**.

23.♗xf5! (Bogoljubov) **23... ♖xf5 24.♘e2 ♗d7 25.♘d4.** The white knight has got to d4 – and now it's decisive **(B)**.

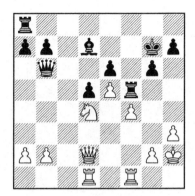

25...♖f7 26.h4! (Bogoljubov) **26...♖af8 27.♖f3.** White has created a great strategic rank a3-h3, with the rook able to move quickly to either flank **(R)**.

27...♔h8. Black, upset at losing the battle for the d4 square, is playing rather haphazardly, almost in a panic. It was necessary to play 27...♖c8 **(R)**.

28.♖c1 ♕d8? (Romanovsky) **29.♔g3!** This is better than 29.g3,

because it leaves the a3-h3 rank open **(R)**.

29...♖g8. *The computer insists on 29...a5, preventing the white queen's maneuver.*

30.♕b4 ♕b8.

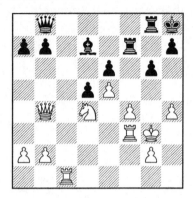

31.♕d6! (Romanovsky) **31... ♕e8.** The queen trade lost quickly: 31...♕xd6 32.exd6 ♖c8 (to protect from ♖c7) 33.♖xc8+ ♗xc8 34.♖c3 ♖f8 (or 34...♗d7 35.♖c7) 35.♖xc8! ♖xc8 36.♘xe6 etc. **(R)**.

"e2 to e4, or Bogoljubov versus Romanovsky". The result of this match that immediately followed the championship left no doubts as to the grandmaster's superiority: +5−1=6. Cartoon by N. Radlov, from his archive. First published in the Begemot satirical magazine (No. 11, 1924).

32.♖c7 ♗c8 33.♖xf7. Most players would have played 33.♖fc3 here, which also leads to a win, because white's position is overwhelming. The game move, however, starts a beautiful forcing combination that quickly wins material for white **(R)**.

33...♕xf7   34.♖c3   ♕e8! (Bogoljubov). 34...♖f8 is bad due to 35.♔h3!, and the capture on f4 is impossible due to ♖f3 **(R)**.

35.♖c7! (Bogoljubov) **35...♖g7.**

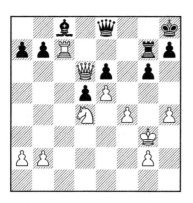

36.♘b5! The first blow. Black can't play 36...♕xb5 because of mate in three. After 36...♖xc7, there's 37.♘xc7 ♕g8 38.♕e7 ♕g7 39.♕d8+ ♕g8 40.♘e8!, winning **(R)**.

36...a6 37.♕c5! Another surprise, which cannot be countered by black in any way. White threatens ♖xc8. After 37...♗d7, there's 38.♘d6, crushing **(R)**.

37...♖xc7 38.♘xc7 ♕f7. Forced, because 38...♕g8 is met with 39.♕e7, following the line after white's 36th move. After 38...♕d8, meanwhile, there's 39.♕d6 ♕xd6 40.exd6

♔g7, and white wins a piece with a peculiar move 41.♘a8! **(B)**.

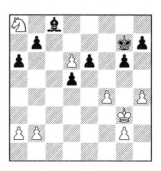

This line is the last point of white's combination **(R)**.

39.♘xd5   ♗d7.   39...exd5 40.♕xc8+ ♔g7 41.e6 ♕e7 42.♕d7 ♔f6 43.♕xd5 is totally hopeless **(R)**.

40.♘f6 ♗c6 41.♕d6 h5 42.♔h3 ♔g7. Black's position is mostly difficult not because he is down a pawn, but because his queen and bishop are very limited in their mobility **(R)**.

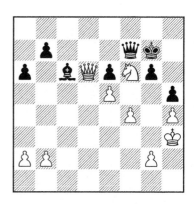

43.g4 ♗f3. If 43...hxg4+, then 44.♔xg4 ♔h6 45.♕d8 ♕g7 (45... ♔g7 46.♔g5) 46.♕d2!, winning, for instance: 46...♕c7 47.h5 gxh5+ 48.♔h4 ♔g7 49.♕c2 etc. **(B)**.

44.gxh5 gxh5. Black could have held for longer after 44...♗xh5 **(B)**.

45.♕d3 ♗g4+ 46.♘xg4 hxg4+ 47.♔xg4 ♔h6 48.♕d8! (Romanovsky) **48...♔h7.** After 48...♕f5+ 49.♔g3 black can't avoid the queen trade: 49...♔h7 50.♕e7+ etc., while any queen move along the h7-b1 diagonal is met with 50.♕h8+ ♔g6 51.h5+ ♔f7 52.♕f6+ and ♕g6+ **(R)**.

49.♕f6 ♕g8+ 50.♕g5 ♕c8 51.h5 ♕c6 52.♕g6+ ♔h8 53.♔g5. Black resigned.

"One of the most interesting games of the match," Bogoljubov concluded, *and... after winning another tournament together with Romanovsky, this time in Leningrad, he returned to Triberg, until the next Soviet Championship.*

Стоят слева направо: М. Вакулин, маэстро И. Л. Рабинович, А. Перфильев, И. П. Голубев, Я. Г. Рохлин, Н. Голубев, П. Колпаков, Л. Я. Травин. Сидят слева направо: маэстро П. А. Романовский, А. Ф. Ильин-Женевский, проф. Б. М. Коялович, проф. А. А. Смирнов, гросмейстер Е. Д. Боголюбов.

The Leningrad tournament was won by Bogoljubov and Romanovsky, while Gotthilf took third place. Ilyin-Zhenevsky: "The play of the Russian chess players showed definite progress, which can mainly be explained by the beneficial effect of Bogoljubov's stay in the USSR." (Krasnaya Panorama, No. 6, 1925.) Published for the first time.
Standing left to right: Vakulin, I. Rabinovich, Perfilyev, I. Golubev, Rokhlin, N. Golubev, Kolpakov, Travin. Sitting left to right: Romanovsky, Ilyin-Zhenevsky, Koyalovich, Smirnov, Bogoljubov

Diagnosis: Chess Fever

4th Soviet Championship: Leningrad, 11th August – 6th September 1925

"Well. If you care for your digestion, here's good advice for you:
do not discuss Bolshevism or medicine during your lunch.
And God forbid you should read Soviet newspapers before lunch."
Mikhail Bulgakov, *Heart of a Dog*

You might have thought that it was time for celebration. The world had never seen such a sharp rise in interest towards chess! In literally two years, the number of organized chess players in the country reached 40,000. The powerful support from the state, which equated chess with other forms of art, was unprecedented as well. The 1925 Soviet Championship was held in the halls of the former Grand Duke. In November, almost the entire world chess elite came to play the international tournament in Moscow – Capablanca, Lasker, Rubinstein, Marshall, Tartakower, Reti, Grunfeld, Spielmann... This was the first chess tournament in history that was funded with state money. They spent an incredible sum – 30,000 rubles! The foreigners were lodged in Moscow's best hotel, the National, the games were held in the Metropol (back then – the Second House of Soviets). The guests were amazed by the fervent fans (more than 50,000 spectators visited the games!) and by the kingly reception. The stunned Capablanca later said in an interview: "... During our entire stay in Moscow we were the guests of the government, and were at all times treated with great courtesy. For example, we were exempted from all hotel expenses, even the most trifling ones, and accommodation in Moscow as well as the train trip to Russia and back was paid for by the Soviet government on behalf of all the players." It's a chess heaven, isn't it?

But something stops me from sharing Capablanca's enthusiasm... Bernard Shaw said that he was welcomed in 1931 "like Karl Marx", and that he admired collectivization, which he described as a chessboard with tiny squares of shabby farms turned into a huge, continuous area that led to incredible results. He added that the Russian revolution hadn't seen any vandalism. Lion Feuchtwanger, after his visit to the USSR, wrote the book *Moskau 1937*, describing Comrade Stalin's "good-hearted guile" and justifying the prosecution of the "enemies of the people". Also, do you know how they sent a delegation of Soviet writers to America right after the war? Stalin asked how much the best American writers were paid for one book. Hearing the answer, $5,000 (the "old", gold-backed dollars), he ordered: "Give [Konstantin] Simonov $10,000. But on one condition: he should spend all of them, until the last cent!" The stunned Americans would remember the "fabulously rich Russian writers" for a long time afterwards... A genius PR move! Of course, if we disregard the fact that our country was ruined and lived on food stamps back then. Still, we are very good at bamboozling gullible foreigners...

Frankly, I have already regretted my decision to paint with such a broad brush. I could have just shown the contours of past battles with small strokes, but I'm also trying to recreate the "historical background" each time. I thought that if we take these tournaments out of their historical context, they would lose the connection with the ground, turn into cardboard cutouts of themselves, and the games alone... You could find millions of games in databases, and many of them would be at least as good as those old Soviet Championship games. Indeed, are

In 1924, the Soviet chess organization got a new head – Nikolai Krylenko, a prosecutor and deputy Russian SFSR People's Commissar of Justice, which largely determined chess's importance for the state.

old games even interesting to modern players if they don't know the living people behind those games, if there's no intrigue, no plot? I want you to use this book as some sort of time-travel portal that brings you back to the almost mythical life of the post-revolutionary Russia, turns you into a contemporary of the player whose game you are watching. I want you to... actually become him, for a time! Do you get it? It's not some guy from the book, it's you who just blundered a knight in a better position! And then it's you who walks on the dark street, tired (the trams have already stopped), and you want to give up on all that and just go to the zoo with your kids tomorrow, and then invite some friends to your house and share a drink... But then you wake up the next day, the evening comes – and you again hurry to the tournament hall, believing firmly that today you will play such a brilliant game that even the swarthy Capablanca will turn pale with envy!

But this chess player doesn't live on a cloud. Even though NEP more or less "brought back" the old way of life and weakened the Bolshevist stranglehold, he's still anxious, especially if he was born in a family belonging to an "enemy class". He remembers the years of Red Terror, the military communism – and, reading the Soviet newspapers in the morning (there are no others), he tries to comprehend what the authorities think, how things will turn out for him personally. And when he sits down at the board, instead of battle courage, the heavy feeling of anguish will occasionally fill his chest... But still, you have to play. Forget that you and your fellow All-Russian Chess Union members were recently labeled "chess Kerenskyists" – and play, play on, proving your right to exist with your successes!

I obviously didn't live back then, I didn't sit in on those chess conferences listening to the fanatical reports of the chief prosecutor, I didn't see how the aggressive mediocrity filled our great country – I just read chess magazines of the time, but they left such a heavy taste in my mouth! Everything is so serious, without a smile, as though they aren't writing about a game, but rather describing the creation of an exemplary commune, whose dwellers must, in their leisure time, study the true proletarian openings, improve their endgame technique under the auspices of chess instructors, and on the weekends sing revolutionary songs and entertain the working people with living chess shows... Bulgakov wrote *Heart of a Dog* in the year of "chess fever".

You know, I really felt a bit sick after reading those magazines (the only reprieve was the privately-owned *Shakhmaty*, but it would be extinguished soon). *64*, with its Sovietization and proletarianization of chess, is a particular offender; this Sharikovism[13] permeates you like radiation... So, I promised you the championships, and I'll give you the championships! And let archive fanatics plough through those conferences with their petty intrigues; in any case, after 1925, the Soviet Championships and chess conferences were held apart, both in time and space. I have no more strength nor desire to dig in this "fossilized excrement", as a poet said – all those reports, decrees, resolutions and declarations. And I value my time, you know. I'd rather take my daughter to the zoo, meet my friends, walk in the sun...

Inhuman Power

Bogatyrchuk: "Ever since the time of military communism, it became clear that universal equal material prosperity was just an unfeasible utopia.

---

[13] Sharik was the dog in Bulgakov's *Heart of a Dog*. The word Sharikovism refers to the Soviet mentality that the dog adopted in the story

The "proletarianization" of chess through the eyes of a cartoonist. Above: "Chess-ball. The integration of chess and checkers circles with physical education circles is planned." Below: "Well damn, where the hell did he put his queen? I should give him a good kick and see what remains of him afterwards..." (Begemot, No. 3, 1925.)

The Bolsheviks decided to correct this false theory of equality in their own way: they declared that equality tacitly existed and then, against the background of everyone's suffering and deprivation, created a class of functionaries that were provided with all of life's necessities. They created a network of so-called restricted "dispensers", open only to a limited number of party higher-ups and functionaries. These dispensers were stocked with foodstuffs and wares looted from the population (we can't call these "seizures" anything else). You could buy any necessities and food there, at well below market prices. The dispensers were either located near state facilities or in the city, under unassuming signboards. Of course, you could enter such a shop only with a special pass. This is the practice described by Orwell in his famous book *Animal Farm*: everyone, of course, was equal, but some were more equal than others. These chosen representatives of the "new class" (as defined by the Yugoslavian communist writer Milovan Djilas) received individual *(as opposed to communal)* apartments, treatment in special restricted resorts and hospitals, and they had everything that the ordinary citizens did not.

Of course, all this inequality was only in its infancy in the time of military communism, and only really came to full bloom much later, but its foundation was laid way back in the twenties. Since the newspapers never printed anything about this side of life under socialism – by contrast, they always insisted that everyone lived happily in the country, without exception – we have gradually learned to accept the pervasive lies of the official side of Soviet reality, the lies described by Pasternak as having "inhuman power". So, to survive, we had to keep our mouths shut, not allowing anyone to learn our true thoughts and feelings. Already in those early years, the true, independent laugh and good-natured humor started to disappear from Soviet daily life, replaced by bleak mediocrity." (From the book *My Life Path to Vlasov and the Prague Manifesto*).

Veterans and First-Timers

From the press: "The All-Union chess competitions opened in Leningrad in the Scientists' House on 10th August with a welcome speech from Comrade A. F. Ilyin-Zhenevsky, the chairman of the 4th Chess Conference organizing committee. Greeting the delegates and tournament participants on behalf of the Leningrad chess and checkers section, Comrade Ilyin-Zhenevsky reviewed the development of chess in Soviet Russia and gave a short description of the work preceding the 4th conference.

Comrade Grigoriev, greeting the conference on behalf of the Executive Bureau of the All-Union Chess Section, noted that this conference was essentially the <u>second</u> All-Union chess conference after the October one, because Soviet society had only truly grabbed the reins of the chess movement at the previous conference...

The Internationale sounds, and the ceremonial part of the assembly was over." (*64*, August 1925.)

Sitting (left to right): Y. Vilner, G. Levenfish, Y. Rokhlin (member of the organizing committee), S. Gotthilf, I. Rabinovich, E. Bogoljubov, A. Ilyin-Zhenevsky, F. Duz-Khotimirsky, P. Romanovsky, A. Sergeyev, V. Nenarokov, B. Verlinsky, A. Rabinovich. Standing: S. Freymann, V. Sozin, V. Eremeev (member of the organizing committee), N. Grigoriev, N. Zubarev, A. Selezniev, A. Kaspersky, N. Kutuzov, S. Vainstein (member of the organizing committee) (64. Shakhmaty i Shashki v Rabochem Klube, No. 17–18, 1925.)

Grekov: "The business part has been postponed; it's going to take place in early November, before the international tournament *(actually, the conference was held in early December, in the midst of the tournament)*. The workers' circle championship will also take place in Moscow, starting on 4th September. Leningrad will host the Soviet Championship Tournament, the inter-city tournament and the Red Army Championship Tournament.

All the best USSR chess players are taking part in the championship, except for two: F. P. Bogatyrchuk, whose results and game quality in the two previous championships were so brilliant, and B. M. Blumenfeld, whose inventive play makes any tournament more interesting. We can only wish that these rare, but dear guests will take part in future serious competitions." (*Shakhmaty*, August 1925.)

Romanovsky: "The greetings are over. The participants are invited to a secluded hall to take part in the last act before the tournament begins: the drawing of lots. Almost all Soviet masters, almost all participants of the last championship, are present. Only Bogatyrchuk is absent – to the great regret of all players, he couldn't play because of his work duties – and the Soviet Champion, the fearsome E. D. Bogoljubov, is still sailing somewhere in the Baltic Sea. *(The grandmaster came late to the first round, only arriving at 7 p.m., almost straight from the steamship.)*

There are only three first-timers: Kutuzov, Kaspersky and Gotthilf. Maestro Freymann's arrival was a bit unexpected – last year's failure seemingly did not discourage him...

Finally, the drawing of lots ends, too *(masters in italics)*: 1. *Freymann*, 2. Kubbel, 3. *Selezniev*, 4. *Bogoljubov*, 5. *Nenarokov*, 6. *Romanovsky*, 7. Zubarev, 8. *Sozin*, 9. *Levenfish*, 10. *Duz-Khotimirsky*, 11. *Vilner*, 12. *Verlinsky*, 13. *Ilyin-Zhenevsky*, 14. Gotthilf, 15. Kutuzov, 16. Grigoriev, 17. *Sergeyev*, 18. Kaspersky, 19. *I. Rabinovich*, 20. *A. Rabinovich*.

The players voted Zubarev, Nenarokov and Romanovsky onto the arbitration court, with Bogoljubov and Levenfish as reserves. Afterwards, the assembly ended with private conversations, evaluations of mutual chances, etc." (*Shakhmaty*, August 1925.)

From the press: "The Scientists' House, hosting the championship and the inter-city tournament, is a magnificent building facing the Neva River; formerly, it was a palace belonging to the "grand duke" Vladimir Alexandrovich. The tournaments are held in the spacious staterooms of the palace, covered by soft carpets and well-furnished. The conference delegates and tournament participants are lodged in the palace as well, in the scientific workers' dormitory.

> **Rokhlin:** "On 2nd July 1925, doing the job I was tasked with, I went to the Scientists' House to get permission to hold the tournaments there. The deputy director coldly listened to my request and then answered tersely, "I won't change the event schedule in my club for the sake of chess."
>
> So I had to resort to extreme measures: I showed the letter I received from Moscow, from the All-Union Chess Section.
>
> "Who is Krylenko?" the deputy director asked, looking at the signature.
>
> "What?" I exclaimed, "You don't know who the Deputy People's Commissar of Justice is?"
>
> This changed everything. The bewildered administrator pushed a chair towards me and asked, "How many rooms do you need?"
>
> Seeing that this "endgame" was won, I said, "There are several All-Union tournaments, large crowds are expected, so we need your House in its entirety."
>
> He agreed..." (*Shakhmaty v SSSR* No. 4, 1977.)

The first round of the Soviet Championship started on 11th August, at 4 p.m. The games are held 6 days a week. Saturday is a rest day, and Tuesday is the play-off day for adjourned games. The games are played from 4 p.m. to 9 p.m. and from 10 p.m. to midnight." (*64*, August 1925.)

Under the Banner of Soberness and Position

Romanovsky: "The first half of the strenuous fight is over. I say "strenuous fight", because all nine rounds of the championship were characterized by an abundance of endgames. Bogatyrchuk, the excellent visionary and creator of beautiful combinations, is sorely missed. What's the matter? Where are all those sharp combination attacks, brilliant mates, subtle, well-calculated sacrifices, pawn storms, everything that defines the Chigorin school, so beloved by the Russian heart? Perhaps the root of evil is point-chasing, caused, in turn, by the excessive desire to obtain new rights or an honorary title? Chasing the "master's third" (*scoring at least one third of total points; automatic qualification for the next championship*), wanting to score 9.5 points (the master's title), finish in the top 7 (automatic qualification for the international tournament) or top 10 (chances to qualify for the international tournament), etc.

The nervous, but sincere, I must even say exceptionally sincere Verlinsky counts every day how many points he has to score to take 9ᵗʰ place – this is not just eccentricity on his part.

Ilyin-Zhenevsky: "Boris Markovich Verlinsky is a curious Moscow player. Fifteen years ago, he achieved great successes in the Russian South and was considered one of the strongest Russian chess players. However, war and revolution put a hold on his career, and when he came to the capital in 1921 or 1922, the Moscow public gave him the cold shoulder. Nobody seriously believed in his chess strength. Verlinsky himself was partly at fault: despite his difficult financial situation, he never played in any serious Moscow tournaments or showed himself otherwise... Since 1923, Verlinsky's creativity has flourished again." (From the book *International Chess Tournament in Moscow.*)

Boris Verlinsky scored a sensational victory against Capablanca at the Moscow International Tournament (1925)!

Win a pawn and exchange queens: this seems to be the latest fad in Russian chess thought, one of the richest in the world. My complaints are also echoed in the words of Gotthilf, one of the talented young Leningrad players; he said that it would be great to play "Teichmann-style": attack, but have a draw in the bag as well.

The circumstances were especially unfavorable. The best Leningrad master in the combination creativity department in my opinion, G. Y. Levenfish, lost the first two games due to nervous, inattentive, shallow play. Getting two zeroes when you still have games with first-rate masters ahead can be quite unnerving. Levenfish is a true chess artist, but while creativity is all very well, circumstances have to be adapted to. The transition from intuition to logic, from sharp combinational thought to cautious point earning, is invisible, and it's usually rationalized by unfortunate circumstances. It's hard for a person to overcome their nature and destroy, solely with the power of the will, the pain that follows a strong physical blow.

> Levenfish was also very vain and did not take defeats from weaker players well.
>
> **Batuev:** "While you're losing, Levenfish is a sweet and witty talker, but if you happen to defeat him, you may incur the wrath of Grigory Yakovlevich – so strong that he'll even stop nodding to you when you meet him. Perhaps he was more tolerant to those he considered equal to himself. Kotov said, "If you evaluate both your own and your opponent's strength correctly, you can endure a loss relatively easily. But if you consider your opponent a worthless loser, of course you'll consider your loss very humiliating and annoying." It's best when a grandmaster treats even a first-category player as an equal. I had the misfortune of defeating Levenfish. He threw the pieces from the table onto the floor and walked off without signing the score sheet, and since that time, he considered me an enemy... He evaluated his own play very highly and even thought that he was worthy of challenging for the world championship!" (*Neva*, No. 9, 1984.)

I'll dare to share some of my creations with the readers. I like combinations, moreover, the chess art charms me most when a strong combination suddenly explodes on the board. The feeling of absentmindedness takes its toll on me, because combination creativity is clearly unattainable in such a state.

Kubbel, the creative wizard, is still on his way to earning the master's title. He got an attack once, against Nenarokov, almost lost the game and now, regretting his decision, is slowly crawling to the coveted pedestal on half-points.

Selezniev is blatantly playing for draws, thinking that his past achievements and a top-10 finish guarantee him a place in the international tournament.

> **Zubarev:** "The 'enigmatic' Selezniev, prizewinner of strong international tournaments, stubbornly explains his relatively poor results in the USSR by the fact that it's easier to take a prize in a strong tournament, because "you don't feel like you are obliged to do so". Sounds paradoxical, but the facts seem to prove his reasoning." (*64*, September 1925.) Selezniev set a new record at this tournament: 14 draws!
>
> From the recollections of the writer **Vadim Safonov**:
>
> "I signed up for the chess circle in the Printers' House, our instructor was A. Selezniev, the maestro (they weren't called "masters" back then) who had returned from abroad. His speech was peppered with foreign

catchphrases. He didn't just declare checkmate, he would coo gently, "Zores-matores."

There were already discussions about Alekhine's chances against Capablanca; Alekhine's combinations were already circulating among the players. But Selezniev, pouring a glass of sparkling lemonade in the cafeteria (there was no custom of ordering cognac at the bar), said softly, "Capablanca is playing devilishly!"" (*Shakhmaty v SSSR*, No. 3, 1975.)

A. Rabinovich is playing in a lively and sharp manner, as always. The spirit of combination is more alive in him than in others. He seems to be less interested in points, as well...

Our current and seemingly

"Stocky, cold-blooded, of average height, completely bald since youth, Nikolai Mikhailovich Zubarev was the epitome of common sense and solidity both in life and chess. A typical master of the positional style... But he didn't like uncertainty and would get lost in complicated, double-edged positions, where it's not enough to rely on general principles, on Lasker's "common sense", and you have to use your intuition." (Panov.) From the brochure International Chess Tournament in Moscow, 1925, and its Participants.

future champion, the esteemed E. D. Bogoljubov, is already very far ahead. He, possibly along with I. Rabinovich, is playing very assuredly and lucidly, without giving in to disappointments or illusions. The championship is played under the banner of soberness and position. The two of them are holding this banner in their hands, and so I think that the second place, occupied currently by our foreign prizewinner *(Rabinovich)*, will ultimately be taken by him.

V. I. Nenarokov is playing quite inconsistently. He is, however, overloaded with work from chess publishers, which hasn't abated for the tournament *(he was also ill for the majority of the competition)*. Freymann is a dangerous opponent this year. He only lacks his past composure; if he still had it, he would probably occupy a higher place than he does now.

Unfortunately, Freymann dropped out of the tournament after the 12ᵗʰ round. Nobody really explained why. In

Grigoriev's words, "This fact, however regrettable, had valid reasons", and *Krasnaya Gazeta* wrote that "Freymann had to leave..." This story looks strangely similar to the equally mysterious departure of Petr Izmailov from the 1929 championship (see the respective chapter).

Zubarev has seemingly not changed since previous tournaments. His goal is to score his "third" to qualify for the next championship. There are many mistakes in Sozin's games and his lack of practice clearly shows. Duz-Khotimirsky is true to himself. Wearing an engineer's cap, he sometimes carelessly throws the pieces around the board, and sometimes, grabbing his head and curling his leg under him, goes out of his way to defeat some experienced opponent.

> **Levenfish:** "The talented Duz seems to have regained his former strength, which makes him dangerous for any maestro. Unfortunately, Duz-Khotimirsky is the *enfant terrible* of any tournament, and his shenanigans make a painful impression both on players and the spectators. But this, too, is curable..." (*Shakhmaty*, August 1925.)

Vilner is calm, probably planning to take eighth, ninth or tenth place. There's always hope on Zhenevsky's smiling face. Grigoriev is fantastic, but not solid enough.

The Moscow champion Sergeyev is tenacious in defense, but he's prone to blunders in this tournament, which is costing him a lot. The skills of Kaspersky and especially Kutuzov are inadequate for such a serious test yet... *(By the way, when Alekhine gave simultaneous displays in Arkhangelsk in 1918, Nikolai Kutuzov won one game against him and drew the other.)*

There is no doubt in my mind that the first half of the tournament was played under the banner of positional structures and plans.

> **Levenfish:** "I consider the prevalence of a positional style over combinations a merit of this tournament, an indicator of its strength, because "brilliancies" rarely occur in games between equals – they are almost always played out in games where one opponent is much stronger."

Hypermodernism was present in the struggles, not as something new, but as a template, so it didn't bring anything integral or especially interesting to chess art.

The influence of modernism was evident in the openings. In the middlegames, where opening structures are evaluated, the most original

Championship organizing committee. Sitting (left to right): Y. Rokhlin, I. Rabinovich, A. Ilyin-Zhenevsky, G. Raskin, S. Vainstein. Standing: F. Tigranov, Alexei Alekhine, V. Eremeev, N. Grigoriev. (64. Shakhmaty i Shashki v Rabochem Klube, No. 16, 1925.)

continuations were found in the Teichmann – Rubinstein – Grunfeld style. The openings created mysteries, which, however, remained unsolved for the whole game...

The opening structures for white were mostly based on the move d2-d4, and one of the players told me frankly – why choose another move if this one guarantees at least a draw? That was a revelation to me, and if everything had really gone so far, I think that it's time to thoroughly search for a remedy against this "American" weapon. White's big win percentage shows that this would not be an easy task. But the fact that controversy does exist is as indubitable as the fact that the chess art is still immeasurable, and its depth can truly be equated with a mysterious abyss." (*Shakhmatny Listok*, August–September 1925.)

Passions in the Palace

Grigoriev: "The Soviet Championship has ended. So many hopes, emotions and passions were tied to it. And the palace of the former duke Vladimir saw so much in that brief time. It hosted this bloodless war that excited its participants and spectators so much. Day after day, everyone gathered at 4 o'clock to sit down at their tables. There aren't many spectators behind the barrier at that point: they come later, when the real fight on the board begins.

However, around 8 o'clock, when there's a break in the games, everything changes drastically. You can't recognize the formerly calm, self-assured fighters. One of them sits red-faced, clutching his head, the other one is so nervous that he can't sit still. The situation behind the barrier changes too: so many curious eyes, and endless noise and whispering.

And then the bell rings. Everyone leaves the boards and runs to the cafeteria. It's lively out there – conversations, emotions. The masters aren't separated by a barrier anymore. They are surrounded and questioned by fans. Not everyone, though. Some of them combine leisure with learning and set up pocket chess sets on the table as they drink their tea: they need to analyze the current position. At 9 o'clock, the bell rings again, calling everyone back to the arena.

The excitement is even greater now. The crowd circles the boards where the end is near, like ravens over a corpse. Verlinsky is vociferous when he loses and beams when he wins.

> **Ilyin-Zhenevsky:** "Many think that Verlinsky is seriously ill because of his deafness and resulting speech impairment *(the consequences of meningitis he suffered from in his childhood)*. My numerous observations and meetings with Verlinsky convinced me that his mental health was perfect, and deafness is more likely an advantage for a chess player – it shields him from the outside noise that disturbs so many players."

Selezniev gets up with a sense of accomplishment, earning his next half-point as "a mark of inner peace". Bogoljubov always looks like an Olympian. You can spot neither sorrow nor joy on I. Rabinovich's face. However, you can see both sorrow and joy on A. Rabinovich's face...

> **Zubarev:** "I. Rabinovich's third place surprised nobody. His exceptionally correct, perhaps somewhat dry play shows his strong ability... The expansive A. Rabinovich is a dangerous adversary for anyone. It was he who ruined Levenfish's hopes, defeating him brilliantly in one of the last rounds. His unnecessary nervousness, depriving his play of consistency needed for great success, is the reason for his relatively poor performance."

Abram Rabinovich won the Moscow championship in 1926, and in 1930 he won the tournament of Moscow masters, although in respect of the

Soviet championships he would now only be a commentator and correspondent. His column in *Vechernaya Moskva* was highly popular. "The old maestro, a most flamboyant person; they don't really make them like that anymore," recalled the writer **Vadim Safonov**. "I constantly encountered him in the chess room of the House of Printers *(today it's the House of Journalists)*. A very sharp chess player, always coming up with all sorts of novelties, he always had lots of them on show, he would set up the pieces and relish crushing any guy suggesting a refutation accompanying his proof with the words "Off to bed, patzer!" no matter who his victim was," (*Shakhmaty v SSSR* No. 7, 1990).

Ilya Rabinovich was the first Soviet master allowed to take part in a tournament abroad (Baden-Baden 1925): "The Baden tournament breached a window to Europe, and the Moscow tournament created a friendly relationship between our players and foreign ones." From the brochure International Chess Tournament in Moscow, 1925, *and its Participants.*

The walls of the palace saw all that, but they can tell you even more: the ovations for Vilner, who was the first to defeat Bogoljubov *(see game 33)*; the noisy, wild delight of the Leningrad youth after one of their own, Model, won the inter-city tournament *(he was awarded the "pre-master title"[14], golden watch and a special prize – a Lenin statuette)*; finally, the informal closing party, where many arrived with their wives or girlfriends; the players didn't just get their "badges of honor" (prizes), but also poured over their battles. And then they scattered among the halls, gathered again at the huge balcony and talked about all things (except chess), breathing in the moisture of the Neva and admiring its expanse.

---

14   In Russian – 'uslovny master', literally 'conditional master'

From the press: "The players who scored 50% or more and didn't have the maestro title were awarded it. They were S. B. Gotthilf, N. M. Zubarev, and A. I. Kubbel.

Three brilliancy prizes were awarded: 1st to B. M. Verlinsky for his game against E. D. Bogoljubov *(game 25)*, 2nd to A. I. Kubbel for his game against F. I. Duz-Khotimirsky *(game 26)*, and 3rd to P. A. Romanovsky for his game against N. D. Grigoriev *(game 27)*.

The prize for a prizewinner's best result against other prizewinners was awarded to B. M. Verlinsky. The prize for a non-prizewinner's best result against prizewinners was awarded to Y. S. Vilner. The prize for a non-prizewinner's best result in the last 3 rounds was awarded to N. M. Zubarev, who scored 2/3." (*Shakhmaty*, August 1925.)

This happened yesterday, but today, the palace of battle resumes its peaceful guise as the quiet, sedate Scientists' House. And it is now, when the battle is already over but memories are still fresh, that we want to comprehend the battle's true significance. And it was very significant, indeed. Outwardly, this All-Union championship was very different from the previous ones, especially the last one. It had a more complete and diverse line-up and truly included all the best chess forces of the Union (we can only regret Bogatyrchuk's absence). But it was better in essence, in quality as well. The Russian masters simply played better. And occasional failures do not matter: they always happen, and they always will. Nobody is free from them, they are not representative. But in general, en masse, our masters displayed huge strength. The prizewinners were not the only ones who showed true mastery; almost every player, including those with poor results, played at least 2–3 great, solid games. Throughout the tournament, Bogoljubov said repeatedly that our playing level had improved considerably. He even suffered two losses, despite being on top form, just as he had been at the previous tournament in Breslau. The growth of our strength was clearly evident in another aspect as well: we saw real competition for first place in this tournament. Yes, Bogoljubov led from start to finish and took first prize, but the distance between him and his competitors was not as immense as it was last year.

Levenfish: "Alekhine won the 1920 Olympiad without any effort. Bogoljubov won the previous championship in such a style that we could not really talk of any "competition"... The predictions of all domestic sibyls were unanimous: "Russian masters cannot compete with the world's grandmasters." But, as though to spite all the "prophets", the fight was as fierce as never before. There were moments when Gotthilf had chances for first prize. And if I hadn't lost by accident to A. Rabinovich in round 17, the result of the championship might have been unsuccessful for the grandmaster. His advantage essentially amounted to a half-point. And only the chivalry of Grigoriev, who refused a draw offered by Bogoljubov to fulfill his tournament duty till the end, increased the gap to a full point."

Zubarev: "Grigoriev is a chess poet. As we know, harsh reality always breaks the dreams of poets. A rich imagination is detrimental to the prosaic counting of points."

Bogoljubov only secured his victory in the last round. His frequent claim that our best masters compare with the best Western masters is completely justified. The fight for the other prize places was even fiercer – it's enough to look at the points difference. And this is great, especially considering that our newly emerging forces Verlinsky, Gotthilf and Ilyin-Zhenevsky fought with the well-known favorites. The great success of the youngest of the three, Gotthilf, should be especially praised: he didn't just confirm his title, but also proved himself a true, strong master, even though it was his first high-level tournament.

Levenfish: "Gotthilf proved that his success in the 10-player 1924 tournament in Leningrad, where he had a chance to overtake Bogoljubov and Romanovsky for a while, was no fluke. Despite his youth, he plays with enviable persistence and composure, understands the position quite well, and does not eschew complications. And the future is there for him. Of all the young players, I place my biggest hopes on Gotthilf."

In addition to Gotthilf, the tournament gave us two other new USSR masters: Zubarev and Kubbel. And this fact is very pleasant: nobody ever doubted their true strength even before they formally got their titles.

Solomon Gotthilf "showed himself a true, good master, even though it was his first tournament at such a level." (Grigoriev.) (Shakhmatny Listok, No. 11, 1930.)

To summarize, it's safe to say that the tournament was a great success." (*Shakhmatny Listok*, September 1925.)

"Verlinsky Defeated Capablanca"

Bogoljubov: "I managed to win the Soviet Championships both this year and last. However, if we compare my results then and now, if we look at both tables, we see that this time my victory was not overwhelming: I was only one point ahead of second place! My performance against the other prizewinners was telling as well: I defeated all my main competitors last year, however, this time my results against prizewinners were more modest: +3–1=3. B. M. Verlinsky, however, who took fourth place, showed an incredible performance against other prizewinners: +5–0=2! So, I didn't enjoy a comprehensive victory this time!

> **Zubarev:** "Verlinsky is the universally-recognized moral victor of the tournament *(he defeated Bogoljubov, Levenfish, Romanovsky, I. Rabinovich and Ilyin-Zhenevsky!)*. He could have taken an even higher place had he not felt that he absolutely had to win every game."
>
> Verlinsky was also named the "moral winner of the championship" by Vladimir Piast, who had covered the tournament for *Krasnaya gazeta* (the poet was a passionate chess fan). In his reports he also wrote about Bogoljubov's play without obsequity. For example: "The worst game, oddly enough, was that played by Bogoljubov and Kutuzov. The latter had to play really badly to allow Bogoljubov to fix his position – and then commit another oversight to hang the exchange and lose the game." Efim Dmitrievich demanded that Piast apologize, and without waiting for an apology called the article about his game "stupid". "Piast then filed a complaint with the local court, and the latter sentenced the champion to public condemnation," wrote chess book collector and historian **Nikolai Sakharov**. "An angry Bogoljubov appealed to the All-Union Chess Section, counting on the support of its chairman Krylenko, who was also state prosecutor of the RSFSR. However, the section's leadership decided to treat the court case against Bogoljubov as a private matter which had nothing to do with his title as Soviet champion." (*Shakhmaty v SSSR* No. 4, 1997.) The story with Piast is recounted in more detail, including an analysis of the said game, in a new book by Grigory Bogdanovich *The Creative Power of Bogoljubov: Volume I: Pawn Play, Sacrifices, Restriction and More* (Elk and Ruby Publishing House, 2020).

How do we explain this fact?

At the start, I managed to get ahead of my main competitors, and after round 13, I led by 2 points. However, the results of other players' games between each other showed that this tournament was different from the last one. Last year, P. A. Romanovsky started with 7 wins in a row, whereas this year, after 6 rounds, he'd already lost two games. G. Y. Levenfish fared even worse: he lost the first two games and drew the third; he was so upset afterwards that he even talked about dropping out of the tournament. However, he managed to redeem himself with careful and strong play and even took second prize. The third favorite, I. L. Rabinovich, endured a rough patch starting with round 9, drawing two games and losing three.

It wasn't just 2nd prize that was at stake. After Ilyin-Zhenevsky, Levenfish, I. Rabinovich and Romanovsky shared 1st-4th places in the Leningrad championship, it was decided that the title of city champion would be awarded to whichever of them scored the most points in the upcoming Soviet Championship. Rabinovich won by default in the last round due to Freymann's withdrawal, and had Levenfish lost to Vilner, Rabinovich would not only have won 2nd prize, but would also have gained the title of champion of Leningrad!

A. I. Kubbel, who was among the leaders until round 13, only drew four games out of the last seven, and lost the other three; instead of sharing 2nd–3rd place, he ultimately shared only 11th–13th. Ilyin-Zhenevsky was unlucky as well: he shared 2nd–3rd place until round 18, but lost the last two games and only finished 6th–8th instead.

Zubarev: "Kubbel is a short-distance player, he cannot endure long tournament struggle; this crisis in the middle was very characteristic of him... More discipline – that's the main slogan Kubbel should follow."

Levenfish: "Without a doubt, Ilyin-Zhenevsky achieved great progress, justifying the master's title awarded to him in the spring. However, fortune helped him a lot in the games against Kubbel and Nenarokov. Bogoljubov also had a hand in this, blatantly playing for a draw *(after two losses in a row, Efim Dmitrievich decided against tempting fate and offered a draw on the 13th move)*. Unlike Gotthilf, Zhenevsky's style suffers from passiveness, and he has to compensate for the lack of initiative with tenacious defense."

These are all examples of how quickly the standings can change. After almost every round, 10 or 11 players went almost toe to toe and constantly switched places, and this is the best evidence that their strength is approximately equal.

№ 49 (140)   Изд. „Мосполиграф". Цена в Москве, провинц. и на ст. ж. д. 10 коп.

А. Ф. ИЛЬИН-ЖЕНЕВСКИЙ—чемпион Ленинграда по шахматам, нанесший поражение чемпиону мира X. Капабланке на международном турнире в Москве. На-днях издании библиотеки „Огонек" выйдет книжка тов. Женевского с впечатлениями о турнире.

фот. А. Шайхета.

"A. F. Ilyin-Zhenevsky, the Leningrad chess champion who defeated the world champion J. Capablanca at the Moscow International Tournament." (Ogonyok, No. 49, 1925.)

The setback suffered by Romanovsky, who had finished in the top two at the three previous championships, is no fluke. Rather, this is more proof that other players have progressed much since last year. Romanovsky, who had got used to winning relatively easily, underestimated the new balance of power, and when he finally realized what was going on, it was too late! Even I could have suffered had I not enjoyed the safety buffer of a two-point advantage by round 14...

All in all, we can safely say that the playing level of this championship was significantly better than in the last one. I daresay that one of the reasons for this was my participation in the previous championship, then my match with Romanovsky and the tournament in Leningrad. I hope that the readers won't confuse my sincere joy about this fact with immodesty.

Zubarev: "What can we say about our champion's play?.. The new thing was that Bogoljubov lost his aura of invincibility. He doesn't cause panic in his opponents as he did last year. I like to think that the main reason for this phenomenon was not Bogoljubov's more complacent game, which is to some extent a factor, but rather the increased playing level of the championship participants, the progress of chess art in the USSR, driven by painstaking work within the country and partially, maybe, by interacting with Western Europe, chiefly through Bogoljubov himself.

Efim Bogoljubov: "I managed to win the Soviet Championships both this year and last. However... this time, my victory was not overwhelming: I was only one point ahead of second place!" (64. Shakhmaty i Shashki v Rabochem Klube, No. 22, 1925.)

This increased playing level of Russian players is especially pleasing to see now, on the eve of the Moscow International Tournament, where our strongest players will take on the world's best. Without a doubt, this tournament will be one of the greatest in chess history.

Concerning the results of the tournament, I'll allow myself to say the following.

I personally hope to make the top five, which will probably feature Capablanca, Lasker, Rubinstein and Vidmar. Concerning the distribution of other prizes, it's hard to say anything concrete. We can only be sure that there will be a fierce fight for all other prizes and places – and not only between the foreign luminaries such as Marshall, Reti, Tartakower and Grunfeld; our maestros Levenfish, Romanovsky, Rabinovich, Duz-Khotimirsky (and maybe someone else as well) will leave their mark, too. I deem it necessary to warn the chess public following the Moscow tournament only through newspapers: when you see some "funny" headline, such as "Verlinsky defeated Capablanca", do not think that someone is pulling your leg... *(Bogoljubov was incredibly spot on: Verlinsky ended up as one of the two Soviet masters who defeated Capablanca!)* Of course, I don't want to say that it's Verlinsky who has the best chance to defeat Capablanca (or Lasker!) – it's certainly possible that another of our maestros will enjoy such luck. *(Ilyin-Zhenevsky!)* The least surprising player to do so would probably be Duz-Khotimirsky, who managed to defeat both the winner and the runner-up in the 1909 St. Petersburg tournament, Lasker and Rubinstein. I also think that the brand-new, but very talented maestro Gotthilf will make a lot of draws against the foreigners. *(Six!)* Let us hope that our maestros can hold their own in this international test and wish them the best possible success with all our heart!" (*Shakhmaty*, September 1925.)

P.S. A Test of Strength

The Moscow International Tournament, as we know, was won by Bogoljubov – in many respects because he knew the playing style of the Soviet masters. After good preparation by playing two Soviet Championships, he, unlike the foreign grandmasters, scored almost 100 percent against them (only drawing with Romanovsky and Bogatyrchuk). In the concluding article, Bogoljubov compares his prediction with the actual result:

Bogoljubov: "Among Russian masters, Romanovsky was the most successful, playing with his characteristic freshness and inventiveness. Even though his imagination sometimes leaves his play insufficiently solid, he compensated that with resilience and tenacity. A number of excellent games are testimony to the high quality of his play.

Ilyin-Zhenevsky's success was the most astounding. Nobody expected such a level of excellence in his play at the tournament. He didn't just compete on equal terms with the Soviet masters, who recently were head and shoulders ahead of him: he even defeated Capablanca and Marshall, i.e. exactly those players whose precise play seemed to be the least comfortable

Boris Efimov's cartoon from the Krasnaya Niva magazine shows the top four players from the Moscow International Tournament: Efim Bogoljubov, Emanuel Lasker, Jose Capablanca and Frank Marshall. The Soviet flag was in the winner's hands – Krylenko's most cherished dream!

for the less practical and perfected style of the Russian masters. Zhenevsky's main strength is doggedness in defense and probably the ability to adapt to his opponent's psychology.

Bogatyrchuk showed in this tournament the qualities that were least expected of him: composure and solidity of play. Earlier, he was known for his sharp attacking style, and we could fear that this would be detrimental against the more experienced opponents. However, he showed that he has made good progress since past tournaments, becoming more cautious and solid. That said, he retained the best parts of his past style as well, and if the position allows, he never loses a chance to win in a brilliant style, though he also scored some wins in great positional style, for instance, against Rubinstein.

Levenfish and Rabinovich performed worse than expected; perhaps this can be explained by some chance personal reasons that stopped them from showing their full strength. They redeemed themselves a bit by good games against Capablanca and their wins – Levenfish defeated Lasker, and Rabinovich won against Rubinstein.

Verlinsky was very steady during the whole tournament. Duz-Khotimirsky was over-imaginative, ignoring the strong technique he was facing. Zubarev didn't play as well as he could because he had to attend to his job and personal matters during the tournament. Gotthilf, who had only recently started playing in serious tournaments, lacked confidence." (*Shakhmaty*, December 1925.)

Bogatyrchuk: "The tournament didn't pique the interest of just chess players. Mosfilm made a film, a comedy called *Chess Fever*, that showed this interest. Capablanca, the conqueror of Moscow girls' hearts, played one of the roles. Capablanca was in love with his own youth and strength. When this film was screened ten years later for participants of the second Moscow International Tournament, I heard sobs nearby – it was Capablanca weeping for his youth, leaving him further and further behind each day. He wasn't a philosopher and couldn't come to terms with the inevitable. "Everyone has to go through that door."

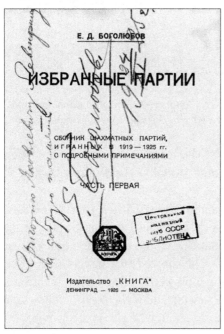

"To Grigory Yakovlevich Levenfish, as a memento. E. Bogoljubov, 24th November 1925." This inscription was made during the Moscow International Tournament. From the Russian Chess Museum library.

There were also questionnaires at the tournament, typical for the Soviet way of life... For instance, you had to name your favorite and least favorite books. In those days, you could still speak more or less freely – with caution, of course – so I named Dostoevsky's *The Devils* among my favorites and wrote that Karl Marx's *Das Kapital* was my least favorite one. Ten or so years later, this answer could have got me into real trouble, but back then, Alexander Fyodorovich Ilyin-Zhenevsky only looked at me reproachfully. He was one of the few communists known to me, sincerely believing in the greatness of their prophet Lenin. You could even argue with him on a delicate subject and express thoughts without fearing that he would denounce you. During the great purge, he was also arrested, but, for reasons unknown to me, didn't get repressed. This communist truly had a human face, but there were very few like him." (From the book *My Life Path to Vlasov and the Prague Manifesto*.)

Meet the Beauty

I'll disappoint the spicy food lovers: this selection is rather glamorous, but without dramatic jalapenos. Well, there's really nothing I could do about that. Almost none of the games that had shocking consequences for the leaders (for instance, Kubbel's undeserved loss to Ilyin-Zhenevsky in round 14, after which he failed to win a single game) or which directly influenced the final places (Romanovsky blundered a piece to Zubarev in round 12, which pushed him into lower-prize territory) were printed in magazines. All in all, only 52 games from this championship survived – even fewer than from the previous one. And nobody said anything about a tournament game collection...

It seems that the new authorities were only concerned with the fight for the "purity of the ranks". It's no coincidence that before the 4th conference, *64*, Krylenko's mouthpiece, sounded the alarm: "The least satisfactory issue is that of chess and checkers literature, which is still almost monopolized by the private, often questionable publishers." How hypocritical should one be to not see the achievements of those "private" publishers. In the first five revolutionary years, not a single chess book was printed in Russia; however, about fifteen were published in 1924 and the same number were already in print!

But that's enough about the sad stuff. Make yourself comfortable – you're going to "meet the beauty" again: the most brilliant games of the tournament, annotated by their authors. Unfortunately, we don't know who awarded the brilliancy prizes – none of the magazines mentioned it. However, since no games won by the champion received any prizes again, we can infer that Bogoljubov was one of the jury members.

First Brilliancy Prize

Levenfish: "Verlinsky's performance was exceptional. His fourth prize was an excellent achievement for a player who was only admitted to masters tournaments last year! Verlinsky's play is inventive, energetic and sharp. The game with Bogoljubov was played very well by Verlinsky, and it was deservedly awarded the first brilliancy prize."

No. 25. Nimzo-Indian Defense E38
Verlinsky – Bogoljubov
Leningrad 1925, round 15
Annotated by B. Verlinsky
1.d4 ♘f6 2.c4 e6 3.♘c3 ♗b4 4.♕c2. Against Romanovsky, I played 4.♕b3, which is probably stronger. *That game continued 4... c5 5.dxc5 ♘c6 6.♘f3 ♘e4 7.e3?! (7.♗d2), and here, instead of 7...0-0, black could have got an advantage with 7...♗xc3+ 8.bxc3 ♘xc5 or 7... ♘xc3 bxc3 8.♗xc5.*

The system with 4.♕b3 was popular in the 1920s, but quickly fell out of fashion and rarely occurs in modern tournament practice.

4...c5 5.e3 *(5.dxc5!; 5.♘f3 – see game 41)* **5...♘c6 6.♘f3.**

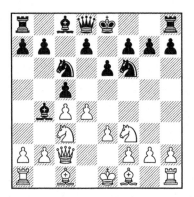

6...d6. There were two continuations that, in my opinion, are more fitting to the development system chosen by black: 1) 6...b6 with the subsequent fianchetto on b7 and 2) 6...cxd4 to open the path to e7 for the dark-squared bishop: 7.exd4 b6 *(7...d5!)* 8.♗d3 ♗b7 9.a3 ♗e7 *(however, after 10.d5 white is better).*

6...d5 was probably the best move.

7.♗d2 0-0 8.a3 ♗a5. *Black could get good counterplay with 8...♗xc3! 9.♗xc3 cxd4 or 8...cxd4!*

9.♗d3. White completes his development, and he is better even at this stage of the game.

9...cxd4. Opening the file, as often happens, is more beneficial for the side that's better developed. The immediate 9...e5 10.dxe5(c5)

dxe5(c5) 11.0-0-0 ♗g4 was worthy of consideration, but even then, of course, white would still have a significant positional advantage *(12. ♗e1!).*

10.exd4 e5. *"Black's position is cramped, but the grandmaster only worsens it with this move, exposing his queen. Bogoljubov completely missed white's ingenious, but somewhat obvious 12th move." (A. Rabinovich)*

Black could also try to extricate himself with 10...d5 11.cxd5 exd5.

11.dxe5 dxe5.

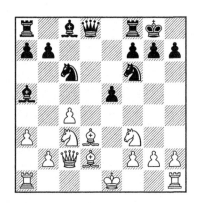

12.0-0-0! ♗g4. 12...h6 was slightly better, which could have been met with 13.h3 and g2-g4 with a very strong attack.

With the game move, black was hoping that white wouldn't go for the exchange sacrifice (see move 14); in that case, black could try and consolidate his position, which became critical due to the queen being in danger.

13.♗g5.

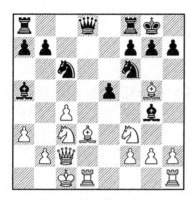

13...♘d4. *Neither Verlinsky nor Rabinovich comment on this move, probably thinking that it was self-evident. However, my pair of "silicon horses" stumbled upon a different move... and take the game into a completely new direction: 13...♗xf3. Give up the queen, just like that?! But they have calculated everything: 14.♗xh7+ (14.gxf3 ♘d4 15.♗xh7+ ♚h8 16.♕d3 ♕b6! didn't give white much) 14...♘xh7 15.♖xd8 ♗xd8! 16.♗xd8 ♘d4 17.♕b1 (there's no other move) 17...♗h5!?*

An incredible position! Trying to save the piece leads to the loss of the queen: 18.♗e7 (or 18.♗c7 ♘b3+ 19.♚c2 ♗g6+ etc.) 18...♖fe8 19.♘d5 ♘b3+ 20.♚c2 (again, there's no

other move!) 20...♗g6+ 21.♚xb3 ♗xb1 22.♖xb1 ♘f8 (23.♘c7? ♖xe7 24.♘xa8 ♘e6, and the white knight is trapped) – black has an exchange for the pawn and a good position.

Indeed, had such a clash happened in the actual game, the first brilliancy prize would have probably gone to Bogoljubov!

14.♘xd4! This is the best move, of course, because the inert rook on h1 plays no role in the battle.

14...♗xd1 15.♖xd1.

15...♕xd4. There's nothing better. 15...♗xc3 could be met with 16.♘f5 ♗a5 17.♗e4, for instance: 17...♕e8 18.♗xf6 gxf6 19.♕e2 with an unstoppable attack.

But 16.♘f5 is actually bad because of 16...♗d4! (closing off the dangerous file) 17.♘xd4 exd4 18.♗xh7+ ♚h8 with an unclear position. The computer recommends 16.♘e6 or 16.♗xh7+, but even in this case, black has better chances than in the actual game (16.♘e6 ♗xb2+ 17.♕xb2 fxe6 18.♗xh7+ ♚xh7 19.♖xd8 ♖axd8 or 16.♗xh7+ ♚h8

17.♘e6 ♕b6 18.♘xf8 ♖xf8 19.♗xf6 ♕xf6 20.bxc3 g6 21.♗xg6 fxg6 22.f3 ♕a6).

16.♘d5! Of course, this is much stronger than the immediate 16.♗xh7+ *(16...♘xh7 17.♖xd4 exd4 with two rooks for the queen).*

16...♘xd5   17.♗xh7+   ♔h8 18.♖xd4 exd4.

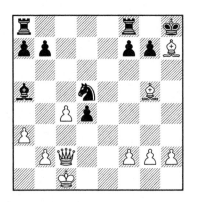

19.♕f5! ♗d8. To meet 20.♗xd8 with 20...♖fxd8 21.♕h5 *(21.cxd5! ♖d6 22.♕e5 ♖ad8 23.♗e4 or 21... ♖ac8+ 22.♔d2 ♖c5 23.♕h3 ♖d6 24.♗e4+, winning)* 21...♘f4 22.♕h4 ♘xg2 etc.

20.f4 ♗xg5 21.fxg5 ♘e7. There's no salvation, and black decides to put a quick end to his suffering.

22.♕h3   ♖fd8   23.♗d3+   ♔g8 24.♕h7+ ♔f8 25.♕h8+ ♘g8 26.♗h7 ♔e7 27.♕xg7. Black resigned.

Second Brilliancy Prize

Romanovsky: "Kubbel refuted Duz's opening structure with a spectacular combination. The latter resigned when all of Kubbel's pieces

– queen, two rooks and bishop – were *en prise.*"

No. 26. Slav Defense D13
Duz-Khotimirsky – A. Kubbel
Leningrad 1925, round 11
Annotated by A. Kubbel

1.d4 d5 2.♘f3 ♘f6 3.c4 c6 4.cxd5. This continuation is rare, white usually plays 4.e3. *The exchange system chosen by white usually leads to a bland game.*

4...cxd5 5.♘c3 ♘c6. "This 'Slav Four Knights Opening' is unlikely to yield any advantage for white: even though black is essentially forced to keep his light-squared bishop in its starting place, his position is not weakened, so he still has good prospects for development." (Alekhine)

6.♘e5 *(this move is usually made after 6.♗f4 ♗f5 7.e3 e6)* **6...e6 7.e3** *(7.♗f4!?)* **7...♘xe5.** This move is linked with black's overarching plan and leads to a lively game.

8.dxe5 ♘d7.

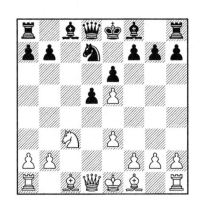

9.f4. *Perhaps white should have taken a risk with 9.e4!? dxe4 10.♕a4*

♕*c7 11.♗f4, and if 11...e3, then*
12.♗xe3 (counting on 12...♕xe5
13.♗b5 a6 14.♖d1 or 13...♗c5
14.0-0-0! ♗xe3+ 15.fxe3, though
after 12...♗c5! 13.♗xc5 ♕xc5, white
still faces certain difficulties).

9...f6. This move looks risky, but
it forces white to make a committal
move – black threatens to isolate the
e-pawn.

10.♕h5+. This check and
pressure on the e6 square look
tempting, but they only make
white's life more difficult, and he
ultimately crumbles. White should
have captured on f6 and continued
piece development.

10...g6 11.♕h3 ♕b6 12.♗d3
(threatening ♗xg6+) **12...♗g7**
13.exf6. Now this is forced, and
black is better, because the white
queen on h3 is out of play, while the
black queen has a great position on
b6. Black also controls the a1-h8
diagonal.

13...♘xf6 14.♗b5+ ♔f7 15.0-0
♖f8 16.♕h4 (the immediate 16.a4
is met with 16...e5 17.♕h4 e4) **16...**
♔g8. Black has castled artificially.

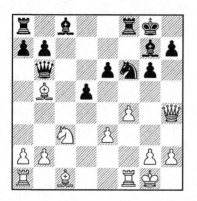

17.a4 a6 18.a5. Kicking the
queen away from the a7-g1 diagonal.
18...♕d6 19.♗a4 ♗d7 20.b3.
This is bad, as black's reply shows
(20.♗c2 or 20.♗xd7 was better).
But white's position is already
difficult

20...♕b4! (fixing the weaknesses
of the b3 and a5 pawns) **21.♗d2**
♖ac8 22.♗xd7. *22.♕h3 ♗xa4*
23.♖xa4 ♕xb3 24.♕xe6+ ♔h8
25.♖b1 ♕c2 26.♖a2 ♕d3 etc. didn't
save the game either.
22...♘xd7.

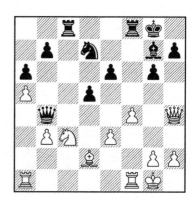

23.♖a4. If 23.♘xd5, then
23...♕xd2 24.♖ad1 (or 24.♘e7+
♔f7 25.♘xc8 ♕xe3+ and ♖xc8,
with two pieces for a rook) 24...
♕xd5! 25.♖xd5 exd5 with more
than enough compensation for the
queen.

23...♕xb3. An obvious move
that required precise calculations.
Black is playing very resolutely.

"Kubbel takes to sharp positions
like a fish to water." (Levenfish)

24.♖b1 ♕c2 25.♖a2 ♕d3
26.♖xb7.

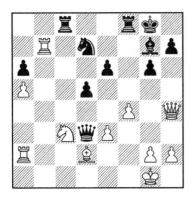

26...♖f7. Calm and solid, avoiding the complications after 26...♗xc3 27.♖xd7 ♖f7 (if 27...♗g7, then 28.♕e7 with a mate in a few moves) 28.♖xf7 ♔xf7 29.♗xc3 etc.

White could only dream of such "complications". There's an even simpler draw after 29.♕xh7+ ♔e8 30.♗xc3.

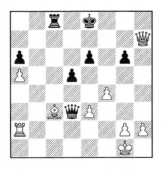

For example 30...♖xc3 31.♖e2! or 30...♕xe3+ 31.♖f2. The attempt to win an exchange with 30...♕b1+ 31.♔f2 ♕xa2+ would be punished: 32.♔g3! ♕a3 33.♕xg6+ ♔d7 34.♕f7+ ♕e7 35.♕xe7+ ♔xe7 36.♗d4, and white's passed pawns are very dangerous!

27.♘a4 (27.♘d1 was better for defense) **27...d4! 28.♕e1 dxe3 29.♗xe3.**

29...♗d4! 30.♖e2? White could have held for longer after 30.♗xd4 ♕xd4+ 31.♔h1 ♕xf4 32.♖a1 ♘e5 etc., but he missed black's problem-like 31st move in time trouble.

30...♖xf4 31.♖xd7. This allows for a spectacular finish, but the game cannot be saved anyway. If, for instance, 31.♘b2, then 31...♗xe3+ 32.♖xe3 ♖f1+! 33.♕xf1 ♕xe3+ 34.♔h1 ♖c1 35.♘d1 ♕d2, winning.

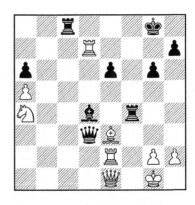

31...♕xe2!! A lethal blow made possible by the king's position in a mating net. 31...♗xe3+ was weaker due to 32.♖xe3 ♕xd7 33.♘b6 etc. White's agony now follows.

32.♖d8+ ♔f7 *(a picturesque position: all black pieces are en prise!)* **33.♖f8+ ♔xf8 34.♕b4+ ♔g8.** White resigned.

Third Brilliancy Prize

Levenfish: "Romanovsky was unrecognizable. The blunder against Zubarev, erroneous combination against I. Rabinovich, very weak games against Bogoljubov, Duz and Verlinsky are so uncharacteristic of our talented master's energetic, inventive style that they must surely be explained away by some unexpected circumstance.

Still, P. A. showed great examples of his creativity in his games against Grigoriev and Vilner."

No. 27. Ruy Lopez C66
Grigoriev – Romanovsky
Leningrad 1925, round 2
Annotated by P. Romanovsky
1.e4 e5 2.♘f3 ♘c6 3.♗b5 ♘f6 4.0-0 ♗e7 5.♘c3 d6 6.d4 ♗d7 7.dxe5. This continuation frees up the d5 and f5 squares from the pressure from black's light-squared bishop. However, black is able to maneuver with his knights more or less freely.

Usually white plays 7.♗xc6 or 7.♖e1.

7...♘xe5. *7...dxe5?! 8.♖e1 ♗d6 9.♗g5 h6 10.♗h4 g5 11.♗g3 ♕e7 12.♘d5 is better for white (Perlis – Wolf, Vienna 1911).*

8.♗xd7+ ♘exd7. In the 1924 championship game between Ilyin-

Zhenevsky and Romanovsky, black recaptured with the f6 knight and got into trouble because he gave up the d5 square too prematurely. *Unfortunately, the game score didn't survive...*

9.♘d4 0-0 10.♘f5 ♖e8 11.♕f3 ♗f8 12.♕g3 ♔h8 13.f3.

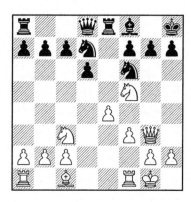

13...h6. Black intends to kick the f5 knight away from its strong position, but it's necessary to play h6 for that. This operation takes too much time, forces some pieces to retreat and weakens the pawn position.

Since the f8 bishop neutralizes the white knight just fine, wasn't it simpler to just immediately launch the counterattack with 13...♘e5 and then c7-c6, ♕c7, ♖ad8, preparing d6-d5? The bishop incursion to g5 can be met with h7-h6.

Both my "silicon horses", despite their differences in temperament, insist on an even more radical solution: the immediate 13...d5!

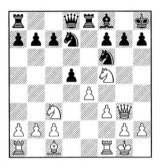

However, while Junior tries to kick the knight away with g7-g6 (14. exd5 ♖e5 15.♕h3 g6 16.♘g3 ♗b4 or 14.♗e3 g6 15.♘h6 ♗xh6 16.♗xh6 c6), Fritz doesn't even touch the g-pawn: 14.♗e3 dxe4 15.fxe4 ♘xe4 16.♘xe4 ♖xe4 17.♖ad1 ♕c8 or 14.exd5 ♘b6 15.♗g5 ♘bxd5 16.♘e4 (16.♖ad1 ♘xc3!) 16...♕d7 17.♗xf6 ♕xf5 etc. It would be interesting to know what Peter Arsenyevich himself thought...

14.♗e3 ♔h7 15.♕h3 (g7-g6 was a threat) **15...♘g8.**

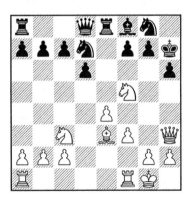

16.♘d5? A bad move. The only way to maintain the pressure was 16.g4!, and if 16...g6, then 17.♘xh6 ♘xh6 18.g5 f6 19.f4!, with a sharp position and mutual chances.

16...♘b6 17.♘f4. The knight is

positioned poorly on f4, so trading it would be a lesser evil for white.

17...g6 18.♘g3 ♗g7. The position has changed drastically. White's forces are pushed away from the fifth rank, and black pieces are poised for counterattack.

19.c3 ♘f6 (the immediate 19...♘c4 was even more energetic) **20.♖ad1 ♘c4 21.♗c1.**

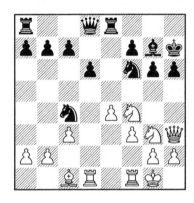

21...c6! (the break d6-d5 is now inevitable) **22.b3 ♕b6+ 23.♖f2 ♘e5 24.♘f1.** If 24.♖xd6, then 24...♖ad8 25.♖dd2 g5 with the subsequent ♘d3.

24...♖ad8 25.♗e3 ♕a5 26.c4 d5! Black breaks through the center, exploiting the white queen's poor position.

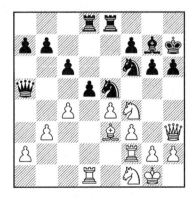

27.exd5 cxd5 28.cxd5 (*if 28.c5 then 28...♘c6 and d5-d4*) **28... ♘xd5 29.♘xd5 ♖xd5 30.♖xd5 ♕xd5 31.♖d2 ♘d3!** After a heated skirmish, the position has been clarified. Black has occupied the d3 square and all open files, and even if nothing else materializes, he still threatens a queenside pawn attack (b7-b5, a7-a5-a4, etc.)

32.♕h4 (*32.♗xa7? ♗d4+!*) **32... b5!** This pawn sacrifice cuts off all the squares for the queen along the fourth rank.

33.♗xa7 (walking into a cunning trap) **33...g5!**

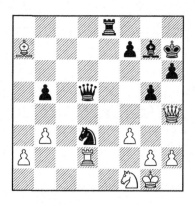

34.♕f2. White lost by force after other moves as well:

1) 34.♕g4 f5 35.♕h5 ♖e7! (not 35...♗d4+ due to 36.♗xd4 ♕xd4+ 37.♔h1 ♘f2+ 38.♖xf2 ♕xf2 39.♕f7+!, and white wins) 36.♘e3 f4! or 36.♗f2 ♗d4! etc. *(37.♖xd3 ♗xf2+ 38.♔xf2 ♕c5+! 39.♔g3 f4+ 40.♔h3 ♕f5+ 41.g4 ♕xd3)*;

2) 34.♕h5 ♖e7! (threatening ♗d4+) 35.♘e3 ♕b7! 36.♖xd3 ♕xa7 37.♔f2 ♗d4 etc.

34...♗c3! 35.♘e3. 35.♖d1 was met with the crushing blow 35... ♖e1!, after which white is forced to play ♖d2 again, giving up an exchange *(36.♕c2 ♗d4+!)*.

35...♕d8. Now white can't save the exchange due to the threat ♘d3xf2.

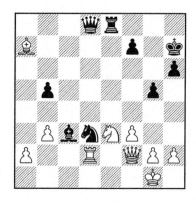

36.♗b6? *36.♕e2 ♘f4! 37.♖xd8 ♘xe2+ 38.♔f2 ♖xd8 39.♔xe2 ♖d2+ lost as well.*

36...♕xb6? After 36...♗xd2 37.♕xd2 ♕xb6 38.♕xd3+ f5! black was up a whole rook. *Here, after 39.♕d7+!, white was up a whole knight. The magazine probably omitted the moves 38...♔g8 39.♔f2, after which 39...f5! is indeed winning (40.♕d5+ ♔h8).*

The subsequent part of the game was not annotated by Romanovsky, who was upset by his mistake (he would later lament his "bout of absentmindedness", because of which, "instead of winning a whole rook, I won only an exchange and prolonged the game for many, many moves". I had to ask the computer for help.

37.♖xd3 ♗d4 38.♖xd4 ♕xd4 39.♘f1 ♕d3 *(39...♕xf2+ 40.♔xf2 ♖a8! was even simpler)* 40.h4 ♖e2 41.♕a7 ♔g7 42.hxg5 hxg5 43.♕c5 ♔g6 44.a4 ♖c2.

45.♕b6+ *(45.♕xb5? ♕d4+ 46.♔h2 ♕h4+ 47.♔g1 ♕f2+, mating)* 45...f6 46.♕e6 ♕d4+ 47.♕e3 ♕xe3+ 48.♘xe3 ♖c3 49.♘d5 *(49.♔f2 b4!)* 49...♖d3 50.♘e7+ ♔f7 51.♘c6 bxa4 52.bxa4 ♔e6 53.a5 ♔d6 54.♘b4 ♖a3 55.♘c2 *(55.a6 ♔c5)* 55...♖xa5. *White could have resigned here, but Grigoriev was an endings expert, and he decided to test his opponent's technique.*

56.♘e3 ♖a2 57.♔h2 ♖e2 58.♘f1 ♔e5 59.♘g3 ♖e1 60.♘h1 f5 61.♘g3 f4! 62.♘h5 *(62.♘h1 ♖f1!)* 62...♔f5 63.g4+ ♔g6 64.♔g2 ♖e7 65.♔f2. *The knight is trapped, and the black king begins a lengthy maneuver.*

65...♔f7 66.♔f1 ♔e6 67.♔f2 ♔e5 68.♔f1 ♖a7 69.♔f2 ♔d4 *(now the knight can be set free)* 70.♘f6 ♖a2+ 71.♔f1 ♔e3 72.♘e4 ♖a5 *(or 72...♔xf3 73.♘xg5+ ♔xg4)* 73.♔g2 ♖d5 74.♔h3 *(74. ♘c3 ♖d2+)* 74...♔xf3 75.♘g3 ♖d1. White resigned.

The Missed Brilliancy Prize

In Levenfish's opinion, he "lost both half a point and the brilliancy prize because of time trouble". He may be right.

No. 28
Levenfish – Zubarev
Leningrad 1925, round 15
Annotated by G. Levenfish

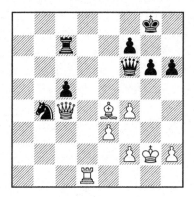

33.♕b5! Beginning a deeply calculated combination.

33...♕e7 34.♕b8+ ♔g7. *It might seem that 34...♔h7 was better, with the idea 35.♗f3 ♖d7 36.♖xd7 ♕xd7, and now 37.♕e5 does not give check, but white could still win the c-pawn with 36.♖a1! ♖d8 37.♖a7 ♖xb8 38.♖xe7 ♔g7 39.♖c7 etc.*

35.♗f3! Not 35.♔f3 because of 35...f5!, and black easily repels the attack.

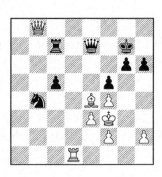

A hallucination: after 36.♗xf5! gxf5 (or 36...♖b7 37.♕c8 ♖c7

38.♕xc7!) 37.♖g1+ ♔f6 38.♕h8+ ♔e6 39.♕e5+ black loses his queen.

35...c4 36.♖d8 c3. Black doesn't see the danger and pushes the pawn. He didn't have a better move though.
37.♖g8+.

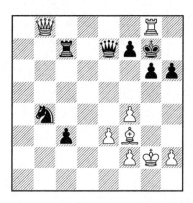

37...♔h7. Very interesting lines could occur after 37...♔f6 38.♕b6+ *(38.♖e8! ♕d7 39.♕xb4 was even simpler)* 38...♘c6, and now it's a mistake to play 39.♗xc6? ♕d6! 40.e4 ♕xc6 (40...♖xc6 41.e5+ ♔e6 42.♖e8+ ♔f5 43.exd6 ♖xb6 44.d7, winning) 41.♕d4+ with a draw.

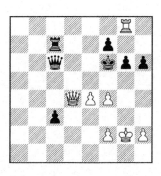

This beautiful line is worthy of being shown in its entirety: 41...♔e6 42.♖b8 c2! 43.♕e5+ ♔d7 44.♕e8+ ♔d6 45.♕f8+! ♖e7 46.♕d8+ ♖d7

(46...♔e6 47.♖b6) 47.♕f6+ ♔c7 (47...♔c5 48.♕c3+ ♔d6 49.♕e5#) 48.♖c8+ ♔xc8 49.♕xc6+. White has the queen, but not the win: 49...♖c7 50.♕a8+ with perpetual check!

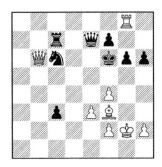

The winning move is 39.e4! c2 40.e5+ ♔f5 41.♕e3 ♕b4 42.♕d3+ ♔xf4 43.♕xc2 etc

Instead of 41...♕b4? black should continue 41...♘xe5 42.♗e4+ ♔f6 43.♕b6+ ♖c6 44.fxe5+ ♔xe5 and black is saved by his strong c2 pawn. Therefore, 39.e4 is no better than 39.♗xc6. The most precise winning move is 39.♖a8!

38.♖h8+ ♔g7 39.♖xh6! ♔f6. The only move *(39...♔f8 40.♖xg6+!).*

40.♗g4! This gets to the goal more quickly than 40.♕h8+ ♔e6

(40...♔f5? 41.♖xg6! f6 42.♖g5+ mating, 41...fxg6 42.♗g4+ or 41...♔xg6 42.♗h5+ also mating) 41.♕e5+ ♔d7 42.♗g4+ etc., because there's an immediate checkmate threat on h8.

40...♕d6 (♕e4+ and ♕c5 both lose) **41.e4 ♕xf4** (after 41...♔e7, 42.♖h8 decides matters) **42.♕d8+.** Cutting off the escape to e7. 42.e5+ was not enough because of 42...♔g5!

42...♖e7 43.♕h8+ ♔g5.

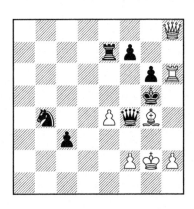

44.♖h5+? I had only 2 minutes left for 12 moves, so I couldn't calculate the lines after 44.♖h3! There was no defense against this move: 44...♕xg4+ 45.♖g3 c2 (or 45...♕xg3+ 46.hxg3 – with the threat of mate in two and capturing the c3 pawn) 46.h4+ ♔f4 47.♕f6+ *(there was a direct checkmate: 47.♖xg4+ ♔xg4 48.♕h6! ♖xe4 49.♕g5# or 48...c1♕ 49.f3#)* or 44...♕xe4+ 45.♗f3 ♕c4 46.♖g3+ ♔f5 47.♗g4+ ♔e4 48.♖xc3, and white wins.

44...gxh5 45.♕xh5+ ♔f6 46.♕h8+, perpetual check.

Solo Wing Run

"Freymann showed that he was no makeweight this year. Getting a better position out of the opening, Romanovsky rushed into attack and snatched a pawn too prematurely. Freymann played the second half of the game with exceptional skill." (*64*).

No. 29. Queen's Gambit D30
Freymann – Romanovsky
Leningrad 1925, round 6
Annotated by S. Freymann and P. Romanovsky

1.d4 d5 2.♘f3 ♘f6 3.c4 e6 4.♗g5 c6 5.e3. This move was too rash. Black now seizes the initiative **(F)**.

5...♕a5+ 6.♘bd2 (this costs a pawn; white should have played 6.♘fd2 – **F) 6...♘e4 7.♗h4 dxc4 8.♕c2.** 8.♗xc4 is met with 8...g5 9.♗g3 g4 and ♘xd2 **(F)**.

8...♘xd2 9.♘xd2 b5 10.♗e2 ♗b4.

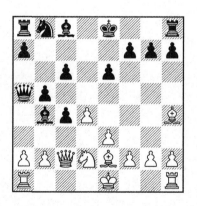

11.a4! A great attacking move. Black has to play very precisely to avoid the pitfalls in his way **(R)**.

11...♗b7? After this move, black's position quickly worsens. 11...♗xd2+ 12.♕xd2 ♕xd2+ 13.♔xd2 ♗d7 (*13...a5!? with the idea of 14.♗f3 ♖a6*) 14.♗f3 etc. was also bad. Black should have played 11...c3 12.bxc3 ♗xc3 13.♖a2 b4 14.0-0 ♗a6, escaping the dangers and retaining the important passed b-pawn **(R)**.

12.0-0 ♕b6. After 12...♗xd2, there's 13.axb5 ♕b4 14.bxc6 ♗xc6 15.♖fd1 c3 16.bxc3 ♗xc3 17.♖db1 (*but not Romanovsky's move 17.♖ac1 because of the reply 17...♗a4!*). White regains the piece and is clearly better **(F)**.

13.♘e4 ♘d7? The third mistake in an already hard-to-defend position! It was necessary to play 13...a5, posing some difficult problems for white. Now, however, the crisis comes very quickly **(R)**.

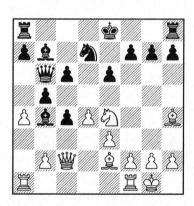

14.a5! ♕a6. 14...♕c7 (*14...♗xa5? 15.♘d6+*) was even worse due to 15.♗g3 e5 (after 15...♕d8, there's 16.♗d6 c5 17.♘xc5 ♗c6 18.♘xe6, and white wins the g7

pawn as well, because 18...fxe6 is followed by a mate in three) 16.a6 ♗c8 17.dxe5 ♘xe5 18.b3 cxb3 19.♕xb3 ♗e7 20.♕c3 with a won position **(F)**.

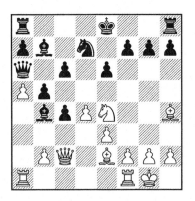

15.b3! c3. Forced. After 15...cxb3 16.♕xb3, the black bishop has no good squares **(R)**.

16.♘xc3 0-0 17.♘e4 c5. White threatened to entomb the queen and bishop forever with 18.♘c5 **(R)**.

18.♘xc5 ♘xc5. White would have met 18...♗xc5 with 19.dxc5 ♕c6 20.f3! ♕xc5 (if 20...♘xc5, then 21.a6!) 21.♕d3 etc. **(R)**.

19.dxc5 ♖ac8.

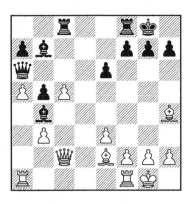

20.♕d3! ♖xc5? There were some practical drawing chances if black gave up the b5 pawn, capturing on c5 with the bishop **(R)**.

21.♕d4 ♖c2 22.♕xb4. *22.♗d1 ♗c3 23.♕d3! won a piece, but Freymann evidently didn't notice that after 23...♗xa1 24.♗xc2 the black bishop is doomed because of the mating threat on h7.*

22...♖xe2 23.♖ac1! e5 (white threatened 24.♕g4 and ♗f6 – **F**) **24.♖fd1 ♕e6.** Defending against both 25.♕xf8+ and 25.♖d6 **(F)**.

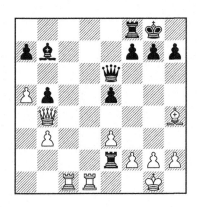

25.a6! A spectacular killing blow! The whole game is very interesting in respect of white's exceptional strength in exploiting his opponent's errors. The black bishop has no good squares. After 25...♗d5, there's 26.♖xd5 *(Freymann planned 26.♕xb5)* and ♕xf8+, while 25...♗c6 is met with 26.♖d6 **(R)**.

25...♗a8 26.♕xf8+ ♔xf8 27.♖d8+ ♕e8 28.♖xe8+ ♔xe8 29.♔f1 ♖a2 30.♖c8+ ♔d7 31.♖xa8 ♖xa6 32.♖f8 ♔e6 33.♖b8. Black resigned.

An instructive lesson

A. Rabinovich: "This whole game was played by Bogoljubov with his characteristic incredible energy, in great style."

No. 30
Bogoljubov – Nenarokov
Leningrad 1925, round 8
Annotated by E. Bogoljubov

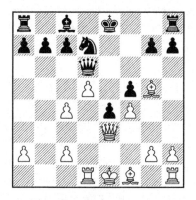

19.g4! An interesting idea to maintain the initiative. If 19...fxg4, then 20.♕xe4+ ♔f7 21.♕e6+ ♕xe6+ 22.dxe6+ ♔xe6 23.c5!, and white has an unstoppable attack for the pawn.

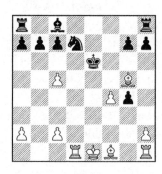

Yes, after 23...♘xc5?, it's indeed unstoppable: 24.♗c4+ ♔f5 25.♖d5+

etc. But after 23...♘f6!, what can white do? He can barely escape with a draw: 24.♗c4+ ♔f5 25.♗d3+ ♘e4 26.0-0 h6 (26...b6? 27.c6!) 27.♗d8 ♗e6 28.♗xc7 ♗d5 or 26.♗xe4+ ♔xe4 27.♔f2 ♔f5 28.♖he1 ♖f8.

So, the correct reply was indeed 19...fxg4! 20.♕xe4+ ♔f7, and white should sound the retreat after that: 21.♗e2 ♘c5 22.♕g2. But the magic of the grandmaster's title was too strong! Only after Bogoljubov was brought down by Vilner and Verlinsky in two consecutive rounds, 14 and 15 (his first losses in the Soviet Championships!), did our masters became more bold in testing his plans; at first, they were too scared of him.

19...h6. This move was both unnecessary and damaging, weakening the pawn structure. It was simpler to reply 19...♘c5 immediately.

20.♗h4 ♘c5 21.g5! h5.

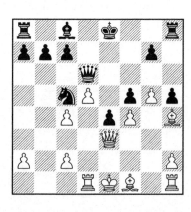

22.g6! *"A sudden spectacular move that cramps black's whole position! This advanced pawn gains incredible strength." (A. Rabinovich)*

22...b6 23.♖g1 ♖h6. Black gains nothing by this; however, it's hard to see any way for him to improve his position *(23...0-0 24.♖g5)*.

24.♗g5! ♖h8 (not 24...♖xg6 due to 25.♗e2) **25.♕d4 ♔f8.**

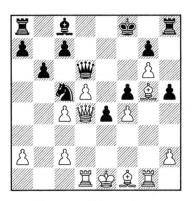

26.♗f6! (the decisive maneuver) **26...♖g8.** *Capturing the bishop is deadly as well: 26...♕xf6 27.♕xf6+ gxf6 28.g7+ ♔g8 29.gxh8♕+ ♔xh8 30.♖d2 ♗d7 31.♖dg2 etc.*

27.♗e5 ♕d7 28.♖g5 e3 29.♗h3 e2 30.♖d2 (30.♔xe2 was even simpler) **30...♘e4(!).** The last attempt. If 31.♗xf5, then 31...♘xg5! *(32.♗xd7 ♘f3+).*

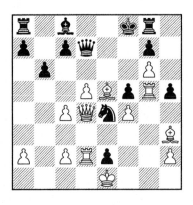

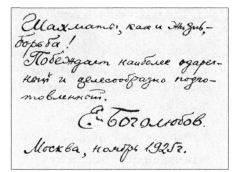

"Chess, like life, is a struggle! He who is most talented and appropriately prepared wins. E. Bogoljubov. Moscow, November 1925."
Autograph from the brochure International Chess Tournament in Moscow, 1925, and its Participants.

31.♕xe4. The simplest, even though the exchange sacrifice 31.♖xe2 may have led to mate even more quickly, for instance: 31... ♘xg5 32.fxg5 a5 (there's nothing better) 33.♕f4 ♖a7 34.♗xf5! ♕xf5 35.♗d6+, with a mate in two.

31...fxe4   32.♗xd7   ♗xd7 33.♗xc7 ♖c8 34.d6 ♖e8 35.♖dd5 ♖e6 36.f5 ♖e8 37.♖xh5 ♗c6 38.d7. Black resigned.

A Brilliant Draw

Levenfish: "The burly Sergeyev showed exceptional tenacity in defense. In the very interesting game with I. Rabinovich, the Moscow champion showed remarkable combinational talent."

No. 31
I. Rabinovich – Sergeyev
Leningrad 1925, round 16
Annotated by A. Rabinovich

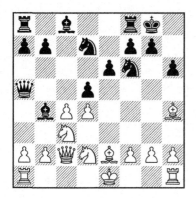

11...dxc4   12.♘xc4   ♛d5!
13.0-0-0. It seems that there's nothing better, because black attacks two pawns at once – d4 and g2 *(13.0-0 ♛xd4 14.♗g3 ♗xc3 15.bxc3 ♛e4).*

13...♗xc3 14.bxc3. And this is probably forced as well: 14.♛xc3 could be met with 14...♘b6, and if 15.♘xb6, then 15...axb6 with an overwhelming attack.

14...♘b6 15.♘d2. *An interesting attempt is 15.♘e3 ♛d8 16.♘g4 ♘bd5 17.♗f3, to avoid moving the c3 pawn*

15...♛d8 16.♘e4 ♘bd5 17.c4.

17...♛c7 (threatening ♛f4+)
18.♗g3. *If white knew what was going to happen, he might have played 18.♗xf6!? ♘xf6 19.♘xf6+ gxf6 20.♖d3 f5 21.♖h3.*

18...♛a5!! An incredibly beautiful combination with a sacrifice of two pieces, which unfortunately only leads to a forced draw.

19.cxd5 ♘xe4. *Junior, unlike the thoughtful Fritz, immediately understood everything after this move and confidently displayed "=" on the monitor.*

20.♛xe4 exd5 21.♛c2 ♗f5!

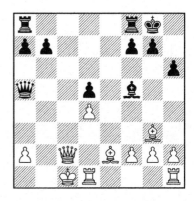

22.♛xf5 (there's nothing better)
22...♖ac8+ 23.♔b1 ♛b4+ 24.♔a1 ♛c3+ 25.♔b1 ♖c6 26.♗b5. 26.♗c7 was also possible, but black still gives perpetual check.

26...♛b4+ 27.♔a1 ♛c3+. Draw.

Without Pause for Breath

Romanovsky managed to create a spectacular combative game, checkmating his opponent with almost all pieces still on the board.

No. 32
Romanovsky – Vilner
Leningrad 1925, round 16
Annotated by P. Romanovsky

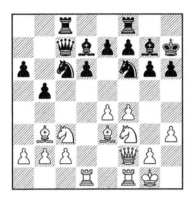

17.e5! ♘e8. After 17...dxe5
18.fxe5 ♘xe5 19.♘xe5 ♕xe5
20.♗d4 ♕c7 (if 20...♕f5, then
21.♗xf6 ♗xf6 22.♕a7!, winning a
piece) 21.♗xf6 ♗xf6 22.♘d5 ♕b7
*(22...♕c6!? 23.♘xf6+ exf6 24.♕xf6
♕xf6 25.♖xf6 ♗f5 was more
persistent)* 23.♘xf6+ exf6 24.♕xf6
♗e8 25.♖d6, black loses a pawn and
falls under a strong attack.
    **18.♘d5 ♕b7 19.♘b6 ♖b8
20.♘xd7♕xd7 21.♕h4.** Threatening
22.e6 with the subsequent ♘g5+.
    21...♕c7

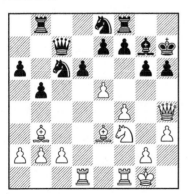

22.f5! gxf5. After 22...♘xe5
23.fxg6+ ♘xg6 24.♕h5 black
couldn't simultaneously defend
h6 and f7 *(the game might have
continued: 24...♘f6 25.♘g5+
♔g8 26.♖xf6! exf6 27.♘xf7 ♖xf7
28.♕xg6).*
    23.e6 f6 *(23...fxe6 24.♘g5+ ♔h8
25.♘xe6)* **24.♕h5 ♖d8 25.♕xf5+
♔g8 26.c3!** Black resigned. There's
no defense against ♗c2.

Sozin's Variation

Boris Vainstein: "The Sozin
Variation was first introduced
to practice in the 1925 Soviet
Championship. The Odessa master
Vilner, a good tactician, consulted
Sozin before the game with
Bogoljubov and deployed a new
move that changed the course of
development of the Meran system."

No. 33. Semi-Slav Defense D49
Bogoljubov – Vilner
Leningrad 1925, round 14
Annotated by Y. Vilner
    **1.d4 d5 2.♘f3 ♘f6 3.c4 c6
4.e3 e6 5.♘c3 ♘bd7 6.♗d3 dxc4
7.♗xc4 b5 8.♗d3 a6.** *"An old-
fashioned move. Most experts in this
currently very fashionable opening
prefer 8...♗b7, and some even try 8...
b4, even though the reputation of 8...
a6 is still high enough."* (Kasparov)
    9.e4 c5 10.e5 cxd4 11.♘xb5.
This move by B. Blumenfeld *(first
tried against A. Rabinovich in the
1924 Moscow Championship)* was

Yakov Vilner was among those who defeated Bogoljubov. Cartoon by N. Radlov (Krasnaya Gazeta, Leningrad, 20th August 1925). Published for the first time.

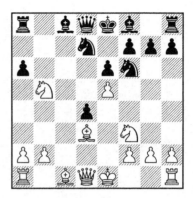

11...♘xe5! A very interesting and probably the best defensive system. White has to go for a forced line with enough counter-chances for black. This move was first pointed out by V. Sozin *(in his annotations to the game Bogoljubov – Thomas; there followed 11...axb5 12.exf6 e5 13.fxg7 ♗xg7 14.♕e2!).*

The capture on e5 was a nasty surprise for Bogoljubov. His choice of variation had been based on the game A. Rabinovich – Gotthilf, played in round 8; there, Alekhine's recommendation 11...axb5 12.exf6 ♗b4+ (12...gxf6! Sozin) 13.♔f1 gxf6 14.♘xd4 ♗b7 was refuted with 15.♗e3!

12.♘xe5 axb5 13.0-0. White sacrifices a pawn for the attack – probably incorrectly. Still, perhaps it was better to go for the forcing line 13.♗xb5+ ♗d7 14.♘xd7 ♕a5+ 15.♗d2 ♕xb5 16.♘xf6+ gxf6 17.♕f3 ♖d8 18.♕xf6? ♖d5.

B. Vainstein wrote in his book The Meran System: *"This annotation clearly shows that Vilner didn't know much about the subtleties of the*

considered a refutation of this whole defensive system. The current game calls this judgement into question.

The first use of 11.♘xb5 on the international arena (Bogoljubov – Thomas, Baden-Baden 1925) caused quite a stir, but Alekhine immediately cautioned: "Blumenfeld's novelty is interesting and deserves detailed study; however, calling it a refutation of the whole Meran system is at best careless. Still, such verdicts are now thrown around quite hastily – this is very characteristic of modern analysis and contrasts sharply with precise, serious work of the times of Steinitz and Chigorin."

system, and in this game he was more or less like a rider sitting on someone else's horse.

Instead of 18...♖d5 (there's probably a misprint in Vilner's text), black should play 18...♖g8 19.♕f3 ♗b4 20.♖d1 ♖g5, and it's hard for white to untangle his pieces."

The move 18...♖d5 is actually not a misprint, but it only leads to a draw: 19.♕xh8 ♖e5+ 20.♗e3 ♕d3! 21.♖d1 ♖xe3+.

13...♕d5! 14.♕f3 *(it was better to play 14.♕e2, without blocking the f-pawn)* **14...♗a6 15.♗g5 ♗e7.**

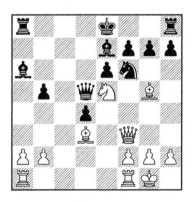

16.♖fc1(?). The rook moves to an open, but useless file. It was better to play 16.♖fe1.

16...0-0 17.♕h3. 17.♕g3 would have also been met with 17...h6, and black's reply would have been even stronger.

This is unlikely, as after 18.♗xh6 ♘h5 19.♘c6! ♕xc6 20.♗h7+ ♔xh7 21.♕d3+ ♔xh6 22.♖xc6 white wins the queen for three minor pieces and equalizes.

17...h6 18.♗f4. Were the e5 knight defended, the bishop sacrifice on h6 would have forced a draw.

18...♗b7 19.♖e1. Precision. The rook is needed on the e-file, not the c-file.

Too late. The prodigal rook's return rectifies nothing...

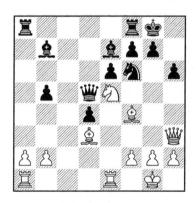

19...♗b4! 20.♖e2 ♖xa2 21.♖f1 ♖fa8 22.f3 ♗f8! 23.♘g4. *After 23.♗e4, there's a pretty line 23...d3! 24.♗xd5 dxe2 25.♖e1 ♘xd5 and black wins.*

23...♘xg4 24.♕xg4 ♕b3! A crushing blow. White's queenside comes crashing down like a house of cards.

"Vilner is in his element, and his play is wonderful." (B. Vainstein)

25.♗b1 ♖xb2 26.♖ee1 d3 27.♖c1 ♖a1.

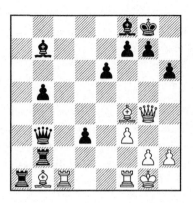

28.♗c2 (or 28.♗xd3 ♖xc1 29.♗xc1 ♕xd3 30.♗xb2 ♗c5+ etc.) **28...♖xc1.** White resigns, since 29.♗xb3 is met with 29...♗c5+, mating, while 29.♖(♗)xc1 ♖xc2 just wins a piece.

Krylenko's Fledglings Learn to Fly

5th Soviet Championship: Moscow, 26th September – 25th October 1927

"The forty-percent spirit is not to be.
Get drunk on chess, ye worker, don't despair!"
A. Bezymensky, *Chess*

It's not without reason that I didn't share Capablanca's admiration for the royal reception in Moscow. Not even a year had passed since the international tournament, held with great fanfare and on a grand scale, before the workers were asked to tighten their belts again. The defense of the state needed to be strengthened. "The working class of the USSR and the whole world is watching most carefully as the English imperialists try to create a united front with the capitalists of other countries and declare war against the Soviet Union!" – the magazine *64* was as intense as the main party press. "The working masses of our country see how great the danger of this war is, and they are preparing to stand in defense of the first workers' state in the world, which is also the fatherland of all the international proletariat and the beacon of social revolution."

The Bolsheviks were always very adept in creating enemies – both real and imagined. Under the pretext of repelling the external threat or fighting the internal counter-revolution, they could easily get their hands on private property and rob NEPmen. Allowing free enterprise to flourish and saving their own power in the process, the successors of the "Kremlin dreamer" now started to slowly fold NEP. As Comrade Stalin explained with his peculiar humor, "The NEP was introduced 'seriously and for the long haul', but... not forever."

Chess suffered, too. "The austerity measures introduced in our country," Krylenko wrote in January 1927, "have hit the chess movement hard as well, destroying the financial resources for a number of organizations. Because of austerity measures, it was necessary to skip the championship and chess conference in 1926."

But the Soviet chess players showed great social awareness. Understanding that it was necessary "to strengthen our air force, build new fighting units and even squadrons", they came up with an

64. Shakhmaty i Shashki v Rabochem Klube magazine, No. 13, 1927.

№ 17.—15 сентября 1927 г.   *Пролетарии всех стран, соединяйтесь!*

ПОПУЛЯРНЫЙ ШАХМАТНО-ШАШЕЧНЫЙ ЖУРНАЛ

ШАХМАТЫ и ШАШКИ 64

ДВУХНЕДЕЛЬНЫЙ ОРГАН
ШАХ. ШАШ. СЕКЦИИ ВСФК
и ШАХБЮРО при КО ВЦСПС

ГОД ИЗДАНИЯ 4-й

В РАБОЧЕМ КЛУБЕ

ПОДПИСНАЯ ЦЕНА:	Адрес издательства: Москва, Воздвиженка, 10. Главная контора подписных и периодических изданий Государственного издательства. Тел. № 5-88-91.	Цена объявлений:
На год с доставкой 5 р. — к. „ 6 м. „ „ 2 р. 60 к. „ 3 м. „ „ 1 р. 35 к. Розничная цена № — 25 к.		Стр. обл. 1 ст. ¹/₂ ст. ¹/₄ ст. ¹/₈ ст. 2-я 20 чер. 12 чер. 6 чер. 3 чер. 4-я 20 „ 12 „ 6 „ 3 „ 3-я 15 „ 10 „ 4 „ 2 „

„Начало Самолета"

Вперед, назад... но вверх и вниз
Не ходят пешки, кони, туры...
И вот рождается эскиз
Еще невиданной фигуры.
Она легка и в даль зовет,
Пространства разрывает путы;
Ее неудержимый лет
Ломает старые дебюты.
И сложат, ужас затая,
Враги подрезанные крылья,
Когда крылатая ладья
Объявит мат их эскадрилье.

* * *

А ты, чтоб враг не подстерег,
Исполнися одной заботы:
Исследуй вдоль и поперек
Свое „Начало Самолета".
И не гроссмейстер, не гигант,
Восстань угрозой Капабланке,
Все удлинняя вариант,
Записанный во **Всекобанке**.

Вл. Вин.

СТРОИМ „САМОЛЕТ ШАХМАТИСТА им. Н. В. КРЫЛЕНКО"

64. Shakhmaty i Shashki v Rabochem Klube magazine, No. 13, 1927.

The Plane Opening
Forward, back... but up and down
The pawns, knights and rooks don't go...
And we come up with a blueprint
For an unprecedented piece.
It's light, it calls us forward,
It tears up the shackles of space;
Its unstoppable flight
Breaks down the old openings.
And, with fear in their hearts,
The enemies shall fold their wings,
When the winged rook
Checkmates their squadron.

And you, to prevent the enemy
*   from blindsiding you,*
Dedicate your efforts to one cause:
Research inside and out
Your "Plane Opening".
Not a grandmaster, not a giant
Will rise up as a threat to Capablanca:
Make the variation longer and longer,
*It's kept in **Vsekobank**.*

Above the headline **Let Us Build the "N. V. Krylenko Chess-Player Plane"** *we see a poem titled "The Plane Opening" by Vl. Vin, encouraging people to donate money to build it to the All-Russian Cooperative Bank.*

initiative: to fund the building of the "N. V. Krylenko Chess-Player Plane"! "By building their own plane, the chess-playing workers of our country will again demonstrate that they do not belong to the ranks of those apolitical amateurs who consider chess an art for the sake of art and who see and want to know nothing beyond that. The workers' chess movement is a part of the whole workers' movement. In days when the workers' state is threatened by war, every member of our organization will set the wooden pieces aside and grab a rifle." And to give this project international scope, they sent "greetings to the Workers' Chess International and a proposal to build the N. V. Krylenko Chess-Player Plane" (*64*).

The "internal enemies" were wide awake, too. The two-times Soviet champion turned out to be a snake nourished in the proletarian's bosom. After failing to obtain an entry visa to Italy because of his Soviet citizenship, Bogoljubov sent a letter to Krylenko in December 1926, telling him that he was renouncing his Soviet citizenship! And this happened after he was invited to join the All-Union Chess Section's Executive Bureau, asked to edit the chess column in *Pravda* and, as an exception, allowed to take part in three tournaments abroad. The reaction was very harsh: "Assuming that Mr. Bogoljubov, following Alekhine's lead and becoming a renegade – not the first and maybe not the last – basically quit the USSR's chess organizations on his own accord, the Chess Section decrees: 1) To strip Mr. E. D. Bogoljubov of his USSR Champion's title; 2) to expel Mr. E. D. Bogoljubov from the ranks of the USSR chess organization..."

Both this document and Bogoljubov's letter have been published numerous times. But the article in *Shakhmatny Listok*, signed by Romanovsky, shocked me. Not with its content – it was more or less characteristic for the era – but rather with its language in general, which sounded like the late 1930s rather than the late 1920s:

> "Every honest person understands the real moral value and strength of a man who sold his citizenship for several hundred fascist liras. It is <u>now</u> obvious to any honest person that the trust and consideration given to the former chess champion of the Soviet Republic was a mistake... Mr. Bogoljubov spat on this consideration and trust the moment the illustrious fascist king Mussolini made one annoyed gesture. However, we are not outraged or angry. Such feelings are too much for a couple of hundred liras that his fascist highness shall pay at the earliest convenience to Mr. Bogoljubov, who showed his true nature..."

I can only wonder what Alekhine thought of all that. From the Chess Section's decree on Bogoljubov, he learned both that he was considered a "renegade" and that the Chess Section "deemed it inappropriate to enter into any kind of talks with Alekhine about his participation in a Moscow International Tournament, considering this master an alien and hostile element for Soviet power." What talks?! Seeing his name in *Shakhmatny Listok* among other possible participants, he wrote to Grigoriev and asked not to invite him: "I'm not going to take part in any chess competitions next year because I'm fully consumed by preparation for my doctor of law exam, which is scheduled for November this year." I think that the underlying reason for this letter was clear: Alekhine wanted to avoid an official invitation – otherwise, he would have had to publicly refuse, which could have been perceived as a deliberate snub by Moscow. So he clearly didn't want to burn all his bridges at that moment! However... the exam likely wasn't the only reason; Alekhine probably feared going to the USSR without "safe conduct" – French citizenship, which he would only obtain in 1927. My hunch was proven right. Here is a diary entry by Sergei Prokofiev made on 22nd December 1925: "I left [Amsterdam] early in the morning... Alekhine traveled in the same railcar, by coincidence, and we talked for the entire trip, mostly about the recently-ended Moscow tournament; Alekhine had decided not to go because he was afraid of the Bolsheviks." (From his book *Diary. 1907–1933 (Part Two)*, Paris, 2002).

The Last Years of the NEP Respite

Bogatyrchuk: "The sixth year of NEP *(1926)* was still tolerable from the material point of view, especially for me. I installed my new X-ray machine delivered from Germany and continued to develop my practice. Thus, I solved my personal problems rather satisfactorily, and I could have just rested on my laurels had I not seen and heard what was going on around me. On the surface, the strangulation of NEP wasn't felt yet, but there were some indirect signs that the noose was tightening on the neck of all our peoples. The most obvious sign was tax pressure on the private sector. The government was clearly facilitating the development of so-called state capitalism. Because of that, many private trading businesses were closing, with state-owned shops opening in their stead. There weren't many goods in these shops, and the quality was below average, but still, there were long lines to buy them. I came under tax pressure as well, but it was still tolerable.

Meanwhile, the GPU (renamed the NKVD at that point) were improving their technique in leaps and bounds. It became known that all post offices now had perlustration departments, reading not only all outbound and inbound letters to/from foreign countries, but even domestic letters written by all those targeted by the NKVD. Many who came into contact with the NKVD told us about that, warning against corresponding with friends and relatives abroad. There were also rumors, which were confirmed soon enough, about the building of concentration camps for "especially hostile elements". These camps were mostly built in the North. The institute of informers came into being, people tasked with informing the NKVD about all dangerous thoughts and views of other citizens. Many became informers voluntarily – not only communists and Komsomol members, but also opportunists and fellow travelers who sympathized with the party; they were only a small percentage of the population, but they did exist. Those with relatives abroad were netted by the NKVD especially easily. An investigator would call such a "candidate informer" and, holding a bundle of perlustrated letters in his hand, say, "You know, there's a lot of material in these letters that can get you arrested and repressed in accordance with the rules that punish you for disclosing classified information to enemies of the proletarian state."

And then, he would quote a couple of innocuous-sounding sentences, which, however, could be construed as compromising. You should understand the position of the future NKVD informants, too. They had nowhere to go and seek protection from these absurd charges. On pain of harsh repression, they couldn't even tell their family members about what had happened. They only told a few people they trusted completely.

"However," the investigator would continue, "you know how benevolent the proletarian power is towards those who want to make amends and help us. We offer you the chance to redeem yourself by informing us about all anti-Soviet views and talk among your colleagues, friends and relatives. You should compile a weekly report about anything you've heard or seen. You should also know that you aren't the only one sending such reports to us. So I would advise against hiding such talk or misrepresenting its meaning, because we will discover the truth, one way or another."

Only very few people had enough willpower and bravery to refuse the offered role. But the NKVD knew about such people's resolve in advance and usually wouldn't even approach them for that "job". They used a devilish move, employing people whose reputation or position made them above suspicion to do this sordid job." (From the book *My Life Path to Vlasov and the Prague Manifesto*.)

We Need a Truly Soviet Champion!

Ilyin-Zhenevsky: "The 5th All-Union Chess and Checkers Conference is opening in Moscow. It was long overdue – two years have passed since the last All-Union Conference.

Молодые участники чемпионата: Ботвинник (17 лет), Макагонов (21 года), Перфильев (22 лет), Раузер (18 лет).

The young participants of the championship: Botvinnik (17), Makogonov (21), Perfilyev (22), Rauzer (18). Actually, Makogonov was 23, and Rauzer turned 19 during the tournament. (Shakhmatny Listok, No. 19, 1927.)

In 1923, we set a tradition to organize the conferences every year. Why then the two-year gap? This is because immediately after the 1925 All-Union Conference, the Moscow International Tournament was organized, depleting our organization's financial and intellectual resources so much that it couldn't organize a new conference in time. Only now do we finally have the opportunity...

The Soviet chess championship will, of course, be the main and most important competition. Since the treason of the last champion, E. Bogoljubov, the USSR has essentially had no champion. The new championship will determine the most worthy player to hold this distinguished title. The fact that there will be no visiting players from abroad at the 5th Soviet Championship is a bonus, rather than a drawback. We need our own, truly Soviet champion, who lives in the USSR, is ideologically close to us and closely tied to our whole public chess life. Bogoljubov, of course, failed to meet those conditions.

Panov: "Towards the end of the Moscow International Tournament, late at night, at about one in the morning, I was walking home and then, at Strastnaya Square, I suddenly saw Bogoljubov at the parking lot for private cars (the "Gnu Antelopes"![15]). Laughing at the top of his voice, drunk, red-faced, with an open fur collar, he was putting two girls of questionable behavior into the car, who giggled cutely, pretended to defend their modesty and struggled for a while, but still sat in the car with that triumphant hamster, and they went quickly towards the hotel.

I walked and thought how Bogoljubov's everyday behavior flew in the face of our Soviet, communistic ethic and was unworthy of a Soviet champion. Of course, we should have immediately extracted Bogoljubov from his petty-bourgeois, burgher surroundings where money was the only king, brought him to the USSR together with his family, given him a job in chess, re-educated him ideologically through constant interaction with the Soviet youth, and then, with his immense talent, he could have done much good. But Bogoljubov remained a typical unprincipled bourgeois professional journeyman, and, the day he first encountered visa troubles, he immediately defected to the enemies of Soviet power and got himself German citizenship. Interestingly, after that his career went downhill, and he traded off his great talent for small money from constant low-quality performances of a foreign professional." (From the book *Forty Years at the Chessboard*.)

In terms of chess ability, we perhaps do not have an equal to Bogoljubov currently, but this is only temporary. We're growing constantly, new talents are springing up, and if the old, sickly chess life still managed to give birth to Chigorin, and then to Alekhine, the young Soviet chess society will surely give us players as great as them.

The line-up of the 5th championship is rife with new young players: Makogonov, Rauzer, Kholodkevich, Rokhlin and, finally, the 16 year-old (!), immensely talented Botvinnik. They will take their first test in this championship. We shall soon see what they can show us. (*Shakhmatny Listok*, September 1927.)

By the way, regarding Botvinnik. When I saw the "**17 year-old** winner" in the annotations to his 1927 championship game against I. Rabinovich in *64*, I didn't pay much attention to that. But then, I saw a photo caption in *Shakhmatny Listok* as well, which said "Botvinnik, **17**". This intrigued me, as it implied that he was born in 1910, and I decided to look through the 1926 magazines. *64*, June: "We should especially take note of Botvinnik, **16**..." *Sh. L.*, July: "A brilliant move that proves the immense chess intuition of the **16 year-**

---

[15]   A reference to a car from another novel by Ilf and Petrov, *The Golden Calf*

old M. M. Botvinnik." (Rokhlin.) But back in July 1926, if he was really born on 17th August 1911, he wasn't even 15 yet. Finally, three Leningrad newspapers, reporting on Capablanca's simultaneous display, listed the **15 year-old** Botvinnik as one of the winners...

The date 17th August 1911 first appeared in a December 1926 issue of *Sh. L.*. The caption also states, "This *(academic)* year, he finishes the second-level school." This, as Yuri Lvovich Averbakh explained, meant that he was in 9th grade – back then, children went to first grade at the age of 8. And if Mikhail was born in 1911, he should have gone to school in 1919. Add nine years,

М. М. Ботвинник.

Mikhail Botvinnik looks older than his actual age on the photos and drawings of that period. (Shakhmatny Listok, No. 19, 1927.)

and you'll get 1928... He also looks too grown-up on all the early photos.

From the recollections of **Boris Vainstein** (you'll read more about him in the annotation to game 40) who first met Botvinnik at that championship: "He looked older than he was – because of his judgement, manner of dress – suit and tie, very neat, unlike me, a student. He spoke slowly, weighing his words, and looked searchingly at the person he spoke to. All in all, he was a very pleasant fellow. He was about four years younger than me, and I was supposed to look down on him being the older one – but I couldn't." (*Shakhmatny Vestnik* No. 8–9, 1993.)

In his memoir, Botvinnik – usually very precise in details – didn't mention when exactly he went to school or how many classes he completed. And how about this? "On 1st June 1924, I became a member of the chess assembly. I had to add three years to my actual age (you had to be 16 or more). The board chairman S. Vainstein, of course, saw through my ruse, but I looked older because of my glasses, so it was quite plausible." Or was it? You can't pass as a 16 year-old youngster when you're not quite 13, but it's certainly more possible when you're 14. To make it even more convincing, Mikhail Moiseevich adds: "I wasn't alone in that regard: Serezha Kaminer was only a bit older than me." Yes, exactly three "missing" years older: Kaminer was born in 1908...

Am I seriously thinking that Botvinnik took a year off his age? Why not? If you can add three years "for a good reason", why can't you take one off? Averbakh thinks that the idea to take a year off could belong to his chess "guardian", Yakov Rokhlin, whose birth year wasn't exactly clear either. In any case, he did help Mikhail to obtain a reference for the university, turning his father into "worker – dental technician"... And the chess authorities were probably only glad to have their own, truly Soviet chess prodigy! By the way, Yakov Gerasimovich helped Botvinnik to take part in this championship as well.

P.S. After this book was published in Russian, **Vadim Faibisovich** found the "Book of Records on Arrivals and Departments in housing block 88 on 25th October Prospect *(Nevsky Prospect's name back then)* in 1919–1921" in the Central State Archive, and it says, "Botvinnik Mikhail Moiseevich, from Minsk Governorate, town of Ostroitsko-Grodetsky, born 17th August 1911". I couldn't find such a town on the Minsk Governorate map, but managed to find the Ostroshitsko-Gorodetky district and the Gorodok Ostroshitsky estate that it contained.

Faibisovich ended his article *The Version Is Not Confirmed* (e3e5.com website, 29th September 2009) with this phrase: "The brothers Isaak and Mikhail Botvinnik were recorded as inhabitants of the Minsk Governorate. Maybe just because it was their father's birthplace. The other question – from where the newspaper reporters got their information – remains open. But one thing is clear: in the 1920s, the age of the sixth world champion did not undergo any documentary changes."

Well, you can't argue with the official record, yet I still have doubts about Botvinnik's year of birth.

Rokhlin: "On 15th September 1927, there was a discussion about the line-up of the 5th championship at the meeting of the Chess Section Council. In my address, I tried to convince the assembly to add Botvinnik to the main list (Misha was only number 2 on the reserve places' list, with V. Rauzer as number 1). However, my proposal raised some objections. Then I went for a desperate gambit: I said that I was withdrawing from the championship in favor of Botvinnik. I remember the Moscow delegates N. Grigoriev and V. Russo immediately agreeing to my withdrawal, but they offered the vacant place to master N. Rudnev, the winner of the Central Asian tournament, rather than to Botvinnik, a first-category player.

Long debates started. The only person to actively support me was Alexei Alekhine (the brother of the future world champion). Krylenko, the chairman, abstained from the vote, and my proposal was rejected by a majority of votes.

After the meeting, when everyone else had left the hall, I remained sitting in my chair, dejected. But then Nikolai Vasilyevich [Krylenko] beckoned me and, saying some encouraging words, added: "Do not despair. I think that the favorite from the Neva, whom you're calling one of the country's best players so boldly, will play in the championship. And you shall retain your place, too..." And Krylenko wrote something down in his notepad. Everything happened as he said." (*Shakhmaty v SSSR*, No. 7, 1977.)

From the press: "On 25th September, the grand Soviet Championship opening ceremony took place in the Red Hall of the House of the Unions. N. D. Grigoriev, opening the proceedings, emphasized in his speech that not even the world championship match between Alekhine and Capablanca, which is taking place currently, reduces the great interest in and importance of the championship, which features an especially strong line-up. Comrade S. S. Levman greeted the championship on behalf of the VtsSPS, pointing out the anti-societal structure of chess competitions in the West and the public impulse that accompanies every chess tournament in our country.

Then the welcoming telegram by Comrade N. V. Krylenko was read.

Proletarian poet A. Bezymensky, who was present at the opening, read his poem *Chess* to us, which, despite being a panegyric for the game of chess, still reminds us: 'That life is similar to a game of chess, but living life is harder than playing chess.'" (*64*, September 1927.)

From the press: "The player assembly that took place after the official opening ceremony decided:

1) To play 6 hours a day instead of 8;

2) To refuse Verlinsky's request to start the championship on 29th September (he is unable to leave Odessa in time due to illness). Since Rosenthal and Rudnev had also withdrawn, the lots were drawn by 21 players. The results of the draw *(masters in italics)*: 1. *I. Rabinovich*, 2. Botvinnik, 3. Perfilyev, 4. Makogonov, 5. *Romanovsky*, 6. *Vilner*, 7. Kaspersky, 8. *Duz-Khotimirsky*, 9. *Nenarokov*, 10. *Ilyin-Zhenevsky*, 11. Pavlov-Pianov, 12. *Bogatyrchuk*, 13. Kholodkevich, 14. *Freymann*, 15. *Sergeyev*, 16. Grigoriev, 17. Rauzer, 18. Rokhlin, 19. *Smorodsky*, 20. *Selezniev*, 21. Model.

Seven honorary prizes (badges) are to be awarded, along with 3 brilliancy prizes...

The Soviet Championship is played in the two halls of the House of the Unions. The venue is not big, but cozy. The players are sitting behind barriers consisting of chairs, along the sides, and the spectators sit in the middle. The spectators usually converge around the tables where the result is already

Слушают поэта А. Безыменскаго, читающаго свою поэму „Шахматы"

Listening to the poet Alexander Bezymensky reading his poem Chess. *(Cover of 64. Shakhmaty i Shashki v Rabochem Klube, No. 20, 1927).*

clear and the position of one of the opponents is hopeless. Even though there aren't many spectators (200–300 people per night), the halls are rather stuffy and noisy. There are many reporters, photographers, and interviewers. The press, however, pays more attention to the tournament than the public. This is unusual for big chess events." (*Shakhmatny Listok*, October 1927.)

Portraits of the Winners

Bogatyrchuk: "Two years have passed since the last championship, and this explains the interest towards this one. This tournament was different in one regard: in addition to the well-known players who'd already taken part in past competitions, seven new players were invited – a whole third of the field; thus the championship was both a competition of renowned players and a test for the youth. The fact that some of them took prizes shows that our young players passed the test with flying colors.

Romanovsky is a known quantity in the USSR's chess life, and his win surprised nobody. In some games, he showed his brilliant combinational creativity (for instance, against Rokhlin and Smorodsky – *see game 38*); others were won with consistent positional play (against Vilner and Selezniev). Without a doubt, he's at his peak strength now, and we can expect even more achievements from him.

Botvinnik: "While still in the train (of course, we rode in economy class), Romanovsky asked, "What if Misha wins?" and laughed. Romanovsky was a remarkable player. His technique was not particularly good, but his inventiveness was inexhaustible, and attacks were always dangerous. He loved chess beyond everything. He was indifferent to money, but loved adoration... Romanovsky, as well as the whole older generation of masters, was jealous of me and not particularly friendly to me. Before my emergence, he and his peers reigned supreme – and then an "upstart" appeared..." (From the book *Achieving the Aim*.)

I'll say a few words about myself as well. During the tournament, many journalists asked me about my views on chess, my tastes in chess art, etc. I'll use this opportunity to answer these questions. I am a disciple and a follower of the so-called "Kiev school" that gave us E. D. Bogoljubov, A. M. Evenson and others. I learned chess mainly through games and annotations of M. I. Chigorin and then, later, A. A. Alekhine. In the small time I can devote to chess, I mostly analyze and study the games of those masters. I follow no modern school in my play, and I think that all the structures of such schools as hypermodernism, superhypermodernism, etc. are totally artificial. I think of my upcoming match with P. A. Romanovsky as a serious test of my entire chess

With his great wins, Fyodor Bogatyrchuk proved that his colleagues didn't call him "Bogatyr Chuk" for nothing. (Shakhmatny Listok, No. 21, 1927.) In East Slavic folklore, a 'bogatyr' was an epic warrior.

understanding, which is not entirely similar to my future opponent's chess philosophy.

The third and fourth prizes were shared by Duz-Khotimirsky and Model. The former is a brilliant combination player with outstanding, original talent. Everyone remembers his wins against the greatest international masters, and it was especially pleasing to see Duz's talent flourish so vividly and with such incredible power; his great wins against Romanovsky *(game 39)* and Nenarokov are true gems of chess art. Unfortunately, Duz has one major flaw

– his play is too inconsistent, and this prevents him from taking the highest places in tournaments, which he most certainly deserves. His co-prizewinner, Model, earned his place with truly excellent play. The distinguishing feature of his specific style is the ability to navigate even the most complicated positions and find incredible winning continuations.

Romanovsky: "Model, the winner of the 1925 Inter-City tournament, has been known in Leningrad for quite a while as one of the strongest amateurs in the former capital. They say that Alekhine once predicted a great future in chess for him. Many of us were sure that he would earn the master's title at the tournament, but nobody expected him to share third place, alongside such a great, inimitable fighter as Duz-Khotimirsky. We think that Model deserved both the master's title and third place. He showed every best bit of his talent more impressively than anyone else in the competition. He stoically

Сидят (слева на право): **Ботвинник, И. Рабинович, Ильин-Женевский, Романовский и Богатырчук.**
Стоят (слева на право): **Модель, Макагонов, Перфильев, Смородский, Фрейман, Селезнев и Раузер.**

Sitting (left to right): Botvinnik, I. Rabinovich, Ilyin-Zhenevsky, Romanovsky, Bogatyrchuk. Standing (left to right): Model, Makogonov, Perfilyev, Smorodsky, Freymann, Selezniev, Rauzer. Photo from Shakhmatny Listok (No. 20, 1927). The Ogonyok magazine (No. 41, 1927) printed it with a caption "Who will become a grandmaster?" – this title was on the line for the first time at the 5th Soviet Championship!

endured all the organizational hardships and built a "stockade" in the table with resounding, elegant wins. His games are full of interesting, subtle ideas, they are very inventive, and his play in general is a reflection of his cheerful, optimistic personality." (*Shakhmatny Listok*, November 1927.)

Botvinnik: "I got to know Model as a chess player in autumn 1927. We played in the 5th Soviet Championship in Moscow and lived together in room 217 of the Liverpool Hotel (now Central) on Stoleshnikov Lane (*the Central Hotel is actually located on Tverskaya Street and was called Luxe back then*). We analyzed games and prepared opening lines together. Model's opening knowledge was not particularly good, so he preferred "non-theoretical" openings – it was he who taught me to play the French and Dutch!

He analyzed masterfully, with great precision and thoughtfulness, and I, 16 at the time, was just a spring chicken in the analysis. "Michel, do not hurry," Abram Yakovlevich would say when I quickly showed him a "forced" long line, and then he would find a hole in my analysis on the second move... I learned the art of analysis from Model as well!

Model played brilliantly in the championship, finishing just a point *(and a half)* behind the winners. Lowering his hands between his knees and bowing his head low over the board, he would completely shut himself off from the outside world – chess was everything for him in those minutes." (From the book *Portraits.*)

The next two players, Botvinnik and Makogonov, like Model, were playing in such a serious competition for the first time. The former, despite his youth, plays very solidly, never losing an opportunity to transition into a better endgame, but his combination skills are very good as well; stylistically, he's similar to the late Kiev maestro A. M. Evenson. Makogonov fully deserved his master's title as well; he's very tenacious in defense and swift in counterattacks.

Romanovsky: "The young Botvinnik's play is not as strong *(as Model's)*, but more solid and balanced. Good composure and deep understanding of various positions made his great success possible. His main flaw is that he's sometimes too formulaic in evaluating the positions, missing the strongest continuations because of that and settling for small advantages, which aren't always enough for a win.

Makogonov is too passive. His play is timid, but based on good positional understanding... To justify his title, he has to infuse his play with more imagination, inventiveness, decisiveness and action in general."

Botvinnik: "This was a very difficult competition: I had to play twenty games. In round 1, I lost to A. Model; in the next round, I brilliantly defeated I. Rabinovich *(see game 36)*. My play was uneven, but I managed to score 5/6 at the finish (my sporting character showed itself!) and shared 5th–6th place with V. Makogonov, exceeding the master's norm by 2.5 points, though this didn't raise any plaudits... By contrast, the Moscow magazine *Shakhmaty* only published all four games I lost *(actually only two – as many as the other magazines)*, and Romanovsky, on the pages of *Shakhmatny Listok*, called my play "balanced". I took it calmly – even back then, I mostly trusted only my own opinion." (From the book *Analytical and Critical Works.*)

Участник шахм. чемпионата СССР
В. И. НЕНАРОКОВ.

Vladimir Nenarokov took a prize place. This was his last success in the national championships. (Novaya Vechernaya Gazeta, Leningrad, 12th August 1925.)

Nenarokov took seventh place; he was very tenacious in defense, but had to concede the higher places to the younger players; his play was affected by physical and nervous fatigue."

Nobody is Left Unnoticed

Bogatyrchuk: "In addition to the three aforementioned prizewinners, Grigoriev also earned his master's title. We welcome his success – he deserved to win this title long ago because of his high-quality, deep and unusual play, but he was haunted by tournament setbacks which prevented him from earning the title. Even in this tournament, the whimsical goddess of luck didn't want to smile on him until the penultimate round, and a number of unfortunately missed wins seemingly precluded him from earning the necessary 10 points. Only great wins in the last two rounds against Romanovsky and Vilner brought him the coveted 50-percent score.

Panov: "A tall, handsome man with jet-black hair and delicate, soulful facial features, which made him look like a French poet, Grigoriev was a master of a versatile, harmonious style – he would readily go for both combination attacks and slow, maneuvering play. However, despite his great theoretical knowledge, deep positional understanding and outstanding endgame technique, he clearly lacked mettle, fire, the will to win. Sporting-wise, he was impractical and lacked time-management skills, which often got him into time trouble. I remember that Grigoriev once thought for 40 minutes on his first move – he couldn't decide which pawn to move." *(So, that's whom Bronstein learned from!)*

Eremeev: "The most amazing thing was that, even in the most severe time trouble, Grigoriev kept completely calm. Without noticing that his flag was already hanging and about to fall, he would coolly light a cigarette. He was completely unfazed by the prospect of losing on time. The most important thing for him was to think the position through and find the best move." (From the book *The First Steps*.)

"A tall, handsome man with jet-black hair and delicate, soulful facial features, which made him look like a French poet, Grigoriev was a master of a versatile, harmonious style." (Panov.) (64, No. 1, 1924.)

He is followed by Ilyin-Zhenevsky, known for his results in international and Russian tournaments; his lack of success can be explained by chance circumstances, because some of his good games show that his playing strength isn't gone. Rabinovich and Freymann didn't earn prizes only because of tournament luck (or should we say, bad luck), because they fully deserved them otherwise. Everyone knows the high class of both those masters.

Pavlov-Pianov shared their score; he's a very solid player who is dangerous for any opponent. We should say that only a stroke of bad luck (a draw was awarded in a completely won game because he repeated moves one time too many) prevented him from earning the master's title.

Romanovsky: "A disappointing thing happened with Pavlov-Pianov. It looked like he was targeted by some kind of curse... Always very nervous, he put much honest, scrupulous work into his play, and it was good, sometimes even very elegant. However, he lacked composure, and Pavlov's play in general needs enrichment – mainly idea-wise."

Sergeyev's result should be considered satisfactory, if we remember that even during the tournament he was still busy with his main, complicated job. We could only wish that, in his next tournaments, the likable Moscow master gets an opportunity to devote more time to chess; I don't doubt that he would be more successful in this case.

Romanovsky: "Sergeyev, as always, played pretty well. His simple, solid positional play is sometimes interrupted by a sudden elegant combination, like in the very difficult endgame against Bogatyrchuk, where he managed to force a beautiful draw with the move g6-g5 despite that leaving his pawn under attack by both the f4 and h4 pawns... If his creativity was a bit more vivid, we could get a complete master who plays equally well at all stages of the game."

When Sergeyev won the strong 1925 Moscow championship (+9=8!), Bogoljubov predicted "brilliant successes in the area of chess art" for him. However, his scientific work (he was an electrical engineer, he later became an associate professor of the Moscow Power Engineering Institute and

Nikolai Pavlov-Pianov. "Only a stroke of bad luck... prevented him from earning the master's title." (Bogatyrchuk.) (64. Shakhmaty i Shashki v Rabochem Klube, No. 7–8, 1927.)

Bogoljubov predicted "brilliant successes in the area of chess art" for Alexander Sergeyev. But Sergeyev, an electrical engineer, chose his scientific work over chess... From the Russian Chess Museum archive (64. Shakhmaty i Shashki v Rabochem Klube, No. 4, 1925). Published for the first time.

was awarded the Order of Lenin) prevented Alexander Sergeyevich from fully developing his chess talent. He never played in the Soviet Championship again.

Perfilyev is a young player who plays in a sharp, combinational style – but, as could be expected from someone of his age, he lacks composure. He has a good future ahead of him, of course, if he works to improve.

The next places were shared by masters Selezniev and Vilner and one of the strongest Leningrad amateurs, Rokhlin. The unsuccessful performance of the first two is fully explained by the fact that they were half-ill during the tournament. In the few days when their health was more or less normal, they played very well, but in their worst days, they would make horrible blunders.

Romanovsky: "Selezniev, who took fourth prize in the big international tournament in Moravska Ostrava, finished at the bottom of the table. Defeating Zhenevsky and Nenarokov in fine style, he unfortunately lost to a number of weaker players and, as usual, couldn't avoid a high draw percentage. His injured leg also gave him a lot of trouble (Freymann joked that Selezniev gave everyone leg odds). But still, the main reason for his lack of success is his style. Selezniev complained that he couldn't compete with the "swindlers" who prevailed at the tournament. But until he pays his respects to

Alexei Selezniev at the Transcaucasian Republics, Ukraine and Uzbekistan masters tournament (Tiflis, 1930).

the modern era and fully embraces the combination element, his results will always be similar to this one."

Actually it wasn't only a matter of his style. As I learned from the book by V. Neishtadt and V. Pak *Prince Myshkin of the Chess Kingdom*, Seleznev was ordered to leave Moscow for three months at the beginning of 1927. Formally, for violating the sporting regime, but in reality it was revenge for Bogoljubov. So he moved to Kharkov to stay with Alexei Alekhine, with whom he had been friends since they were lads. However, life tore them apart in spring 1928, when Alexei publicly condemned his brother for an 'Anti-Soviet' speech in Paris, while

Seleznev tried to talk him out of it: "Stay firm. You absolutely mustn't betray Sashka... I also had to put up with a lot of stuff recently due to Bogoljubov's departure. Oh how they pressured me! And how dare they call me a 'renegade'! So I stopped corresponding with them entirely. And so they sent me here in exile! But I put up with it. I refused to say anything bad about Efim."

Rokhlin's result is satisfactory for the first time; like Perfilyev, he should work more to improve.

Kaspersky needs to put a lot of work into his middlegames; his main flaw is bad understanding of complicated positions. The young Rauzer has a bright future ahead of him; he is talented, without a doubt, but lacks experience – however, both are equally important for tournaments.

Participant of two Soviet championships, Vice-Champion of Belorussia and first category player Anton Kaspersky made a huge effort to promote chess in Minsk. He edited the chess columns in newspapers and magazines and coached young players.

Rokhlin: "Rauzer, the 18 year-old Ukrainian championship runner-up, was overloaded with information from various opening theory textbooks; he once ventured to show us his homemade, huge "card index". However, he couldn't fully demonstrate his creative potential back then...

I went to the tournament very tired because I was overworked – I was in my fourth year of university and also had a lot of organizational and instructional work to carry out. In addition to that, ironically, I was paired with my chess mentor and friend P. Romanovsky in the first round. The heavy defeat in that game strongly affected my psychological state in the next rounds..." (*Shakhmaty v SSSR*, No. 7, 1977.)

Master Smorodsky also spent the entire tournament half-ill; in addition, he was hindered by a lack of preparation – he lives way out in the provinces. We hope that Kholodkevich, who played in such a serious competition for the first time, gained enough tournament experience to serve him in the future.

Andrei Alexandrovich Smorodsky (1888–1954) was a master made of pre-revolutionary fiber. In the All-Russian tournament (1913/14, 6th-7th place) he finished above Bogoljubov, Evenson, Alapin, Freymann and Levitsky... After the revolution, he joined the Red Army, in which he served his entire life. He lived in Tiflis from 1920 and twice won that city's championship (1926 and 1927), as well as winning the All-Army tournament (1933). However, he performed poorly in both of his Soviet championships (1924 and 1927)...

Andrei Smorodsky "was hindered by a lack of preparation – he lives way out in the provinces." (Bogatyrchuk.) From the Russian Chess Museum archive. Published for the first time.

Khrisogon Yustinovich Kholodkevich (1892–1971) took prizes in two Moscow championships: 1926 – 3rd–4th and 1927 – 2nd–3rd. He moved to Moscow in 1924 from Irkutsk, where he had done much to further the development of chess in the city. He was later repressed and spent many years in prison camps. He returned to chess after serving his time, and you can find his games in the chess journals of the 1950s. A curious detail: Kholodkevich played for Lokomotiv in the 1948 Moscow team championship and was even seen on the cover photo of *Shakhmaty v SSSR* (No. 2, 1948).

Now let's discuss the tournament results as a whole. First of all, we should point out the high playing level of all the players: unlike at the previous tournaments, everyone won at least a third of their games. This result is made even more significant by the fact that many participants played in such a serious competition for the first time, yet, despite that, they never feared losing and always played at their full strength. Even the tournament experience and composure of the winners occasionally couldn't help them against the newcomers. This makes the tournament even more valuable...

In conclusion, I should say that despite the unfavorable external circumstances, the organizing committee, represented by the always friendly and amicable V. E. Eremeev, the indefatigable master N. D. Grigoriev and S. O. Vainstein, did everything in their power to satisfy the wishes of the players. We should point out their care and sensitivity and thank them warmly for that." (*Shakhmaty*, November 1927.)

You Can't Hold Tournaments Like That

Romanovsky: "It might seem that, after a two-year gap, the All-Union tournament, awaited so eagerly by the broad strata of chess society, should have included all the best players living in the Soviet State.

The tournament was based on a strict ideological societal foundation. Money prizes were abolished. The winner of the tournament, in addition to the champion's title, was to have been awarded the honorary title of "grandmaster of the USSR". Measures were taken to allow young sprouts of the Soviet Chess School to face experienced masters.

And when the battle-hardened old masters and beardless youth finally arrived, we all saw that there was a breach in the line-up of this tournament, the most important one in the USSR, and this breach devalues the tournament by many percent, no matter which way you look at it.

"Comrades!" we exclaimed. "Yes, we don't have our former luminaries among us, the grand Alekhine and the renegade Bogoljubov, but where is the menace of the Russian masters and the vanquisher of Lasker, Levenfish? *(He will only return to playing in the Soviet Championships in 1933.)* Where is the vanquisher of Capablanca, Verlinsky? Where is Abram Rabinovich, whose games are brilliant and beautiful and sometimes so simple and strong? Where are the inventive A. Kubbel, the dogged Zubarev, the dangerous Gotthilf, and the subtle and original Blumenfeld? Where is Rudnev, who was reborn like a Phoenix from the ashes?"

Eight masters! Their absence is a huge creative blow that demeans the resounding and bright name of victory...

The motley line-up, which always increases the random nature of the outcome, the absence of a number of outstanding USSR masters, the low master's norm requirement *(50%)* – all of these circumstances made the future champion's work hard, but it was made three times harder by the conditions in which the tournament began and continued.

From the outside point of view, it seems that it was never as hard to play as this time. In the cramped halls of the House of the Unions, even a small number of spectators quickly made the air in the hall so stuffy that it was hard to withstand even for a physically robust man. But this was only the beginning. The organizing committee couldn't even provide carpets. All players' pleas were just voices crying in the wilderness. The noise in the hall was unbearable. The spectators didn't restrain themselves, and polite requests by some organizers ("Comrades! The players ask you to be quiet") would melt as quickly as snowflakes on a hot May day. There were no sanctions imposed, so the players suffered a great deal. In the second half of the tournament, the 1.5-hour break, which had provided a reprieve of sorts from the 4 hours in the hot hall, was eliminated, and then it became hopelessly bad. It was explained away by public and commercial interests. Don't the

РОМЭНОВСКИЙ.

E. Mandelberg's cartoon captures Peter Romanovsky's stern disposition perfectly. (Ogonyok, No. 49, 1925.)

players have interests, too? They were forgotten about or outright ignored. There were almost no rest days. On the second day of the conference *(the All-Union Chess Conference was held on 8th to 10th October, at the height of the tournament)*, which was rife with hot, passionate and nervous debate, the most active participants were forced to play as well, and this was the beginning of the collapse by Zhenevsky, who presided over one of the sections; he lost to Botvinnik on that day.

> **V. Neishtadt:** "The conference only ended shortly before the round started. No wonder that some players who took part both in the conference and the tournament cracked under the double pressure, and their conference work affected their tournament performance. Ilyin-Zhenevsky suffered from that – the organizing committee denied his request to move his game to another day. As a result, Zhenevsky got under attack in his game against Botvinnik and, after several weak moves, adjourned the game in a hopeless position." (*Shakhmatny Listok*, October 1927.)

The feeling of powerlessness unbalanced the nervous system, injected the battle with apathy (just let the game end quickly!), drained all physical strength, and, towards the end of the tournament, the most nervous, physically frail or ill comrades were completely exhausted. Vilner, this excellent, inventive, interesting master of the middlegame, was completely destroyed by these conditions. They were especially difficult for him because of his heart condition (asthma). And we, who saw three or four exemplary attacks executed by him, watched brokenheartedly how mercilessly he was crushed by the conditions he was forced to play in.

You might laugh, but even at the Moscow International Tournament the conditions were difficult but still easier than this time.

And so, the tournament lost a lot game-quality-wise – and this is the most valuable aspect of any tournament (who really cares who the champion is? This was not the main reason for spending thousands of rubles on the championship). You can't hold tournaments like that, this is a very bad austerity measure and a strong disservice to chess creativity in the Soviet State.

So, whom did the chess public opinion consider as the main contenders for the championship?

Many hopes were placed on I. Rabinovich, Bogatyrchuk, yours truly and, finally, Zhenevsky.

A smaller number thought Duz-Khotimirsky or Nenarokov could win. Some took interest in Botvinnik.

Before departing to Moscow, I heard another opinion as well: either Romanovsky or Grigoriev(!). Model's name was mooted. Some praised Makogonov. And that's about all. Of course, everyone was trying to guess who would finish last, but this was just that – a guess. Everything was unclear. The motley line-up made everything so foggy that this fog could compete with a good October grey mist in Leningrad.

And so, it began: Perfilyev defeated Rabinovich, then Rauzer did the same. Still earlier, Rabinovich lost to Botvinnik *(see game 36)*, then to Vilner, and finally to Model. This was compounded by draws with some other opponents. There have been probably hundreds of opinions on the reasons for this huge failure of the prominent Leningrad master, the champion of the North-Western region.

Some critics may be singing funeral melodies or even rejoicing at this sad, I repeat, sad setback of Comrade Rabinovich. Many would think that this failure wasn't coincidental. That time is inexorable, and that it's actually not that difficult to defeat or draw with Rabinovich. And many of them are certainly the same people who applauded him after his triumphant return from the Baden-Baden international tournament. Many of them won't understand all the subtleties of Comrade Rabinovich's creativity, just pointing out his zeroes and half-points in the table. Those are the first who should get a rebuke. As for the others, I would advise them to read his outstanding book *Endgame*, recently published by Priboy, and then look closely at the games at... the recently-ended tournament. Rabinovich got ill in the middle of the tournament. Many players would have dropped out in his place. But he valiantly played until the end and gave chess everything he still could... *(I'll add another bit of information: Ilya Leontyevich convincingly won the 1928 Leningrad Championship without losing a single game!).*

Zhenevsky's fiasco, when he lost five games in a row, most of them without much resistance, was of a different nature. In some cases, this tenacious master, who won against Marshall and Capablanca, was basically defeated in bare knuckle combat. What was the matter? Here, we face the tragic creative environment forced upon us by the organizers, for the first time.

"I'm tired, I can't do this anymore!" – that's what he said in reply to my friendly question. This answer probably wouldn't be understood by the brazen spectators who walked freely around the playing hall as though it were a boulevard, but I understood and felt it deeply, because even I felt my strength dropping by the day.

"Another great artist of our chess is dropping out," I thought. Near the end, Duz suffered too – he played brilliantly, and I fell victim to his great style in round 12 as well. He lost a won game against Makogonov, then did the same against Pavlov, and then lost without much struggle to Bogatyrchuk – more evidence of the same phenomenon. He was out of energy.

> **Duz-Khotimirsky:** "I was in good form, just returning from the south where I had played in two local tournaments. I had gained lots of practice and felt physically strong. But I lost several games at the finish, and the Soviet Championship, which I was very close to, eluded me." (From his book *Selected Games*.)

Bogatyrchuk and I were completely exhausted by the end. In the last few rounds, I quickly went for simplifications, ready to agree to a draw at almost any point.

And after four hours of play in the last rounds, we, both soaking wet from perspiration, thinking only of getting to the end at last, agreed to draws with our opponents, and we were almost giddy – because we finally belonged to ourselves once more, instead of this torture hall that didn't understand us, that demanded everything from us and gave nothing. Our minds were literally raped. Nenarokov, who had enjoyed a great start, weakened with each day and finally cracked, like Zhenevsky. He had a drawn position against me but blundered a mate in three. On the same day, he missed a stalemate against Makogonov in a won position. He drew a won endgame against Kaspersky and only took the last prize because Kholodkevich, his last-round opponent, blundered a mate in one in a won position. In general, if we start counting the blunders, we easily see that there really were a whole lot. It seems that no player was completely free from them, and we're only talking about direct, one-move blunders. If we go for miscalculations on the third or fourth move, there's really a ton of them... The vast majority of the games didn't reach their logical conclusion. The value of creativity was just shattered at the tournament...

Rokhlin: "A tragicomedy happened in my game with Rauzer, rare in serious chess practice. In a very complicated position, after some thought, he suddenly exclaimed: "Resign!

"Lean, young, with an angelic face – there was something childish and naive in his image. While his opponent was thinking, Rauzer would walk around the hall, clasping his hands behind his back to prevent himself stooping forward... Vsevolod Alfredovich's play was not consistent. Sometimes his mood would change in the course of a single game. Up to a point, he would play exceptionally strongly, and then suddenly gift his opponent an easy win." (Botvinnik)

There's a mate in four." There was immediately a lot of noise in the hall, but I answered, almost immediately, "I can't see any mating threats here." In reply, Rauzer sacrificed a piece, gave two checks and... stopped. Seeing that my king was in no real danger, he threw the pieces over the board and fled the tournament hall..." (*Shakhmaty v SSSR*, No. 7, 1977.)

Still, despite the high number of accidents, the games in general can be characterized as a big victory for combinational ideas. Model and Freymann played with great fun. My only consolation was in combinations as well. Rokhlin, Rauzer and Perfilyev steered that way too despite many failures. Bogatyrchuk, after a series of draws, finally hit his stride and destroyed Model, Botvinnik *(see game 35)* and Makogonov. There were some sparks of creativity from Vilner. Grigoriev attacked boldly, Botvinnik slowly strangled his opponents... In general, we saw the triumph of imagination – lively, bright, full of ideas, sometimes half-baked, but believing in its ultimate correctness and, because of that, bold, self-assured and winning. From this point of view, the tournament was of course exemplary, and so we can only deeply regret that such masters of combinations as Levenfish, Verlinsky, A. Rabinovich, Kubbel and Blumenfeld were absent from the fights that took place in what was their element...

To finish, I would like to draw two conclusions of a different character. Combinations are slowly but surely clearing new ways to develop – this is first and foremost. And second, it's time to think how to organize our tournaments in such a way that helps the development of creativity, not devalues it. There are so many masters in our country now, but there's no end to stupid, reckless blunders." (*Shakhmatny Listok*, November 1927.)

Bravo, Peter Arsenyevich! Can you imagine? He went against the "party line", challenging Krylenko himself. And he didn't even do that for his own sake – even the conditions didn't stop him from winning – but rather for the sake of chess creativity! And, if we take a broader look, he tried to protect the interests of chess masters, who gradually became increasingly powerless. The abolition of money prizes essentially turned them into proletarians, fully dependent on the authority's will. Ultimately, the Soviet players started playing for "workdays", like on a collective farm, getting meal tickets during the tournaments. Remember the famous quote by David Bronstein, in answer to Baturinsky's reproach that he agreed a draw with Smyslov too soon, despite having white? "Do you really think that I'm going to attack Smyslov for three rubles a day in food stamps?!"

The rebuff to the rebel was given by Semyon Levman – Krylenko's right hand man and his deputy in the magazine *64*.

A Whiff of Bogoljubovism

Levman: "In his article, P. A. Romanovsky allowed himself a number of unacceptable insults against our chess governing body. He attacks the organizers viciously: claiming that the tournament was played in impossible conditions, the organizing committee didn't act in accordance with the players' interests, it was noisy in the hall, etc, etc.. But even these accusations are nothing before the main terrible accusation: the chess governing body put commercial interests before the interests of chess art! Out of material considerations, the Chess Section's Executive Bureau (the organization responsible for the tournament's organization) devalued and demeaned the tournament's importance.

We won't dwell on Comrade Romanovsky's petty attacks here. Perhaps there were some mistakes (they are unavoidable in big projects), but they aren't the important matter here. The important matter is that one of our masters dared to accuse our organization of putting commercial interests before the interests of the chess movement. You can't throw such accusations around freely – you should answer for them.

The Chess Section Council held a colossal event: the All-Union chess championship, the team competitions of oblasts and trade unions, the women's tournament, the Red Army tournament – all in one... Our chess organizations, both Soviet and trade union, spent much money to hold these competitions to the highest possible standards. With great difficulty, the Chess Section Council managed to obtain a venue in the center of Moscow and necessary funds. All participants of the tournaments received paid leave and material support during the tournament. The participants of the Soviet Championship, in addition, received a special fee directly from the Chess Section Council. The 5th Chess Conference cost the Soviet state and trade unions about ten thousand rubles *(to recap, the international tournament alone cost three times more to organize)*. How, in our days of austerity, could we have incurred such expenses if we were pursuing commercial interests?

We know that not all participants of the tournament would agree with Romanovsky's statements. We are sure that Moscow's ordinary chess players *(implying that Romanovsky was being called a kulak chess player!)* present at the tournament will disprove all of Romanovsky's assertions about "impossible conditions". We know that our chess community will never believe the accusations of commercial intent towards the Chess Section Council...

In addition to the formal side of the issue, Comrade Romanovsky's statements have an unpleasant whiff "in substance", as well. Pushing his specific rights as a master, his unhealthy conceit to the forefront – it's not the first time that Comrade Romanovsky has indulged in this. He does not want to take the means and resources of the Soviet chess organization into account; his play is everything, his creativity is the future of the whole chess art. If his play suffers in some way, then the entire chess art suffers, and we should be outraged. He – the championship winner – is allowed to do anything, he can throw around all sorts of baseless accusations, and he should be listened to. This unhealthy conceit, this whiff of Bogoljubovism, has again manifested itself in Comrade Romanovsky's article – perhaps even quite unintentionally. We should stamp that out once and for all. With all

In the 1920s Semyon Levman was an important figure in Soviet chess: he wrote 'instructional' articles and delivered speeches at conferences. He edited chess columns in Pravda and Trud, and, being a famous problem composer, ran the problems column in 64. However, his life changed sharply in 1929: Levman was expelled from the Chess Section's Executive Bureau "for systematically misleading the Executive Bureau over many years in falsely claiming to be a member of the Communist Party, when in reality he was expelled from the Party in 1924". He was also removed from the editorial board of 64 and from editing the column in Pravda. After that, Levman switched careers and became a writer. He became a member of the Writers Union and wrote several novels. He was a war correspondent during World War II and died in hospital in 1943 (either from wounds or from heart trouble).

due respect to the talent of our gifted chess masters, we cannot and do not want to create a privileged place for them in our organization. And, as we fight against the lack of discipline and irresponsible demagogy from the ordinary members of our sections, we should call Comrade Romanovsky to account for his inappropriate and harmful outburst.

By the way, we should also find the answer to another question: why didn't the editors of *Shakhmatny Listok*, printing such an odious article, at least add their own commentary? Do they feel solidarity with the author as well?" (*64*, December 1927.)

The story didn't end there. First, *Shakhmatny Listok* (January 1928) printed Ilyin-Zhenevsky's article "In Defense of the Chess Art", with a preface: "This article, as well as Romanovsky's article "Painful Outcome", expresses the opinion of the entire *Shakhmatny Listok* editorial board." It's a long article so I show just the last part here:

"Comrade Levman is very critical towards the demands from qualified players to establish favorable playing conditions during competitions. He sees either a whim or a manifestation of nervous self-opinion in them. It's both funny and sad. It's as though Comrade Levman heard none of the discussions at the conference about the need for establishing careful medical control during chess competitions. Remember the words of chess master Dr. Bogatyrchuk: "A serious tournament is an incredible strain on the nerves, a lot of sleepless nights, poor food, general weakening of the body." In such conditions, attentiveness towards the competition participants and their demands is an elementary duty of a chess organizer. Comrade Levman's outlook is too simplistic. For him, qualified chess players are merely specialists who perform certain work for a certain reward. For a competition, one has only to give them leave from their main jobs and give them material security, and they do not care how the competition itself is held. Determining the playing time and schedule is the exclusive right of the Organizing Committee. This is a completely wrong and ridiculous opinion. Chess is, above all, an art, and its value is determined by its content *per se*. It's not important *that* you play, it's important *how* you play! Chess art, as any art, can be mighty and beautiful, but in certain conditions, even in the hands of a master, it can be pathetic and impotent. In this regard, the conditions, the specific conditions of the games, play an enormous role. Missing the importance of this point means knowing literally nothing about chess.

But this question also has another aspect. Our qualified chess players are, above all, social activists. With great struggle, in incredibly hard conditions, our chess movement grew and strengthened. And our great achievement was in the fact that ever since the very first pages of our Soviet chess history, which Comrade Levman only heard or read about, this movement adopted a pointedly social nature. Everyone who didn't agree with the new direction of chess development left us. And we can sincerely say to them – good riddance. But this makes us value those qualified chess forces that remained with us and are working in our ranks even more. Relegating them to the role of simple specialists who only know their narrow job is dangerous for the chess art as a whole and wrong from the societal point of view. We don't need chess specialists. Our masters are valuable for us because of their socially beneficial role. From this point of view, Comrade Levman's personal attacks against Romanovsky look ridiculous and pathetic: "pushing his specific rights", "unhealthy conceit", "whiff of Bogoljubovism", etc. It was Romanovsky who wrote the first resolute article condemning Bogoljubov's betrayal. It was also Romanovsky who, despite the difficult conditions, won the championship in question. What anti-societal inclination, what individual demands can we talk about here? Re-read, Comrade Levman, your article one more time, think about it, and <u>you will be ashamed</u>!"

The return shot was delivered by... Bogatyrchuk! The essence of his article "In Defense of the Soviet Chess Championships" (*64*, February 1928) is expressed in the following sentences: "We, the chess players of the provinces, are more vulnerable to various random factors than the well-trained chess players of the center, but we still accept them, and we aren't afraid of them, because we love the chess art with all our hearts and wish it to develop and spread widely. And so we fully support all the events of our chess organization."

I think that the choice of the outlet, as well as the uncharacteristically servile tone, shows that the Kiev player was drifting towards Krylenko (he usually published his articles in the apolitical *Shakhmaty*). To be honest, Bogatyrchuk's behavior was understandable: NEP was slowly folding, and he, a private medical practitioner, didn't want any further heat from the Soviet government. However, it's also possible that Fyodor Parfenyevich was completely honest, and his opinion just happened to coincide with the official position. All in all, the masters from the capital cities have their own truth, and the provincial masters have theirs...

Two Champions: An Economy, Not a Luxury

V. Neishtadt: "The climb to the top is over. The table shows its results. 21 strips, each 20 rounds long, 420 results out of 210 games, 420 numbers showing successes and failures, the progress of these successes and failures along the strips, and the elementary arithmetic calculation that messes up the order in the table set by the initial draw. How simple are the numeric symbols of the tournament struggle! But how much these symbols hide, how much they say and how much, in their simplicity, they keep mum. They don't say anything about blunders, about "tournament luck", the quality of some victories – and why should they, if the very number of wins creates the winner.

And the blunders were numerous. Vilner blundered a piece twice, Selezniev blundered a piece, Sergeyev blundered a full queen; should we even count the pawns?..

A blunder is, of course, unfortunate. But no tournament is free from numerous blunders. A blunder is a necessary element, in a way.

The results of any tournament do not show the <u>absolute</u> strength of the players. There's always some element of randomness – "tournament luck" or "fortune". But blunders do not besmirch the tournament. They are a psychological consequence of chess struggle. Perhaps we could talk about some minimum and maximum number of blunders. There have been, of course, tournaments with excessive blunders, which devalue their results. The Soviet Championship was not devalued by blunders. And two facts make us especially happy: 1) against Romanovsky and Bogatyrchuk, the players blundered more rarely than against others; 2) the young players blundered more rarely than the older ones.

Победители чемпионата СССР

Ф. П. Богатырчук   П. А. Романовский

В марте 1928 г. между ними состоится матч за звание гроссмейстера и чемпиона СССР.
Матч будет играться до 6 выигранных партий, первые 4 ничьи не в счет

"The winners of the Soviet Championship
F. P. Bogatyrchuk   P. A. Romanovsky

In March 1928, they are going to play a match for the titles of grandmaster and USSR
champion. The match is to be played until a player scores 6 wins, while the first four draws do
not count." (64. Shakhmaty i Shashki v Rabochem Klube, No. 20, 1927).

If we want to determine Mr. Luckies and Mr. Unluckies of the tournament,
I think we should point out the "good luck" of Nenarokov, who was gifted at
least 4 points by his opponents, and the "bad luck" of Grigoriev, who gave
away at least 4 points. Duz deserves a special mention: he gave away no more
than 1.5 points, but this was enough to lose first prize.

The young players exceeded expectations. Most thought that Botvinnik
and Makogonov would finish in the middle, and nobody expected anything
from Model (if we count him among the "young" ones as well). However,
all three won prizes, finishing ahead of many older players. The success of
Botvinnik and Model is less surprising: both grew up in Leningrad, nourished
by the previous generation of Leningrad masters. But where did Makogonov,
who lives in a remote chess province, get such self-assurance? What
nourishment did his chess talent receive?

Makogonov's success – three years ago, the previously unknown Sozin emerged as well, but he was alone, while now we have a whole host of youngsters vying for recognition: the 13 year-old Tolya Ufintsov from Omsk *(the future master Anatoly Ufimtsev; I had thought that he was from the industrialist Ufimtsev family, and after the revolution, his parents temporarily changed their surname just in case, but then, in* Shakhmatnoe Obozrenie *(No. 83–86, 1909), I found a mention of A. N. Ufintsev from Tomsk – this was his grandfather, Andrei, despite the slightly different ending)*, and Rauzer, whose great talent is undoubtable, even though he hasn't earned the master's title yet; Perfilyev, whose performance in the championship was very decent (ahead of three masters!); and very good youngsters in the trade union championships (Tischler, Kan), etc., etc. – yes, all this allows us to say that the USSR has new (not just old) gunpowder in its powder flask!..

The climb to the top is over. Two players stepped on to the champion's podium, with 14.5 points in their hands. Two players, sharp as flint. Flint is used to strike sparks. New chess sparks will fly in March. Whose spark will flash brighter? You can't guess..." *(64, October 1927)*.

From the press: "On 25th October, a special session of the Chess Section Council's Executive Bureau took place, chaired by Comrade N. V. Krylenko, to discuss the Soviet Championship match. Since the winners of the tournament, F. P. Bogatyrchuk and P. A. Romanovsky, declined to play the championship match immediately due to exhaustion, the Executive Bureau decreed:

1) The Soviet Championship match is to take place in March – April 1928, in Leningrad;

2) The match will be played until a player gains six points *(the text said six wins, but it was a mistake)*. In the

The poster of the "Live Artistic Chess Game, with participation of the 1927 Soviet Chess Championship winners P. A. Romanovsky and F. P. Bogatyrchuk", which was held on 23rd April 1928 (instead of 26th March, as initially planned) in Moscow, at the 1st State Circus arena. The press run was 3,000 copies! From the RGALI (Russian State Archive of Literature and Art) collection (Moscow).

event of a 5-5 score, the match is considered drawn, the Soviet champion's title remains unawarded, and both opponents receive the grandmaster title;

3) The first four draws do not count;

4) The regulations of the match are based on the Soviet Championship match between Bogoljubov and Romanovsky." (*Shakhmatny Listok*, November 1927.)

In May 1928, *Shakhmaty* reported: "The Soviet Championship match between Bogatyrchuk and Romanovsky is to be played in October in Moscow." While in the previously intended time period, the future opponents played... a living chess game in the State Circus on 23rd April! "Artists were used as pieces, including some very well-known ones. The captured pieces performed a trick from their repertoire. The game ended in a draw on move 34."

This protracted story was only brought to an end in 1929: "In view of the national chess championship being held this year, the match between Bogatyrchuk and Romanovsky shall not take place." (Quote from the typescript "Minutes (stenographic) of the meeting of the Chess Section Council, 8th-9th March 1929".) What was the reason for this decision?

В 1-м Госцирке состоялся вечер живой шахматной игры. Роли фигур исполняли лучшие московские артисты, игру вели мастера Ф. П. Богатырчук и П. А. Романовский. Каждая выбывшая из фигур исполняла номер концертной программы.

Фот. А. Шайхета.

Moscow, 1st State Circus. "The roles of pieces were played by the best Moscow artists, and the game was played by masters F. P. Bogatyrchuk and P. A. Romanovsky. Each captured piece performed a trick." (Ogonyok, No. 20, 1928.)

Bogatyrchuk: "In 1927, I achieved the greatest success in my chess career, sharing first and second place in the 5th All-Union championship with Peter Arsenyevich Romanovsky. Even though we were both only 35 years old, we were already considered "old hands"... As always, I played amateurishly, very inconsistently. For instance, I won five games against the other six prizewinners, but was barely able to scrape 1.5 points against the bottom three players. It was surprising that I managed to share the win...

The tournament regulations stated that in the event of a shared first place, the winners were to play a match to determine a single champion. For me, leaving Kiev always incurred heavy financial damage due to the loss of income from my private practice. I only allowed myself to leave the city once a year, when I took a vacation. So I requested that the All-Union Chess Section compensate, at least partly, my losses in case the match was played outside Kiev. As far as I know, they were ready to satisfy my demand, but then a new complication arose: my co-champion Romanovsky learned that I could receive financial compensation and demanded an equal sum for himself. I do not blame P. A. for this demand, it's possible that he didn't even know why I made such a request. In any event, paying both players to play the match was against the Chess Section's policy – they never paid any appearance fees, only compensating travel and accommodation expenses for those who played outside their home city. So, ultimately, the match was canceled, and we were both declared USSR champions.

After emigrating from the USSR, I couldn't avoid the common fate of all those who stayed abroad. I was struck off the list of Soviet masters, and Romanovsky was declared the sole champion of that year."

The Endurance Test

It's incredible how easily – at least in the 1920s – Krylenko's establishment would lose the games of the country's best players. This time, there was no discussion at all about any tournament book (even though they did find enough money to publish the stenographic transcript of the conference!), and only 85 out of 210 games survived – as before, those that were "lucky" enough to be annotated in chess magazines. Rokhlin would later explain that the tournament took place concurrently with the match in Buenos Aires, so the press "gave its utmost attention" to that, and there was just no space. But why wouldn't *64* at least print all the other games without annotations? This was the first championship in two years, the participants had prepared some novelties and wanted to show their best chess. You should value their creative efforts, save them for the growing fledgling players of the Soviet state... But no, they didn't even care to preserve all the games of the top 7: Romanovsky – 15 games (out of 20), Bogatyrchuk – 10, Duz-Khotimirsky – 6, Model – 7, Botvinnik – 12, Makogonov – 14, Nenarokov – 7. It's especially unfair for Duz and Model: out of 39 games they played, only 13 survived – a mere third! Even though both, as everyone agreed, played with great inspiration...

Of course, because of the unbearable conditions, the creative aspect suffered. Romanovsky didn't exaggerate one bit in his article "Painful Outcome". "The crowd's indiscipline, constant noise, scraping of the feet, stuffiness in the tournament hall – all that creates a very unfavorable environment for chess", *Shakhmatny Listok* reported after round 4. "This explains the lack of quality in many championship games." I. Rabinovich laments the large number of mistakes in his openings review as well: "The participants often made blatant mistakes, and, as a result, the outcome of the games did not always match the quality of chosen openings."

Nevertheless, there are enough beautiful games to choose from. This time, though, I had to prepare the selection myself, based on the round reports and my own taste, because there was a hiccup with brilliancy prizes. At first, as you remember, three brilliancy prizes were to be awarded. According to the historian I. Romanov, "Romanovsky had the most games nominated for the brilliancy prizes, but for some reason – too many years have passed to clarify – no prizes were awarded..." I think that the reason was actually very simple: the Chess Section higher-ups decided to punish Romanovsky for publicizing his grievances, and the best way they could come up with was... not to award any brilliancy prizes!

Clash of the Titans

"It is Sunday, and the game Romanovsky – Bogatyrchuk has attracted a lot of spectators; all their attention is concentrated on this game. The game has turned out to be very intense and has lived up to expectations. Romanovsky has traded queens in the opening and then boldly sacrificed an exchange; many moves have been played before we see that the sacrifice is correct, and white has won three pawns

for the exchange..." (*Shakhmatny Listok*)

No. 34. Ruy Lopez C79
Romanovsky – Bogatyrchuk
Moscow 1927, round 16
Annotated by P. Romanovsky
1.e4 e5 2.♘f3 ♘c6 3.♗b5 a6 4.♗a4 ♘f6 5.0-0 d6 6.d4 b5 7.dxe5 dxe5 8.♕xd8+ ♘xd8 9.♗b3 ♗d6. Another possible, and probably the best move is 9...♘d7 10.♘c3 (*10.a4! I. Rabinovich*) 10...♗d6, threatening to trade one of the white bishops

with ♘c5. *This is Rubinstein's plan, first tried out against Burn (Carlsbad 1911).*

The line with 9...♗d6 is also very rare (there are only thirty or so games in the database). In 1988, it was tried by Spassky twice: against Malaniuk (Rotterdam), and a draw was agreed immediately, and against Beliavsky (Belfort), after 10.♗g5 ♘e6 11.♗xf6 gxf6 12.♘c3 c6 13.♘e2 ♘c5 draw agreed.

10.♗g5 ♚e7. There is no other way to prevent the doubling of black pawns on the f-file.

However, nobody ever played this move – either before or after Bogatyrchuk: this game is literally unique! Black usually plays 10...♗e6 or 10...♘e6.

11.♘c3 c6 12.♖ad1 ♘b7. White again threatened to double the black pawns. With this move, black goes for huge complications, with chances for white.

However, after 12...♗c7 white maintains strong pressure with 13.♘h4 (threatening f2-f4), for instance: 13...h6 14.♗e3! ♘b7 15.f4 ♘g4 16.fxe5

16...♘xe3   17.♖xf7+   ♚e8 18.♘g6!! ♘xd1 19.♘xd1 ♗b6+ 20.♚h1 ♖h7 21.♖f8+ ♚d7 22.e6+ ♚c7 23.e7, winning.

Averbakh once warned me: "You should always check all of Romanovsky's lines that are longer than three moves! His love for beauty often failed him in his analysis." Here, instead of 16...♘xe3?, 16...♗e6 is clearly better, for instance: 17.♘f5+ ♗xf5 18.♖xf5 ♘xe5 or 17.♗xe6 ♚xe6 18.♗d4 ♖ad8, retaining defensive resources. And instead of the suicidal 20...♖h7?, black can equalize with 20...♘c5! 21.♘xh8 ♘xb3 22.axb3 ♗e6 23.♖b7 ♖d8 24.♘c3 ♗d4 25.♘g6 ♖d7 26.♖xd7 ♗xd7, and so, instead of going "for beauty" (18.♘g6?!), white should play the simple 18.♖xc7! ♘xd1 19.♘xd1 ♚d8 20.♖xg7, winning.

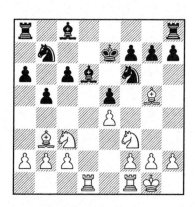

13.♖xd6! ♚xd6! After 13...♘xd6? white could continue the attack in various ways. The simplest was 14.♘xe5 ♗b7 15.♘g4! (15. ♘d3! is not bad either), and if 15...h6, then 16.♘xh6! gxh6 17.♗h4

♘de8 18.e5, with enough advantage.

However, after 18...♚f8! 19.exf6 c5, black's position looks good: 20.a4 c4 21.♗a2 ♖g8 22.f3 ♗c6 or 20.♗d5 ♗xd5 21.♘xd5 ♖d8 (22.♘e7 ♖h7!). Unfortunately, Bogatyrchuk didn't annotate the game, so we'll never know why he decided against capturing with the knight.

14.♖d1+ ♚c7 15.♘xe5 ♗e6 16.♘xf7 ♗xb3 17.axb3 ♖he8. *Perhaps a shorter move was more precise: 17...♖hf8! 18.♗f4+ ♚b6, and here, 19.e5 is bad for white (19...♖xf7 20.exf6 ♖xf6), while after 19.♘g5 ♖ae8 or 19.♘e5 a5, black has a good position.*

18.♗f4+ ♚b6 19.e5 ♖e7! 20.♘g5 ♘g4! After 20...♘d7, there was a very unpleasant reply – 21.♘e6!, and if 21...♘xe5, then 22.♗e3+, and white wins.

21.♘f3 ♖f8 22.♗g3.

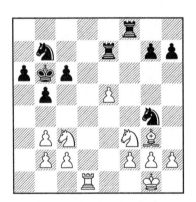

Even though black has managed to drive the white pieces back and has got excellent squares for his rooks, his position remains difficult because of his weak dark squares and

white's well-defended e5 pawn. So it was probably better to give back the exchange with 22...♖xf3 23.gxf3 ♘xe5.

22...♘c5 23.h3 ♘h6 24.♖d6 ♚b7 (not 24...♖e6 because of 25.b4!) **25.♘d4 ♘f5 26.♘xf5!** After 26.♘xc6 ♘xd6 27.♘xe7, black had a very unpleasant reply 27...♘de4!

26...♖xf5 27.b4 ♘e6. 27...♘d7 28.f4 (28.e6 ♘f8) 28...g5 29.e6 ♘f8 30.♘e4 ♘xe6 31.fxg5 ♘xg5 is a bit better; white still has good chances, but in this line he doesn't have his pride and joy, the e-pawn.

The game move is more natural: it stops the f-pawn and threatens to attack the e5 square after ♘f4.

28.♘e4 ♚b6. Black can't let the knight get to c5, after which all of white's problems are resolved. Moreover, the simple 29.♖xe6 was threatened.

29.♘c3 ♚b7 30.♘e4 ♚b6 31.♚f1! The critical moment.

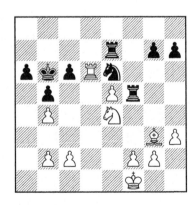

White plans to play f2-f3, put the bishop on the g1-a7 diagonal, seize the c5 square completely and repel the black knight's attack on f4 with the bishop transferring from g3 to d4. Without the king move, this plan is ruined with ♞f4-e2+ with the subsequent exchange of the bishop.

31...h6. Black feared 31...♞f4 32.♗h4 ♜exe5 33.♜d7! g5 34.♞d6, but, giving back the exchange with 34...c5, he got some counterplay. White, however, can parry the black knight's attack in a different way: 32.♞c5! ♜exe5 (32...♜fxe5 33.♞d7+) 33.♜d7!, while if black doesn't capture the pawn immediately, playing 32...a5!, white simply plays 33.c3.

32.f3 ♞f4 33.♗f2+ ♚c7 34.♗d4 ♞d5. Both here and on the next move, the only way to get drawing chances was to sacrifice the exchange back on e5. Black, however, decides against this, and his position quickly gets ruined.

35.c3 ♞b6? 36.♞c5 ♞c4 37.♞xa6+.

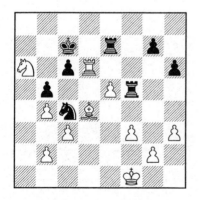

37...♚c8. If 37...♚b7, then 38.♞c5+ ♚c7(b6) 39.♞e6+ ♚c8!

40.♜xc6+ ♚d7 41.♞xg7!! ♜xg7 42.♜xc4 bxc4 43.e6+ etc.

38.♜xc6+ ♚b7 39.♜g6 ♞xe5 40.♞c5+ (40.♜b6+ is even simpler) **40...♚c8 41.♜b6 ♞c4 42.♜xb5 g6 43.b3.** With 43.♚f2, white could keep the connected passed pawns. However, he goes for maximum simplicity.

43...♞d2+ 44.♚f2 ♞xb3 45.♜b6 ♞xd4 46.cxd4. The game was adjourned here, but black resigned without playing. The sealed move was 46...♜g5, after which 47.♞e4, winning the g- and h-pawns, and the simple 47.b5 both win.

The Art of Preparation

"A good exception from the bad round 13 was the game Bogatyrchuk – Botvinnik, won by the former with deep maneuvering play." (*Shakhmaty*)

"Bogatyrchuk got an advantage out of the opening and crushed Botvinnik brilliantly." (*Shakhmatny Listok*)

No. 35. French Defense C17
Bogatyrchuk – Botvinnik
Moscow 1927, round 13
Annotated by F. Bogatyrchuk

1.e4 e6 2.d4 d5 3.♞c3 ♗b4 4.e5! After other moves, 4.exd5 or 4.♞e2, white gets no advantage.

4...c5 5.♛g4! This move is not considered good; that opinion is probably wrong.

5...♚f8. I think that 5...g6 was better, since, as the course of the

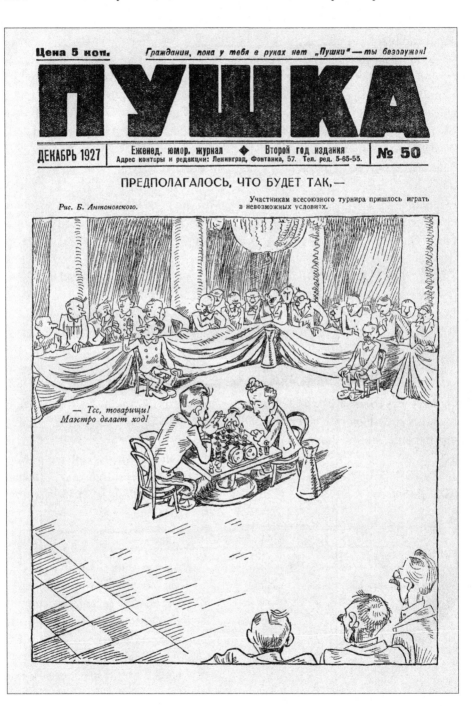

The championship through the eyes of cartoonist B. Antonovsky (Pushka, No. 50, 1927). To the left – as it was supposed to be: "Shush, comrades! The maestro is making his move!" To the right – as it turned out: "A voice in the ear: 'Hey, Comrade Romanchuk, forget 'em pawns! Castle your knight to the corner and then immediately grab at his king!'"

"Romanchuk" is a portmanteau of the two championship winners' last names, Romanovsky and Bogatyrchuk (sitting to the right). Published for the first time.

game shows, black has to constantly be wary of the potential bishop check. *The problem is that it's very hard to finish development and get the h8 rook into play with such a king's position.*

The strongest move here is 5... ♘e7, proposed by I. Rabinovich in his article "What Did the 5th All-Union Championship Give to Opening Theory?" (Shakhmaty No. 1, 1928); this move gradually turned white off 5.♕g4. But not immediately. According to ChessBase, 5...♘e7 was first tested in the games Treybal – Opocensky (Teplitz-Schoenau 1937 and then Prague 1939), and Bronstein – Boleslavsky (Kiev 1944).

6.♘f3 cxd4 7.♘xd4 ♕a5 8.♗d2 ♘c6 9.a3! In the game Vilner – Model, played in round 5, white played a weaker move, 9.♘xc6, after which black even got a better position. *However, the reason for this was not the move 9.♘xc6 per se – it's not bad either – but rather white's imprecise play in the middlegame.*

What's more interesting is the fact that it was... the first time ever that 5.♕g4 was played in tournament practice! Vilner probably didn't like the way in the first round that Model playing black destroyed Botvinnik, who had played 5.a3 (both then and now, this was considered the main line), and he decided to choose another way. In his annotations, Model didn't appreciate the novelty much: "A dubious move that gives black good play in the center." Knowing that Botvinnik followed

Model's advice, Bogatyrchuk decided to "catch" the youngster in this line. A subtle psychological calculation!

The lesson was well-learned. Later, Botvinnik would master this technique perfectly and become a true ace in the art of psychological preparation.

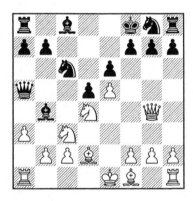

9...f5. Black's position is already shaky, but even here, this move is not the best. 9...♘xd4 10.♕xd4 ♗c5 11.♕f4 ♕d8 probably gave black the best defensive chances – even though white has a certain advantage, it's not that easy to convert.

Black, of course, couldn't play 9... ♘xe5, because he lost a piece after 10.♕g3:

1) 10...♗xc3 11.♗xc3 ♕c7 12.♘b5 ♕b8 13.♗b4+ and ♗d6;

2) 10...♗d6 11.♘cb5 ♕~ 12.♘xd6, and black can't play 12... ♕xd6 due to 13.♗b4 (*after 11... ♕xd2+! 12.♔xd2 ♘c4+ 13.♗xc4 ♗xg3 14.hxg3 dxc4 black equalizes, so the only correct move is 11.♘db5! ♗b8 12.♘xd5 or 11...♘c4 12.♘xd6 ♘xd2 13.♕f4*);

3) 10...♘c6 11.♘b3 and 12.axb4.

10.♕f4 ♘xd4 11.♕xd4 ♗c5 12.♕f4 ♕d8. White is better – but what's next?.. After calm moves, black just develops his knight with ♘g8-e7-g6(c6), attacking the e5 pawn and getting a satisfactory position.

13.♘a4! ♗e7. Black is forced to close off his knight, because after 13...b6 14.♘xc5 and 15.b4, the d2 bishop would take a decisive part in the attack, while 13...♗b6 14.♘xb6 and ♗b4+ is obviously bad for him.

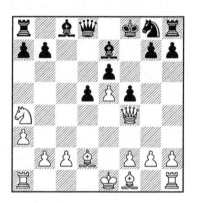

14.g4! Preventing g7-g6: after this move, the g8 knight is trapped forever. Thus, the isolation of the d5 pawn is prepared.

"Black's position quickly crumbles under white's energetic crushing blows." (Model)

14...♘h6 15.♖g1 ♘f7. It's unlikely that black had anything better. 15...g5 was bad: 16.♕f3 f4 17.h4 with the total destruction of the kingside. 15...♗d7 is met with 16.0-0-0 ♗xa4 17.♕xa4 ♘xg4 18.♖xg4 fxg4 19.♕xg4, and white, threatening ♗h3, ♕xe6 and ♖g1,

gets an unstoppable attack for the sacrificed exchange.

However, in the first line, it's better for black to play 16...♔g7! 17.gxf5 ♘xf5 or 16...♗d7 17.gxf5 ♘xf5, and in the second one, 16...g5! is better, because 17.♕d4 ♘xg4, 18.♖xg4 (18. ♘c5!?) 18...fxg4 19.♕xg4 doesn't work anymore due to 19...h5. So it seems that Model was right when he evaluated 15...♘f7 as "bad". The computer quickly draws a line, too.

16.gxf5   exf5   17.♕d4 (threatening   e5-e6)   **17...♗e6.** *"17...♘g5 didn't help either due to 18.♗xg5 ♗xg5 19.♗g2 ♗e6 20.♘c5 etc." (Model)*

18.♘c5 ♕b6. This is much better than trading the knight – after that move, the king's position would be even harder to defend. All in all, black defended most tenaciously in a difficult position.

19.♘xe6+ ♕xe6.

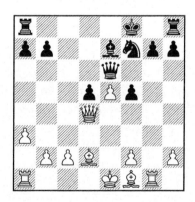

20.0-0-0! *The brave Junior sees this move immediately, while the cautious Fritz doesn't see it at all even after a cup of coffee (for me).*

20...♕xe5 21.♕xe5 ♘xe5 22.♗c3 d4. 22...♘g6 23.♖xd5 f4 24.♖f5+ ♔e8 is clearly bad: white continues the attack and wins the g7 pawn.

23.♗xd4 ♗f6 24.♗g2 g6 25.♗xb7 ♖b8 26.♗h1 ♔g7. After 26...a5 27.♗c3, threatening to meet 27...♔g7 with 28.♖d6, white gets a strong attack. *29.♖xf6 and f2-f4 is a threat as well.*

27.♗xa7 ♖bc8 28.b3 ♖he8 29.♗d4 ♖e7 30.♔b1 ♘g4 31.♗xf6+ ♔xf6 32.♖d2 ♖ce8 33.♗c6 ♖e2 34.♖xe2 ♖xe2.

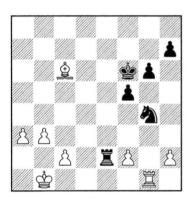

35.a4! Black can't hold back this pawn. After 35...♖xf2, the simplest move is 36.♖xg4, and the a-pawn either promotes, or black is forced to give up his rook for it.

35...♔e5 36.♖d1 ♘xf2 37.♖d5+ ♔e6 38.♖d8 ♘e4 39.a5 f4 40.♗xe4. Black resigned. After 40...♖xe4 41.♖e8+ ♔f5 42.♖xe4, the a-pawn promotes with a check.

As an afterword to this game I provide here a fragment from an article by Bogatyrchuk entitled My Encounters with The World Champion M. Botvinnik (Canadian Chess Chat, January 1960):

"I met Botvinnik for the first time in 1927 in the All Union Championship Tournament. A slender youth of about 15, he was a 'Wunderkind' (wonderchild), discovered by Leningrad chess players. And a wonder, really, he was, as he demonstrated already in this tournament, the first serious competition of his chess career, characteristics of a future world champion; he was not scared to withstand authority, playing equally well with the weak and the strong, and he did not hesitate to use any opening system... provided it was sound, in his opinion... It appeared that only the chessboard and men existed for him when he sat down to play a game. His knowledge of openings, even in that early period, was impressive indeed. It was clear to anyone that stubborn, persistent work was behind his theoretical competence. Even in 1927, a few Russian masters might overplay him. I was one of these fortunates."

Not a Boy, But a Man!

Romanovsky: "In round 1, Botvinnik fell victim to Model's time-trouble tricks. After that game, it was the first time that I saw

Botvinnik losing his composure, which had been characteristic of him since early youth. "I'll probably lose game after game now," he said to me. Perhaps this was the turning point for Botvinnik, after which he re-evaluated the role of tactics in the chess struggle. At any rate, the next day he crushed I. Rabinovich in brilliant tactical style."

No. 36. Dutch Defense A95
I. Rabinovich – Botvinnik
Moscow 1927, round 2

1.d4 e6 2.c4 f5. Many years later, in his *Analytical and Critical Works* (1984), Botvinnik finally revealed who introduced the Dutch Defense to him: "I shared a room with Model during the championship, and he taught me to play this complicated opening."

3.g3 ♘f6 4.♗g2 ♗e7 5.♘c3 0-0 6.♘f3 d5. Black went for the solid Stonewall system. The Ilyin-Zhenevsky variation (6...d6) will become popular after the 7th Soviet Championship (1931).

7.0-0 c6 8.♕c2. This move gives white a small, but steady positional advantage. Contrary to theoretical recommendations, Botvinnik later said that 8.♗g5 was "simpler and better". He played this move in game 22 of the return match against Smyslov (white lost, but not because of a bad opening).

8...♕e8 9.♗f4 ♕h5 10.♖ad1 ♘bd7 11.b3 ♘e4.

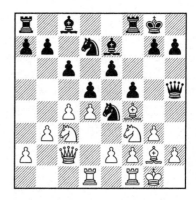

12.♘e5! Now that ♘g4 is no longer a threat.

12...♘g5. Of course, not 12...♘xc3 13.♗f3. In *Shakhmatny Listok* (No. 19, 1927) Botvinnik pointed to 12...♗f6 as the best move, because after the move in the game "now white could simply play 13.f3 ♘h3+ 14.♗xh3 ♕xh3 15.e4 with good play." The same line was shown in *Analytical and Critical Works*, even though after 15...fxe4 16.fxe4 ♘xe5 17.♗xe5 ♗d7! black has a cramped, but solid position. For instance, the attempt to win a pawn 18.exd5 exd5 19.cxd5 is dangerous for white: 19...♗g5! 20.♕e4 (20.♖de1? ♗e3+) 20...♗f5 etc.

13.h4 ♘e4 14.♗f3. "Too indecisive. By playing 14.♘xe4 fxe4 15.f3, white got a better position, because the exchange sacrifice 15...♖xf4 16.gxf4 didn't work," Botvinnik wrote in the magazine; however, after 16...e3! (not 16...♘xe5 17.fxe5 e3 due to 18.f4! and ♖f3) white is in danger of getting attacked. For instance: 17.♕d3 ♗xh4 18.♕xe3 ♗g3 19.♘g4 dxc4! 20.bxc4 (20.♕xe6+? ♔h8) 20...e5 etc.

By the way, the annotation to this move underwent a strange metamorphosis. The magazine notes read: "After a great opening, white, starting with move 14, made a series of weak moves and got a worse position." In the collection *Selected Games 1926–1936* (1938), Botvinnik downgraded the evaluation: "After a good opening…" And in the postwar collections, this phrase was removed altogether!

14...♕e8   15.♘xd7   ♗xd7 16.♔g2 (16.♗g2!?) **16...♗b4!**

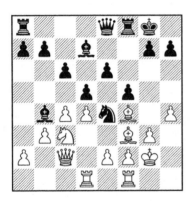

17.♗xe4?! The decisive mistake, in Botvinnik's opinion. He recommended 17.♘b1 "with defending chances", but 17.♘a4!? with the idea ♘b2-d3 is probably more active.

17...fxe4   18.♖h1? This is the decisive mistake! The cold-blooded 18.♗e5! (and if 18...♕h5, then 19.f3) deprived black of the opportunity to play e6-e5 and sacrifice a rook on f4.

18...♕h5 19.f3 ♕g6! "The correct move order was 19...e5! 20.dxe5

♕g6, getting the same position as in the game. But now, white can avoid this" (Botvinnik). However, in this line, white has a great reply 21.♕c1!, preventing the sacrifice on f4 (21...♖xf4 22.h5 ♕g5 23.♘xd5! cxd5 24.♕xf4 or 21...♗xc3 22.h5 ♕f7 23.♕xc3). So, the game move was the strongest one.

20.♔f1. "After 20.♔h2, there's 20...♖xf4, winning," Botvinnik wrote just after the game. Many years later, he changed his opinion: "20.♔h2 was worthy of consideration, avoiding disconnecting the rooks; the king would be safer, too."

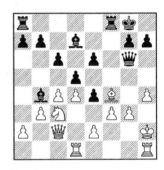

Strangely enough, the young Botvinnik was closer to the truth; however, 20...♖xf4 with great complications wasn't the "winning move". The actual winning line was the computer move 20...exf3! 21.♕xg6 hxg6 22.♖d3 e5! 23.dxe5 (23.♗xe5 fxe2 24.♖e1 dxc4! 25.bxc4 ♗e6) 23...d4! 24.♖xd4 ♗xc3 25.♖d3 (25.♖xd7? fxe2) 25...♗a5 26.exf3 ♗f5 with a piece for two pawns.

I should also add that 20.♕c1 didn't work: without first including 19...e5 20.dxe5, this loses!

20...e5! Winning a pawn with 20...exf3 21.♕xg6 hxg6 and fxe2+ would be aiming too low.

21.dxe5. "White should have played 21.h5, even though after 21...♕f5 22.dxe5 exf3 23.♕xf5 ♗xf5 24.♖c1 d4 25.♘d1 ♗g4! black had a won endgame." In the 1938 collection, Botvinnik finished the line with 25...♗e4, which is actually stronger.

23.e4 doesn't help either because of the precise 23...♕g4! (23...dxe4 is weaker due to 24.♘xe4 with the idea ♕d3 and ♘d6), and if 24.♖h4, then 24...♕xh4 25.gxh4 ♖xf4 – white is doomed because of his badly-positioned pieces.

21...♖xf4! 22.gxf4 ♕g3!!

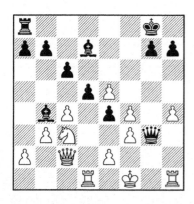

Impressive. Rudolf Spielmann, annotating the game for *64*, awarded double exclamation marks to four black moves in a row (19–22)!

23.♘xe4. After 23.cxd5, Botvinnik showed the spectacular 23...♗c5 24.♘xe4 ♗h3+ 25.♖xh3 ♕g1#. However, there's no direct checkmate after 24.e3, so 23...♗h3+,

winning the queen, is more effective.

23...dxe4 24.♖xd7 (24.♕xe4 ♗c5 25.♖d4 or 25.e3 both lose after 25...♗f5! among other moves) **24...♗c5.** Not 24...e3? because of the crushing 25.♖xg7+!!

25.e3 ♕xf3+ 26.♕f2 ♕xh1+ 27.♔e2 ♕h3! 28.f5 ♕g4+ 29.♔d2 ♖f8 30.e6 ♕xf5. This was all according to the computer's first line! But now, there was also a good alternative: 30...h5! (threatening ♖xf5) 31.♕f4 ♗b4+! 32.♔c1 ♖xf5 33.♕xg4 hxg4, and the pawn promotes.

31.♕xf5 ♖xf5 32.♖xb7 ♖f2+ 33.♔e1 ♖f6.

Mikhail Botvinnik. "Great composure and deep understanding of diverse positions helped him secure his great success." (Romanovsky.) From Y. Neishtadt's archive.

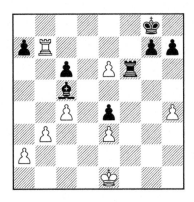

34.b4 (or 34.♖b8+ ♖f8 35.♖b7 ♖e8 36.b4 ♗xe3) **34...♗xe3 35.♔e2 ♗g1 36.e7.** White wants to sell his passed pawn for the biggest possible prize, but this only prolongs the struggle.

36...♔f7   37.e8♕+   ♔xe8 38.♖xg7 ♖g6! 39.♖xh7 ♗d4 40.c5 ♖g2+ 41.♔f1 ♖f2+ 42.♔e1 e3. White resigned.

"The 17 year-old winner executed his attack with great talent and flair. We can place much hope on him in the future." (Spielmann)

The Winning Tabiya

I. Rabinovich: "Model, with admirable persistence (in all 9 games played as white!), used the following development system: 1.♘f3, b3, ♗b2, e3 and d4. Despite the great result (6.5/9), it's hard to say that this system was particularly strong; white's success is mostly explained by the fact that black actively tried to <u>refute</u> this totally acceptable way of development."

Unfortunately, only two of Model's games with white survived,

and only one was annotated by Model himself. Actually, he modified his opening tabiya slightly for this game, playing 1.♘f3, b3, ♗b2, g3, ♗g2, 0-0 and d4, but... this didn't change the result.

No. 37
Model – Sergeyev
Moscow 1927, round 14
Annotated by A. Model

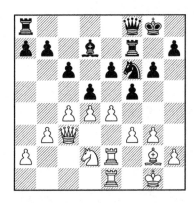

19.b4! White intends to transfer the knight to e5 through b3-c1-d3. It's unlikely that black can stop him.

The machine, both here and on the next move, insists on 19.e5 ♘h5 20.f4, grabbing space – the soulless automaton doesn't understand the adrenaline created by pawn tension!

19...♕h6 (a weak attempt to create kingside counterplay) **20.♘b3 b6.** 20...fxe4 21.fxe4 ♘g4 22.h3 gained nothing for black either.

21.♘c1 ♖d8 22.♘d3 dxe4 23.♘e5 ♖ff8 (23...exf3? 24.♘xf7)

"In 1927, I met Abram Yakovlevich Model – he was 32 then. Since that time, for almost half a century, I never stopped being amazed by his numerous talents: an exceptional mathematician, talented chess master, gifted piano player, stage magician, illusionist, mnemonics expert, poet... He wrote exquisite, witty poems and had an awesome ability to pronounce any word backwards. For instance, Leningrad – Dargninel, Rabinovich – Chivonibar. The most amazing thing was that he could speak this gibberish fluently, without mistakes, and even recite entire poems in it. An incredibly cheerful man, he was always in a great mood. A great master of telling jokes (he knew a lot of them), a good poker player. All in all, whatever he tried, he did well – he was that diversely talented." (Batuev.) (Shakhmatny Listok, No. 21, 1927.)

24.fxe4 ♘g4. The only way to drive the knight away from e5. But now white gets a passed pawn on the e-file, which wins the game quickly.

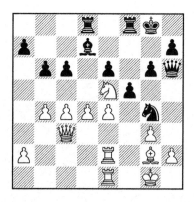

25.♘xg4 fxg4 26.e5! *(now is the right time)* **26...♕g7 27.d5! cxd5 28.cxd5 ♗b5 29.♖d2 exd5 30.♗xd5+ ♔h8 31.♕e3 ♖de8** *(31... ♖f5 32.♗e6!)* **32.♖f2 ♖xf2 33.♕xf2 ♖f8 34.♕e3.**

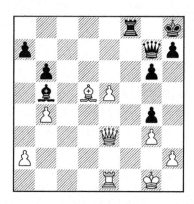

34...h5 35.e6 ♖e8 36.e7. White can't allow ♖e7. *If so, maybe black would have been better off with a different move order: 34...♖e8 35.e6 ♖e7 36.♕f4 h5.*

36...♗d7 37.♕g5 ♔h7 (37... ♕d4+ 38.♔h1 ♔g7 was stronger) **38.♖e5 ♗f5 39.♕e3.** But not 39.♖xf5 gxf5 40.♕xh5+ ♕h6 41.♕f7+ ♔g7, and if 42.♕xe8, then 42...♕d4+ with perpetual check.

39...♕f6 (white threatened ♗c6) **40.b5!**

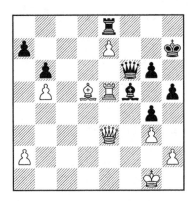

40...♗d7. 40...♗d3 was tempting, but erroneous due to 41.♕f4!, winning at least the exchange.

It's good that his opponent didn't give in to that temptation. Although after 41...♗f5! 42.♕e3 ♗d3 white would've had to settle for a draw, 41.♗g2! ♗xb5 42.♖xb5 ♖xe7 43.♕f2 still won.

41.♕c3. Threatening to win the queen with 42.♖xh5+ ♔g7 43.♖h7+.

41...♔g7 *(41...♕g7 42.♕e1! ♗xb5 43.♗e4 or 42...♕f6 43.a4, and black is in zugzwang)* **42.♗c6 ♗xc6.** The only move. *After 42...♖c8, there's the spectacular 43.♗xd7 ♖xc3 44.e8♘+!*

43.bxc6 ♔f7. The last throes.

44.♕c4+ *(the immediate 44.c7 was possible too)* **44...♔g7 45.♕d4 ♔f7 46.♕d5+ ♔g7 47.c7 ♖xe7 48.c8♕ ♖xe5 49.♕cg8+.** Black resigned.

From Romanovsky's Golden Collection

"The most talked-about game of round 2 was I. Rabinovich – Botvinnik... This "sensation" overshadowed Romanovsky's brilliant win against Smorodsky. The Leningrad master's combinational talent showed itself fully in this game." (*64*)

No. 38
Smorodsky – Romanovsky
Moscow 1927, round 2
Annotated by P. Romanovsky

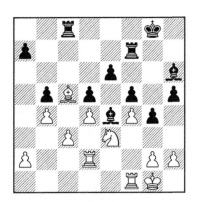

32...a5! 33.bxa5? It was better to play 33.a3, ceding the a-file to black but still putting up stiff resistance.

33...e5! *Interestingly enough, the computer evaluates this position as only slightly better for black, but after 33.a3 thinks that black is clearly better. Maybe the passed pawn on the a-file is a very strong argument for it...*

34.g3 exf4 35.gxf4 ♖a8 36.♗b4 h4.

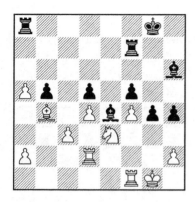

37.h3. Black threatened 37...♗f3 38.♘g2 h3 and ♗xf4.

It seems that 37.a4!? bxa4 38.♖a2 posed black more difficult problems. Now the idea 38...♗f3 39.♘g2 h3 is met with the paradoxical 40.♘h4! ♗e4 41.♖xa4 ♖a6 42.♗c5!, and the attempt to win the knight is dangerous: 42...♖h7 43.♖b4 ♗g7 44.♖b8+ ♔f7 45.♖b7+ ♔e6 46.♖b6+ ♖xb6 47.axb6 ♖xh4 48.b7 ♖h8 49.♗a7 ♗f6 50.b8♕ ♖xb8 51.♗xb8 etc.

Another maneuver still wins – 38...♗d3! 39.♘xd5 ♖e8! (39...♗c4 40.♘b6 or 39...♗xf1 40.♔xf1 ♗f8 41.♖xa4 with equality) 40.♖xa4 ♗c4, for instance: 41.♘b6 ♗xf1! 42.♔xf1 ♗xf4 43.a6 ♗b8, or 41.♗f8 ♗xf1! 42.♗xh6 ♗d3 43.♖a1 ♖e2, or 41.♘e7+ ♖fxe7 42.♗xe7 ♗xf1! 43.♔xf1 ♖xe7 44.d5 ♖a7, and black wins.

37...♖g7 38.♔h2 gxh3! 39.♖df2 ♔f7! Starting an interesting mating combination. In the idea's substance and execution, I consider this combination one of my very best *(don't forget that this is the opinion of*

the "late" Romanovsky – he wrote this in 1954!).

Due to the threat 40...♖g3, white's next move is forced.

40.♖g1 *(40.♖e1 ♖g3 41.♖ee2 ♗f3 42.♘xf5 ♗xf4!)* **40...♖xg1 41.♔xg1 ♖g8+ 42.♔h2.** After 42.♔f1, both 42...♗xf4 43.♖xf4 h2 and 42...h2 43.♖xh2 ♗xf4 44.♖h3 ♗xe3 45.♖xe3 f4 etc. win.

42...♖g3!

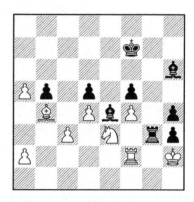

43.a6. The last hope! If 43.♘f1, then 43...♖g2+. Or 43.♘d1 ♔e6 44.a6 ♗f3 45.a7 ♗xf4 46.♖xf3 ♖xf3+ 47.♔g1 h2+ etc.

But instead of 45.a7?, white can save the game with the computer move 45.♘b2! ♗xf4 46.♘d3, for instance: 46...♖g2+ 47.♔xh3 or 46... ♗b8 47.♘c5 ♖g5+ 48.♘e5! ♖g2+ 49.♖xg2 hxg2 50.a7 ♗xe5+ 51.dxe5 d4, and the opposite-colored bishops save white.

So, the correct move after 43.♘d1 is 43...♗f3! 44.a6 (44.♘b2 ♗g2! 45.a6 ♖e3) 44...♗xf4 45.a7 ♖g8+ 46.♔xh3 ♗g4+ etc. By the way, Romanovsky himself showed this line in Shakhmatny Listok, *but changed it in his game collection for some reason.*

43...♖xe3 44.a7. 44.♗d6 ♗g2 45.a7 ♖e1 46.♖xg2 hxg2 47.♔xg2 ♖e2+ and ♖xa2 can't save white either.

44...♖e1 45.♔xh3.

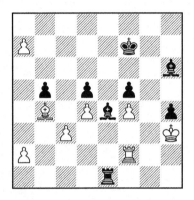

45...♗xf4! 46.♖h2 ♔g6! The king ends the work it started. White resigned: 47.♔xh4 ♖e3 48.♗e7 ♗g3+ 49.♔h3 ♗e1(f2)#.

"Romanovsky played the whole game with great mastery." (*Spielmann*)

Hypnotized by Hypermodernism

"After a complicated strategic battle, Duz-Khotimirsky gained an advantage over Romanovsky and won the game beautifully with an energetic attack." (*Shakhmaty*)

No. 39
Romanovsky – Duz-Khotimirsky
Moscow 1927, round 12
Annotated by F. Duz-Khotimirsky

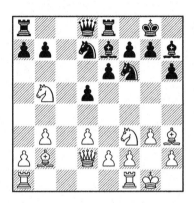

14.♗c3? Hypnosis! Romanovsky is trying to execute Reti's idea – the double attack of the queen and bishop on the g7 square – at all cost, losing the opportunity to seize the open c-file with his rooks immediately.

14...a6 15.♘bd4. Now both the retreat ♗f5-h7 and the reply ♗g2-h3 *(moves 12... and 13)*, preventing the e5 pawn from moving, are more understandable (*black replied 13... ♖e8*).

15...♗d6! 16.b4 (preventing ♗a3) **16...♕e7 17.♕b2 ♖ec8 18.a4.**

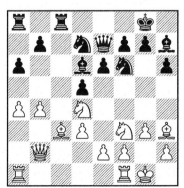

18...g5! An unexpected counter-strike against white's attacking forces. It's necessary to drive away the d4 knight, which dominates black's position.

19.♗g2 e5! 20.♘c2 ♖c7 21.♖fc1 ♖ac8 22.♗e1. *One square too far. By playing 22.♗d2! e4 23.dxe4 dxe4 24.♘fd4 ♗e5 25.e3, white could avoid the e4-e3 push.*

22...e4! The c-file is seized by black, and he goes on a resolute attack.

23.dxe4 dxe4 24.♘fd4 ♘d5 25.♗h3! The bishop's second incursion, again worrying black. This bishop is white's only active piece.

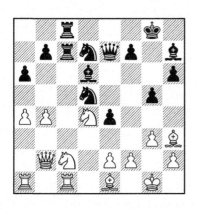

25...e3! 26.♗f5. *Loses by force. White should have tried 26.♘xe3!?, simplifying the position and getting out of the pin: 26...♘xe3 27.♖xc7 ♖xc7 28.fxe3 ♕xe3+ 29.♗f2 or 28... ♘f6 29.♗f5 ♕xe3+ 30.♗f2, and white can still hold.*

26...exf2+ 27.♗xf2 ♕e5! 28.♗xh7+ (28.♗xd7 ♖xc2!) **28... ♔xh7 29.♕b1.** A transparent trap!

29.♘e1 was more tenacious, for instance: 29...♕e4 30.♖xc7 ♖xc7 31.b5 or 29...♘xb4 30.♖xc7 ♖xc7 31.♘ef3 ♕e4 32.♘d2 – the position is shaky, but there's no mate in sight.

29...♔g8. Simple and convincing. Now the c2 knight is pinned, so white has to move the rook away from the c-file.

30.♖f1? White should have played 30.♖e1. The game move allows black to finish the game with a spectacular combination.

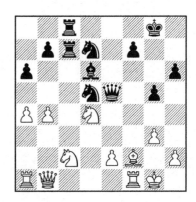

30...♖xc2!! 31.♘xc2 ♘c3 32.♕b3 ♘xe2+ 33.♔g2 ♖c3! White resigned. He either loses his queen – 34.♕xf7+ ♔xf7 35.♗d4+ ♘f4+! – or gets mated in three.

Maestro Von Freymann Keeps His Cool

Romanovsky: "Freymann's games were inconsistent, but rich in ideas. He showed his true mastery in creating and executing ideas in many games."

No. 40. Queen's Gambit D52
Freymann – V. Makogonov
Moscow 1927, round 17

1.d4 ♘f6 2.c4 e6 3.♘f3 d5 4.♗g5 ♘bd7 5.♘c3 c6 6.e3 ♕a5 7.cxd5 ♘xd5 8.♕b3?! "A weak move. White should have played 8.♕d2 *(for instance: 8...♗b4 9.♖c1 h6 10.♗h4 0-0 11.♗c4 ♘xc3 12.bxc3 ♗a3 13.♖b1 with a good position, Alekhine – Nimzowitsch, Zurich 1934)*. Now he is in serious trouble." (Freymann)

8...♗b4 9.♖c1 e5! Tartakower's novelty, used against I. Rabinovich at the 1925 Moscow International Tournament. In the game Levenfish – Freymann (1925 Soviet Championship) black played 9...c5 10.♗e2 b5 11.0-0 c4, and after 12.♕c2 ♘xc3 13.bxc3 ♗a3 14.♖b1 ♘b6 15.e4 slowly lost.

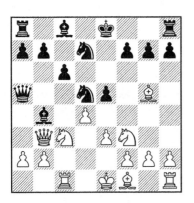

If white now plays 10.dxe5?, then there's 10...♘c5 and ♘a4, while after 10.♘xe5 ♘xe5 11.dxe5 ♗e6! black has an active position. Rabinovich tried 10.a3, but after 10...♗xc3+ 11.bxc3 exd4 12.exd4 0-0 13.♗d3

♖e8+ 14.♔d1 lost his castling rights and quickly crumbled.

And now it's time to open the book *Ferzberi's Traps*. It was written by the great chess writer Boris Samoilovich Vainstein, the older friend and mentor of David Bronstein and the famous and mysterious "grandmaster Ferzberi":

"A group of young Tashkent players, me included, intently sought out any available chess information. The thought that black could so quickly equalize and even get an advantage in the Queen's Gambit seemed illogical and impossible for us. We turned to Dr. Tarrasch's excellent book *Defending Against the Queen's Gambit* and found what we needed: "If now (after 9.♖c1) black advances his c- or e-pawn, white shouldn't capture it, but rather play 10.♗d3, intending to castle."

Checking this line in several games, I was certain that Tarrasch's recommendation was correct and, mustering up the courage, decided to write a letter and send it to Paris, to Tartakower, without even the slightest hope of getting a reply...

I'll never forget the day when the swarthy postman in a Muslim skullcap brought me, an unknown student from Tashkent, an envelope with a French postmark and a Paris stamp. Yes, this was a letter from Tartakower! The forty-degree heat seemed like heavenly freshness to me

Шахматы на Советском Востоке

Группа узбеков из Старого Ташкента (туземной части города) за игрой в шахматы.—
×) рабочий *Ходжаев*, один из сильнейших игроков Ташкента; ××) тов. *Б. Вайнштейн*, один из руководителей шахм. организаций Ташкента. Посредине между
ними тов. *Ф. И. Дуз-Хотимирский* (в узбекском костюме).

*"Chess in the Soviet East. A group of Uzbeks from the Old Tashkent (the native part of town)
playing chess. X) was a worker, Khodzhaev, one of Tashkent's strongest players; XX) was
Comrade B. Vainstein, one of the heads of the Tashkent chess organizations. Between them sits
Comrade F. I. Duz-Khotimirsky (in an Uzbek costume)." (Cover of 64. Shakhmaty i Shashki v
Rabochem Klube, No. 17, 1926.*

when I ran to the club to share my joy
with my friends. The grandmaster
wrote that both Tarrasch's analysis
and our ideas were correct (and
later recommended 10.♗d3 in his
theoretical article about the Moscow
tournament)...

A   year   passed.   Maestro
S. N. Freymann – the mentor of the
Tashkent players – was preparing
for the 1927 national championship
and, in strict confidence, showed
me the refutation of the 10.♗d3
line. Sergei Nikolaevich had found a
wonderful reply 10...h6!, the hidden

power of which is only seen seven
moves later... Armed with this secret
weapon, maestro von Freymann, as
he was called before the revolution,
went to the championship...

Freymann had no opportunity to
test his novelty. However, in one of the
last rounds, his opponent Vladimir
Makogonov chose the Cambridge
Springs Defense. I was in Moscow to
play in some team competition back
then, and I watched this game in the
hall. Freymann sat in deep thought,
grabbing his head in both hands,
and his long beard almost touched

the chessmen. To my abject horror, he led the game, move after move, towards the very position that he recently showed me as won for black. I fidgeted near his table, trying to attract his attention, but Freymann was fully concentrated on the game. Making the move 10.♗d3, he finally got up and went for a walk around the hall, smiling blissfully.

I approached him and said in a tragic whisper, "What are you doing, maestro? You're playing the very same line you refuted! Makogonov only has to make one move – you know which one – and you lose by force!"

"So that's it!" Freymann answered, his face remained quite impassive. "Well, I did notice that the position looked familiar..."

And he walked on..."

10.♗d3? "It's hard to find a satisfactory continuation for white. The game move should have lost." (Freymann)

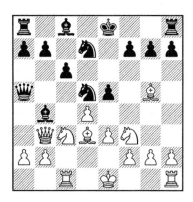

10...exd4. "Black should have played 10...h6! 11.♗h4 exd4

12.exd4 (if 12.♘xd4, then 12... ♘c5, threatening to win a pawn with ♘a4) 12...♘f4. If now 13.♗f1, then 13...0-0, and black gets a very strong attack against the white king that's stuck in the center. But the alternative is even worse: 13.♗c4 ♗xc3+ *(it's also interesting to check the immediate 13...♘xg2+ 14.♔f1 ♘xh4 15.♖e1+ ♗e7, leaving the d4 pawn without protection)* 14.bxc3 ♘xg2+ 15.♔f1 ♘xh4

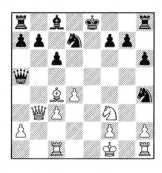

16.♗xf7+ *(16.♘xh4 0-0 17.♘g6? ♕g5)* 16...♔d8 17.♘xh4 ♕g5!, and black wins a piece." (Freymann)

But why can't white play 16.♖e1+, preventing the double attack? For instance: 16...♔d8 17.♘xh4 ♕h5 18.♘g2 ♕f3 19.♖e3 (19.♗xf7? ♖f8) 19...♕f6 – Black has an extra pawn, but he's somewhat behind in development.

"After the game," Vainstein writes, "Freymann had the indiscretion to show Makogonov the winning move, and then, in his annotations for *64*, published the entire line, which, to my knowledge, has never been played in tournaments since."

Vladimir Makogonov. "To justify his title, he would have to infuse his play with more imagination, inventiveness, decisiveness and action in general." (Romanovsky.) (Shakhmatny Listok, No. 21, 1927).

Indeed, there's only a single game in this line in the database: Peev – Atanasakis (Sofia 1967). There followed: 13.♗c4 0-0 14.♗g3 ♗xc3+ (14...♗d6!? 15.0-0 b5, maintaining the initiative) 15.♖xc3 ♘d5 16.♗xd5 ♖e8+ 17.♔d1 cxd5 18.♗c7 ♕a6 19.♕xd5 ♕e2+ 20.♔c1 ♘f6 21.♕a5 b6 22.♕a3 ♗f5 23.♕b3 ♕e4 24.♔d2 ♕e2+ 25.♔c1 ♕e4 with a draw.

11.exd4   ♘7f6   12.0-0   0-0 13.♘e5   ♗e6   14.♕c2 (14.♘c4!? ♘xc3 15.♘xa5 ♗xb3 16.bxc3 ♗xa5 17.axb3, with the bishop pair) **14... h6 15.♗d2 ♕b6.**

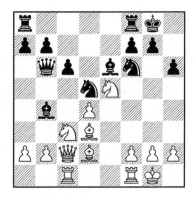

Even though black didn't find the winning move (10...h6!), his position is already better.

16.♘e2 (16.a3!? ♗e7 17.♘xd5 ♘xd5 18.♗e3) **16...♗xd2 17.♕xd2 ♘b4 18.♗b1.** "White's game is strategically bad; 18.a3 ♘xd3 19.♘xd3, and black has a significant advantage. With the game move, white sets a trap, and black walks right into it." (Freymann)

18...♗xa2 (18...♘xa2! 19.♗xa2 ♗xa2 or 19.♘c4 ♕a6) **19.♗xa2 ♘xa2 20.♖a1.**

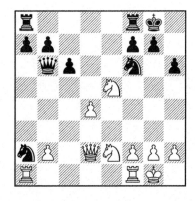

20...♕b3? Loses a piece. Freymann recommended 20...♘b4 21.♘c4 ♘e4, "holding onto the pawn", but after 22.♘xb6! ♘xd2 23.♘xa8 ♘xf1 24.♖xa7 white regained that pawn anyway.

21.♕d3! ♕xb2 (21...♕d5 22.♘f4; 21...♕a4 22.b3) **22.♖fb1 ♘b4 23.♖xb2 ♘xd3 24.♘xd3 ♖fe8.** This is curtains already...

25.♔f1 b6 26.♖c1 ♖ac8 27.♖bc2 ♘e4 28.f3 ♘d6 29.♖xc6 ♖xc6 30.♖xc6 ♘b5 31.f4 ♔f8 32.♘e5 f6 33.♘f3 ♖d8 34.f5 ♘d6 35.♘f4 ♔f7 36.g4 b5 37.♘e6. Black resigned.

A dramatic fight! I think that the unique case of chess amnesia that struck maestro von Freymann deserves a place in the annals of our championships.

Odessa Roulette

6th Soviet Championship: Odessa, 2nd – 20th September 1929

> "From the main platform a cast-iron, slow voice:
> 'Those in favor shall raise their hands.'"
> Evgeny Zamyatin, *We*

Alas, Krylenko was right when he said "Politics is a thing similar to nature: you chase it out the door, and it climbs back through the window." Yeah, I know I said that I wouldn't be writing about chess conferences anymore, about the endless fight against "counter-revolution", "henchmen of the bourgeoisie" and "agents of world imperialism" – but what can I do if Soviet chess was thoroughly politicized? And without knowing the "ideological" underpinnings, you'll never understand why some chess players fell out of favor while others made their careers very quickly, why the *Shakhmaty* magazine was closed, why decent people suddenly started writing indecent things about Alekhine and Bogoljubov, why the language of talented authors shriveled, their thoughts weakened, their humor disappeared completely.

Я.С.ЮРГЕЛЕВИЧ

„ШАХ-БОЙ"

ВОЕННО-ШАХМАТНАЯ ИГРА

ИЗДАНИЕ
Московского Областного Совета Осоавиахима
Москва   1934

A tank instead of a plane! "In 1927, 64's editorial board launched a fundraiser to build the "N. V. Krylenko Chess-Player Plane". 454 rubles 22 kopecks were raised, which was obviously not enough to build a plane. At this moment, when the entire USSR is intensely watching events by the North Chinese border, when all workers are building tanks, planes, etc. to fight back against the impudent Chinese White-Guard bandits, 64's editors are proposing to transfer this money to the builders of the Pravda Readers' Tank. Time waits for nobody!" (64. Shakhmaty i Shashki v Rabochem Klube, August 1929.)
The brochure **Shakh-Boi (Chess Battle)** was published by Osoaviakhim in 1934. The new game is similar to chess, but red oppose white in this game, the board is 12x12, and the following pieces take part: foot soldiers (budenovka hats) x15, machine guns (bullets), cavalry (horses) and cannons (shells) x2 each, tanks (a tank), planes (a plane) and headquarters (a mast) x1 each. From the author's archive.

Why the chess community, so individualistic and diverse, suddenly became so incredibly homogenous. Did everybody just break down at once and unquestioningly submit to the blunt state machine of Bolshevism, which had been grinding down the brightest, the most talented, the freest spirits in Russian society for years?

Of course it didn't. I remember Yuri Lvovich Averbakh telling me that the spine of our civil society was only broken in the mid-1930s, whereas in the 1920s the intelligentsia were not yet afraid to express "alien" views, engage in controversy, defend their opinions. Bogatyrchuk, for instance, could still give a sharp rebuke to Krylenko for his insulting accusations, and Romanovsky could quit the *Shakhmatny Listok* editorial board in protest. And this was not perceived as a heroic deed or a suicidal move, after which a visit from the secret police to both was only a matter of time. No, it was just a normal expression of human dignity, characteristic of Russian society. And, by the way, the magazine printed open letters of both of them. What else could it do? It's necessary to give the person an opportunity to defend themselves

Арабские цифры обозначают красных, римские—фашистов.

1—обозначают вождя,
2—   „   коммуниста,
3—   „   комсомольца,
4—   „   пионера,
I—   „   диктатора,
II—   „   фашиста,
III—   „   юнкера,
IV—   „   бой-скаута.

Shakh-Boi wasn't the first Soviet chess modification. In the 1920s, the game

Komsomol Chess *was invented (see picture). The game is played on a standard chess board, and there are 32 pieces as well – 16 black (Fascists) and 16 red (Communists). There are four types of pieces, with their names very much reflecting the spirit of the times: the red side has Leaders (No. 1 on the board), Communists (No. 2), Komsomol members (No. 3) and Pioneers (No. 4), while black has Dictators (No. I), Fascists (No. II), Junkers (No. III) and Boy Scouts (No. IV).*

There was also a book called **New Revolution Strategic Game "The International"** *For Two or Three Players, Like Chess, with 32 Special Pieces (1925). It was edited by Ilyin-Zhenevsky himself. The rules need to be seen to be believed: "The opponents in this game represent countries divided by classes. The common people of both fighting sides in the initial position are subjugated by their ruling classes and serve to further their imperialistic agendas. However, as soon as agitators and popular leaders infiltrate their ranks, the subjugated classes stop obeying their governments, fraternize, start a revolution, and, if they are successful, declare the International."*

and their honor! Only later, other kinds of letters became fashionable – either repentant, admitting mistakes or delusions – or collective, demanding to shoot or otherwise repress somebody...

We'll discuss the scandalous absence of the joint Soviet champions in the upcoming championship later. But for now, we shall start at Krylenko's article with its unassuming headline, "More about Politics and Chess". In actuality, this is a stunning document of the era! The article shows how strong was the resistance to the forced politicization of chess, how still internally free were the people, who was responsible for pitting the chess "youngsters" against the "old men", who... Anyway, a careful reader will figure everything out.

"Too Much of that Krylenko Thing"

Krylenko: "...The growing activity of the counter-revolutionary groups, often not formally organized yet, but still undeniably counter-revolutionary in their essence, manifests itself in different forms – from organizing counter-revolutionary uprisings and economic sabotage to simple grumblings of the

Seeing this photo in the 64 magazine (No. 2, 1930), I could barely believe my eyes. The leader of the world proletariat, yawning his head off? This is nothing less than sabotage! What was Comrade Krylenko, the executive editor, thinking?! But then it dawned on me: back in those years, Stalin, in his bid for personal power, started turning Lenin into a somewhat comical figure, and Krylenko sensed that trend pretty well. Lenin was playing against the medical scientist and revolutionary Alexander Bogdanov, with the writer Maxim Gorky watching.

classes and groups disgruntled by the revolution. We want to talk about how it manifests itself in our environment.

Chess players, as long as the chess art was a leisure for the old privileged class of bourgeoisie and its henchmen, were a politically amorphous mass. "Chess", they would say, "gives us rest, aesthetic pleasure, peaceful, bloodless fights..."

Alongside this, during the revolution, a big stratum of chess players grew, comprised of the so-called middle intelligentsia, which serves the state apparatus. Having no direct economic ties to the bourgeois class, they, nevertheless, inherited a number of past traditional views, and so, unable to comprehend the full essence and the whole complexity of the revolutionary upheaval, they still see chess as a reprieve from sharp challenges posed to us by the current political life... In this regard, they are similar to the chess players of the past, and these masses, in the current environment of aggravated class struggle, are more or less vulnerable to being used by openly counter-revolutionary groups as a sympathizing sphere, as sympathizing company in these groups' fight against the Soviet authorities...

That's why we cannot be fully indifferent to such a voice, cannot ignore the slogan "Away with politics in chess", which has been voiced louder and louder lately among a certain category of our players...

Shakhmatny Listok surveyed many chess players; this survey, among others, contained a question "How can you explain the dropping sales of our magazine?" Here are some rather "interesting" answers given by our readers:

"Chess is for chess", says one. "The articles of Krylenko and his yes-men only bring decay and divisiveness to our organization and only endanger our movement rather than helping it. The note to Kmoch's article about the match, that Alekhine and Bogoljubov are considered antisocial elements, doesn't make *Shakhmatny Listok* any more successful."

Another one writes, "There never were and never will be separate proletarian and bourgeois chess."

The third one proposes, "...Spare the readers the stupid Krylenko articles, which only take up valuable space." He also says, "Do not cause ridicule from all people who understand this by printing the "communist" games *(games of foreign communists)*."

The next one states, "This is a chess magazine, not a political magazine, so it should only concern itself with chess."

Another one writes, "Too much unnecessary and useless politics that have nothing to do with chess."

And here's another reply: "As an amateur chess player, I demand from my magazine a deeper look at chess: I can read about politics in newspapers and other magazines."

Some of the answers are even more concrete. To the question "Which new columns would you like to see in the magazine", one of the authors answered, "Get rid of the revolutionary column, headed by Comrade Krylenko, and print more chess games... I would like to see Krylenko's articles in other magazines, which are more appropriate for such content than *Shakhmatny Listok*."

The other writes, "Do not bog it down with politics... Too much of that Krylenko thing."

Still others are directly calling for the editorial board's replacement. One writes, "Remove Ilyin-Zhenevsky as the executive editor" and demands to "Invite Alekhine and Bogoljubov to work with the magazine." Or that the main drawbacks of the magazine are the articles by Krylenko and Ilyin-Zhenevsky, because he, as a chess fan, "doesn't want to see any politics in the magazine".

As you may see, this is all very... candid.

All these documents are rather characteristic and, if you like, politically valuable for us. Of course, the political "boldness" of the respondents can only be explained by the anonymous character of the survey. But for us, these answers are political documents first and foremost.

> The "anonymous character of the survey" is a great hallmark of the time. Averbakh remembers a parody remake of the popular song 'Letter to Voroshilov' (the lyrics of the original song were written by the poet L. Kvitko, who was eventually shot) that he'd heard in his childhood: "I wrote a letter to Klim Voroshilov. / Then I thought a bit and didn't sign it."

What do all these answers mean? They mean exactly what we were talking about: in the milieu of our chess players, there's a powerful enough current that strongly opposes introducing political matters to chess. It's united by the slogan "Away with politics in chess", but in actuality, this slogan hides antipathy not towards politics per se – they are fighting against our politics in particular... However, Levenfish's great article in the latest issue of *Sh. L.* shows clearly how our politics can be reconciled with chess art, if there's a will to do so.

> To make clear what exactly Krylenko recommends as a "politically mature" exemplary article, I'll quote the beginning of that article.
>
> **Levenfish:** "The two-month world championship match has ended. The battle between Alexander Alexandrovich Alekhine, representing France, and Efim Dmitrievich Bogoljubov, representing Germany, was decisively won by the "Frenchman". Such a grimace by history. The two best Russian

players, direct successors of Chigorin, joined the camp of the enemies of their motherland and fought, wearing the buffoonish togas of "noble foreigners".

So, we saw a battle between two deserters. Alekhine, a former lawyer and the heir to black-earth estates and Prokhorov factories, was naturally drawn to the white emigrants' "heaven", but why was he followed by a former poor student from Kiev, who was adored by the Soviet chess players as recently as 1925? This situation looks strange at first.

But the answer is simple: he became a petty bourgeois. Settling by chance in Triberg, a small German town, Bogoljubov couldn't extricate himself from the philistine quagmire of the publicans surrounding him and quickly parted with his Soviet passport, which had caused him to lose maybe 100 marks or so. Even a talented chess artist, it seems, can have the soul of a titular councilor *(a transparent hint about Alekhine, who gained the titular councilor title after graduating from law school)*.

Politically alien and hostile to us, Alekhine and Bogoljubov nevertheless remain two of the greatest chess players of our time, and the match between them is a very important event for chess art. We shall evaluate the match strictly from this point of view..." (*Shakhmatny Listok*, December 1929.)

At the latest meeting of the Chess Section Council's Executive Bureau, this question came up in connection with another question: the fate of the *Shakhmaty* magazine, published by N. I. Grekov. All chess players know this magazine, they know its strengths and weaknesses. Among this magazine's strengths are a deep academic approach, good management, the great theoretical value of annotations and articles published there, but this magazine was apolitical on principle and never printed any political articles. However, it systematically printed Alekhine's annotations, he was listed as their full-time employee for quite a while, and the magazine was in constant correspondence with him. For that category of

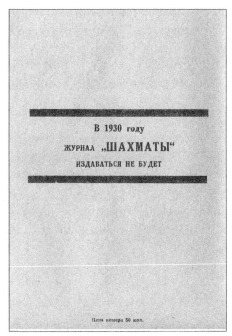

"*In 1930, the Shakhmaty magazine will not be published.*" – *Back cover of the penultimate issue of Shakhmaty (No. 11, 1929).*

"politicians" we wrote about earlier, this journal was a godsend – it was, objectively speaking, a center they grouped around, it was their political banner. In many survey answers, the respondents said that if politics would still have a presence in *Shakhmatny Listok*, they would switch to *Shakhmaty* instead. We'll disappoint them: *Shakhmaty* will cease to exist. The Executive Bureau considered – I personally spoke about that at the last conference, when the question of the *Shakhmaty* magazine was raised – that it was unnecessary to apply any repressive measures to *Shakhmaty*, that we did not have any suspicions about the editor of this magazine, N. I. Grekov – he's a well-known figure in the chess world, and we have no information that could cast any shadow on him. But we only tolerated *Shakhmaty*, and its apolitical attitude wasn't to our taste. That's why we aren't taking any measures to save *Shakhmaty* when its existence is under threat...

> **Panov:** "The whole editorial board of this one and only privately-owned chess magazine in the USSR, *Shakhmaty*, consisted of Grekov alone, and the technical and shipping staff was his wife. Despite that, the magazine was very effective at reporting on Soviet and, especially, foreign chess life; its design was great, it was always published on time, and it's still important even now, as an artifact of the 1920s chess culture.
>
> Grekov managed to get Alekhine, Rubinstein, Tartakower, Spielmann, Nimzowitsch, and Reti to write regularly for the magazine, along with the strongest Soviet masters, whose names, together with the names of foreign luminaries, were printed on the cover as an advertising move." (From the book *Forty Years at the Chessboard*.)

The Executive Bureau has, however, decreed to sharpen the political line in our chess movement even further, and, in reaction to such tendencies and groupings among chess players, to raise the question of the inextricable link between the chess movement and general movement in the country, eradication of the last vestiges of capitalism – old traditional views and political tendencies that still have a place among chess players...

We reiterate: as a reaction to those rising tendencies in the chess environment, the Executive Bureau shall highlight the political content in its activity even more sharply, and shall pursue the slogan "Chess is a weapon of politics" even more acutely. From now on, the proponents of the slogan "Chess is outside politics" shall be considered our enemies." (*Shakhmatny Listok*, December 1929.)

Surrender Your Hard Currency!

Bogatyrchuk: "The first five-year plan of forced industrialization in the USSR, outlined in 1928, needed large funds in gold and foreign currency. The immorality of the Soviet authorities allowed them to use blunt violence, or, to put it in the simplest terms, to rob the people to get the needed resources. The technique was very simple. The intended victim was summoned to an NKVD inspector who demanded that they give up all their savings in gold, foreign currency and gemstones for the sake of industrialization.

"You know," he would say, "that to reach our goals, we have to buy the machinery for factories from capitalists, and the capitalists aren't willing to take our rubles as payment!" And then he would add cynically, "You have surely been saving for a rainy day. That rainy day is today."

If someone didn't agree outright, they would be asked to think further in a "special chamber" that was constantly heated to tropical temperatures. After spending several days in such conditions, the prisoner was ready to give up anything for freedom.

> "Then he dreamt that the hall plunged into darkness, and huge burning letters appeared on the walls, 'Surrender your hard currency!' Then the curtains opened again, and the master of ceremonies said, "I would like Sergey Gerardovich Dunchil to take the stage."
>
> Dunchil turned out to be a comely, but unkempt man in his fifties.
>
> "Sergey Gerardovich," the master of ceremonies said, "you have been sitting here for a month and a half, refusing stubbornly to surrender your remaining currency. Your country needs it, while you personally do not, but still you persist..."
>
> "Unfortunately, I can't do anything with that, because I don't have any currency anymore," Dunchil answered calmly.
>
> "Don't you at least have diamonds?" the artist asked.
>
> "I don't have any diamonds either," he said." (From the novel *The Master and Margarita* by Mikhail Bulgakov.)

As everyone knew that doctors with a private practice didn't trust the ruble, whose exchange rate would drop rapidly at an increasing pace, and started buying foreign currency and gold instead, the NKVD used another dirty trick. The currency sellers were promised a full pardon for illegal trading and even a percentage from the confiscated sums if they ratted on their buyers.

I was once summoned to the NKVD as well, and saw that very trick in action the next day. The arrested were sat on chairs along the walls of a big room, and they let the sellers in; each of them had to go through the rows, look at their faces and point out the buyers.

I had nothing to fear, because it was officially known that I spent all my currency on X-ray equipment, however, even I felt somewhat uncomfortable when the broker who sold currency to me looked in my face. But there are different people in every profession, and my broker was a very honest man. He didn't just look at me sharply: he leaned to my face and whispered, "I'll never say anything to anyone."

More than forty years have passed, but I still can't forget these words. I showed the documents that proved that I spent my currency abroad to the inspector, and he let me go peacefully. He probably considered me small fry with nothing to give. My other colleagues weren't as lucky. Many of them were robbed of big sums of money.

> **Botvinnik:** "My father bought gold before the revolution. When my parents split up, he left all the gold to my mother (more than 1 kilogram). It was kept in an old washbasin for 21 years *(at the start of the war, it was donated to the defense fund)*. In 1932 (if I'm not mistaken), they started to arrest "the formers" in Leningrad, with known financial savings. The prisoners were freed after giving up their savings to the government. I was told by phone that Maria Porfiryevna, my late father's second wife *(Botvinnik's father died in 1931)*, was under arrest.
>
> I asked A. Y. Model for advice – could he help in some way? Soon Abram Yakovlevich gave me the phone number and full name of the inspector who was on the case of my father's widow.
>
> I called that number and was summoned to the "Big House" hosting the NKVD department (at the intersection of Liteiny Avenue and Voinov Street). The inspector, a young, pleasant man, told me quite frankly, "We know that your father bought gold..."
>
> "If Maria Porfiryevna had that gold," I answered, "her family wouldn't live in such poverty. They are most needy, and I financially support them."
>
> Obviously, I couldn't tell them where the gold was really located; my father left it to my mother when he left us in 1920. My mother was ill, and I was her sole provider. If something happened to me, my mother would've been completely helpless if not for those valuables... So, I decided to be cunning. I don't know whether the inspector believed me, but he got an excuse to free Maria Porfiryevna. Three days later, she returned home." (From the book *The Aim Achieved*.)

They also confiscated the last gold and gemstones from Orthodox churches. Without a doubt, the Soviet government will deny this shameless robbery of its own citizens and church relics. I won't be surprised if I someday find an official account of the valuables "voluntarily donated by USSR citizens for industrialization."

But the authorities didn't stop at robbing the haves. With compulsory loans, the government robbed the have-nots as well – workers and clerks. The technique of this so-called "voluntary loan subscription" was simple. A general meeting was called, and some visiting orator would wax poetical – "for the country's industrialization, we should make some sacrifices," etc. – and proposed a resolution in favor of a voluntary loan subscription – some percentage of the monthly salary. This false voluntariness was underscored in a popular joke at the time: "The policeman in his description of the corpse noted that there were no signs of violence on the body except for government bonds."

The economic conditions in the country worsened after NEP folded, and this affected chess competitions, too. In three years (1928–30), only one All-Union championship was held – Odessa in 1929. It was held under a new system of groups, which had more drawbacks than advantages. The main advantage was the fact that many more players than usual could take part – 36. The main disadvantage was a much weaker line-up than usual. There were also some surprises. Botvinnik, by then the strongest player of all, failed to reach the final. The completely unknown Izmailov suddenly shone brightly and just as suddenly disappeared like a meteor; nobody had heard about him before the tournament, then he dropped out and was never heard of again *(he actually played in the 7th Soviet Championship semi-final as well)*. Since people would often disappear without trace in the depths of the NKVD at the time, nobody paid attention to Izmailov's disappearance, and he was only briefly mentioned in the press. Because of this incident, only three players took part in the final. The first prize was won by B. Verlinsky, who had defeated Capablanca in 1925; he repeatedly proved that his congenital physical disability *(actually the complications of meningitis he suffered from in his childhood)* didn't prevent him from playing brilliant chess." (From the book *My Life Path to Vlasov and the Prague Manifesto*.)

The Slogan is "Beat the Masters"

Sozin: "On 1st September, at 7 p.m., the 6th All-Union Chess Championship opened in the conference hall of the Odessa District Executive Committee, contested by 14 masters and 22 very strong first-category players, mostly youngsters who had proved themselves in various competitions in the last two years.

All the players were divided into 4 groups of 9 players *(masters in italics)*: <u>Group I</u> – 1. *Sozin*, 2. Rokhlin, 3. Bernstein, 4. Silich, 5. Panov, 6. Sorokin, 7. *Ilyin-Zhenevsky*, 8. Vygodchikov, 9. *Vilner*. <u>Group II</u> – 1. Pavlov-Pianov, 2. Poliak, 3. *Freymann*, 4. Rauzer, 5. Mudrov, 6. Riumin, 7. Ragozin, 8. *Botvinnik*, 9. *Nenarokov*. <u>Group III</u> – 1. *Model*, 2. *Rudnev*, 3. *Zubarev*, 4. Goglidze, 5. Grigorenko, 6. Ravinsky, 7. *Verlinsky*, 8. Kan, 9. M. Makogonov. <u>Group IV</u> – 1. *Selezniev*, 2. Kirillov, 3. *Grigoriev*, 4. Slonim, 5. Izmailov, 6. *V. Makogonov*, 7. Yuriev, 8. Rosenthal, 9. *Gotthilf*.

> **Grekov:** "Both the line-up and the formula of this championship were vastly different from the previous ones. There were 36 players, but a number of well-known masters were absent, including the three main contenders for the USSR champion's title: F. P. Bogatyrchuk, G. Y. Levenfish, and P. A. Romanovsky." (*Shakhmaty*, September 1929.)
>
> Ilya Rabinovich didn't play either. That spring, he supported the decision of the general meeting of the education workers trade union chess players, who accused Leningrad chess officials of bureaucracy and other sins. An audit found no serious misconduct. Rabinovich was disqualified from chess for three years for making false accusations, missing two national championships in that time.

Three winners of each group progress to the next stage, with two 6-player groups. The outright winners of each of those two groups play a three-game match for the Soviet Championship; if the match is drawn, it continues until the first win.

In the preliminary groups, the participants play 3 games in 2 days, time control is 2 hours per 36 moves and then 1 hour per 18 moves. In the final, the opponents play 1 game a day, with time control of 2 hours per 32 moves and then 1 hour per 16 moves." (*Shakhmatny Listok*, September 1929.)

Kan: "The games were held in two venues: the preliminary groups played in the Odessa city council offices, while the semi-final and final were played in the Sailor's Palace.

First of all, we should point out that the playing conditions in the preliminary groups were rather difficult: it was nearly impossible for many to play 3 games in 2 days. Because of objective, purely financial reasons, the organizing committee had to place the players in a very difficult situation.

The lineup of <u>Group I</u> was the most balanced, so the fights were the most tenacious; as a result, none of the masters in that group progressed to the semi-final. Silich played well; losing a won game against Rokhlin *(see game 48)* deprived him of outright first place. Of the non-masters, we could probably have expected better from Bernstein and Panov.

Sozin: "In the first group, everyone is more or less toe to toe, without getting ahead or falling behind. In the last rounds, the players were rather tired and nervous. "A game of musical chairs," master Grigoriev said about the tournament. "A lottery," many others say. "Is it enough to draw to progress to the semi-final, or do you have to play for a win?" – that's the most important question for the players of all groups. In the first group, the majority of the players decided to play sharply for a win straight out of the opening."

<u>Group II</u> was easily won by master Botvinnik, who didn't lose a single game and had only one dubious position (against Freymann). Poliak was unlucky because of the Berger coefficient; however, some of his wins (for instance, against Rauzer) were rather curious. Master Nenarokov's failure is surprising. Rokhlin got ill at the end of the tournament and didn't play too well. Riumin was considered one of the likeliest candidates for the master's title.

Botvinnik: "In the last round of the quarterfinal, I grew tired by squeezing out a win against A. Poliak – Vsevolod Rauzer asked me to do that the day before.

The 1929 Moscow champion Vasily Panov wasn't immediately admitted to the Soviet Championship. "It seems that my playing style is not completely safe," he explained in 64 (20th June 1929), and then proceeded to paint his self-portrait: "I am a sharp, very aggressive player, striving for complicated and risky games and avoiding drawish lines. I think of Lasker and Bogoljubov as my unattainable idols. My main weaknesses are a lack of self-assuredness, and my impatience and carelessness in detailed calculations, which often cause mistakes and outright blunders. I must say that I'm probably the only chess classicist among the young players. I think that modernism, since it's not a result of the natural evolution of the master's worldview, is just a fancy word describing avoidance of an open, fair fight." From the author's archive.

"If you defeat Poliak, and I defeat Riumin, then I'll overtake Poliak in the coefficient table and qualify for the semi-final."

In the semi-final, you could easily achieve a master's norm; even back then, I greatly respected Vsevolod Arnoldovich and couldn't deny his request. Ultimately, Rauzer brilliantly crushed Riumin with black *(see game 47)* and became a master in the semi-final." (From the book *Analytical and Critical Works.*)

By the way, about Riumin. **V. Eremeev:** "We first met in October 1925 when we hired demonstrators for the Moscow International Tournament. A young man came to me and handed me an application letter. This was Nikolai Riumin, then 16 *(actually 17)* years old. I had already heard of his remarkable chess talent. I consulted with N. D. Grigoriev, the tournament committee chairman, and, despite Riumin's youth, we hired him as a demonstrator.

The Moscow international played a great role in N. Riumin's life. He completely "converted" to chess and decided to fully dedicate his life to it." (*Shakhmaty* Riga, No. 20, 1964.)

Group III was unexpectedly won by Kan, who didn't lose a single game. Verlinsky was extremely lucky, while Ravinsky, on the other hand, was rather unlucky. Master Model finished last – his interesting, but insufficiently solid play met stiff resistance this time.

Finally, in Group IV, we should take note of master V. Makogonov, who started with two losses but still shared first place with master Grigoriev. Out of those who failed to qualify, the Ukrainian champion Kirillov demonstrated nice, aggressive play.

The results were quite unexpected: out of 14 masters, only 5 reached the semi-finals! The youngsters played quite well, and this cannot be explained by luck, either. Too many masters played below par, the first-category players' wins over them were too convincing. The lack of masters' success can be mainly explained by the youngsters' increased chess strength." (*64*, September 1929.)

Sozin: "Such masters as Ilyin-Zhenevsky, Model, Nenarokov and others failed to qualify for the semi-finals; among non-masters, some players qualified who had the least chances, and a number of very talented players who proved their strength in major tournaments, such as Riumin, Panov and Goglidze, were eliminated. How can you explain that? One of the reasons was the tournament formula – 3 rounds in 2 days, which, coupled with adjournment play-offs, forced the players to sit at the board for 8 hours a day..." (*Shakhmatny Listok*, October 1929.)

Botvinnik: "I once did a very nasty thing to Alexander Fyodorovich. It happened in Odessa, at the 1929 Soviet Championship. Ilyin-Zhenevsky shared first place in the quarter-final, but didn't qualify due to coefficients *(that's an error reprinted in many publications: actually, he shared 3rd–4th place)*. Then, N. D. Grigoriev, chairman of the tournament committee, decided to correct things: he gathered all players (about 40) and proposed to let Ilyin play in the semi-finals if everybody agreed.

An 18 year-old youngster raised his hand and said that regulations are the law, and you couldn't violate them. Alexander Fyodorovich left Odessa immediately. He never blamed me for that; he probably realized what character I had."

Grekov: "The group system didn't justify itself, because it was inevitably accompanied by randomness (which started with the composition of the group lineups – naturally, they couldn't all be of equal strength)... The desire to qualify for the next stage forced almost all participants – due to the small amount of games in the groups – to play sharply and riskily for a win. All that adversely affected the game quality." (*Shakhmaty*, September 1929.)

The Unprecedented Failure of the Capital Cities

Kan: "The semi-finals started on 9th September. The playing conditions were more normal, however, many players were too exhausted after the tiresome battles in the initial groups.

Group I was won by Izmailov and Kan, both of whom played with great inspiration and finished ahead of such "crocodiles" as masters Botvinnik and V. Makogonov; the old masters Verlinsky and Freymann won Group II. Master Grigoriev played below his strength.

Botvinnik: "Between the two Soviet Championships (1927 and 1929), I took part in only two tournaments, which weren't particularly strong... After six weeks in the military student camp outside Novgorod, I went to Odessa to play in the next Soviet Championship.

In the camp, I – for the first and only time in my life – played three games blindfolded simultaneously, without much difficulty: N. V. Krylenko forbade blindfold play at the time. *(In fact, not then, but only after the Odessa championship.)* We went to Novgorod and played against the city's chess team. None of this, of course, helped much in preparing for the championship.

Группа участников и членов Оргкомитета чемпионата СССР.

I ряд: Бернштейн, Дуз-Хотимирский, Измайлов. II ряд: Фрейман, Созин, Панов, Поляк, Юрьев В., Верлинский, Макогонов М., Ильин-Женевский, Модель. III ряд: Вильнер, Алехин, Воронин, Койфман, Еремеев, Зубарев, Рохлин. IV ряд: Сорокин, Розенталь, Ботвинник, Готгильф, Равинский, Григоренко, Рюмин, Кириллов, Кан. V ряд: Выгодчиков, Григорьев, Рагозин, Мудров, Макогонов В., Петроковский, Гинзбург, Гоглидзе, Ненароков.

Group of the Soviet Championship participants and Organizing Committee members. (Shakhmatny Listok, No. 19, 1929).
First row: Bernstein, Silich, Duz-Khotimirsky, Izmailov. Second row: Freymann, Sozin, Panov, Poliak, V. Yuriev, Verlinsky, M. Makogonov, Ilyin-Zhenevsky, Model. Third row: Vilner, Alekhine, Voronin, Koifman, Eremeev, Zubarev, Rokhlin. Fourth row: Sorokin, Rosenthal, Botvinnik, Gotthilf, Ravinsky, Grigorenko, Riumin, Kirillov, Kan. Fifth row: Vygodchikov, Grigoriev, Ragozin, Mudrov, V. Makogonov, Petrokovsky, Ginsburg, Goglidze, Nenarokov.

I won the quarterfinal group easily, but then flopped in the semi-final. A difficult playing schedule, bad food, exhaustion and lack of preparation all played their role..." (From the books *Achieving The Aim* and *Analytical and Critical Works.*)

Botvinnik contradicts himself about "bad food". Here's an excerpt from his article about G. Goldberg: "Concurrently with the championship, a team competition took place in Odessa, where Goldberg played. After each round, Grisha became some sort of "ringleader" for the young players, and we went to dinner under his leadership. "Eleven beef steaks and one *razvrat*[16] with

---

[16] *Razvrat* (read as spelled, sounding similar enough to "Rostbrat") means "debauchery" in Russian. – *Translator*

onions" (the menu, of course, featured Rostbratwurst!), he would say to the waiter, with his face dead serious."

The tournament produced six new masters – Vygodchikov (Smolensk), Izmailov (Tomsk), Kan (Moscow), M. Makogonov (Baku), Rauzer (Kiev) and Silich (Vitebsk). All of them, except Vygodchikov, are young players aged 20–23. Only Rokhlin, plagued by bad luck, failed to gain the master's title." (*64*, September 1929.)

Duz-Khotimirsky: "As we know, there were four winners in the semi-finals: new young masters I. A. Kan (Moscow) and P. N. Izmailov (Tomsk), and two frequent participants of the All-Union championships, old masters B. M. Verlinsky (Odessa) and S. N. Freymann (Tashkent). For the first ever time in the Soviet chess movement's history, the capital cities suffered an unprecedented defeat. Of the four semi winners, only Kan defended the honor of Moscow. Even though the other Moscow chess players never thought that he would qualify from the preliminary group, let alone reach the final, Kan showed high class in this tournament. His play was simple and deep at the same time. He won 7 games out of 13 (defeating masters Model, Rudnev, Verlinsky and Botvinnik – *see games 41 and 44*), drew 6 and lost none. Izmailov also showed great talent; he wasn't as enterprising as Kan, but his composure was better. Against the masters, Izmailov, like Kan, got great results (defeated V. Makogonov twice, and Botvinnik and Selezniev once). Both of those young talents fully deserved the esteemed title of Soviet master.

> **Panov:** "Ilya Abramovich Kan was a subtle sports psychologist with deep theoretical knowledge. What amazed me the most in him was his strong character and worldly wisdom: he would always carry an old-fashioned black umbrella, even in good weather. Kan also took great care of his appearance and clothes, even though youngsters were often unkempt back then. Kan was determined, practical and methodical in his approach to chess as well. Preferring maneuvering play with slow accumulation of a positional advantage, he nevertheless didn't eschew sharp situations. In Odessa, his composure and practicality helped him to navigate through the difficult qualification system."
>
> Kan defeated Botvinnik with the Evans Gambit. When he defeated him again at the second Moscow International Tournament (1935), this time in a sharp Vienna Game, the poet **Semyon Kirsanov** wrote (as though in Botvinnik's voice) for a joke "Book of Complaints" in the tournament bulletin the following lines:

Twice Kan played a gambit.
Twice Kan me did beat.
If again I play against Kan,
I will limit myself to the Caro-Kann.

Verlinsky played languidly in this tournament, way below his usual strength. He had a bad start, and only his last-round win against Zubarev helped him reach the semi-final. He had a bad start there as well, losing to Freymann, but then won 4 games in a row, showing great tenacity and composure, and now he is one of the main candidates to win the Soviet Championship.

Freymann's results in the Soviet Championships are fascinating: 4/17 (1924), 5/12 (1925), 9.5/20 (1927), 10.5/13 (1929). If we compare his results this year with the other semi-final participants, he takes first place (2. Kan – 10 points, 3–4. Verlinsky, Botvinnik – 9.5). His play in this tournament was sharp, bold and deep.

After the semi-finals ended, it transpired that Izmailov couldn't take part in the final match tournament because he had to take exams at his college back home." (*Shakhmatny Listok*, October 1929.)

> **Nikolai Izmailov**, the master's son: "This championship could have been the finest hour for Izmailov. He was just 23, on the rise, in his peak form. But, unfortunately, my father didn't play in the final. Why? I tried to find out, but I couldn't. There are several versions.
>
> Duz-Khotimirsky in *Shakhmatny Listok* reported that "he had to take exams at his college". Kan said in *64* that Izmailov dropped out himself. *Pravda* and *Izvestia* wrote that he was ill, and *Komsomolskaya Pravda* cited exhaustion as the reason.
>
> Half a century after the championship, my mother told me that in the mid-1930s, she talked with my father about that (in 1929, they hadn't met yet), and he said that he was healthy and ready to play on, but he was forced to drop out... Now, of course, we can't find out what really happened, but one thing is safe to say: this unfortunate story left a deep scar in Izmailov's soul." (*Shakhmaty v Rossii*, No. 1–3, 1999.)

As to the real reason for Izmailov's withdrawal, we return to this sorry matter in our discussion of the 10th championship in 1937 towards the end of this book.

Kan: "Now let's discuss the final match tournament, which was contested between masters Verlinsky, Kan and Freymann (master Izmailov dropped out).

Grekov: "The tournament regulations didn't say anything about the case of having more than one winner in the semi-final groups. There were two options, hotly debated: use the Berger system again, as in the quarterfinals, or have both winners qualify. The tournament committee supported the second option. Had the Berger system been used, Kan and Freymann would have played in the final."

This tournament should go down in Soviet chess history because of the extremely low quality of the games. It's enough to say that two games out of six were decided by blundering a whole queen: Freymann blundered against Verlinsky in a drawn endgame, and Kan blundered against Freymann in a won position! This can only be explained by the players' exhaustion.

Still, we should praise the good, active play of the tournament's winner. The new Soviet champion Boris Markovich Verlinsky is a player with great experience and big successes. His greatest achievements were 4th place in the 1925 All-Union Championship (6 points out of 7 against the top 8!) and 1st place in the 1928 Moscow Championship. Verlinsky has posted wins against Capablanca, Bogoljubov, Rubinstein, Spielmann, Saemisch and others. By winning this tournament, B. M. Verlinsky earned the title of the first Soviet grandmaster." (*64*, September 1929.)

Do not believe your eyes, dear reader. According to the Chess Player's Handbook (1984), the first Soviet grandmaster was actually not Verlinsky (he's not even in the list), but... Botvinnik (who received that title in 1935). Why is it so? It turns out that the 7th All-Union Chess Conference (1931) abolished the grandmaster title to "eradicate the concepts of 'champion' and 'championship' from active use", and four years later, the title was created anew. Absurd? No, I think the thing was that the goals had changed. In 1931, there was no talk about challenging for the world championship, whereas by 1935, that goal had probably already been set. So, they needed to somehow elevate Botvinnik above the rest of the Soviet masters...

*The most cynical thing is that the resolution "On the All-Union Chess Tournament in Odessa" said, "The USSR champion Comrade B. M. Verlinsky is to be awarded the grandmaster title **for life**."*

The Unwelcome Truth about the Championship

Ilyin-Zhenevsky (Leningrad): "This year, because of the lack of funds, we essentially had no Soviet Championship, because the competition that took part in Odessa hardly looked like a way to determine the strongest chess player in the USSR. Romanovsky and Bogatyrchuk were sorely missed. The quantity of blunders and losses on time was at an all-time high. The chances of some players, both during the whole competition and individual games, jumped like body temperature during a typhoid fever. The results of the preliminary groups were not representative. Who can seriously say that Kan is the strongest player in Moscow, ahead of Zubarev, Panov and Riumin, and Rokhlin is the strongest Leningrad player?

The abnormal game conditions in the preliminary rounds affected the semi-finals as well. On the one hand, we saw how exhausted several players were (Botvinnik's failure), and, on the other hand, we saw the chase for the cheap master's title. It wasn't an accident that almost all first-category players drew their games between each other. It was the surest way towards the necessary 1.5 points. Where is the art? The victory of Verlinsky, who'd been long known as a brilliant player, is the least of all evils. It horrifies me to think what would've happened with the coveted USSR Champion's title had Verlinsky not made it to the final..."

Б. М. ВЕРЛИНСКИЙ
чемпион и гроссмейстер СССР

The first grandmaster of the USSR, Boris Verlinsky. The title was awarded "for life", but the 1931 All-Union Chess Conference abolished the grandmaster title altogether. It would come back to our chess only in 1935. (64. Shakhmaty i Shashki v Rabochem Klube, No. 19, 1929.)

Rokhlin (Leningrad): "The championship had two defining features: the incredible flop of masters and the time-trouble epidemic. The champions of the two capitals, Zhenevsky and Panov, failed undeservedly, the poor performance of Model and Vilner was unfortunate, as well as that of some other masters; in this context, Verlinsky's victory looks like it was written in the stars: Zubarev's indecisiveness helped him reach the semi-final, and then Rokhlin's recklessness helped him into the final. However, after reaching his goal, Verlinsky easily snatched the Soviet Championship. Still, it's good to see several new masters, although the absence of two favorites, Romanovsky and Bogatyrchuk, and the talented Botvinnik's unexpected failure, was disappointing."

Vilner (Odessa): "The championship system with a group stage did not justify itself: it was clearly shown that, in small groups, luck is more important than actual playing strength. This, of course, shouldn't take place in such a serious competition as the Soviet Championship...

However, we should say that the stake on youngsters paid off, the young players played very well in this championship, showing great composure, preparation, etc."

Botvinnik (Leningrad): "I think that our chess governing body made a mistake when they tried to include all masters and all young forces of the Union in the tournament. This inevitably led to the introduction of a group system, with all the obvious consequences. The experience from this tournament showed me that the preliminary groups put such a strain on the nervous system that I, for instance, was completely exhausted by the semi-final – even though I played only 3 games against masters out of 13 games overall.

If we want to hold showcase tournaments to demonstrate the great level of Soviet chess creativity, we should develop a system of regional and republic-level tournaments that limits the number of Soviet Championship participants to 16, with qualified players unable to be replaced by any other candidates."

Panov (Moscow): "I think that the Odessa tournament was a shining example of the struggle for the 8-hour workday and its maximum compactness. The greatest strengths of the tournament: the complete lack of crowd noise (due to the absence of the crowd); turning time trouble and accidents caused by it into an integral part of the game; quick lessons in arithmetic through the Berger table, and the relatively small number of groups (just 4 9-player groups when they could have created 9 4-player groups). Still, I think that the end result was more or less natural: the most consistent and composed players won..."

Bogatyrchuk (Kiev): "I don't think that this tournament could be called successful. A competition that tests the quality of the whole country's chess movement can and should be held with a much more thoughtful and serious approach.

1) The line-up was far from complete: firstly, many, or should I say most of the strongest masters were absent; secondly, the championship's

quality wouldn't have suffered much without a fair number of the players present.

2) The group system is, of course, unfitting for such a serious competition. The preliminary groups looked less like a chess tournament than a steeple chase, which was too difficult for many older masters, because physical stamina was more important than chess skill.

3) The qualifying part was also disappointing. The intensive production of masters looks dubious. As far as we know from their current and past games, only 1, maybe 2 players of the 6 awarded the master's title are really worthy of it; on the other hand, such a player as Rokhlin, who fully deserves his title, failed to obtain it.

Overall conclusion: <u>next year they should organize a tournament that can truly be called a 'championship'.</u>" (*Shakhmatny Listok*, October 1929 – all the above quotes are taken from this issue.)

Placing Stakes on the Youngsters

Krylenko: "The outcome of the Soviet Championship provoked a number of harsh articles in our periodicals, most of them lacking in objectivity. The authors, unwilling to take into account the organizational difficulties, only discussed the shortcomings, failing to notice the known positive aspects that cannot be denied. However, even the negative aspects of this championship will give us valuable experience to prevent us from repeating similar mistakes in the future. It's enough to remember that the organizing committee proposed two formulas at the opening ceremony of the championship: 6 6-player groups (with one game per day), or 4 9-player groups (with three games per two days). Despite the unanimous protests of all Leningrad players, who tried to defend normal conditions for chess creativity, the second formula was selected by the vast majority of votes. This was an error on the part of the organizing committee, but the players have to shoulder a part of the blame, too – they didn't realize how difficult the conditions they committed to would be. The heat also played a major role; none of the "objective critics" noted its influence on the tournament conditions.

Krylenko is not fully right. Judging by the next quote, someone did complain.

L. Frenkel: "Of course, it was tempting for Comrade Pavlov-Pianov to compare himself with Em. Lasker: Lasker lost to Capablanca in Havana "because of the heat", and Pavlov-Pianov lost to his opponents in Odessa because of the heat as well! The young chess players withstood the heat and other burdens better than the older players! It might be so. However, the older players, the "masters", have more composure, tournament experience and so on. And you can't say for sure what's more important for the championship: young strength or maturity, composure and experience." (*64, October 1929.*)

What is the championship's outcome? First of all, we should point out the unequivocal victory of youth, whose chances weren't rated too high in comparison with the 14 masters. The results show that the youngsters played with much inspiration, having a clear goal ahead of them, while our masters, sure of their superiority and "natural" way of things, went for complicated maneuvers that led to an unexpected finish. The ability to get your opponent into time trouble with all other things equal is also one of the coefficients *(sic!)* of tournament success. For this, we should also give credit to our young players. Concerning the "blunders", they were mostly made by those players who were clearly out of form and finished at the bottom of the table. The semi-finals were mostly contested by representatives of the combinational school, who also showed good composure.

м. С. Фрейман

Master Sergei Freymann. "S. N. Freymann also proved his high playing level with this classy success, which is significant as well." (Krylenko.) From Shakhmatnoe Pervenstvo SSSR special edition (No. 9–10, 1938.)

At any rate, those championship participants who met the stated conditions for the master's title <u>will be awarded that title</u>. This is the result of their art, their talent. And no matter how harshly the old masters "criticized" those "young" masters, the chess organizations of the USSR and the wider chess community recognize them. The unfriendly atmosphere created by the "elders", manifesting itself in part in the championship surveys we published *(see the previous section)*, will probably evaporate, and, if it doesn't, then we think that the young masters will disperse it with their play in the following tournaments.

B. M. Verlinsky's victory, considering this line-up, is well-deserved and places him among the leading USSR chess players. S. N. Freymann also proved his high playing level with this classy success, which is significant as well.

However, there were many negative aspects in the championship as well, both organization-wise (the group system, the consequences of using the Berger table, etc.) and, what's even more important, a number of negative sides of our chess players' <u>public life</u>. However, if our younger generation grows further, we probably won't be able to avoid the group system in the future. Still, we have to make adjustments that will create normal conditions for chess creativity. Our society and our governing bodies should seriously think about this.

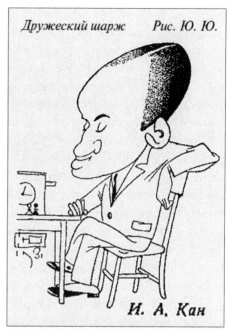

Дружеский шарж   Рис. Ю. Ю.

И. А. Кан

The third prizewinner, Ilya Kan, "was a subtle sports psychologist and opening theory expert" (Panov). Cartoon by Y. Yuzepchuk (1931).

Another negative side is that the Soviet Championship played almost no role in campaigning and propaganda. The Ukrainian chess organization failed to attract interest in the tournament and appreciate its social and political importance. The newspapers printed almost no reports, the Odessa trade unions "slept" through the entire tournament, and the working masses weren't spotted in the luxury halls of the City Council, able to host hundreds of spectators. The tournament participants couldn't understand why Ukraine wanted to host the championship in Odessa so badly...

In conclusion, here are some remarks on the negative aspects of our players' public life.

Many people regretted that the masters Romanovsky and Bogatyrchuk didn't take part in the competition. Of course, it would have been most desirable to have seen them among the players. However, their absence was due to the fact that they believed they were entitled to make unreasonable financial demands on the chess leadership and the organizing committee. Our masters have to end this unpleasant habit of weighing their talents in money terms. They should remember that, turning up at chess tournaments organized by Soviet society, each participant, as a member of an organization, is equal to each other. We have abolished prizes. Out of principle we abolish individual appearance fees, too. We can pay foreign masters to take part in tournaments. That's why we view them as some alien element. We have the right to treat our own tournament participants differently, and anybody who doesn't agree with our requirements, no matter who they are, will not be allowed to compete....

The caste spirit of a small group of persons who got used to only playing each other in tournaments and so forgot about the social importance of the chess movement as a means to raise the whole country's culture level – this is another negative side of our chess life. With this same consideration, we can mostly explain our masters' attempts to excuse their failures by the "greater physical stamina" of the younger players in comparison with the older masters, and their unfriendly attitude towards the youngsters who defeated them. The USSR chess organizations would like to state that in this dispute between the "elders" and the "youngsters", they fully support the latter.

The extra demands from some players towards the organizing committee are also expressions of this same caste spirit. A certain group of persons seems to have gotten used to them being "wooed", their whims being met, etc. We would like to state that the chess movement as a whole is more important to us than the participation of any particular individual in the championship.

Bogatyrchuk: "There was an article "The Results of the 6th Conference" in *Sh. L.* No. 20, and some passages of this article concern me personally. The esteemed author stated that my absence and that of Romanovsky from the latest tournament was explained by the fact that we "made unreasonable financial demands on the organizing committee"... Without going into fundamental debates, which are essentially debates between proponents of so-called "amateurism" and "professionalism", I still deem it necessary to point out that the author's suggestions in the article are somewhat inconsistent with the accepted principles of remuneration of labor.

As far as we remember, along with the resolution that abolished money prizes, another resolution was adopted, concerning "reimbursement of expenses" for players invited to tournaments, which was observed up until the last conference... The reimbursement sums can and should be significantly differentiated, if we want chess players who earn a living by working outside chess to play in tournaments. It's only natural that a player who has a big family to provide for or needs to hire one or even two work replacements at his own expense (chess players can't always use their allocated vacation to play in tournaments) can and should receive much larger compensation than a young man whose adult life has only just begun. I see nothing abnormal with that, and so I did demand and shall be demanding that they reimburse my expenses in future, because even though I would love to cover all my expenses myself, I am unable to do so.

You couldn't say that I requested a particularly exorbitant sum – the reimbursement I requested was no different from the one I received at the previous conference. I would also like to point out that I play in most Kiev championships completely for free, even though this entails certain difficulties for me.

A couple of words about the "unfriendly attitude" towards the young players (it's too early, dear Nikolai Vasilyevich, to rank us among the "elders"!). Throughout my chess career, I have always been more unfriendly chess-wise to those who were equal to or stronger than me, only valuing victories in tournaments with truly strong line-ups. The Kiev chess players know about our efforts to always invite all the strongest players in the city; we think that this is the only right course of action. The shallow successes of young chess players don't help them much in most cases, only strengthening their excessive conceit that harms their further progress. So you should be very wary in praising such 'achievements'."

Romanovsky: "I consider printing N. V. Krylenko's article in issue No. 20 of the *Shakhmatny Listok* magazine a wrong move, both formally and in substance, and I hereby declare my resignation from the editorial board and magazine staff." (*Shakhmatny Listok*, November 1929.)

Our goal is to widen the reach of chess, because for us, chess is first and foremost a means for general cultural development of the masses rather than an end in itself, rather than a self-sufficient art. Those who want to leave these slogans on one side or even forget them altogether are not welcome on our journey. This is another of the conclusions, that we draw from the chess championship." (*Shakhmatny Listok*, October 1929.)

A lottery

Out of 180 games played in the championship, just a bit more than a third (65, including fragments) survived, and very haphazardly at that. A relatively large number of games survived from the second preliminary group, although almost nothing was left from group IV. The same motley picture can be seen with the players, even those who reached the semi-finals. Some players got lucky, some – not so, and some, like Izmailov, had no luck at all: of his 13 games, only two small pieces survived: the opening of his game against Botvinnik and the lost endgame against Grigoriev.

The luckiest one was Botvinnik – all of his 13 games survived! As for the others: Kan had 10 out of 17, Verlinsky 9/17, Freymann 8/17, Rauzer 8/13, Grigoriev and M. Makogonov – 6/13, Vygodchikov and Silich – 3/13, and V. Makogonov and Rokhlin – 2/13. And this is despite Rokhlin performing very well at the tournament. Panov: "In the semi-final, lady luck was outrageously unfair towards Rokhlin – a sharp and elegant player, fully deserving a master's title."

There was no talk about brilliancy prizes at all – they were probably considered another vestige of the past. Many critics, as you remember, lamented the poor quality of the games. Indeed, it was very dispiriting. Quite a few games were completely one-sided, already won in the opening; some interesting games were marred by mutual mistakes; there were some outright blunders as well. Of course, the spectators would have enjoyed all that, but... there were very few spectators at the tournament. Who would go and watch chess instead of heading for the beach in such weather?!

A Dress-Rehearsal for the Final

Sozin: "The young Moscow player Kan is playing superbly in this tournament. Today he scored his fourth point (out of 5), against Verlinsky, no less. Kan attacked on the kingside; in time trouble, white failed to notice the danger of his position and lost a piece."

No. 41. Nimzo-Indian Defense E38
Verlinsky – Kan
Odessa 1929, preliminary group 3
Annotated by I. Kan
1.c4 ♞f6 2.d4 e6 3.♞c3 ♝b4 4.♛c2. 4.♛b3 is a good reply as well; to meet the game move, Alekhine recommends 4...d5.

Concerning 4.♛b3, I can only quote the textbook words from Nimzowitsch himself: "This powerful-looking move actually gives white nothing good. In essence, it's unacceptable for the queen to enter the struggle with the bishop at such an early stage of the game – it's as bad as blocking a passed pawn."

4...c5 5.♞f3. 5.dxc5! is much stronger, intending ♞f3, ♝g5 and ♜d1.

One of the championship games that did not make it to the databases but survived thanks to B. Vainstein's book Ferzberi's Traps *went like this (the names of the players weren't given): 5.dxc5 ♝xc5 6.♝g5? ♝xf2+! 7.♚xf2 ♞g4+ 8.♚e1 ♛xg5 – the knight unpinned itself, and the bishop, which so hurried to pin it, fell!*

5...cxd4 6.♞xd4 ♞c6 7.e3 0-0.
After 7...d5!? 8.♞xc6 bxc6 9.♝d2 0-0 10.♝e2 e5, black is better (Pavey – Keres, New York 1954).

8.a3 ♝xc3+ 9.♛xc3 d5 10.♞xc6 bxc6 11.b3. 11.♝d3 looks more natural. White's opening play is somewhat artificial.

11...♘e4 12.♕c2 f5 13.♗d3 ♗a6 14.0-0 ♖f6. The position has settled: white has two bishops, but black has a kingside attack.

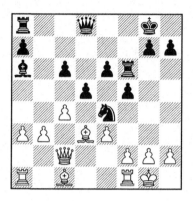

15.♗b2 ♖h6 (a pointless move; black should have played 15...♖g6 immediately) **16.♗e5 ♖g6 17.♖fd1 ♕g5 18.♗f1 ♖e8 19.♖ac1 h5.** This move is the only way to maintain the pressure on the white king's position. **20.♔h1 h4 21.♖e1 dxc4** (creating good play along the d-file) **22.bxc4 ♖d8 23.♖e2 ♘d6 24.♖d2.** *If the computer is to be believed, white just missed a clear advantage: 24.♕a4! ♗xc4 25.f4 etc.*

24...♘f7 25.♖xd8+ ♕xd8 26.♗d4.

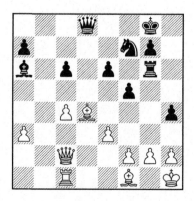

26...c5! After this, the game becomes very sharp. The pawn sacrifice is most probably correct, because black's attack immediately comes alive due to the b7 bishop's threatening position.

Fritz doesn't see this move at all, and Junior advises to meet it with 27.♗xc5 h3 28.f3 ♘e5.

27.♗xc5 ♗b7! 28.h3 (of course, not 28.♗xa7? ♕a8) **28...♘g5.** The immediate 28...♕c7 with the subsequent ♘g5 was stronger.

29.♖d1 ♕c7 30.♗d6 ♕c6 31.♔h2? This blunder loses immediately. White should have played 31.c5 ♘xh3 32.f4, creating a very curious position rich in opportunities. The line shown by N. D. Grigoriev looks very interesting:

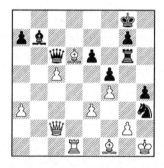

32...♘f2+ 33.♕xf2 h3 34.♖d2 (*white can win here with 34.♔g1! ♗a6 35.♖d2 ♗xf1 36.♕xf1 etc.*) 34...hxg2+ 35.♗xg2 ♖xg2 36.♕xg2 ♕b5, and black wins the queen for bishop and rook, but the path to victory is unclear.

31...♘f7 (now white loses the bishop because of the threat ♖xg2+) **32.♗g3 hxg3+ 33.fxg3 ♘g5 34.♖d4**

♘e4 35.♖d8+ ♔h7 36.♗e2 ♕c7. White resigned.

Following in the Steps of Luminaries

Duz-Khotimirsky: "White played the old McCutcheon Variation suboptimally, made a few weak moves, missed the drawing line and ultimately lost."

No. 42. French Defense C12
Kan – Verlinsky
Odessa 1929, final
Annotated by I. Kan

1.e4 e6 2.d4 d5 3.♘c3 ♘f6 4.♗g5 ♗b4 5.e5 h6 6.exf6. The old move, which is rarely used today. According to the latest theory, the strongest continuation here is 6.♗d2! ♗xc3 7.bxc3 ♘e4 8.♕g4 with sharp play. *This is still the main line of the McCutcheon counterattack.*

6...hxg5 7.fxg7 ♖g8 8.h4 gxh4 9.♕h5 ♕f6 10.♘f3 ♕xg7 11.♕xh4 ♘c6 12.0-0-0.

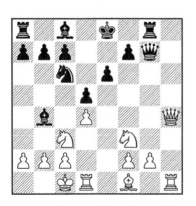

12...♗d7. Now black intends to play ♗e7 and 0-0-0.

Verlinsky was the first to deviate from the game Romanovsky – Bogoljubov (Leningrad (m/12) 1924). There, after 12...♗e7 13.♕f4 ♗d6 14.♕e3 ♘e7 15.♘b5 ♗d7 16.♘xd6+ cxd6 17.♕f4 ♘c8 18.♗d3 ♕g4 19.♕e3 ♘b6 20.♖h4 black gave up his queen for rook, knight and pawn – 20...♕xg2 21.♖g1 ♕xg1+ 22.♘xg1 ♖xg1+, but the game ultimately ended in a draw. The database shows that 12...♗e7 was never played again in serious tournaments; WGM Ludmila Zaitseva tried 12...♗d7 three times in 1995, with all three games ending in a draw.

13.♘b5 ♗a5 (forced, because 13...♗e7? is met with 14.♕f4) **14.♗d3.** The move 14.a3! *(or 14.c3 Sozin)* posed black more problems.

14...a6 15.♘c3 ♗b4 16.♖de1. *A more active plan was worthy of consideration: 16.g3!? ♗e7 17.♕f4 ♗d6 18.♕e3 ♘b4 19.♖h7 ♘xd3+ 20.♕xd3 ♕f6 21.♖dh1 etc.*

16...♗e7 17.♕f4 0-0-0! Black's opening play was excellent. He has at least equalized because of the bishop pair.

18.♕e3. Both 18.♖h7 ♕xg2! 19.♖xf7 ♖df8 and 19.♖g1? ♕xg1+ 20.♘xg1 ♖xg1+ with the subsequent ♗g5 are better for black.

18...♔b8 19.♘e2. *"White should have played 19.a3. Now black trades the d3 bishop, and white's position becomes even worse."* (Botvinnik)

19...♖h8 20.♖hg1. Botvinnik: it was still not too late to play 20.a3, because after 20...♖xh1 21.♖xh1 ♕xg2 black would have had to give up his knight to save the queen:

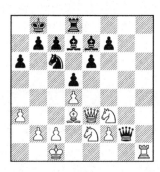

22.♘g3! ♘xd4 23.♘xd4 ♖g8 24.♕e1! (24.♗f1 ♗g5) 24... ♗g5+ 25.♔b1 ♗e3 26.♕xe3 ♖xg3 27.♖h8+ etc.

20...♘b4 21.a3 ♘xd3+ 22.♕xd3 c5. Black launches queenside activity with this move.

23.♕e3 ♗f6 24.c3 cxd4 25.♘exd4 ♖c8 26.g4 ♖h3 27.♕f4+ ♔a8. If 27...e5?, then 28.♖xe5! ♗xe5 29.♘xe5 etc.

28.g5. White allows his opponent to execute a spectacular combination, because he thought that the position resulting from this combination was better for him, despite the lack of a pawn.

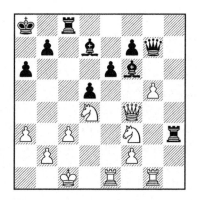

28...♖xf3 29.gxf6 (of course, 29.♕xf3 ♗xd4 and 29.♘xf3 ♗xc3! are bad) **29...♕xg1! 30.♘xf3 ♕xf2 31.♕e3 ♕g2.** The queen exchange guaranteed at least a draw for white in the endgame.

32.♘e5 ♗a4 33.♕d2 ♕g8 34.♕f4 ♗e8 35.♖h1? White overestimates his position. After the calm 35.♔b1, black has no clear plan, because the great positions of the f6 pawn and white knight comprise good compensation for the pawn.

35...d4 36.c4. After 36.♕xd4 ♕g5+ and ♕xf6, black has two connected passed pawns.

36...♖d8

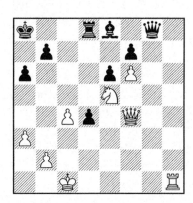

37.♖d1? A new mistake that completely cedes the initiative to black.

But what can white do, on the other hand? Apart from 37.♕g4 ♕f8 38.♕f4, there's nothing good…

37…♗a4! 38.♖e1 ♕h7 39.♕d2 ♔b8 (time trouble!) **40.b3.** White sacrifices a second pawn to repel the mating threats and get some counterplay.

40…♗xb3 41.♔b2 ♗a4 42.♖c1 ♕h3 43.♘d3 ♖g8! 44.♕f4+ ♔c8 45.♕xd4 ♖d8 (the decisive move) **46.♕c5+ ♔b8 47.♖c3.** The last attempt to get some chances for a draw.

47…♕g2+ 48.♔b1.

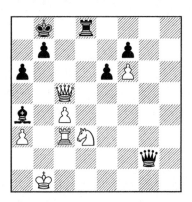

48…♕f1+! The simplest. Instead of winning the piece, black retains his two extra pawns without any counterplay for the opponent.

The knight capture gave white some chances to save the game. The following line is curious: 48… ♖xd3 49.♖xd3 ♕c2+ 50.♔a1 ♕xd3 51.♕f8+ ♔c7 52.♕xf7+ ♗d7 53.♕e7 ♕d6? 54.♕xd6+ ♔xd6 55.c5+, winning.

49.♘c1 ♕xf6 50.♕b4 ♗c6 51.♘d3 ♗e4 52.♔c2 ♕f2+ 53.♔b3 ♗xd3. White resigned.

Alekhine Sends His Regards

Sozin: "Freymann defeated Makogonov with black, using a novelty in the West Indian Defense recommended by Bogoljubov."

No. 43. Indian Defense A50
M. Makogonov – Freymann
Odessa 1929, semi-final group 2
Annotated by S. Freymann
1.d4 ♘f6 2.c4 b6 3.♘c3 ♗b7 4.♕c2 d5 5.cxd5 ♘xd5.

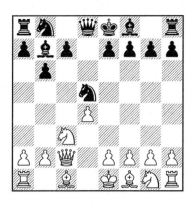

6.e4. *In the final tournament, Verlinsky played 6.♘f3! against Freymann, and after 6…e6 (6… ♘xc3!? Chekhov) 7.e4 ♘xc3 8.bxc3 ♗e7 9.♗b5+ c6 10.♗d3 ♕c7?! (10… c5!? 11.♗b5+ ♗c6 12.a4 0-0 13.0-0 Gheorghiu – Matanovic, Athens 1976) 11.0-0 ♘d7 12.c4! ♖d8 (12… c5 13.d5!) 13.♗b2 0-0 14.e5 g6 15.♗e4! got a better position and won in 33 moves with a direct attack.*

6...♘xc3 7.bxc3 e5. This curious move is not my novelty. In the annotations to Gotthilf – Reti (Moscow 1925), Bogoljubov recommends 8.dxe5 ♕h4 9.♗d3 ♕g4 in this position, with great development for black as compensation for the pawn.

Bogoljubov wasn't the one who came up with this move! It occurred in the game Euwe – Alekhine (Budapest 1921), which, after 8.dxe5 ♕h4 9.♗b5+ ♘d7 10.♘f3 ♕xe4+ 11.♕xe4 ♗xe4

12.♘g5 (the sharp 12.e6!? fxe6 13.♘e5 c6 14.♗xc6 ♗xc6 15.♘xc6 with mutual chances was also possible) 12...♗xg2 13.♖g1 c6 14.♖xg2 cxb5 15.e6 fxe6 16.♘xe6, soon ended in a draw.

8.dxe5. *"8.♘f3 is calmer," V. Sozin advised in the openings review. For instance: 8...exd4 9.♗c4 ♘c6 10.0-0 d3!? (an interesting attempt) 11.♗xd3 ♗c5 12.e5 with equality (Zilberstein – Bronstein, Baku 1972).*

8...♕h4 9.♗b5+. After 9.♗d3, it was possible to play 9...♘d7 10.♘f3 ♕h5 11.♗f4 0-0-0 12.0-0 ♘c5, regaining the pawn, since 13.♖ad1

is met with 13...♖xd3 14.♖xd3 ♗xe4 15.♘e1 ♘xd3 16.♘xd3 ♕g6, and black wins.

9...♘d7 10.♗xd7+. *The root cause of all his troubles: white shouldn't have given up the light-squared bishop. 10.♘f3, following Euwe – Alekhine, was better.*

10...♔xd7 11.♕d3+ ♔c8 12.♕h3+ ♕xh3 13.♘xh3 ♗xe4.

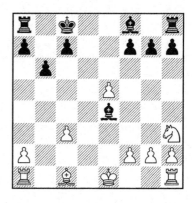

Black is better out of the opening. He has the two bishops, open d- and e-files, and an extra queenside pawn. The white pawns a2 and c3 are weak, as well as the d3 square. So black has winning chances after just 13 moves. Bogoljubov's novelty, at least in this game, justified itself well.

14.0-0 h6. Preventing white's minor pieces from reaching g5.

15.♖e1 ♗f5 16.♘f4 ♔b7 17.♘e2 ♖d8 18.♘d4 ♗d7 19.♗f4 ♖e8. 20.♖ad1 c5 21.♘b3 ♗e6 22.♖a1. *22.♖e2 ♗e7 23.♖ed2 was stronger and more natural. Now black has a real advantage.*

22...♔c6. Intending to attack his opponent's weak pawns after

exchanging rooks on the d-file.
23.♘d2 ♖d8 24.a3 ♖d3 25.♘e4 ♗e7 26.h3 g5.

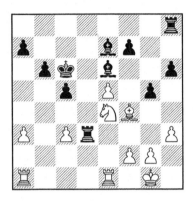

27.♗e3. *He might have tried to save the c3 pawn with 27.♗c1 ♗d5 28.♗b2, but turning the bishop into a pawn is not much fun.*

27...♗d5 28.♘d6 ♗xd6 29.exd6 ♖xc3 30.h4. This loses more quickly, making a decisive attack along the g-file possible *(30.♗c1 ♖c2).*

30...gxh4 31.♗f4 ♖g8 32.♖e7 *(32.g3 ♖f3!)* **32...♖xg2+ 33.♔f1 ♖c2 34.d7 ♖cxf2+ 35.♔e1 ♗c4 36.d8♘+ ♔b5 37.♖b1+ ♔a6.** White resigned: 38.♔d1 ♖f1+ *(38... ♖xf4 with the same idea is even crueler)* 39.♖e1 ♖xe1+ 40.♔xe1 ♖g1+ etc.

An Opening Disaster

Sozin: "Botvinnik lost again, very quickly crumbling against Kan who played the Evans Gambit; after castling prematurely, black got a miserable game, then miscalculated and lost a piece. Botvinnik probably wasted too much energy in the preliminary tournament, playing every game for a win, and now tiredness started to affect his games."

No. 44. Evans Gambit C51
Kan – Botvinnik
Odessa 1929, semi-final group 1
Annotated by I. Kan

1.e4 e5 2.♘f3 ♘c6 3.♗c4 ♗c5 4.b4 ♗b6. Declining the Evans Gambit can hardly be called its refutation. The strongest continuation for black is probably Lasker's line 4...♗xb4 5.c3 ♗a5 6.0-0 d6 7.d4 ♗b6!, and if now 8.dxe5 dxe5 9.♕xd8+ ♘xd8 10.♘xe5, then 10...♗e6!, with a better endgame for black.

Black probably thought that I had specifically prepared some line in the old gambit, and so decided to decline it out of caution. Actually, this was an amusing mistake, because I decided to play the Evans Gambit shortly before the game started, following the advice of old masters F. I. Duz-Khotimirsky and S. N. Freymann. Over the board, I thought for about ten minutes over 4.b4, but my goal was to basically prepare myself: I wanted to keep a serious face and not laugh about my own "insolence".

5.a4 a6 6.♘c3. The usual 6.♗b2 is stronger.

Today, 6.♘c3! is considered the best move – it starts the Sokolsky Attack.

6...♘f6. 6...d6 or 6...♘xb4 were worthy of consideration. If the latter line, 7.♘xe5 could be met with the well-known 7...♕g5!, which gives an advantage to black.

Modern theory prefers Botvinnik's move. This game is the first one in the database to feature 6.♘c3 ♘f6.

7.♘d5 ♘xe4. Both sides go for complications. The game becomes very sharp.

7...♘xd5 8.exd5 e4 9.dxc6 exf3 10.♕xf3 ♕e7+ 11.♔d1 dxc6 is quieter, with only a slight advantage for white.

8.0-0.

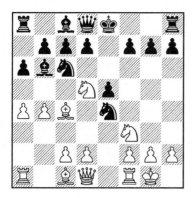

8...0-0? This move loses. Black should have played 8...d6 or 8...♘f6.

But even then, white is better: 8... d6 9.d3 ♘f6 10.♗g5 ♗e6 11.c3 ♗xd5 12.♗xd5 h6 13.♗xf6 gxf6 14.a5 ♘e7 15.♗xb7... 1-0 (Crown – Sergeant, Nottingham 1946).

9.d3! ♘f6 (forced, because 9... ♘d6 is met with 10.♗g5 ♕e8 11.a5, winning) **10.♗g5.** Now white's attack basically plays itself.

10...d6 11.♘d2! Threatening to attack the poor f6 knight for the third time, with ♘e4.

11...♗g4. Black prefers a quick demise. After 11...♗f5, white could play either 12.♘e4 ♗xe4 13.dxe4, threatening ♕f3, or 12.c3 with the same threat.

12.♗xf6 ♕c8 13.♘xb6. 13.♕e1 gxf6 14.b5 won as well. The game move is simpler.

13...cxb6 14.f3 ♗e6 15.♗h4 ♘xb4 16.♗e7 ♕c5+ 17.♔h1 ♖fe8 18.♘e4 ♕c6 19.♗xd6. Black resigned.

Sozin said that Botvinnik "lost again" in the introduction because he sensationally lost playing black to Izmailov two rounds earlier: **1.d4 ♘f6 2.♘f3 e6 3.c4 d5 4.♗g5 ♘bd7 5.♘c3 c6 6.e3 ♕a5 7.♕c2 ♗b4 8.♘d2 0-0 9.♗e2 b6 10.0-0 ♗xc3 11.bxc3 ♗a6 12.♗f4.**

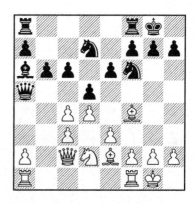

12...♖ac8? (12...♖fc8!) **13.♗d6 c5** (or else 14.♗b4, trapping the queen) **14.♗xf8 ♘xf8.** The game score stops there, so we can only quote Sozin: "Afterwards, Izmailov played badly and missed several simple continuations leading to a quick win, but he still won regardless."

Because of those two opening disasters, one of the main championship favorites failed to qualify for the final match tournament...

The Odessa failure probably left quite a scar on Botvinnik's soul. At any rate, he didn't include a single game from that tournament in his *Analytical and Critical Works*, even though the young Leningrad master won several pretty games in the preliminary group and fought in the semi-final until the bitter end.

Go Forth, Infantry!

This game, played after the loss to Izmailov, shows both Botvinnik's tactical prowess and sporting character.

No. 45
Botvinnik – Silich
Odessa 1929, semi-final group 1

13...h5. Botvinnik explained this move in *Shakhmatny Listok*: "Black's

position is very difficult because of the strong threat e4-e5. Hence, his desperate attempt at counterplay."

14.e5! ♘e8. After 14...♘d7, white wins with 15.♘e4 dxe5 16.fxe5 ♘xe5 17.♗g5 f6 18.♘xf6! (Botvinnik). For instance: 18...♘f7 (kicking the bishop away, to an unprotected square) 19.♗h4 ♘d6 20.dxe6! ♖h6 21.♘g8! ♕xh4 22.♘xh6 gxh6 23.e7 or 18...♘xd3 (more resilient) 19.♘e4 ♕d7 20.♕xd3 exd5 21.cxd5 ♗xd5 22.♗xd8 ♖xd8 23.♘g3!

15.exd6 ♘xd6. Botvinnik writes that "after 15...♕xd6 16.f5! exd5 17.♗f4 ♕c6 *(17...♕f6!? 18.cxd5 ♖xd5 19.♗e4 ♖d7)* 18.cxd5 ♕xd5 19.♖ad1 white has a very strong attack." Actually, after 19...c4! 20.♗e4 ♕c5+ 21.♗e3 ♕e7 he would still have a lot of work to do. However, 19.♗e4! won immediately: 19...♕c4 20.♗xb7+ ♔xb7 21.♕e7+ or 19...♕d7 20.♖ad1 ♕a4 21.♗c2!

16.f5.

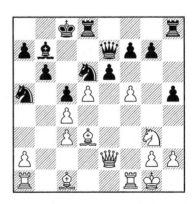

16...e5 17.f6! Preventing his opponent from strengthening the position with f7-f6, after which white's attack could have fizzled out.

17...gxf6 18.♘xh5 f5. "This elegant move seemingly refutes white's plan, because after 19.♗xf5+ ♔b8!, black is better. However, 18...e4 19.♘xf6 ♕e5 20.h3 ♕xc3 21.♘xe4 ♘xe4 22.♗xe4 ♘xc4 23.♗g5 was stronger, even though white is still better." (Botvinnik)

The computer, on the other hand, evaluates the position after 23...♕d4+ 24.♔h2 ♘d6 as roughly equal (25.♗xd8? ♘xe4).

19.♘g7! e4. Black had more chances to create complications after 19...♕h4, for instance: 20.g3 (not 20.♕xe5 ♘axc4!) 20...♕h3 21.♘xf5 ♘axc4 22.♗g5 ♖d7 23.♗f6 ♖h5, but white's threats are still stronger here.

20.♘xf5 ♘xf5 21.♖xf5 ♕d6. In case of 21...♕h4, 22.♗f4 won (22... exd3 23.♕e5 mating, or 22...♖de8 23.♗xe4).

22.♕xe4 ♕xh2+ 23.♔f2. The position has cleared: black is simply a pawn down, and his minor pieces are out of play.

23...♖de8   24.♕g4   ♕h4+ 25.♕xh4 ♖xh4 26.♗f4! ♖f8 27.♗d6 ♖g8 28.♖xf7 ♔d8 29.♖e1. Black resigned.

The Desperado Rook

Here we see a rare case of a desperado rook that is sacrificed to win the game, rather than draw.

No. 46
Izmailov – Grigoriev
Odessa 1929, preliminary group 4
Annotated by N. Grigoriev

1.♔f2. With this move, white places the king on a dark square and moves it away from the g-file. The first circumstance prepares 2.♕xc7, while the second circumstance prevents the threat 1...♖h3, undermining the g5 knight.

1...♖a3!   2.♕xc7. Everything looks good, black's last pawn is weak, too... It's hard to imagine the catastrophe awaiting white very soon.

2...♖xa2+. Now, of course, the white king needs to retreat to a dark square, otherwise a bishop check would cost him the queen.

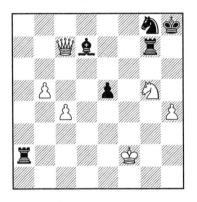

3.♔e3 ♖e2+! White resigned.

Didn't white make a big mistake, choosing the worst square for the king? Actually, the other three moves weren't any better:

1) 3.♔g3 ♖g2+!, winning;

2) 3.♔g1 ♖g2+! 4.♔h1 (or 4.♔f1 ♖2xg5!) 4...♖g4 5.♘f3 e4 etc.;

3) 3.♔e1   ♖e2+!   4.♔d1(!) ♗g4 (this time, the bishop makes a discovered attack on the queen without check, but it's not any more pleasant for white, because black now threatens a discovered check with the e2 rook) 5.♕b6 (other queen moves, for instance to c5 or b8, change nothing, while 5.♘f7+ is simply met with 5...♖xf7) 5...♖a7!, winning the queen or mating.

"Riumin's Box"

I'll start with a funny story from Viktor Lvovich Khenkin: "A while ago, a little old man called Perkovsky used to frequent the chess pavilion

in Gorky Park. He was one of those regulars who made the park games especially lively. He played solidly, but had a distinctive feature: he loved "overprotecting" his king, building bizarre defensive constructions. Such positions were even named "Perkovsky's box". This box often became the place when his poor king died." The narrow tomb built by Riumin for his queen is probably worthy of a special name, too.

No. 47

Riumin – Rauzer
Odessa 1929, preliminary group 2
Annotated by A. Model

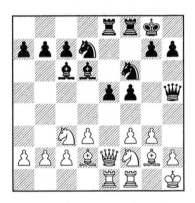

17...♘c5! 18.♘cd1 ♘e6 19.c3 ♘f4!! The knight has finally reached its desired square! White's position, already compromised by the misplayed opening *(1.e4 e6 2.g3 d5 3.♗g2 dxe4 4.♘c3 ♗d7 5.♘xe4? ♗c6 6.f3 e5 7.♘e2 f5)*, is destroyed in a few moves.

20.gxf4 exf4 21.♘e4 (21.♗e3 fxe3 22.♘h3 f4 led to a hopeless position as well) **21...fxe4.**

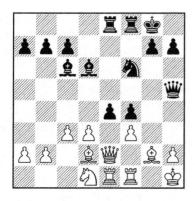

22.fxe4. 22.dxe4 is met with 22... ♘xe4! 23.fxe4 f3! and then like in the game.

22...f3! 23.♗xf3. Forced, because of the threat 23...♕xh2#.

23...♘xe4! 24.dxe4. After 24.♗xh5, black mates in two: 24... ♘f2+ and ♘h3#, while 24.♗xe4 is met with 24...♖xf1+, winning the queen.

24...♖xf3 (24...♖xe4! was even more spectacular) **25.♖xf3 ♖xe4 26.♖f8+** (a last-gasp check) **26... ♗xf8.** White resigned.

The Birth of a Variation

Yudovich: "I didn't play in the Odessa championship, but watched the games with great excitement. Konstantin Alexeevich Vygodchikov, or Uncle Kostya, as I and my friend Sergei Belavenets called him, played in the tournament. The first-category player Konstantin Vygodchikov, who took part in the pre-revolutionary tournaments in St. Petersburg and played Alekhine himself, didn't just teach us the basics of chess. He played training games with us, testing new opening ideas.

I was particularly interested in whether Uncle Kostya managed to uncork my novelty in the Slav Defense. After **1.d4 d5 2.c4 c6 3.♘f3 ♘f6 4.♘c3 dxc4 5.a4 ♗f5 6.♘e5 ♘bd7 7.♘xc4 ♕c7**, I found the move **8.g3** in 1928 and tested it numerous times in my matches with Belavenets.

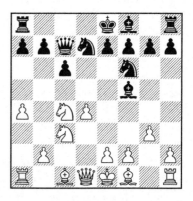

It might seem strange and even immodest for me to say that this line was my invention. Sometime later after the 6th Soviet Championship, Capablanca himself played this system, and it became widely popular.

And still, I like to flatter myself and think that Capa took note of the game Vygodchikov – Vilner that was played at that Soviet Championship and emphatically won by white (8... *g6? 9.♗g2 – the immediate 9.♗f4! ♕c8 10.e4! with the idea of 10...♘xe4 11.♘xe4 ♗xe4 12.♕e2! was stronger – 9...♗g7 10.♗f4 ♕c8 11.♘e3 0-0 12.♖c1 ♖d8 13.♘xf5 gxf5 14.♕b3*

♘f8 15.d5! and so on., but 8...e5! 9.dxe5♘xe5 10.♗f4♘fd7 11.♗g2f6 was stronger, Capablanca – Vidmar, Carlsbad 1929). Perhaps he was also aware of the championship's opening review published in *Shakhmatny Listok* (No. 24, 1929). Our renowned theoretician V. Sozin pointed out my authorship and valued the move 8.g3 highly.

Be that as it may, Belavenets and I were very proud of Uncle Kostya earning his master's title at this tournament. We learned from him, but we were also, in a way, his coaches, his sparring partners."

Oh, how quaint can our memory be. Mikhail Mikhailovich remembered the phrase about his authorship ("The invention of the Smolensk amateur Yudovich"), but forgot Sozin's next sentence: "Curiously, this same move occurred in the game Capablanca – Vidmar from the Carlsbad tournament, which wasn't known in Odessa yet." Since the Carlsbad tournament took place in August, and the Odessa championship started in September, the Cuban, without a doubt, came up with this move himself. So, this is a typical example of a simultaneous invention!

Capablanca popularized this line in the chess world, and it was even tested at the highest level – in the two matches between Alekhine and Euwe. The idea is most enduring and this line has still not been sidelined completely. It's occasionally employed by the strongest grandmasters of the 21st century: Kasparov, Anand, Kramnik, Khalifman, Ivanchuk, Carlsen, Caruana, Grischuk, Ding Liren, Aronian, Mamedyarov... And Morozevich likes playing this line for black!

Payback Time

Yudovich: "This game impressed us greatly. It made rounds in the world chess press back then."

No. 48
Silich – Rokhlin
Odessa 1929, preliminary group 1
Annotated by M. Yudovich

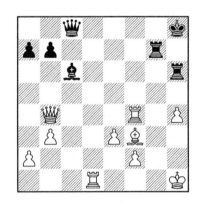

In the course of an attack, black sacrificed three pawns but couldn't quite reach the white king. His last move was ♗d7-c6, with a clear intention to give checkmate on h3.

35.♖f8+ *(35.♕f8+! was curtains)* **35...♔h7.** White has an overwhelming material and positional advantage. The spectacular 36.♕e4+! *(or 36.♖xc8)* won easily: 36...♖hg6 37.♖xc8 or 36...♖gg6 37.♖xc8 ♗xe4 38.♖d7+. It's easy to ascertain that 36...♗xe4 37.♗xe4+ *(37...♖gg6 38.♗xg6+ and ♖xc8)* crushed black as well.

It seemed that the game was in the bag, but... "I wanted to win more quickly," Silich explained later, "so I decided to trade the bishops with check."

36.♗e4+? Incredibly, this natural move leads to disaster. The crushing counterblow **36...♕f5!!** followed, and white had to resign.

"Nothing like that ever happened to me before," Silich said, demonstrating the game. "I felt as though the tournament hall ceiling had fallen in on me!"

This win helped Rokhlin to progress to the semi-final. However, he had to pay back his debt there!

No. 49
Rauzer – Rokhlin
Odessa 1929, semi-final group 2
Annotated by V. Sozin

Rauzer planned an interesting attack, but Rokhlin put up an original and ingenious defense. To continue the attack, Rauzer sacrificed a queen, driving the black king into a mating net that seemed inescapable at first...

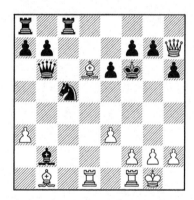

25.e4. *25.♖d5!! was a worthy conclusion to the attack, creating a mating threat on f5. Rokhlin himself pointed out this move soon after the tournament. 25...g6 26.♗xg6! ♖f8 27.♗xf7 leads to pretty lines, for instance: 27...♖xf7 28.♕xh6#, 27...exd5 28.♕g6# or 27...♖g8 28.♗xg8 exd5 (28...♖xg8 29.♗e7#) 29.♗e7+ ♚e5 30.f4#. Only 27... ♕xd6 28.♖xd6 ♖xf7 prevents the*

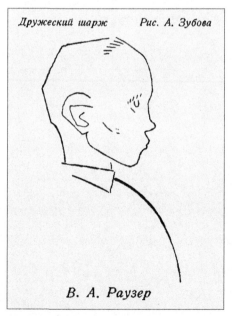

Дружеский шарж   Рис. А. Зубова

В. А. Раузер

Vsevolod Rauzer was among the six new masters who earned their titles at the Odessa championship. Cartoon by A. Zubov (64. Shakhmaty i Shashki v Rabochem Klube, No. 19, 1927).

immediate mate, but after 29.♕c2, there's still no salvation.

25...♘d7 26.♔h1!? ♖h8 27.f4. *The computer prefers 27.e5+ ♗xe5 28.♗xe5+ ♘xe5 29.♕e4.*

27...♖xh7   28.e5+   ♘xe5 29.fxe5+ ♔g5 30.♗xh7 h5 31.♖xf7 ♔h6 32.♗e4 (perhaps *32.♗b1 was better*) **32...♖c8 33.h4 ♕e3 34.♗b1.**

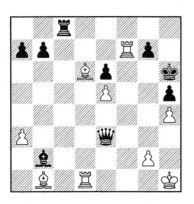

And here, Rokhlin makes a grave mistake that cost him both the game and master's title:

34...♖c4??   After   34...♗xa3 35.♖df1 ♖c1 (*or 35.♖f3 ♕e2*), black should have won.

35.♖f6+! Black resigned: 35... gxf6 36.♗f8# or 35...g6 36.♖xg6+. After winning the game, Rauzer earned the master's title.

"The "accident" that happened to me (as master Botvinnik liked to joke, I "fell under the tram") was quite notorious," Yakov Gerasimovich recalled. But he didn't mourn for long. After defeating Model in a match in December (5.5–4.5), Yakov Rokhlin became the first USSR master to win the title in a qualifying match.

The Splendors and Miseries of the Extras

7th Soviet Championship: Moscow, 10th October – 11th November 1931

"Masters should become brigadiers,
fighting for cultural recreation,
donating their experience and high technique to the masses."
From the 7th Soviet Championship bulletin

Autocratic leaders love parades and rallies. Mass action always looks impressive – if only because of the scale of what's happening. The mass action called the "7th Soviet Championship" also had a concrete goal. Krylenko never even hid it, having already staked on younger players at the Odessa 1929 championship. To eliminate the "elders" even more quickly, he came up with the group system, which, as you remember, was criticized sharply by masters, including the young Botvinnik. Bogatyrchuk called this novelty "steeple-chase", saying that "the group system was unfitting for such a serious competition." But Krylenko stubbornly forged ahead: "If our younger generation grows further, we probably won't be able to avoid the group system in future."

Avoid? Odessa had 36 players, and Moscow now had 80! Nobody was exempted from qualification – even the 43 year-old USSR champion Verlinsky had to play in the semi-finals. "In accordance with the workers' suggestions", there were only two stages this time. Yet in Odessa the finalists had to endure 17 games (8+5+4), while in Moscow this number grew to 26 (9+17). The regulations also provided an insurance policy against any unwelcome accidents: in the final, the games were held daily, from 3 to 8 p.m., then a 1-hour break, and then two more hours of play. The play-off for adjourned games was the next morning. All 17 rounds were held back-to-back, without a single rest day!

The result of this month-long "survival race" was predictable: of the "elders", only Bogatyrchuk and Verlinsky managed to obtain prizes. Long before the tournament ended, the 23 year-old Nikolai Riumin from Moscow and 20 year-old Mikhail Botvinnik from Leningrad got far ahead of the field, leaving their competitors with no chance. Krylenko's bold experiment justified itself. Essentially, a generation change happened at this championship, and masters who had grown up and learned chess under the new authorities started assuming key roles. The term "Soviet Chess School" hadn't been coined yet, but it was already born and started its victorious progress...

First, let's go through the pages of the chess press. After a resplendent celebration of its 10th birthday, *Shakhmatny Listok* rebranded – the former name *("Chess Sheet")* was no longer fitting for the spirit of the time. Thankfully, they didn't change *Listok* to *Front*, as Yakov Rokhlin proposed, but the editorials increasingly smelled of gunpowder and camp dust: "For ten days, the hired highly-qualified traitors, trying to outdo each other in cynicism, told the grim, silent audience of the House of the Unions Column Hall about the confidential plans of our enemies and the long chain of betrayal, treason, sabotage and espionage that had been cut down by the punishing sword of the OGPU."

Shakhmaty v SSSR ("Chess in the USSR"), as the magazine became known from July 1931, would later attack the "enemies of the people" with the same fervor. Together with the *64* magazine, personally edited by Krylenko, who was promoted to Russian SFSR People's Commissar of Justice in May. "Regardless of the individual qualities of the accused," he would edify, "only one method should be used against him: evaluation from the point of view of class expediency." Krylenko evaluated chess masters from the same point of view. "Traitor Zalkind should be expelled from the ranks of Soviet problemists!" That's what *64* wrote about Lazar Zalkind, accused of counter-revolutionary activity and cut down by the "punishing sword of the OGPU". Krylenko was the state prosecutor in that court case. Of course, he knew that the 1929 *Chess Player's Dictionary* called the accused "one of the greatest Soviet problem and study composers, with world renown". But the interests of the class struggle trump any accomplishments!

The editor and publisher of the folded *Shakhmaty* magazine,

В. Е. Еремеев   Н. В. Крыленко

Valerian Eremeev, Nikolai Krylenko
If not for the caption, you would have thought that this was a caricature of Hitler (he only lacks the mustache). However, if we go by Viktor Baturinsky's description, the artist's cartoon was quite accurate: "Nikolai Vasilyevich was a short man with a shaved head. He would always wear a military jacket, fashionable back in the day, and leather or felt boots." Cartoon by Y. Yuzepchuk (64. Shakhmaty i Shashki v Massy, ("Chess and Checkers to the Masses") No. 8, 1932).

Nikolai Grekov, also suffered from that "Krylenko method". They attacked him incessantly, without measuring their language, in retaliation for his firm position and independent views. "Such petty-bourgeois scribbling as the article "Chess" by N. I. Grekov hadn't been seen in our literature for a long time," wrote the bright-eyed Rokhlin, denouncing him from the pages of *Shakhmaty v SSSR*. "You can't just pass by the criminal negligence of the editors: on the very pages of the *Small Soviet Encyclopedia*, there's a shameless example of the alien ideology, hostile to the victorious proletariat, disorienting the wide working masses, imparting the thought that chess is a hundred-percent "apolitical" and separating Soviet chess players from the fighting revolutionary positions of the working class." Thankfully, at least they didn't imprison him...

The condemnation of the author of *Chess and Checkers Almanac* (1931), the only such publication in the USSR, was no less brutal: "The foreword illustrates abject political, literary and just about any other wretchedness... Only blindness and rotten liberalism can explain the very publishing of this pointedly apolitical and trite book... We have to reiterate over and over again that it is necessary to show maximum class vigilance at the front *(! - S.V.)* of chess publications, to fight mercilessly against any expressions of the alien, petty-bourgeois, philistine ideology." Who was the target of this attack? Vladimir Neishtadt, chess historian and journalist, translator of Capablanca's, Lasker's and Reti's books, a member of the USSR Writer's Union. And who were the authors? "Brigade of the Leningrad Chess Committee's Science and Methodical Section, R. Alexandrov, M. Botvinnik, and L. Ramm."

Politicization was rather deleterious for the magazines' quality. Only a small while earlier, the pages had been filled with rich ideas and evaluations, the championship articles had been so lively, the circle of authors so wide! And now everything had changed so quickly: the bland, homogenized, official language, the languid paucity of thought – as though everyone had got infected with the virus of mediocrity. *64* looked especially faceless. I couldn't even understand who exactly was reporting on the championship – not a single article was signed, as though the entire team took turns at the pen, and then forgot who wrote what! There was nothing more I could do, so I looked at the editorial board and chose the biggest name among them... In short, *64* is represented by Nikolai Grigoriev. There's no pluralism in *Shakhmaty v SSSR* either – everything is signed by Samuil Vainstein. As you can understand, it's hard to get any kind of diversity in such a situation – I had to use all my abilities to flavor this bland dish with various sauces, condiments and spices. Don't expect anything grand...

The Boomerang of Lies

Bogatyrchuk: "In two years, the last vestiges of NEP were eliminated, and we fully became the victims of the shark – state capitalism...

In the early 1930s, the "spiderwebization" of the will of the Russian peoples was complete, and this gave start to the era which was probably the darkest in the entire history of humanity. The authorities could literally do anything they wanted to the people, without fearing criticism or protests. The artists sang from the stage, "Wide is my native country, many are the forests, fields and rivers, I don't know any other country where man breathes so freely." And no singer would blush with shame when they sang that last line.

In the NKVD torture chambers, such heinous deeds were committed that even the most inventive torturers of the Middle Ages would have cried with envy had they seen them. And the Kremlin bigwigs, never elected by anyone, had the gall to call themselves people's representatives. A Western person couldn't even imagine that people could have a government hostile to them. Even now, I occasionally hear phrases such as, "If your government is so bad, why don't you overthrow them?"

Late 1920s. "Even when they play chess, the Red Army soldiers are always ready for attack by their capitalist neighbors."

Because of the pervasive lies, the Bolsheviks even developed a special language, where words had meanings different from the common ones. The lyrics of that Dunaevsky song is a prime example. But a free thinker should be glad that although the pursuit of freedom in the souls of Russian peoples can be suppressed, it cannot be fully crushed and eradicated.

At the time of my writing *(the 1970s)*, emigration is growing almost every day, with new defectors and legal emigrants from the USSR. Even more than half a century of terror and strangulation of liberties could not erase the pursuit of the most valuable thing in life – freedom. This fact makes me sure that when our peoples finally throw away the shackles of Marxism, and freedom is reborn, there won't be only faceless robots left in the country – there'll be freedom lovers who shall lead our Motherland to new cultural heights, worthy of the great past reputation of our culture.

Lies, however, have one unpleasant aspect which is often forgotten by the liars. "Lie once, and who believes you again?" Kozma Prutkov once said.

Lies, like a boomerang, hit the liar as well, and people stop believing the liar even in the rare cases when they speak the truth. For instance, during the economic and financial crisis in the USA in the 1930s, the Soviet press gave a largely truthful description of the hardships suffered by Americans. However, nobody in the USSR believed these articles, thinking that it was just idle speculation by Soviet hacks. I personally was astonished when I learned that the Great Depression really did take place. Later, we deceived ourselves in rejecting the descriptions of the Nazi atrocities against the Jews. Nobody, not even Jews themselves, believed these "inventions", and many Jews lost their lives because of this disbelief.

Another negative side of all-pervasive lies is the absolute distrust in others, even your closest friends and relatives. And this distrust leads to a paradoxical opposite extreme: the person starts believing only what they want to believe, casting aside everything else as lies. I can accept that the investigators really believed the accused when they testified against themselves, admitting nonexistent crimes. I am also sure that Stalin sincerely believed that his delusional ideas were true.

All that happened against the backdrop of collectivization, industrialization, five-year plans in four years and songs of encouragement from the loudspeakers. Chess also helped build socialism. In those years, the "propaganda" porcelain collection was supplemented by the **"Collective Farm and Town"** chess set, created at the famous factory in Verbilki (author – E. Tripolskaya) and currently kept in the Russian Chess Museum in Moscow.

Pieces from the "Collective Farm and Town" set (Verbilki, 1930s). Left to right: white bishop, black queen, white king, black bishop. From the Russian Chess Museum collection.

Here's an excerpt from an article by **Natalia Ivanova**, who was the museum's curator for several years (*The Chess Herald* No. 3, 1994[17]):

"The Collective Farm and Town set concerns one of the favourite topics of Soviet propaganda, labor competition between the socialist town and the collectivized countryside. However, the artist E. Tripolskaya's imaginative treatment of it makes us smile now.

The trihedral pyramids for the kings and queens have a painted relief on each face. The country king has a collective farmer carrying a sheaf on one, a combine harvester operator on another, and a mammoth corn cob on the third. Each of the queen's faces represents a collective farm girl. Together they support a giant sheaf of wheat. A red flag inscribed "100%" – perhaps, a report of all plan targets met – represents the bishop. The emblem of a tractor depot stands for the knight (no wonder, as the propaganda idiom of the time referred to tractors as "steel steeds"). Silos stand for rooks, while

---

[17]   The English version of the article in the bi-lingual *The Chess Herald* named the set "Town and Country", but "Collective Farm and Town" is a true rendition of the Russian name

Pieces from the "Collective Farm and Town" set (Verbilki, 1930s). Left to right: white bishop, black queen, white king, black bishop. From the Russian Chess Museum collection.

pawns glorify science, with a retort, an open book and a chemical formula on the faces.

The black, urban king has a worker on each face, all of different trades. Similarly, the factory girls on the queen pyramid. There is another hundred-percent banner for the bishop, while the knight is thoroughly urban, painted all over with turbines, electric transmission lines and factory smokestacks. The rook is also a smokestack. The pawns are even more spectacular than the pieces – gas-masked children, as the 1930s involved all Soviet citizens, from greybeards to toddlers, in paramilitary training programmes, ready for Anti-Aircraft and Chemical Defense, and races in gas masks were something of an entertainment."

In 1931, I went to Moscow again to play in the 7th All-Union Championship. The tournament was a great success for the 20 year-old Mikhail Botvinnik, who won the Soviet champion's title. His success was especially valued by the Bolsheviks because Botvinnik was the only Komsomol member at the championship. He was quickly surrounded with attention and received all possible help to develop his extraordinary chess talent. At this tournament,

I recorded my only ever draw with him, winning two more games in the subsequent tournaments where we played together.

It was in Moscow that I first heard discussions about Stalin being well on the way to one-man dictatorship, even though he wasn't threatening any party higher-ups yet, with the exception of Trotsky, who was expelled from the USSR. I personally wasn't interested in the power struggles at the top of the party. I, like many of my friends, couldn't wait for all those "leaders" to rip each other's throats out. Alas, the process of "ripping the throats out" is still going on, and it's hard to say when it will finally end..." (From the book *My Life Path to Vlasov and the Prague Manifesto.*)

Qualifying Musical Chairs

S. Vainstein: "In the morning of 10th October, the building of the VSFK *(the Highest Physical Education Council, as we noted much earlier in our tale)* on Ilyinka Street is bustling. The participants of the All-Union competitions walk up from all sides, register and then get directed to the 3rd House of Soviets. By 2–3 p.m., the representatives of many republics still haven't shown up, and some delegations have sent telegrams saying that they have been caught up on the way and will only arrive tomorrow. At 6 p.m. the session of the qualifying commission opens, consisting of two Leningrad and two Moscow delegates. With an elaborate voting system, they determine the line-up of the preliminary groups *(the championship was contested in two stages: first, the qualifying tournament – 8 groups of 10 players, and then 2 winners of each group progressed to the finals)*.

At 9:30, the session in the House of the Unions is opened. Even though it is a closed session, the hall is jam-packed with participants and representatives of organizations. The competition rules and regulations are announced, and then the organizing committee proceeds with drawing lots. Ilyin-Zhenevsky, Botvinnik and Riumin are greeted with loud applause. 20 masters and 40 first-category players are taking part in the tournament...

The first round started with a delay because of a lack of clocks, which, as usual, were provided late by the Moscow organizations. The overall picture of the tournament hall is spectacular. Behind the barrier, players sit at the tables, very close to each other, and there's a big crowd in the middle. The games of Riumin, Bogatyrchuk and Botvinnik attract the most interest; the crowd is a bit condescending towards the lesser-known youngsters, but it's clear to everyone that in a few days, when the results of first rounds are published, the spectators will pay more attention to the younger participants...

The interest in the tournament only grows. Some games attract special attention; there are so many people around some tables, especially in critical situations, that even the tournament committee members see nothing...

After three rounds, the table stretches like a long rubber band. Nine players have three zeroes, and it's unlikely to be an accident. A number of players, including some masters, had a bad start and have likely lost all hopes of qualifying for the Soviet Championship proper. There's fierce competition in some groups, while in others the advantage of certain players is quite obvious... Some jokers proposed to print a special poster: "Selezniev vs. Riumin, daily, 11 a.m. to 1 p.m." Indeed, this game was adjourned for the fourth time, but still hasn't ended...

Duz-Khotimirsky dropped out of the tournament due to illness. This unexpected event upset the group balance a bit, because it's impossible to replace a player who'd already played four games... Botvinnik couldn't convert his opening advantage against Konstantinopolsky, got confused in complications and lost an exchange. The resulting rook ending, despite two days of resistance, was hopeless for the Leningrad master...

The most outstanding event of the sixth round was Botvinnik's second loss in a row (to Izmailov, he blundered an exchange in a roughly equal position), and so his qualification chances suffered somewhat...

> **Botvinnik:** "I easily won the first four games and was in a great mood. We played in the October Hall of the House of the Unions, and before the games, we dined where the Column Hall cafeteria is now located. There were long tables with benches, where the players sat. I ate dinner with great appetite and then decided to have another tasty schnitzel (those were the hungry times). I sat down at another table. The waitress immediately brought me a bowl of borscht. I couldn't refuse, or else she would have understood that I had already eaten. So, I had to eat the second bowl of borscht in addition to the schnitzel... And then, I had to play A. Konstantinopolsky. I had an advantage in the opening, but then I felt very sleepy. And by the time I "woke up", my position was already lost. The next day, I was so upset that I lost to P. Izmailov as well (see game 50) – that's what you sometimes get when you eat too much." (From the book *Achieving the Aim*.)
>
> **Nikolai Izmailov:** "After graduating from university, my father started working with geological exploration parties. He had no time for chess anymore, it was pushed into the background. However, he still played in the 7th Soviet Championship in 1931. As fate would have it, he again faced Botvinnik in the preliminary round. Izmailov had a poor start, scoring only 2/5, while Botvinnik had won game after game. But their grudge match was won by the

Siberian master! Nevertheless, he couldn't make it to the final. He shared 3rd place, while Kasparyan and Botvinnik qualified. As an anonymous author wrote in *64. Shakhmaty v Rabochem Klube*, "master Izmailov is isolated from chess life (he works in the taiga), and the lack of tournament practice affected his performance." (*Shakhmaty v Rossii*, No. 1–3, 1999.)

The tournament is heading towards the end. The sporting tensions are huge. There's a large crowd around the tables – they're calculating chances, arguing, discussing things. This day should have clarified matters, but it seems that the situation in some groups has become even more complicated, because Ilyin-Zhenevsky, Bogatyrchuk and Riumin all lost...

Genrikh Kasparyan won his qualification group (a point ahead of Botvinnik) and made it to the Soviet championship final for the first time. On the photo: playing in the Tiflis championship (1928).

And so, after a fierce 9-day struggle, only 8 out of 20 masters progressed to the Soviet Championship proper (*Verlinsky, Bogatyrchuk, Riumin, Freymann, Blumenfeld, A. Kubbel, L. Kubbel, Grigoriev, Selezniev, Izmailov, Rokhlin and Silich all failed to qualify*). This fact vividly shows the colossal growth of our youth's playing level. The All-Union competition exhibited a number of great chess players we never knew about. This result could have been produced only by the bold competition formula, which may need some tweaks here and there, but was generally good...

> Indeed, everything happened by the book. Back in July, *Shakhmaty v SSSR* had written, "Even now, it's clear that mostly young players will qualify for the final, and the old master cadre will be sifted away with the preliminary filtration system."

The winners were distributed in this way: Leningrad – 8 players, Transcaucasia – 3, Ukraine – 2, Moscow – 2, and Belarus – 1. The brilliant victory of Leningrad and Transcaucasia shows the results of systematic qualification work and the rich cadre available to these chess sections. By contrast, Moscow's failure is surprising: it held a number of serious tournaments last year, seemingly producing several young and promising players.

The preliminary groups brought many unexpected results. We have no doubt that the Soviet Championship shall underscore the progress of young players and their importance for our chess movement." (*Shakhmaty v SSSR*, October 1931.)

Guilty Without Guilt

S. Vainstein: "20th October. At 7 p.m., Comrade Krylenko declares the 7th Conference of the USSR Proletarian Chess and Checkers Organizations open. The huge Column Hall, decorated with chess slogans, is filled to the brim. The mood is joyful; no chess and checkers conference ever opened in such a festive atmosphere before. After a short introductory word by Comrade Krylenko, the conference elects its governing bodies. The line-ups of the presidium (31 people), secretariat, editorial board, and mandate commission are announced, as proposed by the VKP(b) faction. Accompanied by loud applause, an honorary presidium is elected, consisting of Comrades Stalin,

The Casualties. Only eight masters out of 20 qualified for the final tournament... Cartoon by E. Dor (64. Shakhmaty v Rabochem Klube, No. 21–22, 1931).

Molotov, Voroshilov, Kalinin, Kuibyshev, Kosior, Kirov, Andreev, Enukidze, Antipov, Shvernik, and Krylenko *(oddly, 64 gives a different list, adding Kaganovich, Ordzhonikidze, Rudzutaks and... Maxim Gorky, who, as we shall see from Bogatyrchuk's report below, "spoke out against chess numerous times"[18]!).*

Comrade Krylenko gives a presentation about the objectives of the chess and checkers organization. His speech, lasting for 1 hour 40 minutes, was listened to with relentless attention.

> **Krylenko:** "...In our epoch, the slogan "Chess and checkers to the masses as a weapon of cultural revolution" has been expanded: "Imbue chess and checkers with political content", transform our chess and checkers players into political workers, conscientious participants of the building of socialism.
>
> In addition to that, we should fight against everything that holds us back, that wants to weaken the political enthusiasm of the masses under any excuse... Are there any tendencies in our organizations to abstain from politics? Comrades, it's no secret – it was published in the press, in my article "Politics and Chess" *(the full name was "More about Politics and Chess" – see the chapter on the 6th Championship)* – that such tendencies are still alive and kicking and will probably stay alive in the future. These tendencies were sharply demonstrated in the formula shown in an anonymous poll in the *Shakhmatny Listok*: "Too much of that Krylenko thing." We wrote, both in our resolutions and articles, that <u>apoliticism was politics too, and a struggle against politics was a political struggle, first and foremost</u>. And that's when our slogan came to be. We said: anyone who stated that political issues should be separated from the issues of general cultural work, from the life of our organizations, was deliberately opposing our political position and, therefore, was our class enemy..."

Some parts of his report were most impressive; he ended it with Stalin's emphatic phrase: "If we don't want to get beaten, we shouldn't get behind." General applause, The Internationale plays, and Comrade Krylenko leaves the podium.

---

[18] Averbakh told me a curious anecdote. After Gorky returned to the USSR, he was asked to write something about chess. Gorky sent a postcard (Averbakh said that he saw it in the *64* editor's office) that said, "I'm not a chess player and, frankly, I see no difference between chess and fishing." There's also another piece of funny testimony. From M. Mikhailov's article "On the Reason of Chess Stagnation" (*Shakhmatny Listok*, 10th February 1930): "No later than in summer 1929, M. Gorky was amazed by the spread of chess circles and asked warily, 'Is that really good?'"

Strangely, the head of Soviet chess said nothing about Vilner. There weren't too many masters in the country back then, and the death of one of them surely deserved a minute of silence to commemorate it.

Rokhlin: "After a long illness, master Yakov Semyonovich Vilner died on 29th June. He was just 32 years old... Since 1923 (the 2nd All-Russian Tournament), Y. S. had played regularly in the All-Union championships. In 1924, he won the Ukrainian championship in nice style (ahead of F. P. Bogatyrchuk); the same year, he shared 6th–8th prizes in the Soviet Championship and received the master's title. In the 1925 Soviet Championship, Y. S. scored 9.5/19, but won a brilliant game against E. D. Bogoljubov. Then his illness worsened (chronic asthma, frequent colds), preventing him from achieving further success.

Y. S. belonged to the combinational school of Soviet masters. He was especially inventive in complicated attacking positions, where his creativity worked with special energy. The original interpretation of new openings (Nimzo-Indian Defense, Alekhine Defense) and fresh theoretical thought in the old openings, coupled with great understanding of the most complicated endgame positions, gave him great strength." (*Shakhmatny Listok*, June 1931.[19])

21st October. The conference was moved to the hall of the USSR Central Executive Committee and held in a businesslike environment. 150 delegates are taking part, regularly attending the conferences and watching the debates attentively... At the evening conference session, Comrade Bogatyrchuk gives a very interesting report. He harshly criticizes himself for the hygiene conditions of chess and checkers competitions, and talks about the huge gap between the goals of the physical education movement and the realities of chess life...

Bogatyrchuk: "It's no secret that chess, in addition to enthusiasts and friends, has many enemies. There are well-known writers, prominent doctors and many public activists as well. Let's remember M. Gorky, who has spoken out against chess numerous times, let's remember the negative attitude towards chess of 90% of neurologists. This negative attitude is based in many cases on the fact that all these people, while not denying the known benefits

---

[19] For a detailed biography of Yakov Vilner, including his best games and his compositions, see *Yakov Vilner, First Ukrainian Chess Champion and First USSR Chess Composition Champion* by Sergei Tkachenko (Elk and Ruby, 2019)

This colorful pastoral by A. Saveliev would grace the wall of the Central Chess Club for years. A funny detail: the Russian Chess Museum has a black and white painting by P. Vasilyev on the same subject; Lenin and the writer Maxim Gorky play chess there as well, with Lenin's wife Nadezhda Krupskaya watching; the only difference is that she doesn't have a cat in her arms in the second painting.

of chess, consider that these benefits are too paltry in comparison with its negative sides.

The latter are mostly tied to playing conditions, hygiene, chess players' everyday life, etc. Here, our situation is quite unpleasant, to put it bluntly. Playing venues are a large part of the problem. The atmosphere of the preliminary tournament is a great example of how little attention is given to this side of things. It's very hard to play, let alone play seriously, in such a hall, and it requires too much energy. Even the spectators are tired towards the end of the games – this should say something about how chess players feel.

In addition to the venue itself, quietness during the game is very important. Currently, the influence of noise on the human psyche is being researched both in our country and abroad. It's already known that the influence of noise is not externally visible, yet quite strong...

Now, let's discuss everyday life. It's only natural that as a result of such an unsanitary environment, we see a certain type of chess player who is completely separated from the physical education movement. His chest is sunken, complexion is pale, clothes are often untidy, he's unkempt in general; a razor blade rarely touches his face, and a cigarette never leaves his mouth (as the saying goes, he smokes like a horse). Ask such a chess player about athletics, or swimming – it would seem so alien to him. Ask his family about such a chess player's everyday life, and you'll likely hear that he's very "peculiar", and they have given up on him, that he's an enemy of tidiness and looking smart – you know, he's a chess player, what else can you expect from him.

What can we say against such facts? Try now to prove that chess is indeed beneficial for one's psyche!.." (*Shakhmaty v SSSR*, December 1931.)

23rd October. The last day of the conference... All items of the agenda have been covered, but Comrade Krylenko makes an extraordinary statement about the incidents with masters Gotthilf and Romanovsky and reads out the documents that prompted the presidium to submit the problem for discussion. The attempts of some delegates to deviate from the <u>principal</u> side of the case with sentimental arguments have been sharply and deservedly rebuked. With an overwhelming majority of the votes, with 13 against and 3 abstained (*oh, wouldn't I like to know who those brave men were!*), the resolution on Gotthilf's exclusion and Romanovsky's disqualification was adopted.

FROM THE CONFERENCE'S RESOLUTION
ON MASTERS ROMANOVSKY AND GOTTHILF

The conference categorically disapproves of Comrade Romanovsky's behavior; Romanovsky surrendered his delegate's mandate and refused to play in the final tournament as a protest: he was unhappy that the resolution of a closed organizing committee meeting on the expected final line-up was not communicated to him... The conference considers fully unsatisfactory the subsequent explanatory letter sent by Romanovsky, where he, with great reserve, explained his behavior as due to illness and, instead of admitting that the decision of the organizing committee was binding on him, still continued to oppose the organizing committee, saying that he, Romanovsky, no longer considers the inclusion of Riumin, as a talented player, "a reason for war against the organizing committee".

Based on the above, the conference decrees: <u>to exclude Romanovsky from the final competition; taking into account his past accomplishments, to limit the penalty to a one-year disqualification.</u>

Concerning Gotthilf, who left the tournament on his own accord only because he, Gotthilf, issued an ultimatum – to provide him with individual accommodation, instead of a dormitory room like all the other players – and this demand was not satisfied: to consider this kind of behavior <u>clearly antisocial and exclude master Gotthilf from the ranks of USSR chess organizations.</u>

P.S. As we say, "there was a similar case in Odessa". Let me remind you that at the Odessa championship, Ilyin-Zhenevsky failed to qualify for the semi-final, and the tournament committee chairman offered to include him as well, if all other participants agreed, but the young Botvinnik said that "regulations are the law, and you can't violate them". Now,

Дружеский шарж   Рис. Ю. Ю.

П. А. Романовский

The inclusion of several masters who didn't qualify was against the rules and drew the ire of Peter Romanovsky. The reaction was very harsh: the conference decreed to exclude him from the final tournament! Cartoon by Y. Yuzepchuk (64. Shakhmaty i Shashki v Massy, No. 5, 1932).

to appease Krylenko, who doted over Riumin, they decided to violate the law – quietly, behind the players' back. And when one of them showed integrity, he was put to the pillory. Krylenko himself let slip that this was indeed a "ritual sacrifice", when he counted "the growth of political consciousness that expressed itself in a concrete example of public solidarity prevailing over individual accomplishments" as one of the conference's best achievements.

Meanwhile, the 29 year-old Solomon Gotthilf, a Leningrad player, was essentially forced to retire. And remember what a great beginning he had recorded: playing at the 1925 Moscow International Tournament, winning the tournament in Leningrad where Carlos Torre participated, sharing 6th–8th places with Ilyin-Zhenevsky and Romanovsky in the Soviet Championship. As you remember, Levenfish wrote of him, "Of all the young players, I place my biggest hopes on Gotthilf."

It turned out that, in preliminary group 2, Kan and Zamikhovsky *(a first-category player from Kiev)* scored an equal amount of points and even equal

Berger table tiebreaks. This prompted the organizing committee to expand the final line-up... On the other hand, Riumin fell victim to the Berger table, as he finished behind Budo on tie-breaks in group 6. If Riumin is included in the final as well, then other players who scored 6 points in their groups – Bogatyrchuk, Verlinsky, Podolny (*a Red Army soldier from Polotsk*) and Grigoriev – also have grounds to qualify for the finals. The organizing committee took the view that since the group system is the only possible one for mass competitions, we should set aside formal rules and make adjustments that improve the quality of the final line-up. This last consideration was especially important after the conference excluded masters Gotthilf and Romanovsky from the finals. So, two options were offered to players: 1) increase the number of players in the final tournament to 20 and play in two groups, with a final, or 2) only include Riumin, Bogatyrchuk, Verlinsky, Kan and Zamikhovsky. As we know, the players unanimously voted for the second option.

Of the principal decrees of the conference, important for the final, we shall highlight the following: 1) increase, based on the new qualification regulations, the norm for awarding or confirming the master's title to 50% (8.5 points); 2) abolish the grandmaster title; 3) abolish the title and name of "champion, championship" and replace it with "premiership" and "winner of the premiership".

> **Zubarev:** "The master's title is not only an honorific one, but also a category title, defining the highest level of chess strength in our qualification system. And since it is so, there's no reason to retain the fancy, but somewhat expressionless "grandmaster" title, which is essentially analogous to the term "champion" which was already abolished in the Soviet physical education movement. So, the decision of the conference that abolished the honorific "grandmaster" title and did away with the terms "champion" and "championship" is completely understandable." (*Shakhmaty v SSSR*, December 1931.)

Thus, the following players shall take part in the All-Union *Premiership*, listed according to the draw (*masters in italics*): 1. Kirillov, 2. Lisitsin, 3. *Ilyin-Zhenevsky*, 4. Sorokin, 5. Kasparyan, 6. *Goglidze*, 7. Budo, 8. Mazel, 9. *Sozin*, 10. Alatortsev, 11. *Verlinsky*, 12. *Kan*, 13. Zamikhovsky, 14. *Bogatyrchuk*, 15. Yudovich, 16. *Botvinnik*, 17. *Riumin*, 18. *Rauzer*." (*Shakhmaty v SSSR*, November 1931.)

The Rise and Fall of Riumin

S. Vainstein: "In the October Hall of the House of the Unions, the participants of the finals, the women's tournament, the Red Army tournaments and checkers masters all sit together. Still, despite the 50 players, it's relatively sparse in the hall in comparison with the bustle of the preliminary groups. The final attracts much interest, there are a lot of spectators. Ilyin-Zhenevsky spotted that Botvinnik had weakened his kingside, sacrificed a knight and crushed his opponent in style.

> **Botvinnik:** "New trials awaited me in the final. I lost to Ilyin-Zhenevsky in the first round *(see game 59)*, then to Sozin in the seventh; I almost repeated my Odessa 'exploits'..."

Tournament standings: Riumin – 7/8 (!), Verlinsky – 6, Bogatyrchuk and Botvinnik – 5.5, Zhenevsky and Kirillov – 5, Zamikhovsky and Yudovich – 4.5...

Round 10. For today, the games were moved to the Business Club and held without paying spectators. The small room that hosts the players is carpeted; it's easy and comfortable to play here...

The tournament was moved to the Polytechnic Museum at Lubyanka. It's somewhat stuffy and cramped here, but the museum has a large foyer with demonstration boards installed. To prevent the public from over filling the tournament hall, a new rule has been introduced: every finished game is immediately demonstrated by one of the players (usually by the winner). These unique lectures attract huge interest and are listened to very attentively, freeing up the hall at the same time...

Round 13. The sporting tension hasn't reached its culmination yet, but the atmosphere in the hall is already heated. It's amazing how the spectators experience certain games and how excited they get with each move. It turns out that chess struggle can excite and captivate not only the players themselves, but others as well, that chess emotions can be stronger and, in any case, more enduring than sporting ones. Today's chess spectators are already savvy enough in complicated positions to be able to judge and criticize the play of our best players.

Riumin and Botvinnik are, of course, in the spotlight again. Both have black, the former against Bogatyrchuk, the latter against Yudovich. Botvinnik overlooks a combination in the opening and loses a pawn. The outcome of the whole tournament seems foregone. However, Bogatyrchuk wastes no time and tries to sharpen play as much as possible. On move 26, he has an extra pawn and significant advantage, but... he's in time trouble. Trying to consolidate his position, he overlooks a counterattack that can change everything. Riumin again shows his mastery of complicated positions and, with several strong moves, obtains a clearly won position. And Yudovich still has no winning plan. After the break, Bogatyrchuk resigns, and Botvinnik's game attracts all the spectators' attention. White plays indecisively (he, like many other players, is already too tired), and black is very strong; unable to withstand the tension, white makes a decisive mistake and resigns due to the loss of his queen.

Botvinnik gets an ovation; he's also greeted with applause when he, according to the new tradition, goes to demonstrate his game together with Yudovich.

Tournament standings: Riumin – 11/13, Botvinnik – 10, Verlinsky – 8, Bogatyrchuk and Yudovich – 7.5...

And it's now round 15. The hall doors were closed at 6 p.m., because the hall was packed. Everyone's eyes are on the Botvinnik – Riumin game *(see game*

Дружеский шарж Ю. Ю.

From the back left to right: Kan, Yudovich (sitting), Kots (a participant in the preliminary tournament) on his knee, Alatortsev, Golts (64's executive secretary), S. Vainstein, Botvinnik, Mazel, Rauzer, Riumin; Mar, Chudova and Girvidz (players of the Soviet Women's Championship), Krylenko; Zubarev and Eremeev (tournament committee members), Kasparyan (crying at Eremeev's feet). In the left corner – Verlinsky and Bogatyrchuk. In the right corner – Romanovsky and A. Rabinovich, Vechernaya Moskva reporter. Cartoon by Y. Yuzepchuk from the games collection of the 7th Soviet Championship

53). If Riumin draws, he remains half a point ahead of his opponent; however, if Botvinnik wins, he overtakes Riumin and, having weaker opponents ahead of him, gets great winning chances. The public is excited, waiting impatiently for each move; Moscow spectators clearly support Riumin.

Both opponents play quite slowly in the opening. Black chooses a line that was rejected by theory and gives away an important central pawn. At the cost of weakening his castled position, Botvinnik retains the pawn and gets the bishop pair. Riumin has a solid, but difficult position, and he's also in time trouble: about 5 minutes left for 12 moves. It's impossible to find the strongest replies; he makes some weaker moves, loses a piece and immediately resigns. There's excited noise in the hall, someone is trying to applaud, but the stewards quickly restore order...

> **Botvinnik:** "My opponent stops the clock. "What time trouble!" a familiar voice says. Our eyes meet – Nikolai Vasilyevich turns his back to me and leaves. Krylenko clearly supported Riumin, a fellow Muscovite." (From the book *The Aim Achieved.*)
>
> **Baturinsky:** "In his memoir, Botvinnik writes that during the decisive game between him and Riumin, Krylenko clearly supported the Moscow player. I wouldn't dare to dispute this impression, but I personally heard Krylenko saying in the early 1930s that Botvinnik was the main hope of Soviet chess in future competitions with foreign luminaries." (From the book *Pages of Chess Life.*)

Only two rounds remain until the end of the tournament. Many players are so tired that they can't withstand long games and do everything in their power to finish the games before the break. The others, by contrast, gather their last ounces of strength to score the points necessary to obtain or confirm the master's title. The struggle for first place between Botvinnik and Riumin ends. The former is still in great form, while Riumin, by his own admission, doesn't hope for anything anymore...

The last round begins an hour earlier, the break was canceled, so play shall last for 8 hours. This was all done to finish the tournament today and let the Leningrad players depart on the night train. But the breaking point has already been reached, and there isn't much fight on most boards; both the winners and losers play unusually fast, and all games end before 7:30 p.m. (Riumin unexpectedly lost his third game in a row). The results are announced to the public, and they reluctantly leave..." (*Shakhmaty v SSSR*, November 1931.)

The "Elders" Might as well Retire!

S. Vainstein: "After the first few rounds, most predicted that Riumin, Bogatyrchuk or Verlinsky would win. And only when Botvinnik and Riumin got ahead of the field, did people start to study their style, their manners, the content of their victories. And it became obvious to most that Botvinnik wouldn't just compete for first place – he had everything he needed to win it. And the closer the tournament got to the finish, the more assured and calm he was in defeating his opponents; his finishing spurt (9/10) is unprecedented in All-Union competitions. He performed brilliantly at a difficult, important tournament and saved his strength so well that he could have easily played another half a dozen intense games...

The most important thing in this spectacular, intense sporting struggle, of course, is not the fact that Botvinnik, rather than Riumin, won it, but rather that the tournament was won by the new generation of Soviet youth, which has prepared for years to reach the greatest heights. And if we look at the tournament from the point of view of a generational struggle, then we should state that there was essentially no struggle, and the gap between the two winners and Bogatyrchuk and Verlinsky is a historical milestone, signifying the triumph of the central chess organization's youth policy.

Botvinnik and Riumin: the former is a student, a Komsomol member, and a future electrical engineer, the latter is a state employee, a chess organization worker who has about ten extracurricular duties; one of them is aged 20, the other is 23, there are so many similarities between them. Nevertheless, they are polar opposites at the chessboard.

Botvinnik is a fully-fledged chess fighter, an expert in opening theory and a great strategist in the middlegame and endgame; he methodically prepares for every game using the Nimzowitsch –

Mikhail Botvinnik won his first Soviet championship at the age of 20. "The logical simplicity of his play makes him similar to Capablanca." (Grigoriev.) Cartoon by Y. Yuzepchuk (64. Shakhmaty i Shashki v Massy, No. 4, 1932.)

Mueller system, thoroughly studying the games of his future opponents and noticing the slightest tactical chances. His games are positional, meaningful, and seamless. In his 12 wins, he only made 2 or 3 mistakes altogether, probably no more – this says everything.

> **Grigoriev:** "A shock worker at his job, in the high-voltage lab of the Elektrotok, a Komsomol member, Botvinnik is graduating from the Leningrad Polytechnic Institute this year, he's the youngest and most talented USSR master. His performance in all the latest tournaments has been successful, and Botvinnik's win in the All-Union tournament was well-deserved. The logical simplicity of his play makes him similar to Capablanca. Riumin, on the other hand, always looks for complications in his games, his playing style is closer to Alekhine's." (*64. Shakhmaty v Rabochem Klube*, December 1931.)
>
> **Panov:** "With his full approval, I characterized Riumin in the 1930s press as a master of counterattack. In this regard, Riumin's play vividly resembled that of the young Lasker. He could defend tenaciously in worse, but complicated situations, and as soon as his opponent made a mistake, he would seize the initiative immediately and launch a counterattack. Later, he became much stronger in positional, maneuvering struggle as well." (From the book *Forty Years at the Chessboard*.)
>
> **Baturinsky:** "Nikolai Nikolaevich Riumin, multiple-times Moscow champion, was the favorite of Moscow spectators. Tall, stooping a bit, with Mongol-like facial features and bushy brows that joined at the nose bridge, he was a talkative, amiable man, dangerous for anyone behind the chessboard."

Riumin, who was still a first-category player early in the year, only started to truly show his immense chess talent after winning the qualifying match against Grigoriev (+6–1=1). He's only a developing player, and it's hard to say whether he has a particular style yet. He's persistent, inventive, performs greatly in complicated positions. He literally destroyed Budo, Sozin and Verlinsky, exploiting their mistakes in the opening, trapped Bogatyrchuk in complications started by Bogatyrchuk himself; in other games he got a cramped position, but would gradually extricate himself and then create an attack. He plays black less assuredly than white, sometimes experimenting in the opening and making psychological mistakes, like in the game against Botvinnik: in that all-important game, he tried to play a line rejected by theory. He clearly got tired towards the end of the tournament, and one loss was enough to unsettle him.

Grigoriev: "Riumin took the lead from the very beginning and was cruising confidently ahead until round 15, and only the crushing loss to Botvinnik pushed him back to second place. The leaders were so far ahead of all the others that Riumin, despite losing in all three last rounds, still finished 1.5 points ahead of third place."

Nikolai Riumin, the runner-up, "always looks for complications in his games, his playing style is closer to Alekhine's." (Grigoriev.) Cartoon by M. Arts (64. Shakhmaty v Rabochem Klube, No. 23–24, 1931.)

Bogatyrchuk and Verlinsky were always considered masters of the attacking style. In this tournament, however, Bogatyrchuk's style wasn't similar to his style of 1927: there were no combinational ideas, examples of creative imagination, or brilliancies. Probably his only seamless combinational game was against Alatortsev; he earned all his other wins and draws in deep endgames, where he showed much tenacity, exceptional mastery and much inventiveness. He had better chances to take clear third place than the others, but he lacked strength and momentum as well.

Bogatyrchuk: "In this tournament, I couldn't maintain my tradition of getting good scores against other prizewinners. Out of 8 games with leaders, I scored just 2.5 points; I got 7.5 points from the bottom nine players, scoring 10/17 in total and sharing third and fourth prizes with Alatortsev (a talented Leningrad master)."

Unbelievable, but true: in the next championship, Bogatyrchuk achieved the exact same result: 2.5 points against the top 8 and 7.5 against the bottom 9!

Verlinsky lost his title won in Odessa. His poor health was probably the decisive factor that stopped him from truly demonstrating his class. And three key losses to the young players (Botvinnik, Riumin, and Kan) showed that his play had serious flaws that cannot be fixed only with routine work...

Panov: "Verlinsky was a tactical, trappy player, he was especially strong in complicated positions, always able to gain a strong initiative. He was less strong in defense and obviously underestimated opening theory, preferring to play only a few lines he knew in great detail."

Дружеский шарж   Рис. Ю. Ю.

Б. М. Верлинский

Boris Verlinsky failed to repeat his Odessa success. Cartoon by Y. Yuzepchuk (64. Shakhmaty i Shashki v Massy, No. 3, 1932.)

Five new masters emerged at the tournament, whose combined age is just 106. The youngest of the five is Mazel, and the "oldest" one is Kirillov (born in 1908). All of them are talented and love chess. Mazel is the most interesting figure; this tournament was his first where he got to play against masters. Alatortsev showed his combinational talent pretty well in Moscow; Yudovich, whose play is generally similar to Botvinnik's, also played well. Lisitsin and Kirillov are weaker than those promising three, and they need to do a lot of work to improve.

Grigoriev: "Some evil tongues said that the latter two were "masters of the last round", but this is simply unfair. To earn the master's title, they had to pass a long ordeal – play 26 games against the USSR's strongest players, and they earned their titles not simply because of one win in the last round."

Botvinnik: "In the last round, I could even have lost – this didn't affect the tournament standings. G. Lisitsin approached me before the game: "Misha, could you agree a draw with me? I'll get the master's title in this case..." Back then, I already treated Lisitsin with respect and decided to draw, but, to avoid rumors, I didn't give a clear answer.

In the game, despite the simplified position, white *(Botvinnik)* still had some advantage. While thinking on my next move, I suddenly heard the tragic whisper of the horrified Lisitsin: "Misha, what are you doing?" After that, I couldn't play anymore and, smiling, extended my hand to the new master." (From the book *The Aim Achieved.*)

Kan, who improved towards the end, and Ilyin-Zhenevsky, who, by contrast, collapsed at the finish, performed below their potential. Zhenevsky played exceptionally sharply in this tournament – he defeated Botvinnik and Sorokin with great sacrificial combinations, played pretty attacks against Budo and Zamikhovsky, but performed rather weakly in many other games. Kan threw away one point in total against Yudovich and Bogatyrchuk, scored many draws, and, had he been more tenacious, he would probably have had as many chances as Bogatyrchuk to take third place. Rauzer lacks individuality; he's too sensitive to external factors and gets too upset with losses, even the smallest things make him nervous. But his opening play reveals systemic, hard work.

Grigoriev: "Rauzer's style was completely uncharacteristic for a young master; he scored a record number of draws, earning the nickname "Soviet Tartakower" from the tournament spectators."

Botvinnik: "At the final stages of the championship, I overtook my main rival Nikolai Riumin by a half-point, but there were two more rounds ahead. And then I reminded Rauzer that he owed me one *(at the Odessa championship, he had asked Botvinnik to defeat his main competitor, A. Poliak)*.

"I can't play good chess... I have bad facial features (?!)" Rauzer suddenly announced.

At first, I was flabbergasted, but then decided to tell a white lie:

РАУЗЕР (слева)   БОТВИННИК (справа)

Rauzer (left) and Botvinnik (right)
After a chat with Botvinnik, Vsevolod Rauzer came to believe in himself and defeated Riumin! Cartoon by Y. Yuzepchuk (Shakhmaty v SSSR, No. 23–24, 1931).

"You know Alexei Alekhine from Kharkov, do you? Does he have good facial features?"

"Of course not..."

"Well, Alexei Alekhine is an Apollo in comparison with his brother Alexander, and Alexander sure can play good chess!"

Vsevolod Alfredovich played a very strong game against Riumin and won."

The remaining six players are those who lacked physical stamina and couldn't score the necessary 8.5 points. It's probably no accident that all three Tiflis players, who performed well in the preliminary round, were among those six. It was also painful to watch Sozin, who lost game after game with incredible blunders; he, of course, is capable of playing better than his poor results show. It's clear that not everyone was able to withstand the nervous pressure of 26 games. The lack of physical fitness adversely affected many players.

We think that the formula of the Soviet Premiership completely justified itself; it gave young players a chance to shine, attracted huge interest from chess fans, and the tournament was replete with great sporting content. The round reports were awaited eagerly, and each issue of *Izvestia* without new information about the tournament disappointed many readers.

> **Grigoriev:** "The periodicals were in no state to cover the tournament or the conference as a whole. So it seemed that publishing the *Bulletin* was a highly useful innovation, and it would have been so, if not for the awful distribution. You could only obtain the bulletin regularly in the tournament hall; the Moscow newspaper sellers got only some of the issues, and, judging by numerous letters, the bulletin never reached the provinces at all..."
>
> *I can only imagine the losses incurred by this "useful innovation".* **V. Eremeev** recalled: "During the tournament, 20 issues were printed, with a huge press run for the time – 10,000 copies of each issue." (From the book *The First Steps.*)

Still, we shouldn't look the other way when discussing the flaws of the system. The most glaring one was the excessive strain on the players' nervous system. Playing for 6–8 hours a day for a month straight, in a smoky room, surrounded by a dense and sometimes unruly crowd, is a difficult task that requires robust health. You shouldn't forget either that the players, upon returning home, cannot even rest – they immediately have to return to their college studies or jobs. So we think that next time, it would be more expedient to expand the preliminary groups, but reduce the size of the finals, holding a match tournament with 4–6 winners. Finally, we should think about participants and spectators, creating conditions that allow them to fully devote themselves to chess creativity.

> **Grigoriev:** "Even the huge halls of the House of the Unions were too cramped for such a massive event, and while the conditions were tolerable for participants, the service for spectators left much to be desired. However, after

the tournament was moved to the Polytechnic Museum, the conditions for participants worsened as well – cramped, stuffy and noisy. Who knows, maybe this was the main reason for a lot of blunders we saw at the tournament."

We must hope that the 8th All-Union Conference will be held in a venue worthy of both the size of the chess and checkers movement and the technical advancements of the first five-year plan, which will be completed by then." (*Shakhmaty v SSSR*, November 1931.)

The Cornucopia

You wouldn't believe it, but the publication of the tournament game collection of the 7th Soviet Championship did not make me happy at all. Earlier, when I leafed through magazines in search for surviving gems, I felt like a treasure hunter; now, though, my job looked more like a search engine, and the joy of findings was marred by the volume of the shoveled "ore". 153 games were played in the final alone; a further 90 games from the semi-finals were also included. There were no prizes for brilliancies or best games (attacks, combinations, endgames...), so the only inputs I could use for guidance were round reports. However, when I tried to extract the quintessence from all of that, I quickly became despondent, realizing that there were too many games worthy of description. And so, I ultimately had to choose the games according to my own taste.

Manuscripts Don't Burn

Let's start with a game that was not featured in any journals or the tournament book. Petr Izmailov, the finalist of the Odessa championship, was particularly "unlucky". Out of his nine games in the semi-final (+3–2=4), only one was published in the periodicals – a loss! The tournament book, edited by Botvinnik, was even more telling: it featured both losses by Izmailov – and nothing else...

Thankfully, one game was saved by Izmailov's son, who wrote an article called "Petr Izmailov's Calvary" for the *Shakhmaty v Rossii* magazine in 1999. The article ended with a beautiful victory against Botvinnik, after which the first Soviet world champion never said a good word about the 1928 Russian SFSR champion in his entire life. Mikhail Moiseevich didn't even know (or pretended not to know) who Izmailov was. "There was a forester in Siberia who went by that name," he said a year before his own death. But in actuality, Petr Nikolaevich was a true prodigy. A graduate of Tomsk University, he worked as a geophysical engineer and managed a prospector team. He spent six or seven months a year in the Siberian wilderness – and still managed to play excellent chess!

No. 50. Queen's Indian Defense E12
Izmailov – Botvinnik
Moscow 1931, semi-final group 4
Annotated by Y. Averbakh
1.d4 ♘f6 2.♘f3 b6 3.c4 ♗b7 4.♘c3 e6 5.♗g5 ♗e7 (5...♗b4 is more active) **6.♕c2 h6 7.♗xf6 ♗xf6 8.e4 d6 9.e5.** A dubious plan: opening up the position is good for black, who has the bishop pair.

According to the database, nobody else has tried that move, preferring 9.♖d1, 9.0-0-0 or 9.♗e2.
9...♗e7 10.♖d1 ♘d7 11.♗d3 ♕c8. 11...dxe5 12.dxe5 ♗xf3?! 13.gxf3 ♘xe5 14.♗e4 would be better for white.
12.♗e4 c6 13.♕e2 ♕c7. Intending to launch a kingside counterattack after 0-0-0.
14.0-0 dxe5 15.dxe5.

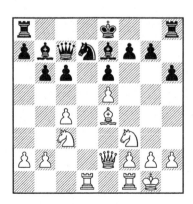

15...0-0-0. 15...g5 looked tempting, counting on 16.♖fe1 g4

17.♘d4 ♘xe5 18.♘db5 ♕b8!, but there was a stronger move for white: 16.♗c2 g4 17.♘d4 ♘xe5 18.♖fe1 ♗f6 (18...♘d7? 19.♘xe6!) 19.♘e4 ♗g7 (19...♗e7 20.♘g3!) 20.♘d6+!, and black is forced to play 20...♔f8 (20...♕xd6?! 21.♘f5 ♕f8 22.♕d2! with the idea ♖xe5 and ♕d7#; *if 22...♗f6, then, of course, not 23.♖xe5? ♖d8, but rather 23.♘d6+ ♔e7 24.♘xb7 ♕b8 25.♕b4+ c5 26.♘xc5!).*

16.♗c2 g5 17.♖fe1 g4 18.♘d4 ♖hg8 19.f4! Izmailov strengthens the e5 pawn, not fearing the opening of the g-file.
19...gxf3 20.♘xf3.

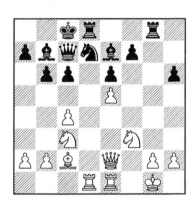

20...♗b4. This loses control over the dark squares. 20...♗a6!? was worthy of consideration.
21.♔h1 ♖g4 22.h3 ♖g3 23.♖d2 ♗xc3 24.bxc3 ♖dg8 25.♕e3 h5 26.a4. After 26.♕h6, black had a strong reply 26...♗a6!, for instance: 27.♕xh5 ♗xc4 28.♕xf7 ♗xa2.

But the last move is dangerous due to 29.♗h7! ♖f8 30.♕e7 ♗d5 31.♔h2, and black has to give up the exchange: 31...♖gxf3 32.gxf3, and after 32...♖xf3, there's a strong reply 33.c4! ♗xc4 34.♕e8+. So, the immediate 28...♗d5 was better.

26...♔b8.

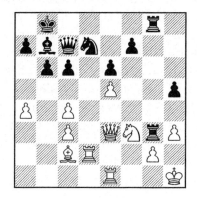

П. Измайлов, дружеский шарж из газеты "Советская Сибирь"

The scoresheet of Petr Izmailov's second win against Botvinnik (in the qualifying group) was preserved by his son and was first published in Shakhmaty v Rossii (No. 1–3, 1999). Cartoon of Izmailov from the Sovetskaya Sibir newspaper.

27.♖ed1!! A brilliant reply! After 27.♕h6, Botvinnik had prepared a combination: 27...c5! 28.♗e4 *(28. ♗h7 ♖xh3+!)* 28...♘xe5! 29.♗xb7 ♕xb7!, winning.

27...♘c5 28.a5! (getting rid of a weak pawn) **28...♕e7 29.axb6 axb6 30.♕f4 ♔c7 31.♔h2.** White threatens ♗h7.

31...♗a6? 31...h4 was necessary, protecting the rook on g3. *But what if white simply plays 32.♘xh4 ? Now 32...♖xc3 is met with the spectacular 33.♘f5! and ♘d6 (33...exf5? 34.e6+ ♔c8 35.exf7 ♕xf7 36.♗xf5+).*

However, since the computer shows that 31...♗a6 was indeed the strongest move, the mistake was made somewhere earlier. Perhaps when Botvinnik tried to prepare a trap for his opponent instead of equalizing with 26...c5.

32.♗h7!

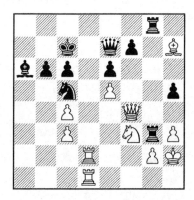

32...♖3g7. A sad necessity. After 32...♖8g7, there's a very unpleasant reply 33.♕f6! ♕xf6 (33...♕f8? 34.♖d8 ♖xg2+ 35.♔h1, winning) 34.exf6 ♖xh7 35.♔xg3

♘e4+ 36.♔h4! (but not 36.♔f4? ♘xd2 37.♖xd2 ♖h6 38.♔e5 h4! 39.♘g5 ♖h5 with a draw) 36...♘xd2 37.♖xd2 ♖h6 38.♘e5 ♖xf6 39.♖d7+ ♔b8 40.♖xf7 with a clear advantage.

But, objectively, this line gave black more practical chances. After the game move, black loses by force.

33.♗xg8 ♖xg8 34.♖d4 ♗c8 35.♕h6 ♘d7 36.♖f4 c5 37.♕xh5 (the rest is simple) **37...♖g7 38.♖g4 f5 39.♖xg7 ♕xg7 40.♖e1 ♗b7 41.♕g5 ♕h8 42.♕e7 ♕h6 43.♕d6+ ♔c8 44.♖d1 ♕f4+ 45.g3!** Black resigned: 45...♕xf3 46.♕xd7+ ♔b8 47.♕d8+ ♔a7 48.♖a1+ ♗a6 49.♕c7+ etc.

A Puzzle for the Computer

S. Vainstein: "Botvinnik seized the initiative against Sorokin in the Orthodox Defense and, gradually improving his position, reached the endgame, where the black pieces essentially got stalemated."

No. 51
Botvinnik – Sorokin
Moscow 1931, round 2

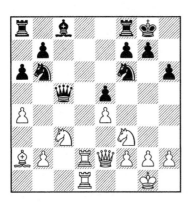

20.♕e3! "This non-obvious move is the strongest one. After the queen trade that can't be avoided (20...♕c7 21.♘xe5), black's positional weaknesses become much more pronounced," Botvinnik wrote in *Analytical and Critical Works*. He adds: "This was the subtlest positional move I'd ever made in my seven years of playing chess." Even Bogatyrchuk, always a harsh critic, praised this move in his article "Botvinnik's Creative Works" (*Shakhist*, 5th October 1936): "Botvinnik's move 20.♕e3!!, even back then, showed that he was a great master."

"Botvinnik is a fully-fledged chess fighter, an expert in opening theory and a great strategist in the middlegame and endgame."
(S. Vainstein)

Indeed... A computer can't come up with something like that even if you give it the whole night. Even Rybka cannot come up with anything better than 20.♖c2... (Well, I wrote that back in 2007. Now in 2020, after a few minutes' thought, Stockfish 9 finds Botvinnik's move and eventually treats these two moves as equally strong, at about +1.00.)

20...♕xe3 21.fxe3 ♗g4 22.a5 ♘c8 (the knight hurries to c6) **23.♖c1 ♗xf3.** After 23...♖e8, Botvinnik recommends 24.h3 ♗e6 (24...♗h5 25.♘h4!, threatening 26.g4) 25.♗xe6 ♖xe6 26.♖d8+, but instead of 24...♗e6?, it's better to play 24...♗xf3, going for the same line as in the game.

24.gxf3 ♘e7.

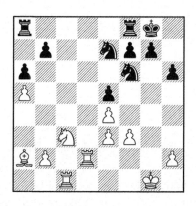

25.♘d5 ♘c6? That's the decisive mistake, not commented on by Botvinnik! Now the white rooks penetrate the seventh rank by force.

Botvinnik writes that "after 25...♘fxd5, white shouldn't play 26.exd5 ♘f5 27.e4 due to 27...♘d6,

and the knight blockades the d5 pawn, but rather 26.♗xd5 ♘xd5 27.♖xd5, after which material gains are guaranteed." However, after 27...♖ac8!, black creates some counterplay. 26.exd5 looks more precise at first: after 26...♘f5, instead of the timid 27.e4, white can play 27.d6!, not fearing 27...♘xe3 due to 28.♖e1 ♘f5 29.♖xe5. But black can play better, too – 26...♖ac8 27.♖c3 ♘f5!, for instance: 28.d6 ♖xc3 29.bxc3 ♖d8 or 28.♖dc2 ♖xc3 29.♖xc3 ♘d6! (and if 30.♖c7, then 30...♖c8).

26.♘xf6+ gxf6 27.♖d7 ♖ab8. Of course, not 27...♘xa5 due to 28.♖cc7.

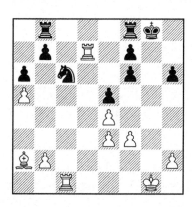

28.♔f2! The point! "White suddenly creates a threat on the other flank: 29.♖g1+ and ♗xf7. As consolation, black gets the a5 pawn." (Botvinnik)

28...♘xa5 29.♖cc7 ♖bc8 30.♖xf7 ♖xc7 31.♖xc7+ ♔h8 32.♗d5 b5!? The best chance (32...♖b8 33.♔g3! or 32...♘c6 33.♖xb7).

33.b3. 33.♖a7 ♘c4 34.b3 won more quickly, but, as Botvinnik wrote, "he was tempted by the idea of stalemating the knight."

33...♖d8 34.♔g3. There was an opportunity to win a pawn with 34.♖c1 ♖d7 35.♖a1 ♘b7 36.♖xa6, but white doesn't deviate from his main idea.

34...f5 35.♔h4 fxe4 36.fxe4 ♖d6 37.♔h5 ♖f6 38.h3 ♖d6.

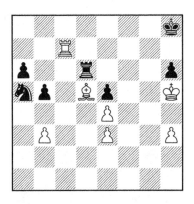

39.h4. A simple change in the move order led to winning the e5 pawn and a much quicker victory: 39.♔g4! ♖f6 40.h4, and black is in zugzwang! For instance: 40...♖f1 41.♖e7 ♖f6 (both 41...♖b1? 42.♔h5 and 41...♖g1+ 42.♔f5 ♖h1? 43.♔g6 lead to mate) 42.♖xe5, and 42...♘c6 is bad due to 43.♖e8+ ♔g7 44.e5!

39...♖b6 40.♔g4 ♖f6 41.♖a7 ♖b6 (41...♘c6? 42.♖xa6) **42.♖e7.** Again preventing the knight from escaping its cage.

42...♖d6 43.♖c7 ♖f6 44.♖a7 ♖b6 45.♖c7 ♖f6 46.♔h5 ♖d6.

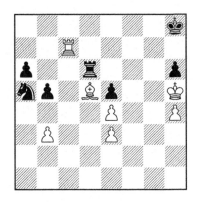

47.♗f7! A tactical nuance: if 47...♔g7, then 48.b4!, winning the knight!

47...♖f6 48.♗g6 ♘xb3 49.♔xh6 ♖f8. After 49...♔g8, Botvinnik showed the following line: 50.♔g5 ♖f8 (50...♖f1 51.♗f5) 51.♗f5 ♖e8 (51...♘d2 52.♗e6+ and ♔g6) 52.♔g6 ♘d2 53.♗d7 ♖b8 (53...♖d8 54.h5 ♘xe4 55.♗e6+ ♔f8 56.♗f7+ ♔e8 57.♗d7+ etc.) 54.♗e6+ ♔f8 55.♖f7+ ♔e8 56.♗d7+ ♔d8 57.♖f8+ etc.

50.♖h7+ ♔g8 51.♖g7+ ♔h8 52.♗f7 ♖xf7 (white threatened 53.♖h7#) **53.♖xf7 ♔g8 54.♔g6 ♘d2 55.♖d7.** Black resigned.

The Somersault of Death

Kan: "The second half of this game, where Riumin masterfully and inventively used all possible chances, is still engraved in the memory of the older generation of players."

No. 52
Sorokin – Riumin
Moscow 1931, round 3
Annotated by N. Riumin

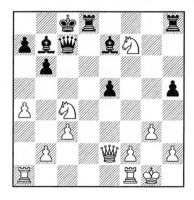

20...♛c6. A desperate attempt to create an attack, but black has either to attack or resign.

21.f3 ♝c5+ 22.♔g2 (22.♔h1 is dangerous due to 22...e4!) **22... h4 23.♞xd8 h3+ 24.♔h1 ♜xd8 25.b4.**

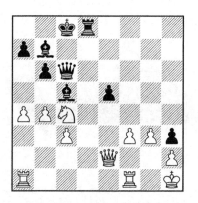

25...e4. *"Understanding that retreating the bishop is tantamount to resignation, black sacrifices another piece, ending up a rook down. The course of the game*

showed that this decision was right – at least in the psychological sense." (Kan)

26.bxc5 ♛xc5 27.♞d2. 27.fxe4! immediately ended all resistance.

27...exf3 28.♞xf3 ♜f8 29.♜f2. Starting from this moment, white made several weak moves in a row. Instead of the highly unnatural game move, it was worth considering 29.♜ae1, threatening to return the piece, but trade queens.

29...a5 30.♜d1 ♔b8. *30...♛xf2 31.♛xf2 ♜xf3 is hopeless because of 32.♔g1.*

31.♜e1 ♔a7. Black, unlike white, has used his time well and has managed to create a solidly defensive, and at the same time active position. Despite having a huge material advantage (rook and pawn), it's hard for white to find a good plan and convert it.

32.♛e3. White seems to be confused. The correct move was 32.♛f1!, with a sure win.

The game move doesn't spoil anything yet either.

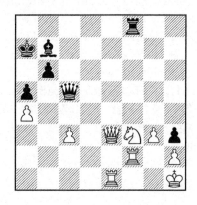

32...♖e8! 33.♕d2 (the only move; white can't play 33.♕xe8 due to 33...♕xf2) **33...♖d8! 34.♕e2 ♖d3.** Cramping white's position even more and threatening 35...♕xc3.

35.c4   ♕d4   36.♕f1   ♗c6! Countering the threat of ♖e7! Black cannot allow white to trade his bishop, the main resource of his attack.

37.♖e7+. The pawn march g3-g4-g5 won.

"Sorokin was probably unsettled by Riumin's inventive tactics." (Kan)

37...♔b8 38.♖e8+ ♔a7 39.♖e7+ ♔b8.

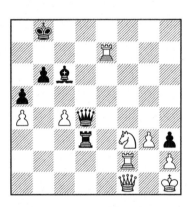

40.g4?? A huge blunder, probably caused by his inability to find a win.

40...♖xf3! 41.♖e8+. Not 41.♖xf3 ♗xf3+ 42.♕xf3 due to 42...♕a1+, with a mate in two.

41...♔a7 42.♖e7+ ♔a6 43.c5+ ♖d3+ 44.♔g1 ♕xg4+ 45.♔g2 ♕xg2+ 46.♕xg2 hxg2. White resigned.

"One of the most exciting games in the history of chess." (Kan)

The Game of His Life

Yudovich: "The 15th round, played on 9th November 1931, will always stay in my memory. Not only because I earned my master's norm that day. The leaders of the tournament played each other in this round. Such an incredible day! Soon after the game started, the doors of the packed hall closed, and hundreds of chess fans camped out at the entrance of the Polytechnic Museum, waiting impatiently for news from the chess battlefield.

Дружеский шарж   Рис. Ю. Ю.

М. М. Юдович

Mikhail Yudovich: "The 15th round, played on 9th November 1931, will always stay in my memory. Not only because I earned my master's norm that day. The leaders of the tournament played each other in this round. Such an incredible day!" Cartoon by Y. Yuzepchuk (64. Shakhmaty v Rabochem Klube, No. 23–24, 1931).

The day before the game, Riumin's friends, me included, advised him to play calmly, without taking risks. "You have black," N. Zubarev told him, "and it's Botvinnik who has to go for complications, because he's behind you in the tournament. Choose some solid opening system, go for simplifications..." But Riumin paid no heed to the recommendations. This just wasn't in his character. Kolya didn't like to wait and maneuver.

In the opening, Riumin went for highly risky complications and got under an attack, which was executed by Botvinnik with great power.

I regularly approached the table where the two great players sat. Botvinnik looked outwardly calm, but his worry was apparent in the deliberately slow piece movements on the board and frequent glances at the chess clock. Botvinnik was pale, he didn't get up from the table. I felt that he put everything he had into this game. He recorded the game very clearly and accurately.

The effusive Riumin's cheeks were feverishly red. Nervous arm movements, quick and therefore messy recording of the moves. He would get up frequently after making a move and walk about the stage.

I rooted for Kolya, almost lost my own game because of that, and I first saw Nikolai Vasilyevich Krylenko looking anxious after coming to watch the games. Riumin was his favorite..."

No 53. Semi-Slav Defense D30
Botvinnik – Riumin
Moscow 1931, round 15
1.d4 d5 2.c4 c6 3.♘f3 ♘f6 4.e3 e6 5.♗d3 ♘bd7 6.0-0 ♗d6. "It was necessary to play 6...dxc4! 7.♗xc4 ♗d6, and white can't stop black from playing the freeing move e6-e5, like, for instance, in game 23 of the first Alekhine – Bogoljubov match," Botvinnik wrote in the book *Selected Games 1926–1946* (1951).

7.♘bd2 e5. I'll quote the methodically important commentary from that book, which Mikhail Moiseevich omitted from *Analytical and Critical Works* (1984) – maybe because in the 1980s this line, with various move orders but still leading to the same position after move 10, had returned to tournament use:

"We can't believe that black didn't know the conclusions of theory, which rejected this dubious move; it's clear that opening up the position is more beneficial for white. We can say for sure that by playing for a win in this game, black consciously went for complications. But he made a two-pronged mistake. First of all, when you face an opponent who knows opening theory well, you should not go for suboptimal lines. Secondly, if you go for complications, they should not entail the risk of immediately losing the game. In this regard, Alekhine's games are very instructive – he would masterfully find a way to complicate the game at exactly the right moment."

8.e4! 0-0. It's easy to see that any pawn capture is beneficial for white (8...exd4? even loses a piece: 9.e5 ♘xe5 10.♖e1).

9.cxd5 cxd5 10.exd5 exd4. 10...♘xd5? 11.♘c4! (11...♕c7 12.dxe5 ♘xe5 13.♘cxe5 ♗xe5 14.♗xh7+ led to a pawn loss).

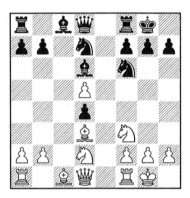

"As a result, a complicated and completely symmetrical position occurred – a rare combination. The d-file is totally cluttered with pieces. As often happens in such open positions, the right move is very important." (Here and further, Botvinnik's notes without a source are from the 1984 book.)

11.♘e4 ♘xe4. Understanding that further symmetry is dangerous (11...♘e5 12.♗g5, and the knight pin is very unpleasant), Riumin decides to sacrifice a pawn for the initiative. The computer agrees!

12.♗xe4 ♘c5. Botvinnik recommended 12...♘f6!, "getting the bishop pair as compensation for the pawn." However, Riumin probably expected me now to play

the exchange line 13.♕xd4 ♘xe4 14.♕xe4 ♖e8, overlooking the fact that there is no longer a bishop tied to defending the d5 pawn.

13.♗c2! ♗g4. At the cost of giving up the bishop pair, black breaks up the white king's pawn cover.

14.♕xd4 ♗xf3 15.gxf3.

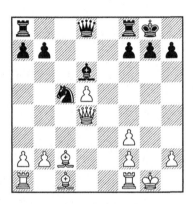

15...♖e8. "A great move!" Botvinnik exclaims in the 1951 book. It's not easy to repel the "cunning threat" 16...♗e5 (17.♕xc5 ♖c8 or 17...♕h4 18.f4 ♕g4+), but white rises to the challenge.

16.♖d1! ♖e2. "This move is seemingly bad, but it contains a subtle trap. For instance, the natural 17.♗d3 is met with 17...♘xd3 18.♕xd3 ♕h4!, winning (19.♕xe2 ♕xh2+ and ♕h1#!). In reply, white finds a great light-squared bishop maneuver to protect the kingside." (Panov)

17.♗f5 g6 18.♗h3 ♘d7. In 1951, Botvinnik awarded this move an exclamation mark, adding, "Black is maneuvering masterfully."

For instance, 18...♛c7 was bad because of 19.♗e3! ♖e8 (19...♗xh2+? 20.♔f1) 20.♖ac1 ♖8xe3 (necessary, to avoid the worst) 21.fxe3 ♛e7 22.♔f1 ♖xh2 23.♗g2 etc.

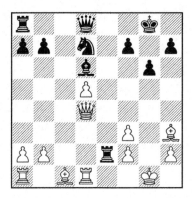

19.♗e3! An inventive attempt to quench his opponent's activity in exchange for a pawn.

19...♗e5   20.♛c4.   20.♛e4! was more aggressive, indirectly protecting the b-pawn (20...♖xb2? 21.♗xd7 or 20...♗xb2? 21.♖ab1 ♗g7 (or else ♛d3) 22.d6!).

20...♖xb2 21.♖ac1. Botvinnik writes that 21.d6! gave "a decisive advantage for white: 21...♖c8 22.♛e4 ♗f6 (22...♗g7 23.♛e7) 23.♛g4! or 21...♘b6 22.♛e4 ♗xd6 23.♛d4!", overlooking the more resilient defense 22...♖b5! in both lines. After 21...♘b6 (best) 22.♛e4 ♖b5! with the idea f7-f5, white would have

The decisive game of the tournament: Botvinnik – Riumin. A unique moment of full symmetry on the board after 10 moves. But white spent 12 more minutes on his moves. S. Vainstein, M. Volkovyssky and N. Zubarev are watching the game. (64. Shakhmaty i Shashki v Massy, No. 2, 1932.)

needed to carry out a lot of work to convert his positional advantage into a full point.

21...♘b6 22.♕e4 ♕d6. The wrong piece: 22...♗d6! would have punished white for his inaccuracy on move 21. And the queen, as we know, is a bad blockading piece.

23.f4 ♗g7 (23...♗f6 24.♗c5 ♕d8 25.d6 is not much better) **24.♗c5 ♕d8 25.♗e7 ♕e8 26.d6 ♕b5.**

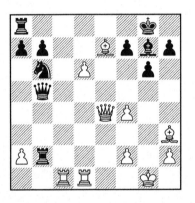

The outcome of this fight is unfortunate for black: the passed pawn will cost him a full piece. But in time trouble (as a reminder, the time control was 2 hours per 30 moves), Riumin continued to struggle in a futile hope for a miracle...

27.d7 ♘xd7 28.♗xd7 ♕b6 29.♕e3 ♕xe3 30.fxe3 ♖xa2 31.♗c8 h5 32.♖d8+ ♔h7. Black resigned.

"Nikolai Riumin was a great master of complicated, double-edged structures. He was without doubt one of the strongest players of the new generation of masters. He loved chess with a passion and

had a friendly personality. After our fierce tournament struggle ended, he kissed me on the cheek at the closing ceremony." (Botvinnik)

The Warning Bell

At first sight, it was the Botvinnik game that started Riumin's downfall: he lost his last two games as well! Had everything gone well, the Moscow player would have been two points ahead before his game against his main rival, which could have made him more sure of himself and, what's more important, not prompted him to go for complicated lines...

No. 54
Riumin – Yudovich
Moscow 1931, round 14
Annotated by M. Yudovich

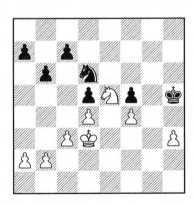

After a sharp struggle, this position had arisen, which was quite unpleasant for me.

White is a pawn up and, naturally, has realistic winning chances. He

should have played 44.♘c6, for
instance: 44...♔h4 45.♘e7! ♔xh3
46.♘xd5 ♔g3 47.♘xc7 ♔xf4 48.c4,
and black will suffer.

But Riumin didn't have enough
time to think this through, so he
quickly played **44.c4?**, and that
suddenly changed the course of the
game. After **44...dxc4+ 45.♘xc4
♔h4!** white himself offered a draw,
because of 46.♘xd6 cxd6 47.♔c4
♔g3! 48.♔d5 ♔xf4 49.♔xd6 ♔g3,
and the pawns promote at the same
time.

Yudovich (left) – Riumin (right)
*After losing to the leader, Riumin lost two
more games in a row. But perhaps it all
started a day earlier, when Botvinnik, pushed
to the edge of the abyss by Rauzer, managed
to survive and even win, while Riumin failed
to defeat Yudovich. Cartoon by Y. Yuzepchuk
(Shakhmaty v SSSR, No. 21–22, 1931).*

*Writing about that tournament
in the* Central Chess Club Bulletin
*(No. 13, 1983), Mikhail Mikhailovich
recalled two other fascinating
endgames.*

Study Embryos

Yudovich: "Leonid Kubbel, who
played in the championship semi-
final, told me that he was planning
to use the ideas from this endgame to
compose a new study.

No. 55
Lisitsin – Yudovich
Moscow 1931, round 16
Annotated by M. Yudovich

Black's only chance is to create
threats to the c4 pawn. 67...♘d4
68.f6 is bad: black is forced to let the
white king occupy the f5 square.

67...♘a3!   68.♘b2   *White
immediately won with 68.♘e5!
♘c2 69.f6 or 68...♔e7 69.♔d3♔f6
70.♘xc6 ♔xf5 71.♘xa5 etc.*

68...♘b1! An unusual raid
behind enemy lines. 68...♘c2 69.♔f4

♘d4 lost to 70.♔g5. Now, however, black can meet 69.♔f4 with 69...♘c3, and if 70.♔g5, then 70...♘e4+! 71.♔g6 ♔e5.

69.♔d3. "White, losing hope of making his passed pawn useful, is now trying to trap the wayward black knight." (Lisitsin)

69...♔e5 70.♘d1. "It's no better to play 70.♔c2 ♘a3+ 71.♔b3 ♘b1 72.♘d3+ ♔xf5 73.♘xc5 ♔e5 74.♘b7 (if 74.♔c2, then 74...♔d4!) 74...♘d2+ 75.♔c3 ♘e4+ 76.♔d3 ♘f2+ 77.♔c2 ♘e4 78.♘xa5 ♘c5 with a draw." (Lisitsin)

Georgy Lisitsin earned his master's title when he drew against Botvinnik in the last round after... offering a draw beforehand! Cartoon by Y. Yuzepchuk (64. Shakhmaty i Shashki v Massy, No. 12, 1932.)

70...♔xf5.

This position attracted the attention of all players, and later, that of many endgame study composers as well. Can white win? Here's what G. Lisitsin wrote in the tournament book:

"A promising position for white, however, there's no clear way to win. The game move (71.♘f2) is refuted very easily. The strongest move was 71.♘e3+!, which after 71...♔e5! could lead to very interesting lines: 72.♘c2 ♔d6! 73.♘a1 ♔c7! 74.♘b3 ♔b6 75.♔c2 ♘a3+ 76.♔c3, and black is saved by 76...♘b5+!, trading both white pawns, or 72.♘f1 ♔f4! 73.♔c2 ♔e4 74.♔xb1 ♔d3! 75.♔b2 ♔xc4 76.♔a3 ♔d3, and white can't win because of his a4 pawn's weakness and bad knight."

The computer shows that 71...♔e5? loses due to 72.♘g4+! ♔f5 73.♘f2 ♘a3 74.♘h3 ♘b1 75.♘g1 and 76.♘e2 followed by ♘g3-e4 or ♘c1-b3. But black could have saved a draw with 71...♔e6 or 71...♔f4.

Therefore, 71.♘e3+? misses the win, whereas the move actually played 71.♘f2! should have won.

71.♘f2 ♘a3! 72.♘e4 *White would have won with the study-like 72.♘h3! with the same idea of ♘g1-e2, and then ♘g3-e4 or ♘c1-b3.*

72...♘xc4 73.♘g3+ ♔g4 74.♔xc4 ♔xg3 75.♔xc5 ♔f4 76.♔xc6 ♔e5 77.♔b6 ♔d6. Draw.

The renowned study composer also got very interested in the following endgame.

No. 56
Goglidze – Budo
Moscow 1931, round 12
Annotated by M. Yudovich

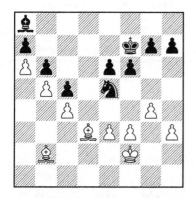

White played **29.♗e2** and won after a long struggle. Vyacheslav Ragozin showed a paradoxical way to victory, which was fully approved by L. Kubbel:

29.♗xe5! fxe5 30.♗xh7! g6 31.h4 ♔g7 32.♗xg6 ♔xg6 33.e4. Black has an extra piece, but the "hermit bishop" on a8 looks pitiful.

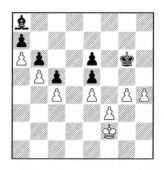

33...♔f6 34.h5 ♔g5 35.♔g3 ♔f6 36.♔h4 ♔g7 37.g5 ♗d5 (the only counter chance; otherwise, the g- and h-pawns will promote) 38.exd5 exd5 39.cxd5 c4 40.d6 c3 41.d7 c2 42.d8♕ c1♕ 43.h6+ ♔f7 44.♕f6+ ♔e8 45.♕c6+ ♕xc6 46.bxc6, winning."

The Poisoned Pawn

S. Vainstein: "Bogatyrchuk elegantly outplayed Goglidze in the Reti Opening; white, masterfully exploiting the weakness of the b6 and d6 squares, gained a decisive advantage and created a mating net for the opponent's king."

No. 57
Bogatyrchuk – Goglidze
Moscow 1931, round 2
Annotated by F. Bogatyrchuk

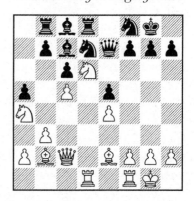

19.♘f5 ♛e8. Of course, not 19...
♛g5 due to 20.f4, winning the queen
(20...exf4 21.h4; 20...♛f6 *is equally*
bad: 21.♘b6 ♛e6 22.♘d5! cxd5
23.exd5 ♛e8 24.d6 etc.).

20.f4 ♘g6 21.♘d6! Forcing the
trade of the dark-squared bishop,
because if the queen moves away, f4-
f5 completely paralyzes black.

21...♗xd6 22.♖xd6!

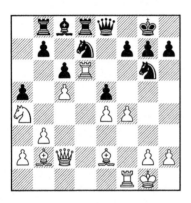

This sudden pawn sacrifice is
the point of white's maneuver that
started on move 19. Black can't
play 22...♘xf4, because this is met
with 23.♖fd1! with horrible threats
♘b6 and ♗g4. For instance: 23...
♘e6 24.♗g4 ♘ef8 25.♘b6 with
black stalemated. Any white move is
winning.

However, after 24...♘f6!, the
computer does not despair, thinking
that black has enough defensive
resources after both 25.♗xe6 ♗xe6
26.♗xe5 ♖xd6 27.♗xd6 ♖d8 and
25.♖xd8 ♘xd8 26.♗xc8 ♖xc8
27.♘b6 ♖c7. Still, such an inventive
tactician as Bogatyrchuk would have
probably come up with something...

Шарж Дани.

Мастер Ф. П. Богатырчук.

"In this tournament, however, Bogatyrchuk's
style wasn't similar to his style of 1927: there
were no combinational ideas, examples of
creative imagination, or brilliancies." (S.
Vainstein.) Cartoon by Dani (Vechernaya
Moskva, 9th September 1933.)

22...b5. Perhaps this was the best
chance for black, but even that was
not enough.

**23.cxb6 ♘xb6 24.♖xd8 ♛xd8
25.♖d1.** *Depriving the bold pawn*
of its deserved laurels: 25.f5! ♘xa4
26.fxg6! ♛b6+ 27.♔h1 ♘xb2 (27...
hxg6? 28.♗xe5) 28.gxf7+ ♔f8
29.♛xb2.

25...♛e7. 25...♛c7 26.♘xb6
♛xb6+ 27.♔h1 lost as well: black
can't capture on f4, either with
the knight (27...♘xf4 28.♗xe5) or

with the pawn (27...exf4 28.♕c3 f6 29.♕c4+ ♔h8 30.♕xc6 ♗e6 31.♕xb6 ♖xb6 32.♖d8+ ♗g8 33.♗c4 ♘e7 34.♗a3 etc.).

26.♘xb6 ♖xb6 27.f5 ♘f4. 27...♘f8 was even weaker due to 28.♕c3, winning an important pawn.

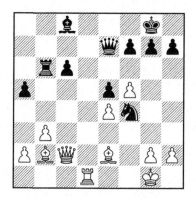

28.♗f1. White could play 28.♗xe5 ♘xe2+ 29.♕xe2 f6 30.♕c4+ ♔h8 31.♗d6, and the black queen has no good squares – black loses at least an exchange, no matter where the queen retreats to.

28...h6 29.g3 ♘h5 30.♕d2 ♕c5+ 31.♕f2. Forcing a trade that's beneficial for white.

31...♕xf2+ 32.♔xf2 ♗b7 33.♖d8+ ♔h7 34.♗c4. Wins immediately, because black can only avoid mate at the cost of at least two pawns.

34...♘f6 35.♗xf7. Black resigned.

Despite the substantial obstacles in the form of numerous tactical subtleties, white logically executed his plan.

We aren't Pawn-Pushers Here!

Panov: "Alatortsev – the master of the classical positional Rubinstein-like style – was renowned for his deep, solid play in closed openings." In this game, he spectacularly destroyed his opponent who snatched the a2 pawn in the Slav.

No. 58
Alatortsev – Zamikhovsky
Moscow 1931, round 5
Annotated by V. Alatortsev

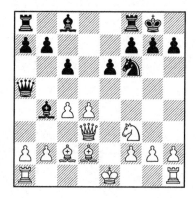

Black is trying to save the game with simplifications, not expecting the blow that awaits him.

13.0-0-0! ♗xd2+ 14.♖xd2 b5. Opening the center with c6-c5 was only good for white because of his advantage in the center and better development. 14...♗d7 was probably best, to play ♖fd8 and then protect g6 with ♗e8.

15.c5 ♕xa2? Now the game is forced. Black should still have played 15...♗d7 and ♖fd8.

But after 16.♘e5 ♖fd8 17.g4! h6

(17...g6? 18.♕f3) 18.h4 white has a strong attack.

16.♘e5 g6. Preventing the threat ♘g4. 16...♖e8 was somewhat better.

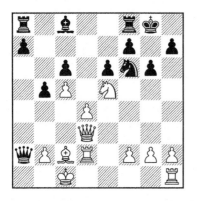

В. А. Алаторцев

Vladimir Alatortsev shared 3rd–6th place in his first ever Soviet Championship, immediately taking his place among the chess elite. Cartoon by Y. Yuzepchuk (64. Shakhmaty i Shashki v Massy, No. 4, 1932.)

17.h4! There's no sense for white to regain the pawn with 17.♘xc6. He goes for mate.

Curiously, the "bone" on c6 didn't even tempt the ever-hungry Fritz – it also goes for mate in this position!

17...♘d5. Threatening ♘b4, taking the bishop.

The computer recommends 17... ♕a1+ 18.♗b1 a5 with counter threats against the king.

18.♗b1 ♕a4! In a hopeless position, black finds a practical chance, counting on the natural 19.h5? ♘b4 20.♕h3, and now not 20...♘a2+? 21.♗xa2 ♕xa2 22.hxg6 ♕a1+ 23.♔c2 ♕a4+ 24.♔b1, and black is out of checks, but rather 20...g5! and then f7-f6 with good defensive prospects.

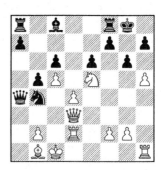

However, white has the more precise 20.♕e4! (targeting h7), and after 20...♘a2+ 21.♗xa2 ♕xa2 22.♕h4! or 20...f5 21.♕h4 ♕a1 22.♖c2!, there are no "good defensive prospects" in sight.

19.♕g3! ♕a5 20.h5 ♕c7 21.♖d3. Now white threatens 22.♖f3 and then 23.hxg6 fxg6 24.♗xg6 hxg6 25.♕xg6+ ♕g7 26.♖g3, winning.

21...♞e7. This allows a pretty ending.

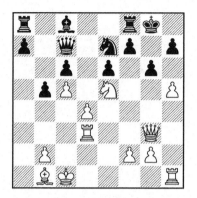

22.hxg6 fxg6 23.♞xg6 ♛xg3 24.♞xe7+ ♚f7 25.♖xh7+! ♛g7 26.♖f3+ ♚xe7 27.♖xg7+. Black resigned.

The Ilyin-Zhenevsky Variation

A. Kubbel: "Excellent play by Ilyin-Zhenevsky throughout the game." A meticulous reader may notice that Botvinnik ended his annotations in the tournament book with the same phrase. I'll say more: he used other annotations by A. Kubbel from *Shakhmaty v SSSR* verbatim as well. The explanation can be found in the line under the list of commentators: "For some games, annotations published in the chess press were partially used."

No. 59. Ruy Lopez C90
Ilyin-Zhenevsky – Botvinnik
Moscow 1931, round 1
1.e4 e5 2.♞f3 ♞c6 3.♗b5 a6 4.♗a4 ♞f6 5.0-0 ♗e7 6.♖e1 b5

7.♗b3 d6 8.c3 0-0 9.d3. "Zhenevsky's patented move. White usually plays 9.h3 with the subsequent d2-d4. However, Zhenevsky had been playing this modest line for many years, mostly getting good results.

Zhenevsky's plan is very inventive. Since white intends to attack the kingside with the well-known system ♞bd2-f1, h2-h3, g2-g4, ♞g3-f5, ♚h1 etc., black, of course, should go for the central counterattack with d6-d5. In this case, white trades on d5 and attacks the weak e5 pawn. The central d3 pawn, like the d6 pawn in the Sicilian, is not weak at all. White eventually finds the right moment to play d3-d4, opening the diagonal for the bishop on c2 and launching a kingside attack." (Botvinnik)

9...♞a5 10.♗c2 c5 11.♞bd2 ♞c6. "Intending to play d6-d5 as soon as possible. This plan is correct in and of itself, but it needs adequate preparation." (A. Kubbel)

12.♛e2 ♖e8 13.♞f1 d5.

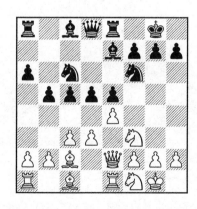

14.exd5. Continuing a five year-old dispute. In the 1926 Leningrad championship, Ilyin-Zhenevsky after 14.a4 ♗e6 (14...♖b8 15.axb5 axb5 16.♘g3 ♗f8 17.♗b3 h6 18.exd5 ♘xd5 19.♕e4 ♗e6 20.♗d2 ♘f6 21.♕xc6! ♗xb3 22.♘e4 ♗d5 23.♕a6 ♗b7 24.♕a7 ♕xd3 25.♘xe5! with equality, Ilyin-Zhenevsky – Rubinstein, Moscow 1925) couldn't outplay the young Botvinnik: 15.d4 cxd4 16.axb5 axb5 17.♖xa8 ♕xa8 18.♕xb5 ♖b8 19.♕e2 dxe4 20.♗xe4 ♘xe4 21.♕xe4 dxc3 22.bxc3 f5! 23.♕e2 e4 24.♘g5 ♗xg5 25.♗xg5 ♕a3 26.f3 ♖b2 27.♗d2 ♕a2 (27...♕c5+! 28.♕e3 ♕xe3+ 29.♖xe3 ♗c4 with an advantage).

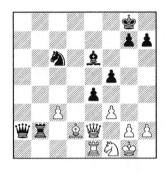

28.fxe4! f4 29.♕d3 ♗c4 30.♕d6 ♗xf1 31.♕xc6 ♗b5 32.♕c8+ ♔f7 33.♕f5+ ♔g8 34.♕c8+ ♔f7 35.♕f5+ ♔g8 36.♕c8+ ♔f7 37.♕c7+! ♔g8 (37...♔e6 38.♗xf4 ♖xg2+ 39.♔h1 ♖g6 40.♗g3 is better for white) 38.♕b8+ ♔f7 39.♕xf4+ ♔g8 40.♕b8+ ♔f7 41.♕c7+ ♔g8.

Alexander Ilyin-Zhenevsky's inspired play against Botvinnik possibly had a psychological subtext. Cartoon by N. Radlov, from his archive. First published in the book 1932 Leningrad Championship.

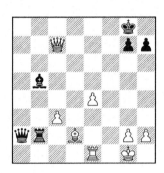

42.c4! ♕xc4 (both 42...♗xc4 43.♕d8+ ♔f7 44.♕d7+ ♔f8 45.♗b4+ ♖xb4 46.♕d6+ and 42...♖xd2 43.♕c8+ ♔f7 44.♕f5+ ♔e7 45.♕g5+ are bad) 43.♕b8+ ♔f7 44.♕f4+ ♔g8 45.h3 h6 46.♖a1 ♗c6 47.♖f1 ♕xe4 48.♕xe4 ♗xe4 49.♖f2 – draw!

14...♘xd5 15.♗d2. The line 15.♘xe5 ♗d6 16.d4 (not 16.♘xc6? ♖xe2 17.♖xe2 ♕c7! Botvinnik) 16...♘xe5 17.dxe5 ♖xe5 18.♘e3 is better for black.

15...♗f8 16.♘g3. After 16.d4, Botvinnik recommended 16...♗g4 17.♕d3 g6!, threatening ♗f5, "and the position opens up in black's favor," but there's a stronger move: 17.h3! ♗xf3 18.♕xf3, with the idea 18...cxd4 19.♗b3 – black's position is under major threat on light squares.

16...♗b7. Botvinnik criticized this move, which "unnecessarily exposes the f5 square" (moreover, he thought that it was "the move that lost the game for black"), and recommended 16...♘f6! However, Rybka insists on 16...♗b7. Who is right? Perhaps Botvinnik's opinion was influenced by the fact that white landed the decisive blow on the f5 square...

17.a4. The immediate 17.♘g5 was more active.

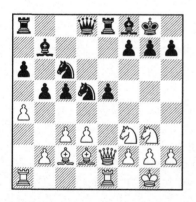

17...b4. "Black had a chance to at least equalize the game with 17...♘f4!" (Botvinnik). However, even the game move doesn't spoil anything yet...

18.♘g5! h6. "Almost forced, because of the threat ♕h5. 18...g6 was bad: 19.♕f3 ♕d7 20.♘3e4 and ♗b3"

(A. Kubbel). While against 18...f6, Botvinnik recommended 19.♘xh7! ♔xh7 20.♕h5+ and d3-d4.

19.♘5e4 g6? "A weak move, exposing black's kingside too much. 19...♘a5 was relatively better, even though white's positional advantage was still obvious." (A. Kubbel)

20.♕f3.

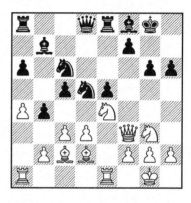

20...f5? "The second weak move, basically provoking a sacrifice on f5, after which white creates an unstoppable attack on the exposed black king. Even here, 20...♘a5 gave better black chances to defend. There was also an interesting line after 20...♖e6 21.♗xh6! ♗xh6 22.♘xc5 ♖e7 23.♗b3!, and white regains the piece, ending two pawns up" (A. Kubbel). The computer's defense gave black even better chances: 22...bxc3! 23.♘xe6 (23.♘xb7? ♕c7) 23...fxe6 24.bxc3 ♘xc3 with incredible complications.

What was Botvinnik thinking when he allowed the knight sacrifice? It turns out that he underestimated it, thinking that "white intended to play

21.♗b3. But that would be met with 21...♘a5 22.♗xd5+ ♗xd5 23.♘f6+ ♕xf6 24.♕xd5+ ♕e6!, and black's game is positionally even won."

21.♘xf5! gxf5 22.♕xf5.

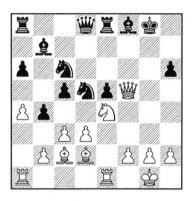

22...♗g7. "Both here and subsequently, black defends with only moves." (A. Kubbel). However, the computer insists on 22...♔h8!? – it looks like the king is walking straight into a mating net, but after 23.d4 ♕c7! 24.♘xc5 ♗xc5 25.dxc5 ♕g7 there's no obvious win.

23.♘xc5 ♗c8 24.♕g6 ♘ce7 25.♕h5 ♘f5 26.d4 ♖f8 27.dxe5. White has four pawns for the piece, and the attack is still growing.

27...bxc3 28.bxc3 ♕e7. The queen trade didn't save the game, but it was better to play 28...♕c7!?, not taking the square away from the knight (29.e6 ♘de7).

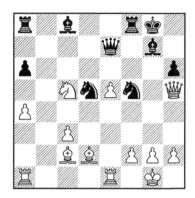

29.e6! "The attack plays itself; black is defenseless." (A. Kubbel)

29...♕xc5 30.♗xf5 ♕e7 (30... ♘e7? 31.♗h7+) **31.♗xh6 ♖xf5 32.♕xf5 ♗xh6 33.♕xd5 ♗b7 34.♕d7 ♗g5.** The queen trade lost a piece: 34...♕xd7 35.exd7 ♔f7 36.♖ab1! (36...♗c6 37.♖b6 or 36... ♗d5 37.♖bd1).

35.♖ab1! ♗c8? (a blunder, but the game couldn't be saved anyway) **36.♕c6.** Black resigned.

White's inspired play may have had a psychological subtext. Remember that story about "a youngster" insisting on adherence to regulations at the Odessa championship, which barred Ilyin-Zhenevsky from playing in the semi-final? I think that the name "Revenge for Odessa" might be very fitting for this game.

A Mirror for the People's Commissar

8th Soviet Championship: Leningrad, 16th August – 9th September 1933

> "Like in a mirror of the horrible night,
> The man is so mad, he doesn't want
> To recognize himself..."
> Anna Akhmatova, *Poem Without a Hero*

Bad examples seem to be truly contagious. As soon as Hitler came to power in January 1933, German chess quickly started to turn into a military-like structure with metal sheen, similarly to Soviet chess. However, Krylenko and his associates, for some reason, didn't have any words of support for that – like, "Great, this is the way, comrades!" No, there was a tidal wave of condemnation on the pages of *Shakhmaty v SSSR* and *64*. Maybe they recognized themselves in the mirror and were horrified by the similarities?

"Irreplaceable leader of the Soviet chess organization, People's Commissar for Justice of the USSR Nikolai Vasilyevich Krylenko." Photo from a unique issue of Shakhmaty v SSSR (No. 10, 1937) – its press run was almost entirely destroyed (we discuss this event later). From M. Sokolov's archive.

Or, on the contrary, they forgot the things they themselves said at the 3rd All-Union Chess Conference (1924) when they started building their power structure? Let's compare them.

"The fascistization of German chess organizations is happening very quickly and exposes the ugliness of all the "charms" of the Hitler regime." Well, Comrade Levman (Krylenko's closest associate) declared in his report at that conference that "the Moscow Chess Section was the first one to step on the path of proletarianization of chess" – yet nothing had changed, the knight continued to make its L-shaped moves, as before.

"Chess was declared a specific weapon of politics." Well, Krylenko said openly in his throne speech that he "considered the chess art a political weapon", and then coined the slogan "Chess is a weapon of politics". And reinforced it in the preface to the book *Flohr – Botvinnik Match* (1934): "Our slogan is, Chess is a weapon of culture, and thus chess is a weapon of politics. Organized chess players cannot be apolitical."

"Under pressure from the National Socialists, all chess communities and unions in Germany have been merged into a single All-German Chess Union." They could just find an old issue of *64* and read the same report by Levman: "No independent chess unions should exist." The All-Russian Chess Union was all but destroyed – with similar pressure from the Bolsheviks.

The chairman of the All-German Chess Union, Josef Goebbels. Photo from the unique tournament book Erster Kongress des Grossdeutschen Schachbundes in Pyrmont 1933 (Berlin 1933), kept in Y. Averbakh's library.

"The events in Germany serve as a great lesson in politics for those who think that chess cannot be used as a weapon of class struggle." This may have been no surprise to Russians after nine years of "proletarianization of chess."

"Jews are not permitted to take part in organizational work and tournaments." The race-based fascism of one country and class-based fascism of the other country both delivered disasters. The Nazis wiped out Jewish populations and Gypsies, while in the country of the Soviets whole strata of society – noblemen, clergy, merchants, intelligentsia, peasants – were just destroyed or sent to the North to live in inhuman conditions. And concerning the chess comrades sent to "concentration camps or prisons of fascist Germany" – let me remind you that concentration camps were in use in our country from 1918, back when Krylenko was the chairman of the Highest Revolutionary Tribunal, and only grew after that...

"Propaganda minister Goebbels was elected honorary chairman of the All-German Chess Union." A real case of the pot calling the kettle black... Goebbels headed the propaganda department and he was the "honorary" chairman. Meanwhile the chairman of Soviet chess was the people's commissar for justice. By a strange coincidence, in January

1933, "for work in exposing sabotage and other counter-revolutionary organizations", he was awarded the Order of Lenin. And a month later, "for exceptional accomplishments in the struggle against the enemies of the Soviet socialist fatherland", he also received the Order of the Red Banner. It seems that Comrade Krylenko worked like Stakhanov outside chess: Stalin rarely rewarded his subordinates with two orders in two months.

Finding Bricks with Ilyich's Method

Bogatyrchuk: "In 1930, their grip on power was so firm that the Bolsheviks finally decided to enslave the peasants – the only class that had been more or less spared from the Bolshevist experiments so far.

There's much said in literature about what happened in the villages during collectivization, and I'm not going to quote any of it here. I will only tell you about the things I saw with my own eyes and heard with my own ears in Kiev and other cities I visited. The state took the bread away from peasants, paying a laughable sum for it. These unfortunate people then had to try and buy it in neighboring cities. But they were in for bitter disappointment: they could buy the bread that was confiscated from them in state shops, but for much higher prices than those which were paid to them. In Kiev, I often saw entire families of destitute people, walking about the streets in futile search for cheap bread. The parents carried the exhausted children on their backs, and the kids who could walk by themselves held out their hands to passers-by, begging for at least a crust of bread.

> **Botvinnik:** "Together with my older comrade Y. G. Rokhlin, we got ready for travel – to Teberda in the Caucasus. We needed to rest and prepare for the 8th Soviet Championship.
>
> Times were hard. The collective farms hadn't consolidated yet, so the food situation was bad *(well, the food situation was hardly decent after the collective farms consolidated)*. There were rumors about a typhus epidemic. My mother didn't want to let me go. However, my cheerful companion managed to convince her: "There's a great insect repellent – naphthalene... We'll 'disinfect' all the passengers."
>
> Rokhlin kept his word. I was dying from laughter when he poured naphthalene all over himself and me, and, while talking with our compartment neighbors, poured some naphthalene into their pockets as well – and then, how sincere was his disgust at bad smells in the train, about which he agreed with other passengers!..

> The road to Nevinnomyssk was pretty uneventful. In the night, we were waiting for the connecting train to Batalpashinsk. We couldn't sleep – kids, blackened and emaciated from hunger, were begging for food: Kuban was suffering from famine. Our exhilaration ended immediately, we couldn't look each other in the eye." (From the book *The Aim Achieved*.)

It's hard to imagine a more blatant injustice than being unable to buy your own bread because the state sells it to you at exorbitant prices. If a private seller dared to sell bread in that manner, he would be immediately arrested and tried for price gouging, facing harsh punishment. However, the state could do anything it wanted.

Once, an emaciated old peasant died with a loaf of bread in his hands, which he held tightly to his chest, probably to save the bread for the children. He'd lain for the whole night on a hillock near my apartment, and nobody dared to take away this precious bread he didn't need anymore. Only in the morning did an ambulance come and take the poor man with his bread away to the morgue. And this all happened in our fertile Ukraine, which was considered "the granary of Europe" not so long ago!

> The famine, known as Holodomor, which killed millions in Ukraine, was a direct consequence of the collectivization and destruction of strong peasant farmsteads – their owners were deported together with their families. The first wave of "dekulakization" happened in winter 1929/30. This was blatant robbery. According to the declassified OGPU reports, half a million peasants were first deported, then about a million more; all in all, four million were "dekulakized" before the war. Not counting thousands more who were killed or sent to camps.
>
> Two decades later, **Boris Pasternak** told Varlam Shalamov, the author of *Kolyma Tales*: "In 1931, I traveled to the Urals as a member of a writers' brigade, and the trip shocked me: beggars in homespun Southern clothes walked around the trains, asking for bread. There were endless echelons with families, kids, screams and crying, surrounded by convoys – the kulaks were being deported to the North, to die. I pointed those echelons out to my friends in the writers' brigade, but nobody could give any coherent reply."

Near our hospital, there was an incomplete building, and the authorities decided to disassemble it and use the materials for another building. The hospital workers, seeing the disassembly on the way to work, called it "finding bricks with Ilyich's method". In these dark times, the disenfranchised Soviet citizen could only laugh bitterly over the "accomplishments" of the Soviet planners. If only they had allowed private initiative, there would immediately have been bricks and other rare commodities. But this would entail the return of "capitalists", whom the Marxists feared more than anything else.

Soviet citizens even had to laugh with caution, out of earshot of secret NKVD informants. It was known that for such jokes, you could be sent away god knows where. Still, what else could a citizen of the "first free country in the world" do but laugh? For criticism or protests, he could easily be branded as "socially alien" or even an "enemy of the people", with all the repercussions. The majority of people slipped into political apathy...

> Do you remember **Osip Mandelstam's** lines from the poem *Kremlin Highlander?*
> *We are living, but can't feel the land where we stay,*
> *More than ten steps away you can't hear what we say.*
> *But if people would talk on occasion,*
> *They should mention the Kremlin Caucasian...*
> This poem, that proved so suicidal for its author, was written in that same 1933.

Could Soviet citizens imagine that the leftist socialists who shouted loudly about freedom being repressed in Tsarist times would become that freedom's destroyers as soon as they gained power? The peoples of Russia paid dearly for their naivety.

In 1933, in Leningrad, I played in my worst Soviet Championship, only taking eighth place. I had only two consolations: the fact that I was selected for the USSR national team to play at the Chess Olympiad in Stockholm *(it's unclear what competition Bogatyrchuk is talking about, because the USSR team never took part in the "bourgeois" Olympiads before the war)*, and that I defeated Botvinnik.

I don't know why, but the Stockholm visit was scrapped, and so I lost my chance to visit Sweden. However, even though I was considered a chess "elder" at my age of 41, I still wasn't planning to retire any time soon." (From the book *My Life Path to Vlasov and the Prague Manifesto.*)

The Fourth "Swallow"

Rokhlin: "On 15th August, the All-Union Chess Tournament begins in Leningrad *(for the first time since 1925!)*. The best representatives of the Soviet chess art earned the right to take part in it after qualifying tournaments.

The first "swallow"[20] of the nascent struggle between the old and new generations was the 1927 tournament in Moscow. This was the time when M. Botvinnik was just testing his strength, and the talented chess youth was represented by A. Model, who shared 3rd–4th place with Duz-Khotimirsky. But the struggle was unequal, and the older generation, spearheaded by Bogatyrchuk and Romanovsky, prevailed.

In 1929, in Odessa, we saw a similar picture. The creative energy of the young players, who had a very good start in the All-Union tournament, steadily declined, and the "elders" – Verlinsky and Freymann – again won the tournament. It was completely obvious that such "paradoxes" as the failure of the whole young generation of masters – Botvinnik, Riumin, Rauzer, Kan (in part) and others – could not happen again.

1931 came. Before the tournament, most predicted that Bogatyrchuk, Verlinsky or Duz-Khotimirsky might emerge as winners. However, the whole chess world was surprised when the tournament was won by young masters – Botvinnik and Riumin – rather than the experienced "elders". Still, those were only the first thunderclaps.

What's characteristic for the current tournament? All the forces of the old generation, except Ilyin-Zhenevsky (A. Rabinovich and Selezniev can't be considered serious contenders), have mobilized. And while the absence of Romanovsky and Levenfish in 1931 sparked some debate – "had they taken part, what places would they have obtained?" – this time, there were no reasons for such idle talk, because the youth gave their opponents – their former mentors – an opportunity to field a full, battle-ready line-up." (*Shakhmaty v SSSR*, August 1933.)

S. Vainstein: "The tournament line-up of the 8th All-Union Premiership consists of the winners of the local qualifying tournaments. On the basis of the results of a masters tournament, Moscow sent Riumin, Duz-Khotimirsky, Kan, Yudovich, and Zubarev; Leningrad sent the winners of a similar tournament: Botvinnik, Romanovsky, Lisitsin, Chekhover, Levenfish (replacing Ilyin-Zhenevsky, who was assigned to work in Prague), Savitsky, and I. Rabinovich; Ukraine sent Kirillov; Uzbekistan sent Freymann; Transcaucasia sent Sorokin *(the only first-category player in the tournament)* and Goglidze. Moreover, the winners of the All-Union Central Council of Trade Unions tournament, Bogatyrchuk and Verlinsky, qualified *(Moscow, February 1933: 1. Bogatyrchuk – 4.5/6, 2. Verlinsky – 4, 3. Riumin – 2.5, 4.*

---

[20]   In Russia, the first swallow is a metaphor for something new happening

Romanovsky – 1), and at the last moment, after the number of participants was increased to 20, two more players were included – Alatortsev, who didn't take part in qualifying tournaments, and Rauzer, who scored as many points as Kirillov." (From the tournament games collection.)

The Starting Fever

S. Vainstein: "The exceptionally strong line-up and great organization of the tournament are attracting a huge number of spectators to the Central House of Physical Education. The games are held in the arena hall and gymnastics hall, both holding up to 500 spectators. The demonstration boards are installed in the left wing; finally, simultaneous displays are held in the foyer during the breaks. No wonder that the presence of so many spectators is not felt; only in the critical moments, when a leader finishes off his opponent or, by contrast, fights until his last breath in agony, does a tight circle appear around the table, when only the clatter of dropped pieces can break that circle...

Peter Romanovsky. He was completely unrecognizable in this championship. Cartoon by N. Radlov (1935). Charcoal, watercolors. From A. Kentler's archive. Published for the first time.

The first days have already overturned many assumptions, and have cast aside many masters who were expected to take top places.

Riumin's unsuccessful performance is a complete surprise – zero wins in the first seven games. He's playing sluggishly and indecisively; he seems to be unprepared for the fights that are necessary to succeed in such tournaments. The extremely poor start after a number of significant successes in the last few years, only rivaled by Botvinnik, has completely unsettled him and, unfortunately, precluded him from competing for the leadership.

Romanovsky sacrificed a piece to Kirillov in round 1 and won with a beautiful, deeply calculated combination. However, a series of five draws followed, and then he blundered a mate in two in a completely won position against Sorokin. It's evident that he's in poor form.

Bogatyrchuk's performance is also relatively poor – we don't see the usual inventiveness and tenacity in his play. He lost to Levenfish in round 3 after careless opening play, and suffered another disappointing loss the next day against Alatortsev *(see game 67)*. He seems to be out of form, too.

Rauzer's success is more pleasing. In an interview before the tournament, Botvinnik was rather complimentary of his play. The game against Alatortsev, where Rauzer deployed a theoretical novelty and literally crushed his opponent, seemingly confirmed that opinion. However, he rather ingloriously lost to Lisitsin afterwards, and then, two rounds later, to Botvinnik *(see game 61)*. Since the fifth round, the Kiev player *(Rauzer)* has been on a winning streak and repeated Botvinnik's record in the first half of the tournament.

> **Rauzer:** "After the 1931 Soviet Championship, where I disappointingly scored too many draws, I analyzed my games and reached the conclusion that I wasn't really winning games myself – it's my opponents who lost because of their own mistakes. My second conclusion was that the fashionable defenses against 1.e2-e4 were inadequate.
>
> In the subsequent period, I worked hard and productively on opening theory. Outwardly, the change in my approach was embodied in the fact that I started playing 1.e2-e4 instead of 1.d2-d4.
>
> In the 1933 Soviet Championship, I surprised my opponents by winning games very consistently, from the very start... Now my guiding principle is to gain an opening advantage with white and then logically convert it and win, and to go for a draw with black. My play is especially inspired when I get at least a small advantage out of the opening. My main flaw is that I don't like to defend." (Special bulletin of the All-Union Young Masters Tournament, 24th December 1936.)

The Moscow "elders" Verlinsky and Duz-Khotimirsky aren't playing too well. The former wouldn't have lost such games to Botvinnik and Savitsky in his earlier days, but here he was completely helpless in difficult positions. Duz's play was completely unrecognizable and leaves us a bit sad. The best Moscow player is Kan, playing confidently and energetically. In the first four rounds, he only lost a half-point, and even that was to Botvinnik... Moscow's lack of success, especially if we remember the victorious ways of Riumin and good performances of Verlinsky and Yudovich at the previous premiership, is the main sensation of the tournament.

Among the Leningrad players, Levenfish attracts the most attention. His table is always surrounded by a dense crowd. He's playing with great intensity and rarely gets up to look at his competitors' games. While the hopes placed on Riumin and Romanovsky have collapsed, the interest towards Levenfish is growing. Despite the lack of serious practice for years, he's already defeated such serious opponents as Bogatyrchuk and Riumin in good style. However, Levenfish's overconfidence occasionally gets him in big trouble.

> **Yudovich:** "Levenfish suffered a sensational loss to Goglidze. White simply but convincingly refuted black's efforts to create an attack, transitioned into a better endgame and won it with precise moves. This game shows master Goglidze in the best possible light." (*64*, September 1933.)

Savitsky, the youngest player of the tournament (both in age and in master's experience), had a brilliant start. In the first-round draw against Riumin, the Leningrad player managed to put him under considerable pressure, and then he won four games in a row!

> **Yudovich:** "Savitsky causes panic. His latest victim is Lisitsin, who played tenaciously, but yet couldn't do anything. You don't need to be a prophet to

Leningrad masters Leonid Savitsky, Vitaly Chekhover and Georgy Lisitsin (Shakhmaty v SSSR, No. 8, 1935).

foretell a great chess future for the young master, who progressed from fifth-category tournaments to the USSR premiership with breathtaking speed."

Chekhover is playing well; Rabinovich and Alatortsev have recovered from a bad start – they are among those players unaffected by losses. Lisitsin lost to Kan in the first round, but quickly improved his standing with technically perfect wins over Rauzer and Alatortsev – he outplayed them both in the opening. All the Leningrad players are performing very well, and they all seem to want to finish in the "international top ten".

Botvinnik and Romanovsky always sit at the same tables. As Romanovsky falls further and further behind first place, the crowd around his table thins, joining the circle around Botvinnik's table. On some days, it's particularly hard for him to play: despite all the natural and artificial barriers, people are literally hanging above him – which is made easier by the Swedish bars along the walls.

Botvinnik had a shaky start, but after round 4 he literally started destroying his opponents. A deep, combinational game against Rauzer, which surely should contend for the brilliancy prize, showed his great form and high playing ability *(see game 61)*. If his strength doesn't fail him, he will surely win this premiership as well.

> **Botvinnik:** "The question of whether I would win the premiership again was of interest to many people, but I think that the most interested person was me. I should readily admit that I was rather skeptical of my winning chances. I was disturbed by flaws in my play uncovered at the Leningrad masters tournament *(March-April 1933; Botvinnik shared 1st–2nd place with Romanovsky, but, in his own words, "played irresolutely, made some blunders")*, the unprecedentedly strong lineup and my special status in the tournament – even second place would have been considered a failure for me...
>
> I couldn't properly prepare for the tournament. Postgraduate studies took up all my free time from my job. I placed all my hopes on a month's vacation that I spent in the Caucasus mountains – in Teberda. Naturally, it would be harmful and useless to spend my entire vacation on preparation. So I worked only on developing some opening ideas, completely eschewing middlegame analysis." *(Shakhmaty v SSSR*, September 1933.)

The first stage of the tournament was characterized by the high quality of games, as well as a lack of blunders and time trouble, which would occasionally distort the normal flow of games later.

Results after 7 rounds: Botvinnik – 6, Savitsky – 5.5, Levenfish and Rauzer – 5, Kan and Lisitsin – 4.5, Bogatyrchuk, Verlinsky and Chekhover

– 4, Alatortsev, Rabinovich, Romanovsky, Sorokin and Yudovich – 3.5, Goglidze – 2.5, Duz-Khotimirsky, Zubarev and Riumin – 2, Freymann – 1.5, Kirillov – 0." (*Shakhmaty v SSSR*, July and August 1933.)

The Ghost Story

It's very hard to find vivid details in the chess magazines of the time. And don't get me started on the memoirs of our great players, emasculated by self-censorship and then completely killed by the editors. Open the books of Romanovsky, Duz-Khotimirsky or Kan, and you'll find a desert, with occasional cacti of honesty. Still, can you blame the authors themselves? We probably should pity them – and us, readers, too.

"'Davy, do you know what they have done?' Levenfish exclaimed despondently when he met Bronstein in the offices of the Soviet state publisher *Fizkultura i Sport*. 'They struck out half of the book, everything spicy and interesting!' But Grigory Yakovlevich didn't get to see his book printed, even in such a mutilated form: it was only published six years after his death. Bronstein's efforts to find the manuscript afterwards were futile – it disappeared without trace."

Genna Sosonko's book *My Testimony*, which I quoted, is one of the most honest in all chess literature. But even Sosonko didn't allow himself to finish the thought: who was behind all of that? Did the editor himself decide to cut up the book so brutally? Did *Fizkultura i Sport* delay the publication for so long? I don't know about Genna, but the answer is obvious to me. It's enough to remember whose relationship with Levenfish was always "very tense" and who was the head honcho of Moscow chess in the early 1960s...[21]

But we digress. I just want to amuse you with a story that happened before round 7. Mikhail Yudovich related it in the *Central Chess Club Bulletin* (No.

---

[21] To avoid accusations of bias, I'll also quote A. Kentler's version: "When I prepared the article "Yes, that very Levenfish" (*Shakhmatny Peterburg* No. 2, 2002), I tried to ascertain the fate of the manuscript. I found out who read the manuscript, where it was kept, I met with the grandmaster's children, etc. I think that Grigory Yakovlevich's sad admission that many things were omitted from the book due to censorship was more likely addressed to Levenfish's own internal censor. He'd been hiding the true details of his biography his entire life. And the fact that the book was only published six years after his death has actually more to do with his last marriage: his widow tried to publish the book of his selected games and memories under two names – his and hers. She didn't succeed."

13, 1983); unlike the officious *Shakhmaty v SSSR* where he worked, he could allow himself some "liberties" here.

Yudovich: "The championship was held in an old mansion on Khalturin Street (close to the Hermitage), and all visiting players lived there as well. Spiral staircases led to the third floor, and every master had a small individual room on it.

> So, Gotthilf's demands for individual accommodation at the previous championship weren't made in vain! However, not everything was so good.
> **Baturinsky:** "The championship was held in the House of Physical Education on Khalturin Street. The visiting players lived in the dormitory of the same building, but the conditions weren't exactly good for rest or preparation. The Kiev master Rauzer suffered especially. He usually went to sleep early, pulled a sheet over his head and begged his neighbors not to make too much noise because he needed to think about his next game plan." (From the book *Pages of Chess Life.*)

There were many Moscow players at the tournament, and, as usual, Nikolai Nikolaevich Riumin was the head of our delegation – he was respected by everybody. We got along very well, supported each other in the days of difficult tournament emotions and disappointments, and would often get together in our free time.

At these gatherings, Fyodor Ivanovich Duz-Khotimirsky, 54 years old at the time, was always the center of attention. He told us about meeting Chigorin, Rubinstein, Alekhine, about his mathematical hobbies. Duz always said that anyone who understands nothing but chess actually doesn't even understand chess. A cheerful man who loved funny jokes, Fyodor Ivanovich was the soul of our chess society...

> If you really want to "hear" Duz, open the January 1933 issue of *64*. His descriptions of Schiffers and Chigorin are vastly different from those printed in the book *Selected Games*. See how the levels of emotion, photographic precision and color in his portrayals contrast with those printed 20 years later.
> **Duz-Khotimirsky:** "The waiter invited me to the cafeteria and pointed me out to some fearsome-looking, huge man. The man had a big gray beard and a head of hair *a la* Karl Marx. His right eye rolled furiously. He addressed me, "Allow me to introduce myself: Emmanuel Stepanovich Schiffers..."
> Then I finally saw M. I. *(Chigorin)*. I was so disappointed: he was even slightly shorter than me! His height notwithstanding, Chigorin impressed me

with his appearance. A copper-red face, dark grayish hair, small beard, dark brown eyes, big, penetrating, with a somewhat severe and sad look, but kind."

Duz-Khotimirsky, 20 years later: "The waiter invited me to the cafeteria, and there, pointing at me, he whispered some words to a venerable, huge old man with a big gray beard. I was a bit intimidated. The man addressed me, "Allow me to introduce myself: Emmanuel Stepanovich Schiffers..."

Then I finally saw Mikhail Ivanovich. He was somewhat short. The face I knew from portraits seemed more friendly and likable to me than in the photos. Dark grayish hair, a small mustache, a square beard, brown eyes, dark, big, with a somewhat severe and sad look."

One day, Nikolai Mikhailovich Zubarev and I sat in Riumin's room late at night. Zubarev, who was performing poorly in the tournament, sighed and showed us his game with Rauzer, where he had obtained a good position but made a mistake in a critical moment.

Suddenly, someone knocked on the door loudly, Boris Markovich Verlinsky ran into the room and nervously explained that he had just been visited by... a ghost.

Holding back his smile, Riumin asked what this ghost looked like and what it was doing in Verlinsky's room. It turned out that the "ghost" in a white sheet appeared when Verlinsky lay down and turned off the light. In a menacing voice, the ghost said, "Lose to Duz tomorrow," and then went away.

We went to Duz's room together. He pretended to be asleep, but his smiling eyes revealed the secret of the ghost to us.

The next day, Verlinsky angrily attacked   Duz-Khotimirsky's

Дружеский шарж   Рис. Ю. Ю.

м. Дуз-Хотимирский

Duz-Khotimirsky was called
Just "Duz", until grey hairs
He was as though made of crystal,
He wasn't at all saddened
By everyday worries.
The old man was so attached to the game
That youth returned to him at the board.
It was also he who named
The opening we know as the Dragon.
We still remember
His Dnipro-deep eyes,
Which hold, clear as crystal,
The purity of the turquoise.

From The Tale of the Thousand Year-Old Game by chess player and poet V. Pokrovsky. The original Russian rhymed. Cartoon by Y. Yuzepchuk (64. Shakhmaty I Shashki v Massy, No. 4, 1933).

position. The supernatural powers were put to shame again, and Duz ultimately had to resign."

It turned out that this championship was the last one for both the "victim" and the "ghost". Verlinsky and Duz still continued to play in tournaments, but never managed to get through the grind of semi-finals again...

Panov: "I got to know Boris Markovich especially well in 1934, during our tour of Tashkent. I had to solve all the financial and household issues for both of us and take great care of Verlinsky, because he was deaf, spoke (if you could call it that) in a harsh, hoarse whisper and understood others by lip reading. Nevertheless, he was a pleasant, interesting companion with a rich inner life. I was especially amazed by the fact that, despite his deafness, Verlinsky was an avid music lover; he would eagerly go to symphony concerts both in Moscow and Tashkent, and he absolutely loved the musical celebrities of the time." (From the book *Forty Years at the Chessboard*.)

The Blunder Epidemic

S. Vainstein: "The three-city physical education contest required us to leave the hospitable halls of the Central House of Physical Education. However, the Sadovsky Club provided an even more imposing, if less comfortable, hall for the tournament. There were a lot of spectators as well, especially in the days when leaders played each other.

These six rounds essentially decided the tournament's outcome. Botvinnik got to be 2 points ahead of Rauzer, and then was able to relax a bit. To his credit, he played brilliantly. He calmly outplayed Zubarev, then checkmated Yudovich after sacrificing two pieces, while Sorokin managed to drop a piece as early as move 12. However, with the black pieces, Botvinnik had to demonstrate all his skills in defense.

> **Botvinnik:** "In round 9, I was put to a serious test. Deciding to rest a bit and reach a "grandmaster draw" with I. Rabinovich, I (as always happens in such cases) got into a difficult situation. Missing an elementary tactic, I lost a pawn, and my position was clearly lost." (*Shakhmaty v SSSR*, September 1933.)
>
> **Yudovich:** "The leaders met: Savitsky – Botvinnik *(see game 70)*. The opening already promised a sharp fight after black's novelty. Indeed, with subtle maneuvering, Savitsky got a superb attack, and only Botvinnik's ingenious defense allowed him to emerge only a pawn down. In time trouble, however, Savitsky suddenly got nervous, made several mistakes and blundered a piece."

Romanovsky played a couple of good games – against Duz and Bogatyrchuk *(see game 62)*, but made a number of blunders in the others. He was very unlucky against Levenfish – first he missed a win, and then missed a mate in two *(game 63)* – but then Freymann returned the favor to him, blundering a knight...

Levenfish and Alatortsev frequently got into time trouble and were only saved by their exceptional inventiveness. Alatortsev managed to wriggle out even when he had almost no time left. In the games against Freymann, Zubarev and Chekhover, he had just 1–2 minutes to make a good many moves versus 10–15 minutes for his opponents, and yet, Alatortsev managed to win all three.

Rauzer's good score in these rounds can't really be used as a quality indicator yet. He subtly exploited Savitsky's opening errors and the extra exchange against the blundering Levenfish, but his win against Duz was quite dubious, and the incorrect piece sacrifice against Sorokin was naive – however, he paid for that naivety with a loss.

By contrast, Lisitsin rarely makes serious mistakes and even more rarely loses an advantage already gained. If he goes for a sacrifice, the combination is always calculated to the very end.

Rabinovich is slowly emerging as one of the most solid contenders. Chekhover played good games against Riumin and Bogatyrchuk, who still can't get a grip on himself. Yudovich and Kan played badly. Riumin's form is still quite unsatisfactory. He has only managed to win one game out of 12 – against Verlinsky, whose performance in this tournament has been disappointing. Freymann has improved a bit, he's considered a threat after defeating Verlinsky and Chekhover. The weakest players have been Verlinsky, Savitsky (1.5/6), Zubarev (1) and Duz (0.5).

The overall impression is much less favorable: many blunders and gross miscalculations, made even by the recognized favorites. It seems that only a few players are able to withstand the daily 7-hour stretches of play...

Results after 12 rounds: Botvinnik – 10.5, Rauzer – 8.5, Levenfish – 8, Alatortsev, Lisitsin, Rabinovich and Chekhover – 7.5, Romanovsky and Savitsky – 7, Bogatyrchuk and Kan – 6.5, Sorokin – 6, Verlinsky and Yudovich – 5.5, Goglidze and Riumin – 4, Freymann – 3.5, Zubarev – 3, Duz-Khotimirsky – 2.5, Kirillov – 2."

The Clock Story

If you remember the last championship, the games were held daily, from 3 to 8 p.m., and then two more hours after an hour-long break; the play-off was held in the morning. Not everyone was able to withstand such a tempo for several weeks straight; towards the end of the tournament, the number of time trouble cases and blunders grew sharply. This time, the players managed to negotiate a less exhausting schedule – with three full play-off days and two rest days. There was a sharp discussion about time control.

Yudovich: "In the old times, many questions, which are total non-issues now, required discussions and special decisions. One such controversial topic was time control. Until the 9th Championship, it was always discussed at the players meeting.

I remember the hot discussions before the 8th championship. Grigory Yakovlevich Levenfish proposed a new time control: 3 hours for 48 moves. He would hotly assure all of us that this innovation would allow more time to think in the critical moments of the games and save us from time trouble. Also, there'd be fewer adjourned games.

Levenfish's eloquence convinced many, but... I've never since seen such horrible time trouble as at the 8th championship. It's understandable psychologically. You think that you have a lot of time and don't hurry too much. And then you have only a few minutes for a lot of moves and have to scramble for time...

The time-trouble records were set by Savitsky, Lisitsin, Duz and... Levenfish himself. Time trouble was his undoing in the game against Kirillov. The latter posted a very bad start, losing nine games in a row (a record for our national championships). But in round 13 with black he destroyed Levenfish, who tried to avoid a draw against the makeweight in time trouble." (*Central Chess Club Bulletin* No. 13, 1983.)

Memory failed the old master – there was only one round played with "Levenfish time control"! It's enough to look at the tournament review to ascertain that.

Yudovich: "Round 10. The games are being filmed today, and so a new time control has been introduced: 48 moves in 3 hours. The experts say that this control prevents time trouble, or, to be precise, not the time trouble itself, but its destructive consequences. This view may actually be correct. The crisis in the game usually comes around the 30th or 40th move – precisely during time trouble with the usual control. Naturally, this affects the results big time."

The innovation didn't help Yudovich himself though: in that round, he got checkmated by Botvinnik after just 25 moves!

Botvinnik: "Because of the film crew, the games started much later than usual. So the time control was changed: 48 moves in 3 hours. I should say that such regulation changes are completely unacceptable – on that day, many games were lost in time trouble because of the unfamiliar control. Luckily for me, my game against Yudovich didn't last long – or else I would've been in severe time trouble, too: my clock was already showing 1 hour 50 minutes!" (*64*, November 1933.)

So, what time control was actually used then? Let's look into the primary sources.

Levenfish: "Every highly-qualified chess player knows about the nervous strain required by any long and serious tournament. Unfortunately, medics were never asked to take part in writing the tournament regulations, even though it's clear that playing from 3:30 p.m. to 8 p.m. and then from 9 p.m. to 11:30 p.m. is quite exhausting. Also, starting the games immediately after lunch violates the basic rules of physiology.

Before the start of the tournament, the majority of the players supported the proposal to play for 6 hours without a break, i.e. from 5 to 11 p.m. But it was rejected by the organizing committee – supposedly because of their inability to provide dinner at such a late time. Basically, nobody even seriously tried to solve this paltry problem.

Time trouble is a scourge of our tournaments. Both in the last and in the current premiership, a lot of games were ruined by time-trouble blunders.

> **S. Vainstein:** "The second half of the tournament was rife with blunders, surprises and time trouble, which most often happened after the break. The game Duz – Savitsky was an especially glaring example: both players were so stupefied in time trouble that one of them persistently blundered his knight, and the other tried to run away from that knight with the same persistence." (*Shakhmaty v SSSR*, August 1933.)

However, we stubbornly copy the poor West European resort tournaments (we should note that the rounds usually start at 9 a.m. there) and set the time control for 16 moves per hour instead of the normal 15. Why? Because there would purportedly be fewer adjourned games, and we wouldn't have to prolong the tournament for an extra day. This same consideration led the organizers to decrease the number of rest days between rounds." (*Shakhmaty v SSSR*, September 1933.)

Dizzy with Success

S. Vainstein: "The points scored in the last seven rounds of the premiership, which moved back to the Central House of Physical Education, look quite unusual: Alatortsev and Riumin – 5.5, Lisitsin and Rabinovich – 4.5, Bogatyrchuk and Levenfish – 4, Botvinnik, Chekhover, Freymann, Kan, Verlinsky, Yudovich and Zubarev — 3.5, Duz-Khotimirsky, Kirillov and Rauzer – 3, Goglidze and Romanovsky – 2.5, and Savitsky and Sorokin – 1.5.

The fact that both the leaders and the rear performed almost identically is no accident: this is the result of exhaustion, when the physically weaker players collapse, and even the most important games are prone to "accidents". The play of Botvinnik, who basically had lost positions in 6 games out of 7...

> Against Duz, Levenfish, Bogatyrchuk, Riumin, Freymann and Goglidze. I remember feeling a sharp pang when I saw that only two of those games survived (against Bogatyrchuk and Freymann), but when I failed to find the games against Verlinsky and Rabinovich as well, where, as Botvinnik himself admitted, he had lost positions too, I felt almost sick. The story about the "lost" loss to Izmailov in the 7th championship was too fresh in my mind to believe in a simple coincidence.

...was affected by other factors as well: he was too self-assured, probably even dizzy with success. He quickly lost the momentum that made him strain, fight for the win, be vigilant. He was psychologically affected by the knowledge that he could easily lose a game at any time without fearing for his first place.

Rokhlin: "Alatortsev's "marathon spurt" created a real panic at the finish. Even Botvinnik, usually unflappable and self-assured, would cast anxious glances at the "reserve player" who was chasing after him, and had Alatortsev not suffered a crushing defeat against Romanovsky, the fate of the premiership would have been decided only in the last round." (*Shakhmaty v SSSR*, August 1933.)

Botvinnik: "After I played the last game, I was introduced to Mikhail Zoshchenko. He was

Вперед к первому месту!

Forward, to first place! "Still, all external circumstances notwithstanding, Botvinnik's finish was inglorious and completely devoid of the effect it had in 1931." (S. Vainstein.) (Shakhmaty v SSSR, No. 10, 1933.)

slender, taciturn, with very sad eyes standing out on his long, swarthy face framed by black, sleek hair – it was hard to believe at first that this man was an author of amusing short stories. He made me feel embarrassed: "You'll achieve much in this life, not only in chess..." It seems that Mikhail Mikhailovich didn't see anything amusing in me." (From the book *The Aim Achieved*.)

Still, all external circumstances notwithstanding, Botvinnik's finish was inglorious and completely devoid of the effect it had in 1931. The impression from his win was a far cry from everyone's expectations after the great performance in the first 12 rounds. The "Pyrrhic victory" against Freymann, the failure of his novelty against Levenfish, the 70-move resistance against Riumin while a piece down *(see game 66)* – all these "achievements", if you can call them that, are rather negative.

Rokhlin: "While being a player of a <u>positional style</u>, Botvinnik proved that he does not avoid the combination element when the situation requires. That's why we can say that in his games, in addition to great theoretical knowledge, Lasker's defensive prowess is coupled with Capablanca's positional understanding.

Of course, Botvinnik, like any great master, has some flaws in his play, resulting from certain coldness of thought, from his frequent desire to send the game down his favorite path of clear positional ideas, which often leads to excessive theorization of a given position, both in the opening and in the middlegame."

Botvinnik: "In some games, I managed to punish my opponents' mistakes with precision I could never have expected earlier. In time trouble, I didn't panic and quickly evaluated even complicated positions. My calculations were almost always correct and deeper than my opponents'. I didn't fear combinations and gladly went for them. The fact that I was in great physical shape helped me immensely. All in all, I shall partly credit my success to the distant Teberda." (*Shakhmaty v SSSR*, September 1933.)

By the way, comparing the original article from 1933 "How I Competed for the Soviet Premiership" with the version printed in Analytical and Critical Works *over fifty years later, I came across an example of whitewashing the "Soviet past", which is characteristic of other authors as well, not only Botvinnik.*

Telling how Duz was planning to "torture" him in a theoretically drawn endgame, Botvinnik originally wrote, "These cute eccentricities are just a vestige of the 'glorious' traditions of Dominic's Cafe, and, of course, they are completely unacceptable in our Soviet chess environment."

In the book, this passage was changed: "He had probably still not shaken off the 'glorious' traditions of Dominic's Cafe (in the old St. Petersburg, there were two popular chess cafes: Dominic's and Platter's, and anything could happen there)."

Alatortsev posted three early losses in the premiership (albeit not in row), but didn't lose heart – this is an enviable quality for many: by contrast, he then started to crush his opponents with doubled energy. At the end of the tournament, he showed much tenacity and ingenuity. He boldly played for a win and energetically achieved his goals.

Alatortsev was awarded a special "youth" prize for a young player who scored the most points against the "elders" (7 points out of 9).

Yudovich: "Winning nine or so games in a row is certainly an indication of high class and great willpower. But I would like to point out a huge flaw in his play; if Alatortsev eliminates it, he might be able to give even more to the art of chess. This flaw is a lack of self-criticism, evident bias in the evaluation of position and opponents." (*64*, September 1933.)

The inscription in the book *The Ways of Chess Creativity*, which **Romanovsky** gave him as a gift during the tournament, says the same thing: "To Vova Alatortsev, the proponent of deep chess ideas. I wish you to never be satisfied with what you've already achieved and be more critical of your own play. Peter Romanovsky, 4th September 1933."

Друж. шарж Ю. Ю.

АЛАТОРЦЕВ:
— Восемь пешек, один я...

"Alatortsev: Eight pawns, but just one of me"... Vladimir Alatortsev finished just one point behind the winner! Cartoon by Y. Yuzepchuk (64, 20th December 1937).

Alatortsev: "I feel obliged to expand my knowledge of openings and endings, and also change my game – to get rid of my propensity to complicate things where it's not necessary." (*Shakhmaty v SSSR*, October 1933.)

Riumin lacks the very qualities that played the critical role in Alatortsev's success – persistence and the will to win. Only after he came to terms with the fact that he wouldn't get a good result and essentially gave up on the tournament, did he manage to show his true strength. He started to play calmly, without strain, and easily created positions desirable for him. His game against Rabinovich is one of the best in the whole tournament *(see game 65)*. All in all, Riumin's finish only confirms that his failure was a chance event, albeit a symptomatic one.

The game between Rabinovich and Levenfish was, without a doubt, the most intense in the whole tournament, captivating the entire hall. This battle was won by Levenfish, whose combination talent prevailed many times in this tournament. Unfortunately, the strain took its toll on him, and he fell unconscious on the tennis court the next day... In general, Levenfish's participation deeply enriched the tournament, and he exceeded all expectations.

Lisitsin and Rabinovich enjoyed a good finish. The former, after a string of logical and beautiful games against Bogatyrchuk, Goglidze *(see game 68)* and Verlinsky, could even have caught Alatortsev, but fell victim to Romanovsky's beautiful combination in the last round. The latter stumbled a bit at the end against Levenfish and Riumin, who managed to successfully find his weak spots.

Rokhlin: "I. Rabinovich achieved a great performance. His once sluggish positional style from past tournaments has greatly evolved, gaining (through games with young players) the necessary harmony and strength. The main flaw in Rabinovich's play is still with combinations, where he often fell victim to the more far-sighted and flexible ideas of his opponents (Levenfish, Riumin and Verlinsky).

The modest Lisitsin played quite "immodestly", overtaking 14 masters and defeating both the experienced representatives of the older generation (Bogatyrchuk, Verlinsky and Duz-Khotimirsky) and his peers (Alatortsev, Rauzer and Chekhover). Lisitsin's style has deepened considerably, but even now, his strongest aspect is still his technique, which is enviable for most of our players."

Players from Leningrad took the first five places in the tournament – a phenomenal success!

Bogatyrchuk improved towards the end, but still played somewhat unsteadily. The wins over Botvinnik *(game 60)* and Kirillov came to him much more easily than they would have had his opponents played as well as they could. And, conversely, we can't say that Lisitsin or Rabinovich were lucky in their games against Bogatyrchuk.

> **Rokhlin:** "Bogatyrchuk suffered the most from the youngsters – he couldn't successfully use his main weapon, the Odysseus-like cunning positional combinations that were once the scourge of all his opponents. It's hard for Verlinsky to compete for the highest places as well, surrounded by such energetic, ingenious and technically strong youth that easily avoids the reefs of his inventive combinations."

Kan, Verlinsky and Yudovich finished the last stretch with a 50-percent result; their play wasn't particularly good or bad. Still, we think that all of them could have achieved more than they did at the tournament.

Rauzer, Romanovsky, Savitsky and Sorokin (and, to a lesser extent, Chekhover and Goglidze) fizzled out long before the tournament ended. The list of their blunders would stretch too far. Romanovsky, nevertheless, managed to win the key games against his pupils Alatortsev and Lisitsin, but he most probably gathered all his remaining strength for these battles.

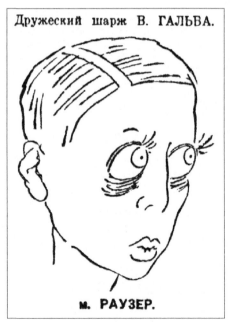

Дружеский шарж В. ГАЛЬВА.

м. РАУЗЕР.

Despite his motto "1.e2-e4, and white wins!", Vsevolod Rauzer occasionally played 1.d2-d4 as well. Cartoon by V. Galba (V. Galberstadt) (64, 5th March 1936).

> **Yudovich:** "Rauzer is an original chess thinker, who, nevertheless, adheres to a reactionary chess ideology. His achievements stem from deep development of opening ideas, but his deliberately provocative sweeping statements (such as "e2-e4 wins", "♝f8-b4 loses", and so on), are unconvincing, unjustified and essentially harmful...
>
> Chekhover is a top-class master. He proved it more with the quality of his wins than his overall result."

Rokhlin: "Despite some individual setbacks, Rauzer showed himself in the best possible light. His deep theoretical preparation and analytical skills give us the right to assert that such a master as Rauzer, if he overcomes his unnecessary subjectivism in evaluation of positions, can and should move the chess science forward.

Chekhover's seventh prize shows that the young player is already a fully-formed master, whose sharp attacking style will be dangerous even for the strongest international players."

The last three half-points that gave Sorokin his master's title came to him at great cost *(he got ill)*, but in general, as the only first-category player, he didn't spoil the overall picture. Zubarev, Duz-Khotimirsky and Kirillov improved towards the end, but after that ill-fated loss to Botvinnik, Freymann immediately lost all remaining interest in the tournament." (*Shakhmaty v SSSR*, August 1933.)

Some Criticism and Self-Criticism

Levenfish: "The Soviet premierships are the most important events in our country's chess life. They require big expenses and take most of the players away from their jobs for almost a month. Finding tournament venues, accommodation and catering for the players is also a difficult task. Nevertheless, the importance of the All-Union tournaments for the development of chess art in the USSR is so obvious that holding them every other year has become absolutely necessary. And the requirements for the proper organization of these unique tournaments should be even stricter.

The premiership's main goal is propaganda – attracting whole society's attention to chess and its role in the country's cultural life, and thus introducing chess to more fans from the masses.

Rokhlin: "More than 15,000 people visited the tournament; they gained the opportunity to become more than passive spectators, and rather to feel like active participants because of skillful mass propaganda work (demonstrations of games by the winners, discussions between masters and the public, lectures and simultaneous displays organized in the tournament hall and outside of it, etc.). The press and radio in all centers of our country paid great attention to the tournament. Some moments in the competition were filmed by the Roskino Leningrad brigade, which is going to produce a special chess movie in the coming days *(it's interesting whether the footage survived)*. All these events

Left to right: Romanovsky, Levenfish, I. Rabinovich.
All three Leningrad leaders were quite dissimilar. Levenfish was tall, slender, respectable,
always elegantly dressed, sarcastic and irritable. He was famous as a talented and witty orator,
with a sometimes poisonous tongue. You really didn't want to irritate him. Rabinovich was
broad-shouldered, portly, unflappable. Excellent complexion, small brush-like mustache; he
would always carry a notepad to write down all his lectures, performances, meetings. Clean
shaven, well-dressed, he was mightily impressive. He always respected his opponents, would
never get angry, it was pleasant to play him. Romanovsky was not tall, always carried a cane.
He had a peculiar way of twitching his head. He didn't care how he was dressed. He often
suffered from sciatica and walked with a limp because of it. He liked to speak in public, but
it was very hard to listen to him: because of some speech impairment, he couldn't pronounce
some sounds at all." (Batuev.) From the book Chess Tournament of USSR Masters with the
Participation of Euwe and Kmoch (Leningrad 1934).

are unknown to the practice of bourgeois countries, where big tournaments have no connection with workers' leisure time."

However, the national premiership has another, equally important goal – to showcase the high-quality achievements of Soviet chess life over the two-year period. The main criterion for these achievements is the quality of tournament games. Unfortunately, organizational mistakes with this premiership led to conditions that were not conducive to improving the quality of the games, which remained rather low on average.

Let's start with the line-up selection. Until now, the selection was based on purely formal criteria. The formal principle, naturally, is completely reasonable when organizing ordinary tournaments, whose goal is the advancement of young players. However, if you organize an All-Union event, you should "look into the roots" of things and, in creating the lists, concern yourself less with geography and arithmetic of random points, and more with determining the true value of the candidates, <u>studying their tournament experience</u> thoroughly. The precedent of the 1931 premiership, when the Executive Bureau included several masters who didn't meet formal criteria, seemed to give a reason to change the old qualification system, but it remained in place, and such interesting players as Model, A. Rabinovich, Grigoriev and Ragozin were left behind. Moreover, three prizewinners – Alatortsev, Rauzer and me – weren't even included in the initial list.

Some words about the regulations *(his comments shown in* The Clock Story *above follow here)*... And, finally, the lack of bonus payments for the players is also evidence of the disregard for quality and a manifestation of unnecessary egalitarianism on the chess front. Playwrights, writers, engineers, and innovators get rewards at competitions, but chess masters do not – despite being called on to create artistic value with maximum possible stress!

The conclusion: our chess organizations do not feel any responsibility for the quality side of their tournaments – and this is what causes everything that's mentioned above.

Let's now turn to the results of the premiership. S. Vainstein's evaluation of the players was on the whole correct, so I'll dwell only on particular details. Botvinnik's superb technique, his characteristic tenacity in defense and subtle positional understanding delivered him the esteemed title of Soviet premiership winner. But he has a serious flaw in his play – he's indecisive in complicated, combination-rich middlegames. Only by overcoming this can Botvinnik count on serious success in international encounters with professional masters armed with the best techniques.

Alatortsev scored 4/10 against prizewinners but 9/9 against the bottom of the table. So he's the one who benefited the most from the motley line-up. His second prize is the result of not just his playing strength, but also drive and willpower.

I am impressed the most by Lisitsin's success; this master raises his level with each tournament he plays. Lisitsin lacks impartiality in evaluation of positions, his chess erudition is insufficient and highlights inadequate work on opening theory, but these shortcomings can be easily rectified. I'm sure that Lisitsin is on the verge of new, even greater success.

Rauzer is a great expert in theory, and has a lot of homespun novelties. He understands the position well, and he's also a good tactician. He could have taken an even higher place, but collapsed at the end of the tournament, unable to withstand the strain. Chekhover played several great combinations, but his play is not solid or resilient enough yet. The only Leningrad player who didn't win a prize, Savitsky, is a very talented chess player, but, unlike Alatortsev, doesn't believe in himself and can't easily recover after defeats.

> The lack of self-belief could have been caused by his heart disease.
> **Volkovyssky:** "In autumn 1932, right after obtaining the master's title in the Leningrad championship, the first terrible bout of heart disease that eventually killed Leonid had him bedridden for several months." (*Shakhmaty v SSSR*, August 1935.)

The Moscow fans had their hopes pinned on Riumin, and they had every reason to do so. Despite his lack of success in this tournament, I consider Riumin the most talented of all the young players. He has everything required for a brilliant chess career; he needs only to improve his playing technique and, what's more important, his fighting qualities – willpower and composure.

Kan, like Chekhover, is a talented combination player, but his play is overly inventive and risky.

Speaking of the "elders", Rabinovich has finally regained his old form and deservedly took a high place.

The winners of the 1927 and 1929 premierships, Verlinsky, Bogatyrchuk and Romanovsky, performed poorly. Verlinsky lost his tactical inventiveness, which was the main trump of his play. Bogatyrchuk was unrecognizable – gone was the freshness and originality of play that once captivated me. They were replaced by industriousness, squeezing out points and waiting for opponents' mistakes. Bogatyrchuk's play gained routine, but lost much of its color.

And, finally, Romanovsky, whom many expected to win the tournament. It's not easy to find the reason for his lack of success. He played some individual games very well, but in many others we can see a certain emptiness and lack of ideas. I think that his investigations into Reti's and Nimzowitsch's ideas are holding back free, unconstrained creativity. Always guided by certain logical frameworks, Romanovsky deliberately steers his talent towards a preplanned path; in chasing chess truth, he limits his natural abilities.

Of the non-prizewinners, Freymann again showed himself as a strong master of ideas, with a distinctive positional understanding. But, as before, he lacks willpower to maintain intensity throughout the struggle. He played some games brilliantly, but he would make inexplicable mistakes in some others that hopelessly ruined won positions for him, while in still others he would just give away points without any resistance.

Мастер С. Н. Фрейман

Sergei Freymann. (Shakhmaty v SSSR, No. 10, 1933).

Concerning myself, I can say that the eight-year hiatus affected my playing technique in a negative way. In a number of games, I got a bad position out of the opening and had to try and equalize in the middlegame, while in others, I failed to convert an advantage in the endgame. Unfortunately, I couldn't rest before the tournament, and so I felt very tired after 10 rounds *(indeed, the 44 year-old Levenfish would surely have benefited from a month in Teberda)*. This explains the mistakes I made in the games against Rauzer, Botvinnik, Kirillov and Zubarev. Towards the end of the tournament, I managed to recover and take third place – the maximum I could do in these circumstances.

I played in the premiership with great interest. Eight years have passed since the Moscow International Tournament, and I wanted to check out myself, my old comrades in arms and, of course, the new generation of masters. Here's my main impression from the tournament. Most "elders" still have a lot to show, while there are many talents among the youth. But both lack playing technique. This lack of technique manifested itself in numerous time trouble cases – the consequence of their inability to manage time well – and in many blunders, which most often occurred after the break.

Opening knowledge and the right opening technique, precise ending play and, most importantly, the ability to win won positions – that's the necessary technical minimum for an average international-class master. Of all the participants, only Botvinnik has great technique, with Rabinovich and Lisitsin a bit behind. While the lack of technique among the non-professional masters, overworked at their main job, is at least explicable, many of our young masters, who basically have chess as their job, don't have that excuse.

The main reason for this lack of technical skills is certainly the fact that we are separated from foreign chess technique. A similar situation occurred during the 3ʳᵈ All-Union Championship in 1924, when Bogoljubov, armed with modern foreign technique, crushed the Soviet masters. But in just that one year of his sojourn in the USSR, our masters learned much from him, and while Bogoljubov won the 1925 championship as well, he did it with much more effort, after an intense struggle. In technology, science and art, we are persistently trying to master the greatest achievements of the bourgeois world. Our chess art should go in the same direction." (*Shakhmaty v SSSR*, September 1933.)

Blunders and Masterpieces

When I opened the tournament book *8ᵗʰ All-Union Chess Premiership*, I was a bit shocked. My critical notes about the previous championship's tournament book were "heeded" both by the collection editor, Ilya Rabinovich, who included only 46 games out of 190 in the book, but by the championship organizers as well, awarding three brilliancy prizes. I knew that thoughts had material power. But that they worked backwards in time as well?..

Of course, kudos to the organizers, but Ilya Leontyevich obviously overdid it. Nobody asked him to completely "throw overboard" the championship games from the ship of history! I meant another thing: annotate the best of them, and print everything else in short notation at the end of the book (if paper was an issue, you could use small print). But ultimately, fewer than half of all games of the 8ᵗʰ championship survived: only 66 completely, and 15 more as endgames. How many interesting games were there that we'll never see?

However, my expectations are probably too high. As you already know, the tournament was rife with time trouble and blunders. "All this taken together," Levenfish wrote, "led to a rather unfortunate fact: the percentage of "printable" games wouldn't be higher than 35–40, and of those that were played consistently well by both players – only about 10, and I don't know of any truly "historically valuable" games played in this tournament. Even in the prize-winning games Rabinovich – Riumin *(see game 65)* and Rauzer – Botvinnik *(see game 61)*, the losing players demonstrated far from perfect technique in defense."

Despite such a harsh evaluation of the brilliancy-prize games, I had decided to start the review with them anyway. But... at the very last moment, as luck would have it, I stumbled upon a mystery story.

"A Gross Blunder"

Yudovich: "Bogatyrchuk's play was unrecognizably pallid, and he only showed the true power of his creativity in the games against Botvinnik and Kan."

No. 60
Bogatyrchuk – Botvinnik
Leningrad 1933, round 15
Annotated by F. Bogatyrchuk

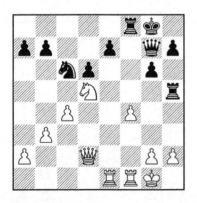

24...g5? *Before letting the winner speak, let's see what I. Rabinovich wrote in the tournament book:* "A gross blunder. However, after the best move 24...e5, white still kept his positional advantage, for instance, with 25.♘b4 ♘d4 (or 25...♘xb4

26.♕xb4 exf4 27.♕xd6) 26.♘d3 ♖hf5 27.fxe5

27...♖xf1+ 28.♖xf1 ♖xf1+ 29.♔xf1 dxe5 30.♕e3 ♘c6 31.♕e4 or 31.♔g1."

Frankly, this line is quite languid, and the final position is almost equal. Moreover, the commentator missed the spectacular 27...♕h6!! (with the idea 28.♕xh6? ♖xf1+ 29.♖xf1 ♘e2+ 30.♔h1 ♖xf1#) that allows black to force a draw: 28.♕d1 ♖xf1+ 29.♖xf1 ♕e3+ 30.♔h1 ♖xf1+ 31.♕xf1 dxe5, and if 32.♘c5 ♘f5 33.♘xb7, then 33...♘g3+ 34.hxg3 ♕h6+ with perpetual check.

Maybe Botvinnik was right when he wrote in the article "How I Competed for the Soviet Premiership", "I just blundered a pawn to Bogatyrchuk. The correct move (which I actually planned to play) was 24...e5!, and black can still resist, even though his position is still much worse"?

Judging by Rabinovich's line – yes, he was. But it turns out that Bogatyrchuk planned to meet 24...e5 in a very different way!

Black's position is already bad, but he still has some defensive resources, and it was unnecessary to give up the pawn. The best move probably was 24...e5, after which white has two possible continuations: 1) the quiet g2-g3 with the subsequent ♕g2, ♖e4 etc. – black would sooner or later be forced to take on f4, dooming the d6 pawn, and 2) the sharp (which, by the way, white intended to play during the game) 25.g4! ♖h4 (the only move) 26.g5 exf4 27.♘f6+

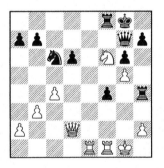

and white has a decisive advantage after both 27...♔h8 28.♖xf4 ♖xf4 29.♕xf4 with a dominant knight on f6, and 27...♖xf6 28.gxf6 ♕xf6 29.♖e4! g5 30.♕d5+ ♔g7 31.♖e6, with a won position.

Thus, even the best defense probably wouldn't have saved the game for black. So I was rather perplexed by the comments in one Leningrad newspaper: "Black could have equalized with e7-e5, but he made a gross blunder."

I'll add that after 27...♔h8, white has an even stronger move: 28.♕f2! ♖h3 29.♕xf4, for instance, 29...♖d3 30.♖e8 ♘e5 31.♘xh7! ♖xe8 32.♘f6, or 29...♘e5 30.c5! ♘d3 31.♕g4, or, finally, 29...h6 30.♖e8! ♖xe8 31.♘xe8 hxg5 32.♕xg5 ♕e7 (forced) 33.♕xg6 etc.

I don't know about you, dear reader, but I have several questions. First of all, why, unlike in the 1931 tournament book, did the editors of the 1933 edition not use the winner's (Bogatyrchuk's) notes? They could have taken them from the same issue of 64 as Botvinnik's annotations to his game with Yudovich (the game was literally on the adjacent page!). Secondly, what stopped Rabinovich from showing Bogatyrchuk's line, at least for comparison? Thirdly, why did Botvinnik, knowing about the refutation of 24...e5, still maintain the legend about a "gross blunder"?

25.♕e2!

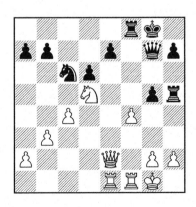

1933 год. VII Всесоюзное первенство. Решающая партия Богатырчук — Ботвинник. Зрители тесным кольцом окружают мастеров: играть трудно, слышны реплики, шум от передвигаемых стульев, гул от находящейся в постоянном движении толпы

"1933. 7th All-Union Premiership. The decisive game Bogatyrchuk – Botvinnik. The spectators surround the masters in a tight circle: it's hard to play, there are loud remarks, the noise of chairs being moved, the hum of the moving crowd." Photo from that same unique issue of Shakhmaty v SSSR (No. 10, 1937) whose press run was almost entirely destroyed. From M. Sokolov's archive. Baturinsky wrote in his book Pages of Chess Life regarding the destruction of the press run "it's not hard to guess the reasons why that happened," hinting at Krylenko's arrest. However, he was only arrested in 1938. I think that the reason was different: this issue, dedicated to the 20th anniversary of the Russian Revolution, overly promoted Krylenko. Right behind portraits of Stalin and Lenin it featured the photo of the same size (and at first glance actually bigger) of the "irreplaceable leader of the Soviet chess organization, People's Commissar for Justice of the USSR Nikolai Vasilyevich Krylenko" that we show earlier in this book. The destruction of the press run suggests that the minister's fate was sealed long before his arrest. The tournament was known as the 7th premiership as the 1920 Olympiad was not counted.

25...♕h6. 25...♖h6 26.♘xe7+ ♘xe7 27.♕xe7 gxf4 28.♕xg7+ ♔xg7 29.♖e7+ ♖f7 30.♖xf7+ *didn't save the game either.*

26.fxg5 ♖xg5 27.♘xe7+ ♔h8 28.♖xf8+ ♕xf8 29.♘xc6 bxc6 30.♕e7. In the opinion of the same commentator, white made an inaccuracy here, which allowed black to "hold" until move 50, while 30.♕e8 won immediately. I don't know why *(these moves are evaluated almost identically by the machine).* Black could have "held" for 20 more hopeless moves after almost any continuation.

30...♛xe7 31.♖xe7 ♖a5 32.a4.

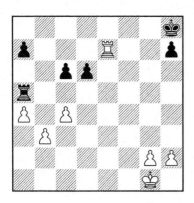

The white rook's dominant position and the weakness of the black pawns render black completely helpless.

32...d5 (32...c5 33.♔f2 ♖a6 34.♖b7! is equally bad) **33.cxd5 cxd5 34.♖d7 a6 35.♖a7 d4.** Desperation. But there was nothing to do anyway, because the threat ♔f2-e3-d4 is unstoppable.

36.♖d7 ♖c5 37.♖xd4 ♖c1+ 38.♔f2 ♖c2+ 39.♔f1 ♖b2 40.♖d8+ ♔g7 41.♖b8 a5 42.♖b5 ♔g6 43.h4 h5 44.♔g1 (the endgame is childishly simple) **44...♔h6 45.♔h2 ♔g6 46.♔g3 ♖b1 47.♔f2 ♔h6 48.♔e3 ♖g1 49.♖xa5 ♖xg2 50.♖b5 ♖g3+ 51.♔f2 ♖g4 52.♖b6+ ♔g7 53.a5 ♖xh4 54.a6 ♖h2+ 55.♔g3 ♖a2 56.b4 h4+ 57.♔xh4 ♔f7 58.b5.** Black resigned.

Years later, in his article *My Encounters with The World Champion M. Botvinnik* (*Canadian Chess Chat*, January 1960) Bogatyrchuk wrote: "I had played unsuccessfully in this tournament. Botvinnik was on top, defeating one opponent after another. His victory in this tournament seemed to be quite secure. Four or five rounds before the end I had to play him. I had to win because of two reasons; first, my situation in this tournament was bad enough and I had to reinstate my reputation. Second, I had to show Botvinnik and other young chess players that the older generation cannot be taken from the account easily...

I had a difficult problem before me, how to win? Which weaknesses had I to make use of in Botvinnik's play? I knew all his games up to this time and I had considered his only weaknesses to be:

1) over-self-confidence, i.e. he did not believe in any chess miracle which could not be foreseen, and

2) he was too dogmatic in his treatment of chess openings and the middlegame.

In other words, he believed in the existence of an absolute chess truth. Thus my plan had to be: to let Botvinnik carry on his plan and try to find some miracle good for me at the end of this plan." (*Minor stylistic adjustments made.*)

Don't Mess with the Dragon

Romanovsky: "Ten minutes after Rauzer's resignation, I encountered Botvinnik, who was uncharacteristically excited. Seeing me, he exclaimed, "Finally, Peter Arsenyevich, I played a game that gave me great pleasure!"

Indeed, Botvinnik's original combination and the whole attack that followed were masterpieces in their own way."

No. 61. Sicilian Defense B74
Rauzer – Botvinnik
Leningrad 1933, round 4

1.e4 c5 2.♘f3 ♘c6 3.d4 cxd4 4.♘xd4 ♘f6 5.♘c3 d6 6.♗e2. Rauzer hadn't yet developed his famous attack with 6.♗g5 preventing the Dragon.

6...g6 7.♗e3 ♗g7 8.♘b3. Taught by Rauzer's experience, Bogatyrchuk used Grigoriev's move 8.♕d2 against Botvinnik in round 15 and got a better position: 8...♘g4 9.♗xg4 ♗xg4 10.♘d5! "In exchange for the bishop pair, white has good knight play in the center, and he can also play c2-c4 to prevent d6-d5 – black's trump card in many Sicilian lines." (Bogatyrchuk)

10...0-0 11.c4 ♗d7 ("this tempo loss is a necessity, because otherwise,

black can't show any activity – neither with f7-f5 nor e7-e6") 12.0-0 f5 13.exf5 ♗xf5 14.♘xf5 ♖xf5 15.♖ad1 ♕d7 16.♗h6 ♗xh6? (16...♗h8) 17.♕xh6 ♖af8 18.♕d2 ♘e5 19.♘e3 ♖h5 20.f3 ("20.c5 is dangerous due to 20...♘f3+ 21.gxf3 ♕h3 22.♘g4 ♖xf3 with a strong attack") 20...♕e6 21.b3 ♕f6 22.f4! ♘c6 23.♖de1 ♕g7 24.♘d5 – see game 60 for the continuation.

8...♗e6 9.f4 0-0.

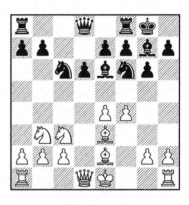

10.0-0. At the 1936 Moscow International Tournament Kan played 10.g4 against Botvinnik and got an advantage after 10...♘a5. Towards the end of the tournament, Botvinnik found an improvement: 10...d5! Levenfish played 11.e5, allowing black to seize the initiative with 11...d4 12.♘xd4 ♘xd4 13.♗xd4 ♘xg4, etc.

Later, after 10...d5! Alekhine tried an interesting novelty in Nottingham – 11.f5 ♗c8 12.exd5 ♘b4 13.d6!?, but Botvinnik forced a perpetual check with the inventive sacrifice of two knights: 13...♕xd6

14.♗c5 ♕f4 15.♖f1 ♕xh2 16.♗xb4 ♘xg4! 17.♗xg4 ♕g3+ 18.♖f2 ♕g1+ etc.

In round 2, Rauzer played 10.♗f3 against Lisitsin (ceding the important c4 square, since white hadn't castled yet), but after 10...♗c4! 11.♕d2 ♖c8 12.♖d1 ♕c7! 13.♘d5? ♕b8 14.♘d4 ♖fe8! fell under a strong attack. "The chess players, who'd often heard from Rauzer that "e2-e4 wins by force", were rather amused by the Kiev player's loss." (Yudovich)

10...♘a5 11.♘xa5. "The point of 10...♘a5 is that after 11.f5 ♗c4 12.e5 ♗xe2 13.♕xe2 dxe5 14.♖ad1 ♕c7 15.♘b5 ♕c4!, white doesn't win a piece," Botvinnik wrote in the book *Selected Games 1926–1946* (1951).

And he showed the best move, found by Spielmann a year later: 12.♗d3! However, it was later determined that black could solve all his problems with 12...♗xd3 13.cxd3 d5 14.♘xa5 ♕xa5 15.e5 d4.

11...♕xa5   12.♗f3   ♗c4 13.♖e1   ♖fd8   14.♕d2   ♕c7 15.♖ac1. Botvinnik, like Tarrasch, recommended 15.♕f2 instead of this passive move, "distracting black from his plan with the threat to capture the a7 pawn"; the computer considers 15...♘d7 the best reply.

15...e5!   16.b3. Of course 16.♘d5? ♘xd5 17.dxe5 is bad due to 17...exf4! However, Botvinnik's move 16.fxe5 dxe5 17.♕f2 "with roughly equal chances" was better.

"But Rauzer probably anticipated how he would methodically exploit the "fatal" weakness of the d6 pawn. How surprised and disappointed he was when instead of positional clarity, a combination storm began at the board!" (Ragozin)

16...d5! Amazingly, Rybka sees neither of black's last moves! And only after a bit of thought does it give the correct verdict: the position is equal.

17.exd5. After 17.fxe5, Botvinnik recommended 17...♘xe4, even though the machine insists on 17...dxe4!, going for incredible complications. But the calculations are so difficult here that it's impossible to go for such a move over the board.

17...e4!

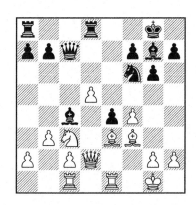

"This was the first of my games that made rounds in the world chess press," Botvinnik writes in *Analytical and Critical Works* (1984), "and this position was studied by such analysts as Tarrasch and Becker. They considered the following continuations:

1) 18.♗xe4 ♘xe4 19.♘xe4 ♗xd5 20.♕d3 (but not 20.♘g3 ♗c3) 20...♕c6 21.♗f2 ♖e8, and 22...♗xg2 after the knight retreats *(but 21...f5! is stronger – this move was already found by Tarrasch, not by Burgess as noted in* My Great Predecessors*);*

2) 18.♘xe4 ♘xd5 19.♔h1 ♘xe3 20.♕xe3 ♗d4 21.♕d2! ♗b2 (or 21...♗e6 22.c4 ♗e5 23.♕c2 ♗xf4)

22.♕b4 ♗xc1 (22...♗d5 23.♖b1 ♕xc2 is also possible) 23.♘f6+! ♔h8! 24.♕c3 ♗d2 25.♕b2 *(Ragozin's line)* 25...♗e6! 26.♘d5+ (26.c4 ♕a5) 26...♗c3 27.♘xc3 ♔g8 28.♘e4 ♕xf4 29.♘f6+ ♔f8, and white gets nothing in either line."

"However, in the second line, white has a strong reply 30.♘d5! ♖xd5 31.♕h8+ and ♕xa8, so it's better to play 22...♕xf4!? 23.♖cd1 ♗e5 24.♘g3 ♗a6 with equality." (Kasparov)

18.bxc4. "White is trying to save the d5 pawn, hoping to use it to win the game. Alas, this hope was unrealistic." (Ragozin)

18...exf3 19.c5 ♕a5.

Rauzer and Botvinnik analyzing the game. Far right – Samuil Vainstein. For the photo, Botvinnik grabbed the e-pawn, as though he'd just played e7-e5. However, if we look at the position closely, we see that the white pawn is already on b3, which means that black played e7-e5 one move earlier. From the author's archive.

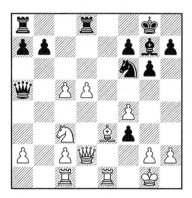

20.♖ed1? "20.d6? was poor defense against the threat of 20...♘xd5 because of 20...♘g4 21.♘e4 *(21.♗d4 f2+!)* 21...♕xd2 22.♗xd2 (or 22.♘xd2 ♘xe3 23.♖xe3 ♗d4) 22...f2+! 23.♘xf2 ♗d4.

The best move **20.♕d3!** was pointed out by Grigoriev, who, as the jury chairman, awarded this game the brilliancy prize, though he doubted this move for a long time, as he evaluated the line 20...♘g4 21.♘e4 f5 22.♘g5 f2+ 23.♗xf2 ♘xf2 24.♔xf2 ♕xc5+ 25.♔g3 ♖xd5 (25...♕xd5? 26.♖e8+!) 26.♕b3 as better for white." (From the 1984 book.) Strangely, this whole line was shown by Ragozin in *Shakhmaty v SSSR*, and Rabinovich mentioned it, too, in the tournament book: "White could also play 20.♕d3!, as Ragozin pointed out." Finally, Botvinnik himself didn't mention Grigoriev as the author of the move in his 1951 book.

I should add that in the 1960s Mikhail Moiseevich indicated the best way to equalize as: 20...b6 21.gxf3 bxc5 or 21.cxb6 axb6.

However, according to Stockfish 20...♘g4 and 20...♖ac8 both make the position totally equal, whereas 20...b6 accords white a slight advantage.

20...♘g4! 21.♗d4. This only accelerates the defeat. Botvinnik said that even the best line 21.♘e4 ♕xd2 22.♗xd2 ♗d4+ 23.♔h1 fxg2+ 24.♔xg2 ♖xd5 didn't save the game, although after 25.h3! black might not win. For instance: 25...♘f6 26.♘xf6+ ♗xf6 27.♗e3 ♖ad8 28.♖xd5 ♖xd5 29.♖b1 ♖d7 (despite the pawn islands, white's position is still viable) or 25...♖e8 26.c4! (but not 26.♘d6? ♖e2+) 26...♖dd8 27.hxg4 ♖xe4 28.♗c3!, and the deadly pin forces a draw (28...♖xf4 29.g5 f6 30.♖d2 or 29...♔f8 30.♖b1 ♔e8 31.♖e1+) – this resembles an endgame study!

21...f2+ 22.♔f1 (22.♔h1? ♖xd5) **22...♕a6+ 23.♕e2.** "After 23.♕d3 ♗xd4 24.♕xa6 ♘xh2+ 25.♔e2 f1♕+! 26.♖xf1 bxa6 white might as well resign, while after 23.♘e2 ♖xd5 24.c3 ♖e8! there's no defense against ♘e3+." (Botvinnik)

23...♗xd4 24.♖xd4.

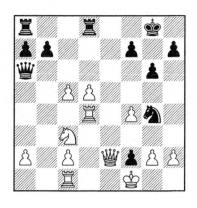

24...♕f6! 25.♖cd1 (or 25.♕d3 ♖e8 26.♘e4 ♘xh2+ 27.♔xf2 ♕xf4+ and ♕xc1+) **25...♕h4 26.♕d3 ♖e8 27.♖e4 f5 28.♖e6 ♘xh2+.** Simpler than Tarrasch's 28...♖ad8 29.♕b5 (29.♕g3 ♕xg3 30.hxg3 ♖xe6 31.dxe6 ♘e3+) 29...♖xe6 30.dxe6 ♖xd1+ 31.♘xd1 ♘xh2+ 32.♔e2 f1♕+.

29.♔e2 ♕xf4. White resigned.

Strangely, the 1990 *Chess* dictionary published in the USSR "awarded" the first brilliancy prize to this game, even though the original jury (Grigoriev, A. Kubbel and Rokhlin) stated clearly in their decision: "All three prizes were awarded *ex aequo*, i.e. on equal terms."

The Beauty of the Struggle

Levenfish: "Some   of Romanovsky's   games   –   against Bogatyrchuk,   Alatortsev   and Lisitsin – were played very well and should be named among the best in this tournament."

No. 62. King's Indian Defense E60
Romanovsky – Bogatyrchuk
Leningrad 1933, round 10
Annotated by I. Rabinovich
1.♘f3 ♘f6 2.b3 g6 3.♗b2 ♗g7 4.c4 0-0 5.e3 d6 6.d4 (transposing into an Indian system) **6...♘bd7 7.♗e2 c5.** 7...e5! was better, and if 8.dxe5, then 8...♘g4.

8.0-0 b6 9.♘c3 ♗b7 10.♕c2. If 10.d5, then 10...♘e4! 11.♕c2 ♘xc3 12.♗xc3 ♗xc3 13.♕xc3 b5!

with a good position for black. With 10.♕c2, white prevents this line and now threatens to play 11.d5!, cramping his opponent's position.

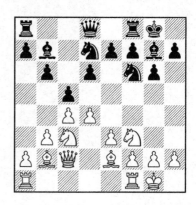

10...♕c7? Black   seems   to underestimate the strength of the move 11.d5! He should have immediately mobilized the e7 pawn, creating counter-pressure in the center: 10...e5! 11.dxe5 (11.♖ad1 ♕e7, while 11.♘b5 ♕e7 12.♘xd6? is met with 12...♗xf3! 13.♗xf3 ♕xd6) 11...dxe5 12.e4 ♘h5, intending, if possible, ♘f4 and f7-f5.

The annotation to the move 12.e4 says, "12.♖ad1 ♕e7 13.♖d2 is better, with an advantage for white." But if it is stronger, why then was the line bracketed? Also, after 13...e4 14.♘g5 ♖fd8 15.♖fd1 h6 16.♘h3 ♘e5, black has good counterplay.

11.d5! ♖ad8. After 11...e5(e6) 12.dxe6! fxe6 13.e4 with strong threats ♖ad1 and ♘g5, black would have had to play passively, because 13...d5? is met with 14.cxd5 exd5 15.exd5 ♘xd5 16.♗c4! with an overwhelming positional advantage

Peter Romanovsky. "He played some individual games very well, but in many others we can see a certain emptiness and lack of ideas." (Levenfish.) (Cover of 64. Shakhmaty i Shashki v Rabochem Klube, No. 16, 1929.)

(the immediate 16.♘xd5! ♗xd5 17.♗c4 ♗xc4 18.♕xc4+ ♔h8 19.♗xg7+ ♔xg7 20.♘g5 wins even more quickly).

12.♖ad1 a6 13.♘g5 ♖fe8 14.f4 e6 15.dxe6 fxe6 16.e4. White's advantage is now clear: he has more space and threatens to attack both in the center (the d6 pawn) and on the kingside (f4-f5).

16...h6. Black should have played 16...♘f8, because 17.e5!? is met with 17...dxe5 18.fxe5 ♕xe5! 19.♘d5 (19. ♘ce4 ♗xe4!) 19...♕xg5 20.♗xf6 (20. ♘xf6+? ♗xf6, threatening mate!)

20...♗xf6 21.♘xf6+ ♔h8 with an advantage for black. If 17.♗f3 or 17.f5, then 17...e5 with better chances of defending successfully than in the actual game.

17.♘h3 ♘f8 18.♗f3.

18...♘6h7. Here, e6-e5 is already bad for black: 18...e5 19.fxe5 dxe5 20.♘d5 ♘xd5 21.exd5 ♗c8! 22.♗e4!!, and the weakness on g6 is very painful.

19.♘e2 (preventing ♗d4+ and then e6-e5) **19...b5 20.♖d2 ♖d7.** And now e6-e5 would have led to trouble for black, because white would return the knight to c3, creating positions similar to those occurring in the notes to black's 18th move. For instance: 20...e5 21.♘c3 ♘e6! 22.♘d5! ♕b8 (after 22...♗xd5 23.exd5, the c2-g6 diagonal opens up; if 22...♕d7(c8), then 23.♗g4!) 23.f5, and if 23...gxf5 24.exf5 ♘d4, then 25.♗xd4 c(e)xd4 26.f6! ♘xf6 27.♘xf6+ ♗xf6 28.♗xb7, and white wins a piece.

Still, the move 20...e5 was possible: unlike the position on move 18, white has to lose a tempo to return the knight to c3, and now it's black to move!

Instead of 21...♘e6, there's a stronger move: 21...b4! 22.♘d5 ♗xd5 23.exd5 exf4 24.♘xf4 ♗xb2 25.♕xb2 ♕g7, and if 26.♘e6, then 26...♕xb2 27.♖xb2 ♖d7 28.♖bf2 ♖f7, holding the position.

21.♖fd1 ♖ed8 22.♗xg7 ♖xg7 23.♘f2! (threatening ♘g4) **23... ♖gd7 24.♕c3 b4 25.♕b2 h5 26.g4! ♖g7 27.♖d3 ♕e7 28.♕d2 hxg4 29.♘xg4 ♕h4 30.♘g3.** Of course, not 30.♖xd6? due to 30...♖xd6 31.♕xd6 ♖d7!, winning.

30...♖gd7 31.♕g2!

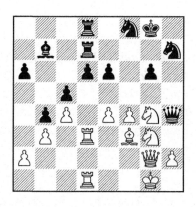

Threatening 32.f5 exf5 33.♘xf5!, and black can't capture the knight

because of a mate in two. *Instead of 32...exf5?, black has 32...♔h8!, for instance: 33.♕b2+ (or 33.fxe6 ♘xe6 34.♘e5 ♘f4) 33...♔g8 34.fxe6 ♘xe6 35.♘e5 ♘f4 with a roughly equal game.*

31...♘f6   32.♘xf6+   ♕xf6 33.♘h5 ♕h4. Addressing 34.f5, which is now met with 34...exf5 35.exf5 ♗xf3 and ♕xh5.

White doesn't have to play cooperative chess though: instead of 35.exf5? he has the more precise 35.♘g3 with the idea 35...f4 36.♘f5.

34.♕g3! ♕xg3+ 35.♘xg3. After the queen trade, white hasn't reduced his pressure one bit; moreover, now he is able to bring out the reserves (the king and the h-pawn).

35...♔f7 36.♔f2 ♘e7 37.♔e3 a5 38.h4 ♖b8 39.f5! gxf5 40.exf5 ♗xf3 41.♔xf3 ♖bd8 42.♖e3 ♔f7 43.♖f1 exf5. If 43...e5, then 44.♘e4!

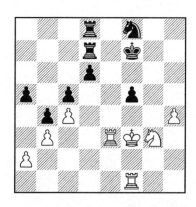

44.♔g2! ♘g6. After 44...d5, the simplest is 45.♘xf5 dxc4 (45...♔g8 46.♘e7+!) 46.♘e7+! ♔g7 47.♖g3+ ♔h6 (other king moves lead to mate) 48.♘g8+ and ♘f6+.

45.♖xf5+   ♔g8.   45...♔g7
doesn't save the game either due to
46.♔h3!, for instance: 46...d5 (46...
♘e5 47.♘e4! with the threat ♖g3)
47.♖e6! ♘f8 48.♘h5+ ♔h8 (if 48...
♔h7(g8), then 49.♘f6+ and ♖c6!)
49.♖h6+, and white, at the very
least, wins the d5 pawn.

*Rabinovich writes that after
47...♖d6 48.♖xd6 ♖xd6 49.cxd5,
"black can't play 49...♖xd5 due
to 50.h5! ♖xf5 51.♘xf5+ ♔f6
52.hxg6, winning." But instead of
50...♖xf5?, black can play 50...♘e7,
making it more difficult for white.
So, it's better to play 48.♘h5+!
♔h6 49.♘f4, and if 49...♖xe6, then
50.♖h5+ ♔g7 51.♘xe6+, forking
the last rook.*

46.♔h3! ♖f8. If 46...d5, then
47.♖g5 ♔h7 48.♘h5 d4 49.♖e6,
and white wins: 49...d3 50.♖exg6,
threatening mate in three; 49...♘f8
50.♘f6+ ♔h6 51.♘g8++ and ♖h6#;
or, finally, 49...♖g8 50.♘f6+ ♔g7 (or
mate otherwise) 51.♘xd7.

47.♖g5 ♔h7 (or 47...♔g7 48.♘f5!
♘f4+ 49.♔g4 ♖xg5+ 50.♔xg5,
winning) **48.♘f5.**

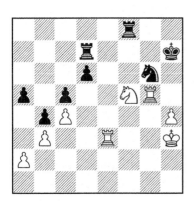

48...♖df7. Black has no defense
against multiple threats: 48...♘e5
49.♖eg3, or if 48...♘f4+ 49.♔g3
♘g6, then 50.♖e6, winning at least
an exchange.

48...♖f6 was relatively better.
There might have followed 49.♖eg3
♖df7 50.♔g4! ♘e5+ 51.♔f4 ♘g6+
52.♔e4 ♖e6+ 53.♔d5! ♖e5+ (53...
♘f4+!? 54.♔c6 d5+ 55.♔b5 ♖ef6
56.♘e3 dxc4) 54.♔c6!! ♖exf5
55.♖xg6 ♖f2 56.♖g2 with an
advantage for white.

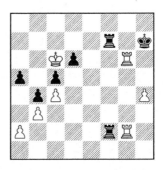

*After 56...♖xa2! 57.♔xd6 ♖a3
(57...♖xg2 58.♖xg2 ♖f3 59.♖b2 is
worse) 58.♖6g3 a4, the path to victory
is very difficult: 59.♔xc5! (59.bxa4
♖xa4 60.♖g5 ♔h6 61.♔xc5 b3 etc.)
59...axb3! 60.♖g5 (60.♔xb4? b2,
and black wins!) 60...♖a5+ 61.♔xb4
♖xg5 62.hxg5 ♖b7+ 63.♔c3 ♔g6
64.♖b2! ♔xg5 65.♖xb3. Still, it's
better to figure out how to win rook
endings in quiet home analysis rather
than in time trouble, hammering on
the clocks...*

**49.♖h5+   ♔g8   50.♖g3! ♖f6
51.♘e7+.** Black resigned: he loses a
piece after 51...♔f7 52.♖h7+ or 51...
♔g7 52.♖hg5.

This game was awarded one of the brilliancy prizes.

Harakiri

"Unfortunately, age and, especially, progressive heart disease caught up with him," I. Romanov wrote in his book *Peter Romanovsky*. "Peter Arsenyevich's play, once confident and stable, now directly depended on his health. In the 8th Soviet Premiership, he was simply unrecognizable. In two games, he blundered a mate in two in won positions. The loss to Levenfish was a particularly strong blow."

No. 63

Levenfish – Romanovsky

Leningrad 1933, round 9

Annotated by M. Yudovich

In that round I played Chekhover. Levenfish and Romanovsky played at the adjacent table. The games went on a long time and were on their way to adjournment. I was thinking over my next move when I suddenly heard the quiet "Ah!", turned around and saw Peter Arsenyevich Romanovsky leaning back helplessly on his chair, and arbiters rushing up to him. Grigory Yakovlevich Levenfish, pale and distraught, sat at the table.

Here's what happened in their game.

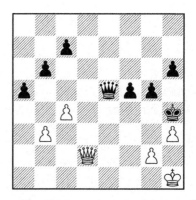

Romanovsky had executed an inventive strategic plan, won two pawns and got an overwhelming position. There followed:

48...♕g3 49.c5 bxc5? (49...f4 won, threatening f4-f3) **50.♕xa5 ♕xb3 51.♕e1+ ♕g3 52.♕e6 h5 53.♕xf5 ♕e3 54.♕d7.**

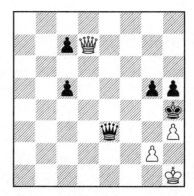

54...c4? Black calculated the "winning" exchanging line. The correct continuation was 54...♕e1+ 55.♔h2 ♕g3+ 56.♔h1 ♕d6.

55.♕xc7 ♕c1+? *(55...♕f4 still drew)* **56.♔h2 ♕f4+.** Everything's all right, but... **57.g3+.** The horrible check! The lurking pawn suddenly struck the deadly blow.

Victim of the Applause

The playing hours after the break weren't harmful only for Romanovsky. His "assailant" suffered in the next game.

No. 64
Verlinsky – Levenfish
Leningrad 1933, round 8
Annotated by G. Levenfish

The extra pawn with an exposed king is not enough for a win. After half an hour of thinking, I found a combination, but I needed to lure the white queen to f6 to execute it.

47...♔g8! 48.♕f6. There's nothing better. If 48.♕e1, then 48...♕f5+ 49.♔g3 ♕d3+ (the spectacular 49...♕xf4+ leads to a draw) 50.♔h4 ♕xb5 51.♕e7 ♕d7.

48...♕d1+? At this moment, N. D. Grigoriev finished his lecture in the adjacent hall, and the public's applause was so loud that I lost my thread of thought. The right move was 48...♕g2+ 49.♔h4 ♕h2+ 50.♔g4 ♕h5+ 51.♔g3 ♕xg5+!

or 50.♘h3 ♕g3+! 51.♔xg3 ♘e4+ *(however, in the second case, black would have still needed some effort to convert the extra pawn in the knight ending!).*

49.♔g3 ♕g1+ 50.♔f3! Now it's impossible to chase the white king to h4, and black is forced to agree to a draw.

The Signature Style

Yudovich: "Riumin finally shined, brilliantly crushing Rabinovich with a spectacular finishing rook sacrifice."

No. 65. Dutch Defense A85
I. Rabinovich – Riumin
Leningrad 1933, round 18
Annotated by N. Riumin

1.d4 e6 2.c4 f5 3.e3. *"A rare guest in modern practice – a development system used back in the days of Steinitz. This system is reasonable and can be quite poisonous, even though white usually prefers fianchettoing the bishop (g2-g3 and ♗g2) in modern practice." (Kan)*

3...♘f6 4.♘c3 ♗e7 5.♗d2. White's system requires a precise move order. It was necessary to play 5.♗d3!, and if 5...0-0, then 6.♘ge2 d6 7.♕c2 ♘c6 8.a3, after which e6-e5 is impossible because the f5 pawn is hanging. I think that this structure is one of the best against the Dutch.

White's passive move *(which was never repeated in tournaments)* allows black to get some active play.

5...0-0 6.♕c2 d6 7.♗d3. Trying to prevent the break e6-e5.

7...♘c6 8.a3 e5! 9.d5. His previous passive moves basically forced white to push this pawn. Indeed, neither 9.♗xf5 exd4 nor 9.dxe5 ♘xe5 10.♗xf5 ♘xc4 cause black any trouble.

9...e4.

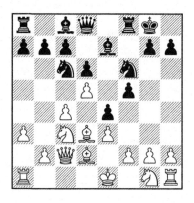

10.♗e2. By playing 10.♗xe4 ♘xe4! 11.♘xe4 fxe4 12.dxc6 bxc6 13.♕xe4, white could win a pawn, but as compensation black got a free open position and the bishop pair.

10...♘e5 11.f4 exf3 12.gxf3. 12.♘xf3 ♘fg4! led to a bad position for white. Black is already better because of a number of weaknesses in white's pawn structure.

12...c6 (preparing to open the c-file in case white castles long) **13.f4 ♘eg4 14.h3 ♘h6 15.♗f3.** White intends to complete development with ♘ge2 and 0-0-0. 15.♘f3 ♘e4 is worse: if 16.♘xe4 fxe4 17.♕xe4?, then 17...♗f5 18.♕d4 ♗f6, winning.

It seems that white should have played 15.0-0-0, even though after 15...cxd5 16.cxd5 ♗d7 17.♔b1 ♖c8 black, naturally, got a strong queenside attack.

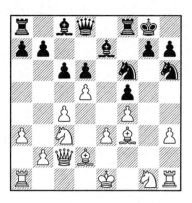

15...♘e4! (this blow disrupts all of white's calculations) **16.♘xe4.** The pawn sacrifice needs to be accepted because of the threats ♗h4+ and ♘f2 (after 16.0-0-0). However, as compensation for the pawn, black deprives white of castling rights, gets a rich attacking position and strong pressure against his opponent's central pawns.

16...fxe4 17.♗xe4 ♗h4+ 18.♔d1. If 18.♔e2, then 18...♘f5! 19.♗xf5 *(19.♔d1!?)* 19...♗xf5 20.e4? ♗xe4, and black wins.

18...♗f5 19.♘f3. 19.♘e2 ♕e8! *(the straightforward attack through the center – 19...♕e7 20.♗d3! ♗xd3 21.♕xd3 ♖ae8 22.♘c3 ♘f5 – gives black nothing: 23.e4 ♘g3 24.♖e1 ♘h5 25.♖f1 etc.)* had its own drawbacks, for instance: 20.♘c3 ♕h5+ 21.♔c1 ♖ae8 – black's attack essentially plays itself (but*

20.♗xf5!? ♘xf5 21.♕d3 was more resilient).

19...♕e7 20.♗xf5 ♘xf5 21.e4.

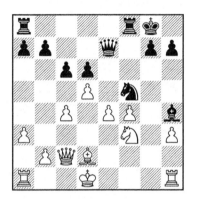

21...♖ae8! Drawing on his last reserves with decisive effect. White can't capture the knight because of the check on e2.

22.dxc6 bxc6 23.c5! An interesting move. White is unable to protect the e4 pawn, but he finds a way to push it forward. 23.♘xh4 ♗xh4 24.♖e1 ♘f3! was bad, because black regains the lost pawn and maintains a strong attack.

23...d5. White threatened 24.♕c4+, and if 24...♔h8, then 25.exf5. After 23...♕xe4 24.♕xe4 ♖xe4 25.♘xh4 ♘xh4 26.cxd6, white had some defense.

24.e5. It seems that white has managed to strengthen his position quite a bit, but this is only an illusion, as we shall see in a few moves.

24...♘g3 25.♖h2 (25.♖g1 ♘e4 is no better: black threatens ♗g3!) **25...♘e4 26.♘xh4 ♕xh4 27.♗c1.** Black would have met 27.♗e3 the same way.

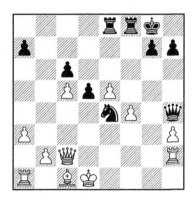

27...♖xe5! 28.fxe5 ♖f1+ 29.♔e2 ♘g3+! *Black had an even more spectacular mate: 29...♕e1+! 30.♔d3 ♖f3+ 31.♔d4 ♘c3!!, threatening ♘b5#, and if 32.bxc3, then 32...♕h4+.*

30.♔d3 ♕e4+ 31.♔d2 ♕f4+ 32.♔c3 ♖f3+. White resigned (*33. ♕d3 ♕c4+ etc.*).

The game was awarded one of the brilliancy prizes.

The Lost Game

"The eighth national championship was only a modest success for Riumin," I. Kan writes in the book *Chess Player Nikolai Riumin.* "It seems that Nikolai Nikolaevich was unfortunately affected by his ailing health, which he paid little attention too. His poor performance was somewhat compensated for by defeating the championship winner, Botvinnik. Here are some details of this game.

Riumin prepared for the championship together with me. And then, in preparation for the game against Botvinnik, we found a

Nikolai Riumin, the favorite of the Moscow fans. From Y. Neistadt's archive.

cunning trap in an opening line that he could play *(in the Dutch Defense)*. And so, the day when Riumin played Botvinnik came...

While I played my own game, I literally pined for any information about the Botvinnik – Riumin game, which was held in the adjacent hall. Finally, I got up and went there to see what was happening, and bumped into Riumin, who was hurrying the other way.

"You know," Nikolai Nikolaevich exclaimed excitedly, not even trying to hide his joy, "you know, he got caught in that trap!"

Riumin won a piece, and then the game, after a very tenacious defense from the inventive tournament leader. Unfortunately, we couldn't

restore the game score. But you can look at the trap idea here.

No. 66
Botvinnik – Riumin
Leningrad 1933, round 16

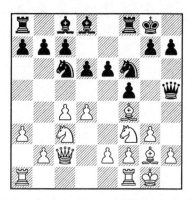

In approximately this position, Riumin played **1...e5! 2.dxe5 dxe5 3.♗xe5? ♘g4!**, and white loses material (**4.♗f4? ♘d4!!**)."

P.S. The Moscow player didn't have it easy. "However, Riumin, very sure of his victory, played so badly that he adjourned the game with very unclear winning chances in a complicated endgame – two rooks and knight versus queen and two pawns. In the next session, Botvinnik tried to resist, but couldn't save the game." (*64*, September 1933.)

The One-Two Pawn Punch

Alatortsev explained his success with "solely the strength of middlegame play", where he "managed to couple moments of strict positional play with timely combinations."

No. 67
Alatortsev – Bogatyrchuk
Leningrad 1933, round 4
Annotated by V. Alatortsev

13...罩fc8. It was better to place the other rook on that square and the f-rook on d8, because the d6 pawn is quite weak in the dark-squared bishop's absence. However, black

wants to undermine the c4 pawn and prepares to double rooks on the c-file.

14.b3 a6 15.罩ad1 罩c7 16.瞥d2 ②c5! White threatened to play ②a4 and 瞥b4! with pressure on two weakness – d6 and b6.

17.f4 罩ac8 18.f5!

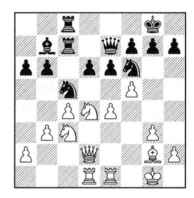

18...罩d8? This accelerates the defeat. But even the relatively better

Vladimir Alatortsev proved his class by winning the Transcaucasian Republics championship in Tiflis (1933). On the photo: a game against Viktor Goglidze.

18...e5 cedes the strong d5 square to white after 19.♘c2!. It's also easy to prepare the movement of the g-pawn, which makes black's position even worse.

18...b5? was bad: 19.cxb5 ♘xb3 20.axb3 ♖xc3 21.♘c6!, winning an exchange. 18...♘cd7 19.fxe6 fxe6 20.♗h3 ♘f8 21.e5 dxe5 22.♖xe5 was equally bad, when there's no 22...♖d8 due to 23.♘c6! etc. *(with 23...♕c5+ 24.♖xc5 ♖xd2 25.♖xd2 bxc5, black can save the exchange, but even Lasker wouldn't be able to defend such a ruined position!).*

19.e5!! *Well done, Junior! The engine saw this move immediately. Fritz, however, missed it completely... This strong one-two pawn punch in the center is reminiscent of Rauzer – Botvinnik (game 61).*

19...♘e8. Or 19...dxe5 20.♘c6! ♖xd2 21.♘xe7+ ♖xe7 22.♖xd2 ♗xg2 (22...exf5 23.♖d8+ ♘e8 24.b4 ♗xg2 25.bxc5! etc.) 23.♔xg2 exf5 24.♖d8+ ♘e8 25.♘d5, winning.

After the game move, black loses a pawn by force.

20.♗xb7 ♘xb7 21.fxe6 fxe6 22.exd6.

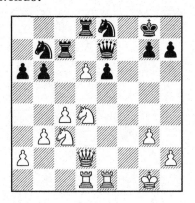

22...♕xd6 (necessary: 22...♖xd6 is met with 23.♘d5!) **23.♖xe6 ♕xe6.** 23...♕c5 24.♘d5! etc. was no better. But the endgame with an extra pawn can be won quickly as well.

24.♘xe6 ♖xd2 25.♖xd2 ♖e7 26.♘f4 ♘f6 27.♘cd5 ♘xd5 28.♘xd5 ♖e1+ 29.♔f2 ♖e6. To answer 30.♘c7 with 30...♖f6+ and a6-a5.

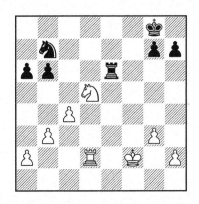

30.♖e2! ♖xe2+. After the forced rook exchange, black has to move the b-pawn, weakening the already weak queenside.

31.♔xe2 b5 32.cxb5 axb5 33.♔d3 ♔f7 34.♔c3 g5 (if 34...♔e6, then 35.♘c7+) **35.♔b4 h5 36.♔xb5 ♔e6 37.♘e3 ♔e5 38.♘c4+! ♔d5 39.a4 ♘c5 40.♘e3+ ♔d4 41.♘f5+ ♔d5 42.b4 ♘e6 43.a5.** Black resigned.

Surprise after Surprise

Yudovich: "Lisitsin surprised everyone, even his fans. Nobody expected him to finish that high in such a strong tournament."

No. 68
Lisitsin – Goglidze
Leningrad 1933, round 16
Annotated by G. Lisitsin

14...c4. Black probably thought that white (because he loses an exchange after 15.bxc4 dxc4) would retreat the bishop to e2, and then intended to play 15...b5, threatening to kick away the c3 knight and then invade the e4 square, gaining a positional advantage. He should have played 14...b5 15.a3 c4 16.♗f5 ♘b6.

15.bxc4! Black probably didn't expect that!

15...dxc4 16.♗xc4 ♗xf3 17.gxf3. It's not hard to see that white has enough compensation for the exchange. He has two active bishops and a strong knight in the center, and he's also able to quickly seize the open g-file, which gives him great chances for a mating attack.

17...b5 18.♗b3 ♘b6 19.♔h1.

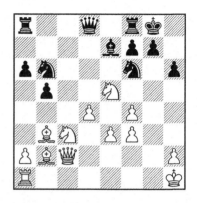

19...b4? The decisive mistake. Black could have held with 19...♖c8 20.♖g1! ♘c4 21.♕g2 ♘e8 22.♘xc4 bxc4 23.♗a4 ♗f6 24.♗a3 ♘d6 25.♘e4 ♘xe4 26.fxe4, and white has a won position, but he still needs to win it!

That's all obvious. However, after the apparently suicidal-looking 23... g6, it's hard to defeat black quickly, for instance: 24.♗c2 ♘g7 25.f5 g5 26.f4 f6 27.♗e4 ♔h8 etc.

20.♖g1! (a new surprise for black!) **20...♘h5.** Or 20...bxc3 21.♕g6 ♘h5 (21...♘e8 22.♘xf7 ♖xf7 23.♕xf7+ ♔h7 24.♕g8#), and then like in the game.

21.♕g6 bxc3 22.♕xh5.

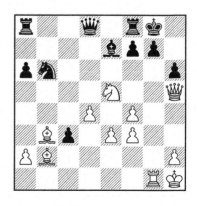

22...♗f6. After 22...cxb2 23.♘xf7, black would have to resign immediately.

23.♘xf7 ♖xf7 (forced, or else a quick mate follows) **24.♗xf7+.** Driving the king into the corner and preparing the finishing combination.

24...♔h8 25.♗xc3 ♕e7 26.♖g6! Black resigned, because he can't avoid getting checkmated or losing his queen: 26...♕xf7 27.♖xh6+ gxh6 28.♕xf7, or 26...♔h7 27.♖xh6+ gxh6 28.♕g6+ ♔h8 29.♕xh6#, or 26...♕f8 27.♗b4 ♗e7 28.♗xe7.

Under Four Attacks!

S. Vainstein: "Such elegant endings as Levenfish vs. Yudovich will always serve as great methodical material for those who aren't yet well-versed in the beauty of chess combinations."

No. 69
Levenfish – Yudovich
Leningrad 1933, round 17
Annotated by G. Levenfish

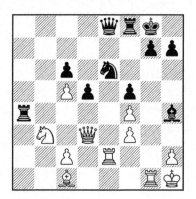

25.♕e3! White was thinking of 25...♘c7 26.♗b2!, and if 26...g6, then 27.♕c3, while after 26...d4, there's 27.♗xd4 *(or 27.♕d3!+−).*

25...♔f7 26.♗b2. Threatening 27.♕xe6+ ♕xe6 28.♖xg7+.

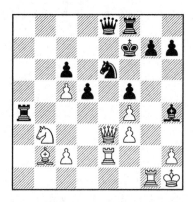

26...♖g8? 26...♗f6 didn't help either due to 27.♗xf6 gxf6 28.♖ge1! ♘g7 (or 28...♘c7 29.♕e7+) 29.♕g1! ♕d7 30.♖e7+.

However, 26...g6!, which wasn't even mentioned by either Rabinovich (in the tournament book) or Levenfish (in his memoir), suddenly creates a dead end for white! How to attack further? You can't attack e6 directly (the bishop is guarding the e1 square), and all critical squares are covered on the long dark diagonal. No matter what white plays, black is fine.

27.♕e5! ♗f6. After 27...g6, there's 28.♖ge1! again.

After 28...♕d7 (28...♗xe1?? 29.♕f6#) 29.♕xe6+ ♕xe6 30.♖xe6 ♗xe1 31.♖xe1 ♖b8!, there's still much play left in the position, for instance: 32.♗e5 ♖b5 33.♗d6 ♖b7, and you can't crack black's defense without the king's support.

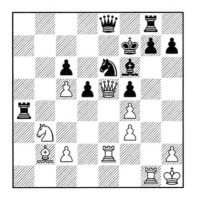

28.♖xg7+!! Under four attacks. *This one move over the board redeems all the flaws in his home analysis...*

28...♗xg7   29.♕xf5+   ♔e7 30.♖xe6+ ♔d8 31.♖xe8+. Black resigned.

The Savitsky Enigma

Gotthilf: "Savitsky's pursuit of an opening initiative was always based on opening knowledge, understanding the spirit of openings and concrete analysis of lines."

No. 70. Indian Defense A50
Savitsky – Botvinnik
Leningrad 1933, round 11
Annotated by L. Savitsky
1.d4 ♘f6 2.♘f3 b6 3.g3 ♗b7 4.c4 e5! Botvinnik's move, recommended by him back in 1928 and finally used in an actual game.

This move had already occurred in the Teichmann – Alekhine match (Berlin 1921). Alekhine's note: "A

sudden counter-strike reminiscent of the Budapest Gambit, leading to equality."

5.dxe5 ♘g4 6.♗g2. This move equalizes immediately. Trying to refute black's move with 6.♗h3? ♘xe5 7.♘xe5 ♗xh1 8.f3 loses to 8... ♕e7!

Alekhine agrees: "White has nothing better. After 6.♕d4, black gets an advantage after 6...h5 7.♕f4 g6 etc.". But 7...♗c5! is much stronger!

6...♘xe5 7.♘bd2 ♗e7 *(Alekhine preferred 7...♘xf3+ 8.♘xf3 ♗b4+)* **8.0-0.**

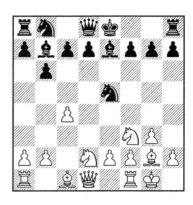

8...♘g6? This is a mistake. The right move was 8...♘xf3+ 9.♘xf3 0-0 with the subsequent ♘a6-c5 and an equal game. With the move played, black wanted to avoid the piece trade, but gets a very difficult position because of it.

9.♘b1!! *"The knight that just developed retreats to head for c3 (the goal is d5!) This one example should be enough to convince you that Leonid indeed had great opening knowledge."* (Gotthilf)

9...0-0 10.♘c3 ♞a6 11.h4! ♗f6. Forced, because white threatened to drive away the knight with h4-h5. If 11...♖e8, then 12.h5 and h5-h6.

12.h5 ♞e7 13.♕c2 ♞c5 14.♗e3 ♖e8? Black should have played 14...h6, for instance: 15.♗xc5 bxc5 16.♘g5 ♗xg5 17.♗xb7 ♖b8 18.♗f3 with an advantage for white.

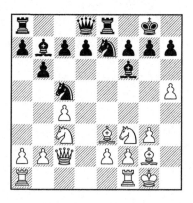

15.♖ad1. White had an interesting, but inadequate attack after 15.b4. For instance: 15...♗xc3 16.♘g5 ♗xa1 (16...g6 17.♕xc3 ♗xg2 18.♕f6 ♖f8 19.♗d4, *mating; however, 17...♘f5! was more resilient, and if 18.hxg6 hxg6 19.♗f4, then 19...♗xg2 20.♔xg2 f6!?)* 17.♕xh7+ ♔f8 18.♖xa1! ♞g8 (18...♞e6? 19.h6!) 19.h6 ♕f6!, and black repels the attack.

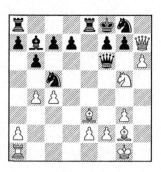

Savitsky overlooked the strong reply 20.♕b1! (threatening ♘h7+), which made black's position critical: 20...♔e7 (20...♕e5 21.h7 g6 22.♕d1!, threatening ♗d4 and forcing 22... ♕g7(h8) 23.bxc5 ♗xg2 24.hxg8♕+ ♔xg8 25.♔xg2 etc.) 21.h7 ♞h6 22.♗xb7 ♞xb7 23.♕e4+ ♔d8 24.♗d4 ♕e7 25.♕xb7 with a won position.

However, his evaluation of the move 15.b4 was correct: instead of 16...♗xa1?, black repelled the attack with 16...♗xg2! 17.♕xh7+ ♔f8 18.♔xg2 ♗xa1 19.♖xa1 ♞e6!

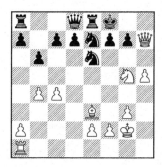

Unlike in Savitsky's line, the light-squared bishops are already traded off, and 20.h6 doesn't lead to the goal: 20...♞g8 21.♘xe6+ ♖xe6 22.♕xg7+ ♔e7 23.♗g5+ ♞f6, and black wins!

15...♗xc3 16.♗xc5 ♗f6 17.♗d4 ♗xd4 18.♖xd4 ♞c6 19.♖g4. This looks threatening, but in actuality it is refuted by the subsequent queen maneuver.

19...♕f6! 20.♘g5 ♕h6! *Rokhlin didn't compare Botvinnik's defensive skills with Lasker's for nothing!*

21.♗d5 (21.♕f5 was better; the game move gives black an important tempo) **21...♖e7 22.♕f5 ♖f8.**

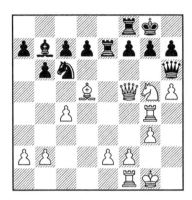

23.♗e4? White gained a decisive advantage and could convert it with 23.♖e4! (found by A. N. Chistyakov, Moscow), threatening ♗xc6 and ♖xe7. For instance:

1)   23...♖f(e)e8   24.♕xf7+, winning;

2)   23...♖xe4   24.♘xf7!!   ♕f6 25.♘g5+ or 24...♕e6 25.♘h6+!;

3)   23...♕xh5   24.♖h4! ♕g6 25.♕xg6 hxg6 26.♔g2, and there's no good defense against 27.♖fh1 and ♖h8#;

4) 23...g6 24.♕f6 ♖e6 25.♘xe6 fxe6 26.♖xe6 ♖xf6 27.♖e8++ and ♖g8#.

So Black is forced to give up an exchange: 23...♖e6 24.♗xe6 dxe6 (24...fxe6 25.♕g4) 25.♕f4 e5 26.♕h4 f5 27.♖e3, and white should win.

However, instead of 26...f5?, the computer finds 26...♘d4!, forcing 27.♖xe5 f6 28.♕xd4 fxe5 29.♕xe5 ♕xh5, and black holds.

So, is 23...♖e6 a refutation? If white captures with the bishop, it is. But after 24.♘xe6! dxe6 25.♖xe6!, black can't hold.

For instance: 25...♘d4 26.♖xh6! ♘xf5 27.♗xb7, and to avoid 27...♘xh6 28.♖d1 ♘g4 29.♖d7 c5 30.♗d5 a5 31.♖b7, black has to capture with the pawn, compromising his pawn structure: 27...gxh6 28.♖d1 ♘d6 29.♗d5 ♖e8 30.e3 and so on.

23...♖e5! Forcing white to capture on h7. After that, all the attacking pieces are traded away, and white is left with nothing.

24.♕xh7+   ♕xh7   25.♗xh7+. Or   25.♘xh7   f5!   26.♘xf8 fxg4 27.♗xc6 ♗xc6 28.♘g6 ♖xe2 with an advantage for black.

25...♔h8   26.♗d3   ♘b4!   27.f4 ♖e7.

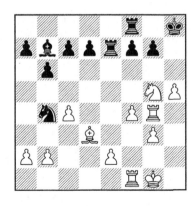

28.h6? White is confused, and his position quickly becomes hopeless.

White could still defend with 28.f5! f6 29.♘e4 ♖fe8 30.♘c3 or even 30.♖ff4!?, threatening h5-h6, and if 30...d5, then 31.♘c3.

28...gxh6 29.♖h4 ♔g7 30.♘f3 *(essentially, only this is the losing move; 30.f5! f6 31.♘e4)* **30...♘xd3 31.exd3 ♖e3 32.♘d4 f5.** *Black is also imprecise. It was simpler to play 32...♖xg3+! 33.♔h2 ♖g2+ 34.♔h3 f5.*

33.g4 fxg4 34.♖xg4+ ♔h7 35.♘c2.

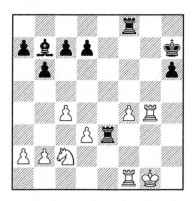

35...♖e2. *35...♖h3! won an exchange and the game immediately: 36.♘e1 h5 37.♖g2 (37.♖g5? ♖h1+). Now, white could hold with the simple 36.♖f2...*

36.♖e1?? ♖xc2. White resigned. The last ten moves by both opponents were made in severe time trouble.

The collapse of the 22 year-old Leningrad master Leonid Savitsky was probably the biggest drama of the whole championship. After a sensational start (5.5/7!) he slowed down a bit, but still remained in the leading group. Had he won that game, he would have narrowed the gap with Botvinnik to one point. The loss turned out to be catastrophic for him! In the last eight games, Savitsky scored just 2 points...

An Old Horse Doesn't Spoil the Furrows

9th Soviet Championship:
Leningrad, 7th December 1934 – 2nd January 1935

"There are some eras that say that they don't care about humans,
that humans should be used as bricks and mortar,
that you should build out of humans, not for them."
Osip Mandelstam, *Humanism and Modernity*

Seeing the title, someone would surely add, "but he can't plough too deeply". Well, if we're talking about a typical country horse, this might be true, but you work with your head on the dark and light squares, and this extends the career of chess "plough-pullers" immensely.

"The ability to play chess (master-strength chess, at that) is retained well into old age," Fyodor Bogatyrchuk reminded readers in the *Moscow International Tournament Bulletin* (No. 1, 1935). "This is only logical if we remember that the human brain ages more slowly than the body. Nevertheless, courtesy of some of our chess press, there's now a widespread, football-like if I may put it that way view of the chess masters. The master is not evaluated as an example of a particular trend in chess, as an expert in chess art, but rather from the point of view of his physical stamina in running a certain distance. If you manage to last the distance, run it without panting, and score 50 percent, then you're still a master. If you didn't manage that, you're done for."

This article was likely written in response to the discussions "on masters and mastery" – that was the title of an editorial in *Shakhmaty v SSSR* (March 1934), which sparked a noisy campaign, possibly initiated by Krylenko himself. At first glance, the main goal was just to tighten the requirements to obtain the master's title, to avoid the "overproduction" of masters, but the true purpose was, without a doubt, to purge the ranks of the masters. Instead of immediately reintroducing the grandmaster's title that was abolished in 1931 (and rehabilitated only a year later), the reformers declared that masters were some kind of a "superclass", and... started to change life to meet their framework.

In the very next issue, this important initiative was supported by the luminaries of Soviet chess –Botvinnik, Levenfish and Romanovsky: "No bourgeois state can even come close to us regarding the number of masters. We have 43 chess masters... However, we should not be dizzy with success. The second five-year plan is the five-year plan of improvement, the five-year

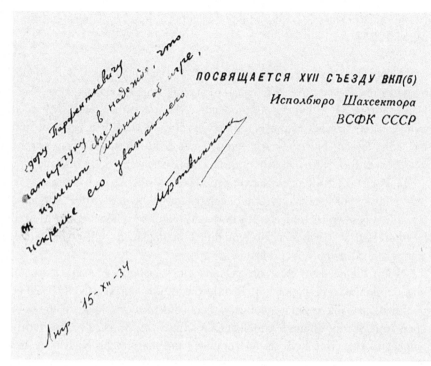

ПОСВЯЩАЕТСЯ XVII СЪЕЗДУ ВКП(б)

Исполбюро Шахсектора

ВСФК СССР

Dedication on the book Botvinnik – Flohr Match (1934), which Botvinnik gave as a gift to Bogatyrchuk during the 9th Soviet Championship: "To Fyodor Parfenyevich Bogatyrchuk, in the hope that he would change his opinion about the play of M. Botvinnik, who deeply respects him. Leningrad, 15th December 1934." This unique document was sent to me by Andrei Eremenko (Kharkov). Book from the archive of B. Schippan (Germany).

plan of high-quality indicators. We should strive, as Comrade Pyatakov said at the 17th Party Conference, for our Soviet brand to be better than the foreign one. This is true for the "brand" of Soviet chess masters as well. We should admit openly that, in this regard, the situation is not good enough."

Listing the criteria that will "allow the master's title to truly become an academic degree", the authors recommended only awarding this title for life to masters aged 50 or more, and everyone else should be periodically sifted through strict qualification procedures: "The Highest Qualification Committee cleanses the masters' cadre and demotes those who do not satisfy the demands to candidate master..."

Afterwards, Nikolai Zubarev, the HQC chairman, proposed demoting "some masters, who had achieved no success in the last three years, directly to first category." And Vladimir Alatortsev reminded his colleagues that "the qualification committees should base their work on the wise slogan of Comrade Stalin, 'Cadres decide everything'."

Only one master dared to challenge the "general line" – at least publicly (*64*, August 1934):

"...The chess organization (of course, I'm talking about our, Soviet organization) is not interested just in having professional masters – it's mainly interested in having masters among the non-professionals. We need more masters among engineers, doctors, professors, qualified workers, and fewer among such players who spend their whole life on the 64 squares of the chessboard. There are several assumptions that prove this point of view:

1) For the USSR chess movement, chess is not an end in itself, but only a means for general cultural development of the masses, for creating a sensible way of recreation, etc. It's only natural for the chess organization to be interested in developing more qualified chess players, masters included, among all walks of life, all professions.

2) For the needs of chess propaganda, the social and scientific status of masters is also very important. If only professional players could become qualified chess players in our country, then a dim view would be taken of our chess organization in maintaining such a situation... We need to constantly emphasize that Botvinnik is an engineer, and, despite his youth, he has achieved some success in his profession, that Romanovsky is an outstanding financial officer, that Levenfish is the chief engineer in a trust, that Ilyin-Zhenevsky is a remarkable diplomat, etc. It's important to stress that for all these people, chess is no more than, as the English say, a *hobby (the word was written in English)*. So, the chess organization should not forget about such masters when holding big competitions – moreover, it should take great care of their interests. Our non-professional masters can only develop their skills at such competitions, because at other times they are so busy with their scientific and public work that they don't have spare time to study chess...

We should also consider the rules for retaining the master's title taking into account the caring attitude towards our non-professional masters. We have no doubt that this title should be kept for life. Obtaining the master's title is another thing – any strict measures are acceptable here... But if this title is awarded, it should be kept for life. The master's title is equivalent to that of Academy of Sciences member in any field, and it should only be taken away after some serious offence.

It's completely wrong to keep the master's title for life only upon reaching the "advanced age" (50 years!), as one article in *Shakhmaty v SSSR* said – its author, most probably, is of the Young Pioneer's age. There are known cases of masters resuming their careers after five or more years of inactivity and immediately achieving great success. On the other hand, masters older than

50 have also put in great performances in tournaments. We shouldn't consider age or the level of activity of a master – only whether or not he deservedly got his title...

So, let's have more difficulties in obtaining the master's title! More care towards non-professional masters! For the lifelong, esteemed title of Soviet master!

F. P. Bogatyrchuk, Radiology Assistant Professor."

Alas, that was a voice crying in the wilderness. The lifelong master's title was awarded only to players who were older than 50. An exception was made only for Verlinsky (the only one to receive a personal pension as well) and Selezniev. "After running down the list with his eyes, Krylenko looked questioningly at Eremeev: "What about Selezniev?" "He's totally taken to the bottle!" shrugged Valerian Evgenievich. "I know," the chess leader snarled gloomily. This pitiless and unsentimental minister who would send his former party colleagues off for execution or a stay at the GULAG with a wave of his hand suddenly turned soft: had he not exiled Selezniev from Moscow the latter wouldn't have picked up this sin. In essence, Selezniev was the nicest person you could meet, smart and erudite. So Krylenko added Selezniev so the list of lifelong masters." (From V. Neishtadt and V. Pak, *Prince Myshkin of the Chess Kingdom*.)

In August 1935, "due to a lack of necessary sporting achievements in the last five years", Gotthilf, Izmailov, Kirillov, A. Kubbel, M. Makogonov, Model, Rosenthal, Rokhlin, Sergeyev, Silich, Sorokin and Vygodchikov were stripped of their masters' titles and demoted to first category. "I can only imagine my father's feelings about that," Nikolai Izmailov wrote in *Shakhmaty v Rossii* (No. 1–3, 1999). "This purging was a huge blow for non-professional masters who could not regularly play

Mikhail Makogonov – one of the players who was stripped of his master's title and relegated to first category during the "purge" of 1935. On the photo: at a tournament in Tiflis (1933).

in tournaments because of their day job, and especially for Petr Izmailov. In these five years, he only once (in 1931) played in an All-Union tournament. Wouldn't it have been more correct to give him and other 'demoted' masters the time and opportunity to prove their titles?"

Bogatyrchuk advocated cultural development through chess, basically repeating what Krylenko had said in the previous few years; he didn't understand (or wasn't willing to understand?) that after the Botvinnik – Flohr match (November-December 1933), the situation had changed, and the higher-ups were now more concerned with world chess domination – and so they didn't need amateur masters anymore. Now they needed battle-hardened professionals who were able to defeat the strongest Western masters and prove the superiority of the Soviet way of life – and all resources were devoted to achieving that aim!

In 1935 and 1936, two big international tournaments were held in Moscow, with much fanfare. Botvinnik brilliantly lived up to the hopes in both: he shared the win with Flohr in the first one, while in the second one he finished only behind Capablanca, who was experiencing his second youth back then. Then, the triumph in Nottingham followed... But when in 1937 Botvinnik declined the invitation to the 10th Soviet Championship because he had to work on his candidate's degree thesis, he received a threatening telegram from Krylenko: "I'll discuss your behavior with the Central Committee." This was a reminder to the best Soviet chess player that he had more important things to do in life than work on his academic career!

The powerful ideological underpinnings of the Soviet chess boom could be seen in Krylenko's mouthpiece (64), which announced at that time: "The exceptional mass popularity of chess in our country, with hundreds of competitions, tournaments of giant factories, the collective farm Spartakiads, the growth of the chess movement in the national republics, the results of two Moscow International Tournaments and, finally, Botvinnik's victory in Nottingham – all that has compelled the whole world to recognize that chess culture can only truly flourish in the country of victorious socialism."

I can't speak for "the whole world", but Alekhine's renewed interest in "the country of victorious socialism", which culminated in his telegram with "sincere greetings to the Soviet chess players on the occasion of the 18th anniversary of the October Revolution", had emerged back in early 1935. It's even strange that his article "Prospects for the Moscow Tournament" wasn't published in the USSR. This was a true panegyric to Soviet chess from "the remnant of the White Guard", as Alekhine was called in *Shakhmaty v SSSR* just half a year before that (see below).

Alekhine: "'Catch up and overtake'... We should impartially admit that in the area of chess, this slogan wasn't just an empty phrase; they achieved both in a relatively short period of time. They 'caught up' in one regard and even 'overtook' in others. They **caught up** because they produced one or two high-class masters (Botvinnik and, probably, Riumin) who have full grounds to honorably represent their country in any international competition; in addition to those two outstanding players, they have a whole generation of younger masters who successfully compete with such experienced chess artists as Romanovsky, Levenfish and I. Rabinovich, who are, of course, rightful members of the average international class.

And they **overtook** others in the average strength of amateur players, which has been clearly and repeatedly shown in the last few years in encounters with foreign guests.

...Of the Soviet masters, I think only Botvinnik has a chance of competing for first place. However, almost all the Russian players have good chances of winning prizes, especially Riumin. The coming weeks shall show how close these assumptions are to the truth and how close the USSR, which already has the strongest amateur players, is to becoming first in the quality and sporting results of its best chess players as well." (*Posledniye Novosti*, Paris, 22nd February 1935.)

Death to the Enemies of the Revolution!

Bogatyrchuk: "In early winter 1934, the 9th All-Union Championship was held, again in Leningrad. On my way there, an agitated man entered my train compartment and said, pointing at a newspaper, "Have you heard? Kirov has been murdered!" He added grimly: "Now it is starting..."

It was clear what "it" was – intensification of the terror. Indeed, soon after arriving in Leningrad, I read in a newspaper that 300 former White Guards had been executed in prisons as a part of the Red Terror. Even those who had lived through the horrors of the Civil War and the terror back then were shocked by this senseless barbarity – especially considering that Kirov was murdered by a young party member rather than some "reactionary". But the authorities and their leader, Stalin, had completely lost all pretenses of benevolence and mistreated their subjects as they pleased. A wave of terror swept over the whole of Russia, destroying thousands of innocent lives. As Khrushchev implied later, it's possible that the murder was organized by Stalin himself, who wanted a free license to destroy his party rivals. The subsequent trials of Zinoviev and other VKP(b) leaders confirm this hypothesis.

Fyodor Bogatyrchuk greets the foreign participants of the 1935 Moscow International Tournament on behalf of the Soviet players. Left to right: Flohr, Lasker, Capablanca, Eremeev, Riumin, I. Rabinovich, Levenfish, Chekhover, Romanovsky, Lisitsin, Bogatyrchuk, Kan, Alatortsev, Botvinnik. Cartoon by N. Radlov (Krokodil, No. 3, 1935). Published for the first time.

Anyway, the dark prediction of my traveling companion fully came true: the floodgates opened, and rivers of blood flowed out of them again; only this time, this was the blood of the creators and inspirers of Bolshevism rather than its enemies.

At first, we thought that the tournament would be canceled, but it went ahead as scheduled." (From the book *My Life Path to Vlasov and the Prague Manifesto*.)

A strange detail: the letter of mourning published in *Shakhmaty v SSSR* on behalf of the players and organizing committee members wasn't signed by Bogatyrchuk, yet Romanovsky and Botvinnik were among the signatories, even though they neither played in the tournament nor organized it. I won't print this letter, titled **"Our Leader, the Best Friend of Chess Players, Comrade Kirov Has Died"**, in full, but I'll quote the final part – to show you the spirit of the times, as it were:

"By destroying the enemies of the Soviet Union, sweeping aside all obstacles, the working class and collective-farm peasants of our great Soviet country advance with iron steps towards new victories, with guidance from the Bolshevist party led by the great Stalin!

Close ranks around our Leninist party!

Death to the enemies of the revolution!"

The chess magazines became increasingly politicized. Here's a quote from an article "Chess Champions in the Role of Fascist Lackeys" by **L. Spokoiny** (*Shakhmaty v SSSR*, July 1934), describing the world championship match between Alekhine and Bogoljubov that was held in Germany:

"Both heroes of this match were worthy of their masters. They knew exactly what was expected from them. Both of those crooks had been talking in great length about their loyalty to National Socialism at the fascist rallies held when they traveled from town to town. Alekhine declared that he was ready to give his life for a National-Socialist Russia. Bogoljubov parroted after him, saying that soon all peoples would follow in Germany's footsteps. We shouldn't be surprised by such proclamations. All the morals and politics, all the principles and convictions of those two are only defined by their passion for money. When you take the fascist money, you speak the fascist language! In the old times, a genius could be a philistine at the same time, as Marx and Engels showed in the examples of Goethe or Hegel; however, in the contemporary celebrities of bourgeois society, great talent in special areas is coupled with total cretinism and degeneracy of their shared moral appearance. Contempt and disgust – that's all we feel towards those "international" remnants of the White Guard."

Grigoriev *(concerning the attribution of articles in* 64, *see the end of the preface to the 7th championship)*: "On 7th December in Leningrad, the 9th All-Union Premiership started, with 20 players participating – the strongest representatives of Soviet chess art. After several qualifying competitions held in Moscow, Leningrad, Tiflis and Central Asia, the following players were admitted to the tournament (listed in the order determined by the drawing of lots): 1. Dubinin (Gorky; *only he and Veresov were first category players*), 2. Chekhover, 3. Levenfish, 4. I. Rabinovich, 5. Alatortsev, 6. Lisitsin (all Leningrad), 7. Yudovich, 8. Kan (both Moscow), 9. Bogatyrchuk (Kiev), 10. Ragozin (Leningrad), 11. Mazel, 12. Belavenets (both Moscow), 13. Veresov (Minsk), 14. Riumin (Moscow), 15. V. Makogonov (Baku), 16. Ilyin-Zhenevsky (Leningrad), 17. Panov (Moscow), 18. Freymann (Tashkent), 19. Rauzer (Kiev), and 20. Savitsky (Leningrad). As we may see, of the strongest players of the Soviet Union, only two are absent – the Soviet champion Botvinnik, who was sent to play at the Hastings international tournament, and distinguished master Romanovsky, who was excused from playing because of ill health.

> Peter Arsenyevich was among the first Soviet sportsmen to receive the title Distinguished Master of Sport, on 5 June 1934.
> **Romanovsky:** "After 1933 and until 1945, I didn't play in the All-Union championships. I had to drop out of the 11th championship (1939) because of illness. My participation in the 1935 Moscow International Tournament was only possible because I adhered to a very strict medical regimen due to progressing heart disease." (From the book *Selected Games*.)
> Romanovsky's health was in fact impacted by two tragedies in quick succession in his family life. In January 1933 his first wife died, leaving him with three daughters. At the end of that year he remarried, but then his second wife died while giving birth to his fourth daughter in 1935.

Due to Botvinnik's inability to participate in this premiership, the winner of this tournament, to confirm his Soviet champion's title, pledges to play a match with Botvinnik in 1935." (*64. Shakhmaty i Shashki v Massy*, January 1935.)

> I'll run ahead a bit here and say that this match never took place. Either because there were two winners in the tournament, or because of Krylenko's stance, who, according to Botvinnik, said around this time, "No matches, period!" At any rate, the match is not mentioned either in the chess press of the time or in Botvinnik's or Levenfish's memoirs – as though this clause was never included in the championship regulations in the first place.

Levenfish: "Among the All-Union championships, the 9th Premiership stands out. A thoroughly filtered line-up allowed the organization of a balanced, strong tournament without whipping boys and also-rans. It's enough to compare the line-ups of the 1929, 1931, 1933 and 1934 championships and the final tables of those tournaments to prove the truth of that statement. The participation of also-rans brings an element of randomness into any competition. There have been cases when a master has scored just 30% against other prizewinners but took a high place because of his great performance against the weakest players *(not-so-subtly hinting at Alatortsev, the runner-up of the previous championship, who scored just 3/9 against the top half but got a perfect 10/10 against the lower half)*. Such accidents were unthinkable in the 9th Premiership. There were almost no "free points" and relatively few so-called "grandmaster" draws. Most games were very combative. I think that in general, the tournament was both stronger and more balanced than the previous championships.

Unfortunately, M. M. Botvinnik, the winner of the 1931 and 1933 premierships and one of the strongest contemporary masters, was absent. His participation would undoubtedly have attracted more interest in the tournament – from both the chess and sporting points of view. Playing Botvinnik is first and foremost a strict opening theory test. The 7th and 8th Soviet premierships showed that the overwhelming majority of our masters couldn't withstand this difficult test, and their games against Botvinnik were essentially the technical "proof" of a bad opening. On the other hand, the 9th Premiership shows great progress among our youth and the growth of their theoretical knowledge. Thus, Botvinnik's participation would have been twice as interesting..." (*Shakhmaty v SSSR*, January 1935, and the book *9th All-Union Chess Premiership*.)

A Huge Intrigue

Levenfish: "Sporting-wise, the tournament was very successful. There had never been such an intense struggle for the prizes in any previous Soviet Championship. The top 8 players qualified for the Moscow International Tournament, which began just two months after the All-Union championship. Thus, in addition to the usual fight for prizes, there was fierce competition for the coveted top eight places. The leadership changed several times, the results were unclear up to the very last round, and so the public, filling the halls of the Central Chess Club, were extremely excited.

> **Yudovich:** "The small club halls couldn't accommodate everyone who wanted to visit the tournament. It was hard for the spectators and even harder for us players. It was hot and noisy. Thankfully, the organizers held several

rounds offsite in the Houses of Culture of the biggest Leningrad factories."
(*Central Chess Club Bulletin* No. 13, 1983.)

Throughout the tournament, huge crowds of spectators would gather around the tables, arguing hotly about the leaders' chances. The buzz grew with every round and reached its apogee towards the end; but a spurt in the last few rounds helped the Leningrad players to grab six prizes out of eight (in the absence of Botvinnik and Romanovsky!).

The tournament was quite volatile because of the draw: the last five numbers and number one belonged to players who indeed finished at the bottom of the table. And so, the leaders who played that group went on a "streak" and quickly got ahead. Alatortsev started this streak, leading for the first half of the tournament. Then Bogatyrchuk started his ascent. He continued his roll with wins against Alatortsev, Riumin *(see game 76)* and Rabinovich, and seemed unreachable. Yet he stumbled, unable

Grigory Levenfish: "The hardest thing for me was playing openings with black – the result of falling many years behind in theory." (64, 5th July 1935.)

to cope with the pressure from the Leningrad youth. He barely managed to draw against Chekhover, but three losses against Lisitsin *(game 77)*, Savitsky *(game 84)* and Ragozin knocked the stuffing out of him.

> **Bogatyrchuk:** "I played very well in the initial rounds, and I led the tournament with five rounds to go, two points ahead of second place. My victory was so certain that I even received a telegram from the Kiev chess players, congratulating me beforehand. But, alas! They forgot what an incorrigible amateur I was. In the last rounds, I lost to two players from the bottom of the table and also scored two draws, which allowed Levenfish and I. Rabinovich to overtake me by a half-point." (From the book *My Life Path to Vlasov and the Prague Manifesto*.)

After round 15, Chekhover objectively had the best chances to win. He had already scored 9.5 points, played with all his main competitors, and in the last four rounds he had to play Makogonov, Panov, Ilyin-Zhenevsky and Freymann. But at the finish, Chekhover was completely exhausted and should have lost all four of those games. Only luck allowed him to draw with Makogonov *(see game 71)* and Freymann and finish in the coveted top 8.

> **Rokhlin:** "Chekhover was reminiscent of Model at the 1927 championship. Similar cunning play, similar energy bursting over the edge and similar losses to the weakest players." (*Shakhmaty v SSSR*, January 1935.)

Bogatyrchuk's and Chekhover's collapses helped me immensely. After round 18, I thought that I would get clear first place. Rabinovich, despite his brilliant finish *(6/7!)*, should have finished a point behind me. However, the situation changed on the day for completing adjourned games before the last round. Ragozin lost to Rabinovich in a completely drawn rook endgame, and the distance between us decreased to a half-point. In the last round, Panov, who posted a fine finish as well, played a great game against me, and I barely managed to get a draw, while Rabinovich easily defeated Ilyin-Zhenevsky and caught up with me.

The most positive outcome of the tournament is, of course, the high game quality. This is explained by the balanced and strong line-up and intense struggles. But the young masters' growing technique also played a role. I think that the time control after the 45th move, proposed by me back in 1923 and finally accepted, after much discussions, for this tournament, was also important. The lack of two time controls (after moves 37 and 52) and, therefore, time trouble no longer happening twice, plus the normal 6-hour workload, the maximum acceptable for such intense mental work as playing chess, sharply decreased the number of blunders and mistakes, especially among the prizewinners. Several masters (including Rabinovich, Savitsky and Panov) told me after the tournament that they felt very fit.

At any rate, there was nothing similar to the 1933 championship, when Botvinnik saved some very dubious games at the finish. Each half-point was earned in battle, especially in the second half of the tournament.

Since the 6-hour time control displayed a number of great advantages, I propose, to avoid the objections against it, to enhance it with a 30-minute break (after 4 playing hours) for rest and tea time, but without a sealed move or analyzing the position."

In summer 1934, many championship participants played in the Leningrad masters tournament featuring M. Euwe and H. Kmoch. Sitting: Alatortsev, Kmoch, Levenfish, I. Rabinovich, Lisitsin, Euwe, Chekhover. Standing: Yudovich, Romanovsky, Golubev, Riumin, Kan, Botvinnik.

The Magnificent Eight

Levenfish: "Rabinovich's play was not only parsimonious, but also quite aggressive, he didn't shun sharp complications. However, in the first half, this strategy didn't get the necessary tactical support, and in critical moments against Dubinin, Alatortsev and Bogatyrchuk, he couldn't find the right continuation and lost. But this didn't break Rabinovich's will: still playing in the same style, he crushed Makogonov, Mazel, Belavenets *(see game 75)* and deservedly shared first place – the greatest success in his entire chess career.

> **Bogatyrchuk:** "Master I. Rabinovich is the epitome of an academic approach to chess. Among the Soviet players, only Rauzer can rival him in that regard. However, studying Rabinovich's latest games shows that his creativity is not just based on routine, but rather on a very high level of mastery, which places I. Rabinovich in the same rank as the USSR's strongest chess masters." (*Moscow International Tournament Bulletin*, No. 1, 1935.)

I felt much better than in the tournament featuring Euwe *(Leningrad, August 1934: 1. Botvinnik – 7.5/11; 2–3. Romanovsky and Riumin – 7; 4. I. Rabinovich – 6.5; 5. Kan – 6. 6. Euwe – 5.5; 7–8. Kmoch and Yudovich – 5; 9–10. Alatortsev and Lisitsin – 4.5; 11. Levenfish – 4. 12. Chekhover – 3.5),*

Grigory Levenfish and Ilya Rabinovich running towards the finish line (Shakhmaty v SSSR, No. 6, 1934).

even though I got only partial leave from my job. The hardest thing for me was playing openings with black – the result of falling many years behind in theory. Six of my eight wins were with the white pieces, while all three of my losses were with black. All my wins were played well and consistently. My technique when trying to win won games is still subpar, and I drew the strategically won games against Alatortsev, Rabinovich and Riumin because of that...

> **Rokhlin:** "Levenfish was always set to eventually regain his old chess level, because he had never lost the freshness of combinational thought. With deep understanding of the laws of the chess struggle, and especially his ability to thoroughly analyze every position, he managed to score a number of spectacular wins."

Bogatyrchuk and Riumin, who shared 3rd and 4th prizes, both display chess individuality. Unlike in the 1933 championship, Bogatyrchuk came to this tournament in a fresh, combative mood. His play was excellent: bold and inventive in attack, solid and tenacious in defense. He faltered towards the finish – either because he couldn't withstand the tension of such long struggle,

"Riumin's multiple talents always appealed to me." (Levenfish.) Cartoon by N. Radlov (1935). Charcoal, watercolors. From A. Kentler's archive. Published for the first time.

or because he got upset when he started losing – this is always tricky for a leader to deal with.

Riumin's multiple talents always appealed to me. He's one of the few young players who's equally strong in attack and defense. He takes to difficult, complicated positions like a fish to water, maintaining pressure for hours and waiting for a tactical blow. That's how he won a difficult game against Rabinovich and saved half a point against me. At the same time, Riumin never loses an opportunity to launch a crushing attack, as happened, for example, against Panov and Mazel *(see game 78)*. Riumin's style is similar to Lasker's, and that says everything.

Grigoriev: "Riumin had just 2.5 points after round 7, and it seemed that he wouldn't be a contender for the top places; however, his brilliant finish *(including five wins in a row!)* helped him take third place. Unfortunately, Riumin's great talent and rich chess erudition don't always deliver success. His play is often sluggish and indecisive. In non-tournament games, Riumin usually plays his best chess when he gets into a difficult position; likewise, in tournaments he only starts playing at his full strength when his standing is somewhat compromised. To become more successful, Riumin should abandon this 'method'." (*64*, January 1935.)

Alas, this was Riumin's last Soviet Championship. Shortly before, he had performed well in the tournament featuring Euwe and Kmoch, but in the 1935 Moscow tournament, despite beating none other than Capablanca at the start, he finished in mid-table. In 1936, Riumin's successes were very modest; when he started agreeing one draw after another in the All-Union Young Masters Tournament, he was jokingly called "the Moscow Schlechter". The reason for the drop in his performance was progressive lung disease, which first forced him to stop playing in serious tournaments, and, in 1942, claimed his life...

As editor of the magazine *Shakhmaty v SSSR* **Vladimir German** recalled: "Kolya Riumin was a huge favorite with the editors. He was a true poet of the chess art. Chess fans studied and continue to study his brilliant combinations. When commentating a game or analyzing a position for a magazine or newspaper, Riumin would write so conscientiously and comprehensively that his articles became true revelations for our readers. Kolya was a very good, gentle and nice man, who always tried to help everybody. He was willing to labor day and night, and it required a huge effort on our part to force him to observe the part-time work regimen arranged for him and convalesce from his terrible illness," (*Shakhmaty v SSSR* No. 5, 1967).

The next four places were shared by the young Leningrad players – Alatortsev, Lisitsin, Ragozin and Chekhover. Alatortsev's play is very temperamental, but inventive in attack; he chooses only certain opening systems (the Queen's Gambit, the French Defense) that he's been developing for years. But in games against stronger opponents, his weaknesses manifest themselves more vividly: the risky nature of his ideas, poor defense, mediocre endgame play and, what's more important, overestimation of both his position and his abilities.

It turns out that the young master was experiencing a serious creative crisis at the time.

Alatortsev: "I think that I rightfully took 2nd place in the 8th Soviet Championship, and so I asked them to organize a match between me and Botvinnik. My goal was to learn, first and foremost – I think that a match would have shown the flaws in my style most vividly, and Botvinnik is quite adept at improving his opponents' play. After efforts to organize this match came to nothing, I lost the desire to improve my play further, concentrating on my work in engineering and planning. This

Vladimir Alatortsev's play was affected by a two-year hiatus from chess, when he, by his own admission, "fully immersed himself in engineering projects". From the author's archive.

hiatus was almost two years long." (Special bulletin of the All-Union Young Masters Tournament, 19th December 1936.)

The exceptionally talented Chekhover has improved considerably, and only poor health prevented him from taking one of the first prizes. He plays great combinations and is generally very dangerous in attack. At this tournament, he showed tenacity in defense as well (for instance, against Riumin). His endgame technique has improved, too.

Lisitsin and Ragozin are masters of defense first and foremost. Lisitsin feels the position very well, converts his advantage without mistakes, and his endgame play is very precise. However, he occasionally plays without inspiration and just gives points away, as happened in the first half of the tournament. To gain better success, Lisitsin needs to strengthen his will to win. He should strictly adhere to tournament discipline.

Ragozin subtly and originally understands the position – he is similar to Nimzowitsch in that regard. He's a very good tactician, but lacks the necessary composure and willpower."

Below the Prizewinners

Levenfish: "The next four places were shared by Moscow players Belavenets, Kan and Yudovich, and Makogonov representing Azerbaijan. All of them are solid, positional masters. For Belavenets, this is his first All-Union tournament, and, unable to withstand the long struggle, he faltered at the finish, even though he didn't lose a single game in the first half of the tournament *(he was a serious contender for the top places, but lost two games at the finish – to Kan and his friend Yudovich)*. Belavenets' result is not indicative of his true playing strength, and I think that his next performances will be more successful. Kan is tenacious and inventive, but doesn't like to analyze the position too deeply; Yudovich has subtle positional understanding, but he's too cautious and fears complications. Makogonov's positional play is very good, but he can get confused in tactical complications, as his games against Ragozin and Chekhover show *(see game 71)*.

13th–14th places were shared by Panov and Veresov, who represents Belarus. This is their first All-Union tournament; both of them are distinctly combinational players, both are very dangerous in attack but weak in defense. Panov needs to balance his style, and then his great talent will surely show itself fully. Veresov has to deepen his strategic positional evaluation; tactically, he's already stronger than many masters. Only a lack of opening theory and disregard for purely positional maneuvering have stopped him

This tournament was Leonid Yakovlevich Savitsky's swan song: half a year after the championship, he died, aged just 24... Judging by the cartoon from N. Radlov's archive, first published in the book 1932 Leningrad Championship, he had a recalcitrant personality. In 1931, he was banned from chess for three months "for rude behavior" (he insulted a Chess Committee member), "seeing that he already had a reprimand for a similar offense." To the right – photo from Shakhmaty v SSSR (No. 8, 1935).

from obtaining the master's title. *(Veresov's result was unique: +9–10, with no draws!)*

The next two places were shared by Savitsky and Mazel. Savitsky, the great opening expert, is very dangerous in attack, but weak in defense and endgames. Towards the end, he regained his footing and shared the prize for best performance in the last 6 rounds with Panov (4.5/6).

> This tournament was Leonid Yakovlevich Savitsky's swan song: half a year after the championship, he died, aged just 24...
>
> **Gotthilf:** "I remember the irrecoverable days of our trip to that last tournament in Voronezh. We quickly run up the gently sloping stairs of the three-story hotel. We stop at the top landing, and suddenly the silence is broken by a distinct, agonizing asthmatic wheeze. This is so unexpected that you involuntarily look around, not believing that it is this blooming boy who is panting so heavily, clutching his chest; he's always so vivid, joyful, happy and lively for everyone around.

"What's up with you, Lyonia?"

"My heart is no good. Completely messed up. I have to be very careful – even a common cold can put me in a hospital bed for ages."

A minute later, everything is forgotten. Again, there are jokes, laughter, Lyonia's words that he invented himself...

He wasn't one of those rare lucky ones whose talent thrived by itself. From the very first steps of his chess career, Lyonia was used to hard work; he had completely mastered the high art of analysis, he was heading towards perfection with assured steps, and death took him just before he could reach his goal." (*Shakhmaty v SSSR*, August 1935.)

Unfortunately, Mazel, an original positional master, brought a dissonance to the overall combative atmosphere of the tournament. He started by offering draws to everyone after just 10–15 moves. When he was warned for that, he started to successfully compete with Lisitsin in showing up late to the games. In the last round, when the fate of all the prizes was to be decided, he arrived 1 hour late to his game against Bogatyrchuk, started playing *a tempo* and blundered a piece. I hope that the Moscow chess organizations will come to a proper assessment of Mazel's behavior. *(His hopes were met: "for an unacceptable attitude towards his tournament responsibilities", Mazel was issued a strong reprimand.)*

17th place was unexpectedly occupied by Rauzer, the great expert in opening theory and endgames, the sophisticated analyst. Rauzer is so infected with dogmatism that he tries to replace free thinking with ready-made patterns. For instance, he's convinced that 1.e2-e4 wins by force, and 1.d2-d4 inevitably leads to a draw, and so he always plays for a draw in the latter opening with black. In addition, after losing all chances in the first half of the tournament, Rauzer played rather sloppily in the second half, forgetting, like Mazel, that neglect of tournament responsibilities discredits a master even more than a poor performance.

> **Rauzer:** "I think that I am getting accused of dogmatism by those of my opponents who don't properly appreciate my approach to chess games. I think that you have to play soundly, scientifically, according to a plan. And against those who play unscientifically, I have a good score – for instance, Ragozin or Riumin; by contrast, my score against Zhenevsky or Konstantinopolsky is rather poor." (Special bulletin of the All-Union Young Masters Tournament, 24th December 1936.)

The three last places were taken by Dubinin, Ilyin-Zhenevsky and Freymann. None of them could withstand the intense tournament atmosphere, but for different reasons. Dubinin only got his first category last year, it was his first tournament of such magnitude, and he tired in the second half. His positional understanding is very original, he plays solidly, but he gets confused in tactical complications. His talent and style guarantee that Dubinin will surely earn his master's title soon.

> **Grigoriev:** "Dubinin had a relatively good start, got a record result against the top 8 – 5.5 points *(he defeated Rabinovich, Lisitsin, Ragozin and Chekhover!)*, but scored just 1.5 points against the 11 non-prizewinners."

Ilyin-Zhenevsky hadn't played serious chess since 1932 because he was abroad, tasked with important diplomatic jobs, so his lack of practice was very evident. He did play some good games (against Lisitsin and Belavenets), but they couldn't save him from numerous blunders and oversights. For Freymann, because of his age *(52)* and poor health, it wasn't easy to play in a long, intense tournament consistently. However, the new time control struck the final blow against this sophisticated chess thinker. Six uninterrupted hours of play proved to be too much for the chess veteran, and Freymann made most of his blunders, costing him more than one won game, in the last two hours." (*Shakhmaty v SSSR*, January 1935, and the book *9th All-Union Chess Premiership.*)

Дружеский шарж Ю. Ю.

м. Раузер

"Rauzer is so infected with dogmatism that he tries to replace free thinking with ready-made patterns." (Levenfish). Cartoon by Y. Yuzepchuk (All-Union Young Masters Tournament, No. 3, 1936).

The Victory of the "Old Guard"

Rokhlin: "More than 15,000 spectators visited the halls of the Central Chess Club during the tournament. However, interest in the tournament wasn't confined to the spectators – enthusiasts from Leningrad, who literally besieged the old Grand Duke's palace in the last decisive round because the halls were packed to the brim – but it spread among the wide working masses and Soviet society at large as well. The best proof of that consists of daily reports on the tournament on the pages of both the national and local press, as well as regular news flashes on the biggest radio stations of Moscow, Leningrad and other cities, which were also listened to by foreign chess fans...

We can draw one indisputable conclusion from the tournament results: the talented chess youth, admittedly without Botvinnik this time, suffered for the first time in years from the "weapon" of their experienced teachers and were pushed back from their leading positions, which they had seemed to occupy securely. Both Riumin and Alatortsev lost to Bogatyrchuk *(see game 76)*, Ragozin and Kan lost to Levenfish *(games 73 and 72)* and Rabinovich, and Belavenets lost to Rabinovich *(game 75)*, while only Chekhover and Lisitsin managed to maintain some balance. Thus, the representatives of the older generation, especially Levenfish and Bogatyrchuk (as I. Rabinovich only gradually improved), proved that their strength was still great.

Levenfish: "However, it would be wrong to jump to the conclusion that the old masters' cadre is superior to the new one. The point difference is very small – there are only 2 points between 1st and 12th places – and therefore much was dependent on tournament luck; but, what's more important, the older masters only managed to win after a fierce struggle. The two players who especially suffered against the younger generations were Bogatyrchuk, who lost three games at the finish – to Lisitsin *(see game 77)*, Ragozin, and Savitsky *(game 84)*, and Levenfish, who was almost deprived of his championship chances by Chekhover, Yudovich and Veresov *(game 74)*. I think that the tournament results

Г. Я. Левенфиш

Grigory Levenfish, returning to chess after an eight-year hiatus, managed to win the Soviet Championship at his second attempt! Cartoon by Lis (N. Lisogorsky), from the Moscow International Tournament Bulletin (No. 23, 1935).

showed that the strength was approximately equal, while the experience and better technique of the older masters prevailed." (From the book *9th All-Union Chess Premiership*.)

Grigoriev: "The victory of the 'old guard' is quite telling and shows that our young players, undoubtedly very talented, still sometimes lack tournament experience and a will to win. They should learn these qualities from the 'elders'." (*64*, January 1935.) For the record: Levenfish was 45 years old then, Rabinovich 43, and Bogatyrchuk 42...

What are the reasons for this unexpected failure of the younger generation? If we think more deeply, there's nothing unexpected in that; by contrast, we can see that this phenomenon was only logical. Our youth, "spoilt" by the truly great achievements of Soviet chess thought, and being, in political parlance, "dizzy with success", lost their way and a "sense of self-criticism", without which no artist, even the most genius, can make progress. And with the current level and depth of chess technique, not progressing is tantamount to regressing. The greater the master's talent and potential, the more systematic and deeper the work he needs to do. Can we say that Riumin, Alatortsev, Kan, Lisitsin and the others came to the All-Union tournament "armed with the latest modern technique"? Of course not. This is first and foremost their own fault, because it's no secret that many young masters quietly (and sometimes even openly) thought that if there's no Botvinnik, they'll win first place easily. This entailed superficial theoretical preparation, disregard for their opponent's strength, "intuitive" play, etc. A part of the fault should be shouldered by the chess organizations as well – they still haven't created specialized working conditions for continuous educational and creative work of the chess master, despite an acute need.

If Hastings was an instructive examination for M. M. Botvinnik *(after sharing 5th–6th place, the Soviet champion humbly said "I flopped in Hastings"),* then the 9th All-Union tournament gave the Soviet masters an opportunity to test their chess weapons for the last time, find a number of weak and vulnerable spots in our youth's play, and recognize the need to prepare for the Moscow tournament very seriously. We should hope that the Soviet masters, learning the lessons of the latest tournaments, will do everything in their power to hold the banner of Soviet chess art high at the upcoming international tests; the whole chess world is going to be watching." (*Shakhmaty v SSSR*, January 1935.)

Brilliancies Without Prizes

His championship win inspired Levenfish to go for an experiment unprecedented in Soviet chess literature: he annotated all the tournament games himself! This delayed the publication of *9th All-Union Chess Premiership* for two years, but made it more stylistically and ideologically valuable. The downside of such a method, tried by Tarrasch and Alekhine before, is, in my view, a certain academic approach to the annotations, which is of course unavoidable when you annotate others' games. Also, to be frank, I think that nothing can compare with the annotations by the players themselves, especially made shortly after the game, when they still remember all the nuances of the battle, and the lines they show haven't been corrected by home analysis. Such express notes aren't always too great from purely analytical and stylistic points of view, but they often contain the truths of life, original ideas, diversity of approaches to solving chess problems; even the mistakes are touching in their sincerity!

And so, I tried to find the annotations by the players themselves from magazines, even though there were only a few of them – about two dozen altogether. What a pity! In Levenfish's opinion, the game quality at this championship was much higher than at previous ones: "Almost every participant played at least 3–4 consistent, rich games, and there's a number of games that could have been the gem of any international tournament. Unfortunately, the three brilliancy prizes remained unawarded. The jury would have had their work cut out, because at least 25 games could have contended for those prizes."

Rokhlin laments the fact that "together with the brilliant works of chess art, we saw some parodies of mastery, draws completely devoid of content, gross blunders, miscalculations and "time-trouble tightrope walking", despite the seemingly comfortable time control." Well, come on. Even world championship matches aren't completely free from all those things; and concerning "time-trouble tightrope walking" – sometimes you play your most beautiful moves when your flag is hanging.

Hocus-Pocus

Baturinsky: "At the chessboard, Chekhover was an inventive tactician, always ready to sacrifice something. I was once present at the postmortem of the game between him and Makogonov, a solid, positional player. The opponents couldn't agree on the evaluation of the position. And then Chekhover said, "You, Vladimir Andreevich, always try to place the pieces in such a way that they protect each other.

And I am always trying to put them *en prise!*"

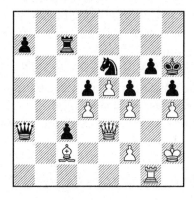

No. 71
Chekhover – V. Makogonov
Leningrad 1934/35, round 16
Annotated by G. Levenfish

The game was adjourned here, and everyone thought that it was hopeless for white. Indeed, after 46...♕e7 47.♕g3 ♕f7 48.♖d1 ♖c4 49.♕e3 ♕e7 50.♔h3 ♕b4, white could resign. But Makogonov was too sure of his victory and carelessly played **46...♕b4,** after which he was struck by a bolt out of the blue:

47.♖xg6+! ♔**xg6 48.♗xf5+!** Even if this combination is not completely correct, white still has nothing to lose. Black's psychological shock was so strong that he ultimately failed to find the strongest reply to white's spectacular combination.

48...♔f7. After 48...♔xf5 white has a perpetual check: 49.♕d3+ ♔xf4 50.♕g3+ ♔e4 51.♕e3+ ♔f5 52.♕d3+ and so on..

49.♕g3 ♘**f8.** *Black won with for example 49...♕xd4! 50.♕g6+ ♔f8 51.♕xe6 ♕xf2+ 52.♔h3 ♕e3+ 53.♔h2 ♕xf4+ 54.♔h3 ♕e3+ 55.♔h2 ♕b6 etc.*

50.e6+ ♔**e8 51.♗g6+** ♔**d8.** After 51...♘xg6 52.♕xg6+ ♔e7 53.♕f7+ ♔d6 54.♕f8+

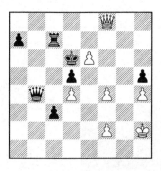

54...♔xe6!! (54...♖e7 55.f5 leads to complicated and unclear play) 55.♕xb4 (55.f5+ ♔d7 56.♕xb4 c2 57.♕b5+ ♔e7 58.♕b4+ ♔f7) 55... c2 56.♕e1+ ♔f7 57.♕c1 a5 and then a5-a4-a3-a2-a1♕ and c1♕ black wins.

Actually, there's no win in this line: 58.f5! a4 59.♕h6 c1♕ 60.♕h7+ ♔f6 61.♕g6+ with perpetual check (the "bracket" line in the above paragraph after 58.♕e2+! is drawn as well). However, 54...♖e7! leads to a win: 55.f5 ♔c7 56.♔g2 (56.f6 ♕d6+) 56...♕d6 57.♕h6 c2 etc.

52.♕g5+ ♔**c8 53.♗f5!** ♕**e7.** This is not bad, but 53...♔b7 won much more easily.

54.♗h3!

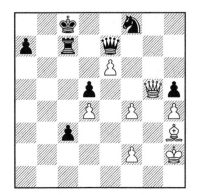

54...c2? Black is obviously panicking after Chekhover's inventive trickery. After 54...♕xg5 55.e7+ ♔b7 56.exf8♕ ♕e7 57.♗c8+ ♔b8!, white should resign.

55.♕xd5 ♔b8 56.♕b3+ ♖b7 57.♕xc2. White has eliminated the c-pawn. He is still a full rook down, but in this mindboggling endgame the absolute value of pieces means nothing.

57...♘xe6 58.♕f5 ♕xh4? The last mistake. 58...♕d6 led to a won endgame: 59.♕xe6 ♕xe6 60.♗xe6 ♔c7 61.f5 ♔d6, and the a-pawn should win the game for black.

For instance: 62.♔g3 a5 63.♔f4 a4 64.♔g5 a3 65.♔xh5 ♖b2 66.♔g6 ♖xf2 etc.

59.♕e5+! ♔a8 60.♕xe6.

"In the evenings, after the games ended, the talented Leningrad musician, chess master and chess composer Vitaly Chekhover would entertain listeners by playing the piano and singing frivolous songs, of which he knew many." (Baturinsky.) Cartoon by Y. Yuzepchuk (VTsSPS Championship, No. 10–11, 1938.)

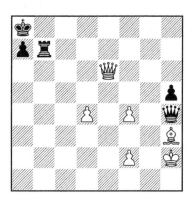

60...♕xf2+. *After 60...♕xf4+! 61.♔g1 ♖b1+ 62.♔g2 (62.♗f1 ♕g4+) 62...♕c1! black could still win, for instance: 63.♕d5+ ♔b8 64.♕e5+ ♔b7 65.♔g3 (65.♕e7+ ♔b6) 65...♕c7 66.♗g2+ ♔b6 67.f4 ♕xe5 68.dxe5 ♖g1! 69.f5 ♔c7 70.♔f3 ♖xg2!*

61.♗g2. And now, the endgame is drawn.

61...♕xf4+ 62.♔h1 ♕h4+ 63.♔g1 ♕xd4+ 64.♔h1 ♕h4+ 65.♔g1 ♕d8 66.♔h1 ♕h4+ *(66...♔b8 67.♕e5+)* **67.♔g1 ♕d4+ 68.♔h1 ♕h4+ 69.♔g1 ♕d8 70.♔h1 ♔b8 71.♕e5+.** Draw. A most fascinating game.

Saving a desperate position always looks like a small miracle. And, even though a strict critic frowns upon such games, the public loves them!

The First Time Over the Board

Every player dreams of playing a study- or problem-like idea in an over-the-board game. But not everyone achieves that dream.

No. 72
Levenfish – Kan
Leningrad 1934/35, round 10
Annotated by G. Levenfish

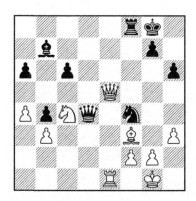

36...♕c3! Brilliant! After the trade on c3, the endgame is better for black, for instance: 37.♕xc3 bxc3 38.♖c1 ♘xh3+ 39.♔f1 ♘g5 40.♗e2

♘e4 or 38.♘d6 ♘d3 39.♖e2 ♘b4! 40.♘xb7 c2 41.♖e1 ♘d3, winning. In addition, black threatens 37... ♘xh3+ and 37...♕xb3.

However, in the first variation, after 41.♔g1! the f2 pawn is poisoned (41... ♖xf2?? 42.♗f3; 41...♘xf2 42.♘d6), while the threat f2-f3 followed by ♖xc3 and ♘a5 grants white a clear advantage, so the right continuation is 38...c5! 39.♖xc3 ♘xh3+ with approximate equality. Further, although the commentator's second continuation is better for black, after 41.♖xc2 (instead of 41.♖e1) 41...♘xc2 42.♗xc6 much fight remains in the game.

White's position looks quite difficult, and many masters would have forced a draw with ♖e1-e3-e1. *(Actually, after 37.♖e3! ♕c1+? white wins with 38.♔h2.)*

37.♘d6!! One of the best combinations I've ever managed to create over the board. The idea of the combination – deflection and interference – had only occurred in problems before, not in over-the-board games. The main line leads to an endgame that required a precise calculation. The combination is even more valuable because I had to consider my opponent's counter-combination as well.

37...♘xh3+ (37...♗a8 would have been met with 38.♕e7, threatening ♕xf8+) **38.♔h2 ♘g5!** To meet 39.♘xb7? with 39...♖xf3!

39.♗g4! ♕xe5+. After 39... ♗a8, white won with 40.f4 ♖xf4 (40...♕xe5 41.fxe5, and the pawn promotes) 41.♕e8+ ♔h7 (41...♖f8? 42.♕xf8+) 42.♗f5+.

40.♖xe5 ♗a8.

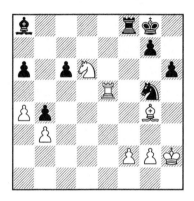

41.f4!! The idea behind the combination is so subtle that many spectators and even other players watching the game thought that it was just a blunder.

41...♖xf4. Black has no choice. If 41...♘f7, then 42.♗e6, and if 41...♘h7, there's 42.♗e6+ ♔h8 43.♘f7+ ♔g8 44.♘xh6++ ♔h8 45.♘f7+ ♔g8 46.♖h5!

42.♗f5! Here's the key move of the whole combination. The rook can't retreat, while white now threatens to checkmate on e8 or win the a8 bishop.

Oddly enough, it was even better to allow the rook to go back: 42.♗e2! ♖f8 43.♗xa6+−.

42...♖xf5? Unfortunately, the psychological shock caused by this unexpected turn of events prevented Kan from finding the strongest move 42...g6, after which white would have played 43.♖e8+ ♔g7 44.♖xa8 gxf5 45.♖xa6. The calculation of this

endgame was the most difficult part of checking if the combination on the 37th move was correct. The endgame is won, as the following lines show: 45...c5 46.a5 ♘e4 47.♖a7+ ♔f6 (47...♔g8 48.♖a8+ ♔g7 49.a6! ♘xd6 50.a7) 48.♘e8+ ♔e6 49.a6 ♖f1 50.♖h7 ♖a1 51.a7 ♔e5 (51...♘g5!=) 52.♖e7+ ♔f4 (*he had to play 52...♔d4 53.♘c7 c4 54.bxc4 b3 55.a8♕ ♖xa8 56.♘xa8 b2 57.♖b7 ♔c3 58.♘c7 ♘c5! – 58.♔c2? ♘b5 – 59.♖b8 ♘d7 with drawing chances*) 53.♘c7 ♘f2 54.♘d5+! ♔g5 55.♖g7+, with a mate in two.

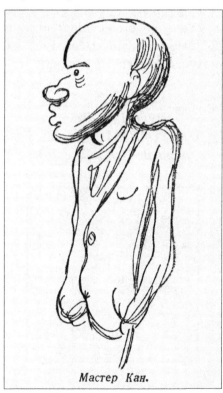

Мастер Кан.

"Kan is tenacious and inventive, but doesn't like to analyze the position too deeply." (Levenfish.) Cartoon by N. Radlov (Tridtsat Dnei, No. 5, 1935). Published for the first time.

43.♘xf5 ♚f7 44.♘d6+. The bishop on a8 falls, and so black resigned.

The Queen is Checkmated!

No matter what learned men say, I contend that chess is like literature: every genre is good, except boring ones. Grigory Yakovlevich probably understood that well, and so he wouldn't refuse himself (or the spectators) the pleasure of playing for a checkmate. I'll say more: even his losses were spectacular!

No. 73
Levenfish – Ragozin
Leningrad 1934/35, round 12
Annotated by G. Levenfish

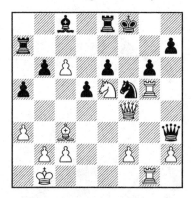

27.♘xg6+! *The position is so rich with combination motifs that it even featured a spectacular dual – 27.♖xf5+! After 27...e(g)xf5 (27... ♕xf5 28.♕h6+) 28.♘d7+!, there are a lot of mating variations. Try to find them yourselves, as an exercise.*
27...hxg6 28.♖xg6 ♕h7 (white threatened to give a check on g8,

trade on e8, and then continue either ♖g8 or ♕b8+) **29.♕g5 e5 30.♗xe5!** The bishop is taboo: after 30...♖xe5, there's 31.♕d8+ *(31...♚f7 32.♖f6# or 31...♖e8 32.♖g8+ ♕xg8 33.♖xg8+ ♚xg8 34.♕xe8+ ♚g7 35.♕xc8).*

30...♗e6. Now, when black manages to finally get all his pieces into the game, he gets a mate in four:

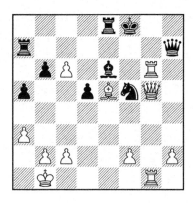

31.♕f6+ ♗f7 32.♖g8+! ♕xg8 33.♖xg8+ ♚xg8 34.♕h8#. *The king is checkmated!*

No. 74
Veresov – Levenfish
Leningrad 1934/35, round 15
Annotated by G. Levenfish

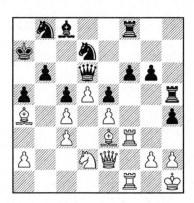

30.g4!! A brilliant, far from obvious move. After 30...hxg3 31.♖xg3 ♖g8 32.♕xh5 gxh5 33.♖xg8, the white rooks invade black's camp with decisive force.

30...♖hh8 31.g5 ♔a8? Black is confused. It was better to play 31...♖h7 *(for instance: 32.♕f2 ♖hf7 33.♕xh4 f5! 34.exf5 gxf5 35.♕h5 f4, and black could still defend).*

Levenfish gives no more notes, and I can understand him: this is a case when a "silent film" is more eloquent than any voice-over text.

32.♕f2 fxg5 33.♗xg5 ♖xf3 34.♘xf3 ♗a6 35.♘d2 h3 36.♕g3 ♗c8 37.♖f7 ♘a6 38.♗e7 ♕b8 39.♗c6+ ♔a7 40.♗f6 ♖f8 41.♖xf8 ♘xf8 42.♗xe5! *The queen is checkmated!*

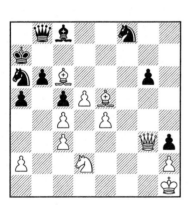

Black resigned. Veresov again showed his tactical prowess.

The Knight Invasion

Levenfish called this game "an outstanding achievement for Ilya Rabinovich," adding "the skillful combination of positional maneuvering and tactical shots makes it one of the best in the whole tournament."

No. 75. Benoni Defense A44
Belavenets – I. Rabinovich
Leningrad 1934/35, round 15
Annotated by G. Levenfish

1.d4 c5 2.d5 e5 3.e4 d6 4.♘c3 g6 5.♗e3? This move wasn't well thought-through *(5.♗b5+).* White wants to prevent the line with ♘h6, f7-f6, ♘f7 by playing ♗e3 and ♕d2, not noticing that his maneuver will only lose several tempi.

Зарисовка А. ШАБАД

И. РАБИНОВИЧ.

This championship was Ilya Rabinovich's finest hour. Drawing by A. Shabad (Moscow International Tournament Bulletin, No. 10, 1935).

Rabinovich came up with an original system 5.h4 ♘h6 6.h5 g5 7.♘ge2 ♘a6 against Riumin and got a good game. However, the attack h2-h4-h5 seems too premature.

5...♘h6 6.♕d2 ♘g4! 7.♗g5? White should have admitted his error and continued development with 7.♗e2, but he persists, losing tempo after tempo.

7...f6 8.♗h4 ♗g7 9.f3? Another significant weakening of the position (9.♗b5+). White again fails to anticipate his opponent's reply.

9...♘h6. Now 10.♕e2 is met with 10...♘e3 11.♗f2 ♘xf1, and black has the bishop pair and a good position. So white tries to save the f1 bishop from being traded.

10.♗b5+ ♔f7! 11.♕e2 ♘e3!

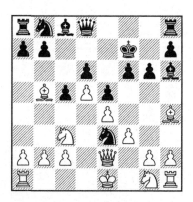

An unexpected move. Black calculated that trying to trap the knight (h2-h3, ♖h2, ♗f2) requires a lot of time. In addition, he's threatening to win the b5 bishop. Thus, black has enough time to protect the knight with f6-f5-f4.

12.g4 ♔g7 13.♗d3 a6 14.a4 ♕c7. Preparing f6-f5. Seeing that, white abandons his efforts to win the knight and trades it instead.

15.♘d1   ♘xd1   16.♔xd1 (white can't capture with the rook because of 16...♕a5+, or with the queen because of 16...c4) **16...b5!!** Unexpected and very strong.

17.axb5 ♖a7!

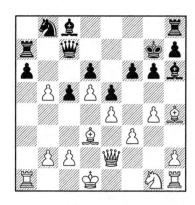

Now we see the deep meaning behind black's maneuver. 18.bxa6 is met by 18...♘xa6 19.♗xa6 ♕b6, regaining the bishop and invading the opponent's camp with major pieces.

18.b6 *(18.♖b1!?)* **18...♕xb6 19.c3 ♗d7 20.♘h3 ♖f8 21.♔e1 ♔h8 22.♔f1 f5.** This long-prepared pawn break threatens the kingside.

23.♔g2 ♖b7 24.♖ab1 ♕c7 25.g5 *(the white bishop will suffer after this move; 25.♘g5!)* **25...♗g7 26.♘f2 ♗b5 27.♗xb5 ♖xb5 28.♖hf1 ♘d7 29.♘d1 ♕d8.**

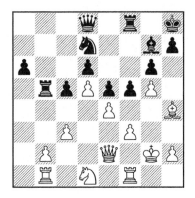

Black's attack on both flanks at once is very artistic.

30.♔h3 ♘b6 31.♘e3 ♛d7 32.♔g2 ♖b8 33.♖f2 f4 34.♘c4 ♘xc4 35.♛xc4 ♗f8 36.♖a1 ♗e7!

Fyodor Bogatyrchuk lost a very real chance to become a two-times Soviet champion... Cartoon by A. Zhitomirsky (Trud, 28th February 1935).

(threatening 37...h6) **37.♔h1.** *Of course, it was unnecessary to hang the bishop, but after 37.♖xa6 h6 38.♖d2 hxg5 39.♗f2 g4!, white's position still comes apart at the seams.*

37...♛h3. White resigned.

The Sicilian Vendetta

In the 7th Championship, Riumin brilliantly defeated Bogatyrchuk in a Scheveningen Sicilian. In the next championship, they went for the same line out of principle and drew. This time, the Kiev maestro claimed revenge.

No. 76
Bogatyrchuk – Riumin
Leningrad 1934/35, round 3
Annotated by F. Bogatyrchuk

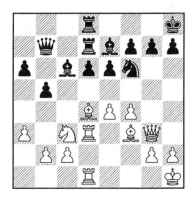

21.♘d5! This unexpected (*at the time*) cavalry attack disorganizes black's position. Of course, he can't play 21...exd5, because after 22.exd5, there's no salvation from 23.dxc6 (22...♗xd5 23.♗xd5 ♛xd5? 24.♗xf6).

21...♘e8 (the only move) **22.♘xe7 ♖xe7.** White has managed to trade away black's crucial defensive piece and obtain the bishop pair, which should give him a decisive advantage due to the weakness of the d6 square.

23.♕e1 ♖ed7 24.♗c3 d5. It's now or never, because this move becomes impossible after 25.♗a5. Black chooses to die in an open battle rather than from asphyxiation.

25.e5 d4. Otherwise, after 26.♗d4 white would get a decisive attack by relocating his pieces to the kingside.

26.♗xc6 ♕xc6 27.♗a5.

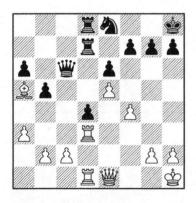

27...♘c7. *"Now black is going through a rough patch. After 27... ♖c8, he feared 28.c3, however, after 28...dxc3! 29.♖xd7 c2 30.♖xf7! ♔g8! 31.♖xg7+ ♔xg7 32.♖c1 ♕c4, black gets a promising position for the pawn." (Levenfish.)* A debatable view: after 33.♗c3 and f4-f5, the black king is under attack (33...♕xf4 34.♖xc2 and ♖f2).

28.♕f2 h6 29.h3 ♔g8 30.♔h2 ♔h7. *"Until the 45th move, black was in time trouble, which explains his subsequent weak play. Instead of the aimless king moves, he had to play ♖d5 and ♖8d7, after which it's unclear how white could improve his position." (Levenfish)*

31.♖1d2 g6 32.♖d1 ♔g7 33.♖1d2 (the moves are, of course, repeated to gain some time) **33... ♔h7 34.♖d1 ♔g7.**

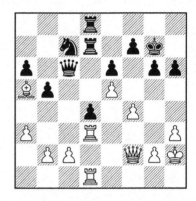

35.c3! White wins a pawn with this move. Black can't play 35... dxc3 due to 36.♖xc3 ♕b7 37.♖xc7, winning a piece.

"If the black king were on g8, and his rook were on d5, then he could save the game with 35...dxc3 36.♖xc3 ♕a8! 37.♖xd5 ♘xd5 38.♗xd8 ♘xc3." (Levenfish)

35...♖c8 36.♖xd4 ♖xd4 37.♕xd4. On the previous move, white could have traded the bishop for the knight and transitioned into a major-piece endgame with an extra pawn, but he thought that the bishop could be used to attack the king and finish the game more quickly.

37...♘d5 38.b3 ♚h7.
Unfortunately, black can't play 38...
♘xc3? due to 39.♖c1, winning a
piece.

**39.♖c1 ♚g7 40.c4 bxc4
41.bxc4.** This is stronger than
41.♖xc4, because it drives the knight
away from its exceptionally strong
position.

41...♛a4 42.♗d2 ♘e7. Black
couldn't play 42...♛xa3 due to
43.cxd5 ♖xc1 44.♗xc1 ♛xc1 45.d6!
♛c8 46.d7 ♛d8 47.♛d6 a5 48.♚g3!
a4 49.♛c6 a3 (or 49...♚f8 50.♛c5+!)
50.♛c8 etc.

43.♛d3 ♘c6.

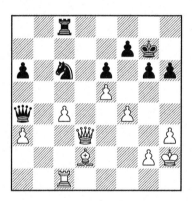

44.♛e3! (already targeting
h6) **44...♖b8 45.f5.** The decisive
breakthrough. After 45...exf5, there's
46.♛xh6+ ♚g8 47.♗g5 and ♗f6,
crushing.

45...g5 46.fxe6 fxe6 47.h4 (the
most energetic) **47...♛b3 48.♛e4
♘e7 49.hxg5 hxg5 50.♛g4(!)
♖h8+ 51.♚g1 ♚f7 52.♖f1+ ♘f5
53.♖xf5+ exf5 54.♛xf5+.** Black
resigned, because he loses his rook to
checks, and then mate is inevitable.

Crushing the Leader

Lisitsin's play was very strong
and inspired in round 14. According
to Levenfish, "Bogatyrchuk
didn't manage to recover from the
devastating loss he suffered that day
by the end of the tournament."

No. 77. Reti Opening A15
Lisitsin – Bogatyrchuk
Leningrad 1934/35, round 14
Annotated by G. Levenfish
**1.♘f3 ♘f6 2.c4 d6 3.g3 e5
4.♗g2 ♘c6 5.d4 ♗d7.** Starting the
maneuver to trade the g2 bishop. It

*"Lisitsin's games are clear, consistent and
calm, which is pleasant for those chess fans
who love a masterful chess landscape."
(Bogatyrchuk). Cartoon by Lis (Moscow
International Tournament Bulletin, No. 6,
1935).*

has a serious flaw: it requires three tempi and doesn't solve any problems in the center.

6.♘c3 ♗e7 7.0-0 ♕c8 8.b3 ♗h3 9.♗b2 ♗xg2 10.♔xg2 ♕d7. Black's position is already difficult. 10...0-0 is met with 11.♘d5! After 11...♘xd5 12.cxd5 ♘xd4 13.♘xd4 exd4 14.♗xd4, white seizes the a1-h8 diagonal and puts some pressure on the c7 pawn. So, black would have to play 11...e4, and after 12.♘g5 h6 13.♘h3 ♘h7, he has a satisfactory position due to the threat f7-f5.

11.♕d2.

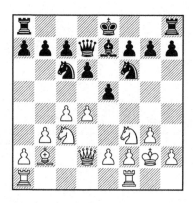

11...e4? Black noticed that after 11...0-0-0 12.d5 ♘b8 13.♕e3 *(13.♘b5!)* 13...b6 14.a4, white gets a strong attack on the king. He should have taken a risk and castled short, because the game move is a direct mistake that leads to a loss of a pawn.

12.♘g5 ♕f5 13.d5 ♘e5 14.♕f4! Not only defending against the threat 14...♘xd5, but also winning a pawn, because after 14...♕xf4 15.gxf4 ♘g6 16.e3, the e4 pawn is

lost anyway. Black gives up the pawn and preserves the queen, hoping for some complications.

14...♕g6 15.♘gxe4 ♘h5 16.♕c1 f5 17.♘d2 ♗g5 18.♕c2!

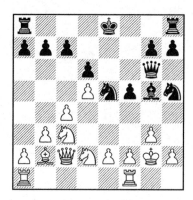

White is willing to allow f5-f4, but only if queens are traded. Black still had to castle: after 18...0-0 19.♔h1 f4 20.♕xg6 hxg6 21.♘ce4 ♗h6, he could still put up stiff resistance. *(After 21...♗h6? that is unlikely: 22.♗xe5! dxe5 23.g4 f3 24.e3 ♘f6 25.g5, and black loses a piece; however, after 21...♗f6, his position is still quite unpleasant.)*

Instead, Bogatyrchuk, who played rather nervously the whole game, launches a desperate attack, which Lisitsin easily repels.

18...♘f4+ 19.♔h1 *(19.gxf4? ♗xf4+ 20.♔h1 ♕h5)* **19...♕h5 20.f3!** *"The cornerstone of white's defense. Now the attack is stopped, and white's counterattack quickly decides matters." (Rokhlin)*

20...♕h6. Black is forced to attack, because all the bridges for retreat have been burned. After 20...

♘h3, there's the simple 21.♕xf5, threatening ♔g2.

21.gxf4! ♗xf4 22.♖f2 ♗xd2.

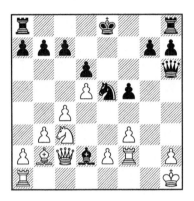

23.♘b5! *"This crushing move was brewing for a while. Now black is hanging by a thread." (Rokhlin)*

23...0-0-0. After 23...0-0, there's 24.♘xc7 and ♘e6, while 23...♗e3 is met with 24.♘xc7+ ♔d7 25.♘xa8 ♗xf2 26.♕xf5+ ♔d8 27.♗xe5 dxe5 28.♕xe5, crushing.

23...♗a5 24.b4 c6 25.♘d4 ♗xb4 26.♘xf5 is bad as well.

24.f4! *"The piece is doomed. Black can't play 24...♘g4 due to 25.♕xf5+ and ♕xg4." (Rokhlin)*

24...♗e3   25.fxe5   ♗xf2 26.♕xf5+ ♔b8 27.♕xf2. All this was precisely and sharply calculated by Lisitsin. Black is destroyed.

27...a6   28.♕a7+   ♔c8   29.e6. Black resigned.

Procrastination is the Thief of Time

Levenfish: "One of master Riumin's virtuoso games that gained him fans among the widest chess circles."

No. 78. English Opening A41
Mazel – Riumin
Leningrad 1934/35, round 5
Annotated by I. Kan
1.c4 e5 2.♘c3 ♘c6 3.♘f3 d6. This and the next move by black are characteristic of the eccentric development system used by Riumin.

4.d4 f6. *"This defense deserves full attention. Black avoids trades and creates a solid position." (Levenfish)*

Isaak Mazel was strictly reprimanded for "an unacceptable attitude towards his tournament duties" (he offered everyone draws right out of the openings and frequently came late to his games). Cartoon by Y. Yuzepchuk (Moscow International Tournament Bulletin, No. 22, 1935).

Dedicated to master Mazel
"There's certainly much in common..."

However, there are only seven games in Megabase with the same first four moves. Two of them were won by white, both after 5.g3, while Kan's recommendation, 5.e4, was only tested once, unsuccessfully.

5.e3. A meek developing move that doesn't pose black difficult problems. 5.e4 with the subsequent ♗e3 is stronger. In this case, black had to contend with his opponent's positional threat to close off the center (d4-d5) and launch a queenside attack (c4-c5).

5...♘h6 6.b3. *"Since white is intending to castle long, he shouldn't have weakened his pawn barrier. A more healthy plan was 6.♗d2, 7.♘d5 and 8.♗c3." (Levenfish)*

6...g6 7.♗b2 ♗g7 8.♕d2 0-0.

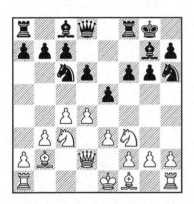

The critical moment. White played the opening without trying to seize the initiative, and now he should be mindful of black's possible aggression after short castling (♘f7, f7-f5 etc.). Perhaps that was the reason why white decided to castle long.

9.0-0-0 ♘f7 10.♗e2 ♖e8 11.♔b1? *"Losing two important tempi. With opposite-sides castling, such a waste of time is especially dangerous, and this game should serve as a good illustration. It was necessary to prepare for the pawn storm immediately: 11.h4, ♘h2, g2-g4 etc." (Levenfish)*

11...♗f5+ 12.♔a1. After 12.e4, black has an unpleasant reply 12...♗h6, forcing white to retreat to e1 with the queen.

12...♘b4 13.♖c1 *(a good alternative was 13.a3 ♘c2+ 14.♔a2 exd4 15.♘xd4 ♘xd4 16.♕xd4) 13...c5 14.dxc5 ♕a5!*

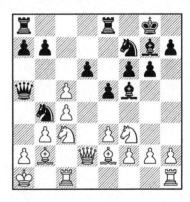

Black didn't of course play 13... c5 to trade queens on d8. The queen incursion is an important link in the chain of Riumin's combination blows.

15.cxd6. For better or worse, white had to play 15.a3. For instance, after 15...dxc5 16.♘a2 ♘c6, the black pieces are more active, but white wouldn't have been comprehensively crushed as in the game.

15...e4! 16.♘d4. *The practical Junior recommends 16.♘a4!? with the idea 16...exf3 17.♗xf3 ♘c6 18.♕xa5 ♘xa5 19.♗c3 ♘c6 20.♘c5! ♘xd6 21.♗d5+ ♔h8 22.♘xb7 ♘xb7 23.♗xc6, getting three pawns for the knight.*

16...♘xa2! *"That's the secret of black's combination! He regains all the sacrificed material and exposes the white king." (Levenfish)*

17.b4. White simply has no other reply due to the threat 17...♘xc3+.

17...♘xb4+ 18.♔b1 ♘e5. The cavalry reserve joins the fight with a decisive effect.

19.♘xf5 gxf5 20.♖hd1 ♖ed8 21.♗a1 ♘ed3.

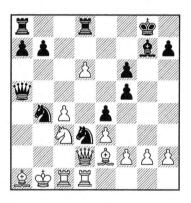

22.♗xd3. *The immediate 22.♘d5! was more resilient, forcing some simplifications: 22...♘xc1 (22...♕a4 23.♘xb4; 22...♖xd6? 23.♗xd3) 23.♖xc1 ♘c6 24.♕xa5 ♘xa5 25.♘e7+ ♔f8 26.♘xf5 etc.*

22...♘xd3   23.♘d5. The last attempt to get at least some counterplay. After 23.♖c2, black had

a choice between capturing on d6 or giving a check on b4.

23...♕a3! Riumin prefers, of course, to continue the attack rather than gain material. The position of the white king makes such a decision obvious

24.♘e7+ ♔h8! 25.♘xf5 ♖ac8! *(exclamation marks awarded by Levenfish)* **26.♕a2.** *White overlooks a chance to complicate things with 26.♖c3 ♕c5 27.f3!, for instance: 27...♖c6 28.fxe4 ♖b6+ 29.♔c2 ♘b4+ 30.♔b3, and the discovered check gives nothing.*

26...♕b4+ 27.♗b2 ♖c5 28.♕a3 (defending against the threat 28...♖a5, but losing a knight) **28...♕xa3 29.♗xa3 ♖xf5.** White resigned.

The Ragozin System

Yudovich: "This game had an enormous influence on the development of strategy and tactics in the Queen's Gambit."

No. 79. Queen's Gambit E33
Riumin – Ragozin
Leningrad 1934/35, round 4
Commentary by V. Ragozin
1.d4 ♘f6 2.c4 e6 3.♘c3 ♗b4 4.♕c2 d5 5.e3 0-0 6.♘f3 ♘c6. Developing the knight before c7-c5 contradicts the usual interpretation of the Nimzo-Indian Defense and starts a system that was later named the Ragozin Defense: black wants to concentrate his efforts on preparing the e6-e5 break, or, if that doesn't

work, on searching for queenside counterplay, as happened in this game.

7.a3 ♗xc3+ 8.♕xc3 ♗d7. The natural-looking 8...♘e4 is just bad. In the game V. Makogonov – Ragozin (Tbilisi 1934), after 9.♕c2 ♗d7 10.♗d3 black had to retreat the knight back to f6, because 10...f5 would have led to a severe weakening of the center.

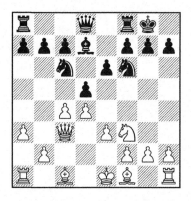

9.b4. *"Black, making his waiting move, counted on this active lunge that, however, weakened the light squares. 9.b3 and ♗b2 was the correct plan."* (Levenfish)

Black would have faced a harder time after 9.♗d3, which I planned to meet with 9...a5, and if 10.0-0, then 10...a4 and ♘a5-b3. *For instance: 11.♗d2 ♘a5 12.♘e5 dxc4 13.♘xc4 ♘b3 with a complicated struggle (Keres – Kotov, Moscow 1946).*

9...a5! In the game Flohr – Romanovsky (Moscow 1935), black went for an original, but ineffective maneuver: 9...dxc4 10.♗xc4 b5 (10...

a5! Flohr) 11.♗xb5 ♘xb4 12.♗xd7! ♘bd5 13.♕c2 ♘xd7 14.e4, and the weakness of black's queenside pawns soon showed.

10.b5. Black still manages to break down this menacing pawn chain. So the correct move was 10.♖b1.

"I must add that the entire opening was a revelation to Riumin. After the game, Riumin, Belavenets and I searched for flaws in Ragozin's plan for ages, but couldn't find anything substantial." (Yudovich)

10...♘a7 11.a4 c6! *"A light-square break, typical for this line."* (Levenfish)

12.♗a3 ♖e8 13.♖b1 dxc4.

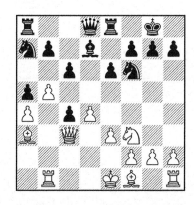

14.b6? This pawn sacrifice is unfounded. After 14.♗xc4 cxb5 15.axb5 ♘d5 16.♕d3, white had an acceptable position.

14...♘b5!? *"A very Ragozin-like move. Less adventurous players probably would have preferred 14...♘d5 or 14...♘c8."* (Yudovich)

15.axb5 cxb5 16.♘e5. White will eventually have to return the piece. However, this was the most opportune time to do so. After 16.♗xc4 bxc4 17.♕xc4 ♖c8 and 18...♗c6, black of course still had a very strong position, but wouldn't keep his material advantage.

16...b4! 17.♕c1. After 17.♗xb4, there's 17...♘d5 and ♘xb4, with black winning at least a pawn.

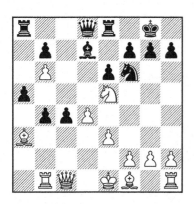

17...♗b5! Black is fighting to save his formidable pawn phalanx. If he were forced to play 17...bxa3, then after 18.♕xa3 and ♗xc4 white would equalize easily.

18.♗e2. White has nothing more energetic. 18.♗xb4 axb4 19.♖xb4 ♕d5! 20.f3 ♖ec8 21.♘xc4 *(21. ♕c3 ♖a2)* 21...♖c6 is dangerous, as white can't escape from the pin *(22. e4 ♘xe4!)*. 18.♗xc4 ♗xc4 looks calmer (this black move is stronger than 18...♖c8 19.♗xb5! with more than enough compensation for the queen) 19.♕xc4 bxa3 20.♕b3 ♘d5 21.♕xa3 ♖a6, but black still kept a material advantage.

In the second line, the correct move is 20.♕a4, because after 20.♕b3?

black has a very strong reply 20...♕d5!

18...♖c8 (18...♘d5 was probably even stronger) **19.♗xb4.** Otherwise, black bolsters his pawns with 19...♘d5.

19...axb4 20.♖xb4.

РАГОЗИН

Vyacheslav Ragozin's Soviet Championship debut was successful. Cartoon by Y. Yuzepchuk (Moscow International Tournament Bulletin, No. 22, 1935).

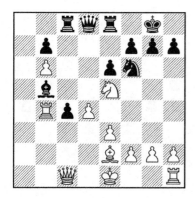

20...♗a6! (20...♕d5 is now bad due to 21.♗f3) **21.0-0.** White can't avoid losing a pawn, for instance: 21.♗f3 ♘d5! 22.♗xd5 exd5 23.0-0 ♖e6, then f7-f6 and ♖cc6.

21...♘d5 22.♖b1 ♘xb6 23.♕a3 f6 24.♘f3 ♘d5 25.♘d2 f5 26.♘f3 ♕e7 27.♕a5 ♕d6 28.♘e5 b5. Black finally pushes this pawn forward, too. However, the position is still far from winning, because white manages to stop the further movement of pawns.

The computer is sure that the c-pawn could move forward even without any support: 28...c3! 29.♗b5 (or 29.♗d3 c2) 29...♕d8! 30.♕a3 c2 etc.

29.♗f3 ♖e7 30.♖fc1 ♖ec7 31.♖a1 ♖a7.

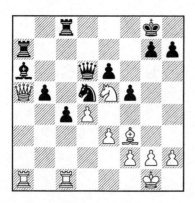

32.♘d3. This knight move is met with an interesting refutation.

32...♖ca8! 33.♘c5. After 33.♗xd5 ♕xd5 34.♘b4 black had 34...♕xg2+ and ♗b7+ with promising simplifications *(instead of 34.♘b4?, white has a better reply: 34.♘f4 ♕d6 35.♖ab1).*

33...e5 34.♗xd5+ ♕xd5 35.♖ab1. White misses black's next move. However, 35.♘xa6 ♖xa6 36.♕xa6 ♖xa6 37.♖xa6 b4 was also hopeless: white can't stop the passed pawns.

35...♗b7 36.e4 ♕xc5. White resigned.

A Trap for... Flohr

Levenfish: "This game is very important for the theory of the Slav Defense. Its importance is evident even because of this one fact: it wasn't published abroad, so Flohr didn't know it, and in the 1936 Moscow International Tournament, Ragozin caught him with the same line."

No. 80. Slav Defense D19
Belavenets – Veresov
Leningrad 1934/35, round 5
Annotated by S. Belavenets
1.d4 d5 2.c4 c6 3.♘f3 ♘f6 4.♘c3 dxc4 5.a4 ♗f5 6.e3 e6 7.♗xc4 ♗b4 8.0-0 0-0 9.♕e2 c5 *(9...♘bd7!)* **10.♖d1 ♘c6.** Black is playing a system recommended by Kmoch. Now white gains nothing with 11.dxc5 ♕e7 or 11.d5 exd5

12.♘xd5 ♘xd5 13.♖xd5 ♛f6 with equality *(I. Rabinovich – Kmoch, Leningrad 1934).*

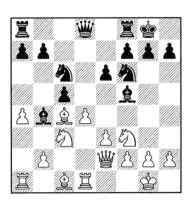

11.♘a2! Intending to gain at least the bishop pair. Black should have probably accepted that, playing 11...♛b6 or 11...♛a5 *(11...♛e7!),* because after the game move, he immediately gets into trouble.

"One of the lines that Belavenets and I prepared together. We spent a lot of time working on this position, but Sergei was the first one to test this novelty in practice." (Yudovich)

11...♗a5?   **12.dxc5**   **♛e7 13.♘d4! ♛xc5.** There's nothing else: otherwise, white plays 14.♘xc6 and b2-b4, holding onto the pawn.

Flohr played 13...♖fd8 against Ragozin at the 1936 Moscow tournament (it turned out that it was Euwe's move, prepared for his match with Alekhine), but after 14.b4! ♗c7 15.h3 ♘e5 16.♗b2 a5 17.♖ac1! he lost as well. Ragozin was well-prepared, because before that championship he had worked

on the lines after ♘a2 together with Belavenets and Yudovich...

14.b4! This combination, based on pinning the black pieces, wins by force.

14...♘xb4. The only move; black can't play 14...♗xb4 due to 15.♘xc6 bxc6 16.♘xb4 and ♗a3, winning an exchange.

15.♗a3! 15.♘b3 ♛e5! 16.♗b2 ♛c7 17.♘xa5 ♘xa2! doesn't work.

15...♖fc8   **16.♖dc1**   **♛b6 17.♘xf5(!) exf5 18.♖ab1 ♘xa2.** Hoping to get two rooks for the queen after 19.♖xb6 ♘xc1. However, white has another continuation that gives him a decisive material advantage.

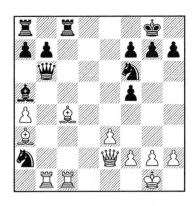

19.♗xf7+! **♔xf7** *(19...♔h8?* *20.♖xc8+ and ♖xb6)* **20.♕xa2+** **♔g6.** 20...♕e6 is bad due to 21.♖xb7+ ♘d7 22.♖xd7+ ♔f6 23.♗b2+ ♗c3 24.♖xc3 ♕xa2 25.♖c6+ ♔g5 26.♖xg7+ ♔h5 27.♖xh7+, with a mate in two.

21.♖xb6 ♗xb6. *"After the great combination started on move 11, white won the queen for rook and knight."* *(Levenfish)*

22.h3 ♖xc1+ 23.♗xc1 ♖d8 24.♕b3 ♖d7 25.♗b2 ♖d6 26.♗e5 ♖d2. Accelerates the loss, but the game is still hopeless. For instance, after 26...♖c6, white would have eventually played g2-g4 and opened up the black king's position.

27.♗xf6 gxf6 (not 27...♔xf6 28.♕c3+) **28.♕g8+ ♔h6 29.♕f7 ♖d6?** (blundering a rook at the end) **30.♕f8+!** Black resigned.

A Round of Miniatures

Can you believe it? Both of the next two short games were played in the same round, both started with the Exchange Ruy Lopez with a b-pawn capture, and in both, the attack began after the pawn break e4-e5!

No. 81. Ruy Lopez C68
I. Rabinovich – Savitsky
Leningrad 1934/35, round 7
Annotated by G. Levenfish
1.e4 e5 2.♘f3 ♘c6 3.♗b5 a6 4.♗xc6 bxc6. 4...dxc6 is just as good. 5.♘xe5 is met with 5...♕g5 and ♕xg2.

5.0-0 ♕f6 (original, but not bad) **6.d4 exd4 7.♘xd4 ♗b7 8.♘c3 ♗c5?** The correct move here is 8...0-0-0 with a good position.

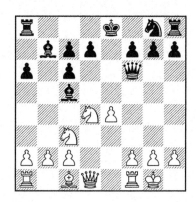

9.e5! ♕g6 (not 9...♕e7 10.♘f5 ♕f8 11.♘e4 ♗b6 12.♘ed6+; *11...0-0-0 12.♘xg7)* **10.♘de2 ♘e7?** Black misses a hidden threat. 10...♕h5 could have saved the game.

11.♘f4! ♕f5 12.g4! Winning a piece. After 12...♕xe5, there's 13.♘d3 ♕d4 14.♗e3 or 13...♕d6 14.♘e4. Black resigned.

A funny game – the shortest in the whole tournament.

No. 82. Ruy Lopez C73
Bogatyrchuk – Freymann
Leningrad 1934/35, round 7
Annotated by G. Levenfish
1.e4 e5 2.♘f3 ♘c6 3.♗b5 a6 4.♗a4 d6 5.♗xc6+ bxc6 6.d4 exd4 7.♘xd4 ♗b7. This move is overly attack-minded and is inappropriate here. Black should have played 7...♗d7, guarding the c8-h3 diagonal.

8.♘c3 ♘f6 9.0-0 ♘d7? This knight excursion is totally

inappropriate with the pieces underdeveloped and king stuck in the center *(9...c5!?)*.

10.♕g4 ♕f6 11.♗e3 g6? Castling long would have been a logical continuation of the previous moves. After 11...0-0-0 12.♘b3 ♕g6 13.♕e2 black's position is not particularly great, due to the threat 14.♘a5, but at least he could put up some resistance. Now, however, a crushing defeat follows.

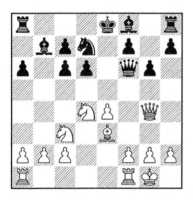

12.♖fe1 ♗g7. Planning to castle short.

13.e5! dxe5. After 13...♘xe5 14.♗g5 0-0 15.♕g3 black loses his queen *(actually, only a knight: 15... ♘f3+ 16.♘xf3 ♕f5)*.

Black could avoid losses with the paradoxical move 14...♕e7!, after which white had a pleasant choice: expose the enemy king with 15.♗xe7 ♘xg4 16.♗xd6+ or make the opponent "play checkers": 15.♕g3 f6 16.♗d2 c5 17.♘b3 g5.

14.♗g5 ♕d6 15.♖ad1! ♕b4. 15...f5 16.♘xf5 gxf5 17.♕xf5 ♖f8 18.♕h3 doesn't help either.

However, 15...c5! does help (16. ♘b3 ♕e6). Strangely, both Freymann over the board and Levenfish in his analysis missed this simple defense.

16.♗e4! 0-0 (After 16...♕xb2 sacrifices such as 17.♘e6 could follow) **17.♘b3.** Black resigned.

A Calling Card for Two

Levenfish: "Alatortsev again played his system in the French, sacrificing the g7 and h7 pawns. His opponent, Rauzer, could have won the game at several points, but got confused and lost."

No. 83. French Defense C18
Rauzer – Alatortsev
Leningrad 1934/35, round 4
Annotated by V. Rauzer
1.e4 e6 2.d4 d5 3.♘c3 ♗b4 4.e5 c5 5.a3 ♗xc3+ 6.bxc3 ♘e7 7.♕g4 ♕a5. *"This risky move was often used by Alatortsev, and, of course, it wasn't a surprise for Rauzer"* (Levenfish). The main moves are 7... *♕c7 or 7...0-0.*

8.♗d2 ♕a4 *(8...0-0 is safer)*
9.♕xg7 ♖g8 10.♕xh7 cxd4.

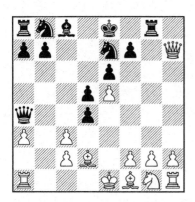

11.♘f3. In a later round, Bogatyrchuk defeated Alatortsev with 11.♘e2. However, 11.♘f3 is much more active and also reinforces the e5 pawn and the whole kingside.

In Levenfish's opinion, it was in the game against Bogatyrchuk that the whole "Alatortsev system" was refuted: 11.♘e2! ♘bc6 12.f4 ♖g6? (12...b6 is more tenacious) 13.h4! ♗d7 14.h5 ♖g8 15.h6 0-0-0 (15... ♖g6? 16.♕h8+ ♖g8 17.♕xg8+!) 16.♕d3 ♖g6 17.h7, and white won.

11...dxc3 *There is a different move order in Megabase, but it's unimportant here: 11...♘bc6 12.h4 dxc3 13.♗xc3 ♗d7.*

12.♗xc3 ♘bc6 13.h4? Having an extra pawn, white attempts to win the exchange as well. The calculation itself is correct, but white doesn't see that after winning the exchange the white king is in danger, his queen is cut off, and all light squares are weakened, especially the b5-f1 diagonal.

Upset by the loss, Rauzer is too self-critical. Actually, his combination gives him a won position and the moves 13.h4 and 14.h5 really deserve exclams.

13...♗d7 14.h5? At least now, white had to stop on his wrong way and play 14.♘g5 0-0-0 15.♘xf7.

This line allowed black to go for complications with 15...♘f5!?, for instance: 16.♘xd8 ♕xc2 (not 16...♕e4+ 17.♔d2!) 17.♗d2 ♕e4+ 18.♗e2 ♖xd8 with decent compensation for the exchange.

14...0-0-0 15.♖h4 ♖g4! (not 15...d4 16.♘xd4 with the threat ♗b5, and if 16...♘xe5, then 17.♘f5) **16.♗b5.** It's better to avoid winning **this** exchange!

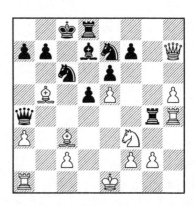

16...♕xb5! *Trying to keep the exchange via 16...♕f4 led to simplifications that were worse for black: 17.♗d2 ♕e4+ 18.♕xe4 ♖xe4+ 19.♖xe4 dxe4 20.♗xc6 ♗xc6 21.♘g5.*

17.♖xg4 ♘f5! 18.♖d1. Only here did white understand how difficult his position was, and he spent 50 minutes choosing between 0-0-0 and ♖d1. If 18.0-0-0, then 18...♕c5 with the subsequent ♕xf2, threatening ♘e3 (after 19.♖d3 ♕xf2 20.♗d2, this threat doesn't exist and white has a clear advantage).

18...♗e8 19.♕h8 d4 20.♗d2 ♘ce7 (threatening 21...♕c4 and ♗b5) **21.♗g5** (21.h6!+−) **21... ♕a5+ 22.♖d2** Definitively giving up his advantage. It was better to play 22.♗d2 ♕c7 23.♖b1.

22...♗b5.

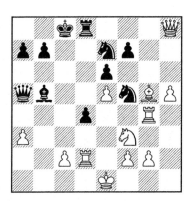

23.♕xd8+! After 23.♕f6 ♕xa3, black's attack doesn't stop, while the white queen remains out of play. Now, white gets two rooks for the queen after great complications. However, the light squares, which weakened after winning that ill-fated exchange, remain weak until the very end of the game.

In reality, the queen sac should lose! Whereas 23.♕f6 ♕xa3 24.♕xf7 or 23...♕c3 24.a4! retained approximate equality. 23.♕h7 ♕c3 24.♗xe7 also

led to incredible complications. White could still hold with precise play, but it's very hard to find these long chains of defensive moves over the board: 24...♘e3?! 25.fxe3 dxe3 26.♗xd8 exd2+ 27.♘xd2 ♕e3+ 28.♔d1 ♕g1+ 29.♘f1 ♕xf1+ 30.♔d2 ♕e2+ 31.♔c1 ♕xg4 32.♗f6! or 24...d3! 25.cxd3 ♖xd3 26.♕g8+ ♔c7 27.♗d8+ ♔c6 28.♕e8+ ♔c5 29.♗e7+ ♘xe7 30.♕xe7+ ♔c6 31.♕d6+!

23...♕xd8 24.♘xd4 ♕h8! The only move (actually missing the win, black should win after 24...♕c7!).

25.♘xf5 exf5. If 25...♕xe5+, then 26.♘e3; if 25...♘xf5, then 26.♖d8+.

Let's continue the first line: 26... ♕a1+ 27.♘d1 (27.♖d1 ♕c3+) 27... ♕e5+ 28.♘e3 with an equal position. In fact the game position here is now also equal.

26.♗f6 ♕xh5 27.♖h4 ♕g6 28.♗xe7 ♕xg2.

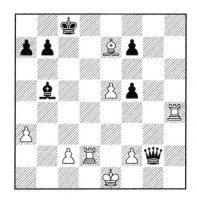

29.c4. *"From the "general considerations" point of view, this move is undoubtedly the best:*

white has defended against mate, attacked a piece with tempo and also set a trap: 29...♗c6 is met with 30.♖h8+ ♔c7 31.♗d8+ ♔c8 32.♗b6+, mating. However, white should have moved contrary to the "general considerations" and won the game with purely problem-like motifs – blocking and a discovered check: 29.♖h8+! ♔c7 30.♗d8+ ♔c6 31.♖h6+ ♔c5 (the b5 square is blocked) 32.♗e7+ ♔c4 33.♖h4+ ♔c3 34.♗b4+ ♔b2 35.c4+, winning the bishop and the game" (Levenfish).

Alas, 31...f6! (instead of 31...♔c5?) 32.♖xf6+ Kc5 33.♗e7+ ♔c4 34.♖d3 ♕e4+ and perpetual check unravels this pretty combination.

29...♗a4. Since checks are now useless for white, black gets some winning chances.

30.♖h8+. At that moment, white was already in severe time trouble, and the goal of the subsequent useless checks was to gain time (30.♖hd4!?).

30...♔c7   31.♗d8+   ♔c6 32.♖h6+? Of course, it was better to leave the king on c6, where it blocked its own bishop. But this is another time-trouble move!

He should have played 32.♖d6+ ♔c5 33.♖h4=.

32...♔c5   33.♖h4. Or 33.♗e7+ ♔xc4 34.♖h4+ ♔b5 35.♖b4+ ♔a5. *But 35.♖d7! was more resilient.*

33...♗c6   34.♔e2 *(this loses immediately)* **34...♗f3+!** *Or the even more forceful 34...♕f3+! 35.♔f1 f4.*

35.♔e3   ♗g4   (*35...♗e4!–+*) **36.♔f4 ♔xc4.**

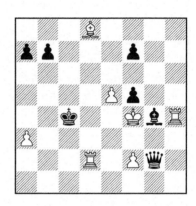

37.♗c7. This protects the e5 pawn, but gives up a3. *37.♔g5! ♔c3 38.♗a5+ ♔b3 39.♔f6 might still save the game!*

37...♔c3   38.♗a5+   ♔b3 39.♖d3+. White is trying to save everything in time trouble, but blunders a full rook.

39...♔a4   40.f3   ♔xa5   41.fxg4 ♕e4+. White resigned.

"The game clearly shows the strengths and weaknesses of both players." (Levenfish)

Young, But Not Green

Levenfish didn't call Savitsky "a master of attacking style" for nothing. It was very dangerous for any player to fall under his attack on a good day! Towards the end of the tournament, Leonid was on the ascent: the day before, he had defeated Freymann, and the day after, he would defeat Rauzer.

No. 84. Ruy Lopez C78
Bogatyrchuk – Savitsky
Leningrad 1934/35, round 17
Annotated by L. Savitsky

1.e4 e5 2.♘f3 ♘c6 3.♗b5 a6 4.♗a4 ♘f6 5.0-0 ♗c5. *"A move often played by Alekhine and analyzed by Savitsky in detail." (Levenfish)*

6.d3. A harmless move, which can't even be seen as an effort to refute black's structure. White should've played 6.♘xe5 ♘xe5 7.d4 ♘xe4 8.♖e1 ♗e7 9.♖xe4 ♘g6 with subsequent castling or 6.c3 ♗a7! 7.d4 ♘xe4 8.♕e2 f5 9.dxe5 *(9.♘bd2! Ilyin-Zhenevsky)* 9...0-0 etc.

6...d6. An inaccuracy. Black should have played 6...b5 and d7-d6. After the game move, black has to cede the e5 square.

7.d4! exd4 8.♘xd4 ♗d7 9.♘xc6 bxc6 10.♘c3. White should have played 10.♗g5 first *("with 10...h6 11.♗h4 g5 12.♗g3 ♘xe4 13.♖e1 d5 14.♘c3 f5, black keeps the pawn, however, after 15.♘xd5! cxd5 16.♕xd5! white's attack is unstoppable" Levenfish).* Now black equalizes.

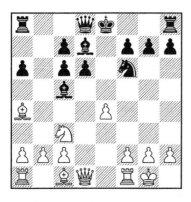

10...♘g4! This move pursues two goals: first of all, black avoids the pin on g5, and, secondly, prepares the eventual push f7-f5, which is the main advantage of this line.

11.♕f3. Black threatened 11...♕h4. If 11.h3, then after 11...♘e5, ♕h4 and ♗xh3 is still a threat. 11.♗xc6 doesn't work because of 11...♕h4, winning at least an exchange.

11...0-0 12.♗f4 ♕e7. White couldn't and still can't capture on c6.

13.♖ae1 ♖ae8 14.♕g3. White should have played 14.e5, with an equal game. After the game move, black obtains the initiative.

Levenfish corrects him: "Here, 14.e5 dxe5 15.♗xc6 was refuted by 15...♘xf2! 16.♗e3 ♘g4!" (or 16.♖xf2 ♗xf2+ 17.♔xf2 ♕c5+ 18.♗e3 ♕xc6).

14...f5!

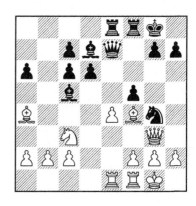

15.h3. After 15.♖e2, black had 15...fxe4, for instance: 16.♖xe4 ♕xe4!! 17.♘xe4 ♖xe4 with a decisive attack.

15...g5! 16.hxg4. If 16.♗xg5, then 16...♕xg5 17.hxg4 f4 18.♕d3 f3! 19.gxf3 ♗xg4 20.fxg4 ♕xg4+ 21.♔h2 ♖e5, winning.

Actually, 21...♖e5? is an error due to 22.♕g3; black wins with 21...♖xf2+! 22.♖xf2 ♗xf2 etc.

16...gxf4 17.♕xf4 fxg4 18.♕g3 h5! 18...♕e5 19.♕xe5 ♖xe5 20.♔h2? doesn't work due to 20...g3+! 21.♔xg3 ♖g5+ 22.♔h2 ♗xf2, but white has 20.g3!, with some defensive prospects.

19.e5. The only way to complicate things and counter the terrible threat h5-h4 and g4-g3.

19...h4 20.♕d3 ♗f5.

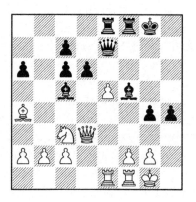

21.♕e2. *That's the decisive mistake! After 21.♕d2!, 21...g3 is not a threat because of 22.♘e4 ♗xe4 (22...h3? 23.♘xc5; 22...♗b6 23.♗xc6) 23.♕xe4, and the rook leaves the doomed square, for instance: 23...♖xf2 24.♖xf2 ♗xf2+ 25.♔h1 ♕g7 26.♗xc6 ♖xe5 27.♗d5+ etc..*

21...g3 22.♘d1 *(forced: 22.♘e4? ♕xe5)* **22...gxf2+.** 22...h3 and ♕h4 won immediately. The game move gives white a short reprieve.

23.♘xf2 ♕g5 24.♔h1 ♖xe5 25.♕c4+. This loses immediately. White could have prolonged the struggle with 25.♕d1.

25...♗e6 26.♖xe5 ♕xe5 27.♕xh4 ♗xf2! 28.♕h6 ♖f6. White resigned.

"The whole game was played very strongly by Savitsky." (Levenfish)

Gamarjoba, Genatsvale[22]!

10th Soviet Championship: Tbilisi, 12th April – 14th May 1937

"I doubt whether in any other country in the world,
even Hitler's Germany, thought be less free,
more bowed down, more fearful (terrorized), more vassalized."
Andre Gide, *Return from the U.S.S.R.*

Exquisite farce and irony delivered by fate: in the year when catastrophe started in the country, the Soviet chess championship was hosted by the home city of the "Kremlin Highlander"... and of another notorious Georgian madman who would soon move to Moscow and accept the baton of murder from his predecessor...

The first attempt to host the country's main tournament beyond the "two capitals" (Odessa 1929) was, as you remember, widely criticized, and the chess officials didn't attempt such an experiment again until the 10th championship. Not many chess fans know that this championship was first scheduled for September 1936 in Kiev, with only "Grandmaster M. Botvinnik and the winners of the last premiership, masters G. Levenfish and I. Rabinovich", receiving personal invitations. This was printed in *Shakhmaty v SSSR* in December 1935, after which the magazine... just forgot about the tournament for a year and a half! It suddenly "remembered" the competition only in April 1937, matter-of-factly stating that the championship had started.

And what about *64*, the first "chess newspaper" in the world? Until a certain time, it kept everyone updated, but then something went very wrong. The first report, on 30th October 1936, was quite upbeat: "The Council of People's Commissars' All-Union Committee for Physical Education and Sport has decreed to hold the 10th All-Union Chess Championship in Leningrad, from 3rd to 27th December", with the organizing committee chaired by Krylenko. Two weeks later, readers learned that the same esteemed authority had approved "the Chess Section's decision to increase the number of championship participants from 18 to 20". But on that day, instead of the promised championship, a Young Masters Tournament started in Leningrad, whereas the championship, without any explanation, was moved to 1937!.. No further information was reported for three months, and only on 24th February, like a jack-in-the-box, did sudden news appear that the All-Union

---

[22] This is Georgian for 'greetings, my friend!'

Master Viktor Goglidze was the first person to propose holding the championship in Tbilisi. The photo was taken at the 1941 Georgian SSR championship. V. Mikenas is sitting beside Goglidze. G. Kasparyan and A. Pirtskhalava are standing. Goglidze is playing black against Sorokin. The Chief Arbiter Vakhtang Karseladze is sitting beside Sorokin.

premiership "is scheduled to take place in Tbilisi." Then, after a further month of silence, there was a tiny article by A. Palavandishvili, a tournament committee member, who joyfully declared that "the local press had already informed the workers of Georgia about the upcoming tournament." And who informed all the other workers of the country? "The local press" as well?

It seems that, this time, the choice of the championship's host city wasn't made by Krylenko. But by whom, then? Let's try and pull out the threads.

My research tells me that the first one to voice the Tbilisi idea was Viktor Goglidze, immediately after the Young Masters tournament: "To add to my gratitude for running a great tournament, I would like to propose holding the All-Union championship in Tbilisi in spring 1937. Under the gracious Georgian sky, in the best possible circumstances created by my hospitable fellow countrymen, the Soviet masters will be able to create the best works of their chess art."

Could Goglidze personally guarantee "the best possible circumstances"? Of course not. So, he was basically voicing somebody else's idea. I actually have a version. The master's brother, Sergo Goglidze, was the right-hand-man of Lavrentiy Beria, back then Georgia's head honcho (and they were both executed on the same day in 1953), while the organizing committee of the 10th championship was chaired by Solomon Milstein, until 1936 the chairman of the Georgian Communist Party Central Committee's secret department; later, he became a state security lieutenant general and was also executed soon after Beria...

Another indirect piece of evidence that Krylenko wasn't involved with the championship consists of the uncharacteristically reserved reports on the championship in *64* and special issues of the newspaper: almost nothing but games and technical reports on the rounds. Also conspicuously absent was the lack of praise for the organizers, even though everyone agreed that the tournament was organized perfectly!

The Troupe Gathers

Lisitsin: "On 11th and 12th April, almost all participants of the All-Union tournament gathered in the capital of the decorated country of Georgia, Tbilisi *(Tiflis until 1936)*. Only Ragozin arrived late; due to an illness, he left Leningrad later than the other participants.

The beautiful Georgia met the guests cordially. After we passed the Yevlakh station, we totally forgot about the Northern snow and cold. The

На белых и черных конях выезжают участники чемпионата по направлению к Тбилиси. В первом вагоне «международники» — участники международных турниров. Старается выиграть темп чемпион Москвы Кан. Второй чемпион Алаторцев упражняется в контроле времени; на руке у него собственное «точное время». Далее мирно беседуют Левенфиш и Рагозин. В том месте, где вагон слегка деформировался — Рабинович И. Далее опытные кавказцы Чеховер и Лисицын. Ильин-Женевский

The championship participants head to Tbilisi pulled by black and white horses. The first train car is titled "International Car", for the players of international tournaments. The Moscow champion Kan is trying to win a tempo. The second champion, Alatortsev, is taking exercises in time control, having his own "precise time" on his wrist. Then, Levenfish and Ragozin converse peacefully. The car is slightly deformed around I. Rabinovich. Then, we see the experienced "Caucasians", Chekhover and Lisitsin.
Ilyin-Zhenevsky is smoking; you can barely see him behind the tobacco smoke. Lilienthal is on the steps (they forgot to issue a travel ticket to the grandmaster, but this didn't stop him from making himself quite comfortable).

tender Southern sun and blossoming green trees as though said, "Dear guests, you're visiting sunny Georgia." Alas, we didn't get to observe the beautiful landscapes that much: the time of chess battles was fast approaching. Only on the rest days and on their way back could the players see the Georgian Military Road, the Kura and Aragvi, the ancient Mtskheta and Gori – the birth town of the great Stalin.

The opening ceremony took place in the office of the Committee for Physical Education and Sports. The chairman, Comrade Milstein, made a short introductory speech, saying that hospitable Georgia would provide all the necessary conditions for productive and creative work. During the discussion of the regulations, time control debates went on for a long time. The majority of participants agreed with the Leningrad delegation, who proposed a 6-hour control (3 hours for 48 moves) and then adjourning for the day, instead of 5 hours for 40 moves with an hour-long break and two more hours of play *(as a reminder, the previous championship was played with a 6-hour control as well, but for 45 moves)*. On the same day, a telegram was sent to the chairman of the All-Union Chess Section, N. V. Krylenko, with a request to change the approved regulations. Since permission from Moscow arrived only on 14th April, the first round was played with the previous time control...

Дружеский шарж Ю. Ю.

курит; его почти не видно за клубами табачного дыма. На ступеньках Липивнталь (гроссмейстера позабыли обеспечить проездным билетом, но это не помешало ему устроиться с комфортом). Далее в специальных вагонах едут ленинградцы Раузер и Будо и москвичи — Панов, Белавенец и Юдович. В последнем вагоне Бондаревский (Ростов н/Д.). Макагонов (Баку) и Константинопольский (Киев). Без плацкарты — кандидат Толуш.

Then, on the second drawing, there are dedicated cars for the Leningrad players (Rauzer and Budo) and Moscow players (Panov, Belavenets and Yudovich). In the last car, there are Bondarevsky (Rostov-on-Don), Makogonov (Baku) and Konstantinopolsky (Kiev). Reserve player Tolush has no seat booked. Cartoon by Yuri Yuzepchuk (10th All-Union Chess Championship, No. 1, 1937.)

The draw gave the following numbers to the players: 1. Ilyin-Zhenevsky, 2. Kan, 3. Rauzer, 4. Rabinovich, 5. Goglidze, 6. Panov, 7. Ragozin, 8. Budo,

The All-Union Young Masters Tournament was a selection stage for the 10th Soviet Championship. From left to right: Riumin, Konstantinopolsky, Alatortsev and Golidze. The sign behind I. Rabinovich reads: "Big selection of French, Italian and Spanish openings". Drawing by V. Galba from the tournament bulletin.

Chekhover and Ragozin under Levenfish's supervision treat the wounds on their knights. Rauzer and Kan try to tell their tournament fortune using the table. Drawing by V. Galba from the bulletin of the All-Union Young Masters Tournament.

9. Bondarevsky, 10. Lilienthal, 11. Makogonov, 12. Kasparyan, 13. Levenfish, 14. Chekhover, 15. Ebralidze, 16. Konstantinopolsky, 17. Belavenets, 18. Lisitsin, 19. Yudovich, 20. Alatortsev.

Prizes were awarded to the first seven places. To obtain the master's title, the first-category players *(Bondarevsky, Budo and Ebralidze)* had to score the qualifying norm – 9 points.

The organization of the championship was exceptional. It was held in a beautiful, spacious building – the concert hall of the Shota Rustaveli Theater. The audience hall was prettily decorated. On the stage, adorned with fresh flowers, stood 10 chess tables, lit by lamps with green silk lampshades. The floors were mostly carpeted, damping the noise. Contact between the audience and the players was maintained through big demonstration boards, with spotlights directed on them from each side. The audience hall was always packed.

The Georgian public and local press took great interest in the Soviet Championship. All newspapers gave thorough reports about each round in both Georgian and Russian.

> **From the press:** "Interest in the tournament is growing every day. *Zarya Vostoka, Vecherniy Tbilisi, Kommunist, Musha* ('Worker') – all the newspapers are dedicating lots of space to it. Portraits, bios, and player quotes fill the newspaper columns. Some newspapers printed entire pages dedicated to the chess premiership before the opening." (*Special issue 10th All-Union Chess Championship* No. 1, 1937.)

Unfortunately, not all the strongest chess players of the Soviet Country could take part in the championship. M. Botvinnik, P. Romanovsky, N. Riumin and F. Bogatyrchuk declined to play, citing various reasons. The names of these comrades would, of course, have graced the tournament and increased interest even further." (*Shakhmaty v SSSR*, May 1937, and the book *10th All-Union Chess Premiership*.)

A Visit to the People's Commissar

The reasons why the first three declined to take part are well-known. Botvinnik was preparing to defend his candidates thesis, while Romanovsky and Riumin had serious health troubles (heart for the former, lungs for the latter). But why didn't Bogatyrchuk come? He never wrote about that himself. But, most probably, chess was the least of his concerns back then. Since the last championship, two secretaries of the chess section had been arrested in Kiev, and Bogatyrchuk himself had to testify twice, once even at the NKVD!

Bogatyrchuk: "Upon returning to Kiev *(after the 1935 Moscow International Tournament)*, I learned terrible news. N. S., the secretary of the chess section (I was its chairman) had been arrested by the NKVD, and his wife ran to find me, pleading to help her. N. S. was a father of five, a very humble and quiet man. I've never seen him interested in anything besides chess and his family, and, of course, he would have never even thought of taking a political stance against the Soviet authorities.

Asking about reasons for the arrest in local organizations was, of course, totally hopeless. So I decided to take the bull by its horns: to travel to Moscow and ask for help from Krylenko – then the all-powerful People's Commissar of Justice and Chairman of the All-Union Chess Section. As I knew, he sometimes helped chess players who got into trouble. When I told him what had happened, he suggested that I visit him. I had heard a lot about the show trials he presided over, so I never expected miracles. But I thought, why not?

He lived near the center, in an unassuming apartment block *(on Novinsky Boulevard)* where other Soviet officials seemed to live as well. The guard who let me in was presumably forewarned about my visit. He brought me in an elevator (an incredible luxury at the time) to the floor where the justice commissar lived. The apartment was modest, only slightly better than my own apartment in Kiev. I encountered the legendary chieftain and USSR's chief prosecutor many times when he discharged his chess duties. He was an average-height, somewhat plump man with an open, even amiable, but strong-willed face, which didn't betray the cruelty and ruthlessness with which he demanded capital punishment for the proverbial "enemies of the people". His face and manners were completely at odds with the stories about the bloodlust he showed towards the generals and officers who had fallen into his hands at the front *(probably referring to the last few months of Russia's involvement in the First World War, November 1917 to March 1918, when Krylenko occupied the position of Army Chief Commander and was engaged in destroying the Tsarist army, which was accompanied by multiple excesses)*. All in all, he was one of those "executioners with a human face" whom I read about in literature. Even the fanatical adherents of some idea who had no qualms about signing the death warrants for thousands of imagined and true enemies can still shed tears for their mortally-wounded cats or dogs.

Krylenko listened to me and then went to an adjacent room with a government phone. About 15 minutes later, he returned and said that he had talked with Balitsky, the chairman of the Ukrainian NKVD, but, unfortunately, he couldn't do anything now, because N. S. had confessed to his crime the day before. He said the word "confessed" with an indescribable shade of sympathy: who, if not him, knew all the methods used to obtain such "confessions". It was cruel irony that, during the Yezhov purge, he himself was forced to "confess" to his anti-Soviet activities and was liquidated together with other "enemies of the people".

Krylenko said nothing to me about the nature of N. S.'s crime, but added that he asked to "go soft" on N. S. This request was granted, and N. S. was only sent into exile for two years." (From the book *My Life Path to Vlasov and the Prague Manifesto*.)

The trouble, as always, came from an unexpected source. "In summer 1937," Bogatyrchuk wrote in his book, "the newspaper *Kommunist*, the central organ of the Ukrainian Communist Party, printed a thunderous article by three local communist-supporting chess players: Pogrebyssky, Poliak and Konstantinopolsky, with an intriguing title "The Squanderer of People's Money", accusing me of spending large sums of money on organizing a chess club, tours by Lasker and Capablanca, and other "unnecessary" events..."

I managed to unearth this article! It turned out that Bogatyrchuk got both the year and the name wrong (that's why nobody managed to find it before): the article "Remove the Brakes from the Ukrainian Chess Movement" was printed in June 1936. I first published it in the second volume of my book in Russian *Fyodor Bogatyrchuk: the Dr. Zhivago of Soviet Chess* (the chapter "Only Friends Can Betray"). You'll find the story of Bogatyrchuk's "interrogation" at the Ukrainian Communist Party Propaganda Department in the same book.

And in early 1937, "the second secretary of my chess section, N. G., who was sent to Kiev from Moscow, was arrested, too." Bogatyrchuk was summoned to the NKVD to testify. Thankfully, he managed to convince the investigator of his innocence. However, on 20ᵗʰ January, a meeting of Kiev chess players was held, where Bogatyrchuk was criticized: he "didn't show the necessary vigilance", displayed "myopic leadership", etc. And, even though there were no further repercussions, the summons to the NKVD was probably the last straw for him. Six days after the meeting, he would write... a "resignation letter" from chess!

The chess community only learned about that in April, during the Soviet Championship, when *64* printed a letter from a member of the Ukrainian Chess Section, **N. Bulkovstein**, unassumingly titled "On Empathy and Attention":

"Why is master Bogatyrchuk, a prizewinner of all previous Soviet Championships, not among the participants of the All-Union Chess Championship? The historical background to this question deserves the attention of our public and physical education authorities. It's telling for the work of the Ukrainian chess and checkers organization.

In the second half of last year, the *Kommunist* newspaper warned about the unsatisfactory state of chess work in Ukraine, and the errors made by Comrade Bogatyrchuk in his work as the chairman. The ensuing self-criticism turned out to be very valuable for the improvement of chess work in Ukraine. The only error made was that the Ukrainian Committee for Physical Education and Sport executives stood aside, not separating the useful, Bolshevist criticism from petty squabbling, couldn't unify the chess organization, or improve the mores and mutual relations.

As a result, on 26th January, master Bogatyrchuk sent a statement, addressed to the chairman of the Ukrainian Committee for Physical Education and Sport, Comrade Korytnyi, notifying him that he had **retired from chess activity and declines to play in the All-Union championship** *(highlighted by me. - S.V.)*

Not considering the author's excuses about being overburdened with medical work valid and legitimate, we are not going to defend master Bogatyrchuk's actions. His statement deserves only disapproval, because chess work and playing in the Soviet Championship is not just Bogatyrchuk's personal affair. Bogatyrchuk played in the Soviet Championship as a Ukrainian master, his play is well-renowned, and our chess cadre should learn from his games.

Definitely, had we posed the question to Bogatyrchuk at the time in such a way, had he been criticized locally but also defended from groundless "criticism", had we simply treated him with empathy – we don't doubt that Bogatyrchuk would have retracted his statement. However, the executives of the Ukrainian organization had a different opinion: nobody reacted to his statement that was so unusual in our circumstances, and the question of Bogatyrchuk's participation in the Soviet Championship was never even raised at the Ukrainian chess section meetings.

This story shows that the Ukrainian Committee for Physical Education and Sports does not value people either. The Committee chairman, Comrade Korytnyi, who ignored Bogatyrchuk's statement for two months, didn't even deem it necessary to talk personally with the strongest Ukrainian master.

It's even more puzzling that the chess section of the All-Union Committee for Physical Education and Sports, upon learning of Bogatyrchuk's refusal to take part in the championship, just tacitly acquiesced and did not even react to that situation. And we really need to get to the bottom of it." *(64*, 24th April 1937.)

This unique document sheds some light on the attitude of the local sports authorities (and Krylenko himself) towards Bogatyrchuk. It's very telling that there was no public reaction to this letter.

However, just two weeks after filing his statement about "retirement from chess activity", Fyodor Parfenyevich played in the match between the Ukrainian SSR and Moscow with great success, crushing both Moscow champions – Kan and Alatortsev. And in the summer, he won the Ukrainian championship! But he never played outside Kiev in the Soviet Union again.

At the Start

That's the title of N. Polevoy's report in the special issue of *64* dedicated to the championship (No. 2, 19th April 1937). The series was not continued, and it's a real pity: on the backdrop of languid writings in *64* and *Shakhmaty v SSSR*, devoid of all color, this sketch looks like a vivid spot of real life, which had only recently filled the chess (and non-chess) magazines. Who was N. Polevoy? This pseudonym was used by the well-known Leningrad journalist and chess player Nikolai Feldman ("Polevoy" is basically a translation of his last name from German into Russian – "Field man"). After the war, he moved to Moscow, became a candidate master and wrote for *Shakhmaty v SSSR*. He wrote a lot of articles about chess at collective farms and two brochures: *Chess and Checkers* and *All-Union Collective Farm Workers' Tournament* (both 1951).

Polevoy: "If you ask the players what matter concerns them the most now, the majority will surely reply: "The weather! When is it going to get warmer?" The weather question is not just a whim. Panov fell ill and didn't play on the first day. Ilyin-Zhenevsky had to stop his game against Alatortsev because of health problems. And everyone looks up, into the gloomy sky.

The heat in the hotels has been turned off because spring has already come. It's cold.

But if we forget about the weather – the welcoming hosts cannot do anything about this flaw – then we have to admit that the Georgian chess organization has done everything in its power to use the championship to popularize the chess art in the decorated republic.

I remember last year's All-Union tournaments in Leningrad. The Leningrad newspapers only dedicated tiny articles to them. A handful of spectators gloomily walked about the huge empty halls.

Here in Tbilisi, however, a lot of work has been done: they held lectures at the factories and offices, mobilized the chess community, newspapers dedicate whole pages to the tournament. The championship is at the center of attention of the Tbilisi public.

Moving the tournament to Georgia, additional expenses, long travels for the majority of participants – all this chess pilgrimage to faraway Tbilisi has been justified by the rise of the chess movement we've encountered here.

All the invited players arrived. However, the "desertion" of a well-loved participant, master Bogatyrchuk, from the chess front is inexplicable. They said that he didn't even provide an explanation for his absence. Ebralidze was signed up to the tournament instead.

> From the article by **V. Faibisovich** "A little about G. I. Ravinsky" (e3e5. com website, 2019) I learnt that the later famous coach Grigory Ravinsky was due to play in this championship. He had won one of the three groups of the All-Union tournament that was a qualifier for the final of the championship. However, unexpected circumstances intervened:
>
> "In December, the Control-Audit Department (CAD) of the People's Commissariat of Finances started to audit the activities of the State Sports Committee. As a result of the audit, employee of the Mass Chess Bureau G. I. Ravinsky was accused of wasting money (you can read about it in the *Spartak* newspaper dated 15th April 1937). It seems that the accusation was empty and didn't lead to any long-term consequences. But it was sufficient to exclude him from the list of participants of the final of the All-Union championship."

Tolush once joked that the Moscow player Kots achieved his greatest success when he was present at the All-Union tournament draw as a reserve. Now Tolush himself has to swallow the same pill. But he isn't dismayed: he has taken up reporting instead and says that it's more pleasant to watch others make mistakes than to make them yourself.

The draw determines the order of participants. The debates about the chances of winning or achieving the coveted master's norm (nine points!) are rather heated. As we know, it's best to talk about winning chances after the tournament is over. Now, though, most Tbilisi newspapers are fairly cautious in their predictions, naming... three quarters of the field as the possible winners.

What more can we say, if the old guard is full of vigor and energy, while the young masters have already gained a lot of experience?

Take Rabinovich from Leningrad – he's happy, healthy and calm. His triumphant air portends nothing good... for him. He was warned back in

Leningrad: if you're too sure of yourself, you will underestimate your opponents. This prediction came true in the very first round, when Belavenets, full of internal tension, masterfully defeated Rabinovich.

Levenfish is focused. His games are watched with special attention. Lilienthal is not well, nervous and reacts badly to losses. After losing to Makogonov, he's ready to say "it's all over". The championship participants take much care of him, they cheer him up warmly and in a friendly manner. However, over the board, they pull all the stops against him.

Chekhover *totally confidentially, not for publication*, told me that he's going to win first prize, because he will play well against some players, while others will play badly against him. However, there seems to be some unfortunate misunderstanding: Budo played well against Chekhover, and Chekhover played badly against Bondarevsky. Chekhover seeks

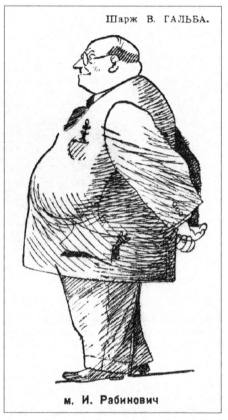

Шарж В. ГАЛЬБА.

м. И. Рабинович

Soviet champion Ilya Rabinovich is full of hope. Cartoon by V. Galba (USSR Chess Premiership, No. 8, 1938).

consolation in playing the piano. All the players listen to his impromptu performances during leisure time with pleasure, not even trying to compete with him here.

Kan, after his start, is already afraid of returning to Moscow. Belavenets and Yudovich feel like all of Moscow is watching them.

Panov: "The two "chess Ajaxes" – Sergei Belavenets and Mikhail Yudovich – moved from Smolensk to the capital in 1930. Friends since school, they grew together as chess players as well, collaborating on chess theory and training each other *(Panov fell victim to one of their opening novelties – see game 90)*. Both were masters of an elegant positional, maneuvering style; the only difference was that Belavenets was mainly a strategist, while Yudovich was more of a tactician. Their personalities were

Chekhover's sad melodies attract a wide, kindred audience. Left to right: Kan, Chekhover, Rabinovich, Lisitsin, Rauzer (below), Lilienthal, Kasparyan and Ebralidze. Cartoon by Y. Yuzepchuk (64, 30th April 1937.)

different as well. Belavenets was very tenacious and stubborn in attack and defense, relentlessly "squeezing" the win out of the smallest advantages. He had a philosopher's mind. I remember two of his sporting adages quite well: "Chess is a tragedy of one tempo!" and "You can't win a game without heavy stress!"

Yudovich, on the other hand, is an exceptionally cunning, tricky tournament psychologist, able to find the key to any player and provoke him into some dubious activity that draws him into deeply-hidden traps. As a fighter, he's not as persistent as Belavenets, but he never avoided complicated, sharp struggle and eagerly went for it, while Belavenets preferred purely maneuvering play." (From the book *Forty Years at the Chessboard.*)

Ragozin arrived ill, but recovered and claimed a great start.

Lisitsin is already annotating his future games for *Shakhmaty v SSR* (not a joke: he shoulders a big journalistic workload).

All in all, everyone is full of energy and desire to fight for every point – no, even every half-point."

The Three-Year Old Khvanchkara

Levenfish: "The spring months – April and May – are very pleasant in Tbilisi. There's no oppressive summer heat, but it's already warm, everyone goes without coats, and after 1st May, by an unwritten law, everyone wears white linen clothes...

On rest days, the welcoming hosts drove us to the picturesque environs – Kojori, Mtskheta, the Georgian Military Road. However, I preferred walking around the unfamiliar city. I hadn't been to Tbilisi for twelve years. The old city hadn't changed much, but in that time a new city had grown, with great buildings, parks and embankments. Once I turned into a quiet side-street and saw some carts with huge barrels near a warehouse. When I asked the guard about the cargo, he proudly answered, "They brought the three-year old Khvanchkara from the state farm."

I didn't know much about Georgian wines, but had already heard great things about Khvanchkara, so I immediately bought a dozen bottles. When they were delivered to me in my hotel two hours later, the hotel manager happened to be walking by, and asked, "Which wine did you buy?"

I answered nonchalantly, "The three-year old Khvanchkara."

The manager suddenly jumped, as though zapped by electricity, and a real pandemonium ensued. The manager, his deputy, the restaurant manager, the chef – everyone immediately ran to the warehouse to buy wine. The duty administrator pleaded for them to buy some for him as well. When I asked this poor man, who had to stay at his post, what was going on and why there was such a commotion, he looked at me like at a naive boy and answered, "Katso *(friend)*! Good wine for a Georgian is the same thing as a beautiful woman for a Frenchman!"

Друж. шарж ГАЛЬБА.

Г. Я. Левенфиш

Grigory Levenfish doesn't yet know that this year will be the most successful one of his career. Cartoon by V. Galba (64, 24th March 1937).

Then I understood everything and asked no further questions.

Tolush, who had just obtained his master's title, went to the tournament as a reporter. We decided to go home through Vladikavkaz, along the Georgian Military Road. In Vladikavkaz, we played a successful alternating simultaneous display, ate some Terek trout with great pleasure and then went back to Leningrad." (From the book *Selected Games and Memories*.)

Meanwhile, in Siberia

While Tbilisi hosted captivating chess battles, far away, in Tomsk, the earthly journey of Petr Izmailov, the participant of the 6th championship who had been "purged" from the ranks of the Soviet masters two years earlier, came to an end.

Nikolai Izmailov: "In April 1936, my father played in the All-Union first-category tournament – the Savitsky Memorial, held in Leningrad. Who would have thought that this would be Izmailov's very last tournament?

My mother remembered that on the day of his arrest, father called her from his work and assured her that she should not worry: he'd come home later than usual because he was invited to the local NKVD department to clarify some minor issues. This was the last time they talked. He never left the walls of the NKVD again...

Two years ago, I was finally able to review my father's case file. I was astonished by the sheer absurdity of what I read. He was accused of being a member of a "counter-revolutionary Trotskyist-fascist terrorist organization" (what a word salad!), headed by Galakhov, the Industrial Institute professor; this organization's goal was to overthrow the existing government and establish a fascist dictatorship, with none other than Hitler's closest ally Rosenberg as the ruler – the same Rosenberg who was sentenced to death at the Nuremberg trials after the war!

This organization allegedly planned the assassination of Stalin and his closest associates. Even father's trip to his last tournament was construed as an attempt to establish communication with an analogous organization in Leningrad: he purportedly took part in a meeting discussing the assassination of Zhdanov there...

My father's case was heard in a closed session of the field court of the USSR Supreme Court Military Board on 28th April 1937. The session protocol says that "the presiding official asked the defendant if he pleaded guilty, and the defendant pleaded not guilty." And then, "In his last words, the defendant stated that he was never a member of any counter-revolutionary organization..."

The protocol impassively states that the hearing lasted for just 20 minutes. In 20 minutes, without any prosecuting or defense attorneys, without witnesses, a man's fate was decided. The infamous *troika* sentenced Petr Nikolaevich Izmailov to capital punishment – execution by shooting with confiscation of all personal belongings.

There was a certificate with the old "Confidential" stamp in the case file, stating that the sentence was carried out on the same day, 28ᵗʰ April. And then, 20 years later, another, final certificate was added to the case file – I have appended a copy to this article.

More than 60 years have passed since my father's death. His name was finally cleared, international tournaments are held in his memory, and recently, a chess club has opened in Tomsk, named after Petr Izmailov – Siberia's first chess master." (*Shakhmaty v Rossii*, No. 1–3, 1999.).

Nikolai Izmailov then published a small book in Irkutsk in 2006, *The Truth About My Father* (an English translation of this work by Elk and Ruby Publishing House is pending). Originally made "for friends" and not for sale, it contained a big revelation regarding the real reason why the Tomsk master did not take part in the final of the 6ᵗʰ Soviet Championship of 1929.

Nikolai Izmailov: "So, why were the reports by the chess and central press so inconsistent? Where is the truth?

The last photo of Petr Izmailov, taken from his case file No. 12236. Published by his son in the book The Truth About My Father (Irkutsk, 2006).

I'll allow myself to state my own opinion, corroborated many years later by my mother's memories, which I never published before.

As we recall, four players made it to the final: two experienced masters *(Boris Verlinsky and Sergei Freymann)* and two representatives of the younger generation, who, according to the press, showed much promise *(Ilya Kan and Petr Izmailov)*.

Without a doubt, Verlinsky and Freymann were considered the favorites – they were objectively stronger and more experienced than their opponents...

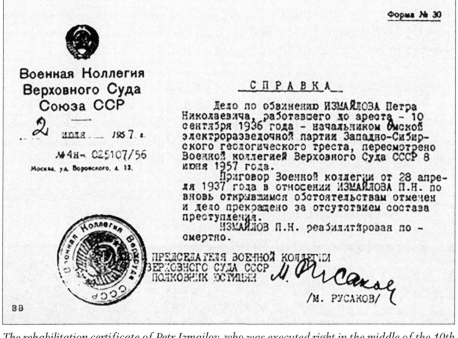

The rehabilitation certificate of Petr Izmailov, who was executed right in the middle of the 10th championship.

CERTIFICATE

The case of IZMAILOV Petr Nikolaevich, who worked as head of the Omsk Electrical Exploration Party of the West Siberian Geological Trust before his arrest on 10th September 1936, was sent for retrial to the USSR Supreme Court Military Board on 6th June 1957.

The sentence of the Military Board dated 28th April 1937 concerning IZMAILOV P. N. has been overturned because of newly-found circumstances, and the case has been closed for lack of evidence.

IZMAILOV P. N. is rehabilitated posthumously.

Signed: Deputy Chairman of the USSR Supreme Court Military Board, Colonel of Justice M. Rusakov. Dated 2 July 1957. From N. Izmailov's archive.

But we know a lot of examples – both generally in sport and particularly in chess – when the strongest do not win, and instead the winner is the one who is stronger at that particular moment, or perhaps even luckier rather than stronger. The final was a short tournament, and an element of surprise or luck could have played its role – don't forget that there were already a lot of surprises at that tournament.

And so, my father and Kan had a chance to win, too – even though they were rather minuscule; my father had already gotten lucky numerous times at that tournament. The results of both games against master V. Makogonov and the game against master Selezniev were hanging by a thread, and, frankly, my father was just lucky to win them. Luck was also on my father's side in the semi-final game against M. Botvinnik: Botvinnik made a very uncharacteristic miscalculation in the opening and couldn't save the game. Maybe luck would have helped him in the final as well – who knows?

I reiterate: Verlinsky and Freymann had every chance of winning, but still, you couldn't discount the possibility of any finalist winning the tournament – including my father.

But our chess higher-ups couldn't allow that. **They couldn't allow the son of a clergyman to win the USSR Championship** (*highlighted by me – S.V.*) Such a scenario just couldn't fit in their heads. The son of a clergyman just couldn't be a champion of our Soviet state of workers and peasants. Moreover, N. Krylenko himself, the head honcho of all the country's chess life at the time, was, as we know, present at the tournament, and he couldn't allow that.

So, in 1997, when I looked through my father's case file in the Tomsk FSB archive, I saw that his non-proletarian background was referred to numerous times in the file. The case documents clearly stated that he descended from an alien stratum of society, and this was, without a doubt, used as an aggravating factor.

It was unthinkable for a person with such a background to become the Soviet champion at that time, and even though my father's victory was quite unlikely, they did everything to prevent it altogether. How could they do that? The simplest and most reliable way was to make my father drop out. And they did that... He was ordered to leave the tournament, in a harsh, categorical tone, and my father had no choice other than to comply.

Perhaps that's why the reasons for my father's "voluntarily quitting" the tournament varied so wildly in different newspapers?"

One might wonder how come Romanovsky twice managed to become Soviet champion when he came from an entire dynasty of clergymen? Well, he was simply lucky. Romanovsky gained such success from the very beginning of the championships (1920, 2nd place; 1923, 1st place; 1924, 2nd place), that nobody even thought about his origins. Moreover, he was a loyal Soviet citizen, demonstrating this frequently, attacking in the press both Alekhine and Znosko-Borovsky... Whereas Izmailov was an outsider, seemingly apolitical, from somewhere in Siberia and, yes, the son of a priest. I think his son was right in his judgement.

The Style of a Complete Grandmaster

Levenfish: "Did the ability of the Soviet masters improve in the last two and a half years? That's the main question that the 10th championship is meant to have answered. I think that, in general, the answer to this question is yes.

Konstantinopolsky, Ragozin, Goglidze, Makogonov, and Belavenets showed in this tournament that they have improved considerably and could successfully compete with foreign masters. Based on the first 10 rounds, we could also add Yudovich to the same group; he led confidently in the first half of the tournament. However, it turned out that in addition to great talent and wide chess erudition, Yudovich has a purely sporting flaw: he endures losses badly and collapses towards the finish.

Yudovich: "I had a good start to the tournament, but, as always, finished badly... Now, my most important goal, in track-and-field parlance, is to

"Our Leningrad correspondent, artist V. Galba, got interested in preparation for the Leningrad masters tournament. "I studied the secrets of tennis," Levenfish said. "The most difficult and important thing is to get the ball over to the opponent's half of the court, the rest will come." Lisitsin always thought that a great composer was dying in him (or maybe had already died) – he's inspired by radio. Ilyin-Zhenevsky went to Kislovodsk one month before the tournament – it seems that the Narzan spas are beneficial for training." (64, 15th April 1937.)

"improve my breathing", i.e. to learn to keep my play steady during the whole tournament. I hope that the bad finish in this tournament will be my last bad finish period." *(64*, 15th May 1937.)

I managed to win the champion's title only because I worked intensively to eliminate the flaws in my play, and I played better in this tournament than in the last one. This is true in regards of opening preparation, the purely positional method of playing, which I avoided before without any good reason, and endgame technique.

> **Levenfish** expanded on his preparation method on the pages of *Pravda* (11th May 1937): "In the last two years I have worked hard to improve my play. Above all, I overcame my lack of opening theory caused by my absence from chess in 1925–1933, when I exclusively concentrated on my day job. Because of that, I often lost in the past with black even though I almost never lost with white. In this tournament, though, I had almost no difficulty playing black. I adopted Botvinnik's approach to preparing for the games. It consists of analyzing the style of each opponent and selecting an opening and game character that would be unpleasant for them. Finally, I managed to balance my style. Before I would strive to conclude the battle with a combination. Now, though, I just as eagerly play positional games and tricky endings."

The play of I. L. Rabinovich, who shared first and second place in the 9th championship with me, seems to have stabilized. I often watched his games. The same solid interpretation of openings, the same composure and patience in positional maneuvering, the same solid restraint in the endgame. But the young masters learned all that from Rabinovich, and they surpassed him in opening and middlegame play. And so, he now had to fight for every half-point instead of being guaranteed full points.

The adherents of the open game – Rauzer, Panov, and Ilyin-Zhenevsky – showed nothing. This fact alone shows that the <u>one-sidedness of play and voluntary abandonment of analysis in the huge and interesting areas of the Queen's Gambit and Indian defenses does not justify itself in any way</u> *(compare that to Romanovsky's opinion below, also underlined by me).* Indeed, Rauzer was completely helpless when his opponents managed to take him outside his scope of analyzed lines. *(The* 64 *editorial board awarded Rauzer a special prize "for a set of valuable theoretical novelties".)*

Panov always attacks and never systematically defends. Sometimes he does manage to destroy an opponent, but often he just loses by himself without much resistance.

Kasparyan suffers from the same flaw; both for white and black, he just can't help but play the "mysterious" moves g2-g4 and g7-g5.

Ilyin-Zhenevsky would go for complications, but often miscalculated.

The Moscow champions Alatortsev and Kan, and VTsSPS champions Lisitsin and Chekhover, showed nothing. Nevertheless, Lisitsin won four games in a row at the finish and managed to cling onto a prize place. As we know, chess "business" is often more important for Lisitsin than chess art... *(Is this a hint at the "big journalistic workload" mentioned by Polevoy?)*

Of the three first-category players, only Bondarevsky managed to earn the master's title. His great chess talent is indubitable. He's young, plays with great temperament and prefers furious attacks to difficult defense. His game with Panov, where he checkmated his opponent after sacrificing three pieces, drew the plaudits of hundreds of spectators *(see game 86)*. If Bondarevsky manages to balance out his style, he'll soon join the front row of the Soviet masters.

> **Bondarevsky:** "I should note that, up until now, I haven't been working sufficiently on chess theory. The reason is the lack of incentive in the form of playing stronger opponents... The championship showed me the shortcomings in my play. Firstly, indecisive interpretation of cramped positions without enough counterplay, where tenacious defense is necessary. Secondly, poor opening knowledge, which led to bad positions with black and resulting time trouble.
>
> On the other hand, I became even more convinced of my earlier view that I feel very confident in sharp positions." *(64, 30th May 1937.)*

Budo is a subtle positional player; his endgame technique is good. He could have obtained the master's title, were it not for his overly risky play in several games. His game against Makogonov is one of the best in the tournament *(see game 94)*, and his prize for the best result

Igor Bondarevsky was the only first-category player who managed to earn a master's title.

against prizewinners *(awarded by the* Musha *newspaper, where Goglidze was the editor of the chess column)* was well-deserved.

Like Bondarevsky, Budo qualified for the championship after his brilliant victory at the Savitsky Memorial, the All-Union first-category player tournament (Leningrad, April 1936), which proved to be the highlight of his career. Even though Alexander Semyonovich Budo wasn't particularly successful in either of his appearances at the highest level (1931 and 1937), he set a unique "record" described by **Vadim Faibisovich** (*Shakhmatny Peterburg*, No. 2, 2002):

"The total number of All-Union championship participants from 1931 to 1991 exceeded 200. For clarity, we should make one qualification: these tournaments were twice played according to the Swiss system. I think that in these cases we can only count those who finished in the top 20. Then we get the number 218. This is a very broad spectrum: from nine world champions to Yuri Nikitin, known only to well-versed chess fans. All of them were eventually grandmasters or masters. All – except one..."

Ebralidze lacks nerve and technique. Until he treats the first and learns the second, he can't count on much success, despite his apparent chess talent.

This was the only Soviet Championship appearance of Archil Silovanovich Ebralidze – three-times Tbilisi champion by that time, the future master, four-times Georgia champion, and the translator of textbooks by Lasker, Capablanca and Euwe into Georgian.

Bronstein: "Archil Ebralidze was a rare soul, highly educated, loved culture madly. By today's standards, he would have been a dissident, because he was always trying to understand the world philosophically... After my

Archil Ebralidze "lacks nerve and technique... despite his apparent talent." (Levenfish.) The photo was taken at the 1928 Georgian championship.

departure from Tbilisi *(in 1943)*, Ebralidze found and fostered the talent of a young Tbilisi player, Tigran Petrosian, and imparted his playing style and a part of his chess philosophy to him." (from unpublished notes entitled *Georgian Memories*).

The tournament showed the great modernization of our masters' style, which is getting closer to the style of a complete grandmaster.

A meeting between the new generation of young masters and foreigners would surely be of great interest. Considering the creative progress of our youth, the prospects of such a meeting should be favorable for us." (*64*, 15th May 1937.)

In the special issue (No. 11), **Levenfish** was more nuanced in his description of the young masters:

"Up until now, many talked about young masters as a single unit. However, we should divide the young masters into two groups – both by age and by tournament experience.

In my view, Alatortsev, Ragozin, Panov and Kan, for instance, belong to the first group. Konstantinopolsky, Belavenets and Goglidze are the second group. We should point out that the second group, who became masters later than the first, have already overtaken the first.

Of the "old guard", I was the only one who managed to withstand the onslaught of youth. Of the members of the first group, I can say the same thing only about Ragozin.

The championship highlighted a nascent third group of young masters, a third wave. Bondarevsky is the first among them. I wouldn't be surprised if this wave becomes the most successful of all."

Alarming Tendencies

Romanovsky: "Before the championship started, many predicted that Levenfish would win. Among other candidates, Ragozin, Kan and even Chekhover were named, the latter – mostly because of his actually unconvincing victory in the Young Masters tournament, where the overall game quality wasn't particularly high *(Leningrad, December 1936: 1–2. Chekhover and Rauzer – 8.5/14; 3. Kan – 8; 4–5. Konstantinopolsky and Ragozin – 7.5; 6. Alatortsev – 7; 7. Riumin – 5.5; 8. Goglidze – 3.5).*

Those who foretold Levenfish's victory were right. However, the explanations for those predictions were flimsy at best. They mostly cited Levenfish's many years of experience. Of course, experience does play a major role in sporting success, but it cannot be the key factor, especially in the All-Union competitions. In this case, it was already clear in the first five or six rounds that the battle between Levenfish and his "less experienced" opponents was based on entirely different considerations. Experience was probably the thing Levenfish benefited the least from. Budo, Yudovich, Konstantinopolsky, and even Ebralidze showed him that it was impossible to defeat them solely through erudition.

We should search for the reasons of Levenfish's win in other places. Had Levenfish tried to solve problems facing him solely through technical means, he probably wouldn't have lost to Kan *(see game 96)* and Belavenets, but, on the other hand, he wouldn't have won the tournament, either.

The battle for superiority that Levenfish had to fight was built on different principles from the outset.

This principled approach emerged in conjunction with the creative (and, in a way, anti-creative) tendencies shown by many participants of the premiership. The biggest of those tendencies is the desire to avoid defeat, first and foremost. Because of that, many games of the tournament ended in senseless draws after 16 or even 13 moves...

Because of these tendencies, Levenfish was faced with rather thankless work. It's not that simple to defeat a master who is ready to settle for a draw at any moment *(the future champion started the tournament with three draws!)*. We have to say that Levenfish sometimes had to resort to experimental continuations to avoid this drawing threat, looming from the very first opening moves. A debatable issue arises: did this playing for a draw justify itself from the sporting point of view? Konstantinopolsky, Goglidze, and Belavenets are probably ready to give an affirmative answer. And if it is so, then they might be unhappy with our attitude towards such point-chasing. However, what would Budo and Ebralidze say, seeing how their fellow young first-category player and future master Bondarevsky started scoring points right out of the gate?

Ultimately, only the resolute struggle to win the initiative led Levenfish to first place and delivered Bondarevsky his master's title. Who knows – maybe Levenfish's work would have been even harder had such a talented player as Konstantinopolsky, who shared 2nd–3rd place in the tournament, tried to break his drawing streak in the first half of the tournament with some full points – perhaps even at the cost of a couple of losses.

Konstantinopolsky: "I often see evaluations of my play that are not, in my opinion, completely fair. For some reason, people think that I come to each tournament with a solid stock of opening novelties and theoretical findings. In actuality, I only studied openings seriously until 1935, and then, seeing substantial flaws in my middlegame and endgame play, I started studying those stages of the game.

It may sound strange, but when I play an unfamiliar opening, I feel much better than after going down well-trodden theoretical paths. And so, despite sharing master Rauzer's views on white's advantage because of his first-move rights (1.e2-e4 wins!), I still play a wide variety of openings to study the diverse kinds of middlegames arising from these openings.

The big number of draws is explained by my desire to spread my energy equally along the long, hard distance." *(64, 15ᵗʰ May 1937.)*

Друж. шарж Ю. Ю.

м. А. Константинопольский.

Alexander Konstantinopolsky managed to share 2nd–3rd place in his first ever Soviet Championship! He would never again finish in the top three. Cartoon by Y. Yuzepchuk (64, 15th May 1937).

Another tendency, which, unfortunately, looks increasingly "similar" to a style, is the <u>self-limiting of creative scope with routine structures, based on the much vaunted d2-d4 with the subsequent or first fianchettoing of the king's bishop with g2-g3</u>. Both g-pawns – white and black – had a lot of work to do at this tournament. A routine opening, a routine clash in the center – and then a draw or another blunder, which have, sadly, also became routine. Some blunders, by Alatortsev, Ragozin, Makogonov, Panov, Zhenevsky, Ebralidze, Kasparyan, Budo, Yudovich, and Kan are just inexplicable.

With the general tendency towards a cautious, narrowly strategic playing style, these numerous mistakes make a strange, unpleasant impression. Let's, however, close our eyes to technical flaws and imagine that there weren't any. Then we shall vividly see the contours of a style that, frankly, can't be considered complimentary for our masters. This style is well-known. Raise it to the second power, and we'll get the routine, technically brilliant and rich compositions of Flohr, Fine, Stahlberg and some other foreign grandmasters.

We don't think that the latter's creative path is the saving beacon that our masters should strive for in searching for the greatest achievements." (*Shakhmaty v SSSR*, May 1937.)

The Debate Gets Personal

The champion's reply followed quite soon. It was voiced at his meeting with the Moscow players in the Central Park of Culture and Recreation.

Levenfish: "The distinguished master P. A. Romanovsky stated that the masters haven't been progressing lately – that by contrast, their creativity had even dropped somewhat. This opinion is wrong. Both the young masters and the "international players" – the USSR masters who have already played in international tournaments – have improved. Contrary to Romanovsky's assertion, the opening repertoire of the Soviet masters hasn't narrowed, either. Many games were played logically and in a good style. The championship also saw a lot of well-executed endgames.

Romanovsky says in his article that some players went for compromises and peaceful draws instead of fighting. This is true to some extent, but it does not allow us to reach any conclusions about a decline in fighting spirit. There is another possible reason. By the will of the All-Union Chess Section, the participants of the 9th Soviet Premiership who didn't gain prizes found themselves unwelcome at big competitions for two and a half years *(a criticism of Krylenko?)*. The chess section constantly referred to that unchanging prizewinner list of the 9th premiership when selecting players for other competitions.

It was the rightful fear that a lost half-point would prevent them from reaching a prize place and, therefore, deprive them of the right to play in further tournaments that forced some players to go for "riskless" draws instead of adopting a creative approach.

> **Lisitsin** and **Sokolsky:** "Many draws in tournaments of recent years, particularly in the 10th Soviet Championship, were caused by the fear of performing poorly at the tournament and then suffering from a "first-class burial" – i.e. being excluded from big competitions for two or three years. This fact is one of the main reasons why a "cautious" style gained a foothold in Soviet tournaments... There's no need to prove the harmfulness of the excessively cautious tactics, leading to games devoid of all content and dull draws. The Soviet masters should play aggressively, inventively, ingeniously, and style doesn't matter." (*Shakhmaty v SSSR*, July 1937.)

We should do away with the system of inviting only a small, limited group of masters to all tournaments. We have to hold more "intermediate-level" competitions, without too much hype and sporting fever; such competitions can be a good school for all our masters and will see more interesting fights." (*64*, 30th May 1937.)

That's How You Should Play Chess!

Romanovsky: "Levenfish's victory is a victory of a master who managed to blend the strict requirements of modern strategy and technique with the creative ideas of old masters. His "dark-squared suite" in the game against Alatortsev reminds us of Tarrasch's logical and purposeful strategy. The crushing win against Makogonov was played with the energy of Pillsbury's strategic attacks. His unique tactics in the games against Budo and Bondarevsky are similar to the original thoughts of Chigorin, as well as his defensive concept against Kasparyan. *(Both the "suite" and the "crushing win" were published in Levenfish's book. You might ask why I left the mentions of the games not featured in this book intact? Well, to make it easier for you to find them in Megabase without wasting your time sifting through all 190 games.)*

Ragozin remained true to himself. Above all, he's a tactician, and it's very pleasant to see his great success in this tournament. He proved that his tactical superiority was enough to defeat the wise strategic ways of draw advocates. He managed to save some dubious positions (against Yudovich, for instance), and defeated the eventual champion when he needed it the most.

Konstantinopolsky is an interesting and original master, and if he was more enthusiastic, he would probably have played even more creative games. He's not a fully-formed player yet, and the future will show which way he's going to choose. He has every opportunity for that.

The next prizewinners – Makogonov, Goglidze, Lisitsin and Belavenets – didn't show any new features in their chess interpretation.

Makogonov's play is very thoughtful and logical. His mounting successes tell us that his characteristic sober, healthy positional evaluation is taking robust, stable forms in his play. He's very masterful in exploiting small positional advantages, and his game against Lilienthal is a great example of a correctly executed strategic plan. Makogonov even led the tournament for a while, but, after failing to withstand Panov's sharp onslaught, lost his leadership and ultimately dropped to fourth place.

The reasons for this collapse became known only many years later. From the book *Vladimir Makogonov* by **Valery Asriyan:**

"The participants are going down the homestretch... Levenfish and Makogonov are ahead with 10 points, Konstantinopolsky has 9.5, Belavenets and Yudovich 9. Everyone thinks that Mak has the best chance of first place. He has the easiest run in: two games out of four are against the rear – Budo, who isn't even a master, and Panov... And only he alone knew: the run in would be incredibly difficult, if he managed to play on at all. His most dangerous opponent loomed over him: fever. Not the "tournament fever", but a real one (he had endured sporadic bouts of fever ever since he was struck by malaria as a child, but it was the first time he suffered from fever during a tournament). The bout lasted only for a few days, but that was enough for two

Vladimir Makogonov's brilliant performance was marred by a bout of fever that cost him two losses at the finish. From the author's archive.

tragic losses. He first lost to Panov, and then, two rounds later, to Budo. And only in the last round, when the fever finally subsided, did he manage to play at full strength and defeat Bondarevsky... He often reminisces about the Tbilisi championship. Sometimes proudly ("How well I played in Tbilisi!"), but more often bitterly ("I was in the lead. Oh, if not for that fever!")."

Back then, however, **Makogonov** never said a word about his illness:

"I am satisfied with my result as a whole, even though my finish was poor. Exhaustion and a lack of training probably played its role.

I should again recall the almost complete neglect of the masters from the periphery. I propose holding the Soviet Championship in two stages. First, we would hold big qualification tournaments, in 2–3 groups with 14–16 players in each, inviting all the masters and many first-category players. The next year, the winners of these groups form the line-up of the Soviet Championship. This system would allow every master to take part in All-Union competitions; moreover, many first-category players would be included as well, and from this cadre, new Soviet masters would emerge." (*64*, 15th May 1937.)

The very next championship was held under this formula!

Goglidze, as well as Konstantinopolsky and Yudovich, recorded 12 draws. At the finish, he managed to defeat the underperforming Kasparyan *(see game 99)* and Ebralidze, and he could look back at all the earned half-points with pleasure.

His sporting result is much better than expected, especially after his flop in the Young Masters tournament. Despite his success, Goglidze would still have to think about his creative methods. They are unlikely to bring him new laurels in his career, and if he wants to climb higher or at least stay at the heights he has reached, he needs to re-evaluate his approach to the struggle. *(As we shall see, Goglidze did not "think about his creative methods": this was his last appearance in Soviet Championships.)*

Mikhail Yudovich's successful debut (1931, shared 3rd–6th place) remained his best achievement in the Soviet championships. Cartoon by Y. Yuzepchuk (64, 20th April 1937).

Goglidze: "I wanted to vindicate myself after a poor performance in the Young Masters tournament, and so I played very reservedly and sometimes even too cautiously, and I lost good chances to take second place because of that. Still, I managed to make up for a lack of success at that tournament. For instance, I defeated both of its winners – Rauzer and Chekhover." (*64*, 15th May 1937.)

Of the Moscow players, only Belavenets played relatively well, showing that while he could be defeated, the usual methods of this championship wouldn't have worked on him.

Yudovich, despite a good start, finished very poorly, and Kan, with his languid play that lacked initiative, couldn't do much.

Alatortsev blundered rooks twice, even though one of those mistakes happened in an already lost position. The reasons for his poor performance are, however, more complex than those blunders. He just couldn't cope with the difficult strategic environment of the tournament and couldn't satisfactorily employ his previously energetic style against it. Rauzer, Rabinovich, Chekhover, Ilyin-Zhenevsky, Budo – the Leningrad five who failed to obtain prizes. Rauzer performed better than the others, barely missing the prizes. Maybe he could have achieved more if he'd taken a couple of years of rest from his opening analysis, which only hinders the expression of his outstanding talent.

Друж. шарж Ю. Ю.

м. В. Раузер

Vsevolod Rauzer: "Maybe he could have achieved more if he'd taken a couple of years of rest from his opening analysis, which only hinders the expression of his outstanding talent." (Romanovsky.) Cartoon by Y. Yuzepchuk (64, 5th May 1937).

Panov: "He was an enthusiastic opening researcher, who made a great contribution specifically to the theory of 1.e4; Rauzer always played this move as white, considering it the strongest one. I once asked him about his work schedule, and when he answered, I was stunned by his fanaticism. 'You know,' he said, 'I usually get up at 6 a.m., get to my analysis board and work until night, with short breaks for eating. Unfortunately,' Rauzer sighed, 'I just can't make myself work on theory of the game for more than 16 hours a day! My head can't endure more.'"

We shouldn't be surprised that such overexertion eventually led to a mental condition. "Unfortunately, Rauzer's nervous system wasn't too durable," Botvinnik recalled, "and his game results didn't match his potential abilities. He had some strange quirks. This eccentricity gradually turned into an illness, and shortly before the war, his chess ability went downhill." This championship was the last for Vsevolod Rauzer. He died at the very beginning of the siege of Leningrad (he moved there from Kiev in 1936), aged just 33...

Panov's interesting play brought him great victories over the prizewinners, but, as a whole, he couldn't cope with the "equalization strategy" either.

We should also pay special attention to the results of Bondarevsky and... Grandmaster Lilienthal, whose paltry two wins out of 19 leaves one feeling sad. Looking through Lilienthal's games unfortunately leads to one conclusion: it wasn't because we progressed, it was because he regressed. It's useless to guess the reasons, but some conclusions have to be drawn.

Bondarevsky's talent is very attractive, however, pure talent is not enough to achieve complete mastery. In some positions, he's completely helpless, for instance, against Yudovich and Kan. His draws with Budo and Ebralidze are unconvincing, but formally, he managed to score the necessary amount of points. He needs to widen his strategic horizons. His quick and inventive attacks require more sound strategic foundation. While we want to advise some participants of the tournament to look through the games of Morphy, Zukertort, Chigorin, Pillsbury, and Janowski, Bondarevsky needs to thoroughly study the thoughts of Tarrasch and Rubinstein.

Still, some of Bondarevsky's ideas are so interesting that, addressing some players, I want to say simply, 'That's how you should play chess!'" (*Shakhmaty v SSSR*, May 1937.)

P.S. The Gauntlet is Thrown

Immediately after the tournament ended, Mikhail Botvinnik congratulated Levenfish on his Soviet Championship win and challenged him to a match: "My post-graduate studies prevented me from taking part in the championship. However, this autumn I will eagerly challenge for the title of Soviet Champion in a match with G. Y. Levenfish, if the All-Union Chess Section provides me with this opportunity." (*Pravda*, 11th May 1937). Two weeks later, a decision was made to hold the match. It was to begin on 15th September. To win the match, a player needed to win 6 games, and draws did not count. As you might see, everything was very serious: the world championship match between Capablanca and Alekhine had the same formula.

I'll get ahead of myself and say that the battle was indeed epic. In addition, this was the first (and most extensive) Soviet Championship match in the history of Soviet chess. I'll have to dedicate a separate chapter to it...

The Players' Versions

"The premiership provided a lot of creative, wholesome material. We need to immediately publish the best and most instructive games of the tournament in a book, and do it as soon as possible, without delay." Unfortunately, Romanovsky's appeal wasn't heeded: the tournament book, like the previous time, was only printed two years later, after the next championship had ended! The reason for the delay was the same.

After writing the 9th premiership book alone, Levenfish was sure that his project "is unlikely to find followers, because analyzing almost 200 games, filled with complicated struggle, and, with a few exceptions, never annotated before, is a rather difficult task." But he was mistaken! Georgy Lisitsin was unfazed by the 190 games, and the title page of the book *10th All-Union Chess Premiership* was adorned with a sentence, very characteristic of the time, "I dedicate my first work to the XVIII Conference of the Great party of LENIN-STALIN" (a similar sentence was written in red on Botvinnik's first games collection: "Dedicated by the author to the twentieth anniversary of the Lenin-Stalin Komsomol").

How could the young master complete such a formidable task? "The secret of this "achievement," B. Blumenfeld wrote in *64* (20th November 1939), "is a "businesslike" approach. Most of the premiership games were already annotated in the tournament bulletin. Why then waste time, so valuable for a busy man, to create your own annotations if you could just follow the ready-made template? And if there is no such template, you can always make some "simplified" notes. So, the "work" of master G. M. Lisitsin is not a proper work by contestants."

In general, the book's quality was good, which is not surprising: it went through serious editorial control by... Levenfish! But there's one "but": you don't want to eat too many pieces of fruit of this "rather difficult task" – you will quickly get bored. To diversify the "menu", I had to dig into the periodicals in search for the players' comments. It was a real effort, sure, but now the dishes are going to be exclusive!

Riumin's Favorite

Riumin: "The tournament participants submitted a record amount of games for the traditional competition run by the *64* newspaper – 24... I think that the best one was between Konstantinopolsky and Rabinovich, strategically seamless and rich with energetic struggle. It required a lot of inventiveness and calculation of complicated lines from white, and it was played in a bold and precise way. I award the prize to A. M. Konstantinopolsky."

No. 85. *King's Indian Defense E60*
**Konstantinopolsky –
I. Rabinovich**
Tbilisi 1937, round 19
Annotated by A. Konstantinopolsky

1.♘f3 ♘f6 2.c4 g6 3.b3 ♗g7 4.♗b2 d6 5.d4 0-0 6.g3 ♘bd7 7.♕c2 ♖e8 8.♗g2 e5. In a roundabout way, black has reached the usual King's Indian structure with a pawn stronghold on e5.

9.0-0 c6. Perhaps it was better to play 9...e4 10.♘g5 e3 11.f4 ♘f8. Black has good tactical chances, and it's not that easy to reach his e3 pawn. Meanwhile, after 9...c6, he has a cramped position, as often happens in this opening.

10.e4 ♕c7. Overprotecting the e5 square, black plans to put the d7 knight on f8 and develop the c8 bishop. Still, he had a more energetic plan: 10...exd4 11.♘xd4 ♘c5 12.♘c3 a5, then ♕b6 and ♗d7.

11.♘bd2.

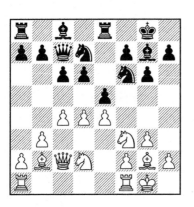

11...♘h5(?). Of course, this was played to prepare f7-f5. White is planning to play the c4-c5 break, which exposes the weakness of the d6 square, so that the d2 knight can reach it through c4. By protecting the e5 pawn one more time, black tries to stop him. However, the knight is positioned quite awkwardly there, and this fact will later give white a motif for his decisive combination.

11...b6 looks stronger, to meet 12.c5 with 12...dxc5! 13.dxe5 ♘g4. On the other hand, trying to close down the position with 11...c5 gave white an obvious advantage after both 12.d5! ♖f8 13.♘h4 and then f2-f4 and 12.dxc5 dxc5 13.♘b1! ♘b8 14.♘c3 ♘c6 15.♘d5 ♘xd5 16.cxd5 ♘d4 17.♘xd4 exd4 18.f4!

12.♖ad1. 12.c5 is too premature: 12...dxc5 13.dxe5 (13.dxc5 b5!, preventing the knight from reaching d6) 13...♘xe5 (13...b6 14.♘c4 ♗a6 is also possible) 14.♘xe5 ♗xe5 15.♗xe5 ♕xe5, with an advantage for black.

12...b6 13.♖fe1 ♘f8. Black thinks that c4-c5 is still impossible. It was still bad to play 13...c5 14.dxc5 dxc5 15.♘b1! with an initiative for white.

The best move was 13...♗b7!?, and if 14.b4 (preparing c4-c5), then 14...exd4 (14...a5 15.c5! with beneficial complications) 15.♗xd4 a5! 16.♗xg7 ♘xg7 17.a3 axb4 18.axb4 ♘e5, and it's not easy for white to attack the weakness on d6.

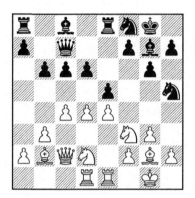

14.c5! White manages to execute his plan. 14...exd4 is simply met with 15.cxd6 ♕xd6 16.♘c4 and ♗xd4; or 14...bxc5 15.dxe5 dxe5 16.♕xc5 with strong pressure.

"A brilliant move that required deep calculations from white." (Riumin)

14...dxc5! And now, it's very hard to calculate who benefits the most from the capture on e5, because it was clear that the pawn would soon fall. If 15.dxc5, then after 15...b5!, the d2 knight can't reach d6, and black gets a good position.

15.dxe5! Probably the most difficult move in the whole game. To win the e5 pawn, black has to trade away his g7 bishop, which severely weakens the kingside. This weakness and the h5 knight's awkward position allows white to get a strong attack for the pawn.

15...♗a6. Now the knight reaches d6. However, even after

15...♗e6 16.♘c4 ♗xc4 17.♕xc4 ♖ad8 18.♕c1! (threatening g3-g4) white maintains a dangerous initiative *(18...♘e6!? 19.♗h3 ♗f8 Lisitsin).*

16.♗f1 ♗xf1 17.♖xf1 ♘d7. And so, the e5 pawn is defenseless.

18.♘c4 ♖e7 19.♕d2 b5. This is necessary, because white threatened 20.g4.

20.♘d6 ♘xe5 21.♘xe5 ♗xe5 22.♗xe5 ♖xe5. Black has achieved his goal, but it's now clear that the pawn sacrifice is correct. White can play, for instance, 23.♕c3 f6 24.f4 ♖e7 25.♕xc5, immediately regaining the pawn, but black can trade queens in this case (25...♕b6). So white chooses a more resolute continuation.

"The position suited both players. Konstantinopolsky went for it, hoping to exploit the knight's bad position on h5; Rabinovich, winning a pawn, thought that his opponent was already doomed, as usual." (Lisitsin)

23.f4 ♖e7.

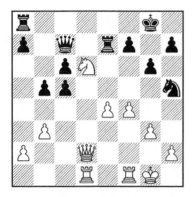

Here, white could maintain a clear positional advantage with 24.e5, however, after 24...♞g7, black had a chance to defend successfully. The following combination wins the game by force:

24.f5! ♜d8! Black pinned a lot of hope on this move *(24...♜f8 25.g4 ♞f6 26.♛f4 is most unpleasant)*. After 25.g4?, he intended to play 25...♞f6 26.fxg6 ♞xe4!, because both 27.gxh7+ ♚xh7 and 27.gxf7+ ♜xf7! 28.♜xf7 ♛xf7 29.♞xf7 ♜xd2 deliver nothing good for white.

25.f6 ♜e6. Loses at least an exchange. 25...♜e5 26.g4 and 25...♜ed7 26.e5 followed by g3-g4 are even worse. The main line of the combination involved the trade of the queen for two rooks: 25...♜xe4 26.♞xe4! ♜xd2 27.♜xd2. Black should have gone for that line, because white would have needed much more effort to win than in the actual game. Still, the threat g3-g4 and the black king's bad position (because of the pawn wedge on f6!) is enough for white to win,

as we may see from the following analysis.

Black should play 27...h6! (defending against 28.g4 ♞f4 29.♜xf4!), and after 28.♜fd1 he has the following defenses:

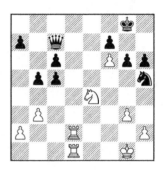

1) 28...♛e5 29.♜d8+ ♚h7 30.♜8d7 ♞xf6 (everything else loses too: 30...♛xe4 31.♜xf7+ ♚g8 32.♜e7 ♛d4+ 33.♜xd4 cxd4 34.f7+ and ♜xa7; or 30...♛e6 31.♜e7 ♛g4 32.♞f2 ♛c8 33.♜xf7+ ♚g8 34.♜fd7 etc.; or, finally, 30...♚g8 31.♜e7 ♛b8 32.♜dd7) 31.♞xf6+ ♛xf6 32.♜f1! ♛e6! 33.♜fxf7+ ♚g8 34.♜fe7!, and black is defenseless;

2) 28...g5 (28...c4 and ♛b6 leads to similar positions) 29.♜d8+ ♚h7 30.♜8d7! (only with this rook, because the d1 rook protects the king from checks in some lines and supports the movement of the f6 pawn after the f7 pawn is captured in others) 30...♛b6 (if 30...♛e5, then 31.♜xf7+ ♚g6 32.♜e7, and after 32...♛b8, there's 33.g4 ♞xf6 34.♜d6, while 32...♛f5 is met with 33.♜f1) 31.g4! (not letting the king get out of the mating net *(but again 31.♜xf7+ ♚g6 32.♜e7 is simpler)*) 31...c4+

32.♔f1 ♛e3 (32...♘f4 33.♖xf7+ ♔g8 34.♖g7+ ♔f8 35.♖dd7, winning) 33.gxh5, and white should win, because black can't capture the knight.

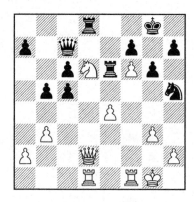

26.♘xb5! ♖xd2 27.♘xc7 ♖ed6. Not 27...♖xd1 28.♖xd1 ♖xf6 because of 29.♖d8+ ♔g7 30.♘e8+ etc.

28.♖xd2 ♖xd2 29.g4 ♘xf6. This knight finally falls. The rest is simple.

30.♖xf6 ♖xa2 31.♖xc6 ♖e2 32.♘d5 ♔g7 33.♖xc5 ♖xe4 34.h3 ♖e5 35.b4 h5 36.gxh5 ♖xh5 37.♔g2 ♖e5 38.♖a5 ♔h6 (the a-pawn cannot be saved) **39.♔f3 f5 40.♘c7 ♖e4 41.b5 ♖b4 42.♖xa7 ♖b3+ 43.♔f4.** Black resigned. After 43...♖xh3, white wins a rook: 44.b6 ♖b3 45.b7 and then ♘a6.

The Gem of Tbilisi

Riumin: "Without a doubt, the game Panov – Bondarevsky would have been a candidate for the "Most Beautiful Game" award. His opponent's passive play was effectively exploited by Bondarevsky, who destroyed white's castling position after sacrificing three pieces."

No. 86. French Defense C09
Panov – Bondarevsky
Tbilisi 1937, round 14
Annotated by I. Bondarevsky

1.e4 e6 2.d4 d5 3.♘d2. This line has become fashionable again lately. *"Tarrasch's flexible plan, later developed by Geller and Karpov, but poorly studied at the time."* (*Kasparov*)

3...c5 4.exd5 exd5 5.♗b5+ ♘c6. Black avoids the usual 5... ♗d7 6.♛e2+ ♛e7, which results in an endgame that is drawish in character, but still requires precise play from black (*after 7.dxc5 ♛xe2+, Bondarevsky had earlier lost to Kan in round 10*).

6.♘gf3 (6.♛e2+ is stronger) **6... ♛e7+.** *This game saw the very first use of this rare move in tournament practice. However, the next black win in this line happened only in 2001, by Korchnoi; Viktor Lvovich went on to win a couple more games with black afterwards. And Bondarevsky himself won against the same line with white in 1964!*

7.♗e2 (7.♛e2 ♛xe2+ 8.♗xe2 ♗f5 leads to equality; or 8.♔xe2 a6!) **7...♛c7.** *More logical than 7...cxd4 8.0-0 ♛c7 9.♘b3 ♗d6?! 10.♘bxd4 (Keres – Capablanca, AVRO 1938).*

8.0-0 ♘f6 9.♖e1 ♗e6 10.dxc5 ♗xc5 11.♘b3 ♗b6 12.♘fd4 0-0 13.c3 ♘e5.

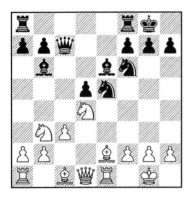

14.h3? Unnecessarily weakens the position, even though it's hard to find a good plan for white. 14.♗f4 is bad due to 14...♘f3+ 15.♗xf3 ♕xf4 16.♘xe6 fxe6 17.♖xe6 ♗xf2+ 18.♔xf2 ♘g4+ etc.

Of course, going for such a position with white is a terrifying prospect, but after 19.♔e2!, the computer confidently gives long lines where white wins. The strength of 14.♗f4! is shown even more clearly in Lisitsin's line 16.♖xe6! fxe6 17.♘xe6 ♗xf2+ (or 17...♕h4 18.♘xf8 ♕xf2+ 19.♔h1) 18.♔h1 ♕f5 19.♘xf8 ♖xf8 20.♕e2 ♗b6 21.♖d1.

14...♘c4 15.♗d3 ♖ae8 16.♘e2. White is worse. He's trying to regroup with 17.♘bd4 and then, if possible, b2-b3 and ♗a3. However, black's reply shows that this plan is clearly wrong.

16.♕c2 and ♗d2 still kept the position viable.

16...♗xh3! 17.♗f4. If 17.gxh3, then 17...♖xe2! 18.♖xe2 ♕g3+ 19.♔h1 ♕xh3+ 20.♔g1 ♘g4 21.♗f4 g5!, and there's no defense

against mate or big material losses *(here, after 22.♕f1! ♕xd3 23.♗h2, white can still resist for some time, however, 20...♕g3+ 21.♔f1 ♕f3! wins immediately).* After 18.♕(♗) xe2, the win would have been even simpler. For instance: 18.♗xe2 ♕g3+ 19.♔h1 ♕xh3+ 20.♔g1 ♗xf2+ 21.♔xf2 ♘e4+ 22.♔g1 ♕g3+ 23.♔h1 ♘f2#.

17...♕d7. *Missing a spectacular queen sacrifice: 17...♖xe2! 18.♗xc7 ♗xf2+ 19.♔h2 ♖xe1 20.♕xe1 ♗xe1 21.♖xe1 ♘xb2 with three extra pawns.*

18.gxh3. *"The decisive mistake, after which white is crushed. It was better to play 18.♗xc4 ♕g4! (or 18...dxc4 19.gxh3 ♕xh3 20.♘bd4) 19.♗xd5 ♘xd5 20.♕xd5 ♖xe2 21.♖xe2 ♕xe2 22.♗g3 ♗e6 23.♕d2, and white could still resist."* *(Lisitsin)*

18...♕xh3 19.♗xc4. Probably the strongest move for white. Black threatened ♘xb2 with a complete rout. Another threat was 19... ♗xf2+! 20.♔xf2 ♘g4+ 21.♔g1

♘ce3!! 22.♗xe3 ♕h2+ 23.♔f1 ♘xe3#.

19...♕g4+! 20.♔f1. Best. 20.♗g3 is met with 20...♖xe2 21.♖xe2 (21.♕xe2 ♕xg3+ 22.♔h1 ♕h3+ 23.♔g1 ♘g4 with inevitable mate) 21...♕xg3+ 22.♔f1 ♕h3+ 23.♔e1 (23.♔g1 ♘g4; *this is bad because of 24.♕xd5, one winning move is 23...dxc4!*) 23...dxc4 24.♘d4 ♘e4 25.♖xe4 (preventing the mate on h1) 25...♕h1+ 26.♔d2 ♕xe4, winning.

25.♖e3 is more resilient, not giving the rook away (25...♕h1+ 26.♔e2 ♕h4 27.♕g1).

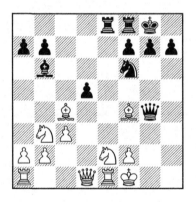

20...♗xf2! 20...♗f3 21.♘bd4 ♗xd4 22.♕xd4 ♖xe2 23.♗g3 ♖xb2 24.♔g1 dxc4 was enough to win, but black goes for checkmate.

21.♔xf2. Accepting the latest sacrifice was forced. Among other things, black threatened 21...♖xe2.

21...♘e4+ 22.♔f1 ♕f3+ 23.♔g1 ♕f2+! After the immediate 23...♖e6, white had 24.♖f1 ♖g6+ 25.♘g3, and black can only give perpetual check.

24.♔h1 ♖e6.

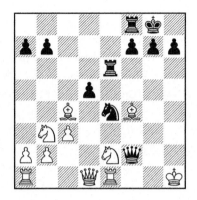

25.♗xd5. Leads to mate. 25.♕d3! prolonged the struggle; there could have followed 25...dxc4 26.♕e3 cxb3 (26...♕h4+!? 27.♔g2 ♕g4+ *with a decisive attack*) 27.♕xf2 ♘xf2+ 28.♔g2 (28.♔g1 ♘d3 29.♖ed1 ♘xb2 *is a bit better*) 28...♘d3 29.♔f1 ♘xe1 30.♖xe1 bxa2 31.♖a1 ♖fe8, winning.

25.♕xd5 ♖g6 also led to checkmate, for instance: 1) 26.♕xe4 ♕h4+ 27.♗h2 ♕xe4#, 2) 26.♖g1 ♕h4+ 27.♗h2 ♘f2#, or 3) 26.♘g3 ♘xg3+ 27.♗xg3 ♖h6+ etc.

25...♕f3+ (the immediate 25...♖g6 was also possible) **26.♔h2 ♖g6 27.♗xf7+ ♖xf7 28.♕d8+ ♖f8 29.♕d5+** (traditional pre-mortem checks) **29...♔h8 30.♘g3 ♕f2+.** White resigned due to inevitable mate.

In 1966, Bondarevsky, when asked about his most memorable win, said, "My game against Panov in the 10th Soviet Championship. I sacrificed three minor pieces, and the whole attack wasn't just about forcing moves."

Just a Masterpiece

Lisitsin: "Levenfish managed to retain enough energy for a good finish. In round 17, he brilliantly showed his will to win, his determination to claim the honorable title of the Soviet Country's chess champion in the game against Goglidze. This creative work, like the game Panov – Bondarevsky, is a true masterpiece in every sense of the word."

No. 87. Nimzo-Indian Defense E32
Levenfish – Goglidze
Tbilisi 1937, round 17
Annotated by G. Levenfish

1.d4 ♘f6 2.c4 e6 3.♘c3 ♗b4 4.♕c2. This move was considered the strongest back then. Now white plays 4.e3 or 4.a3 more often.

4...0-0. Goglidze chooses the so-called Leningrad system. 4...d5 is the simplest way to equality.

5.e3 d6 6.a3 ♗xc3+ 7.♕xc3 ♘bd7. Strengthening the e5 square is the main defensive idea.

8.♗d3 b6 9.♘e2 ♗b7 10.0-0 e5. The light-squared bishop trade 10...♗e4 11.♘g3 ♗xd3 12.♕xd3 was just a waste of time. 10...c5 was probably best.

11.♘g3 ♖e8 12.b3! (the only way – not b2-b4) **12...d5 13.♗b2 c5?** Looks very strong, because black is threatening to exert powerful pressure along the c-file, but in actuality, opening the a1-h8 diagonal with the game move was an error.

Black should have prevented that with 13...e4 14.♗c2 c6 15.f3 exf3 16.gxf3 h5!, with some counterplay. **14.dxe5 ♘xe5.**

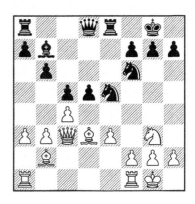

15.♖fd1! White prepares an escape route for the d3 bishop. Black can't trade it now, because after 15...♘xd3 16.♖xd3, the d5 pawn can't be defended.

15...♕c7 16.♗f1!! Protecting the g2 square and covering the first rank. The importance of this move will be seen later.

Yes... The computer would rather freeze than think of something like that!

16...♖ad8 17.cxd5 ♖xd5. Both 17...♘xd5 18.♖xd5 ♗xd5 19.f4 and 17...♗xd5 18.e4 ♗xe4 19.♖xd8 ♕xd8 20.♖e1 led to a loss of material.

18.e4! *"From here and until the end, white executes a brilliant attack, which makes this game one of the best in the whole tournament."* (Romanovsky)

18...♖xd1 19.♖xd1 ♘g6. 19...♗xe4 is met with 20.♖e1 and f2-f4, winning a piece, while after

19...♘xe4, there's 20.♘xe4 ♗xe4 21.♖e1.

20.♘f5! ♖d8. White threatened 21.♘xg7.

After 20...♗xe4, this blow was indeed decisive, but 20...♖xe4 21.♘xg7 ♖f4! is better for black. So, instead of taking on g7, white should play 21.♕d2 ♘e8 22.♗b5!

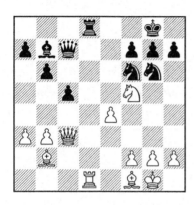

21.♕g3! This combination became possible because of the move 16.♗f1.

"This move and the next don't just add an elegant artistic decoration to the attack: they are decisive in their strategic strength." (Romanovsky)

21...♖c8. The only move. After 21...♕c8, there's 22.♘e7+ ♘xe7 23.♗xf6 g6 24.♖xd8+ ♕xd8 25.♕g5 ♔f8 26.♕h6+ ♔e8 27.♗b5+, while 21...♕b8 is met with 22.♘h6+ ♔f8 (22...gxh6 23.♗xf6 ♖e8 24.e5!) 23.♗xf6 gxf6 24.♖d7! ♘e7 25.♗b5! with the decisive threat 26.♕g8+! ♘xg8 27.♖xf7#.

22.♗e5! ♕c6. 22...♕xe5 loses to 23.♕xe5 ♘xe5 24.♘e7+ ♔f8

25.♘xc8 ♗xc8 26.♖d8+, with white an exchange up.

23.f3! (calm before the storm) **23...c4.** There's no defense against the terrible threat ♖d6 (23... ♘e8 24.♖d6, winning the queen: 24...♘xd6 25.♘e7+). Black is desperately trying to save the game.

24.♗xc4 b5.

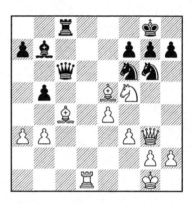

25.♗f1. 25.♗xf7+ ♔xf7 26.♘d6+ won as well. However, the game move is calmer – black has nothing to do anyway.

25...♕c5+ 26.♗d4 ♕c2 27.♖e1 ♘e8 28.♗xb5 ♕xb3 29.♗xe8 ♖xe8 30.♘xg7 ♖d8 31.♘f5 ♕c4 32.♕g5! Black resigned. After 32... ♖xd4, there's 33.♕h6, mating.

Capablanca Style

Lisitsin: "The leader defeated Ilyin-Zhenevsky with a brilliant, deeply calculated pawn sacrifice. Such surprise combinations are characteristic of Levenfish's deep style."

No. 88
Levenfish – Ilyin-Zhenevsky
Tbilisi 1937, round 13
Annotated by G. Levenfish

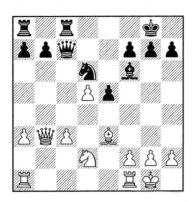

19.c4! The only move that gives white any chances, and it also starts a fascinating combination. Black threatened b7-b5.

19...♘xc4 (the meek 19...b6 is met with 20.♖fc1 and a3-a4-a5) **20.♘e4!!** A completely unexpected pawn sacrifice; 20.♘xc4 ♕xc4 21.♕xb7 only led to equality.

20...♕e7? The unexpected change of decorations took my opponent by surprise. After 20...♘d6 21.♖fc1 ♕d7 22.♘xd6 ♕xd6 23.♖xc8+ ♖xc8 24.♕xb7 white is better; 20...♗e7 21.♖fc1 with a very unpleasant pin *(21...♘a5 22.♕b5! ♕d8 23.d6).*

After 20...♘xe3 21.fxe3, white has a strong blockading position for the pawn. 21...♗e7 can be met with the following combination:

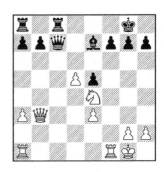

22.♖xf7! ♔xf7 23.d6+ ♕c4 24.♕xb7 ♔g8 25.dxe7 ♖ab8 26.♖d1!!
The cool 26...♕f7! brings white down to earth: 27.♕xb8 ♖xb8 28.♖d8+ ♕e8 29.♖xb8 ♕xb8 30.♘d6 ♕b1+ with perpetual check. But this is only half the problem: the whole combination is refuted with 24...♔g6! (25.dxe7 ♖ab8 and ♕xe4).

Later, in his book, Levenfish came to the conclusion: "It seems that the correct move is 20...♘xe3 21.♘xf6+ gxf6 22.fxe3 ♕b6, transitioning into a drawn four-rook endgame (if 23.♕d3, then 23...♔h8 24.♖f3 ♖g8)".

21.d6.

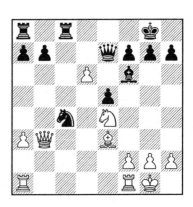

21...♕e6. 21...♘xd6 22.♗c5 ♖xc5 23.♘xc5 b6 24.♘a6 ♘f5 was better, giving black some drawing chances.

After 25.♕f3! that is highly unlikely: 25...e4 26.♕xf5 ♗xa1 27.♖xa1 with a knight for two pawns. Instead of 24...♘f5?, there's a better move: 24...e4 (for instance: 25.♖ac1 ♗e5 26.♖c7 ♕h4 27.g3 ♕f6).

22.♘c5 ♕xd6. After 22...♖xc5 23.♗xc5 ♘d2, instead of 24.♕xe6 fxe6, with black regaining the exchange with ♘b3, white plays 24.♕xb7!

Here, after 24...♖d8, black regains the exchange as well, but in worse conditions: 25.♕xa7 ♘xf1 26.♖xf1 ♕d5 27.a4, and the passed pawn is rather dangerous.

23.♕xc4 ♗e7. Perhaps black had hoped to regain the piece after 23...b6, but overlooked the saving move 24.♘e4.

24.♕e4 ♖xc5 25.♗xc5 ♕xc5 26.♕xb7. The rest is a matter of technique.

26...♖c8 27.a4 f5 28.♖ad1 ♗f6 29.♖d7 a5 30.♕d5+ ♔h8 31.♖d1 ♕b4 (a trap: if 32.♖d8+, then 32...♗xd8 33.♕xd8+ ♕f8) **32.♕b5 ♕c3.** Black resigned, spotting that he is now mated in three after 33.♖d8+.

Betting on His Own Loss

Panov: "This game was preceded by a funny "backstage story". We met in one of the last rounds. Makogonov's play had been highly inspired, and he even had some chances of winning first prize before our game. I, however, had a poor start, and only found my game near the finish. Fearing for his result, Makogonov, for some strange reason, decided to play safe and made a bet with another tournament participant – a bottle of good, expensive Georgian wine. The other player bet on Makogonov winning

Друж. шарж Ю. Ю.

м. Панов

"Panov's interesting play brought him great victories over the prizewinners," (Romanovsky), but nothing more. Cartoon by Y. Yuzepchuk (tournament bulletin, No. 2, 1937).

that important game. Makogonov, however, bet that he would lose to me (!); he probably wanted to console himself with the blessed Caucasian drink if he lost or make a redemptive sacrifice to the chess gods if he won.

The player who made the bet immediately came to my room and, laughing, told me about Makogonov's strange choice. I always try to help my comrades, so I decided to do everything in my power to help Makogonov win the cherished bottle and punish the other player for indiscreetly revealing the secret.

The game was very sharp, even wild, and ended with a beautiful finale. But I wasn't invited to the wine tasting for some reason..."

No. 89
Panov – V. Makogonov
Tbilisi 1937, round 16
Annotated by V. Panov

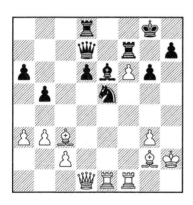

31...♛c8! A cunning move! 31... ♖df8 was bad because of the simple 32.♗xe5 dxe5 33.♛xd7 ♗xd7 34.♗d5 *(or 33...♖xd7 34.♖xe5)*. Now

black threatens to meet 32.♗b2 with 32...♖c7, after which white can't play either 33.♖e2 ♗g4 or 33.♖f2 ♞g4+.

The line 33.♖e2 ♗g4 led to a draw. After 34.♛d5+ ♔f8 35.♖e4!, black has to play 35...♗f5! (but not 35...♖xc2? 36.♗xe5 or 35...♖c5 36.♛d2 ♖xc2? 37.♛h6+), and then, after 36.♖e2 he again has to play 36...♗g4, because the capture 36...♖xc2? loses here as well: 37.♗xe5! ♖xe2 38.♗xd6+ ♖xd6 39.♛xd6+ ♔g8 (39...♔f7 40.♖f2!) 40.f7+ ♔xf7 41.g4 etc.

32.♛d4! Preventing 32...♖c7, which is now met with 33.♗a5, and preparing the decisive combination.

32...♖fd7. With the idea of transferring the bishop to f7, blocking the dangerous pawn, but allowing white to execute his plan *(32...♗f5!?).*

33.♖xe5! dxe5.

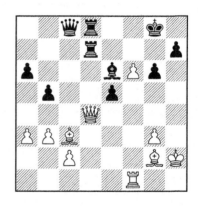

34.f7+! Black overlooked this spectacular Zwischenschach *(the computer finds it in a split second!).* After the immediate 34.♛xe5, black had 34...♖f7. Now he can't escape the mating net!

34...♖xf7 (or 34...♔f8 35.♗b4+ ♖e7 36.♕xe5) **35.♕xe5 ♔f8 36.♕g7+ ♔e7.** If 36...♔e8, then 37.♕g8+ ♔e7 38.♗b4+ ♖d6 39.♖xf7+ ♗xf7 40.♕xc8.

37.♗b4+. Black resigned. After 37...♔d7, there's a mate in two, while if 37...♖d6, then 38.♖xf7+ ♗xf7 39.♕e5+ ♕e6 40.♗xd6+.

However, in the next game, a dashing attack only brought woes to Panov.

The Anti-Chatard

Riumin: "Evaluating all the theoretical novelties submitted for the *64* competition, I think that the Panov – Yudovich game deserves the award the most. The defensive system for black in the Chatard Attack, developed by masters Yudovich and Belavenets, has a sound idea behind it, is logical, backed by concrete lines and, as a whole, is a consummate opening development, more valuable than any of the other novelties."

Lisitsin: "In this game, the f7 pawn's progress was particularly impressive: it managed to cross three files, six ranks, capture two pieces on the way and promote on the h1 square on move 15 (!)."

No. 90. French Defense C13
Panov – Yudovich
Tbilisi 1937, round 5
Annotated by M. Yudovich
Belavenets and I prepared for this championship together. We developed opening set-ups, searched for new continuations and found them. We knew very well that Panov usually played 1.e4, and that he always plays the Chatard Attack in the main line of the French.

And so, we developed a new line in the Chatard for black – very complicated and sharp, with multiple combinational blows and sacrifices – especially for Panov. After the draw, it turned out that both Belavenets and I had black against Panov – he played him in round 3, and my game was in round 5.

"So," I told Sergei, "fate has it that you'll be the first to test our secret weapon..."

1.e4 e6 2.d4 d5 3.♘c3 ♘f6 4.♗g5 ♗e7 5.e5 ♘fd7 6.h4. *"The Chatard Attack, one of the sharpest lines of the French Defense, became widely known after Alekhine's great win against Fahrni in Mannheim." (Riumin)*

6...f6! An old move, which was prematurely consigned to the archives. As our research shows, this move calls the correctness of the Chatard Attack into question.

Two years later, in the game Alexander – Milner-Barry, white tested the maneuver 7.♕h5+!, which was later developed by the Belorussian master V. Silich and gave white better chances (see, for instance, the game Spassky – Guimard, Gothenburg 1955). So, 6...c5 is now considered the best reply for black, immediately counterattacking in the center.

ДУЭТ СМОЛЕНСКИХ БЛИЗНЕЦОВ

Шарж Ю. Ю.

Юдович:
Я — мастер начала.

Белавенец:
Я — мастер конца.

Близнецы хором:
Все знают
Юдовича—Белавенца.

Юдович:
Наш всяк сотворенный
Вдвоем вариант —
В оправе теории
Чудный брильянт.

Белавенец:
И труд бескорыстный
Мы вносим в дебют:
Очками в таблице
Секреты цветут.

Близнецы хором:
В груди — благородства
Бушует пожар:
Отдам ему славу,
Возьму гонорар.
А червь сердце точит:
Он, правда, мой брат, —
Но как бы совместный
Зачесть результат?...

но как бы совместный
Зачесть результат?...

7.♗d3. Alekhine recommended this at the New York 1924 tournament as the best move that gives white a strong attack *(after 7... fxg5 8.♕h5+ ♔f8 9.♖h3)*. However, black has an energetic blow c7-c5, which apparently refutes the whole attack.

Duet of the Smolensk Twins

Yudovich:
I'm the master of the opening.

Belavenets:
I'm the master of the ending.

Twins together:
Everyone knows
Yudovich–Belavenets.

Yudovich:
Every line created
By us together
Is an amazing diamond
In the frame of theory.

Belavenets:
And we work selflessly
For the sake of openings:
Our secrets grow into
Points on the table.

Twins together:
There's a fire of chivalry
In our chests:
I'll give him the glory,
And I'll take the royalties.
Ah, but there's a doubt in the heart:
Yes, he's my brother indeed,
But is there any way
To count our result together?..

Cartoon by Y. Yuzepchuk (USSR Chess Premiership, No. 6, 1938).

In the game against Belavenets, Panov avoided Alekhine's recommendation after a long think, played 7.exf6, and the game ended in a draw.

"What would you have done had I played 7.♗d3?" Panov asked Belavenets after the game. Of course, Sergei couldn't disclose our idea: he avoided the question and quickly walked out of the tournament hall.

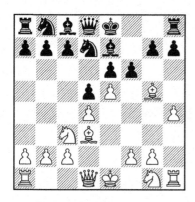

7...c5! *"A novelty by Yudovich and Belavenets!" Lisitsin and Riumin were convinced. Actually, this move had been successfully tested back in 1926 in the game Woinarski – Purdy from an Australian championship*

8.♕h5+. After 8.exf6 ♘xf6 black is better, because white's center is defenseless.

8...♚f8 9.♘xd5!? We had analyzed this move thoroughly. If 9.exf6 ♘xf6 10.♗xf6 ♗xf6 *(as was played in the aforementioned Australian game)*, then black's position is excellent.

Here, white would have gained good counterplay after 11.dxc5.

Instead, he chooses "an unclear attack with colossal material losses. This way is even harder if we remember that black knows the line very well because of his home analysis." (Lisitsin)

9...fxg5. Bold and correct. However, even after 9...exd5, black can equalize, for instance: 10.e6 ♕e8 11.exd7 ♗xd7 12.♕xe8+ ♚xe8 13.♗e3 cxd4 14.♗xd4 ♘c6 15.♗e3 ♘b4!

10.♖h3 g4! An important moment. After 11.♕xg4 exd5 12.♖f3+ ♘f6 black keeps his extra piece and repels all the threats.

11.♘f4 ♘xe5! (white threatened 12.♘xe6+ or 12.♘g6+) **12.dxe5 gxh3.**

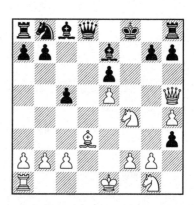

13.♗xh7. White had three other possible continuations:

1) 13.♘g6+ hxg6 14.♕xh8+ ♚f7 15.♕h7 ♕xd3! 16.cxd3 h2 17.0-0-0 h1♕ 18.♘f3 ♕xg2 19.♖g1 ♕xf3 20.♕xg6+ ♚f8, and the king escapes the checks;

2) 13.♘gxh3 ♚g8 14.0-0-0 ♕f8 15.♗c4 ♕f7 16.♕g4 ♘c6, and white's attack is repelled;

3) 13.0-0-0 h2 14.♘gh3 h1♕ 15.♖xh1 ♚g8 with incredible complications, probably beneficial for black.

In this line, after 16.♘g5! black might as well resign: 16...♗xg5 17.hxg5 h6 18.♕g6. So, the correct move here is 14...♘c6!, and Lisitsin's analysis shows that black's threats are more dangerous: 15.♗xh7 ♕xd1+ (the immediate 15...♖xh7! is even stronger) 16.♔xd1 ♖xh7 or 15.♘g6+ hxg6 16.♕xh8+ ♚f7 17.♗xg6+ ♚xg6 18.♘f4+ ♚f7! 19.♕h5+ ♚g8! 20.♖xd8+ ♘xd8 21.♕e8+ ♗f8 22.♘g6 h1♕+ 23.♚d2 ♘f7!

Perhaps white can still improve in this line. However, this game shows that black's idea (9...fxg5!) was correct.

13...♖xh7 14.♕xh7 h2!

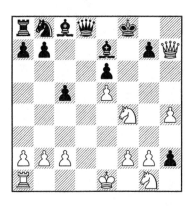

A rarity in a real game: a second queen appears on move 15.

15.♚e2 h1♕ 16.♘g6+ ♚f7 17.♘h8+ ♕xh8! The simplest. After 17...♚e8 18.♕g8+ ♚d7 19.♖d1+ ♚c7, some complications could have

occurred *(20.♖xd8 ♗xd8 21.♕xg7+ ♗d7, curtains)*.

18.♕xh8 ♘c6 19.♕h5+ ♚g8 20.♘h3 ♕xg2. Avoiding the trap 20...♕xa1? 21.♕e8+ ♗f8 22.♘g5 ♘xe5 23.♕h5 with a draw.

21.♕e8+ ♗f8 22.♘g5 ♘xe5 23.c4. Desperation! If 23.♕h5, then 23...♕g4+, and black threatens b7-b6 and ♗a6+.

23...♕g4+ 24.♚f1 ♕xc4+ 25.♚g1 ♕g4+ 26.♚f1 ♗d7! White resigned.

Of course, Panov was upset by this defeat, but he was always very calm and correct at the chessboard. When Vasily Nikolaevich shook my hand, he said, "Such a good idea you invented! However, I still think that the bishop move to d3 is good!"

Opening Scrollwork

Lisitsin: "The opening in the Belavenets – Lisitsin game was so sharp and complicated that the two players spent more than three hours on their first nine moves! Belavenets precisely refuted his opponent's adventurous opening plan."

No. 91. Queen's Pawn Opening D02
Belavenets – Lisitsin
Tbilisi 1937, round 15
Annotated by S. Belavenets

1.d4 ♘f6 2.♘f3 d5 3.c4 ♗f5. A rare move, rejected by theory.

4.♕b3. The simplest way for white to gain an advantage is 4.cxd5 ♘xd5 5.♕b3 ♘c6 6.♘bd2, threatening e2-e4. The game move gives white nothing good.

4...♘c6! 5.♘c3. It's bad to take on b7 due to 5...♗d7! 6.cxd5 ♖b8 7.♕a6 ♘b4 8.♕c4 e6!, and black's initiative compensates for the sacrificed material.

5...e5. Black goes for complications, avoiding the quiet 5... e6 6.c5 ♖b8 etc.

Lisitsin accords this move a question mark in the tournament book, with a terse note: "Sharp, but not solid."

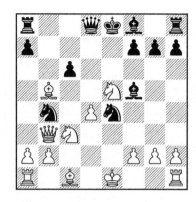

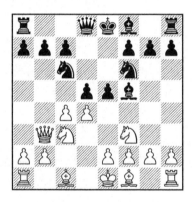

6.cxd5! The only move. After 6.dxe5 dxc4 7.♕a4 (otherwise ♘b4-d5) black is better.

6...♘b4? Black should have stopped in time and transitioned the game onto positional rails with 6... ♘xd4 7.♘xd4 exd4 8.♕a4+ c6, with roughly equal chances.

7.e4! *"This simple move, as it soon turns out, destroys all the imaginary towers built by black." (Lisitsin)*

7...♘xe4 8.♗b5+ c6 9.dxc6 bxc6 (all of black's moves are forced) **10.♘xe5!**

Georgy Lisitsin "is already annotating his future games for Shakhmaty v SSSR." (Polevoy.) Jokes aside, he would even write the entire tournament book on his own! Cartoon by Y. Yuzepchuk (tournament bulletin, No. 2, 1937).

It's hard to believe that such a wild position could occur in the Queen's Gambit after just 10 moves. Black's pawns on f7 and c6 are under attack, and he can't adequately defend both.

10...♝e6. Admitting his helplessness. However, there's nothing better. If 10...♛xd4 (10...♛e7 11.♞xc6; 10...♛f6 11.♞d5!), then 11.♝xc6+ ♚d8 12.0-0!, and black inevitably loses something. 10...♛c7 11.♞xc6 ♞xc6 12.♛d5! (11.♞d5 ♛a5! 12.0-0 ♝e6 13.♞xc6 ♛xb5 is worse, and it's very hard for white to win *(after 14.♞c7+ ♚d7 15.♞xb5 ♝xb3 16.♞e5+ ♚e7 17.axb3, the computer sees no difficulties with winning))*.

"After playing 5...e5?, black counted on this move, but forgot about one interesting resource for white." (Lisitsin)

11.♞xc6! ♛b6 (after 11...♝xb3, 12.♞xb4+! ♚e7 13.♞c6+ regains the queen) **12.♞xb4+ ♛xb5 13.♛xe6+.** The simplest – now black has no hope of drawing with opposite-colored bishops.

13...fxe6 14.♞xb5 ♝xb4+ 15.♚e2 ♚d7. 15...♜c8 is met with 16.f3! and ♚d3 with full consolidation; black gains nothing.

16.f3 ♞f6 17.♞c3. White is two pawns up, and black has no serious counterplay; only the ensuing time trouble complicates things.

White finally converted his advantage on move 58.

New Wine in old Wineskins

Yudovich: "I won't forget my last meeting with Ilyin-Zhenevsky over the board. He was a great man, one of the organizers of the Soviet chess movement. He was sincerely overjoyed by the successes of the young players. He would often talk to me, even back when I was a rookie debuting at the 7th championship. Noticing that I wore worn-out, old boots and summer clothes in November, Alexander Fyodorovich got me orders for footwear and warm clothes. This might seem like a small thing, but it was a big deal in 1931.

In Tbilisi, Ilyin-Zhenevsky played in the championship for the last time. He took part in the very first Olympiad, back in 1920, and then played in seven more national championships. Against me, Alexander Fyodorovich chose his favorite Dutch Defense. The game was quiet and ended in a draw. When we analyzed the possible lines, he talked about his plans for the future.

"I'm very busy," he said, "but I want to write a book about Alekhine. He's not an enemy, just a very confused man. So talented! I spoke with him many times. I'm gathering the materials right now."

He couldn't put his plan to fruition. Alexander Fyodorovich died in 1941, he was forty-seven years old...

Very busy with party and diplomatic work, Ilyin-Zhenevsky couldn't study systematically. But he was excellent in the positions where he could obtain an initiative. The next game is an example of that."

No. 92. Philidor Defense C41
Rauzer – Ilyin-Zhenevsky
Tbilisi 1937, round 3
Annotated by A. Ilyin-Zhenevsky

1.e4 e5 2.♘f3 d6 3.d4 exd4. *Ilyin-Zhenevsky usually played 3... ♘f6 4.dxe5 ♘xe4. But shortly before the championship, he faced a strong novelty 5.♘bd2! in the match against Sokolsky (this move is still considered the main line) and decided to capture with the pawn instead.*

4.♘xd4 ♘f6 5.f3. A dubious novelty. The idea is to eventually play c2-c4 and seize the important d5 square. This move is correct only if black plays passively.

"Ever the tireless experimenter, Rauzer tried to pour new wine into old wineskins in the Philidor Defense. But his attempt was unsuccessful." (64)

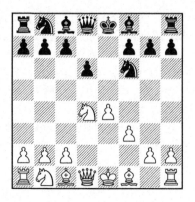

5...d5! Black prevents white's plan and starts energetic piece play, where white's weakened kingside should play its role.

6.e5 ♘fd7 7.f4. If 7.e6, then simply 7...♘f6 8.exf7+ ♚xf7, which is better for black.

7...♘c6 8.♘xc6 (black threatened ♘dxe5) **8...bxc6 9.♗d3?** And this is a serious mistake 9.♗e3 is better.

9...♛h4+ 10.g3 ♛h3 11.♛f3 *(white can't drive the queen away: 11.♗f1 ♛e6 and then f7-f6)* **11... ♗c5 12.♗e3 0-0 13.♘d2.**

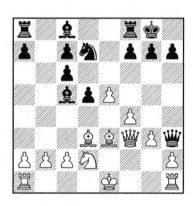

13...f6! The move that exposes the weaknesses in white's position. There's no good defense against the threat f6xe5.

14.exf6. *"Tantamount to suicide."* (Grigoriev.) *"White could defend with 14.♗xc5 ♘xc5 15.♗f1 ♛e6, even though he still couldn't avoid material losses: 16.♛e3 ♘d7 17.♘f3 fxe5 etc." (Lisitsin)*

14...♖e8 15.♘f1 ♘xf6! Black could have won a piece with 15... ♗xe3 16.♘xe3 d4

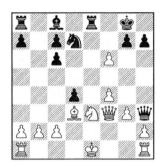

but then white had some tactical chances after 17.♗c4+ ♔h8 18.fxg7+ ♔xg7 19.0-0-0 ♖xe3 20.♕xc6.

Not just "some", but very tangible: 20...♞b6 (20...♖b8?? 21.♕d5) 21.♕c5! ♞xc4 22.♕xd4+ and ♕xc4 with three pawns for the piece.

16.♔d2. White should have accepted the loss of the exchange with 16.0-0-0 ♗g4 17.♕f2 ♗xe3+ 18.♞xe3 ♗xd1, but his position is still lost.

16...♗g4 17.♕f2 d4 18.♗xd4 ♖e2+! White resigned: after 19.♗xe2, there follows 19...♞e4+ 20.♔e1 ♞xf2 21.♗xg4 ♕xg4 22.♗xf2 ♖e8+, curtains.

The quickest win in the whole championship.

Punishment for Routine

This game was also a miniature. The reasons for the quick loss of the only "supermaster" in the championship were shown by the sophisticated diagnostician Yudovich: "The hypnotic sway of natural moves affects even grandmasters!"

Ragozin – Lilienthal
Tbilisi 1937, round 16
Annotated by G. Lisitsin

After making "developing" moves which were, however, inappropriate for the current situation (a7-a5, ♗a6), black lost his advantage in the center and got into a very difficult situation.

14.♖d4! ♞c5. 14...f5 weakened black's position too much.

"The decisive mistake. Black should have tried 14...f5, for instance: 15.♗xe4 fxe4 16.c5+ ♔h8 17.♕d1 ♖ad8 18.♕d2, even though white still has a positional advantage." (Lilienthal)

15.♕c2 ♞e6 16.♖h4 ♞f8 17.♖d1 ♖ab8 18.c5! Fixing the weaknesses of black's pawn position (the c7-c6-d7 triangle) and threatening to relocate the rook from h4 to a4 to attack the a5 pawn.

"A very subtle move!" (Lilienthal)
18...h6.

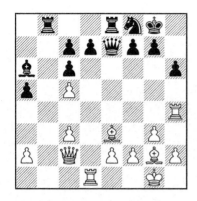

19.♖a4 ♗b5 20.♖g4! Very subtle! Now white threatens 21.♗xh6 and 21.c4; 20.♖xa5 ♖a8! won a pawn, but still gave black chances to resist.

20...♔h8. Both 20...♘g6 21.c4 ♗a6 22.♖e4 ♕d8 23.♖ed4 ♘f8 (23...♘e5! *is more tenacious*) 24.♗xc6 and 20...♕e6 21.♗h3! were rather bad.

21.c4 ♗a6 22.♕c3! Black resigned. He has no good defense against mate or ♕xa5xc7.

Budo's Heroic Feat

Lisitsin: "Up until round 18, the battle for the Soviet Championship wasn't over, because Konstantinopolsky, Makogonov and Belavenets were in hot pursuit of Levenfish. All of them suffered crushing defeats, and this enabled Levenfish to win the tournament and the title of Soviet champion with one round to spare.

Makogonov played a mediocre Grunfeld Defense against Budo. White gained a positional advantage and then converted it very precisely,

For the fourth prizewinner of the 1936 Moscow tournament, Andor Lilienthal's result was disastrous. In round 2, he failed to outplay Genrikh Kasparyan with black.

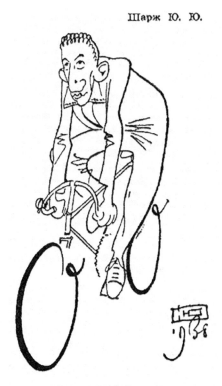

Шарж Ю. Ю.

Будо «финиширует».

"*Budo at the finish*"
Alexander Budo was awarded a special prize for the best result against prizewinners by a non-prizewinner. Cartoon by Y. Yuzepchuk (USSR Chess Premiership, No. 13–14, 1938).

without mistakes. This win got Budo a special prize for the highest score against prizewinners among non-prizewinners – the talented Leningrad first-category player caused them a lot of trouble in the 10th championship."

No. 94. Grunfeld Defense D97
Budo – V. Makogonov
Tbilisi 1937, round 18
Annotated by A. Budo
1.d4 ♘f6 2.♘f3 g6 3.c4 ♗g7 4.♘c3 d5 5.♕b3 dxc4. The goal of

this move is to create piece pressure on white's center.

6.♕xc4 0-0. Black could also play 6...♗e6 7.♕b5+ ♘c6 8.e4, however, white's position is still better.

7.♗f4 c6 8.e4 ♗e6. *Later, Boleslavsky demonstrated that black could get good counterplay with 8... b5 or 8...♕a5 with the idea b7-b5. In 1944, both of these moves were tested against... Makogonov: 8...♕a5 by Boleslavsky himself, and 8...b5 by Tolush. After sharp struggles, both games ended in draws.*

9.♕d3 ♘e8 10.♗e2 ♘d6 11.0-0 ♘a6 12.♖ad1 ♕a5.

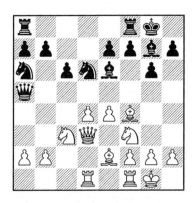

This position is very hard to evaluate. At first glance, black's development is harmonious, and his queenside chances are more realistic than white's possible kingside and center activity.

13.♕d2! A subtle move. It suddenly turns out that black's piece pressure has reached its limit, and his pieces are insecure. The continuation 13...♘c4 14.♕c1 c5 15.d5 ♘xb2 16.♕xb2 ♗xc3 17.♕xb7 loses a piece. 14...♕b4 15.b3 ♘d6 16.♗h6 *(16.e5! ♘c8 17.♘e4 is stronger)* is not particularly tempting either.

So, instead of 12...♕a5, black probably should have preferred 12...♗c4, trading away the bad bishop *(11...♗c4 was good as well).*

13...♖fd8 *(here, however, 13...♗c4 is bad because of 14.♘d5!)* **14.♘g5 ♗c4 15.e5 ♗xe2 16.♕xe2 ♘f5?** This loses. 16...♘b5 17.♕e3 gave black some chances to defend.

However, after 17.♕c4 e6 18.♘ge4! (Lisitsin), black would have a hard time.

retreat of the g5 knight) **18...f6.** *"It's only a matter of taste whether 18...♘c7 19.♕e3 ♔h8 is better." (Grigoriev.) However, involving the knight in defense does look more solid.*

19.♘e6. There was probably a quicker win: 19.♕c4+ ♔h8 20.♘e6 ♖e8 or 20...♖d7 21.♘xg7 ♔xg7 22.♗xh6+ ♔xh6 23.♕f7.

19...♖e8 20.♘xg7 ♔xg7 21.♕e3 ♘f7 22.d5! ♘b4. Giving white an opportunity to exploit the hanging knight on b4; however, the game was lost anyway.

23.e6 ♘d8 24.♗h6+.

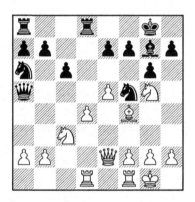

17.g4! ♘h6. Not 17...♘xd4 18.♕c4 ♕b4 19.♕xf7+ ♔h8 20.a3!, and the queen has no good squares to retreat to: after 20...♕c5, there's 21.♖xd4 and ♘e6; or 20...♕xb2 21.♕c4, and there's no 21...♕xc3 because of 22.♘f7+, mating. 18...♘e6 19.♘xe6 fxe6 20.♕xe6+ is also bad: if 20...♔f8, then 21.♗g5 ♕c5 *(21...♕c7 22.♘e4!)* 22.♖d6 ♖e8 23.♖d3!

18.h3 (another threat: to win the h6 knight after 19.♕e3 and the

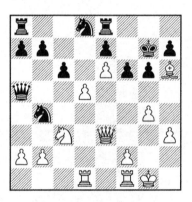

24...♔h8. 24...♔g8 25.d6 exd6 26.♘e4 *(26.♖xd6 is simpler)* 26...♕e5 *(nor can he save himself with the more stubborn 26...♖xe6 27.♘xf6+ ♔f7 28.♘e4 ♘d5 29.♕f3+ ♔e8 30.♘g5 and so on)* 27.♗f4 ♘d5 28.♗xe5 ♘xe3 29.♘xf6+ ♔f8 30.♗xd6+ ♔g7 31.♘xe8+.

25.d6 exd6 26.♕f4! ♖xe6 27.♖fe1! Precise. 27.♖de1 didn't lead to the goal because of 27...♘d5 28.♖xe6 ♘xe6 *(after 28.♕xd6!, there's still no salvation for black).*

27...♔g8 28.♖xe6 ♘xe6.

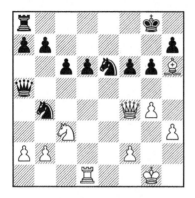

м. В. Алаторцев.

Vladimir Alatortsev only scored 1.5 points against the top 8 and "blundered rooks twice, even though one of those mistakes happened in an already lost position." (Romanovsky.) Cartoon by Y. Yuzepchuk (tournament bulletin, No. 3, 1937).

29.♕xd6! (not 29.♕xf6? due to 29...♕e5) **29...♖e8 30.♖e1** (30.♕d7 is also possible) **30...♔f7 31.♖xe6.** Black resigned.

"Budo played the entire game in great style; unfortunately, Makogonov's play was below his usual level." (Grigoriev)

Let Him Suffer!

The tournament was highly prolific from the creative point of view. There were so many interesting combinations, original plans, elegant endgames and cunning traps that you can't possibly list all of them...

No. 95
Ragozin – Alatortsev
Tbilisi 1937, round 13
Annotated by M. Yudovich

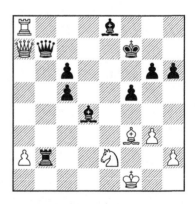

This position attracted the attention of the tournament players for several days.

43.♕a3? Around the 30th move, the opponents had got into severe time trouble and were blitzing out their moves.

43...♕b4 44.♕a7+ ♕b7 45.♕a3 ♕b5 46.♕a7+ ♕b7 47.♕a3 ♕b4 48.♕a7+ ♕b7. Finally sighing with relief, Ragozin crossed the time-control line and adjourned the game *(it's not hard to see that the current position is the same as that on the diagram)*.

When the move was sealed and handed to the arbiter, Bondarevsky came to the board and, saying "Now it's all over," showed the following line: **49.♘xd4 cxd4** *(49...♖b1+ 50.♔f2!)* **50.♕xb7+ ♖xb7 51.♖xe8 ♔xe8** (51...♖b1+ 52.♖e1) **52.♗xc6+ ♖d7 53.♔e2 g5 54.♔d3 f4 55.gxf4.** Alatortsev, who, in the heat of the battle, thought that his position was won, was stunned.

"Did you seal the move ♘xd4?" he asked Ragozin.

"Of course," Ragozin answered calmly.

The second session was to take place three days later. And for all these three days, Alatortsev was tormented by that thought: did he really seal that move?..

When the envelope was opened, it turned out that white had sealed the move... **49.♕a3?** Here is how the game ended:

49...♕e7 50.♖a7 ♖b7 51.♖xb7 ♕xb7 52.♕a5 ♗d7 53.a4 ♗e6 (53...g5 is stronger) **54.♔g2 ♕d7 55.h4 g5 56.hxg5 hxg5 57.♘xd4 cxd4 58.♕c5 d3 59.♗xc6 ♕d8 60.♗f3.**

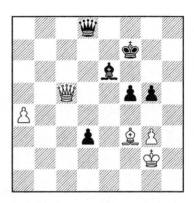

60...g4? *"The idea of trading queens is fundamentally wrong. Black should have played 60...d2 61.♗d1 ♕d3, and, combining the threats to the white king involving the d2 passed pawn, black should win."* (Lisitsin)

61.♗d1 ♕d5+. And here, black should have played 61...♕h8.

This move led to a draw after 62.♕c7+ ♔g6 63.♕d6!; however, 61...♕g5! indeed won: 62.♕c7+ ♔g6 63.♕f4 (forced) 63...♕xf4 64.gxf4 ♗d5+ etc.

62.♕xd5 ♗xd5+ 63.♔f2 ♔e6 64.♔e3 ♗e4 65.♗b3+ ♔e5 66.♗c4 d2 67.♔xd2 f4 68.gxf4+ ♔xf4 69.♔e1. Draw. What a stressful game!

A Tactical Dessert

The next three combinations would probably fit into any textbook. The theme for the first two is deflection (the elimination of defense), and the third one is the cross-pin.

No. 96
Kan – Levenfish
Tbilisi 1937, round 14
Annotated by I. Kan

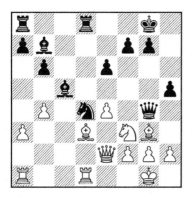

18.♕f1! Black seems to have overlooked this cunning reply *(black had just attacked the white queen with his knight).* Now he can't capture on f3 because this lost a piece.

Ilya Kan was the only non-prizewinner who managed to defeat Grigory Levenfish.

18...♗e7? The decisive mistake. It was possible to avoid material losses by retreating the bishop to f8. However, after 19.♘e5 ♕g5 20.f4 white still had an attack.

19.♘xd4! Starting a forced line. Even black's best moves still lead to a lost position.

19...♖xd4   20.♗e2   ♖xd1 21.♕xd1 ♕g5 22.h4 ♕f6 23.e5. Disrupting the link between the queen and e7 bishop and winning a piece.

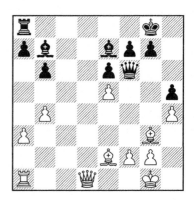

23...♕g6 24.♕d7 ♗xg2. Alas, ♕e4 is again impossible (see moves 20 and 21) because of white's reply ♗f3.

25.♔xg2   ♗xh4   26.♕d3 ♕xd3 27.♗xd3 ♗g5. Formally, black is only one pawn below full compensation. However, white wins without much trouble because his bishop pair are very active.

Black fought until the bitter end, only resigning on move 51.

No. 97
Belavenets – V. Makogonov
Tbilisi 1937, round 8
Annotated by G. Lisitsin

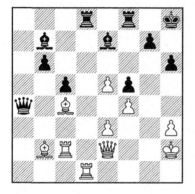

28.♖g1? This allows black to execute an interesting combination

to eliminate the defense. After 28.♖a1 ♕c6 29.♖g1, white could still resist.

28...♗f3!! 29.♕f2 *(or 29.♗b5 ♗xe2 30.♗xa4 ♗d1 31.♖c4 b5!)* **29...♗h4!! 30.♕xf3** *(30.♖g3 ♖d1)* **30...♕xc2+ 31.♖g2 ♕xc4.** The rest is simple *(white resigned on move 42)*.

No. 98
V. Makogonov – Chekhover
Tbilisi 1937, round 5
Annotated by M. Yudovich

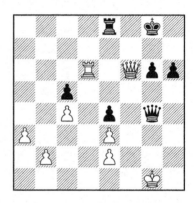

I approached the board when black gave a queen check on g4. Where should the king go? Without thinking, Makogonov played **36.♔f2?** Strangely, this loses. 36.♔f1 was the correct move.

There followed **36...♖f8 37.♖d8 ♕h4+!**, and white had to resign. Were the king on f1, there could have followed: 36...♖f8 37.♖d8 ♖xd8 38.♕xd8+ ♔f7 39.♕c7+ ♔f6 40.♕xc5 with winning chances.

This spectacular cross-pin has been included in textbooks.

The study-like endgame against Makogonov was the only consolation for Vitaly Chekhover. From the author's archive.

A Dual in the Study

There was a sweet study-like endgame. It lived for a long time until its creator decided to critically look at his brainchild... And the results upset him greatly.

No. 99
Goglidze – Kasparyan
Tbilisi 1937, round 16
Annotated by V. Goglidze

41.♘xg4!? *"An elegant combination that suddenly forces a quick finale." (Grigoriev.) "A beautiful, deeply calculated combination." (Lisitsin.) However, when Goglidze prepared a collection of his games for publication (Tbilisi, 1949), he found a "small, but significant flaw" in white's plan.*

It was better to sacrifice the knight on e4, for instance: *41.♘e4! fxe4 (forced) 42.♕g8+ ♕g7 43.f5+!, and black has no defense against multiple threats (43...♔f6 44.♕e8! exd3 45.cxd3 h5 46.♕e7+ etc.).*

41...fxg4 42.♕g8+ ♕g7? Black didn't appreciate all the subtleties of the position. He could have saved the game with 42...♔h5!!, for instance:

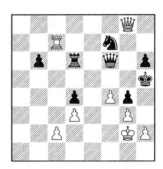

43.♕xf7+ ♕xf7 44.♖xf7 ♖c6, and black regains the pawn, while if 43.♖xf7, then 43...♕e6 44.♔f1 ♕d5 with unpleasant threats for white.

After 44...♕d5?, white is actually better: 45.♕e8! ♕h1+ 46.♔e2 ♕xh2+ 47.♔d1 ♕g1+ 48.♔d2 ♕f2+ 49.♔c1 ♕e3+ (forced) 50.♕xe3 dxe3 51.♖e7. The right way is 44...♖d7! 45.♖f8 ♕xg8 46.♖xg8 ♖c7, and black should hold.

Unfortunately, 43.h3!? doesn't work due to 43...gxh3+ 44.♔xh3 ♘g5+! 45.fxg5 ♕f1+, with perpetual check.

43.f5+! ♔f6.

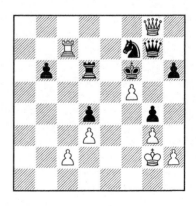

44.♕e8! The finishing move of the combination. Black has no defense against the threat ♕e7+.

44...h5 45.♕e7+ ♔xf5 46.♕xd6 ♘xd6 47.♖xg7 ♔f6 48.♖h7 ♘f5 49.♖c7. Black resigned.

"Archil, take the rook!"

Lisitsin: "The ending of the interesting game Ebralidze – Ragozin featured an episode that's unlikely to ever be repeated."

No. 100
Ebralidze – Ragozin
Tbilisi 1937, round 2
Annotated by M. Yudovich

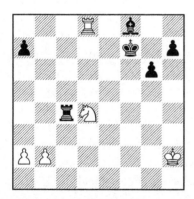

39.b3. Since the move 39... ♖c7? is impossible (for some reason, it's recommended in the tournament book) due to 40.♖xf8+ ♔xf8 41.♘e6+, Ragozin should have played 39...♖b4, but in time trouble, he decided to go for a "combination".

39...♗e7 40.♖d7 ♖c7??

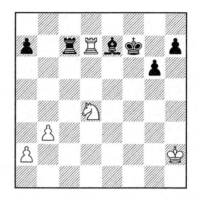

At this moment, I looked at Ragozin carefully. We sat opposite him. Slava was imperturbable, even though he immediately saw that he had blundered a rook – the e7 bishop is pinned! Ebralidze was in deep thought – he had about half an hour on the clock. Time control was 3 hours for 48 moves.

"Ragozin was so calm and self-assured that Ebralidze flinched internally and probably didn't believe his own eyes." (Belavenets.) Cartoon by A. Petrakovsky (tournament bulletin, No. 9, 1937).

The spectators in the hall were startled, the noise gradually grew, there were even some shouts in Georgian. Chief arbiter N. Zubarev called to order, Ebralidze even rose his arm, asking everyone to calm down...

I must admit that at this moment, I made a seemingly surefire bet with Belavenets. I said that Ebralidze will capture the rook, while Belavenets, ever the wise psychologist, thought that the move 41.♖xc7 wouldn't take place.

The noise in the hall didn't subside. Ebralidze thought for about ten minutes, and during this whole torture, Ragozin sat completely calmly, "thinking" about the position intently.

And then, the impossible happened: Ebralidze played 41.♖d5?? A storm erupted in the hall. A famous Georgian writer who was sitting beside us couldn't stand it anymore: he jumped up and loudly, in violation of all tournament rules, asked Ebralidze: "Archil, why didn't you take the rook?"

"Why did you think Ebralidze wouldn't take the rook?" I asked Belavenets. Here's what he answered:

"It's all simple. Ragozin was so calm and self-assured that Ebralidze flinched internally and probably didn't believe his own eyes. I saw in his face that he was worried by this rook move, and so he's wasn't going to take the rook."

Yes, a miracle happened... Only after putting the rook on d5 did Ebralidze snap out of his trance and realize what had just happened. He was stunned.

41...♗f6 42.♘b5 ♖c2+ 43.♔g3 a6 44.♖d7+ ♔e8 45.♖c7 (and now it's white who loses the rook on that fatal square) **45...♗e5+.** White resigned.

Late at night, at the dinner, I asked Ragozin why he put the rook on c7.

"Anything can happen in time trouble," Slava answered. "I saw that I couldn't play ♖c5, but I still wanted to activate the rook. I made the move and immediately noticed that I had blundered. But I managed to get a hold on myself. And then I felt Ebralidze looking at me intently. I kept my cool and looked down at the score sheet, checking how many moves were left until time control. It's psychology. And my self-assured look worked..."

Running into a Brick Wall

Soviet Championship Match: Moscow – Leningrad, 5th October – 11th November 1937

*"The grandmaster was met with applause.
A small club hall was adorned with multicolored flags."*
Ilf and Petrov. *The Twelve Chairs*

Chess history is rife with coincidences. The Soviet Championship match Botvinnik – Levenfish started on the same day – 5th October – as the Alekhine – Euwe world championship return match. Moreover, the turning point of both matches happened in game 6, again played on the same day (16th October). After winning three games in a row, Botvinnik (in Moscow) and Alekhine (in Leiden) took the lead 4-2 with two draws... Unbelievable!

Another analogy comes to mind as well. At the world championship in Baguio (1978), Karpov faced Korchnoi, who, like Levenfish long ago, was two decades older than his opponent. And what happened next? In a desperate situation, both veterans managed to win three games out of four at the finish and equalize the score, 5-5...

But enough of the coincidences, they are beside the point. The Botvinnik – Levenfish match has a special place in the modern history of chess. The winner of Nottingham, the universally-recognized candidate for the world championship, suffered a fiasco in a match against a master who wasn't formally a member of the world elite. That was a shock! The opinion of "wide circles of the chess public" was expressed by Eugene Znosko-Borovsky in the Riga-based Russian-language newspaper *Segodnya*: "It's not even because Botvinnik failed to win the match: the fact that he lost 5 games out of 13 is worse, and even worse is the fact that he sometimes played quite badly, making mistakes and outright blunders which we thought he was incapable of."

However, the match result didn't cause the same stir inside the USSR. Everyone knew Levenfish's playing strength and fighting spirit. Peter Romanovsky warned: "Those who think that the result of this match can be easily predicted are making a big mistake. There'll be a fierce struggle. If it ends in someone's favor score-wise, the winner's advantage won't be that big." So Botvinnik was considered the hands-down favorite only in the West...

Some might be surprised by the bloodshed in the match: only three draws out of 13 games! But it was a common occurrence back then. Alekhine's first match with Bogoljubov and both his matches against Euwe were incredible slugfests, with fans getting all worked up. The modern world championships, with their draws galore, can't be compared with them... But maybe not everything is lost yet? And perhaps sometime in the future we'll get to experience an incredible month, full of delight and despair, like the one Botvinnik and Levenfish gifted to chess fans in 1937?!

Reading Coffee Grounds

Lasker: "Soviet chess players are riveted watching Botvinnik and Levenfish. They are fighting for the Soviet Union championship, which Levenfish won at the last tournament. Levenfish played the whole tournament in brilliant style, but Botvinnik did not take part in it. This win is a great achievement by Levenfish.

It's not necessary to mention Botvinnik's achievements: they speak for themselves. In Moscow and Nottingham, the best of the best chess masters were playing, and nobody could demonstrate superiority over him.

The match between Botvinnik and Levenfish will be extremely interesting. Levenfish plays very strongly and uses every opportunity provided to him.

Leningrad, 30th October 1937. I managed to find this unique photo in the archive of 64. Based on the position on the demonstration boards, it's easy to determine that this is game 11, and Levenfish is thinking over his 29th move, ♗b1. The banner says: "Long live the best friend of physical education practitioners Comrade Stalin!"

In Tbilisi, he lost only three games out of 19, one of them in the last round, having already won first prize. Defeating such a master is a difficult task for any chess player, regardless of who he is. This task would have been easier if he didn't have to watch the safety of his own position. But in this case, Levenfish will surely launch an attack.

Botvinnik is even more dangerous in attack than Levenfish. We should not forget the fact that Botvinnik is a world championship candidate. If it turns out during the game that the position of both players is equally impregnable, which can be expected, then Botvinnik is less likely than Levenfish to try and attack the opponent's fortress, because in chess, like in war, it's always easier to defend than attack with equal forces. The decision to attack a solid position is usually too risky. Chess players of all the world will be watching to see how Botvinnik tries to solve this task." (*64*, 5th October 1937.)

Ilyin-Zhenevsky: "Even though recent years showed a certain convergence between the chess outlook of Botvinnik and Levenfish, we can still see differences in their methods of position evaluation and creative tendencies, characteristic of their strategic plans.

> **Levenfish:** "Two years ago, Botvinnik and I were chess antipodes. But in recent years, our styles have changed somewhat. Botvinnik's playing style changed towards strengthening tactics, while I improved on my strategy. Nevertheless, I interpret the position very differently from my opponent.
>
> I intend to spend at least two months on preparation. This is necessary, because everyone knows that the opening repertoire is very important if you're going to compete with Botvinnik." (*64*, 24th May 1937.)

Botvinnik represents strict rational playing methods. Any thought expressed by him at the board is based on a deep, clear, mindful internal foundation. The amount of risk in Botvinnik's games is minimal.

Levenfish's interpretation of the struggle is sharper and more temperamental. He sometimes consciously avoids natural, logical continuations, especially in positions that are not to his personal taste. Levenfish is able to create sudden complications, to choose a line that can't be completely calculated over the board.

The technical level of both is very high. If they have a clear target to attack, they usually execute the attack with near perfection. The deep calculation technique of both is well-honed." (*Shakhmaty v SSSR*, June 1937.)

Bogatyrchuk: "Sensation seekers will surely be disappointed at this very interesting competition. There will be no stunning sensations, the struggle will be based on subtleties, imperceptible nuances, the exploitation of minimal advantages. The strongest player will win, without a doubt.

The job of an analyst who tries to make some kind of prognosis based on individual games played by the opponents is very difficult. The only thing that's possible for us is to characterize the creative traits of both masters and reach some subjective, personal conclusions based on these characteristics.

The strength of an outstanding player is defined by three main factors: 1) intuition; 2) deep calculation; and 3) the ability to switch to defense at the right time. A fourth factor, which some consider the most important one, is knowledge, especially in the

Друж. шарж
Ю. Ю.

Опытнейший мастер Ф. П. Богатырчук

"The struggle will be very intense" – this was the diagnosis of the "experienced master F. P. Bogatyrchuk" (he was a medical doctor). "No matter who wins, we will bear witness to a whole lot of beautiful chess symphonies." Cartoon by Y. Yuzepchuk (Shakhmaty v SSSR, No. 4, 1938).

area of opening theory, but it will not play a major role, since both opponents are among the best theoreticians of the Soviet Union.

The most shaky concept in chess is intuition. Maybe we're just unable to put a finger on what we call "intuition"; we can't find a solid scientific foundation for it, based on experience, positional understanding, deep calculation, etc. A chess position can sometimes be so complicated that it's impossible to precisely calculate all the branching lines after a decisive move; here, intuition comes to the rescue, which, in addition to the aforementioned factors, also requires courage and self-confidence.

M. M. Botvinnik is an unsurpassed master of intuitive positional decisions. Let's take the move 16...d5! from his famous game with Rauzer at the 1933 All-Union Premiership *(see game 61)*. Tarrasch and Becker note: "A bold, very precisely and deeply calculated sacrifice." We think that this statement is wrong. In making his move, Botvinnik, without a doubt, mostly acted out of general positional considerations, his intuition, but surely not calculation. It's enough to look at the incredibly complicated, incalculable lines after the next 4–5 moves to ascertain that it was plain impossible to make this move solely based on calculations. Looking through Botvinnik's games, we often see such creative impulses that cannot be explained by deep calculation alone...

However, in addition to intuition, Botvinnik is capable of deep and very precise calculation... It's enough to look at the game with Riumin from the 2nd Moscow International Tournament to see how great Botvinnik's calculation skills are.

A year earlier, in the article "Botvinnik's Creative Works" (*Shakhist*, 5th October 1936), Bogatyrchuk defined his style with a sniper's precision:

"Botvinnik's style is, above all, a solid one, devoid of recklessness and based on a deep understanding of positional subtleties. It's interesting to point out that Botvinnik usually goes for risky-looking continuations only after some deep think, making one nonchalant move after another to buy time and then deliver a crushing blow... Botvinnik's style involves bold, precise and deep calculation, based on calm confidence. If we add deep opening knowledge to that, it would be completely right to consider him one of the world's best chess players."

The third component of success – the ability to switch to defense at the right time – is still a relative weakness in his play. We know only two games that Botvinnik managed to save with tenacious defense in a hopeless position: against Goldberg in one of the Leningrad championships and against Lisitsin at the 2nd Moscow International Tournament. In many games, he was unable to process the changed situation and lost because of that. The game against yours truly from the same tournament is indicative in this regard... We should not doubt that we shall soon see Botvinnik's masterful defenses as well, because his remarkable talent progresses with every year.

G. Y. Levenfish, the best representative of the older generation, adheres to the view that there's only one correct way in every position – and he's always searching for this way in every situation, persistently and inquisitively.

Levenfish avoids situations that are impossible to calculate; we won't find any incredible, incomprehensible complications in his games, but there are a lot of truly stunning calculations. In the openings, Levenfish usually avoids pawn breaks, preferring piece maneuvers...

But, on the other hand, Levenfish is so strong in those combinations that can be calculated! Let's recall his exceptional mastery in creating the winning combination against Kan (9th All-Union Premiership – *see game 72)*...

Levenfish is also exceptionally strong in situations when he's forced to suddenly switch from attack to defense. Everyone, including Botvinnik, has something to learn from him in the art of defense – and I'm sure that Botvinnik will learn from him in the upcoming match.

All in all, the most dangerous positions for Botvinnik are those that require a quick switch from attack to defense, and for Levenfish – those where he needs to make an intuitive decision; in all other regards, their chances are approximately equal. The struggle will be very intense. No matter who wins, we will bear witness to a whole lot of beautiful chess symphonies." (*Shakhmaty v SSSR*, September 1937.)

An Ode to Koktebel

Do you remember that, after the 1933 championship, where Levenfish played after an eight-year hiatus, he lamented: "Unfortunately, I couldn't rest before the tournament, and so I felt very tired after 10 rounds"? I quipped then, "indeed, the 44 year-old Levenfish would surely have benefited from a month in Teberda." (As you remember, Botvinnik spent a vacation there before that tournament.)

Чемпион СССР Г. Я. Левенфиш и м. С. В. Белавенец на пляже в Коктебеле.

"Soviet Champion Grigory Levenfish and master Sergei Belavenets at Koktebel beach." (64, 30th September 1937).

This time, the opponents seemingly switched roles. After Nottingham, Botvinnik quit chess for a year, fully dedicating himself to academic work, while Levenfish worked intensively on both his opening preparation and physical shape...

Botvinnik: "I missed the 1937 Soviet Championship in Tbilisi because I was defending my candidate's thesis. Ilyin-Zhenevsky criticized me harshly for that, and Krylenko even sent a threatening telegram ("I'll discuss your behavior with the Central Committee")... Then, Krylenko cooled down. Beforehand, he would say, "No matches!" but in summer 1937 he declared that I would play a match against the national champion. We needed to determine the strongest Soviet chess player! Levenfish was in his late forties. Together with Romanovsky, he was the strongest representative of the pre-revolutionary generation of masters. His technique was outstanding, and he had a strong sporting character, so his chess career was longer than Romanovsky's.

We played until six wins; in case of a 5-5 tie, the match was to be drawn, and the champion retained his title. I didn't play particularly well: deep inside, I underestimated my opponent, but the main reason, of course, was that I had devoted all my time to research for the thesis." (From the book *Achieving the Aim.*)

Levenfish: "The Zenit sports society gave me a lot of help. I was able to rest and prepare for two months, and even had a coach for a month. For training, I invited the young talented master Serezha Belavenets, whose style was somewhat similar to Botvinnik's. The Leningrad Writers' Union kindly provided two package trips to their holiday center in Koktebel, and soon we headed off to Crimea.

The wonderful Koktebel beach consisted of fine, pretty shingle of bizarre shapes, polished by the sea. There were even some agates and cornelians there. Tourists avidly collected them. This "stone fever" is at first quite acute, but it slowly subsides towards the end of the trip. Suitcases can't hold the heavy load, so you reluctantly have to choose only the best specimens.

This picturesque corner of Crimea was once "discovered" by the poet Maximilian Voloshin. The museum in his house is still intact. Koktebel is the best place for swimming and bathing on the entire Crimean coast. The holiday center was in decent shape, and the writers' company was interesting and funny: Zoshchenko, Lavrenev, Marvich, Chukovsky-junior, Rakhmanov and others. Belavenets soon won the hearts of everyone.

During the day, we would go to the beach and work on analysis, and then swim during breaks.

Of course, in such an environment, analysis couldn't just be "dry" and boring.

My main goal was to find a defense for black against the Queen's Gambit – Botvinnik's main weapon. Of course, it was hard to patch all the numerous holes in my play in a month, but our collaboration was beneficial both for me and my coach...

> The excessive self-criticism can be explained by the deference Grigory Yakovlevich felt towards his opponent. In his memoirs, **Levenfish** is restrained in his evaluation of Botvinnik, but here's what he wrote in *64* a year before the match (5th November 1936):
>
> "The games of the young Botvinnik are already striking, his technique is unprecedented among our players... Botvinnik is becoming one of the best chess theoreticians in the world. He already puts up a fight in the opening, and, upon winning that fight, merely has to finish his opponent off... Botvinnik's style is having a huge influence on the young generation of masters... Botvinnik's influence has affected the play of older masters as well. To stand their ground against younger players, they have had to re-evaluate their views: to deepen their opening knowledge and improve their playing technique, especially in the endgame... **The Soviet chess style, surprising all foreign masters facing it for the first time, has developed under Botvinnik's influence. This is a combination of a scientific approach to openings, aggressive pressure at the very start of a complicated and idea-rich middlegame, and subtle endgame technique.**" *(Highlighted by the author.)*

From Koktebel, I went directly to Moscow to play the match. In the train, an unfortunate accident happened – I lost my wallet with money and my passport. I borrowed some money from the writers who traveled on the same train. The loss of my passport was bigger trouble – I had to register in the hotel. Thankfully, newspapers had already printed some reports on the start of the match, so the police chief greeted me very courteously, called the hotel and gave me a new passport in two days." (From the book *Selected Games and Memories*.)

13 Rounds that Stunned the World

From the press: "Long before 6:30 p.m., the entrance of the Polytechnic Museum is besieged by an organized army of chess enthusiasts. Oh, if not for that horrible poster, "All tickets sold out"! The lucky ones (or, more precisely, the chess players with deep positional calculation skills) who managed to buy the match tickets beforehand proudly walk up the wide staircase leading to the Grand Auditorium. Each spectator enters with the feeling as though they should sit at the board themselves. The seats are arranged in the amphitheater, so the stage and the small chess board are visible from anywhere. The big demonstration boards are well-placed. The stage looks very peaceful – beautiful draping flowers. But soon it shall become the arena of fierce chess battles, with fifteen hundred eyes watching intently, holding their breath.

All the rows and aisles are filled. Exactly on the dot of 6:30 p.m., the Soviet champion G. Y. Levenfish, the decorated grandmaster M. M. Botvinnik and the match chief arbiter N. V. Krylenko appear on stage. The hall applauds them. When the silence returns, Krylenko gives a short introductory speech about the importance of the match and the lessons that should be learned from it. After he notes that Botvinnik has demonstrated his strength to the best representatives of the bourgeois chess art not in words only, but in actual

С особым удовольствием буду играть именно с Г. Я. Левенфишем, так как это разносторонний и глубокий шахматист.

Из матча с таким противником можно извлечь хорошие уроки.

Борьба с одним из пяти сильнейших шахматистов мира, каковым несомненно является Ботвинник, настолько для меня интересна, что даже спортивный результат не заслоняет ее глубокого шахматного содержания.

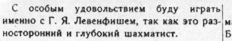

"I am especially pleased to play against Grigory Yakovlevich Levenfish, because he's a versatile and deep chess player.
You can learn many lessons by playing a match with such an opponent." (Mikhail Botvinnik)
"The struggle against one of the five strongest players in the world, which Botvinnik undoubtedly is, is so very interesting to me that even the sporting result is not as important as the deep chess content." (Grigory Levenfish) (64, 5th October 1937.)

deeds, too, the spectators applaud the Soviet grandmaster. Botvinnik and Levenfish sit down at the board to battle it out over 64 squares and determine who is the strongest player of the Soviet country.

Krylenko starts Levenfish's clock. The Soviet champion makes the first move of the first game, 1.c2-c4. After a short think, Botvinnik replies with 1...♘g8-f6.

The struggle for the Soviet Championship begins." (*64*, 10th October 1937.)

Levenfish: "The sporting struggle in the match was very sharp. In the first game, I played quite sluggishly in the opening and middlegame. Botvinnik maneuvered greatly, got an advantage and won *(see game 101)*. I decided to add more tactical pepper to the next game. This game was one of the best in the whole match *(game 102)*. I played an interesting combination with a piece sacrifice and won. The influence of this game was felt for the entire match. In the third game, my opponent's maneuvers on the kingside were too methodical, and he couldn't react to the events on the other side of the board. Botvinnik's desperate counterattack was unsuccessful *(game 103)*. In the fourth game, I used the defense that I developed together with Belavenets. The game ended in a draw after 21 moves. The next game was also drawn.

The sixth game was the turning point of the match *(game 104)*. I played the opening inaccurately and got behind in development. Botvinnik could have gained some decent queenside pressure, but chose a direct attack on the king instead, which was uncharacteristic of his style. The attack was repelled, and white got a weak isolated d4 pawn, which he soon lost. I could have transitioned into a technically simple rook endgame. However, I spent a lot of time on difficult defense and got into severe time trouble. After some weak moves, the game was adjourned in a drawn position. The thought that I had missed a win and that my opponent's third loss could have been decisive unsettled me. Even though I could have still kept my lead with a draw, I was already upset. After a sleepless night, I tried to complicate things without any justification in the final session, got into time trouble and lost that ill-fated game...

I lost the seventh game as well. And the eighth game was even worse. Botvinnik maneuvered poorly in the opening, and after move 20, black got an overwhelming position, which he could have won in various way. Again, a series of weak moves followed, white seized the advantage, and I lost the third game in a row after the adjournment *(game 105)*.

Averbakh: "I remember that in 1937, when Botvinnik played Levenfish for the Soviet Championship, the Moscow boys supported the latter. Maybe because Botvinnik was considered the favorite.

By the way, that was my first time in the National Hotel. Here's how it happened. A group of chess-playing boys were walking down Gorky Street (it now has its old name restored, Tverskaya Street). And then Boris Waxberg came up with:

"Guys! Levenfish is staying in the National! How about we go to him and show our analysis in the Sicilian?"

I have to provide some explanation: back then, Moscow players had thoroughly analyzed a line which later became known as the Moscow Variation: 1.e4 c5 2.♘f3 d6 3.d4 cxd4 4.♘xd4 ♘f6 5.f3 e5 6.♗b5+.

And we acted on that proposal! After some effort, we managed to get past the mustachioed, striped guards at the hotel entrance and took the elevator. Waxberg timidly knocked on Levenfish's door. Rokhlin opened it.

"We need to see Grigory Yakovlevich!" Waxberg bravely said, and we hesitantly followed him into the room.

We were totally bewildered by what we saw. On the couch, hunched over the chess board, sat Levenfish and... Botvinnik! We said our greetings, then there was a pause. Waxberg got a grip on his senses first.

"Grigory Yakovlevich!" he said to Levenfish. "We want to invite you to the Young Pioneers' Stadium! And you too, Mikhail Moiseevich!" he added. And we departed proudly..." (From the book *Centre-Stage and Behind the Scenes*, in the introduction to the 2nd game. This quote is not included in the abridged version published in English, which doesn't include any of the 64 games published in the Russian version.)

The 4-2 score looked disappointing. However, in a match, the score is not as important as feeling good. The games showed me that I could successfully compete with Botvinnik if I managed to shake off the psychological shock caused by my bad performance. The break after the match was moved to Leningrad helped me immensely.

I started the ninth game in a combative mood. I chose the sharp Nimzowitsch System against the French, with a pawn sacrifice. Botvinnik didn't expect this system, however, his opening play was still masterful. Black kept his king in the center and seized the key squares. The critical moment came on move 25. White offered two minor pieces for a rook. Botvinnik needlessly declined to go for complicated but advantageous combinations, and the game ended in a draw.

I met master Alatortsev in the Leningrad chess club. Among other things, we discussed the eighth game, and Alatortsev pointed out the move 8...c5 to me. I analyzed the move at home, found it acceptable, and used in game 10. The element of surprise worked: Botvinnik's reply condemned him to difficult defense, and he ultimately lost.

"Levenfish played very solidly and deservedly defended his Soviet champion's title. He should certainly be considered one of the 10 strongest players in the world." (Fine). Cartoon by N. Radlov (1935). Charcoal, watercolors. From A. Kentler's archive. Published for the first time.

Oddy enough, on the postcard, published in 15,000 copies, the artist missed a letter in Botvinnik's surname! From the author's archive.

In game 11, Botvinnik chose a sharp line in the Grunfeld Defense. To avoid his possible home preparation, I traded queens early. Losing two tempi on this operation, I barely managed to equalize. The last move before time control was a mistake, black overlooked a simple combination and lost a pawn. Soon the game transitioned into a rook + 2 pawns vs. rook + pawn ending. The limited material created a lot of technical difficulties, but this time, I didn't lose my chances and won after 78 moves.

In game 12, I chose a difficult defense and made a serious inaccuracy on move 6, which Botvinnik exploited masterfully. He got two active bishops and kingside pressure. White played very strongly in the middlegame and the finishing attack. This game was Botvinnik's best achievement in the match *(game 106)*.

In game 13, Botvinnik chose the Grunfeld again. I found an improvement in the opening line, but Botvinnik was prepared and sacrificed a pawn. I accepted the sacrifice, repelled black's attempts to regain the pawn and weakened the pawn cover of black's castled position. The critical moment came on move 30, after the exchange sacrifice that forced black to choose the lesser evil. Accepting the sacrifice gave white strong pawns and an attack. Botvinnik declined it, which created a strong passed pawn for me and then a hopeless endgame for black. The game was adjourned, but Botvinnik resigned without resuming it *(game 107)*. The match ended in a draw, +5–5=3, and I managed to retain my champion's title.

The match attracted much interest both in the USSR and abroad. Many games were highly praised in the foreign chess press. A games collection was published in Hungary, in the German language." (From the book *Selected Games and Memories*.)

Dust in the Eyes

The fact that Botvinnik didn't include a single game from this match in his 1949 games collection shows how deeply he was disappointed. But in his memoir, which was published after Levenfish's death and was first called *Only the Truth*, he took his revenge for this humiliation... I remember that many were perplexed as to why Botvinnik included a rather gross episode from his childhood in the book: how he "got a bellyache" on the street and how, after running to the toilet, he "prematurely decided that his aim was achieved". But I think that this was a genius psychological move! What should the reader think? If the author openly talks about such things, then he would write only the truth about other events as well – even the most unsightly ones...

Botvinnik: "Before moving to Leningrad, I led, but then Caissa, the goddess of chess, turned her back on me – she probably thought that I shouldn't have taken a break from chess. Still, before game 13, the score was 5-4, and the champion was behind. However, the game was adjourned in a lost position for me. I was so unhappy with my play in the match that I didn't even analyze the game. I called the arbiter N. D. Grigoriev in the morning and said that I was resigning, and that the match was over.

"Don't hurry," Nikolai Dmitrievich said. "You should go and play. I spent the whole night at the board and found a unique endgame – pawn versus queen. Although Levenfish does have a single line that leads to a win, it's impossible to find over the board. I'll dictate the analysis to you..."

"I'm sorry, but you're the arbiter, and the tournament regulations clearly state that the players should not consult anybody..."

"That's why I deem it necessary to help you," Grigoriev said. "I know that your opponent has been using help from a group of masters since the beginning of the match, while you are alone..."

Nikolai Dmitrievich was right. I didn't even discuss the matter with Slava Ragozin *(who was Botvinnik's friend and sparring partner)*. Before the match, I warned Grigoriev that this clause would harm the more scrupulous player.

"Thank you, but I played badly – why should I be so small-minded? There are many more competitions ahead... I resign."

"I didn't expect any other answer!"

"Andy," as Grigoriev was known to his friends, probably wanted to show me his attitude towards the regulation violators...

Grigoriev didn't just dislike the result of the match because my opponent was helped by a whole brigade. The Soviet chess players needed a leader, someone in whom to place their world championship hopes. And then, a new champion emerged – Levenfish. The situation became complicated, and the match result only worsened the situation. However, the question of whether Botvinnik was able to represent Soviet chess on the world stage was not a hypothetical one. It was a troubled time at the chess Olympus...

A tournament in the Netherlands was scheduled for autumn 1938: a double round-robin for the eight strongest players of the world; the selection was very strict – not even Lasker, after his failures in Moscow and Nottingham in 1936, was invited. Levenfish insisted that he should have gone to represent the Soviet Union, but his request was denied, and I was tasked with playing at the AVRO tournament, featuring the world champion Alekhine, Capablanca, Euwe, Keres, Reshevsky, Fine and Flohr." (From the book *Achieving the Aim*.)

Achieving the Aim

Sosonko: "In 1937, Levenfish again wins the national championship. And Botvinnik again didn't play in it. He challenges Levenfish to a match. The match ends in a draw, and Grigory Yakovlevich retains the Soviet champion's title. It's his greatest triumph, and he dreams of playing at an international tournament. Botvinnik had already played abroad twice – in Hastings and Nottingham – and even Ragozin, whose successes were pale in comparison with Levenfish's, was allowed to play in Semmering.

But sporting success was not the decisive factor for selecting the Soviet player for the AVRO tournament. Botvinnik's personal contacts, friendships in the highest circles, his youth and political loyalty, finally, the "Soviet chess needs only one leader" mindset definitely tipped the balance in his favor. Later, Botvinnik would say very clear, but harsh words: "I was lucky in my life. As a rule, my personal interests aligned with the public interest – this is probably the true definition of happiness. And I wasn't alone – I had support in my struggle for the public interest. But not everyone I met was as lucky as me. Personal interests of some people did not align with the public interest, and these people interfered with my work. And then conflicts arose."

> **Smyslov:** "I still remember the games of the Levenfish – Botvinnik match well. Grigory Yakovlevich was in brilliant form, he played very well – he didn't lose the match and kept his champion's title. As we know, that championship was "recommended input" for the AVRO tournament. But Mikhail Moiseevich ultimately went there, and Grigory Yakovlevich didn't have such influential contacts, that's what decided matters. Also, Botvinnik was a very upright young man, while Levenfish was already in his late forties;

yes, Mikhail Moiseevich played brilliantly back then, but I'm talking from the point of view of legitimacy..."

Bronstein: "I remember Grigory Yakovlevich telling me that Capablanca sent him a personal letter of invitation to the AVRO tournament, but Botvinnik interfered; he was like a hammer-wielding warrior, standing in a circle and waving his hammer above his head, repelling everyone. And he did."

Sergei Prokofiev, an avid chess fan, was not always just a passive observer. He occasionally wrote articles on chess. His article about the AVRO tournament for TASS never saw the light of day, but here's an excerpt: 'We can say many things about other participants, but I would like to mention a Soviet player who, despite not playing in Amsterdam, would have caused much destruction there. I'm talking about Levenfish, who showed exceptional fighting qualities in his drawn match against Botvinnik.'" (From the book *My Testimony*, including the quotes by Smyslov and Bronstein.)

Levenfish: "I thought that my victories in the 9th and 10th Soviet Championships and a draw in the match against Botvinnik, gave me the right to play in the AVRO tournament. However, despite my expectations, I was not sent to it.

My mental state could have been described as suffering a psychological knockout. All efforts of recent years had been wasted. I was confident in my abilities and, without a doubt, I would have fought honorably at the tournament. But I had turned 49, and it was obvious that the following years would affect my playing strength adversely, and I had lost the last opportunity to prove myself. I called an end to my chess career, and, even though I did play in some tournaments afterwards, I only rarely played with real inspiration and sporting interest." (From the book *Selected Games and Memories*.)

Are the Soviet Chess Players Really that Strong?

The reason for this unexpected question in the title of an article by well-known Russian-French master and journalist Eugene Znosko-Borovsky was, as strange as it may sound, the Botvinnik – Levenfish match. And the subtitle "Levenfish's Triumph and Botvinnik's Downfall" reflected the impression the match left in the West.

Znosko-Borovsky: "The chess world got an incredible surprise. Botvinnik, who was considered the most worthy and rightful candidate for the world championship, was everyone's favorite in the recently-ended match with Levenfish, and his victory seemed a foregone conclusion – it was thought that he would win easily. But what then happened? The match was drawn, which essentially means full defeat for the "decorated grandmaster", because his opponent gains everything: he retains the Soviet champion's title, which he had recently won and had to defend from his opponent, and is awarded the grandmaster title, which, until now, was Botvinnik's sole privilege in the USSR.

This status-quo was questioned even before the match.

Flohr: "While in Moscow, I read in newspapers that Levenfish would be awarded the grandmaster's title if he drew against Botvinnik. I think that his outstanding success in the

Master Eugene Znosko-Borovsky (1888–1954) was one of the best Russian chess writers of his time.

All-Union chess championship in Tbilisi is reason enough to award the title to him, because the line-up of the Tbilisi tournament was as strong as a big international event. I can't imagine that the list of the strongest chess players in the world can be complete without the Soviet champion's name. There are several grandmaster-strength players in the Soviet Union, with Levenfish and Ragozin first and foremost among them." (*64*, 5th June 1937.)

Later, Flohr would observe with pleasure, "The match proved my view was right. Even though it was drawn, it's obvious that Levenfish is the hero of the match."

To complete the picture, I'll quote the opinions of two more future AVRO tournament participants.

Reshevsky: "Levenfish played very well in his match against Botvinnik, and it's probably his greatest success. I think that Levenfish deserves the grandmaster's title."

Fine: "Levenfish played very solidly and deservedly defended his Soviet champion's title. He should certainly be considered one of the 10 strongest players in the world."

I remember Levenfish well from before the war, when he, a twenty year-old student, turned up at the St. Petersburg Chess Assembly. He was just five years younger than me and three years older than Alekhine. So, I can't help but sincerely celebrate his latest success, I should be glad that his strength didn't decline – by contrast, he has become significantly stronger in the last few years, leading the young and ardent army of Soviet chess players. However, my feelings are mixed – they aren't all very rosy.

Commenting on the match result and congratulating Levenfish, one chess publication emphasizes the significance of his success by citing Botvinnik's well-known exceptional strength. Allow me to turn this statement on its head: it's Levenfish's strength which is well-known. And this overturns the whole perspective, the whole evaluation of the match.

Youth is a great time, but it's also dangerous. It often brings disappointment, because too many hopes are placed in it, too much is expected... To develop an outstanding player, it's not enough to have youthful fervor and fresh talent, you need many other things that only come with age: a huge work rate, monstrous self-control, strong nerves, good health and, what's most important, a rich reserve of chess ideas.

Botvinnik seemed like the strongest player of the whole young generation, because he had recorded no setbacks in his career – that's the sign of a true world champion. He only slipped up once, taking no prizes in Hastings two years ago, but that can be easily explained by his lack of experience of playing and living abroad. His complaints sounded a bit comical back then: the tournament committee "didn't rent a room" for him beforehand! However, his successes were brilliant: he won several Soviet Championships, drew a match with Flohr, finished among the leaders in many international tournaments...

And now, we see this brilliant player in a completely new, unflattering light. It's not even because Botvinnik failed to win the match: the fact that he lost 5 games out of 13 is worse, and even worse is the fact that he sometimes played quite badly, making mistakes and outright blunders which we thought he was incapable of. We've never known such a Botvinnik before, never knew that he existed, but this version of Botvinnik was brought forth by the ill-fated match.

However, who would have expected his opponent to play with such power that broke down all resistance and pushed him to make mistakes? There's no arguing, the facts speak for themselves *(he lists Levenfish's tournament results in the last quarter of a century)*. As we can see, these results don't really place him among the world's leading players. And could we have believed that he would suddenly improve so much at the age of 48 that he had become the equal of Botvinnik?

Had Levenfish only achieved success against Botvinnik, we could have said that the latter was just out of form. But the fact that he is the recognized champion of the USSR casts doubt on the true level of the Soviet masters, which had been praised a lot lately. The inconsistency of young Soviet masters is obvious and incredible: today's winner can be tomorrow's tail-ender. Here's Ragozin, a top-three player in the USSR, going to the Semmering tournament. He was greeted like a possible winner or at least a joint winner. But he finished next to last.

Will we excuse his failure, like Botvinnik's in Hastings, by the fact that he was not accustomed to life abroad? But then, by the same coin, shouldn't we excuse the foreign masters who perform below their strength in the USSR based on the fact that they weren't accustomed to life in the Soviet Union?

All our conjectures and assumptions are shaky because they are based on singular, random observations. If the young Russian players play in international tournaments too rarely, this might hinder their growth and ruin them. And nobody will be more disappointed than me if Russian chess fails to flourish as much as it initially seemed it would. At any rate, we should wait for the next big international tournament in Moscow, scheduled for early 1938: it should check Botvinnik's form, Levenfish's true strength, and put the whole Soviet chess art to the test." (*Segodnya*, Riga, 23rd November 1937.)

Alas, the Moscow International Tournament (there were rumors that the organizers planned to invite even Alekhine) didn't take place. And the AVRO tournament, held in the Netherlands in the autumn, only allowed Botvinnik's form to be "checked", as we know...

The Joust with Open Visors

Before you partake of the masterpieces and dramas of this incredible fight, I should warn you: the annotations you'll see were written during the match itself and immediately published in *64*. Of course, both opponents annotated the best games in their games collections afterwards, but, as often happens, tried to show themselves in a more positive light, hiding their own mistakes and highlighting their opponent's ones. I already pointed out that only the lines and ideas shown immediately after games are of historical value; later commentaries are only interesting from the analytical point of view – they are similar to Garry Kasparov's attempts to find some "absolute truth" in *My Great Predecessors*...

Botvinnik's poor form is evident in his annotations as well; some inaccuracies were deleted from *Botvinnik's Chess Games*, while others only from *Analytical and Critical Works*. The traces of analytical eraser are seen in Levenfish's collection, too, even though they weren't as obvious. I admit that to avoid cluttering the annotations, I have added all the small corrections to the main text. The comparative analysis was interesting from the

"A Grandmaster Draw". +5–5=3, in Levenfish's favor.
Cartoon by Y. Yuzepchuk, stylized as an antique woodcut (64, 20th November 1937).

psychological point of view as well. While Botvinnik, who was in a position of power, annotated his games in an increasingly bold and self-satisfied way, the notes of Levenfish, who was pushed to the periphery of chess and public life, became increasingly terse and dry.

Finally, let me re-introduce you to your guide in the turbulent flow of the match struggle: the pre-game texts were written by one of the Soviet chess luminaries, Peter Romanovsky.

To Battle!

Peter Romanovsky: An action-packed, sharp battle! For a whole month, thousands of chess hearts have been beating rapidly, awaiting the result of every game of this interesting, intense fight with trepidation. Botvinnik wins – some sigh with relief, others read or listen to the news with disappointment. Levenfish wins – the former are dejected, while the latter perk up.

There were neutral fans as well. When Botvinnik resigned in the rook ending of game 11, while masters were still discussing the possibility of a win while admitting it may end in a draw, some elderly chess player rapturously applauded the winner.

He applauded even as the club lights were turning off. "Surely a Levenfish fan", the annoyed supporters of the young grandmaster thought as they looked at him; but they were wrong. This old enthusiast had a neutral view, which he expressed loudly, saying without really addressing anybody in the emptying hall: "Everything is going just perfectly: the young have their opportunities, but respect to the elders[23]."

However, we think that, in the final stages of the match, especially after game 10, the number of Levenfish supporters grew considerably, and that was only natural.

After a dramatic episode in game 6 and two more wins in a row for Botvinnik, everything seemed perfectly clear, and Levenfish's situation looked precarious. His two wins in Leningrad again overturned the whole picture, again attracted maximum attention of thousands of fans. These victories, scored in an incredibly difficult moment, definitely affected a lot of neutral fans. Game 13, the last one, was also quite spectacular. It's beautiful in its subtle creative content and in the inspired way the Soviet champion played it.

The match has ended... Even if neither the Botvinnik fans (first and foremost) nor the supporters

of our second grandmaster are fully satisfied with the sporting result of this match, they are probably both very happy with its creative result.

Almost every game was full of fierce struggle, and in such cases, it usually takes interesting, creative forms.

Let's retrace the course of the match. The first game was a shining example of Botvinnik's deeply planned play; he punished Levenfish step-by-step for his somewhat sluggish approach. Levenfish was too cautious in this game, even timid.

No. 101. Queen's Indian Defense E17
Levenfish – Botvinnik
Moscow (m/1), 5th October 1937

1.c4 ♘f6 2.♘c3 e6 3.♘f3 b6 4.g3 ♗b7 5.♗g2 ♗e7 6.0-0 0-0 7.b3. "White, wishing to avoid a well-trodden path, chooses a sluggish move. His bishop will be passive on b2, and this also takes away the b3 square from the queen, which is useful in some lines. The simple 7.d4 is much better." (Belavenets and Yudovich).

7...d5 8.cxd5 (8.d4!?) **8...exd5 9.d4 ♘bd7 10.♗b2 ♖e8 11.♖c1.** For the world championship match against Bronstein (1951), Botvinnik prepared the novelty 11.♘e5!

11...c6! 12.♕d2. "12.♕c2 ♗d6 13.♖fe1 with the subsequent e2-e4 was more precise," Botvinnik wrote in *64*. This pawn move in the center is the only way for white to show more activity.

12...♘e4. The line 12...♗b4

13.♕d3 ♘e4 14.♘d2 is also possible. It was rejected by Botvinnik because of 14...f5? 15.♘dxe4 fxe4 16.♘xe4 dxe4 17.♕c4+, but the correct move is 14...♘xd2! 15.♕xd2 ♕e7 and ♘f6, with equality.

13.♕c2. "White can't play 13.♘xe4, because after 13...dxe4 14.♘e1 (14.♘e5?? ♘xe5) 14...♗g5 15.e3 ♗a6 he loses an exchange." (Botvinnik)

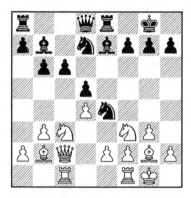

13...♘xc3! The complications after 13...f5 14.♘xe4 fxe4 15.♘e5 ♘xe5 16.dxe5 and f2-f4 were dangerous for black.

14.♗xc3 ♗d6. 14...♘f6 is probably more precise (Belavenets and Yudovich), provoking 15.♘e5 to then break with 15...♗d6, ♖c8 and c6-c5, while if 15.♖fe1, then 15...♖c8 16.♘d2 ♗f8, conserving an important tempo.

15.♖fe1 ♘f6 16.♘d2 (now 16.♘e5 ♖c8 is not good for white) **16...♗f8 17.♗b2.** After the hasty 17.e4 dxe4 18.♘xe4 ♘d5, it's not that simple to drive the knight away.

17...♖c8 18.♕d3. "Getting the queen away from the rook's aim. But this waste of time only allows black to improve his position. White should have played 18.e4 dxe4 19.♘xe4 ♘d5 20.♘c3 ♖xe1+ 21.♖xe1 ♘b4 22.♕d2 ♗a6 23.♖e3 with the subsequent a2-a3. At any rate, this was the only opportunity to gain chances of equality." (Belavenets and Yudovich). The fastidious Rybka mostly approves of this recommendation.

18...♖c7 19.♖cd1 g6. Seizing the f5 square and preparing to relocate the bishop on g7.

20.♘b1?! Inexplicably passive! 20.e4 was asking to be played, and after 20...dxe4 21.♘xe4 ♘d5 22.♘c3 ♖xe1+ 23.♖xe1 ♗c8 24.♘xd5 cxd5, the position is completely equal.

20...♗c8! "The bishop is transferred to f5, after which e2-e4 is impossible for white. If 21.♘c3 ♗f5 22.e4, then 22...dxe4 23.♘xe4 ♘xe4 24.♗xe4 ♖ce7 25.f3 ♕d5! 26.♗xd5 ♖xe1+!" (Belavenets and Yudovich)

21.♗a3 ♗f5 22.♕a6. There's no choice: 22.♕d2 lost a pawn (22...♗xb1 23.♗xf8 ♗xa2), while 22.♕f3 lost a full piece (22...♗xb1 23.♗xf8 ♗e4).

22...♗g7 23.♘c3 h5! 24.♗c1.

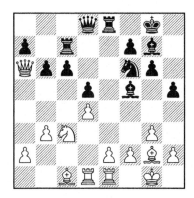

24...♞e4! 25.♘xe4. It was impossible to avoid the trade. After 25.♘a4, Botvinnik showed the line 25...b5 26.♘c5 ♞c3 27.♖d2 ♗xd4! 28.♖xd4 ♖xe2!, crushing. Of course, 26.f3!? bxa4 27.fxe4 ♗xe4 28.♕xa4 ♗xg2 29.♔xg2 is stronger, but... despite the equal material, white can't hold after 29...♖ce7 30.e3 ♕d7 – his pawns are too weak.

25...dxe4 26.h4. "If 26.h3, then 26...♖d7 27.♗e3 *(27.e3 c5!)* 27...♗xd4 28.♗xd4 ♖xd4 29.♖xd4 ♕xd4 30.♕xa7 e3! with a decisive attack." (Botvinnik)

26...♖d7 27.♗g5 ♗f6 28.♗xf6 ♕xf6.

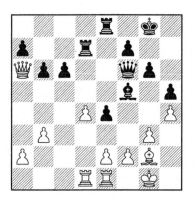

29.♕c4. "After 29.e3, there could follow 29...g5 with an attack or 29...♗g4 30.♖c1 c5 31.dxc5 ♖d2 32.♕f1 bxc5 33.♖xc5 ♕b2, threatening ♗e2." (Botvinnik)

The same line is shown in *Analytical and Critical Works*, even though after 31.♖xc5! white had an extra pawn and a won position. But there's a more important point. It turns out that 29...g5 gave nothing either: 30.hxg5 ♕xg5 31.♖c1! h4 32.♖xc6 hxg3 33.fxg3 ♕xg3 34.♕e2, protecting everything just in time. So white missed a real opportunity to save the game with 29.e3!

29...♖ed8 30.♖c1 ♖d6 31.♕c3. Now 31.e3 is too late: 31...g5! 32.hxg5 ♕xg5 33.♕e2 h4 34.♖c2 ♖g6 35.♕f1 ♖dd6!

31...♕xd4   32.♕xd4   ♖xd4 33.♖xc6 ♖d2.

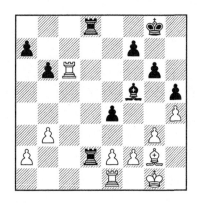

"The active position of his pieces and the weakness of white's queenside pawns gives black a decisive advantage." (Belavenets and Yudovich)

34.a4 ♖b2 35.♖c3. After 35.♖c4, there's 35...e3! 36.b4 (36.fxe3 ♗e6) 36...♗e6 37.♖f4 ♖dd2 or 37.♖c7 a6 38.♖a7 ♗c4.

35...♖d4 36.♖e3 ♖b4 37.♖c1 ♖2xb3 38.♖xb3 ♖xb3 39.♖c4 ♖b1+ 40.♔h2 ♖b2 41.♗f1. 41.♗xe4 ♖xe2 42.♗xf5 ♖xf2+ and ♖xf5 is bad, but 41.♔g1! ♖xe2 42.♔f1 ♖a2 43.♗xe4 prolonged the struggle.

41...♖a2. The sealed move, but white resigned without resuming the game.

"Levenfish played this game in an uncharacteristically timid style, which made black's task easier," Botvinnik wrote later. "Maybe this happened because he couldn't create complicated combinations, where he was especially strong. Neither was there a simple position with a white advantage where he could show his good technique. Complicated positional struggle wasn't really his strong point."

The Little Humpbacked Horse[24]

In the second game, Botvinnik created incredible complications with his bold opening knight jump to e5. In the grand fight that ensued, Levenfish showed his brilliant tactical abilities. The battle, filled with beautiful combinations, ended with an artistic demonstration of knight double attacks.

---

[24] A 19th century fairytale poem by Petr Pavlovich Yershov

No. 102. Grunfeld Defense D94
Botvinnik – Levenfish
Moscow (m/2), 7th October 1937
Annotated by G. Levenfish

1.d4 d5 2.c4 c6 3.♘c3 ♘f6. In the game Capablanca – Rabinovich (Moscow 1935), there followed 3... dxc4 4.e3 e5 5.dxe5 ♕xd1+ 6.♔xd1 ♗e6, with a better position for black.

And just a week later, in the sixth game of the return match, Alekhine stunned Euwe with the line 3...dxc4 4.e4! e5 5.♗xc4 exd4 6.♘f3!!?

4.e3 g6 5.♘f3 ♗g7 6.♗d3. 6.♕b3 is more fashionable (*this line was often played in the 10th Soviet Championship*).

6...0-0 7.0-0 e6. Perhaps it was better to delay this move for a bit and play 7...b6 (*see game 105*).

In game 4, black played 7...♘bd7. Botvinnik noted: "This move also allows white to keep his positional advantage."

8.b3! A strong move: white immediately exploits the weakening of the a3-f8 diagonal.

8...♘bd7 9.♕e2 ♖e8 (9...♕e7 is bad because of 10.a4 with the subsequent ♗a3) **10.♗b2.**

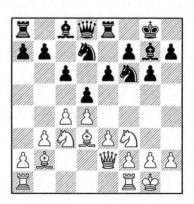

10...b6. Black could play 10...e5 11.dxe5 ♘xe5 12.♘xe5 ♖xe5, and white gains nothing with 13.♘xd5 due to 13...♘xd5 14.♗xe5 ♗xe5, but playing 13.cxd5 ♘xd5 14.♘e4 ♖e8 15.♗xg7 ♚xg7 16.♕b2+ f6 17.♖ad1 he retains a small advantage because of black's weakened kingside.

11.♖ad1 ♗b7

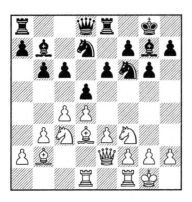

12.♘e5. A committal move, because the game becomes very sharp after that. However, white had no other active moves. He gained nothing after 12.e4 dxe4 13.♘xe4 ♘xe4 14.♗xe4 ♘f6 15.♗c2 ♕c7 with the subsequent c6-c5.

12...♘xe5 13.dxe5 ♘d7 14.f4 ♕e7. The only possible plan for black is to break white's center with f7-f6. This move can't be played immediately though: 14...f6 15.cxd5 exd5 (15...cxd5 16.exf6 ♘xf6 17.e4) 16.e6! ♖xe6 17.f5 gxf5 18.♗xf5 ♖e7 19.♕h5 ♘f8 20.♘e4 with a strong attack.

A purely positional interpretation is to prepare f7-f6 with 14...a6, intending, after 15.cxd5 exd5 16.e4

d4 17.♘b1 c5 18.♘d2 b5, to prevent ♘c4.

15.cxd5 exd5. The only right move: black will soon gain a protected passed d4 pawn as compensation for white's strong pawn center. 15...cxd5? 16.♘b5 is bad.

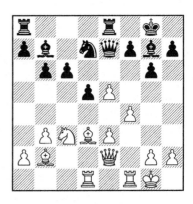

16.e4! White should hurry with this move, because after 16.♗c2 or any other preparatory move, black will play f7-f6.

16...d4 17.♘b1 c5 18.♘d2. The knight's tour to d6 looks tempting, but it costs three tempi, which allows black to prepare to undermine white's center. 18.♗c4 was worthy of consideration, for instance: 18...g5 19.e6 fxe6 20.f5 ♘e5 (20...♘f8 21.e5!) 21.♗xe6+ ♚h8 with mutual chances or 18...♚h8 19.♘d2 g5 20.♕h5 ♖f8 (if 20...gxf4, then 21.♗xf7 ♖f8 22.e6 ♘f6 23.♕f5) 21.♖f3.

After 21.♖f3, 21...gxf4 is good (so 21.♘f3 is probably better), and in the bracketed line, black has an unpleasant reply 23...♗c8.

18...g5! Of course, not 18...f6 due to 19.e6 with the subsequent f4-f5.

The correct move order is 19.♗c4+ ♚h8 20.e6, because after 19.e6, black can play 19...♕xe6! (20.♗c4 ♗d5).

After the game move, black intends to attack white's center and create some counterplay along the g-file, because the opening of this file is forced.

19.g3 gxf4 20.gxf4 ♚h8 21.♘c4 ♖g8. After 21...f6 22.♘d6 fxe5, the simplest for white is 23.♘xe8 ♖xe8 24.f5; he shouldn't take the bishop, because the knight gets stuck on b7.

22.♚h1 f6 23.♘d6.

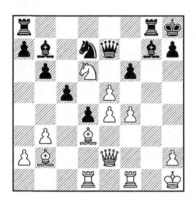

23...fxe5! This piece sacrifice is planned, but in any event necessary. 23...♗c6? is bad because of 24.♗c4.

24.♘xb7 exf4! This is much stronger than trying to regain the piece with 24...♖gb8 (after 25.♗c4 ♖xb7 26.♗d5 ♖ab8 27.♗xb7 ♖xb7, black has lost an exchange, and white seizes the initiative). The b7 knight is out of play, and in this sharp position, each tempo is important.

25.e5! The best move! White gives up a pawn to prevent ♘e5 and open the diagonal for his bishop.

25.♖xf4 was bad due to 25...♘e5, and if white wants to keep the piece, he should play 26.♗a6, after which black's attack has good chances of succeeding, because all three white minor pieces are far from the battlefield.

In his game collection, Levenfish shows 26...♗h6 27.♖f5 ♘g4 "with strong threats."

However, after 28.♖f3 Fritz is quite aggressive. It additionally even suggests an adventurous plan to extricate the knight: 28.e5!? ♘e3 29.♘d6 ♖af8 (29...♘xf5 30.♘xf5 is better for white, while he is also threatening 30.♘f7+) 30.♖xf8 ♖xf8 31.♗c1! ♕xe5 32.♗xe3 ♗xe3 33.♘c4.

25...♗xe5 (25...♘xe5 26.♕e4 is bad) **26.b4?** A serious mistake. White should have played 26.♗e4 with roughly equal chances. Black has three pawns for the piece, and the b7 knight is out of play. Black now gets an opportunity to block the center.

26...♘f6 27.♕f3 ♘g4 28.♖d2. Black threatened 28...♘xh2 29.♚xh2 ♕h4+ 30.♕h3 f3+.

28...♖ab8   29.♗e4   d3! The strongest continuation. After playing that, black had to have his 34th move in mind.

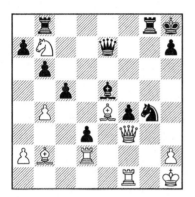

30.♕xd3. The only move. 30.♗xe5+ loses to 30...♘xe5 and ♖xb7.

Belavenets and Yudovich thought that "30.♖g1! was probably enough for a draw," but in their line 30...♗xb2 31.♖xb2 ♘e5 32.♕xf4 ♖xg1+ 33.♔xg1 ♖g8+ 34.♖g2, black had a strong reply 33...♖f8! with a mating attack.

However, the unassuming computer move 30.h3 could lead to an amusing draw by perpetual check: 30...♗xb2 31.hxg4 ♗d4 32.♖h2 ♖xg4! 33.♖xh7+ ♕xh7 34.♗xh7 ♖h4+ 35.♔g2 ♖xh7 36.♖h1 ♖g8+ 37.♔f1 ♖g3!

30...♖xb7   31.♗xb7   ♕xb7+ 32.♕f3   ♕xf3+   33.♖xf3   ♗xb2 34.♖xb2 ♘e5! Only this move gives black winning chances.

35.♖f1. After 35.♖c3, black wins with 35...c4 36.♖e2 ♘d3! 37.♖xc4 f3, while 35.♖xf4 ♘d3 36.♖bf2 cxb4!

leads to a rook ending with white two pawns down.

35...♘d3. *The subsequent part was played in mutual time trouble.*

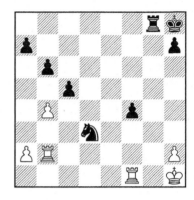

36.♖g2. A waste of time. White should have played 36.♖d2, but after 36...c4 37.b5 ♖g5 38.a4 ♔g7 the king gets to the center, and black's winning chances are great.

However, two other rook retreats could probably save white: 36.♖c2! ♘xb4 37.♖d2 c4 38.♖xf4 c3 39.♖d7 (Belavenets and Yudovich) or 36.♖e2 c4 37.b5 ♖g5 38.♖g1!

36...c4   37.♖c2. After 37.♖xg8+ ♔xg8, white has to give away his rook for the c-pawn. 37.♖d2 was somewhat more precise, but it didn't save the game either.

37...b5   38.a3   f3   39.♖d2   ♖g2! (the decisive move) **40.♖xg2 fxg2+ 41.♔xg2 c3 42.♔f3.** Here, the game was adjourned, and white resigned without resuming play. After 42...c2 43.♔e3 c1♕+ 44.♖xc1 ♘xc1 45.♔d2 ♘a2 46.♔c2 ♔g7 47.♔b2 ♘xb4 white regains the piece, but a hopeless pawn endgame awaits him.

The Favorite Knocked Down

In the third game, Botvinnik's evaluation was not deep enough, and this allowed Levenfish to show his subtle understanding of strategic weaknesses. The queenside attack was impeccable. Botvinnik showed his combinational talent in defense; sacrificing a rook, he managed to prolong the seemingly hopeless game for a number of moves.

No. 103. Nimzo-Indian Defense E34
Levenfish – Botvinnik
Moscow (m/3), 9th October 1937
Annotated by G. Levenfish
1.d4 ♘f6 2.c4 e6 3.♘c3 ♗b4 4.♕c2 d5 5.cxd5 ♕xd5 6.e3 *(in games 5 and 7, white played 6.♘f3)* **6...c5 7.a3.** Even though white forces a minor piece trade and gets the bishop pair, this move is still a loss of tempo. Perhaps 7.♗d2 is stronger.

7...♗xc3+ 8.bxc3 b6 9.♘f3 ♘bd7 10.c4. Euwe played the same move against Botvinnik in Nottingham. In the future, white gets a dynamic pawn center which, however, can be attacked by black.

10...♕d6 11.♗b2 ♗b7 12.♗e2.

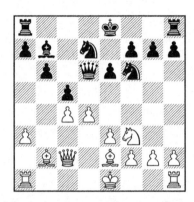

Nikolai Krylenko watching the game. Photo from the aforementioned issue of Shakhmaty v SSSR (No. 10, 1937) that was destroyed. From M. Sokolov's archive. Published for the first time.

12...cxd4. Against Euwe, Botvinnik played more weakly: 12...♖c8 13.0-0 ♗e4? 14.♕c3 0-0 15.♖ad1 ♖fd8, and after 16.d5! got a worse position. The game move is certainly stronger.

13.exd4   0-0   14.0-0   ♘g4. Otherwise, white will obtain a better position after 15.♘e5.

15.h3 ♗xf3 16.hxg4 ♗xe2. A logical move that deprives white of the bishop pair and, what's more important, weakens the already weak c4 pawn. If black tries to keep the bishop on the h1-a8 diagonal with 16...♗b7, then white plays 17.g5, and if 17...♕f4, then 18.♗d3 ♕xg5 19.♗xh7+ ♔h8 20.♗e4, and white is better.

17.♕xe2 ♖ac8 18.♖fd1 (white has to play energetically, or else the weakness of the e4 pawn will make itself felt) **18...♖c7.**

19.d5! e5. After 19...♖fc8, white would have played 20.a4 exd5 (not 20...♖xc4 because of 21.dxe6, winning a piece) 21.cxd5 ♖c2 22.♖d2.

20.♖e1. White wants to provoke f7-f6, which limits the black queen's mobility and creates fertile ground for tactical complications after g4-g5.

20...f6. It was necessary to play 20...♖fc8 and transition into an equal four-rook endgame after 21.♗xe5 ♘xe5 22.♕xe5 ♕xe5 23.♖xe5 ♖xc4 24.♖e7. Black overestimates his position.

21.a4! (starting a dangerous queenside attack) **21...h6.** Too methodical. Black blocks the g4 pawn, prevents g4-g5 and prepares to besiege the c4 pawn, not noticing the serious situation brewing on the queenside.

Levenfish is more categorical in his games collection: "A rare case of Botvinnik misevaluating the position."

22.a5 bxa5 (or else black gets a weak pawn on b6) **23.♗a3 ♘c5 24.♖eb1.**

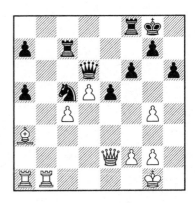

24...a6. If 24...♕a6, then 25.♖b5 ♖fc8 26.♗xc5 ♖xc5 27.♖axa5 ♕xa5 28.♖xa5 ♖xa5 29.d6, and the two passed pawns quickly decide matters.

25.♕e1! ♖fc8. If 25...a4, then 26.♕a5 ♖fc8 27.♖b6 ♕d7 28.d6 ♖c6 29.♖xc6 ♕xc6 30.♗xc5 ♕xc5 31.♕xc5 ♖xc5 32.d7.

26.♕xa5 ♕d7 27.♖b6 ♘d3. The best practical chance. White threatened 28.d6, winning a piece. If 27...♘e4, then 28.f3 ♘g5 29.♖d6 and c4-c5.

"This loses. Black should have played 27...♘e4, and if 28.f3, as Levenfish recommends in 64,

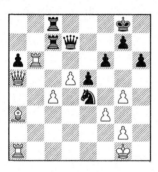

then 28...♖xc4! 29.fxe4 ♕xg4, and white has no good defense against the threat ♖c2. For instance: 30.♕e1 ♖c2 31.♕f1, with chances only for black." (Belavenets and Yudovich)

Strangely enough, in his game collection, Levenfish ignored this drawing recommendation and awarded 27...♘d3 an exclamation mark.

28.d6 ♘f4 (white threatened 29.♕d5+) **29.dxc7 ♕xg4 30.g3 ♘e2+ 31.♔h2 ♘f4 32.♔g1.** White repeats moves until the break.

Why didn't black claim a draw? "At the time, the rule was different. Threefold repetition of the position wasn't enough: to claim a draw, both players had to repeat the same moves

or move sequences three times in a row." (Botvinnik)

32...♘e2+ 33.♔h2 ♘f4 34.♔g1 ♘e2+ 35.♔g2 ♘f4+ 36.♔g1 ♘e2+ 37.♔g2 ♘f4+ 38.♔g1 ♘e2+ 39.♔h2 ♘f4 40.♔g1 ♘e2+ 41.♔g2 ♘f4+ 42.♔g1 ♘e2+ 43.♔h2 ♘f4 44.gxf4 ♕xf4+ 45.♔g2 ♕g4+ 46.♔f1 ♕xc4+ 47.♔e1 ♕e4+ 48.♔d2 ♕d4+.

49.♔c2! ♖xc7+. If 49...♕xa1, then 50.♕d5+ ♔h7 51.♕d3+ e4 52.♕xe4+ ♔h8 53.♖b8 ♕a2+ 54.♔d1 ♕g8 55.♕b7 (were the queen on d3, 55.♕d8 would have won immediately).

50.♔b1 ♖c3 (or 50...♕d3+ 51.♔a2 ♖c2+ 52.♗b2 ♕c4+ 53.♖b3) **51.♖b4!** If 51.♗b2, then 51...♕d3+ 52.♔a2 ♕c4+, drawing.

51...♕d3+ 52.♔a2 ♖c2+ 53.♗b2 ♖xf2. And so, for the first time in chess history, the game reached a curious endgame: queen, two rooks and bishop versus queen, rook and five pawns.

54.♖c1 ♔h7 55.♖b3 ♕e4 (if 55...♕e2, then 56.♕d5, threatening ♖c8)

56.♕xa6 h5 57.♖c7 ♖g2 58.♕d3 ♕xd3 59.♖xd3 ♔h6.

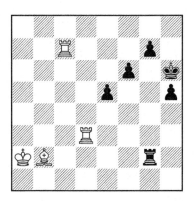

60.♔b3 (the king is the strongest piece against the pawns) **60...h4 61.♖c2 ♖g4.** After 61...♖g1, the king approaches the black pawns through c4 and d5.

62.♖f2   ♔h5   63.♔c2   ♖g1 64.♗a3. 64.♔d2 would be met with 64...♔g4 65.♔e2 h3, and white can't play 66.♖d7 g5 67.♖xf6 h2.

64...e4. If 64...♔g4, then 65.♗c5 h3 66.♖xf6 ♖g2+ 67.♖f2 ♖xf2+ 68.♗xf2 h2 69.♖g3+ ♔h4 70.♖xg7+ ♔h3 71.♖g3+ ♔h4 72.♔d2 h1♘ 73.♖f3+.

65.♖e3   ♔g4   66.♖xe4+   ♔g3 67.♖ff4. Black resigned.

The Turning Point

After two draws, a most dramatic episode happened in game 6. Botvinnik played very boldly for the entire game, trying to avenge his two losses in a row. He sacrificed a pawn and got a strong initiative, but at the critical moment he failed

to overcome Levenfish's masterful defense. Lacking a pawn in the endgame, it was now Botvinnik who had to search for drawing chances. Suddenly, Levenfish made an incredible blunder and... lost.

No. 104
Botvinnik – Levenfish
Moscow (m/6), 16th and 17th October 1937

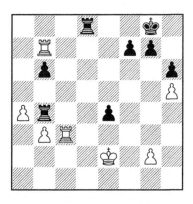

40.g4. "An important move, preventing the black rook from defending the g7 square along the g-file if white attacks it along the seventh rank" (Botvinnik in *64*).

40...♖f8. "The mistakes already made deprived black of winning chances, and the simplest continuation was to force a draw with 40...♖d3. For instance: 41.♖b8+ ♔h7 42.♖cc8 g6 or 41.♖c8+ ♔h7 42.♖xf7 ♖bxb3 43.♖cc7 ♖b2+" (Levenfish).

41.♖bc7. The sealed move. 41.♔e3(e1) also guaranteed a draw.

41...f5 42.♖e7 f4. The simplest way to force a draw was 42...♔h8!

(43.♖cc7 ♖xb3 44.♖xg7 ♖a8), but Levenfish wants to complicate things.

After 42...e3, Botvinnik showed the line 43.g5! ♖g4 (43...hxg5 44.♖cc7 ♖f6 45.♖xg7+ ♔h8 46.♖h7+ ♔g8 47.h6) 44.g6 f4 45.♖cc7 ♖g2+ 46.♔f1 ♖f2+ 47.♔e1 ♖d8 48.♖xg7+ "with a draw", but after 46.♔f3! white actually wins: 46...♖f2+ 47.♔e4 ♔h8 (or 47... ♖d8 48.♖xg7+ ♔h8 49.♖h7+ ♔g8 50.♔e5! etc.) 48.♖xg7 ♖e8+ 49.♖ce7 ♖xe7+ 50.♖xe7 (50...e2 or 50...♔g8 – 51.♔f5).

43.♖cc7 f3+ 44.♔f1. "44.♔e3 is bad due to 44...♖xb3+ 45.♔xe4 ♖b4+ 46.♔e5(d5) ♖ff4" (Botvinnik).

A double mistake! First of all, only 46...♖xg4 wins (46...♖ff4?=), and secondly, 44.♔e3 is actually not bad: instead of 45.♔xe4?, the king just has to go to d4 or f2, and it's a draw.

44...♖d8. "44...♖f4 loses to 45.g5! ♔f8 (45...hxg5 46.♖xg7+ and h5-h6) 46.♖xg7 etc. This line shows the point of 40.g4" (Botvinnik).

45.g5! A sort of psychological attack, which unexpectedly succeeds.

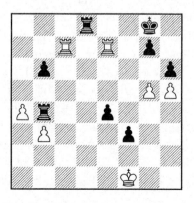

45...♖d1+? 45...e3! 46.♖xe3 ♖f4 47.g6 f2 48.♖c1 ♖f5 etc. led to a draw.

46.♔f2 ♖d2+ 47.♔e1 ♖e2+. Or 47...f2+ 48.♔xd2 f1♕ 49.♖e8+ ♕f8 50.♖xf8+ ♔xf8 51.♔c3 – the rook is trapped!

48.♔f1 hxg5 49.♖xg7+. Black resigned. After 49...♔f8, there's 50.h6, winning.

Botvinnik's Hat Trick

The seventh game was overshadowed by the fatal mistake of the previous game. Having two well-positioned bishops and chances to gain an advantage, Levenfish showed timidity and indecisiveness at the key moment. Botvinnik's knights dominated his opponent's passive bishops and he won the game.

The eighth game was also won by Botvinnik, with subtle and beautiful play in a difficult rook endgame. This game is one of the best in the whole match.

No. 105. Grunfeld Defense D94
Botvinnik – Levenfish
Moscow (m/8), 20th and 21st
October 1937

1.d4 d5 2.c4 c6 3.♘c3 ♘f6 4.e3 g6 5.♘f3 ♗g7 6.♗d3 0-0 7.0-0 b6 8.b3 ♗b7. In game 10, Levenfish improved upon this line with 8...c5! (Alatortsev's idea) and won an important game. "The most precise move order was shown by Kotov, also against Levenfish (Moscow 1949):

8.cxd5 cxd5 9.b3." (Botvinnik, *Analytical and Critical Works.*)

9.♗a3! More active than 9.♗b2, which was played in game 2.

9...♖e8 10.♖c1 e6 11.♕e2. "Too slow. The energetic 11.♘e5 ♘bd7 12.f4 gave white an obvious advantage" (Belavenets and Yudovich). After Botvinnik's suggestion 12...♘xe5 13.fxe5 ♘d7 14.♕e2 it did, but 12...c5!? with counterplay is better.

11...♘bd7.

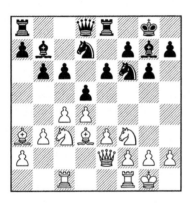

12.♖fd1. Annotating the game for *64* (24th October 1937), Botvinnik deservedly criticizes this move, recommending instead 12.♘e5 ♘xe5 13.dxe5 ♘d7 14.f4, "like in the second game of the match". After 14...f6 "with serious counterplay for black", recommended by Belavenets and Yudovich, there's 15.cxd5 exd5 16.e6! (16...♖xe6 17.f5).

However, Rybka insists on 12.♗d6! with the subsequent bishop transfer to g3. Perhaps it "spied on" the idea in the game Botvinnik – Goglidze (7th Soviet Championship, 1931).

12...♕b8! Defending the d6 and e5 squares and preparing the break c6-c5.

13.h3 a6 14.♗b2. Botvinnik thought that "the last attempt to get some advantage was 14.e4," but the computer meets it with the same "human" answer 14...c5! (with the idea of 15.e5 ♘h5 16.g3 ♗h6 17.♖c2 ♗f8=).

14...c5! 15.cxd5 exd5 16.♗b1 ♕a7!

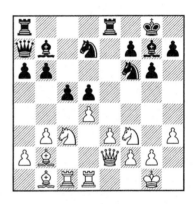

17.dxc5. Virtually forced. Otherwise, after 17...♖ac8, black threatened to attack on the queenside with c5-c4 and b6-b5.

17...bxc5 18.♘a4. White couldn't stop d5-d4 with 18.♕f1 (Botvinnik) because of 18...♘h5! (19.♘a4 d4 or 19.♘e1 ♗c6, and the threat d5-d4 is looming again).

18...d4 19.♘d2. "19.♘xc5 ♘xc5 20.♗xd4 doesn't work due to 20...♗xf3 21.♕xf3 ♘fd7, with an extra piece for black." (Botvinnik.) While 19.b4 loses a pawn: 19...♘d5! 20.bxc5 ♘f4 21.♕d2 ♘xh3+ 22.♔f1 dxe3 23.fxe3 ♗xb2 24.♘xb2 ♘xc5.

19...♘d5?! Losing a chance to surprise his opponent with 19...♘h5! There's a nuance now: 20.♘c4(f1)? is bad due to 20...♗xg2, and if 20.♕f1, then 20...♘b6! 21.♘xb6 (21.♘xc5? dxe3, crushing) 21...♕xb6, and black is better.

20.♘c4! Botvinnik (and Belavenets and Yudovich as well) thought that "20.♘f1 was stronger, not weakening the pressure on the c5 square." But in this case, black gets an initiative with 20...♘f4 21.♕g4 ♘e6! and ♖ad8.

20...♗c6. "If black immediately plays 20...♘f4, then 21.♕g4 ♘xg2 22.e4! (not 22.♕xd7 ♘h4 with complications." (Botvinnik.)) Here, 22.♕xd7! is actually correct (after 22...♘h4 23.♘d6! ♘f3+ 24.♔h1, black simply loses a piece), but after 22.e4? ♗c6 23.♕xg2 ♗h6! 24.♗a3 (24.♖c2? ♗xe4) 24...♗xc1 there's still a lot of play. But, what's more important, black doesn't even have to capture on g2: he can play 21...♘e6 instead, maintaining equality (22. ♕g3 ♗d5=), because the dangerous-looking 22.♘d6 is met with 22...h5! 23.♕e2 (23.♕h4? ♗f6 24.♕g3 ♗e5, and black wins) 23...♗xg2 etc.

Botvinnik was also mistaken in his opinion that "the immediate 20... ♗h6 was repelled with 21.♕g4 ♘7f6 22.♕h4." Instead of 21...♘7f6?, black should play 21...dxe3! 22.♕xd7 exf2+ 23.♔xf2 (23.♔f1? ♖ad8 24.♕g4 ♕b8 is bad) 23...♖ad8! (not 23...♗xc1? 24.♖xc1 ♖ad8 25.♖e1!, and white is better) 24.♖xd5! (the

only move; 24.♕g4? ♗e3+ etc.) 24... ♖xd7 25.♖xd7 with equality.

21.♕f3.

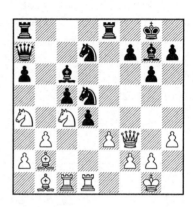

21...♘b4?! The correct move was 21...♕c7!, after which Botvinnik recommended 22.e4 ♘5f6 23.♖e1 as the best defense, "even though black's advantage is indisputable after 23...♗xa4." It's even more indisputable after 23...♖e6!, increasing the pressure on the e4 pawn (Belavenets and Yudovich), so the best continuation for white was 22.exd4 ♘e3 23.d5 ♘xd1, rejected by Botvinnik because of the "mating threat on e1" (24.♖xd1 ♗xa4 25.♗xg7 ♔xg7 26.bxa4, and the strong passed pawn in the center serves as good compensation for the exchange).

22.♕g3 ♗xa4 23.bxa4 dxe3? This hands the advantage to white. After 23...♘c6, black still kept some pressure.

24.♗xg7 ♔xg7? Worsening his position. 24...exf2+ 25.♕xf2 ♔xg7 is bad as well due to 26.♘d6 ♖e7 27.♗e4 ♖d8 28.a3 ♘f6 29.♘f5+!

(Belavenets and Yudovich), but black still had 24...e2 25.♖e1 ♔xg7, "and white regains the e2 pawn with roughly equal play." (Botvinnik)

25.fxe3 ♘f6 26.a3 ♘bd5. After 26...♘c6, white had a pleasant choice between 27.♖d6 ♕c7 (27...♖ac8? 28.♕f3) 28.♕g5 ♘d7 29.♖cd1 and 27.♘d6 ♖e6 28.♗a2 ♘h5 29.♕e1!

27.e4 ♘b6 28.♘d6! (28.e5 ♘h5 and ♘xc4) **28...♖e6 29.e5.**

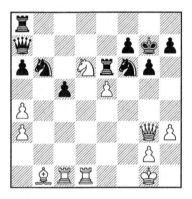

29...♘e8? A bad error unnoticed by the commentators. 29...♘h5!?, eliminating the "thorn" on e5, still gave some defending chances. For instance: 30.♕f3 (30.♕e3 ♘d7 with the idea 31.♘c4 ♘xe5!) 30...c4! (the immediate 30...♖xe5 is worse because of 31.a5 ♘c8 32.♘c4! ♖e6 33.g4 ♘f6 34.g5 with a tight squeeze) 31.♔h1 ♖xe5 32.a5 ♘a4! 33.♘xc4 ♖e6 34.♘d6 ♖f8 (34...♖b8 35.♕xf7+!) 35.♗c2 ♘c5, and, despite losing a pawn, black's position is full of life – 36.♕f2 ♕c7 37.♗xg6 hxg6 38.♖xc5 ♕e7.

30.a5 ♘a4. "Neither 30...♘c8 31.♗f5 nor 30...♘d7 31.♗f5 ♖e7

32.♗e4 is better," Botvinnik wrote in *64*, but many years later (in *Analytical and Critical Works*) he changed his evaluation: "30...♘d7 is preferable, and white probably should play 31.♘c4, keeping up the pressure, but not 31.♗f5 ♖e7 32.♗e4 because of an exchange sacrifice pointed out by Belavenets and Yudovich: 32...♘xd6 33.♗xa8 ♘f5 34.♕f3 ♘xe5. The knight is out of play on a4..."

Amusingly, all three of them failed to notice that 32.♗e4 was an error. After the spectacular 32.♗xg6!!, black could as well resign: 32...fxg6 33.♘f5+ ♔f7 34.♘xe7 ♔xe7 35.♕h4+ ♔e6 36.♕e4! or 32...hxg6 33.♘f5+ ♔f8 34.♕h4!

31.♘c4. Declining to win an exchange with 31.♗f5 ♖e7 32.♘c8 is hard to explain. But this is nothing compared with the mistake on the next move.

31...♖b8 32.♕f2? After 32.♖d2, black wouldn't have lasted for long...

32...♖xb1 (of course!) **33.♖xb1 ♘c3 34.♖bc1 ♘xd1 35.♖xd1.** White has now lost most of his advantage, but not his fighting spirit. "In the next part of the game, Botvinnik shows his incredible battle prowess." (Belavenets and Yudovich)

35...♕c7 36.♖d5 ♖c6 37.♕d2 ♕e7 38.♖d7 ♕e6 39.♕d5! The c-pawn is stopped, and so the rook is free in its actions, hence Botvinnik offers a queen trade.

39...♕xd5 40.♖xd5 ♔f8.

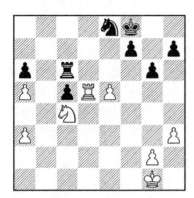

41.♖d7! The sealed move. White has to cut off the king, because after 41...♔e7 and ♔e6, black could take a breather.

41...♖c7. As a "best chance", Botvinnik recommended to prepare f7-f6 with 41...h5 (42.♔f2 f6 43.♔f3! ♖c7 44.♖d8 fxe5 45.♖a8, and "white has big winning chances"), but Rybka found a more solid way: 41...♖e6! 42.♔f2 ♖e7 43.♖d8 ♔g7 44.♔f3 f6 etc.

42.♖d8 ♔e7 43.♖d6! The point! Black can't play 43...♖d7 because of Botvinnik's line 44.♖xa6 ♖d4 45.♘b6 ♘c7 46.♖a7 ♔d8 47.a6 c4 48.♖xc7 ♔xc7 49.a7 ♖d8 50.a8♕ ♖xa8 51.♘xa8+ ♔b7 52.♔f2, with a won pawn endgame.

Annotation from *Analytical and Critical Works*: "Now it's clear that all the maneuvers of the white rook (41.♖d7 and 42.♖d8) prepared this interesting decisive blow (by the way, all the analysts missed it, claiming that white had no advantage in the adjourned position)."

43...♖a7 44.♖c6 ♔d7.

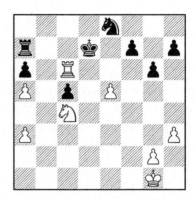

45.♖b6! The pawn is poisoned: 45.♖xc5? ♖c7 46.♘b6+ ♔e6 with a draw.

45...♔e7 46.♔f2 f6 47.♔e2 ♖a8 48.♖c6. There was an alternative: 48.♖b7+ ♔e6 49.♖xh7 fxe5 50.♘b6 ♘f6 51.♖c7 etc.

48...fxe5 49.♖xc5 ♘d6 50.♖c7+! ♔e6 51.♘xd6 ♔xd6 52.♖xh7 ♖b8? Botvinnik said that 52...♔e6 "didn't save black either because of 53.g4, preventing the black king from getting to f5." However, after 53...♖c8!, white still had a lot of work to do, whereas now he wins easily.

53.♖g7 ♖b2+ 54.♔f1 e4. Or 54...♖b1+ 55.♔f2 ♖b2+ 56.♔g3 ♖b3+ 57.♔g4 etc. Black attempts to use his last chance – the passed e-pawn, but...

55.♖xg6+ ♔e5 56.♖xa6 ♖a2 57.♖a8 ♔f4 58.a6 ♖a1+ 59.♔e2 ♖a2+ 60.♔d1 ♖xa3 61.a7 ♔e3 62.h4 ♖d3+ 63.♔c2 ♖d7 64.g4 ♖c7+ 65.♔b3 ♖d7 66.♔c3 ♖c7+ 67.♔b4 ♖d7 68.♔c5. Black resigned.

The Last Ounces of Strength

Levenfish played the ninth game with an air of hopelessness, starting it with 1.e2-e4, which probably didn't feature in his initial plans for the match. With determined, strong play Botvinnik seized the center with a pawn avalanche, got a position where the correct move would have resulted in an unstoppable mating attack on Levenfish's king, and then... everything suddenly transitioned into an equal ending and a draw.

This setback, in turn, probably affected Botvinnik. In game 10, he walked into home preparation, got confused, played badly and quickly lost. Still, the situation was better for him. He led 4-3, even though Levenfish now had some chances to mount resistance.

In game 11, Levenfish again got into a critical position, but fortune was on his side this time. Botvinnik didn't just fail to exploit the advantages of his position – he overlooked a simple combination and lost a pawn. Levenfish played a brilliant rook endgame with an extra pawn, which can be used as a textbook example. The score was equalized – 4-4. The attacks in both of the last two games are executed elegantly and energetically: by Botvinnik in game 12 and by Levenfish in game 13.

No. 106. English Opening A25
Botvinnik – Levenfish
Leningrad (m/12), 3rd November 1937

1.c4 e5 2.♘c3 ♘c6 3.g3 g6 4.♗g2 ♗g7 5.e3 d6 6.♘ge2 ♗e6. "A risky opening experiment," Levenfish self-critically admits in *64*, adding that "6...♘ge7 was the right move." However, in the future, this line became relatively popular and is now known as the Bremen-Hort Variation.

7.d4! A cold shower – this move is still considered the best reply. Black counted on 7.b3 ♕d7 8.d4 ♗h3, with equality. Negative emotions probably affected the choice of the next move.

7...♗xc4. 7...♗d7 (Botvinnik) or 7...exd4 8.♘xd4 ♗d7 were more prudent.

8.d5 ♘b8. "The lesser evil, since white's pieces aren't positioned particularly great in this line." (Levenfish.) There was an alternative: 8...♗xe2 9.♕xe2 ♘ce7 (or ♘b8) 10.♕b5+.

9.♕a4+ b5 10.♘xb5 ♗xb5 11.♕xb5+ ♘d7.

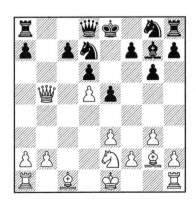

12.e4(?). According to I. Rabinovich (*Shakhmaty v SSSR* No. 11–12, 1937), Botvinnik said after the game that this move "could lead to white losing all his positional advantage. He should have played 12.♘c3! first."

12...♘e7 13.0-0 0-0 14.♘c3 ♖b8 15.♕e2 c5! "If white doesn't take this pawn, then black has a good, free position, while after the trade, the black knight gets to the central d4 square. That's where white's inaccuracy on move 12 made itself felt," Botvinnik wrote in *Analytical and Critical Works*, where he annotated this game for the first time.

16.dxc6 ♘xc6 17.♗e3 ♘c5?! "Black had to meet white's quickly-growing kingside attack (after f2-f4) with rapid queenside counterplay: 17...♘d4 18.♕d2 (or 18.♗xd4 exd4 19.♘d5 ♘b6 with opposite-colored bishops) 18...♕a5 19.♖fc1 ♘b6 20.b3 ♖fc8 with equality." I must add that 19.f4 didn't work due to 19...♘b6 (20.b3? ♕xc3!).

18.♕d2 ♘e6 19.♖ac1 ♘ed4.

20.f4! **♕a5** (20...f6?! 21.♘d5) **21.f5 f6 22.♖f2.** "White gives additional protection to the b2 pawn, freeing up his queen, and prepares the maneuver ♗f1-c4." (Rabinovich)

22...♔h8. Black prevents the bishop transfer for now, preparing to meet 23.♗f1 with 23...gxf5 24.exf5 d5; this line didn't work earlier because of 25.♘xd5.

23.♕d1! "A great move that forces either a beneficial exchange operation for white or a kingside attack." (Levenfish)

23...♖bd8. The trade 23...gxf5 24.exf5 only weakened the light squares. To illustrate that, Levenfish shows the "losing" line 24...♖fd8 25.♗d5 ♘e7 26.♗xd4 ♘xd5 27.♘xd5 ♕xd5 28.♗xa7 ♕xd1+ 29.♖xd1 ♖b7 30.♗c5 ♖bd7 31.♖fd2, missing a strong reply 26...♗h6!, which radically changes the evaluation:

27.♖b1 (the point is that the d4 bishop has no escape squares!) 27...♘xd5 28.♘xd5 ♕xd5 29.♗xa7 ♕xd1+ 30.♖xd1 ♖b7 31.♗c5 ♖c8!, and after 32.♗xd6 ♗e3, white loses an exchange.

Of the last four games, Levenfish won three and lost one – and managed to draw the match!
Cartoon by Y. Yuzepchuk (Shakhmaty v SSSR, No. 5, 1938).

However, all these brilliancies remain offscreen if white plays Rabinovich's move 25.g4! d5 26.g5! fxg5 27.♗xg5 ♖d6 28.f6 ♗f8 29.♕h5!, with a winning attack.

24.fxg6 hxg6 25.♕g4 (the computer already shows the line here) **25...♘e7 26.♗f1 d5.** The attempt to prevent 27.♗c4 with 26...♖c8 is refuted by 27.♕h4+ ♔g8 28.♗h3! (if the rook retreats, there follows 29.♗xd4 exd4 30.♗e6+).

27.♘xd5 ♘xd5 28.exd5! ♘f5 (28...♕xd5?? 29.♕h3+ and ♗c4) **29.♗c5?!** This doesn't miss the win entirely, but complicates it. Rabinovich's move won immediately: 29.♖xf5! gxf5 30.♕h5+ ♔g8 31.d6! ♖f7 32.♗c4 ♖dd7 33.♗xf7+ ♖xf7 34.d7!

"A miscalculation, typical for me in this game," Botvinnik laments. However, according to Levenfish, "both opponents were in severe time trouble here."

29...♗h6.

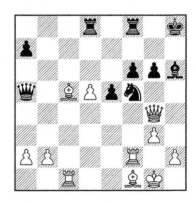

30.b4! "Launching a combination that wins by force." (Rabinovich.)

Actually, almost all roads led to Rome by that point: 30.♗xf8, 30.♖c3, 30.♕xg6...

30...♕a3 31.♕xg6 ♕xc1. If 31... ♗xc1, then 32.♖xf5 ♗g5 33.♕h5+ ♔g8 34.♖xg5+ etc.

32.♖xf5 ♗g5 (32...♗g7 33.d6!) **33.h4! ♖g8** (33...♗e3+? 34.♔h2) **34.♕h5+ ♗h6 35.♖xf6 ♔h7 36.♕f5+.** White repeats moves to gain some time. There was an elegant win: 36.♖xh6+! ♕xh6 37.♗d3.

36...♔h8 37.♕h5 ♔h7 38.♕f5+ ♔h8 39.♕h5 ♔h7. "Here black lost on time, but in the heat of time-trouble the opponents made one further move each: **40.♖f7+ ♖g7.** In this position, hopeless for black, the match arbiter N. D. Grigoriev asked the players to stop the game..." (Rabinovich)

The Winning Point

Together with games 1, 2, 3 and 8, these two games (*the 12th and 13th*) are examples of the highest class. The opponents, trading wins at the finish, ultimately drew the match.

No. 107. Grunfeld Defense B14
Levenfish – Botvinnik
Leningrad (m/13), 9th November 1937
Annotated by G. Levenfish
1.d4 ♘f6 2.c4 g6 3.♘c3 d5 4.♗f4 ♗g7 5.e3 0-0 6.♕b3. More precise than in game 11, where white played 6.♘f3.

6...c5. A pawn sacrifice, obviously prepared beforehand; the normal continuation here is 6...c6 7.♘f3 ♕a5 8.♘d2, with a freer position for white.

7.cxd5. After 7.dxc5, I feared the following during the game: 7... ♘a6 8.cxd5 ♘xc5 9.♕c4 b6, with a dangerous attack for the pawn.

According to Botvinnik, 7...♘e4! 8.cxd5 ♕a5 9.♘e2 ♘xc5 is stronger (Capablanca – Flohr, AVRO 1938) 10.♕d1 ♘ba6!

7...cxd4 8.exd4. *As often happens in modern chess, the game transposed from the Grunfeld Defense (D83) into the Panov Attack in the Caro-Kann (B14).*

8...♘bd7 9.♗e2 ♘b6 10.♗f3 ♗f5. Now white holds onto the pawn. It could be regained with 10...♗g4, but after 11.♗xg4 ♘xg4 12.♘f3 ♘f6 13.d6! exd6 14.0-0, white is better.

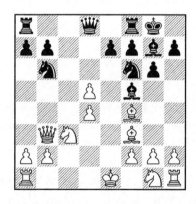

11.♖d1! Necessary, because of the threat ♗d3-c4. 11.a4 ♗d3 12.a5 ♗c4 13.♕b4 doesn't work due to 13...♘bxd5.

11...♕d7 (threatening ♖d8, regaining the d5 pawn) **12.h3.** The threat g2-g4 forces black to significantly weaken his kingside pawn chain.

12...h5 13.♗e5. White is trying to hold onto the extra pawn.

13...♖fd8 14.♗xf6 exf6. After 14...♗xf6 15.♘ge2, the dark-squared bishop has no prospects *(15...e6? loses a piece after 16.g4!).* Now the bishop has the good d6 square, where it blocks the white pawns.

15.♘ge2 ♖ac8 (black prepares to relocate his bad knight) **16.0-0 ♘c4 17.♘g3 ♘d6.** If 17...♗h6, then simply 18.♘xf5 ♕xf5 19.♗e4 ♕d7 20.♖fe1.

18.♖fe1 ♗f8.

weakens the kingside dark squares and the e5 square.

22...f5 23.♘c3 b5 24.a3 a5 25.♕g3 b4. If 25...♗d6, then 26.♕g5.

This just blunders a pawn to 26... ♗xa3! But 26.♕d3 is stronger; if 26... b4, then 27.♘b5!

26.axb4 axb4 27.♘e2 ♔h7. Now we see the point behind the move 25.♕g3. 27...♕xd5 would have been met with 28.♘f4 and ♘xh5+. 27... ♖c2 28.♕b3 ♖dc8 29.♘c3 is also bad.

"The simple 27...♗d6 gave black a good defense." (Riumin)

28.♘f4 ♖e8 (with the threat ♖e4) **29.♕f3 ♖cd8 30.♖e5.**

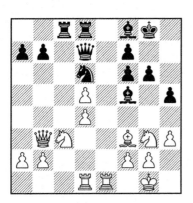

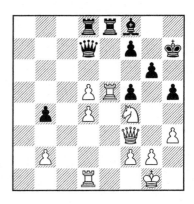

19.♗e4! Prevents a possible opposite-colored bishop endgame in the future and prepares an important strategic maneuver.

19...♗xe4 20.♘gxe4 ♘xe4 21.♘xe4. After the routine 21.♖xe4 ♗d6 22.♖de1 a6, black's position is impregnable.

21...♔g7 22.♕f3! Forcing f6-f5 (if 22...♗e7, then 23.d6), which

30...♗g7. After 30...♗d6, there's a spectacular combination 31.♘xh5! ♗xe5 32.dxe5 gxh5 33.♕xh5+ ♔g7 34.♕g5+ ♔f8 (34...♔h7 35.♖d4) 35.♕h6+ ♔e7 36.d6+. Amusingly, three black pieces block the escape squares for the king. And if 35... ♔g8, then 36.♖d3! f4 37.♖xf4! Black is helpless, despite the extra rook.

31.♖de1! This exchange sacrifice is the culmination of white's entire plan that started after 21.♘xe4 *(in Levenfish's book: "started on the 19ᵗʰ move")*.

31...♖c8. After 31...♗xe5 32.dxe5 ♕c7 33.♕e3, it's hard for black to stop the maneuver ♕d4, d5-d6 and ♘d5 with a decisive advantage. Still, it was better than the game move.

32.d6. There is no defense against this move. Now white threatens 33.♖e7, and black's reply is forced.

32...♖f8 33.♖d5! ♖fe8 34.♖xe8 ♖xe8 35.♘d3 ♖d8 36.♘c5 ♕c6 37.d7!

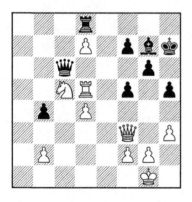

37...♗xd4. After 37...♗f8, an amusing ending would have followed: 38.♖xf5 ♕xf3 39.♖xf3 ♗xc5 40.♖xf7+ ♔g8 41.dxc5 ♔xf7 42.c6 ♔e7 43.c7 with a won endgame.

38.♖xd4 ♕xc5 39.♕d5 ♕xd5. Black could prolong the struggle, but without any chances, after 39...♕e7. A curious ending could occur after 39... ♕c1+ 40.♖d1! ♕xb2 41.♕xf7+ ♔h6 (or 41...♕g7 42.♕e8 ♕f6 43.♖e1) 42.♕e7! ♕c2 43.♕xd8 ♕xd1+

44.♔h2 ♕d6+ 45.g3 ♕d4 46.♕f8+ ♔h7 47.♕e7+ ♔h6 48.♕e3+.

40.♖xd5 ♔g7 41.♔f1. Black resigned, because the pawn endgame after 41...♔f6 42.♔e2 ♔e6 43.♖d4 ♖xd7 44.♖xd7 ♔xd7 45.♔d3 ♔d6 46.♔c4 is obviously hopeless.

Remember Botvinnik mentioned Grigoriev's line with the "queen versus pawn" endgame (in the section Dust in the Eyes)? There is no such line in Grigoriev's analysis in Shakhmaty v SSSR, *No.2, 1938.*

"We should expect," **Romanovsky** concludes his article, "that the Soviet chess masses will gladly congratulate G. Y. Levenfish. Levenfish's grandmastership is a brilliant and fair outcome of both many years of his chess activity and the Soviet forms of the chess movement, which gave him opportunities for constant improvement.

It's obvious that Botvinnik can't be satisfied with the result of this match – he challenged for the Soviet Championship and failed to obtain it. However, without a doubt, he will be able to benefit from this match as well. We know Botvinnik as a player who is able to critically assess his own game and, based on this criticism, work clearly and consistently on eliminating his shortcomings.

This match revealed Levenfish's strong will and, by contrast, Botvinnik's obvious psychological instability in the decisive moment of the match. Time trouble and, as a

The grandmaster's initiation. Cartoon by Y. Yuzepchuk (64, 30th December 1937).

consequence, his total confusion led to him losing several games in the last stage of the match.

I want to hope and believe that Botvinnik's failure shall serve as an even greater incentive for his successes in the future than the unforgettable historical wins in Moscow and Nottingham." (*Shakhmaty v SSSR* No. 10, 1937.)

Championship Tables

All-Russian Chess Olympiad, 1920

#	Players	1	2	3	4	5	6	7	8	9	10	11	12	13	14	15	16	Pts	Prize
1	A. Alekhine (Moscow)	◆	=	=	1	1	1	1	=	=	=	=	1	1	1	1	1	12	I
2	P. Romanovsky (Petrograd)	=	◆	1	0	=	1	1	0	1	1	1	0	1	1	1	1	11	II
3	G. Levenfish (Petrograd)	=	0	◆	0	1	1	=	=	=	1	1	1	=	1	=	1	10	III
4	I. Rabinovich (Petrograd)	0	1	1	◆	0	0	0	=	1	=	1	1	1	=	1	1	9.5	IV
5	N. Grigoriev (Petrograd)	0	=	0	1	◆	1	1	0	0	0	0	1	1	1	1	1	8.5	V–VII
6	A. Kubbel (Yamburg)	0	0	0	1	0	◆	0	=	=	1	=	1	1	1	1	1	8.5	V–VII
7	A. Rabinovich (Vilno)	0	0	=	1	0	1	◆	=	=	1	0	1	0	1	1	1	8.5	V–VII
8	B. Blumenfeld (Saratov)	=	1	=	=	1	=	=	◆	=	0	0	1	0	1	=	=	8	
9	D. Daniuszewski (Lodz)	=	0	=	0	1	=	=	=	◆	0	=	=	0	1	=	1	7	
10	A. Ilyin-Zhenevsky (Moscow)	=	0	0	=	1	0	0	1	1	◆	0	=	1	0	=	1	7	
11	N. Zubarev (Moscow)	=	0	0	0	1	=	1	1	=	1	◆	0	0	0	1	0	6.5	
12	N. Pavlov-Pianov (Moscow)	0	1	0	0	0	0	0	0	=	=	1	◆	1	=	1	1	6.5	
13	N. Tselikov (Moscow)	0	0	=	0	0	0	1	1	1	0	1	0	◆	0	0	1	5.5	
14	A. Mund (Nizhny Novgorod)	0	0	0	=	0	0	0	0	0	1	1	=	1	◆	=	0	4.5	
15	D. Pavlov (Mogilev)	0	0	=	0	0	0	0	=	=	=	0	0	1	=	◆	=	4	
16	I. Golubev (Petrograd)	0	0	0	0	0	0	0	=	0	0	1	0	0	1	=	◆	3	

All-Russian Championship Tournament, 1923

#	Players	1	2	3	4	5	6	7	8	9	10	11	12	13	Pts	Prize
1	P. Romanovsky (Petrograd)	◆	0	1	1	=	1	=	1	1	1	1	1	1	10	I
2	G. Levenfish (Petrograd)	1	◆	=	1	0	1	1	1	1	=	=	=	1	9	II
3	F. Bogatyrchuk (Kiev)	0	=	◆	=	1	0	1	0	=	1	1	1	1	7.5	III–V
4	F. Duz-Khotimirsky (Moscow)	0	0	=	◆	1	=	1	=	1	0	1	1	1	7.5	III–V
5	V. Nenarokov (Moscow)	=	1	0	0	◆	0	=	1	1	1	1	=	1	7.5	III–V
6	A. Kubbel (Yamburg)	0	0	1	=	1	◆	0	1	0	1	0	1	=	6	
7	A. Ilyin-Zhenevsky (Petrograd)	=	0	0	0	=	1	◆	1	=	0	=	=	1	5.5	
8	I. Rabinovich (Petrograd)	0	0	1	=	0	0	0	◆	1	1	1	1	0	5.5	
9	N. Grigoriev (Moscow)	0	0	=	0	0	1	=	0	◆	1	1	=	=	5	
10	N. Zubarev (Moscow)	0	=	0	1	0	0	1	0	0	◆	=	1	0	4	
11	Y. Vilner (Odessa)	0	=	0	0	0	1	=	0	0	=	◆	0	1	3.5	
12	K. Vygodchikov (Smolensk)	0	=	0	0	=	0	=	0	=	0	1	◆	=	3.5	
13	S. Lebedev (Simbirsk)	0	0	0	0	0	=	0	1	=	1	0	=	◆	3.5	

3rd Soviet Championship Tournament, 1924

#	Players	1	2	3	4	5	6	7	8	9	10	11	12	13	14	15	16	17	18	Pts	Prize
1	E. Bogoljubov (Triberg)	♦	1	1	1	1	=	=	=	=	1	1	1	1	1	1	1	1	1	15	I
2	P. Romanovsky (Leningrad)	0	♦	1	=	=	1	1	1	0	0	1	1	=	1	1	1	1	1	12.5	II
3	F. Bogatyrchuk (Kiev)	0	0	♦	=	1	=	1	1	1	=	0	=	1	1	=	1	1	1	11.5	III–IV
4	G. Levenfish (Leningrad)	0	=	=	♦	0	=	=	=	1	1	=	1	1	=	1	1	1	1	11.5	III–IV
5	I. Rabinovich (Leningrad)	0	=	0	1	♦	=	0	=	=	0	1	0	1	1	1	1	1	1	10	V
6	Y. Vilner (Odessa)	=	0	=	=	=	♦	0	=	1	1	1	=	=	1	0	=	1	=	9.5	VI–VIII
7	V. Nenarokov (Moscow)	=	0	0	=	1	1	♦	=	1	1	=	1	0	0	1	=	0	1	9.5	VI–VIII
8	A. Selezniev (Triberg)	=	0	0	=	=	=	=	♦	=	1	0	=	1	=	1	=	1	1	9.5	VI–VIII
9	V. Sozin (Novgorod)	=	1	0	0	=	0	0	=	♦	1	0	1	=	0	1	1	1	1	9	
10	B. Verlinsky (Moscow)	0	1	=	0	1	0	0	0	0	♦	1	1	1	1	=	=	0	1	8.5	
11	F. Duz-Khotimirsky (Moscow)	0	0	1	=	0	0	=	1	1	0	♦	0	=	1	1	1	1	0	8.5	
12	A. Rabinovich (Moscow)	0	0	=	0	1	=	0	=	0	0	1	♦	1	1	1	0	1	=	8	
13	A. Ilyin-Zhenevsky (Leningrad)	0	=	0	0	0	=	1	0	=	0	=	0	♦	=	=	1	1	1	7	
14	N. Grigoriev (Moscow)	0	0	0	=	0	0	1	=	1	0	0	0	=	♦	=	1	1	=	6.5	
15	S. Rosenthal (Minsk)	0	0	=	0	0	1	0	0	0	=	0	0	=	=	♦	=	1	=	5	
16	A. Sergeyev (Moscow)	0	0	0	0	0	=	=	=	0	=	0	1	0	0	=	♦	0	=	4	
17	S. Freymann (Turkestan)	0	0	0	0	0	0	1	0	0	1	0	0	0	0	0	1	♦	1	4	
18	A. Smorodsky (Tiflis)	0	0	0	0	0	=	0	0	0	0	1	=	0	=	=	=	0	♦	3.5	

Soviet Championship Match, 1924

Players	1	2	3	4	5	6	7	8	9	10	11	12	Points
E. Bogoljubov (Triberg)	=	1	=	1	1	1	=	0	1	=	=	=	6 (2)
P. Romanovsky (Leningrad)	=	0	=	0	0	0	=	1	0	=	=	=	2 (2)

The match was played until 6 points were scored, with the first four draws not counting.

4th Soviet Championship, 1925

#	Players	1	2	3	4	5	6	7	8	9	10	11	12	13	14	15	16	17	18	19	20	Pts	Prize
1	E. Bogoljubov (Triberg)	◆	=	1	0	1	=	=	1	1	=	0	1	=	=	1	1	1	1	1	1	14	I
2	G. Levenfish (Leningrad)	=	◆	0	0	1	=	0	=	0	1	1	=	1	1	1	1	1	1	1	1	13	II
3	I. Rabinovich (Leningrad)	0	1	◆	0	0	0	=	1	1	=	=	1	0	1	1	1	1	1	+	1	12.5	III
4	B. Verlinsky (Moscow)	1	1	1	◆	=	=	1	1	=	1	0	=	=	1	0	0	1	0	=	1	12	IV
5	F. Duz-Khotimirsky (Moscow)	0	0	1	=	◆	=	=	1	1	1	=	=	0	=	=	0	1	1	1	1	11.5	V
6	S. Gotthilf (Leningrad)	=	=	1	=	=	◆	0	=	0	=	=	1	1	=	=	=	1	0	+	1	11	VI–VIII
7	A. Ilyin-Zhenevsky (Leningrad)	=	1	0	=	0	1	◆	0	0	=	=	0	1	=	=	1	1	1	+	=	11	VI–VIII
8	P. Romanovsky (Leningrad)	0	=	0	0	0	=	1	◆	1	1	1	0	1	=	1	1	1	=	0	1	11	VI–VIII
9	A. Rabinovich (Vilno)	0	1	0	=	0	1	1	0	◆	1	0	0	0	=	1	1	=	1	=	1	10	
10	A. Sergeyev (Moscow)	=	0	=	0	0	=	=	0	0	◆	1	=	=	=	=	1	=	1	1	+	10	
11	Y. Vilner (Odessa)	1	0	=	1	=	=	=	0	1	0	◆	=	0	=	1	1	0	1	0	=	9.5	
12	N. Zubarev (Moscow)	0	=	0	=	=	0	1	1	1	=	=	◆	0	=	0	=	=	1	=	1	9.5	
13	A. Kubbel (Yamburg)	=	0	1	=	1	0	0	0	1	=	1	1	◆	=	0	=	=	=	=	=	9.5	
14	A. Selezniev (Moscow)	=	0	0	0	=	=	=	=	=	=	=	=	=	◆	=	1	=	1	=	=	9	
15	N. Grigoriev (Moscow)	0	0	0	1	=	=	=	0	0	0	0	1	1	=	◆	0	1	0	+	1	8	
16	A. Kaspersky (Minsk)	0	0	0	1	1	=	0	0	0	=	0	=	=	0	1	◆	0	=	+	=	7	
17	V. Sozin (Novgorod)	0	0	0	0	0	0	0	0	=	0	1	=	=	=	0	1	◆	1	=	1	6.5	
18	V. Nenarokov (Moscow)	0	0	0	1	0	1	0	=	0	0	0	0	=	0	1	=	0	◆	1	=	6	
19	S. Freymann (Tashkent)	0	0	–	=	0	–	–	1	=	–	1	=	=	=	–	–	=	0	◆	–	5	
20	N. Kutuzov (Arkhangelsk)	0	0	0	0	0	0	=	0	0	0	=	0	=	=	0	=	0	=	+	◆	4	

5th Soviet Championship, 1927

#	Players	1	2	3	4	5	6	7	8	9	10	11	12	13	14	15	16	17	18	19	20	21	Pts	Prize
1	F. Bogatyrchuk (Kiev)	◆	0	1	1	1	1	1	=	=	=	=	=	1	=	1	1	1	=	=	=	1	14.5	I–II
2	P. Romanovsky (Leningrad)	1	◆	0	=	=	=	1	0	1	0	1	=	1	1	1	1	1	1	=	1	1	14.5	I–II
3	F. Duz-Khotimirsky (Moscow)	0	1	◆	1	=	0	1	=	0	=	1	0	=	1	1	1	=	=	1	1	1	13	III–IV
4	A. Model (Leningrad)	0	=	0	◆	1	0	0	1	=	1	1	1	1	1	1	1	1	1	1	0	0	13	III–IV
5	M. Botvinnik (Leningrad)	0	=	=	0	◆	1	=	1	1	1	0	1	1	=	0	=	1	=	1	=	1	12.5	V–VI
6	V. Makogonov (Baku)	0	=	1	1	0	◆	=	1	1	=	0	=	=	0	1	=	=	1	1	1	1	12.5	V–VI
7	V. Nenarokov (Moscow)	0	0	0	1	=	=	◆	1	1	=	=	=	=	1	1	0	0	1	=	=	1	11	VII
8	N. Grigoriev (Moscow)	=	1	=	0	0	0	0	◆	=	=	0	1	1	1	1	=	=	1	0	1		10.5	
9	A. Ilyin-Zhenevsky (Leningrad)	=	0	1	=	0	0	0	=	◆	=	1	=	1	1	0	0	1	0	=	1	1	10	
10	I. Rabinovich (Leningrad)	=	1	=	0	0	=	=	=	=	◆	1	=	=	0	0	1	=	1	0	=	=	9.5	
11	S. Freymann (Tashkent)	=	0	0	0	1	1	=	1	0	0	◆	0	1	1	1	0	0	1	0	1	=	9.5	
12	N. Pavlov-Pianov (Moscow)	0	=	1	0	0	=	=	=	=	=	1	◆	0	0	1	1	1	=	0	=	=	9.5	
13	A. Sergeyev (Moscow)	=	0	=	0	0	=	0	0	0	=	0	1	◆	1	=	=	1	1	1	=	=	9	
14	A. Perfilyev (Leningrad)	0	0	0	0	=	1	0	0	0	1	0	1	0	◆	1	0	=	1	1	=	1	8.5	
15	Y. Vilner (Odessa)	0	0	0	0	1	0	1	0	1	1	0	0	=	0	◆	=	0	0	1	1	1	8	
16	A. Selezniev (Moscow)	0	0	0	0	=	=	1	0	1	0	1	0	=	1	=	◆	=	=	=	=	0	8	
17	Y. Rokhlin (Leningrad)	=	0	=	0	0	=	0	=	0	=	1	0	0	=	1	=	◆	=	1	0	1	8	
18	A. Kaspersky (Minsk)	=	0	=	0	=	0	=	=	1	0	0	=	0	0	1	=	=	◆	0	1	=	7.5	
19	V. Rauzer (Kiev)	=	=	0	0	0	0	=	0	=	1	1	1	0	0	0	=	0	1	◆	1	0	7.5	
20	A. Smorodsky (Tiflis)	=	0	0	1	=	0	=	1	0	=	0	=	=	=	0	=	1	0	0	◆	0	7	
21	C. Kholodkevich (Moscow)	0	0	0	1	0	0	0	0	0	=	=	=	=	=	0	0	1	0	=	1	◆	6.5	

6th Soviet Championship, 1929

#	1st Preliminary Group	1	2	3	4	5	6	7	8	9	Pts
1	**Y. Rokhlin (Leningrad)**	♦	1	=	=	=	0	=	1	1	5
2	**V. Silich (Vitebsk)**	0	♦	=	1	1	1	=	1	0	5
3	**K. Vygodchikov (Smolensk)**	=	=	♦	=	=	1	=	0	1	4.5
4	A. Ilyin-Zhenevsky (Leningrad)	=	0	=	♦	=	1	=	1	=	4.5
5	V. Panov (Moscow)	=	0	=	=	♦	=	0	1	1	4
6	V. Sozin (Novgorod)	1	0	0	0	=	♦	=	1	=	3.5
7	N. Sorokin (Tiflis)	=	=	=	=	1	=	♦	0	0	3.5
8	A. Bernstein (Moscow)	0	0	1	0	0	0	1	♦	1	3
9	Y. Vilner (Odessa)	0	1	0	=	0	=	1	0	♦	3

#	2nd Preliminary Group	1	2	3	4	5	6	7	8	9	Pts
1	**M. Botvinnik (Leningrad)**	♦	1	=	1	1	=	1	1	1	7
2	**S. Freymann (Tashkent)**	0	♦	=	1	1	1	1	1	1	6.5
3	**V. Rauzer (Kiev)**	=	=	♦	0	1	1	1	1	=	5.5
4	A. Poliak (Moscow)	0	0	1	♦	1	1	1	1	=	5.5
5	N. Riumin (Moscow)	0	0	0	0	♦	1	1	1	1	4
6	V. Nenarokov (Moscow)	=	0	0	0	0	♦	=	1	1	3
7	V. Ragozin (Leningrad)	0	0	0	0	0	=	♦	=	1	2
8	S. Mudrov (Moscow)	0	0	0	0	0	0	=	♦	1	1.5
9	N. Pavlov-Pianov (Moscow)	0	0	=	=	0	0	0	0	♦	1

#	3rd Preliminary Group	1	2	3	4	5	6	7	8	9	Pts
1	**I. Kan (Moscow)**	♦	1	=	=	1	1	=	1	1	6.5
2	**B. Verlinsky (Moscow)**	0	♦	1	1	=	1	=	=	1	5.5
3	**M. Makogonov (Baku)**	=	0	♦	=	1	=	1	1	1	5.5
4	N. Zubarev (Moscow)	=	0	=	♦	1	1	=	1	0	4.5
5	V. Goglidze (Tiflis)	0	=	0	0	♦	=	=	1	1	3.5
6	N. Rudnev (Samarkand)	0	0	=	0	=	♦	1	0	1	3
7	D. Grigorenko (Kharkov)	=	=	0	=	=	0	♦	=	0	2.5
8	A. Model (Leningrad)	0	=	0	0	0	1	=	♦	=	2.5
9	G. Ravinsky (Leningrad)	0	0	0	1	0	0	1	=	♦	2.5

#	4th Preliminary Group	1	2	3	4	5	6	7	8	9	Pts
1	**N. Grigoriev (Moscow)**	♦	=	1	0	1	=	=	1	1	5.5
2	**V. Makogonov (Baku)**	=	♦	0	1	0	1	1	1	1	5.5
3	**P. Izmailov (Tomsk)**	0	1	♦	1	=	0	1	=	1	5
4	V. Kirillov (Kharkov)	1	0	0	♦	1	1	0	1	1	5
5	S. Rosenthal (Minsk)	0	1	=	0	♦	=	1	1	=	4.5
6	S. Gotthilf (Leningrad)	=	0	1	0	=	♦	=	0	=	3
7	A. Selezniev (Stalino)	=	0	0	1	0	=	♦	=	=	3
8	S. Slonim (Moscow)	0	0	=	0	0	1	=	♦	1	3
9	V. Yuriev (Leningrad)	0	0	0	0	=	=	=	0	♦	1.5

#	1st Semi-Final Group	1	2	3	4	5	6	Pts
1	**P. Izmailov**	◆	=	1	=	1	=	3.5
2	**I. Kan**	=	◆	1	=	=	1	3.5
3	M. Botvinnik	0	0	◆	=	1	1	2.5
4	K. Vygodchikov	=	=	=	◆	=	=	2.5
5	V. Makogonov	0	=	0	=	◆	=	1.5
6	V. Silich	=	0	0	=	=	◆	1.5

#	2nd Semi-Final Group	1	2	3	4	5	6	Pts
1	**B. Verlinsky**	◆	0	1	1	1	1	4
2	**S. Freymann**	1	◆	0	1	1	1	4
3	V. Rauzer	0	1	◆	1	0	1	3
4	N. Grigoriev	0	0	0	◆	1	=	1.5
5	M. Makogonov	0	0	1	0	◆	=	1.5
6	Y. Rokhlin	0	0	0	=	=	◆	1

Final Match Tournament

#	Players	1	2	3	Pts	Prize
1	B. Verlinsky	◆◆	11	1=	3.5	I
2	S. Freymann	00	◆◆	11	2	II
3	I. Kan	0=	00	◆◆	0.5	III

P. Izmailov was unable to take part in the final match tournament.

7th Soviet Championship, 1931

#	1st Preliminary Group	1	2	3	4	5	6	7	8	9	Pts
1	**Rauzer (Kiev)**	◆	=	1	1	1	1	1	1	=	7
2	**Yudovich (Moscow)**	=	◆	1	=	1	=	1	1	1	6.5
3	Bychek (Voronezh)	0	0	◆	=	=	1	1	1	1	5
4	Fogelevich (Moscow)	0	=	=	◆	0	1	1	1	1	5
5	Rosenstein (Crimea)	0	0	=	1	◆	0	1	1	1	4.5
6	Gribin (Vladivostok)	0	=	0	0	1	◆	=	=	1	3.5
7	Moskalev (Kozlov)	0	0	0	0	0	=	◆	=	1	2
8	Rokhlin (Leningrad)	0	0	0	0	0	=	=	◆	1	2
9	Valdaev (Kostroma)	=	0	0	0	0	0	0	0	◆	0.5

Fyodor Duz-Khotimirsky withdrew due to illness (he defeated Valdaev and drew with Bychek, Rokhlin and Fogelevich).

#	2nd Preliminary Group	1	2	3	4	5	6	7	8	9	10	Pts
1	**Goglidze (Tiflis)**	◆	=	=	=	=	1	1	1	1	1	7
2	**Kan (Moscow)**	=	◆	=	0	1	1	1	1	1	1	7
3	**Zamikhovsky (Kiev)**	=	=	◆	0	1	1	1	1	1	1	7
4	Stepanov (Leningrad)	=	1	1	◆	0	0	0	1	1	1	5.5
5	Ebralidze (Tiflis)	=	0	0	1	◆	0	=	=	1	1	4.5
6	Rosenkrantz (Urals)	0	0	0	1	1	◆	=	0	=	1	4
7	B. Vainstein (Tashkent)	0	0	0	1	=	=	◆	1	0	1	4
8	Bautin (Nizhny Novgorod)	0	0	0	0	=	1	0	◆	=	1	3
9	Gaiduk (East Siberia)	0	0	0	0	0	=	1	=	◆	1	3
10	Garrison (Makhachkala)	0	0	0	0	0	0	0	0	0	◆	0

#	3rd Preliminary Group	1	2	3	4	5	6	7	8	9	10	Pts
1	**Ilyin-Zhenevsky (Leningrad)**	◆	1	1	1	0	=	0	1	1	1	6.5
2	**Mazel (Minsk)**	0	◆	=	1	=	1	1	1	=	1	6.5
3	Silich (Vitebsk)	0	=	◆	0	0	1	=	1	1	1	5
4	Kots (Moscow)	0	0	1	◆	1	0	0	1	1	1	5
5	Freymann (Tashkent)	1	=	1	0	◆	0	1	1	0	0	4.5
6	Tanin (Moscow)	=	0	0	1	1	◆	1	0	0	1	4.5
7	Aistov (Stalingrad)	1	0	=	1	0	0	◆	0	1	=	4
8	Eremin (Kazan)	0	0	0	0	0	1	1	◆	=	1	3.5
9	Morozkov (Tomsk)	0	=	0	0	1	1	0	=	◆	0	3
10	Veresov (Minsk)	0	0	0	0	1	0	=	0	1	◆	2.5

#	4th Preliminary Group	1	2	3	4	5	6	7	8	9	10	Pts
1	**Kasparyan (Tiflis)**	◆	0	=	1	1	1	1	1	1	1	7.5
2	**Botvinnik (Leningrad)**	1	◆	=	0	0	1	1	1	1	1	6.5
3	Grigorenko (Kharkov)	=	=	◆	1	0	0	1	0	1	1	5
4	Izmailov (Tomsk)	0	1	0	◆	=	1	=	=	=	1	5
5	Konstantinopolsky (Kiev)	0	1	1	=	◆	0	1	=	0	1	5
6	Lebedev (Moscow)	0	0	1	0	1	◆	=	0	1	1	4.5
7	Akshanov (Tiflis)	0	0	0	=	0	=	◆	1	1	1	4
8	Blumenfeld (Moscow)	0	0	1	=	=	1	0	◆	0	1	4
9	Khodzhaev (Tashkent)	0	0	0	=	1	0	0	1	◆	=	3
10	Kogan (West Siberia)	0	0	0	0	0	0	0	=	0	◆	0.5

#	5th Preliminary Group	1	2	3	4	5	6	7	8	9	10	Pts
1	**Sorokin (Tiflis)**	♦	=	1	=	1	1	=	=	1	1	7
2	**Alatortsev (Leningrad)**	=	♦	=	1	0	=	1	1	1	1	6.5
3	**Bogatyrchuk (Kiev)**	0	=	♦	=	1	=	=	1	1	1	6
4	Slonim (Moscow)	=	0	=	♦	=	1	1	1	1	0	5.5
5	L. Grigoriev (Rostov-on-Don)	0	1	0	=	♦	=	=	=	=	1	4.5
6	A. Kubbel (Leningrad)	0	=	=	0	=	♦	1	1	0	1	4.5
7	Kutuzov (Arkhangelsk)	=	0	=	0	=	0	♦	1	1	1	4.5
8	Mikhailov (Penza)	=	0	0	0	=	0	0	♦	=	1	2.5
9	Ordel (Kharkov)	0	0	0	0	=	1	0	=	♦	=	2.5
10	Kuryshkin (Moscow)	0	0	0	1	0	0	0	0	=	♦	1.5

#	6th Preliminary Group	1	2	3	4	5	6	7	8	9	10	Pts
1	**Gotthilf (Leningrad)**	♦	=	=	1	=	1	=	1	1	1	7
2	**Budo (Leningrad)**	=	♦	=	=	=	=	1	1	1	=	6
3	**Riumin (Moscow)**	=	=	♦	=	1	0	=	1	1	1	6
4	Selezniev (Stalino)	0	=	=	♦	=	1	=	=	=	1	5
5	Myasoedov (Leningrad)	=	=	0	=	♦	1	1	0	=	1	5
6	Oistrakh (Kharkov)	0	=	1	0	0	♦	1	=	1	1	5
7	Noskov (Ufa)	=	0	=	=	0	0	♦	1	=	1	4
8	Baev (Rostov-on-Don)	0	0	0	=	1	=	0	♦	=	=	3
9	Kiselev (Urals)	0	0	0	=	=	0	=	=	♦	1	3
10	Adrianovsky (Chibisovka village)	0	=	0	0	0	0	0	=	0	♦	1

#	7th Preliminary Group	1	2	3	4	5	6	7	8	9	10	Pts
1	**Romanovsky (Leningrad)**	♦	=	=	=	1	=	1	1	1	=	6.5
2	**Kirillov (Kharkov)**	=	♦	1	1	0	1	=	=	1	1	6.5
3	N. Grigoriev (Moscow)	=	0	♦	=	1	0	1	1	1	1	6
4	Panov (Moscow)	=	0	=	♦	1	=	=	=	1	1	5.5
5	L. Kubbel (Leningrad)	0	1	0	0	♦	1	0	1	=	1	4.5
6	Tolush (Leningrad)	=	0	1	=	0	♦	0	1	=	1	4.5
7	Grechkin (Saratov)	0	=	0	=	1	1	♦	0	0	1	4
8	Stashevsky (Mogilev)	0	=	0	=	0	0	1	♦	1	=	3.5
9	Perevoznikov (Tashkent)	0	0	0	0	=	=	1	0	♦	1	3
10	Veizer (Tiflis)	=	0	0	0	0	0	0	=	0	♦	1

#	8th Preliminary Group	1	2	3	4	5	6	7	8	9	10	Pts
1	**Sozin (Novgorod)**	♦	=	0	1	=	1	1	=	1	1	6.5
2	**Lisitsin (Leningrad)**	=	♦	0	=	1	=	1	1	1	1	6.5
3	**Verlinsky (Moscow)**	1	1	♦	0	1	0	0	1	1	1	6
4	Podolny (Polotsk)	0	=	1	♦	=	1	=	=	1	1	6
5	V. Yuriev (Leningrad)	=	0	0	=	♦	1	=	1	=	1	5
6	Nekrasov (Orenburg)	0	=	1	0	0	♦	0	1	1	1	4.5
7	Kaspersky (Minsk)	0	0	1	=	=	1	♦	=	0	=	4
8	Ratner (Kiev)	=	0	0	=	0	0	=	♦	=	1	3
9	Shumilin (Khabarovsk)	0	0	0	0	=	0	1	=	♦	1	3
10	Bogdanov (Petrozavodsk)	0	0	0	0	0	0	=	0	0	♦	0.5

Final Tournament, 1931

#	Players	1	2	3	4	5	6	7	8	9	10	11	12	13	14	15	16	17	18	Pts	Prize
1	M. Botvinnik	♦	1	1	=	1	1	1	1	1	0	1	=	1	1	1	0	=	1	13.5	I
2	N. Riumin	0	♦	=	1	1	=	=	=	=	0	1	0	1	1	1	=	1	1	11.5	II
3	V. Alatortsev	0	=	♦	0	=	1	=	1	=	1	=	0	1	1	1	=	1	0	10	III–VI
4	F. Bogatyrchuk	=	0	1	♦	0	0	=	0	=	=	1	=	=	1	1	1	1	1	10	III–VI
5	B. Verlinsky	0	0	=	1	♦	1	0	1	1	1	1	0	0	=	=	1	1	=	10	III–VI
6	M. Yudovich	0	=	0	1	0	♦	1	1	0	1	=	=	=	1	1	=	1	=	10	III–VI
7	I. Kan	0	=	=	=	1	0	♦	0	=	1	1	0	=	=	1	1	=	1	9.5	
8	I. Mazel	0	=	0	1	0	0	1	♦	1	1	1	=	0	0	=	1	=	1	9	
9	V. Rauzer	0	1	=	=	0	1	=	0	♦	0	=	=	1	1	1	=	=	=	9	
10	A. Ilyin-Zhenevsky	1	0	0	=	0	0	0	0	1	♦	0	=	1	1	=	1	1	1	8.5	
11	V. Kirillov	0	1	=	0	0	=	0	0	=	1	♦	1	=	1	0	=	1	1	8.5	
12	G. Lisitsin	=	0	1	=	1	=	1	=	=	=	0	♦	0	0	1	1	=	0	8.5	
13	N. Sorokin	0	0	0	=	1	=	=	1	0	0	=	1	♦	1	=	0	0	=	7	
14	A. Zamikhovsky	0	0	0	0	=	0	=	1	0	0	0	1	0	♦	=	1	1	1	6.5	
15	V. Goglidze	0	=	0	0	=	0	0	=	0	=	1	0	=	=	♦	0	1	1	6	
16	V. Sozin	1	0	=	0	0	=	0	0	=	0	=	0	1	0	1	♦	0	=	5.5	
17	A. Budo	=	0	0	0	0	0	=	=	=	0	0	=	1	0	0	1	♦	=	5	
18	G. Kasparyan	0	0	1	0	=	=	0	0	=	0	0	1	=	0	0	=	=	♦	5	

Romanovsky and Gotthilf didn't play in the final.

8th Soviet Championship, 1933

#	Players	1	2	3	4	5	6	7	8	9	10	11	12	13	14	15	16	17	18	19	20	Pts	Prize
1	M. Botvinnik (Leningrad)	•	1	1	1	=	1	=	0	=	=	0	1	1	1	1	=	1	1	=	1	14	I
2	V. Alatortsev (Leningrad)	0	•	=	0	=	0	=	1	=	0	1	1	1	1	1	1	1	1	1	1	13	II
3	G. Levenfish (Leningrad)	0	=	•	=	1	0	1	1	1	1	1	=	1	1	=	0	1	=	=	0	12	III–V
4	G. Lisitsin (Leningrad)	0	1	=	•	=	1	1	1	0	0	0	1	=	0	1	1	=	1	1	1	12	III–V
5	I. Rabinovich (Leningrad)	=	=	0	=	•	0	=	1	1	0	0	0	1	=	1	1	1	1	1	1	12	III–V
6	V. Rauzer (Kiev)	0	1	1	0	1	•	=	=	0	1	=	1	1	1	0	0	0	1	1	1	11.5	VI
7	V. Chekhover (Leningrad)	=	=	0	0	=	=	•	1	1	1	1	0	=	0	1	1	0	1	1	=	11	VII
8	F. Bogatyrchuk (Kiev)	1	0	0	0	0	=	0	•	1	0	1	=	1	=	1	1	=	1	1		10.5	VIII
9	I. Kan (Moscow)	=	=	0	1	0	1	0	0	•	1	1	0	=	=	0	1	0	1	1	1	10	IX
10	P. Romanovsky (Leningrad)	=	1	0	1	=	0	0	1	0	•	=	=	=	=	0	0	1	=	1	1	9.5	X–XI
11	N. Riumin (Moscow)	1	0	0	1	1	=	0	=	0	=	•	1	=	=	=	=	0	1	=	=	9.5	X–XI
12	B. Verlinsky (Moscow)	0	0	=	0	1	0	1	0	1	=	0	•	1	0	=	1	0	=	1	1	9	
13	M. Yudovich (Moscow)	0	0	0	=	0	0	=	=	=	=	=	0	•	1	=	1	1	=	1	1	9	
14	L. Savitsky (Leningrad)	0	0	0	1	=	0	1	0	=	=	=	1	0	•	1	1	1	=	0	0	8.5	
15	N. Sorokin (Tiflis)	0	0	=	0	0	1	0	=	1	1	=	=	=	0	•	0	1	0	=	=	7.5	
16	V. Goglidze (Tiflis)	=	0	1	0	0	1	0	0	0	1	=	0	0	0	1	•	1	=	=	0	7	
17	S. Freymann (Tashkent)	0	0	0	=	0	1	1	0	1	0	1	1	0	0	0	0	•	0	=	1	7	
18	N. Zubarev (Moscow)	0	0	=	0	0	0	0	=	0	=	0	=	=	=	1	=	1	•	0	1	6.5	
19	F. Duz-Khotimirsky (Moscow)	=	0	=	0	0	0	0	0	0	0	=	0	0	1	=	=	=	1	•	=	5.5	
20	V. Kirillov (Kharkov)	0	0	1	0	0	0	=	0	0	0	=	0	0	1	=	1	0	0	=	•	5	

9th Soviet Championship, 1934/35

#	Players	1	2	3	4	5	6	7	8	9	10	11	12	13	14	15	16	17	18	19	20	Pts	Prize
1	G. Levenfish (Leningrad)	•	=	=	=	=	=	=	1	0	=	1	1	0	0	=	1	1	=	1	1	12	I–II
2	I. Rabinovich (Leningrad)	=	•	0	0	0	=	1	=	1	1	1	=	1	1	1	1	=	0	1	=	12	I–II
3	F. Bogatyrchuk (Kiev)	=	1	•	1	1	0	0	=	=	=	0	=	1	=	1	0	1	=	1	1	11.5	III–IV
4	N. Riumin (Moscow)	=	1	0	•	=	=	0	=	=	=	1	=	0	1	1	1	=	=	1	1	11.5	III–IV
5	V. Alatortsev (Leningrad)	=	1	0	=	•	0	=	0	0	=	0	=	1	1	=	1	1	=	1	1	10.5	V–VIII
6	G. Lisitsin (Leningrad)	=	=	1	=	1	•	0	0	=	1	=	1	1	1	1	0	=	0	0	=	10.5	V–VIII
7	V. Ragozin (Leningrad)	0	0	1	1	=	1	•	=	0	=	1	1	0	=	=	=	=	0	1	1	10.5	V–VIII
8	V. Chekhover (Leningrad)	1	=	=	=	1	1	=	•	=	1	=	=	1	0	1	=	0	0	0	=	10.5	V–VIII
9	S. Belavenets (Moscow)	=	0	=	=	1	=	1	=	•	0	=	0	1	0	=	=	=	1	1	=	10	
10	I. Kan (Moscow)	0	0	=	=	=	0	=	0	1	•	1	0	1	=	=	1	1	1	0	1	10	
11	V. Makogonov (Baku)	0	0	1	0	1	=	0	=	=	0	•	=	1	1	1	=	0	1	1	=	10	
12	M. Yudovich (Moscow)	1	=	=	=	=	0	0	=	1	1	=	•	0	0	=	=	1	=	=	1	10	
13	G. Veresov (Minsk)	1	0	0	1	0	0	1	0	0	0	0	1	•	1	0	1	1	1	0	1	9	
14	V. Panov (Moscow)	=	0	=	0	0	0	=	1	1	=	0	1	0	•	0	0	1	1	1	1	9	
15	I. Mazel (Moscow)	0	0	0	0	=	0	=	0	=	=	0	=	1	1	•	1	=	1	1	=	8.5	
16	L. Savitsky (Leningrad)	0	0	1	0	0	1	=	=	=	0	=	=	0	1	0	•	1	1	0	1	8.5	
17	V. Rauzer (Leningrad)	=	=	0	=	0	=	=	1	=	0	1	0	0	0	=	0	•	1	0	1	7.5	
18	P. Dubinin (Gorky)	0	1	=	=	=	1	1	1	0	0	0	=	0	0	0	0	0	•	1	0	7	
19	A. Ilyin-Zhenevsky (Leningrad)	0	0	0	0	0	1	0	1	0	1	0	=	1	0	0	1	1	0	•	=	7	
20	S. Freymann (Alma-Ata)	0	=	0	0	0	=	0	=	=	0	=	0	0	0	=	0	0	1	=	•	4.5	

10th Soviet Championship, 1937

#	Players	1	2	3	4	5	6	7	8	9	10	11	12	13	14	15	16	17	18	19	20	Pts	Prizes
1	G. Levenfish (Leningrad)	•	=	0	1	0	1	1	1	=	1	=	=	0	=	1	=	1	1	1	=	12.5	I
2	A. Konstantinopolsky (Kiev)	=	•	=	=	=	=	=	0	=	1	=	1	1	=	1	1	=	=	1	=	12	II–III
3	V. Ragozin (Leningrad)	1	=	•	=	=	=	1	=	=	=	=	1	=	1	0	0	1	=	1	1	12	II–III
4	V. Makogonov (Baku)	0	=	=	•	1	=	1	1	=	=	1	=	1	1	0	0	=	0	1	1	11.5	IV
5	S. Belavenets (Moscow)	1	=	=	0	•	=	1	=	=	=	=	1	0	=	=	=	1	1	0	1	11	V–VII
6	V. Goglidze (Tbilisi)	0	=	=	=	=	•	=	1	=	1	=	=	=	=	=	0	=	1	1	1	11	V–VII
7	G. Lisitsin (Leningrad)	0	=	0	0	0	=	•	=	1	1	1	=	1	=	1	=	1	=	=	1	11	V–VII
8	V. Rauzer (Leningrad)	0	1	=	0	=	0	=	•	=	1	0	=	=	1	1	1	0	1	1	=	10.5	
9	M. Yudovich (Moscow)	=	=	=	=	=	=	0	=	•	0	1	=	1	=	1	1	=	=	0	=	10	
10	V. Alatortsev (Moscow)	0	0	=	=	=	0	0	0	1	•	1	=	=	=	0	1	=	1	1	1	9.5	
11	I. Bondarevsky (Rostov-on-Don)	=	=	=	0	=	=	0	1	0	0	•	=	0	=	1	=	1	1	1	=	9.5	
12	I. Rabinovich (Leningrad)	=	0	0	=	0	=	=	=	=	=	=	•	1	=	0	1	1	=	=	1	9.5	
13	I. Kan (Moscow)	1	0	=	0	1	=	0	=	0	=	1	0	•	=	1	=	=	=	=	=	9	
14	A. Lilienthal (hors concours)	=	=	0	0	=	=	=	0	=	=	=	=	=	•	=	1	1	0	=	=	8.5	
15	V. Panov (Moscow)	0	0	1	1	=	=	0	0	0	1	0	1	0	=	•	1	=	0	0	1	8	
16	A. Budo (Leningrad)	=	0	1	1	=	1	=	0	0	0	=	0	=	0	0	•	0	1	=	=	7.5	Special prize
17	A. Ilyin-Zhenevsky (Leningrad)	0	=	0	=	0	=	0	1	=	=	0	0	=	0	=	1	•	1	=	=	7.5	
18	V. Chekhover (Leningrad)	0	=	=	1	0	0	=	0	=	0	0	=	=	1	1	0	0	•	=	1	7.5	
19	G. Kasparyan (Erevan)	0	0	0	0	1	0	=	0	1	0	0	=	=	=	1	=	=	=	•	=	7	
20	A. Ebralidze (Tbilisi)	=	=	0	0	0	0	0	=	=	0	=	0	=	=	0	=	=	0	=	•	5	

Soviet Championship Match, 1937

Players	1	2	3	4	5	6	7	8	9	10	11	12	13	Pts
G. Levenfish (Leningrad)	0	1	1	=	=	0	0	0	=	1	1	0	1	6.5
M. Botvinnik (Leningrad)	1	0	0	=	=	1	1	1	=	0	0	1	0	6.5

The match was played until six wins. In case of a 5–5 score, it would be a draw.

A. Alekhine – 1920

B. Verlinsky – 1929

P. Romanovsky – 1923, 1927

M. Botvinnik – 1931, 1933

E. Bogoljubov – 1924, 1925

I. Rabinovich – 1935

F. Bogatyrchuk – 1927

G. Levenfish – 1935, 1937

Championship Rankings

There was already an attempt to calculate the points percentage of the first ten Soviet championships (*64*, 24th August 1937). However, those numbers were untrue. The table titled "Sporting Results of the Soviet Masters" lacked not only Alekhine and Bogoljubov but everyone who was excluded from the list of masters in 1935. Also, the results of the 1929 and 1931 championships weren't included in full, which is, in my opinion, wrong, because in both cases, the qualifying and final stages were parts of a **single** competition. So here is my version.

Player	Tournaments	W	L	D	Games	Pts	Percentage
Bogoljubov	2	24	2	10	36	29	80.6%
Alekhine	1	9	0	6	15	12	80.0%
Botvinnik	4	46	12	20	78	56	71.8%
Romanovsky	7	61	22	28	111	75	67.6%
Levenfish	7	59	19	42	120	80	66.7%
Bogatyrchuk	6	52	22	39	113	71.5	63.3%
Izmailov	2	9	4	9	22	13.5	61.4%
Konstantinopolsky	2	10	4	14	28	17	60.7%
Verlinsky	5	48	29	21	98	58.5	59.7%
Alatortsev	4	36	20	27	83	49.5	59.6%
Riumin	4	29	16	27	72	42.5	59.0%
Lisitsin	4	34	20	29	83	48.5	58.4%
Makogonov V.	4	29	18	24	71	41	57.7%
Rabinovich I.	8	57	37	45	139	79.5	57.2%
Gotthilf	3	11	6	18	35	20	57.2%
Kan	5	38	26	16	100	56	56.0%
Yudovich	4	26	17	39	82	45.5	55.5%
Model	2	13	10	5	28	15.5	55.4%
Belavenets	2	11	7	20	38	21	55.3%
Makogonov M.	1	5	4	4	13	7	53.8%
Rauzer	6	44	36	35	115	61.5	53.5%
Kubbel A.	4	22	18	17	57	30.5	53.5%
Mazel	3	17	14	14	45	24	53.3%
Ragozin	3	15	12	19	46	24.5	53.3%
Duz-Khotimirsky	5	33	28	26	87	46	52.9%
Silich	2	8	7	7	22	11.5	52.3%
Rabinovich A.	3	21	19	11	51	26.5	52.0%
Zamikhovsky	1	11	10	5	26	13.5	51.9%
Chekhover	3	18	17	22	57	29	50.9%
Bondarevsky	1	5	5	9	19	9.5	50.0%
Sorokin	3	13	14	17	44	21.5	48.9%

Nenarokov	5	26	28	22	76	37	48.7%
Grigoriev	6	37	40	27	104	50.5	48.6%
Panov	4	18	20	17	55	26.5	48.2%
Goglidze	4	20	23	29	72	34.5	47.9%
Ilyin-Zhenevsky	9	49	56	49	154	73.5	47.7%
Selezniev	5	14	18	41	73	34.5	47.3%
Kirillov	3	19	22	12	53	25	47.2%
Savitsky	2	12	16	10	38	17	44.7%
Sozin	4	21	29	20	70	31	44.3%
Vilner	5	22	31	23	76	33.5	44.1%
Kasparyan	2	12	18	15	45	19.5	43.3%
Zubarev	5	19	30	24	73	31	42.5%
Veresov	2	11	16	1	28	11.5	41.1%
Freymann	7	29	47	17	93	37.5	40.3%

Bibliography

Books and tournament game collections

Alatortsev V. A. et al *The Championship of Leningrad 1932 (Pervenstvo Leningrada 1932 goda)*. Leningrad-Moscow, 1932

Von Alechin A. *Chess Life in Soviet Russia (Das Schachleben in Sowjet-Russland)*, Berlin 1921

Asriyan V. A. *Vladimir Makogonov*, Moscow 1990

Averbakh Y. L. *Centre-Stage and Behind the Scenes (Shakhmaty na stsene i za kulisami)*, Moscow 2003

Baturinsky V. D. (editor) *Botvinnik's Chess Games*, Vol. 1 *(Shakhmatnoe tvorchestvo Botvinnika)*, Moscow 1965

Baturinsky V. D. *Pages of Chess Life*, 2nd edition *(Stranitsy shakhmatnoy zhizni)*, Moscow 1990

Belavenets L. S. (editor) *Master Sergei Belavenets*, Moscow 1963

Bogatyrchuk F. P. *My Life Path to Vlasov and the Prague Manifesto (Moy zhiznenniy put k Vlasovu i Prazhskomu manifestu)*, San Francisco 1978

Botvinnik M. M., Vainstein S. O., Nenarokov V. I. (editors) *7th All-Union Chess Tournament (VII Vsesoyuzniy shakhmatny turnir)*, Leningrad–Moscow, 1933

Botvinnik M. M. *Selected Games 1926–1946*, 2nd edition *(Izbrannye partii 1926–1946)*, Moscow 1951

Botvinnik M. M. *Achieving the Aim (K dostizheniyu tseli)*, Moscow 1978

Botvinnik M. M. *Analytical and Critical Works. 1923–1941 (Analiticheskie i kriticheskie raboty. 1923–1941)*, Moscow 1984

Botvinnik M. M. *Analytical and Critical Works. 1928–1986 (Analiticheskie i kriticheskie raboty. 1928–1986)*, Moscow 1987

Botvinnik M. M. *The Aim Achieved (U tseli)*, Moscow 1997

Botvinnik M. M. *Portraits (Portrety)*, Moscow 2000

Bychkov L. A. *Chess in Gorky (Shakhmatny Gorkii)*. Gorky, 1985

Chess Encyclopedia (Shakhmaty. Entsiklopedicheskiy slovar), Moscow 1990

Chess Player's Dictionary (Slovar shakhmatista), Leningrad 1929

Dlugolensky Y. N., Zak V. G. *People and Chess (Lyudi i shakhmaty)*, Leningrad 1988

Duz-Khotimirsky F. I. *Selected Games (Izbrannye partii)*, Moscow 1953

Dvorkovich V. Y. (editor) *Andre Lilienthal*, Moscow 1989

Eremeev V. E. *The First Steps (At the Dawn of Soviet Chess) (Pervye shagi (na zare sovetskikh shakhmat))*, Moscow 1968

Estrin Y. B. (editor) *Vasily Panov*, Moscow 1986

Goglidze V. A. *Selected Games (Izbrannye partii)*, Tbilisi 1949

Ilyin-Zhenevsky A. F. *International Chess Tournament in Moscow (Player's Diary) (Mezhdunarodniy shakhmatny turnir v Moskve (dnevnik uchastnika))*, Moscow 1926

Ilyin-Zhenevsky A. F. *Memoirs of a Soviet Master (Zapiski sovetskogo mastera)*, Leningrad 1929

Ivanov S., Kentler A., Faibisovich V., Khropov B. *The Chess Annals of St. Petersburg. 1900–2005 (Shakhmatnaya letopis Peterburga. 1900–2005)*, St. Petersburg 2005

Kan I. A. *Chess Encounters (Shakhmatnye vstrechi)*, Moscow 1962

Kan I. A. *Chess Player Nikolai Riumin (Shakhmatist Nikolai Riumin)*, Moscow 1968

Kasparov G. K. *My Great Predecessors* vol. 1 and 2 *(Moi velikie predshestvenniki)*, Moscow 2003

Konstantinopolsky A. M. *Alexander Konstantinopolsky*, Moscow 1985

Levenfish G. Y. *9th All-Union Chess Premiership (IX Vsesoyuznoe shakhmatnoe pervenstvo)*, Moscow–Leningrad 1937

Levenfish G. Y. *Selected Games and Memories (Izbrannye partii i vospominaniya)*, Moscow 1967

Levin K. *Mikhail Botvinnik*, Moscow 1951

Linder V. and Linder I. *Two Lives of Grandmaster Alatortsev (Dve zhizni grossmeistera Alatortseva)*, Moscow 1994

Lisitsin G. M. *10th All-Union Chess Premiership (Desyatoe vsesoyuznoe shakhmatnoe pervenstvo)*, Leningrad 1939

Neishtadt V. I., Pak V. N. *Prince Myshkin of the Chess Kingdom (Knyaz Myshkin shakhmatnogo tsarstva)*. Donetsk, 2007

Panov V. N. *Forty Years at the Chessboard (Sorok let za shakhmatnoy doskoy)*, Moscow 1966

Rabinovich I. L. (editor) *8th All-Union Chess Premiership (VIII Vsesoyuznoe shakhmatnoe pervenstvo)*, Leningrad–Moscow 1935

Raskin G. L. (editor). *International Chess Tournament in Moscow 1925 and its Participants (Mezhdunarodny shakhmatny turnir v Moskve 1925 g. i ego uchastniki)*. Moscow, 1925

Romanov I. Z. *Peter Romanovsky*, Moscow 1984

Romanovsky P. A. *Selected Games (Izbrannye partii)*, Moscow 1954.

Selected Games of Ragozin (Izbrannye partii Ragozina), Moscow 1964

Sosonko G. *My Testimony (Moi pokazaniya)*, Moscow 2003

Vainstein B. S. *Ferzberi's Traps (Lovushki Ferzberi)*, Moscow 1990

Vainstein B. S. *The Merano System (Meranskaya sistema)*, Moscow 1956

Yudovich M. M. (author and editor) *Vyacheslav Ragozin*, Moscow 1984

Tournament bulletins

10th All-Union Chess Championship (Desyatiy vsesoyuzniy shakhmatny chempionat), Moscow 1937

Bulletin of the 7th All-Union Chess and Checkers Conference (Bulleten VII Vsesoyuznogo shakhmatno-shashechnogo sezda), Moscow 1931

Bulletin of the Moscow International Chess Tournament (Bulleten Moskovskogo mezhdunarodnogo shakhmatnogo turnira), Moscow 1935

Championship of the VTsSPS (Pervenstvo VTsSPS). Moscow, 1938

Chess Championship of the USSR (Shakhmatnoe pervenstvo SSSR). Moscow, 1938

The All-Union Young Masters Tournament (Vsesoyuzniy turnir molodykh masterov), Moscow 1936

The Third Moscow International Chess Tournament (Tretiy moskovskiy mezhdunarodniy shakhmatny turnir), Moscow 1936

Printed in Great Britain
by Amazon

41503775R00295